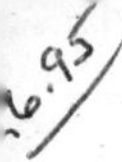

CLYMER®

YAMAHA

YZ50-80 MONOSHOCK • 1978-1990

The world's finest publisher of mechanical how-to manuals

INTERTEC PUBLISHING

P.O. Box 12901, Overland Park, Kansas 66282-2901

FIRST EDITION
First Printing February, 1981
Second Printing September, 1981

SECOND EDITION
Revised by Ron Wright to include 1981-1982 models
First Printing October, 1983

THIRD EDITION
Revised by Ron Wright to include 1983-1985 models
First Printing April, 1986

FOURTH EDITION
Revised by Ron Wright to include 1986 models
First Printing December, 1986
Second Printing April, 1988

FIFTH EDITION
Revised by Ron Wright to include 1987-1988 models
First Printing May, 1990
Second Printing May, 1992
Third Printing April, 1994
Fourth Printing June, 1996
Fifth Printing March, 1998
Sixth Printing June, 2000

Printed in U.S.A.

CLYMER and colophon are registered trademarks of Intertec Publishing.

ISBN: 0-89287-495-3

Library of Congress: 89-46353

Technical assistance by Curt Jordan, Jordan Engineering, Santa Ana, California and Anaheim Motorcycles, Anaheim, California.

Technical illustrations by Steve Amos.

COVER: Photographed by Michael Brown Photographic Productions, Los Angeles, California. Assisted by Tim Lunde. Motorcycle ridden by Trey McFarland. Special thanks to T & O Yamaha, Lawndale, California, for their assistance. Helmet courtesy of Simpson Sports, Torrance, California.

The following books and guides are published by Intertec Publishing.

CLYMER SHOP MANUALS
Boat Motors and Drives
Motorcycles and ATVs
Snowmobiles
Personal Watercraft

ABOS/INTERTEC/CLYMER BLUE BOOKS AND TRADE-IN GUIDES
Recreational Vehicles
Outdoor Power Equipment
Agricultural Tractors
Lawn and Garden Tractors
Motorcycles and ATVs
Snowmobiles and Personal Watercraft
Boats and Motors

AIRCRAFT BLUEBOOK-PRICE DIGEST
Airplanes
Helicopters

AC-U-KWIK DIRECTORIES
The Corporate Pilot's Airport/FBO Directory
International Manager's Edition
Jet Book

I&T SHOP SERVICE MANUALS
Tractors

INTERTEC SERVICE MANUALS
Snowmobiles
Outdoor Power Equipment
Personal Watercraft
Gasoline and Diesel Engines
Recreational Vehicles
Boat Motors and Drives
Motorcycles
Lawn and Garden Tractors

CONTENTS

QUICK REFERENCE DATA

RECOMMENDED LUBRICANTS AND FUEL

Engine oil	Yamaha Yamalube "R", Castrol R
Transmission oil	SAE 10W/30 "SE" or "SF" motor oil
Front fork oil	
1978-1982	20 wt. fork oil
1983-on	10 wt. fork oil
Air filter	Foam air filter oil
Drive chain	Chain lube
Control cables	Cable lube
Control lever pivots	10W/30 motor oil
Swing arm assembly	Lithium soap base grease
Steering head, wheel bearings	Wheel bearing, waterproof type bearings
Fuel	Premium grade—research octane 90 or higher
Brake fluid	DOT 3 or DOT 4

GAS/OIL PREMIX RATIO

Model	Premix ratio with Yamalube "R"	Premix ratio with Castrol R
YZ5	20:1	20:1
YZ60		
1981	16:1	20:1
1982	24:1	20:1
YZ80		
1978	20:1	20:1
1979-1980	32:1	20:1
1981	16:1	20:1
1982-on	24:1	20:1

RATIO 16:1

Gasoline U.S. gal.	Oil Oz.	cc
	8	237
2	16	473
3	24	710
4	32	946
5	40	1183

RATIO 20:1

Gasoline U.S. gal.	Oil Oz.	cc
1	6.4	190
2	12.8	380
3	19.2	570
4	25.6	760
5	32	945

(continued)

GAS/OIL PREMIX RATIO (continued)

RATIO 24:1		
Gasoline	Oil	
U.S. gal.	Oz.	cc
1	5.3	157
2	10.7	316
3	16	473
4	21.2	627
5	26.6	786

RATIO 32:1		
Gasoline	Oil	
U.S. gal.	Oz.	cc
1	4	118
2	8	237
3	12	355
4	16	473
5	20	591

TIRE INFLATION PRESSURE

Front	1.0 kg/cm² (14 psi)
Rear	1.0 kg/cm² (14 psi)

FUEL TANK CAPACITY

Model	U.S. gal.	Liters
YZ50	0.8	3.0
YZ60		
1981	0.8	3.0
1982	0.9	3.3
YZ80		
1978-1981	1.2	4.6
1982	1.4	5.2
1983-on	1.3	5.0

CLUTCH/TRANSMISSION OIL CAPACITY

Model	Drain/refill	Rebuild
YZ50	600-650 cc	650-700 cc
YZ60	650-700 cc	700-750 cc
YZ80		
1978	600-700 cc	650-700 cc
1979-1981	650-700 cc	700-750 cc
1982-1986	625-675 cc	675-725 cc
1987-on	650 cc	700 cc

MAINTENANCE TORQUE SPECIFICATIONS

Item	N·m	ft.-lb.
Cylinder head nuts or bolts		
YZ50	10	7
YZ60	30	21
YZ80		
1978-1980	13-15	9-11
1981-1982	30	21
1983-on	25	18
Fork bridge bolts		
YZ50	15	11
YZ60	16	12
YZ80		
1978	24	17
1979-1979	23	16
1980-1981	15	11
1982	18	13
1983-1985	23	17
1985-on	18	13
Rear axle nut		
YZ50	40	29
YZ60	45	32
YZ80		
1978	70	49
1979-1980	75	54
1981	70	49
1982-on	85	61

FRONT FORK OIL CAPACITY*

Model	cc	oz.
YZ50	75	2.5
YZ60	78	2.6
YZ80		
1978	83	2.8
1979-1980	150	5.07
1981-1982	188	6.4
1983	260	8.8
1984-on	272	9.2

* Each fork leg capacity.

FORK OIL LEVEL (1982-ON)*

Model	Standard mm (in.)	Minimum mm (in.)	Maximum mm (in.)
YZ80 (1982)	160 (7.87)	**	**
YZ80 (1983)	173 (6.81)	**	**
YZ80 (1984-1987)	157 (6.18)	**	**
YZ80 (1988-on)	157 (6.18)	130 (5.12)	180 (7.09)

* Distance from top of fork tube.
** Not specified.

DRIVE CHAIN SLACK

Model	mm	in.
YZ50	5-10	3/16-7/16
YZ60	5-10	3/16-7/16
YZ80		
1978	50-55	2-2 1/8
1979	45-50	1 25/32-2.0
1980	50-55	2-2 1/8
1981-1982	15-20	19/32-25/32
1983-1986	30-35	1 3/16-1 3/8
1987	15-20	19/32-25/32
1988-on	30-35	1 3/16-1 3/8

COOLANT CAPACITY AND SPECIFICATIONS* (1982-ON YZ80)

Model	Liter	U.S. qt.
YZ80 (1982)	1.1	1.2
YZ80 (1983)	0.45	0.48
YZ80 (1984-1985)	0.38	0.40
YZ80 (1986)	**	**
YZ80 (1987-on)	0.49	0.52
Radiator cap pressure test	0.95-1.25 kg/cm² (14-1-8 psi)	
Cooling system pressure test	1.1 kg/cm² (16 psi)	

* Coolant and water mix ratio: 1:1 (50% water; 50% coolant).
** Not specified by Yamaha.

SPARK PLUG TYPE* AND GAP

Model	Type	Gap mm (in.)
YZ50	NGK B9ES	0.6-0.8 (0.024-0.031)
YZ60	Champion N-2	0.7-0.8 (0.028-0.031)
YZ80		
1978	NGK B8ES	0.5-0.6 (0.020-0.024)
1979-1982	NGK B8ES	0.7-0.8 (0.028-0.031)
1983-1985	Champion N-84	0.6-0.7 (0.024-0.028)
1986-1987	Champion N-84	0.5-0.6 (0.020-0.024)
1988-on	NGK B9EG	0.5-0.6 (0.020-0.024)

* Standard heat range spark plugs.

IGNITION TIMING (WITH DIAL INDICATOR)*

Model	mm	in.
YZ50	1.65-1.95	0.065-0.077
YZ60	0.85-1.15	0.033-0.045
YZ80		
1978	2.0	0.08
1979	0.8	0.031
1980	1.0	0.039
1981-1983	0.8	0.031
1984	0.62	0.024
1985	0.8	0.031
1986-1987	1.16	0.046
1988-on	0.78	0.031

* All dimensions taken before top dead center (BTDC).

CARBURETOR PILOT AIR SCREW ADJUSTMENT

Model	No. of turns
YZ50	1 1/2
YZ60	
1981	1 1/2
1982	1 1/4
YZ80	
1978-1979	1 1/2
1980-1981	1
1982-1983	1 1/2
1984-on	1 3/4

CLYMER®

YAMAHA

YZ50-80 MONOSHOCK • 1978-1990

CHAPTER ONE

GENERAL INFORMATION

This detailed, comprehensive manual covers all 1978-1990 Yamaha YZ50, 60 and 80 models.

Troubleshooting, tune-up, maintenance and repair are not difficult, if you know what tools and equipment to use and what to do. Anyone of average intelligence and with some mechanical ability can perform most of the procedures in this manual.

The manual is written simply and clearly enough for owners who have never worked on a motorcycle, but is complete enough for use by experienced mechanics.

Some of the procedures require the use of special tools. Using an inferior substitute tool for a special tool is not recommended as it can be dangerous to you and may damage the part.

Table 1 lists model coverage with engine and frame serial numbers.

Metric and U.S. standards are used throughout this manual. Metric to U.S. conversion is given in **Table 2**.

MANUAL ORGANIZATION

This chapter provides general information and discusses equipment and tools useful both for preventive maintenance and troubleshooting.

Chapter Two provides methods and suggestions for quick and accurate diagnosis and repair of problems. Troubleshooting procedures discuss typical symptoms and logical methods to pinpoint the trouble.

Chapter Three explains all periodic lubrication and routine maintenance necessary to keep your Yamaha operating well and competitive. Chapter Three also includes recommended tune-up procedures, eliminating the need to constantly consult other chapters for the various assemblies.

Subsequent chapters describe specific systems such as the engine, clutch, transmission, fuel, exhaust, liquid cooling, suspension, steering, and brakes. Each chapter provides disassembly, repair, and assembly procedures in simple step-by-step form. If a repair is impractical for a home mechanic, it is so indicated. It is usually faster and less expensive to take such repairs to a dealer or competent repair shop. Specifications concerning a particular system are included at the end of the appropriate chapter.

NOTES, CAUTIONS AND WARNINGS

The terms NOTE, CAUTION and WARNING have specific meanings in this manual. A NOTE provides additional information to make a step or procedure easier or clearer. Disregarding a NOTE could cause inconvenience, but would not cause damage or personal injury.

A CAUTION emphasizes areas where equipment damage could occur. Disregarding a CAUTION could cause permanent mechanical damage; however, personal injury is unlikely.

A WARNING emphasizes areas where personal injury or even death could result from negligence. Mechanical damage may also occur. WARNINGS *are to be taken seriously.* In some cases, serious injury and death has resulted from disregarding similar warnings.

SAFETY FIRST

Professional mechanics can work for years and never sustain a serious injury. If you observe a few rules of common sense and safety, you can enjoy many safe hours servicing your own machine. If you ignore these rules you can hurt yourself or damage the equipment.

1. Never use gasoline as a cleaning solvent.
2. Never smoke or use a torch in the vicinity of flammable liquids, such as cleaning solvent, in open containers.
3. If welding or brazing is required on the machine, remove the fuel tank and rear shock to a safe distance, at least 50 feet away.
4. Use the proper sized wrenches to avoid damage to fasteners and injury to yourself.
5. When loosening a tight or stuck nut, be guided by what would happen if the wrench should slip. Be careful; protect yourself accordingly.
6. When replacing a fastener, make sure to use one with the same measurements and strength as the old one. Incorrect or mismatched fasteners can result in damage to the vehicle and possible personal injury. Beware of fastener kits that are filled with cheap and poorly made nuts, bolts, washers and cotter pins. Refer to *Fasteners* in this chapter for additional information.
7. Keep all hand and power tools in good condition. Wipe greasy and oily tools after using them. They are difficult to hold and can cause injury. Replace or repair worn or damaged tools.
8. Keep your work area clean and uncluttered.
9. Wear safety goggles during all operations involving drilling, grinding, the use of a cold chisel or anytime you feel unsure about the safety of your eyes. Safety goggles should also be worn anytime compressed air is used to clean a part.
10. Keep an approved fire extinguisher nearby. Be sure it is rated for gasoline (Class B) and electrical (Class C) fires.
11. When drying bearings or other rotating parts with compressed air, never allow the air jet to rotate the bearing or part; the air jet is capable of rotating them at speeds far in excess of those for which they were designed. The bearing or rotating part is very likely to disintegrate and cause serious injury and damage.

SERVICE HINTS

Most of the service procedures covered are straightforward and can be performed by anyone reasonably handy with tools. It is suggested, however, that you consider your own capabilities carefully before attempting any operation involving major disassembly of the engine or transmission.

1. "Front," as used in this manual, refers to the front of the motorcycle; the front of any component is the end closest to the front of the motorcycle. The "left-" and "right-hand" sides refer to the position of the parts as viewed by a rider sitting on the seat facing forward. For example, the throttle control is on the right-hand side. These rules are simple, but confusion can cause a major inconvenience during service.
2. Whenever servicing the engine or clutch, or when removing a suspension component, the bike should be secured in a safe manner. An excellent support for YZ models is a wooden box or motocross workstand. A sturdy box can be made with 3/4 in. plywood that will last a long time.
3. When disassembling any engine or suspension component, mark the parts for location and mark all parts which mate together. Small parts, such as bolts, can be identified by placing them in plastic sandwich bags. Seal the bags and label them with masking tape and a marking pen. When reassembly will take place immediately, an accepted practice is to place nuts and bolts in a cupcake tin or egg carton in the order of disassembly.
4. Finished surfaces should be protected from physical damage or corrosion. Keep gasoline and brake fluid off painted surfaces.
5. Use penetrating oil on frozen or tight bolts, then strike the bolt head a few times with a hammer and punch (use a screwdriver on screws). Avoid the use of heat where possible, as it can warp, melt or affect the temper of parts. Heat also ruins finishes, especially paint and plastics.
6. No parts removed or installed (other than bushings and bearings) in the procedures given in this manual should require unusual force during disassembly or assembly. If a part is difficult to remove or install, find out why before proceeding.
7. Cover all openings after removing parts or components to prevent dirt, small tools, etc. from falling in.

8. Read each procedure *completely* while looking at the actual parts before starting a job. Make sure you *thoroughly* understand what is to be done and then carefully follow the procedure, step by step.
9. Recommendations are occasionally made to refer service or maintenance to a Yamaha dealer or a specialist in a particular field. In these cases, the work will be done more quickly and economically than if you performed the job yourself.
10. In procedural steps, the term "replace" means to discard a defective part and replace it with a new or exchange unit. "Overhaul" means to remove, disassemble, inspect, measure, repair or replace defective parts, reassemble and install major systems or parts.
11. Some operations require the use of a hydraulic press. It would be wiser to have these operations performed by a shop equipped for such work, rather than to try to do the job yourself with makeshift equipment that may damage your machine.
12. Repairs go much faster and easier if your machine is clean before you begin work. There are many special cleaners on the market, like Bel-Ray Degreaser, for washing the engine and related parts. Follow the manufacturer's directions on the container for the best results. Clean all oily or greasy parts with cleaning solvent as you remove them. See *Washing the Bike* in this chapter.

WARNING
Never use gasoline as a cleaning agent. It presents an extreme fire hazard. Be sure to work in a well-ventilated area when using cleaning solvent. Keep a fire extinguisher, rated for gasoline fires, handy in any case.

CAUTION
If you use a car wash to clean your YZ, ***don't*** *direct the high pressure water hose at fork seals, steering bearings, carburetor hoses, suspension linkage components or wheel bearings. The water will flush grease out of the bearings or damage the seals. After washing your bike, remove the wheels and clean the wheel drums (if so equipped) of all water and dirt.*

13. Much of the labor charges for repairs made by dealers are for the time involved during in the removal, disassembly, assembly, and reinstallation of other parts in order to reach the defective part. It is frequently possible to perform the preliminary operations yourself and then take the defective unit to the dealer for repair at considerable savings.
14. If special tools are required, make arrangements to get them before you start. It is frustrating and time-consuming to get partly into a job and then be unable to complete it.
15. Make diagrams (or take a Polaroid picture) wherever similar-appearing parts are found. For instance, crankcase bolts are often not the same length. You may think you can remember where everything came from—but mistakes are costly. There is also the possibility that you may be sidetracked and not return to work for days or even weeks—in which the time carefully laid out parts may have become disturbed.
16. When assembling parts, be sure all shims and washers are replaced exactly as they came out.
17. Whenever a rotating part butts against a stationary part, look for a shim or washer. Use new gaskets if there is any doubt about the condition of the old ones. A thin coat of oil on non-pressure type gaskets may help them seal more effectively.
18. If it is necessary to make a clutch cover or ignition cover gasket and you do not have a suitable old gasket to use as a guide, you can use the outline of the part and gasket material to make a new gasket. Apply engine oil to the gasket surface of the part. Then place the part on the new gasket material and apply pressure with your hands. The oil will leave a very accurate outline on the gasket material that can be cut around.

CAUTION
When purchasing gasket material to make a gasket, measure the thickness of the old gasket and purchase gasket material with the same approximate thickness.

19. Heavy grease can be used to hold small parts in place if they tend to fall out during assembly. However, keep grease and oil away from electrical and brake components.
20. A carburetor is best cleaned by disassembling it and cleaning the parts with a spray carburetor cleaner. Never soak gaskets and rubber parts in these cleaners. Never use wire to clean out jets and air passages. They are easily damaged. Use compressed air to blow out the carburetor only if the float has been removed first.
21. Take your time and do the job right. Do not forget that a newly rebuilt engine must be broken in just like as a new one.

WASHING THE BIKE

Dirt bikes get dirty, and if you are riding your YZ and maintaining it properly, you will spend a good deal of time cleaning it. After each riding session, wash the bike. It will make maintenance and service procedures quick and easy. More important, proper cleaning will prevent dirt from falling into critical areas undetected. Failing to clean the bike or cleaning it incorrectly will add to your maintenance costs and shop time because dirty parts wear out prematurely. It's unthinkable that your bike could break down during a race or on a trail ride because of improper cleaning, but it can happen.

When cleaning your YZ, you will need a few tools, shop rags, scrub brush, bucket, liquid cleaner and access to water. Many riders use a coin-operated car wash. Coin-operated car washes are convenient and quick, but with improper use, the high water pressures can do your bike more damage than good.

NOTE

A safe biodegradable, non-toxic and non-flammable liquid cleaner that works well for washing your bike as well as removing grease and oil from engine and suspension parts is Simple Green. Simple Green can be purchased through some hardware, garden and discount supply houses. Follow the directions on the container for suggested dilution ratios.

When cleaning your bike and especially when using a spray type degreaser, remember that what is sprayed on the bike will rinse off and drip onto your driveway or into your yard. If you can, use a degreaser at a coin-operated car wash. If you are cleaning your bike at home, place thick cardboard or newspapers underneath the bike to catch the oil and grease deposits that are rinsed off.

1. Place the bike on a stand.
2. Remove the air filter unit as described in Chapter Three. Insert a dry rag into the carburetor throat to keep water from getting inside the engine. Cover the rag with a plastic wrap or plastic bag.
3. Check the following before washing the bike:
   a. Make sure the gas cap is screwed on tightly.
   b. Make sure the oil fill cap is tight.
   c. Plug the silencer opening with a large cork or rag.
4. Wash the bike from top to bottom with soapy water. Use the scrub brush to get excess dirt out of the wheel rims and engine crannies. Concentrate on the upper controls, engine, side panels and gas tank during this wash cycle. Don't forget to wash dirt and mud from underneath the fenders.
5. Remove the gas tank, side panels and seat. Wrap a plastic bag around the ignition coil and CDI unit. Concentrate the second wash cycle on the frame tube members, outer airbox areas, suspension linkage, monoshock and swing arm.
6. Direct the hose underneath the engine and swing arm. Wash this area thoroughly. If this area is extremely dirty, you may want to lay the bike on its side.
7. The final wash is the rinse. Use cold water without soap and spray the whole motorcycle again. Use as much time and care when rinsining the bike as when washing it. Built up soap deposits will quickly corrode electrical connections and remove the natural oils from tires, causing premature cracks and wear. Make sure you thoroughly rinse the bike off.
8. If you are washing the bike at home, remove the plastic bag and rag from the carburetor throat and start the engine. Idle the engine to burn off any internal moisture. Idle the bike long enough to use the gas remaining in the float bowl. This will

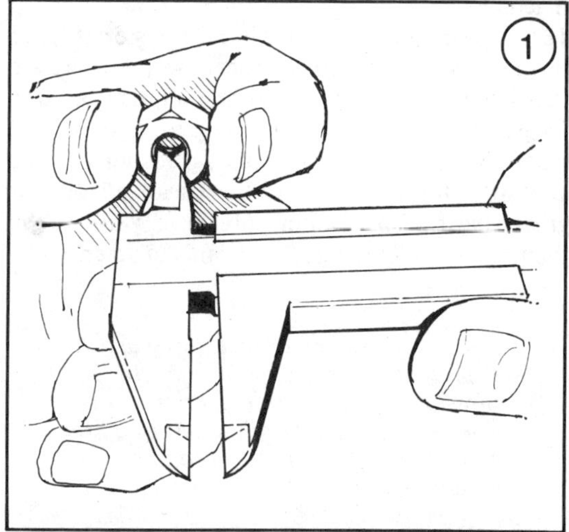

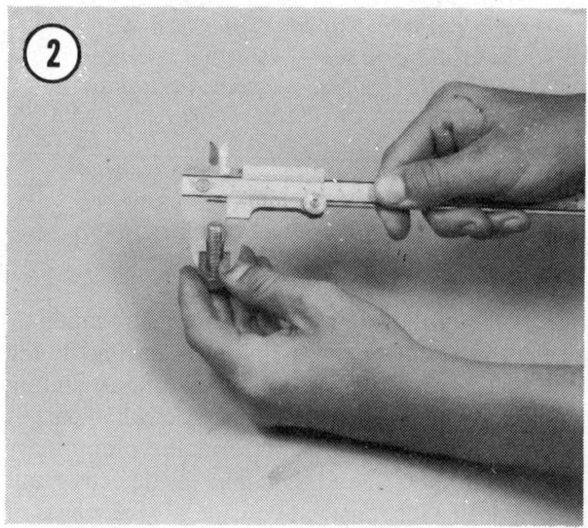

prevent fuel leakage problems when cleaning the carburetor later.

9. Before taking the bike into the garage, wipe it dry with clean shop rags. Inspect the machine as you dry it for further signs of dirt and grime. Make a quick visual inspection of the frame and other painted pieces. Spray any worn-down spots with WD-40 or Bel-Ray 6-in-1 to prevent rust from building on the bare metal. When the bike is back at your work area you can repaint the bare areas with touch-up paint. A quick shot from a paint can each time you work on the bike will keep it looking sharp and stop rust from building and weakening parts.

TORQUE SPECIFICATIONS

Torque specifications throughout this manual are given in Newton-meters (N•m) and foot-pounds (ft.-lb.).

Table 3 lists general torque specifications for nuts and bolts that are not listed in the respective chapters. To use the table, first determine the size of the nut or bolt by measuring it. **Figure 1** and **Figure 2** show how to do this.

FASTENERS

The materials and designs of the various fasteners used on your Yamaha are not arrived at by chance or accident. Fastener design determines the type of tool required to work the fastener. Fastener material is carefully selected to decrease the possibility of physical failure.

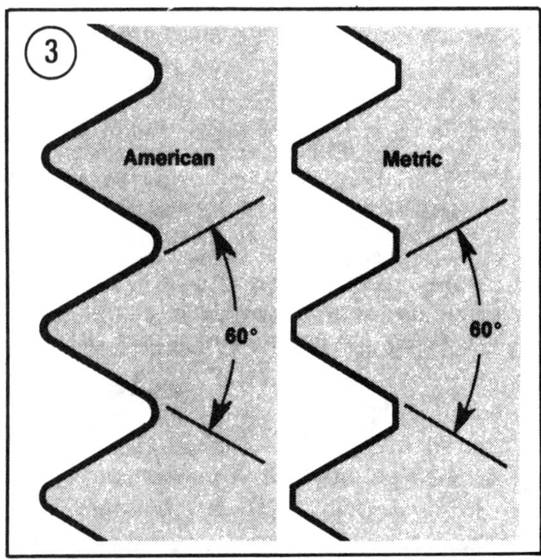

Nuts, bolts and screws are manufactured in a wide range of thread patterns. To join a nut and bolt, the diameter of the bolt and the diameter of the hole in the nut must be the same. It is just as important that the threads on both be properly matched.

The best way to tell if the threads on 2 fasteners are matched is to turn the nut on the bolt (or the bolt into the threaded hole in a piece of equipment) with fingers only. Be sure both pieces are clean. If much force is required, check the thread condition on each fastener. If the thread condition is good but the fasteners jam, the threads are not compatible. A thread pitch gauge can also be used to determine pitch. Yamaha motorcycles are manufactured with ISO (International Organization for Standardization) metric fasteners. The threads are cut differently than those of American fasteners (**Figure 3**).

Most threads are cut so that the fastener must be turned clockwise to tighten it. These are called right-hand threads. Some fasteners have left-hand threads; they must be turned counterclockwise to be tightened. Left-hand threads are used in locations where normal rotation of the equipment would tend to loosen a right-hand threaded fastener.

ISO Metric Screw Threads

ISO (International Organization for Standardization) metric threads come in 3 standard thread sizes: coarse, fine and constant pitch. The ISO coarse pitch is used for most all common fastener applications. The fine pitch thread is used on certain precision tools and instruments. The constant pitch thread is used mainly on machine parts and not for fasteners. The constant pitch thread, however, is used on all metric thread spark plugs.

ISO metric threads are specified by the capital letter M followed by the diameter in millimeters and the pitch (or the distance between each thread) in millimeters separated by the sign ×. For example a M8×1.25 bolt is one that has a diameter of 8 millimeters with a distance of 1.25 millimeters between each thread. The measurement of the inside bore indicates the proper wrench size to be used. **Figure 2** shows how to determine bolt diameter.

Machine Screws

There are many different types of machine screws. **Figure 4** shows a number of screw heads requiring different types of turning tools. Heads are also designed to protrude above the metal (round) or to be slightly recessed in the metal (flat). See **Figure 5**.

Bolts

Commonly called bolts, the technical name for these fasteners is cap screw. Metric bolts are described by the diameter and pitch (or the distance between each thread).

Nuts

Nuts are manufactured in a variety of types and sizes. Most are hexagonal (6-sided) and fit on bolts, screws and studs with the same diameter and pitch.

Figure 6 shows several types of nuts. The common nut is generally used with a lockwasher. Self-locking nuts have a nylon insert which prevents the nut from loosening; no lockwasher is required. Wing nuts are designed for fast removal by hand. Wing nuts are used for convenience in non-critical locations.

To indicate the size of a metric nut, manufacturers specify the diameter of the opening and the thread pitch. This is similar to bolt specifications, but without the length dimension. The measurement across 2 flats on the nut (**Figure 1**) indicates the proper wrench size to be used.

Self-locking Fasteners

Several types of bolts, screws and nuts incorporate a system that develops an interference

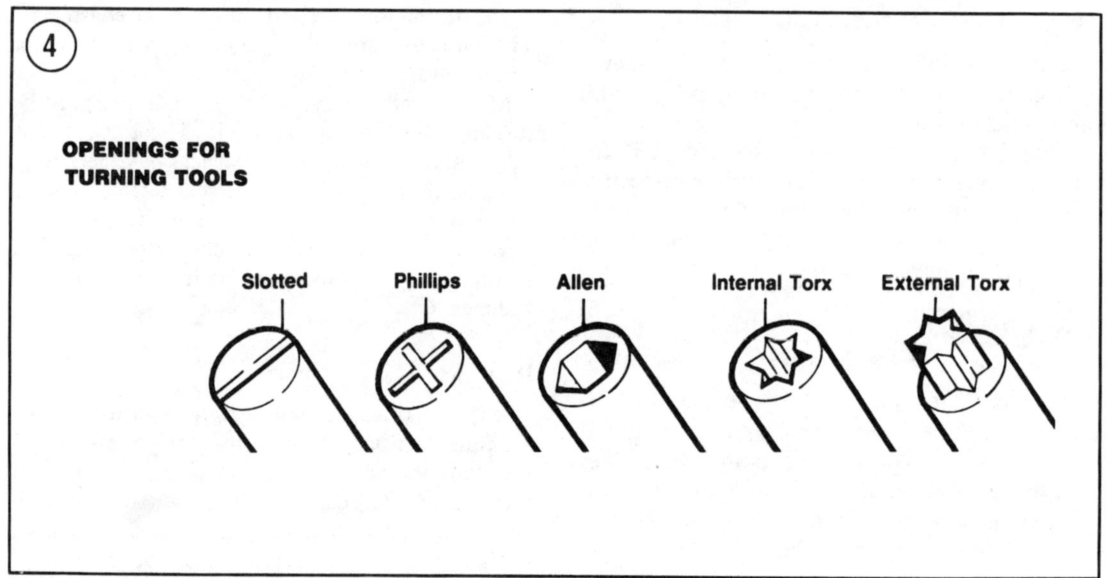

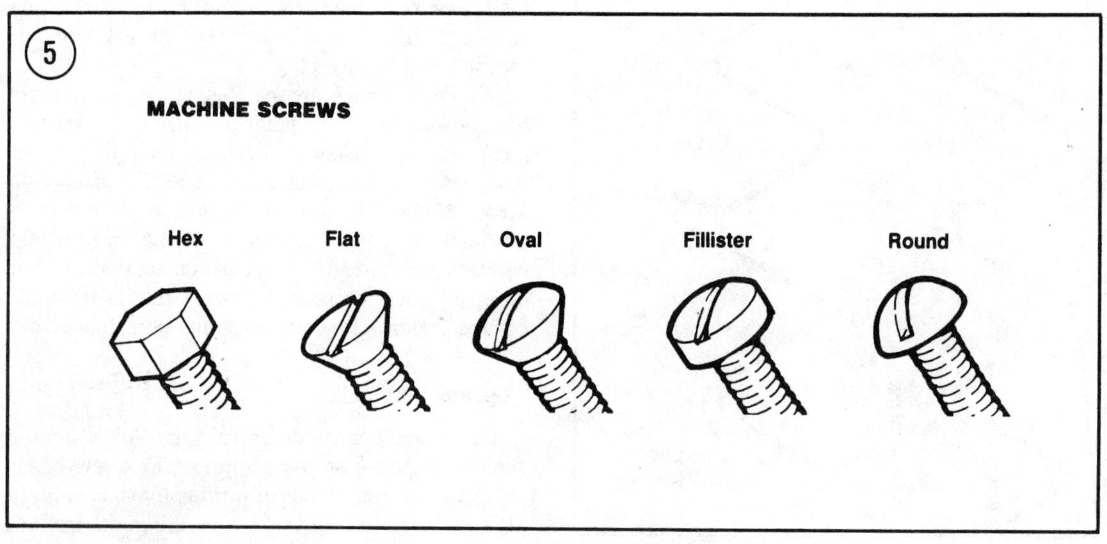

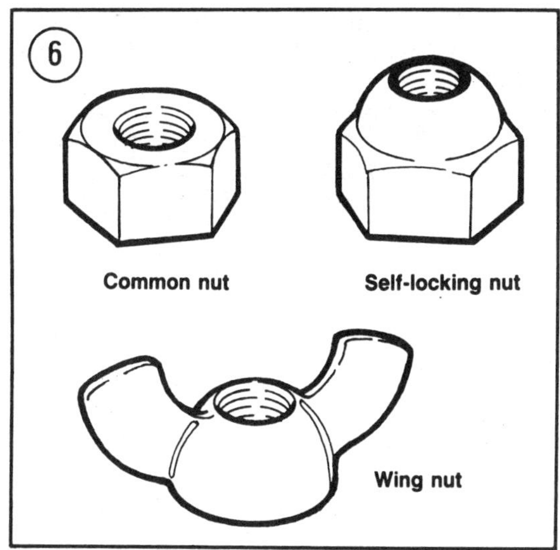

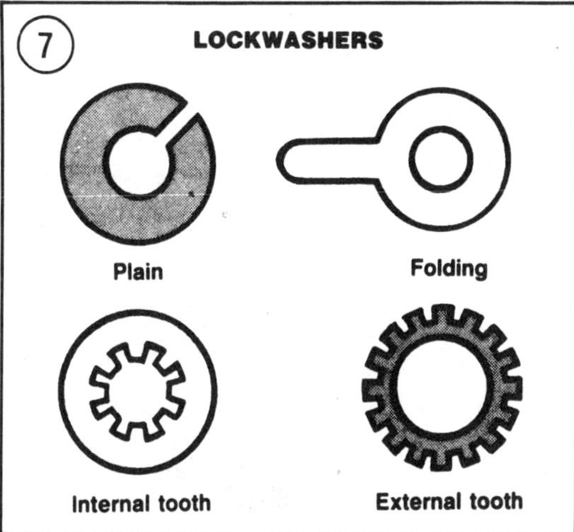

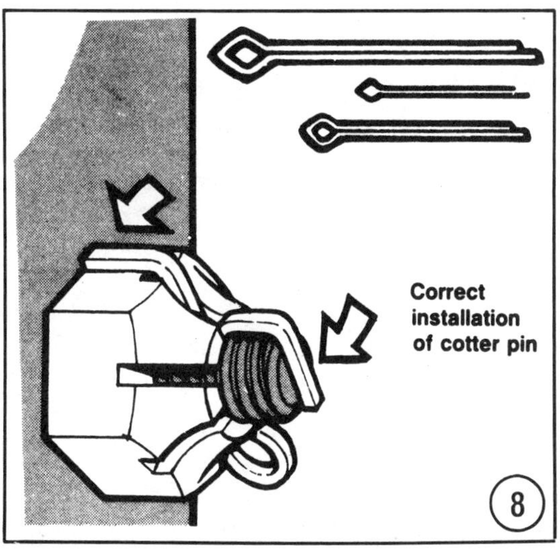

between the bolt, screw, nut or tapped hole threads. Interference is achieved in various ways: by distorting threads, coating threads with dry adhesive or nylon, distorting the top of an all-metal nut, using a nylon insert in the center or at the top of a nut, etc.

Self-locking fasteners offer greater holding strength and better vibration resistance. Some self-locking fasteners can be reused if in good condition. Others, like the nylon insert nut, form an initial locking condition when the nut is first installed; the nylon forms closely to the bolt thread pattern, thus reducing any tendency for the nut to loosen. When the nut is removed, the locking efficiency is greatly reduced. For greatest safety, it is recommended that you install new self-locking fasteners whenever they are removed.

Washers

There are 2 basic types of washers: flat washers and lockwashers. Flat washers are simple discs with a hole to fit a screw or bolt. Lockwashers are designed to prevent a fastener from working loose due to vibration, expansion and contraction. **Figure 7** shows several types of lockwashers. Washers are also used in the following functions:

a. As spacers.
b. To prevent galling or damage of the equipment by the fastener.
c. To help distribute fastener load during torquing.
d. As seals.

Note that flat washers are often used between a lockwasher and a fastener to provide a smooth bearing surface. This allows the fastener to be turned easily with a tool.

Cotter Pins

Cotter pins (**Figure 8**) are used to secure special kinds of fasteners. The threaded stud must have a hole in it; the nut or nut lock piece has castellations around which the cotter pin ends wrap. Cotter pins should not be reused after removal.

Circlips

Circlips can be internal or external design. They are used to retain items on shafts (external type) or within tubes (internal type). In some applications, circlips of varying thicknesses are used to control the end play of parts assemblies. These are often called selective circlips. Circlips should be replaced during installation, as removal weakens and deforms them.

Two basic styles of circlips are available: machined and stamped circlips. Machined circlips (**Figure 9**) can be installed in either direction (shaft or housing) because both faces are machined, thus creating two sharp edges. On splined shafts, circlip ends must be in full support areas (**Figure 9**). Stamped circlips (**Figure 10**) are manufactured with one sharp edge and one rounded edge. When installing stamped circlips in a thrust situation (transmission shafts, fork tubes, etc.), the sharp edge must face away from the part producing the thrust. When installing circlips, observe the following:

a. Compress or expand circlips only enough to install them.
b. After the circlip is installed, make sure it is completely seated in its groove.

LUBRICANTS

Periodic lubrication assures long life for any type of equipment. The *type* of lubricant used is just as important as the lubrication service itself, although in an emergency the wrong type of lubricant is better than none at all. The following paragraphs describe the types of lubricants most often used on motorcycle equipment. Be sure to follow the manufacturer's recommendations for lubricant types.

Generally, all liquid lubricants are called "oil." They may be mineral-based (including petroleum bases), natural-based (vegetable and animal bases), synthetic-based or emulsions (mixtures). "Grease" is an oil to which a thickening base has been added so that the end product is semi-solid. Grease is often classified by the type of thickener added; lithium soap is commonly used.

Clutch/Transmission Oil

Oil for your YZ's clutch and transmission and 4-cycle motorcycle and automotive engines is graded by the American Petroleum Institute (API) and the Society of Automotive Engineers (SAE) in several categories. Oil containers display these ratings on the top or label.

API oil grade is indicated by letters; oils for gasoline engines are identified by an "S". The clutch and transmissions used on YZ models covered in this manual require SE or SF graded oil.

Viscosity is an indication of the oil's thickness. The SAE uses numbers to indicate viscosity; thin oils have low numbers while thick oils have high numbers. A "W" after the number indicates that the viscosity testing was done at low temperature to simulate cold-weather operation such as 5W.

Multi-grade oils (for example 10W-40) maintain the same viscosity at high and low temperatures. This allows the oil to perform efficiently across a wide range of engine operating conditions. The lower the number, the better the engine will start in cold climates. Higher numbers are usually recommended for engine running in hot weather conditions.

Grease

Greases are graded by the National Lubricating Grease Institute (NLGI). Greases are graded by number according to the consistency of the grease; these range from No. 000 to No. 6, with No. 6 being the most solid. A typical multipurpose grease is NLGI No. 2. For specific applications, equipment manufacturers may require grease with

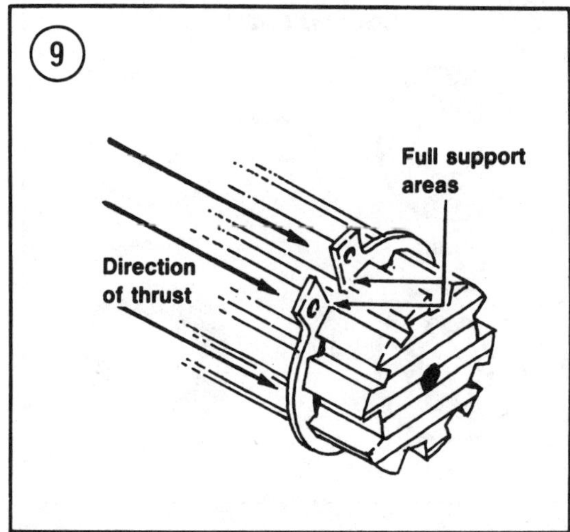

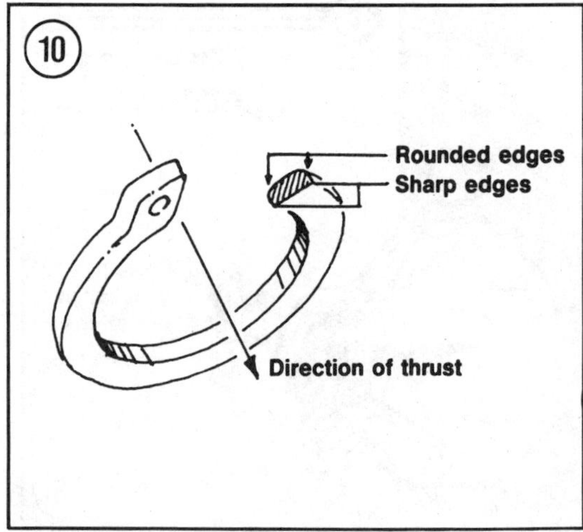

an additive such as molybdenum disulfide (MOS2).

PARTS REPLACEMENT

Yamaha makes frequent changes during a model year, some minor, some relatively major. When you order parts from the dealer or other parts distributor, always order by frame and engine numbers. Frame numbers are stamped on the steering head on the right-hand side (**Figure 11**). Engine numbers are stamped on the top of the left- or right-hand crankcase (**Figure 12**). Write the numbers down and carry them with you. Compare new parts to old before purchasing them. If they are not alike, have the parts manager explain the difference to you. **Table 1** lists frame and engine serial numbers for YZ models covered in this manual.

11

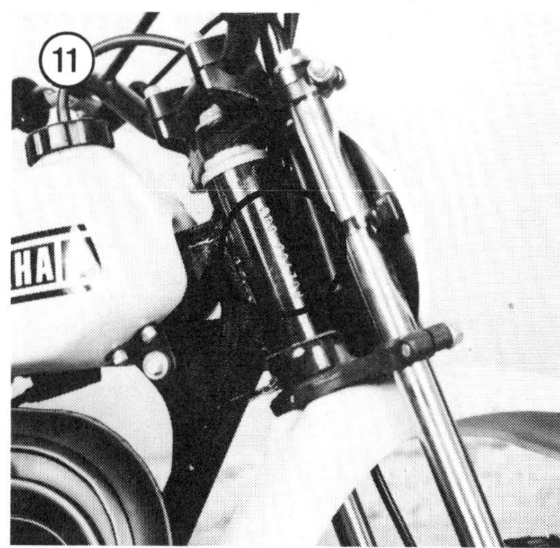

12

NOTE

If you purchased a used YZ model (that is covered in this manual), and you are not sure of its model or year, use the bike's engine or frame serial number and the information listed in ***Table 1****. Check the first two numbers and single letter of your bike's serial number. Then compare the number with the engine and frame serial numbers listed in* ***Table 1****. If your bike's serial number is listed in* ***Table 1****, cross-reference the number with the adjacent model number and year.*

BASIC HAND TOOLS

Many of the procedures in this manual can be carried out with simple hand tools and test equipment familiar to the average home mechanic. Keep your tools clean and in a tool box. Keep them organized with the sockets and related drives together, the open-end combination wrenches together, etc. After using a tool, wipe off dirt and grease with a clean cloth and return the tool to its correct place.

Top quality tools are essential; they are also more economical in the long run. If you are now starting to build your tool collection, stay away from the "advertised specials" featured at some parts houses, discount stores and chain drug stores. These are usually a poor grade tool that can be sold cheaply and that is exactly what they are—*cheap*. They are usually made of inferior material, and are thick, heavy and clumsy. Their rough finish makes them difficult to clean and they usually don't last very long. If it is ever your misfortune to use such tools, you will probably find out that the wrenches do not fit the heads of bolts and nuts correctly and will damage the fastener.

Quality tools are made of alloy steel and are heat treated for greater strength. They are lighter and better balanced than cheap ones. Their surface is smooth, making them a pleasure to work with and easy to clean. The initial cost of good quality tools may be more but they are cheaper in the long run. Don't try to buy everything in all sizes in the beginning; do it a little at a time until you have the necessary tools.

The following tools are required to perform virtually any repair job. Each tool is described and the recommended size given for starting a tool collection. Additional tools and some duplicates may be added as you become familiar with the vehicle. Yamaha motorcycles are built with metric standard fasteners—so if you are starting your collection now, buy metric sizes.

Screwdrivers

The screwdriver is a very basic tool, but if used improperly it will do more damage than good. The slot on a screw has a definite dimension and shape. A screwdriver must be selected to conform with that shape. Use a small screwdriver for small screws and a large one for large screws or the screw head will be damaged.

Two basic types of screwdriver are required: common (flat-blade) screwdrivers (**Figure 13**) and Phillips screwdrivers (**Figure 14**).

Screwdrivers are available in sets which often include an assortment of common and Phillips blades. If you buy them individually, buy at least the following:

a. Common screwdriver—5/16×6 in. blade.

b. Common screwdriver—3/8×12 in. blade.

c. Phillips screwdriver—size 2 tip, 6 in. blade.

Use screwdrivers only for driving screws. Never use a screwdriver for prying or chiseling metal. Do not try to remove a Phillips or Allen head screw with a common screwdriver (unless the screw has a combination head that will accept either type); you can damage the head so that the proper tool will be unable to remove it.

Keep screwdrivers in the proper condition and they will last longer and perform better. Always

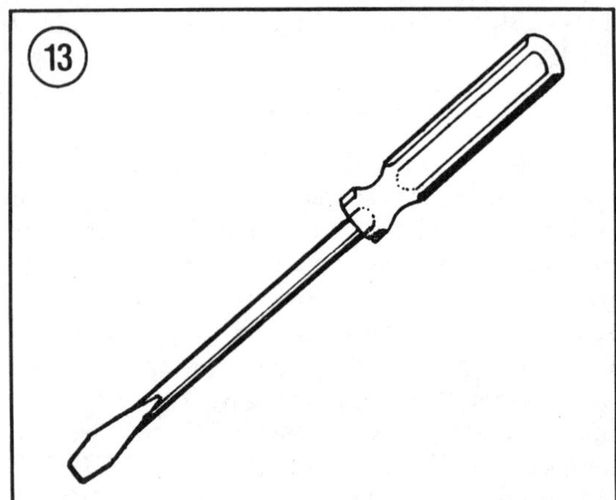

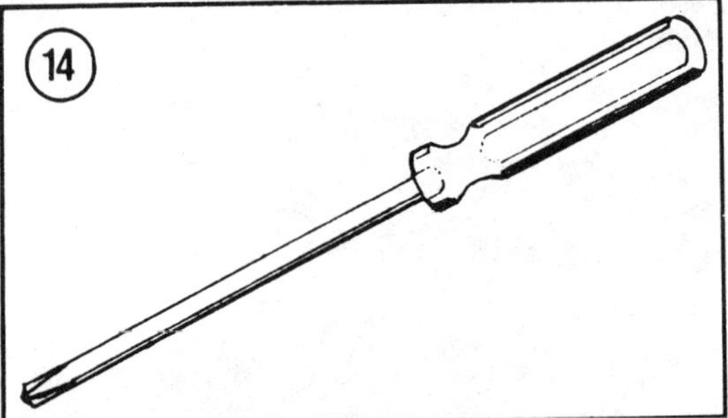

15

FRONT

SIDE

CORRECT WAY TO GRIND BLADE

CORRECT TAPER AND SIZE

TAPER TOO STEEP

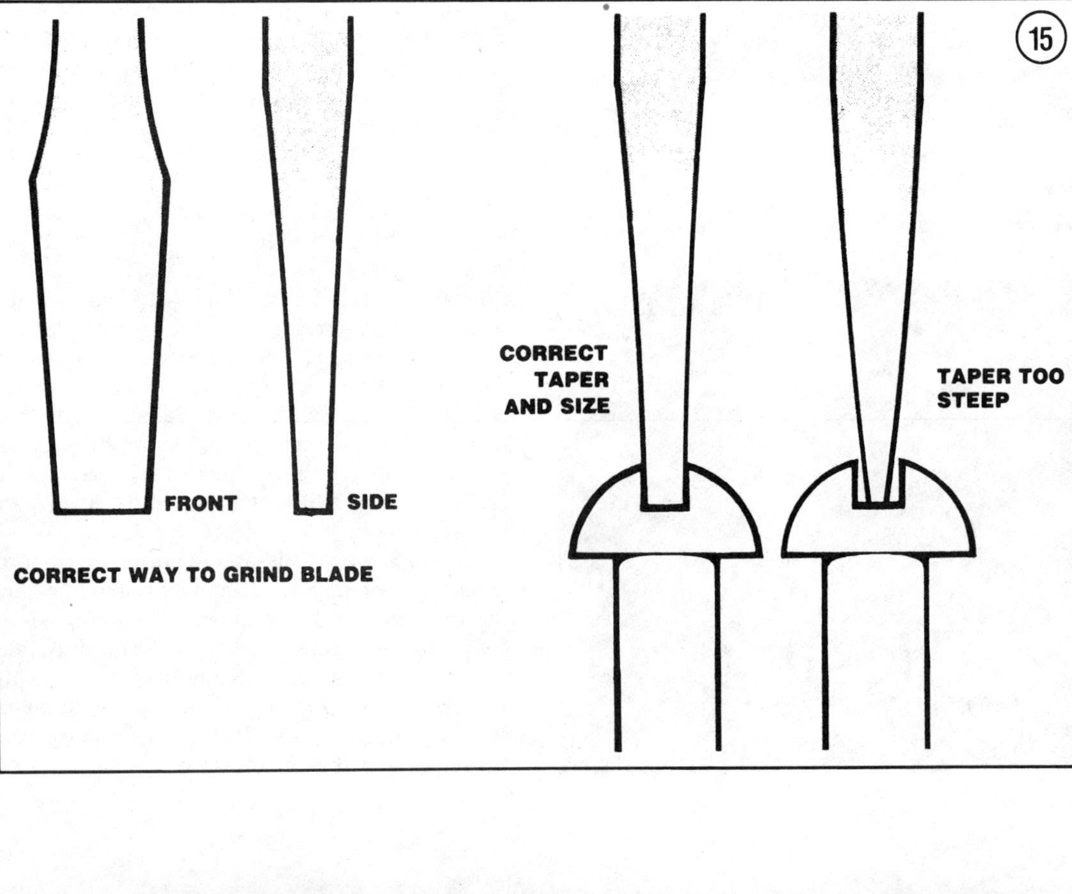

keep the tip of a common screwdriver in good condition. **Figure 15** shows how to grind the tip to the proper shape if it becomes damaged. Note the symmetrical sides of the tip.

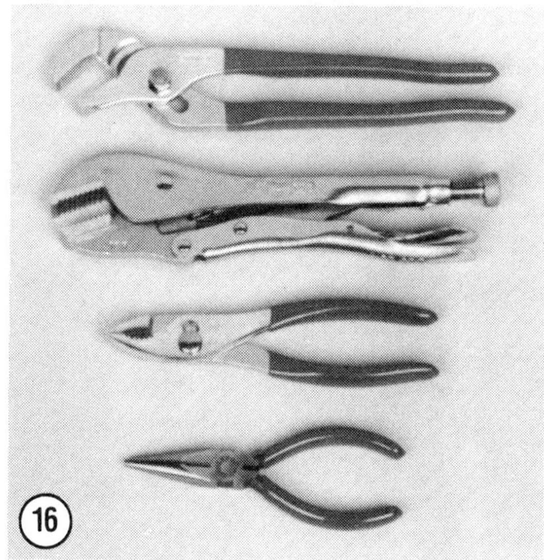

16

Pliers

Pliers come in a wide range of types and sizes. Pliers are useful for cutting, bending and crimping. They should never be used to cut hardened objects or to turn bolts or nuts. **Figure 16** shows several pliers useful in motorcycle repairs.

Each type of pliers has a specialized function. Slip-joint pliers are general purpose pliers and are used mainly for holding things and for bending. Vise Grips are used as pliers or to hold objects very tightly like a vise. Needlenose pliers are used to hold or bend small objects. Channel lock pliers can be adjusted to hold various sizes of objects; the jaws remain parallel to grip around objects such as pipe or tubing. There are many more types of pliers.

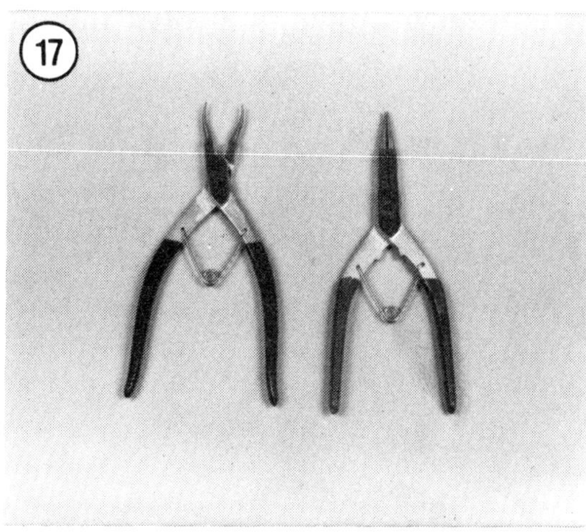

17

Circlip Pliers

Circlip pliers (**Figure 17**) are special in that they are only used to remove circlips from shafts or within engine or suspension housings. When purchasing circlip pliers, there are two kinds to distinguish from. External pliers (spreading) are used to remove circlips that fit on the outside of a shaft. Internal pliers (squeezing) are used to remove circlips which fit inside a gear or housing.

WARNING
Because circlips can sometime slip and "fly off" during removal and installation, always wear safety glasses.

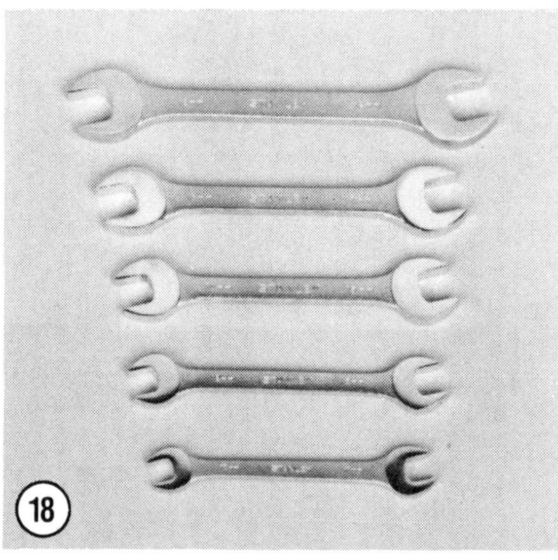

18

Box and Open-end Wrenches

Box and open-end wrenches are available in sets or separately in a variety of sizes. The size number stamped near the end refers to the distance between 2 parallel flats on the hex head bolt or nut.

Box wrenches are usually superior to open-end wrenches (**Figure 18**). Open-end wrenches grip the nut on only 2 flats. Unless a wrench fits well, it may slip and round off the points on the nut. The box wrench grips on all 6 flats. Both 6-point and 12-point openings on box wrenches are available. The 6-point gives superior holding power; the 12-point allows a shorter swing.

Combination wrenches which are open on one side and boxed on the other are also available. Both ends are the same size. See **Figure 19**.

Adjustable Wrenches

An adjustable wrench can be adjusted to fit a variety of nuts or bolt heads (**Figure 20**). However, it can loosen and slip, causing damage to the nut and perhaps to your knuckles. Use an adjustable wrench only when other wrenches are not available.

Adjustable wrenches come in various sizes.

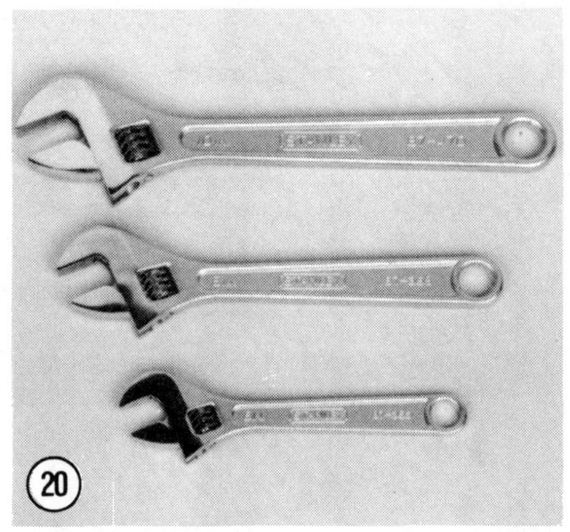

20

Socket Wrenches

This type is undoubtedly the fastest, safest and most convenient to use. Sockets which attach to a ratchet handle (**Figure 21**) are available with 6-point or 12-point openings and 1/4, 3/8, 1/2 and 3/4 inch drives. The drive size indicates the size of the square hole which mates with the ratchet handle.

21

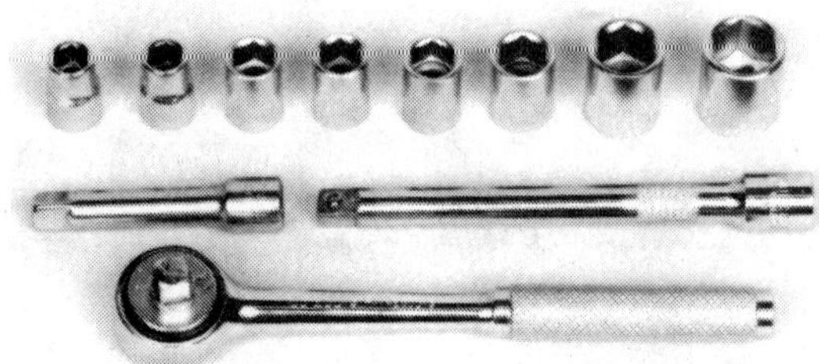

Torque Wrench

A torque wrench (**Figure 22**) is used with a socket to measure how tightly a nut or bolt is installed. They comc in a wide price range and with either 3/8 or 1/2 in. square drive. The drive size indicates the size of the square drive which mates with the socket.

Impact Driver

This tool makes removal of tight fasteners easy and eliminates damage to bolts and screw slots. Impact drivers and interchangeable bits (**Figure 23**) are available at most large hardware and motorcycle dealers. Sockets can also be used with a hand impact driver. However, make sure the

19

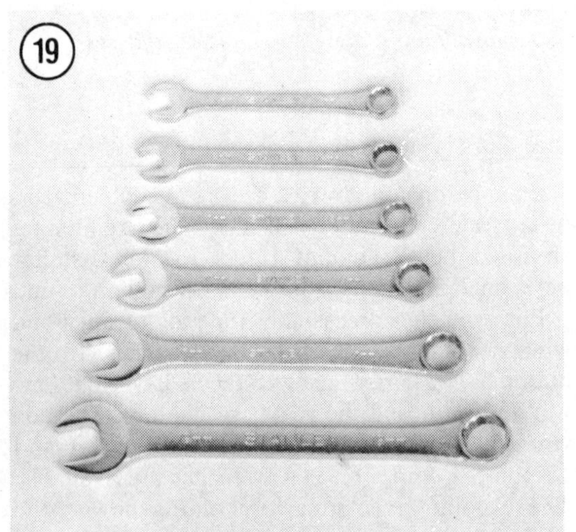

22

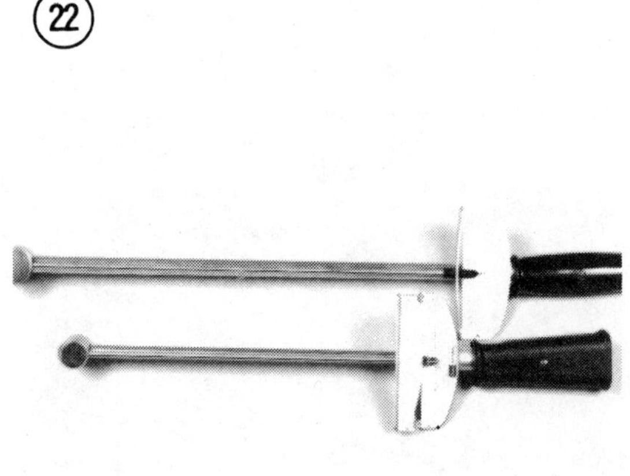

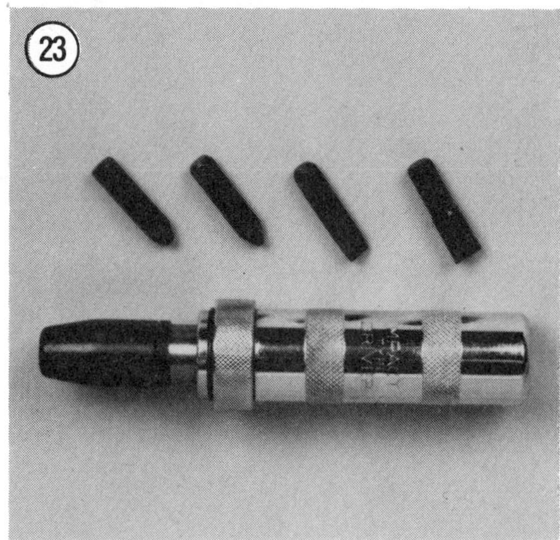

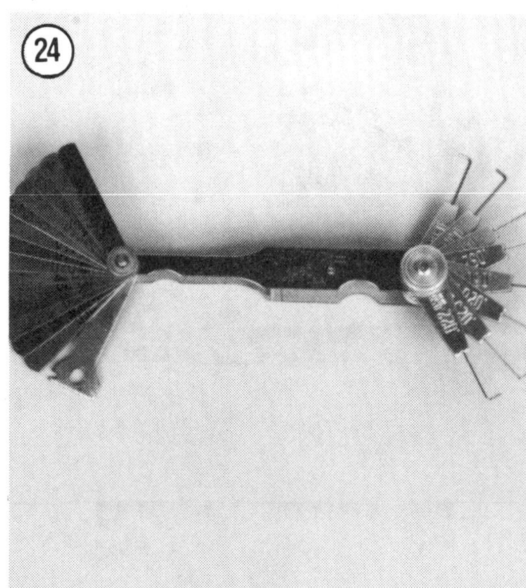

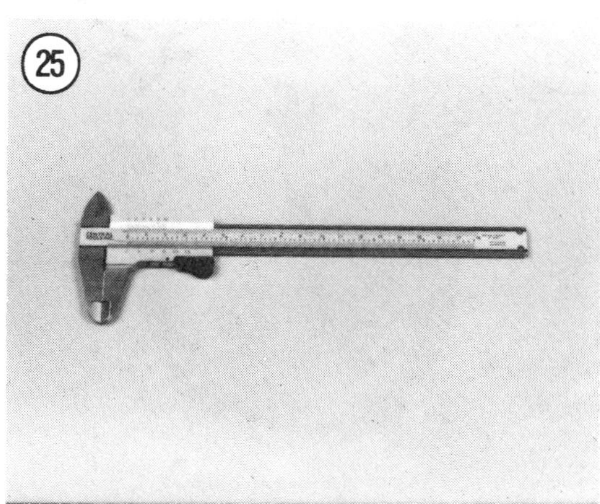

socket is designed for impact use. Do not use regular hand type sockets, as they may shatter during use.

Hammers

The correct hammer is necessary for repairs. Use only a hammer with a face (or head) of rubber or plastic or the soft-faced type that is filled with buckshot. These are sometimes necessary in engine teardowns. *Never* use a metal-faced hammer, as severe damage will result in most cases. You can always produce the same amount of force with a soft-faced hammer.

Feeler Gauge

This tool has both flat and wire measuring gauges and is used to measure spark plug gap. See **Figure 24**. Wire gauges are used to measure spark plug gap; flat gauges are used for all other measurements.

Vernier Caliper

This tool is invaluable when reading inside, outside and depth measurements to within close precision. It can be used to measure clutch spring length and the thickness of clutch plates, shims and thrust washers. The vernier caliper can be purchased from large hardware stores, motorcycle dealers or mail order houses. See **Figure 25**.

Spoke Wrench

This special wrench is used to tighten spokes (**Figure 26**). It is available at most motorcycle shops.

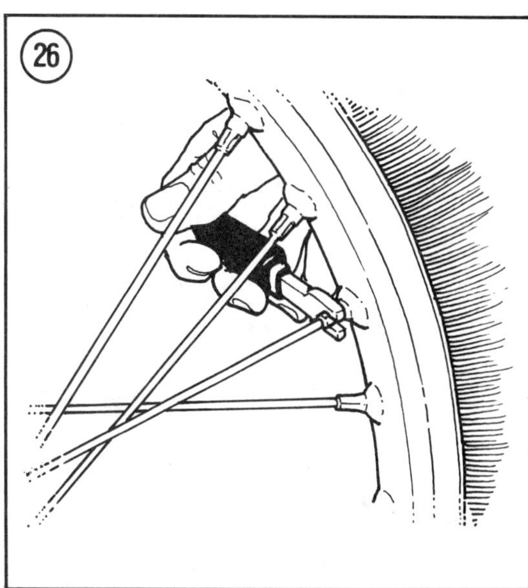

The Grabbit

This is a special tool that is very useful as a holding tool especially in the removal and installing of the clutch nut and the drive sprocket nut. It is called the Grabbit (**Figure 27**) and can be ordered through your Yamaha dealer.

Tire Levers

When riding and maintaining a dirt bike, you must learn how to change tires. To prevent from pinching tubes during tire changing, purchase a good set of tire levers (**Figure 28**). Never use a screwdriver in place of a tire lever. Refer to Chapter Eleven for their use. Before using a tire lever, check the working end of the tool and remove any burrs. Don't use a tire lever for prying anything but tires.

Flywheel Puller

All models require the use of a flywheel puller (**Figure 29**) for ignition timing and points

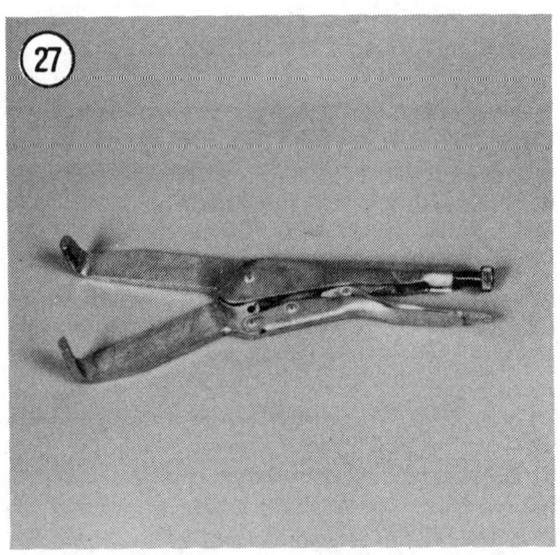

27

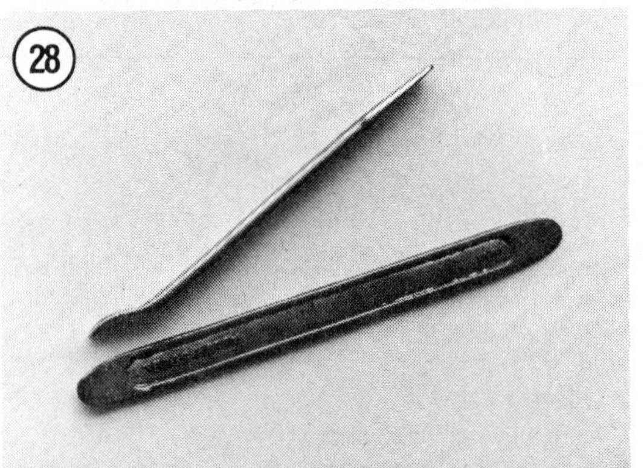

28

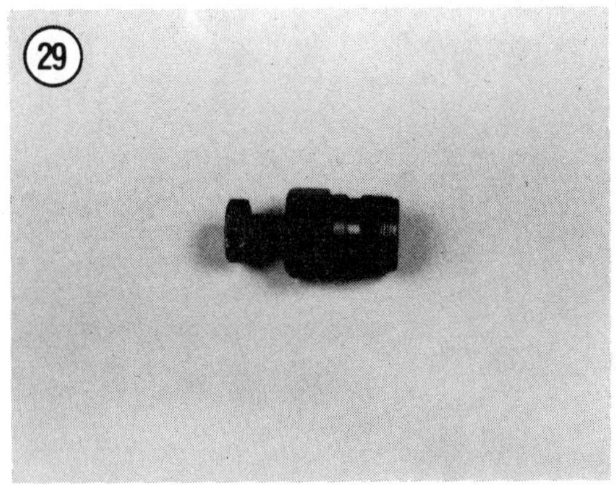

29

30

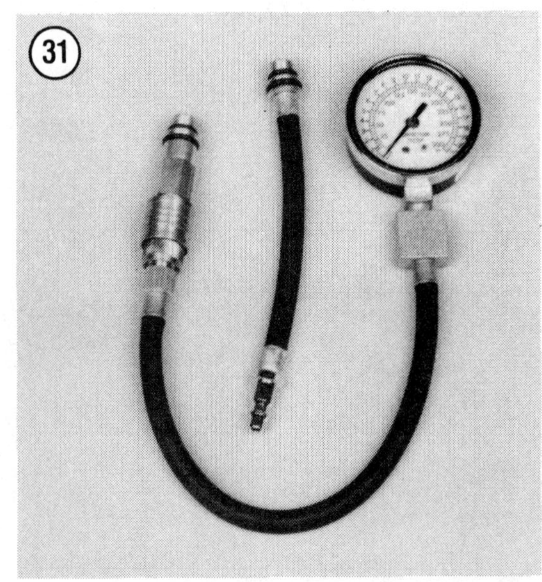

31

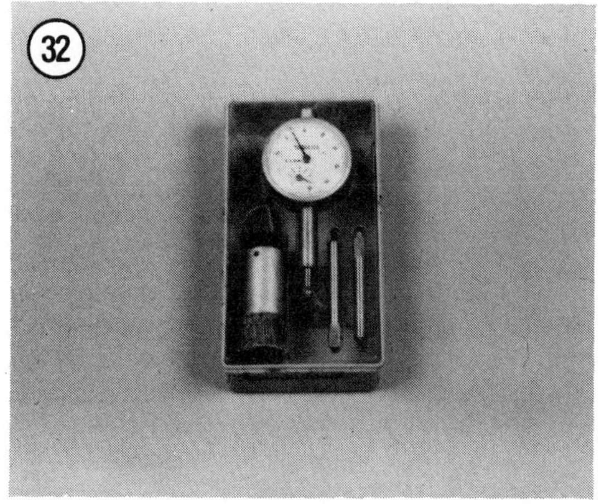

32

33

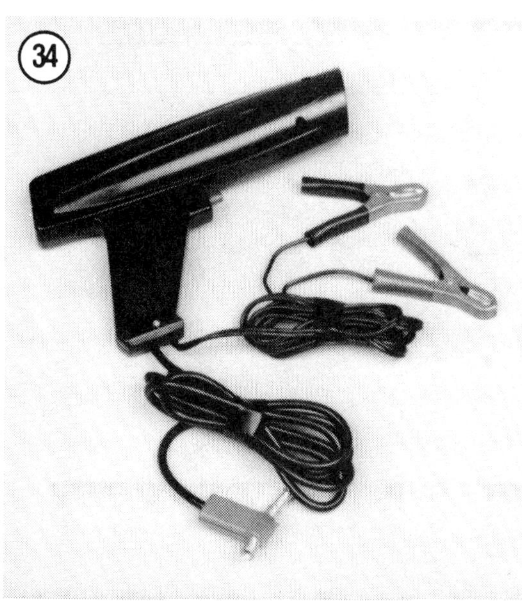

34

replacement (if so equipped). In addition, when disassembling the engine, the rotor must be removed before splitting the crankcases. There is no satisfactory substitute for this tool. Because the rotor is a taper fit on the crankshaft, makeshift removal often results in crankshaft and rotor damage. Don't think about removing the rotor without this tool.

Special Tools

A few special tools may be required for major service. These are described in the appropriate chapters and are available either from a Yamaha dealer or other manufacturers as indicated.

TEST EQUIPMENT

Multimeter or VOM

This instrument (**Figure 30**) is invaluable for electrical system troubleshooting and when adjusting the ignition timing on models with breaker points. Multimeters are available at electronic hobbyist stores and mail order houses.

Compression Gauge

An engine with low compression cannot be properly tuned and will not develop full power. A compression gauge (**Figure 31**) measures engine compression. The one shown has a flexible stem with an extension that can allow you to hold it while kicking the engine over. Open the throttle all the way when checking engine compression. See Chapter Three.

Dial Indicator

Dial indicators (**Figure 32**) are precision tools used to check dimension variations on machined parts such as transmission shafts and axles and to check crankshaft and axle shaft end play. Dial indicators are available with various dial types for different measuring requirements. For motorcycle repair, select a dial indicator with a continuous dial (**Figure 33**). This type of dial is required to accurately measure ignition timing.

Strobe Timing Light

This instrument is useful for checking ignition timing. By flashing a light at the precise instant the spark plug fires, the position of the timing mark can be seen. The flashing light makes a moving mark appear to stand still opposite a stationary mark.

Suitable lights range from inexpensive neon bulb types to powerful xenon strobe lights. See **Figure 34**. A light with an inductive pickup is recommended to eliminate any possible damage to ignition wiring.

When using a strobe timing light to check the ignition timing on your YZ, you will also need a 6-volt battery to connect to the timing light.

EXPENDABLE SUPPLIES

Certain expendable supplies are also required. These include grease, oil, gasket cement, shop rags and cleaning solvent. Ask your dealer for the special locking compounds, silicone lubricants and lube products which make vehicle maintenance simpler and easier. Cleaning solvent is available at some service stations.

WARNING
Having a stack of clean shop rags on hand is important when performing engine and suspension service work. However, to prevent fire damage from spontaneous combustion from a pile of solvent soaked rags, store them in a sealed metal container until they can be washed or discarded.

WARNING
To prevent from absorbing solvent and other cleaners into your skin while cleaning parts, wear a pair of elbow-length, petroleum-resistant rubber gloves. These can be purchased through industrial supply houses or large hardware stores.

MECHANIC'S TIPS

Removing Frozen Nuts and Screws

When a fastener rusts and cannot be removed, several methods may be used to loosen it. First, apply penetrating oil such as Liquid Wrench or WD-40 (available at hardware or auto supply stores). Apply it liberally and let it penetrate for 10-15 minutes. Rap the fastener several times with a small hammer; do not hit it hard enough to cause damage. Reapply the penetrating oil if necessary.

For frozen screws, apply penetrating oil as described, then insert a screwdriver in the slot and rap the top of the screwdriver with a hammer. This loosens the rust so the screw can be removed in the normal way. If the screw head is too chewed up to use this method, grip the head with Vise Grips and twist the screw out.

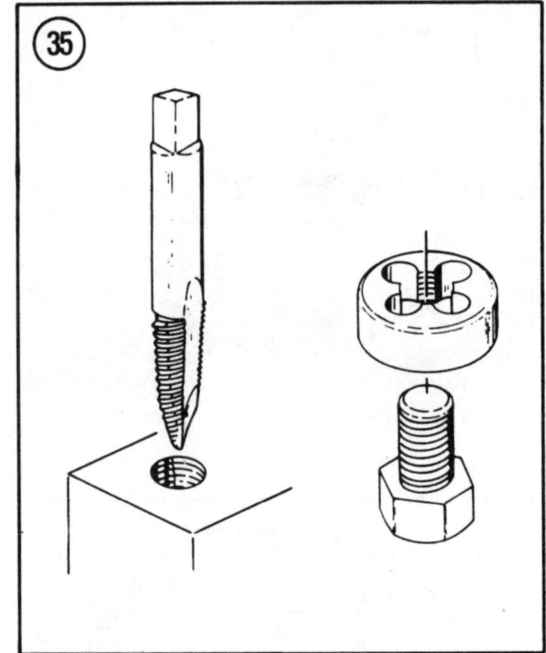

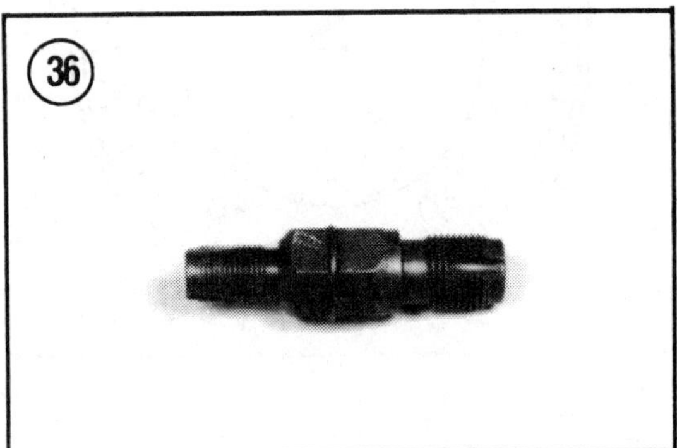

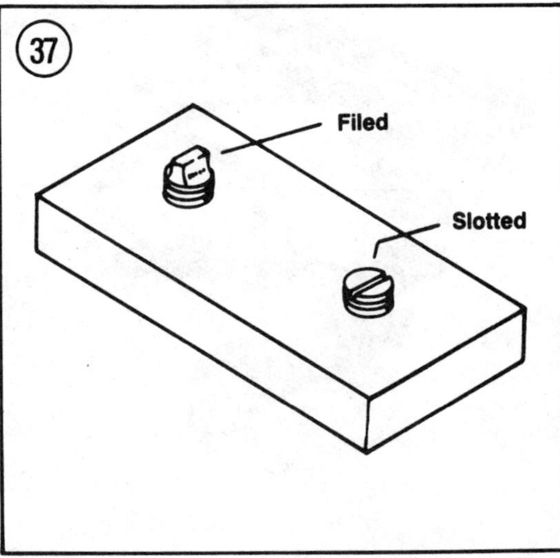

Avoid applying heat unless specifically instructed, as it may melt, warp or remove the temper from surrounding parts.

Remedying Stripped Threads

Occasionally, threads are stripped through carelessness or impact damage. Often the threads can be cleaned up by running a tap (for internal threads on nuts) or die (for external threads on bolts) through the threads. See **Figure 35**. To clean or repair spark plug threads, a spark plug tap can be used (**Figure 36**).

Removing Broken Screws or Bolts

When the head breaks off a screw or bolt, several methods are available for removing the remaining portion.

If a large portion of the remainder projects out, try gripping it with Vise Grips. If the projecting portion is too small, file it to fit a wrench or cut a slot in it to fit a screwdriver. See **Figure 37**.

If the head breaks off flush, use a screw extractor. To do this, centerpunch the exact center of the remaining portion of the screw or bolt. Drill a small hole in the screw and tap the extractor into the hole. Back the screw out with a wrench on the extractor. See **Figure 38**.

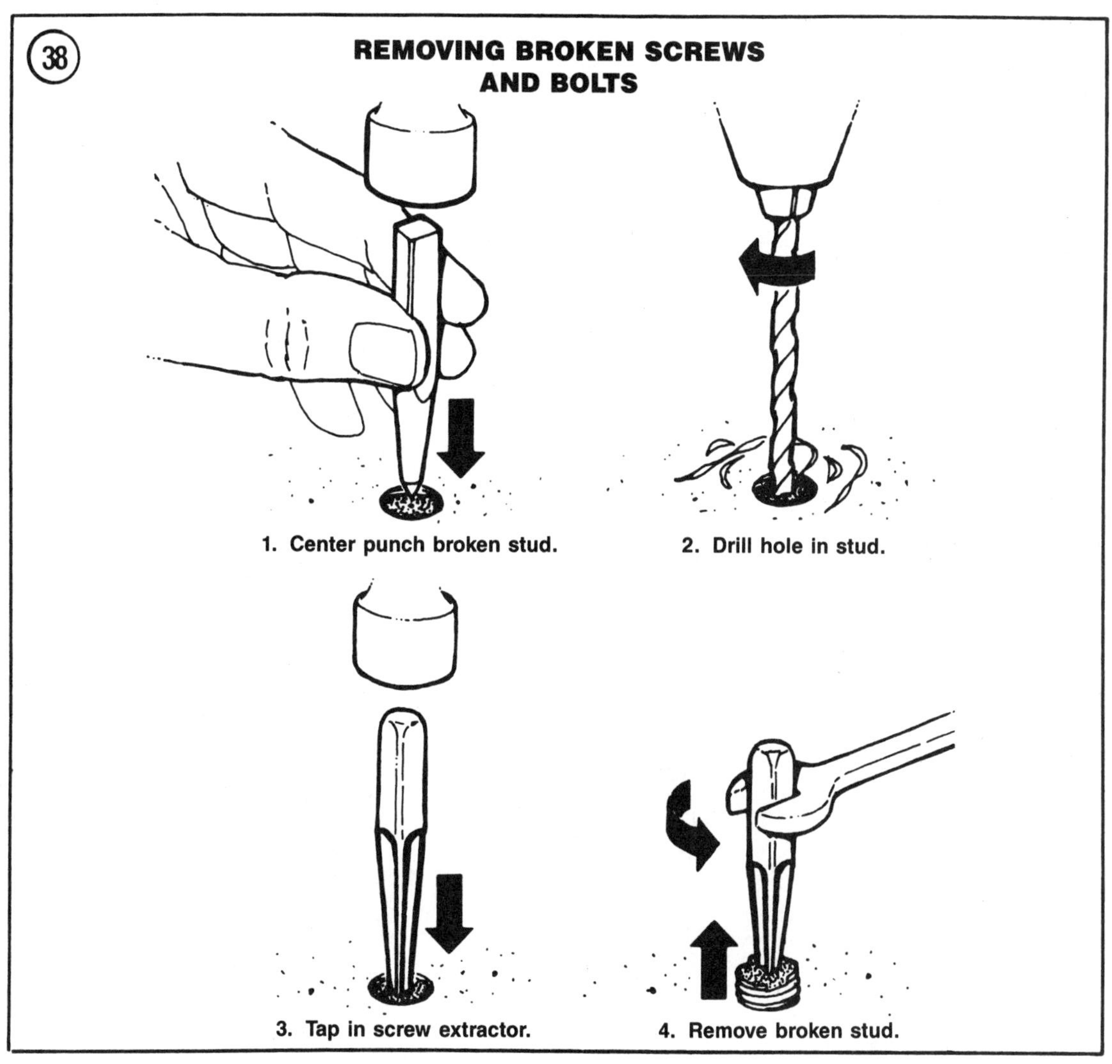
38
REMOVING BROKEN SCREWS AND BOLTS
1. Center punch broken stud.
2. Drill hole in stud.
3. Tap in screw extractor.
4. Remove broken stud.

Tables are on the following pages.

Table 1 ENGINE AND CHASSIS NUMBERS

Model number and year	Engine/frame serial No. start to end
YZ50G (1980)	3R0-000101-on
YZ60H (1981)	4V0-000101-on
YZ60J (1982)	5X1-000101-on
YZ80E (1978)	2J5-000101-on
YZ80F (1979)	2X6-000101-on
YZ80G (1980)	3R1-000101-on
YZ80H (1981)	4V1-000101-on
YZ80J (1982)	5X2-000101-on
YZ80K (1983)	22W-000101-on
YZ80L (1984)	39K-000101-on
YZ80N (1985)	58T-000101-on
YZ80S (1986)	1LR-000101-on
YZ80T (1987)	2HF-000101-on
YZ80U (1988)	2VE-000101—2VE-023100
YZ80W (1989)	3MK-000101-on
YZ80A (1990)	2VE-023101-on

Table 2 DECIMAL AND METRIC EQUIVALENTS

Fractions	Decimal in.	Metric mm	Fractions	Decimal in.	Metric mm
1/64	0.015625	0.39688	33/64	0.515625	13.09687
1/32	0.03125	0.79375	17/32	0.53125	13.49375
3/64	0.046875	1.19062	35/64	0.546875	13.89062
1/16	0.0625	1.58750	9/16	0.5625	14.28750
5/64	0.078125	1.98437	37/64	0.578125	14.68437
3/32	0.09375	2.38125	19/32	0.59375	15.08125
7/64	0.109375	2.77812	39/64	0.609375	15.47812
1/8	0.125	3.1750	5/8	0.625	15.87500
9/64	0.140625	3.57187	41/64	0.640625	16.27187
5/32	0.15625	3.96875	21/32	0.65625	16.66875
11/64	0.171875	4.36562	43/64	0.671875	17.06562
3/16	0.1875	4.76250	11/16	0.6875	17.46250
13/64	0.203125	5.15937	45/64	0.703125	17.85937
7/32	0.21875	5.55625	23/32	0.71875	18.25625
15/64	0.234375	5.95312	47/64	0.734375	18.65312
1/4	0.250	6.35000	3/4	0.750	19.05000
17/64	0.265625	6.74687	49/64	0.765625	19.44687
9/32	0.28125	7.14375	25/32	0.78125	19.84375
19/64	0.296875	7.54062	51/64	0.796875	20.24062
5/16	0.3125	7.93750	13/16	0.8125	20.63750
21/64	0.328125	8.33437	53/64	0.828125	21.03437
11/32	0.34375	8.73125	27/32	0.84375	21.43125
23/64	0.359375	9.12812	55/64	0.859375	21.82812
3/8	0.375	9.52500	7/8	0.875	22.22500
25/64	0.390625	9.92187	57/64	0.890625	22.62187
13/32	0.40625	10.31875	29/32	0.90625	23.01875
27/64	0.421875	10.71562	59/64	0.921875	23.41562
7/16	0.4375	11.11250	15/16	0.9375	23.81250
29/64	0.453125	11.50937	61/64	0.953125	24.20937
15/32	0.46875	11.90625	31/32	0.96875	24.60625
31/64	0.484375	12.30312	63/64	0.984375	25.00312
1/2	0.500	12.70000	1	1.00	25.40000

Table 3 GENERAL TORQUE SPECIFICATIONS*

Thread size	N•m	ft.-lb.
Bolt		
6 mm	6	4.5
8 mm	15	11
10 mm	30	22
12 mm	55	40
14 mm	85	61
16 mm	130	94
Nut		
10 mm	6	4.5
12 mm	15	11
14 mm	30	22
17 mm	55	40
19 mm	85	61
22 mm	130	94

* Use these torque figures for all fasteners not individually listed.

CHAPTER TWO

TROUBLESHOOTING

Diagnosing mechanical problems is relatively simple if you use orderly procedures and keep a few basic principles in mind.

The troubleshooting procedures in this chapter analyze typical symptoms and show logical methods of isolating causes. These are not the only methods. There may be several ways to solve a problem, but only a systematic approach can guarantee success.

Never assume anything. Do not overlook the obvious. If you are riding along and the bike suddenly quits, check the easiest, most accessible problem spots first. Is there gasoline in the tank? Is the fuel shutoff valve in the ON position? Has the spark plug wire fallen off?

If nothing obvious turns up in a quick check, look a little further. Learning to recognize and describe symptoms will make repairs easier for you or a mechanic at the shop. Describe problems accurately and fully. Saying that "it won't run" isn't the same thing as saying "it quit climbing a hill and won't start," or that "it sat in my garage for 3 months and then wouldn't start."

Gather as many symptoms as possible to aid in diagnosis. Note whether the engine lost power gradually or all at once, what color smoke came from the exhaust and so on. Remember that the more complicated a machine is, the easier it is to troubleshoot because symptoms point to specific problems.

After the symptoms are defined, areas which could cause problems are tested and analyzed. Guessing at the cause of a problem may provide the solution, but it can easily lead to frustration, wasted time and a series of expensive, unnecessary parts replacements.

You do not need fancy equipment or complicated test gear to determine whether repairs can be attempted at home. A few simple checks could save a large repair bill and lost time while the bike sits in a dealer's service department. On the other hand, be realistic and do not attempt repairs beyond your abilities. Service departments tend to charge heavily for putting together a disassembled engine that may have been abused. Some won't even take on such a job—so use common sense, don't get in over your head.

OPERATING REQUIREMENTS

An engine needs 3 basics to run properly: correct fuel/air mixture, compression and a spark at the right time (**Figure 1**). If one basic requirement is missing, the engine will not run. Two-stroke engine operating principles are described in Chapter Four under *Engine Principles*. The ignition system is the weakest link of the 3 basics. More problems result from ignition breakdowns than from any other source. Keep that in mind before you begin tampering with carburetor adjustments and the like.

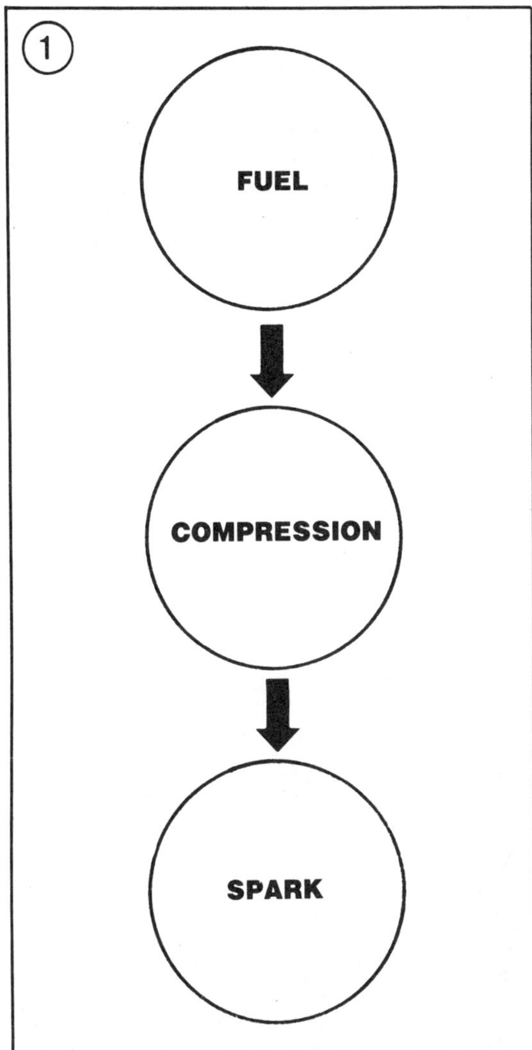

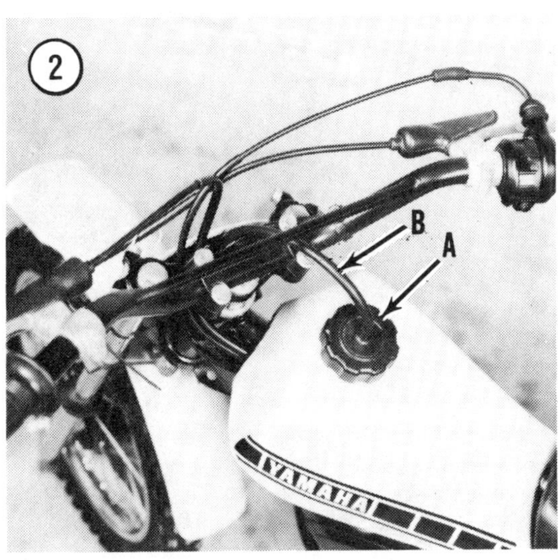

If a bike has been sitting for any length of time and refuses to start, check and clean the spark plug and then look to the gasoline delivery system. This includes the tank, fuel shutoff valve and fuel line to the carburetor. Gasoline tends to lose its fire-power after standing for long periods. Condensation may contaminate it with water. Drain the gas and try starting with a fresh tankful.

TROUBLESHOOTING INSTRUMENTS

Chapter One lists the instruments needed and detailed instruction on their use.

STARTING THE ENGINE

When your engine refuses to start, frustration can cause you to forget basic starting principles and procedures. The following outline will guide you through basic starting procedures.

Starting a Cold Engine

1. Shift the transmission into NEUTRAL.
2. Apply the front brake and rock the bike back and forth. This will help to mix the fuel in the tank.
3. Turn the fuel valve to ON.
4. Pull the choke lever OUT.
5. With the throttle completely *closed*, kick the engine over.
6. When the engine starts, work the throttle slightly to keep it running. Push the choke lever IN as required.
7. Idle the engine approximately for a minute or until the throttle responds cleanly and the choke is pushed all the way IN.

Starting a Warm or Hot Engine

1. Shift the transmission into NEUTRAL.
2. Turn the fuel valve to ON.
3. Push the choke lever IN.
4. Open the throttle slightly and kick the engine over.

STARTING DIFFICULTIES

When the bike is difficult to start, or won't start at all, it does not help to kick away at the kick starter. Check for obvious problems even before getting out your tools. Go down the following list step-by-step. Do each one. If the bike still will not start, refer to the appropriate troubleshooting procedures which follow in this chapter.

1. Is there fuel in the tank? Remove the filler cap (A, **Figure 2**) and rock the vehicle. Listen for fuel sloshing around.

WARNING
Do not use an open flame to check in the tank. A serious explosion is certain to result.

2. If there is fuel in the tank, pull off a fuel line at the carburetor. Turn the fuel valve (**Figure 3**) to RES and see if fuel flows freely. If none comes out and there is a fuel filter installed in the fuel line, remove the filter and turn the fuel valve to RES again. If fuel flows, the filter is clogged and should be replaced. If no fuel comes out, the fuel valve may be shut off, blocked by foreign matter, or the fuel cap vent (B, **Figure 2**) may be plugged. If the carburetor is getting usable fuel, turn to the electrical system next.
3. Make sure the kill switch button is not stuck or working improperly or that the wire is not broken and shorting out. See **Figure 4** or **Figure 5**.

NOTE
*If the bike does not start after a spill, check that the kill switch housing was not damaged. This problem is more common on models that have the kill switch installed on the left-hand side (**Figure 5**). After a spill, the clutch lever housing may have hit against the kill switch housing and caused the kill switch to short to ground.*

4. Is the spark plug wire on tight (**Figure 6**)? Push it on and slightly rotate it to clean the electrical connection between the plug and the connector.
5. Is the choke (**Figure 7**) in the right position? The knob should be pulled OUT for a cold engine and pushed IN for a warm engine.

ENGINE STARTING

An engine that refuses to start or is difficult to start is very frustrating. More often than not, the problem is very minor and can be found with a simple and logical troubleshooting approach.

The following items show a beginning point from which to isolate engine starting problems.

Engine Fails to Start

Perform the following spark test to determine if the ignition system is operating properly.

CAUTION
Before removing the spark plug in Step 1, clean all dirt and debris from the plug base. This is more of a problem on air-cooled engines as dirt is easily trapped by the cylinder head fins. Dirt that falls into the cylinder will cause rapid piston, piston ring and cylinder wear.

CLYMER RACE TIP
If you are checking the spark plug at the track, more than likely there is dirt underneath the fuel tank. When the spark plug is removed, dirt could fall from the tank and into the cylinder. If you do not have time to remove the fuel tank, wrap a large clean cloth around the fuel tank. Then remove the spark plug and check or replace it as required. Remove the cloth after reinstalling the spark plug.

1. Remove the spark plug.
2. Connect the spark plug wire and connector to the spark plug and touch the spark plug base to the

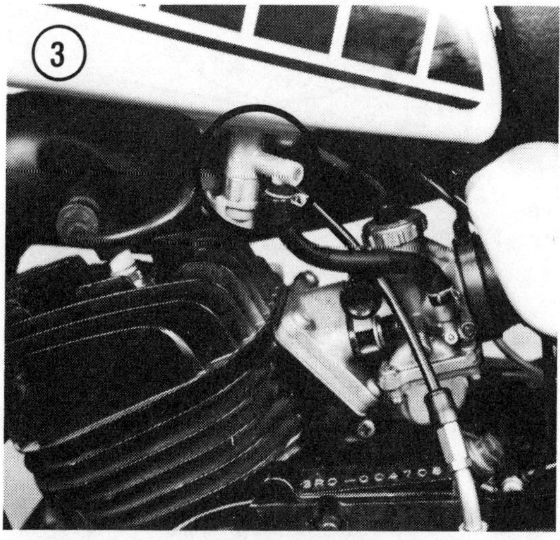

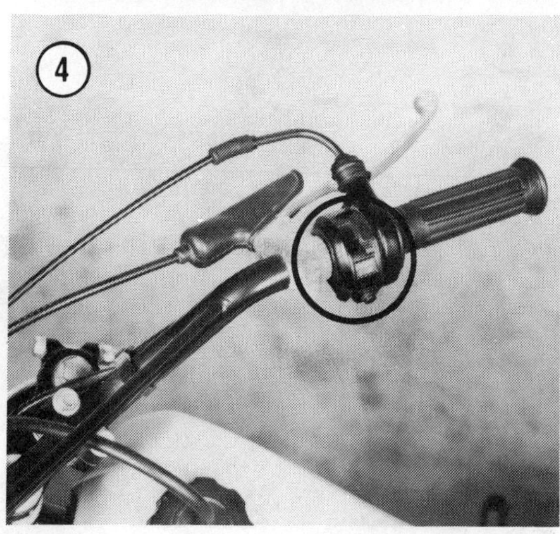

cylinder head to ground it (**Figure 8**). Position the spark plug so you can see the electrode.

3. Crank the engine over with the kickstarter. A fat blue spark should be evident across the spark plug electrode.

WARNING
Do not hold the spark plug, wire or connector or a serious electrical shock may result.

4. If the spark is good, check for one or more of the following possible malfunctions:
   a. Obstructed fuel line or fuel filter.
   b. Leaking head or cylinder base gasket.

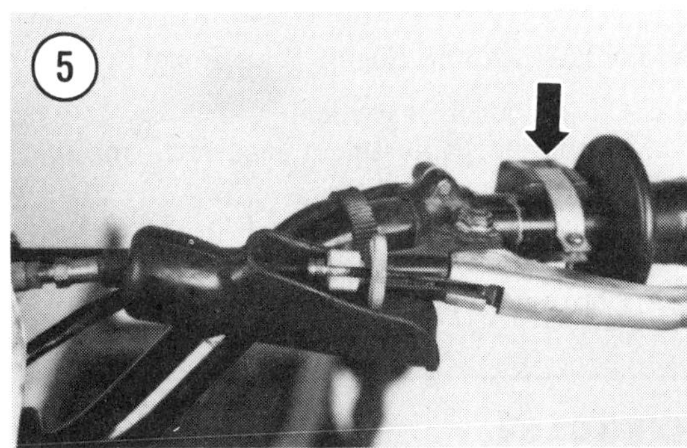

5. If spark is not good, check for one or more of the following:
   a. Weak ignition coil.
   b. Weak CDI unit (YZ60 and YZ80).
   c. Loose electrical connections.
   d. Dirty electrical connections.
   e. Loose or broken ignition coil ground wire.
   f. Incorrect contact breaker point gap (YZ50).

2

Engine is Difficult to Start

Check for one or more of the following possible malfunctions:
   a. Fouled spark plug.
   b. Improperly operating choke.
   c. Contaminated fuel system.
   d. Improperly adjusted carburetor.
   e. Loose electrical connections.
   f. Dirty electrical connections.
   g. Weak CDI unit (YZ60 and YZ80).
   h. Incorrect contact breaker point gap (YZ50).
   i. Weak ignition coil.
   j. Poor compression.

Engine Will Not Crank

If the engine will not crank because of a mechanical problem, check for one or more of the following possible malfunctions.
   a. Defective kickstarter and/or gear.
   b. Seized piston.
   c. Seized crankshaft bearings.
   d. Broken connecting rod.

ENGINE PERFORMANCE

In the following check list, it is assumed that the engine runs, but is not operating at peak performance. This will serve as a starting point from which to isolate a performance malfunction.

The possible causes for each malfunction are listed in a logical sequence and in order of probability.

Engine Will Not Idle

a. Carburetor incorrectly adjusted.
b. Pilot jet clogged.
c. Obstructed fuel line or fuel shutoff valve.
d. Fouled or improperly gapped spark plug.
e. Head gasket leaking.

Engine Misses at High Speed

a. Fouled or improperly gapped spark plug.
b. Improper carburetor main jet selection.
c. Carburetor main jet and/or needle jet clogged.
d. Obstructed fuel line or fuel shutoff valve.
e. Ignition timing incorrect.

Engine Overheating

a. Incorrect carburetor jetting or fuel/oil ratio mixture.
b. Incorrect ignition timing (YZ50).
c. Ignition timing incorrect due to improper timing or defective ignition component(s) (YZ60 and YZ80).
d. Improper spark plug heat range.
e. Intake system or crankcase air leak.
f. Water cooling system inoperative (water-cooled system).
g. Damaged or blocked cooling fins (air-cooled system).
h. Dragging brake(s).

Smoky Exhaust and Engine Runs Roughly

a. Clogged air filter element.
b. Carburetor adjustment incorrect—mixture too rich.
c. Carburetor float damaged or incorrectly adjusted.
d. Choke not operating correctly.

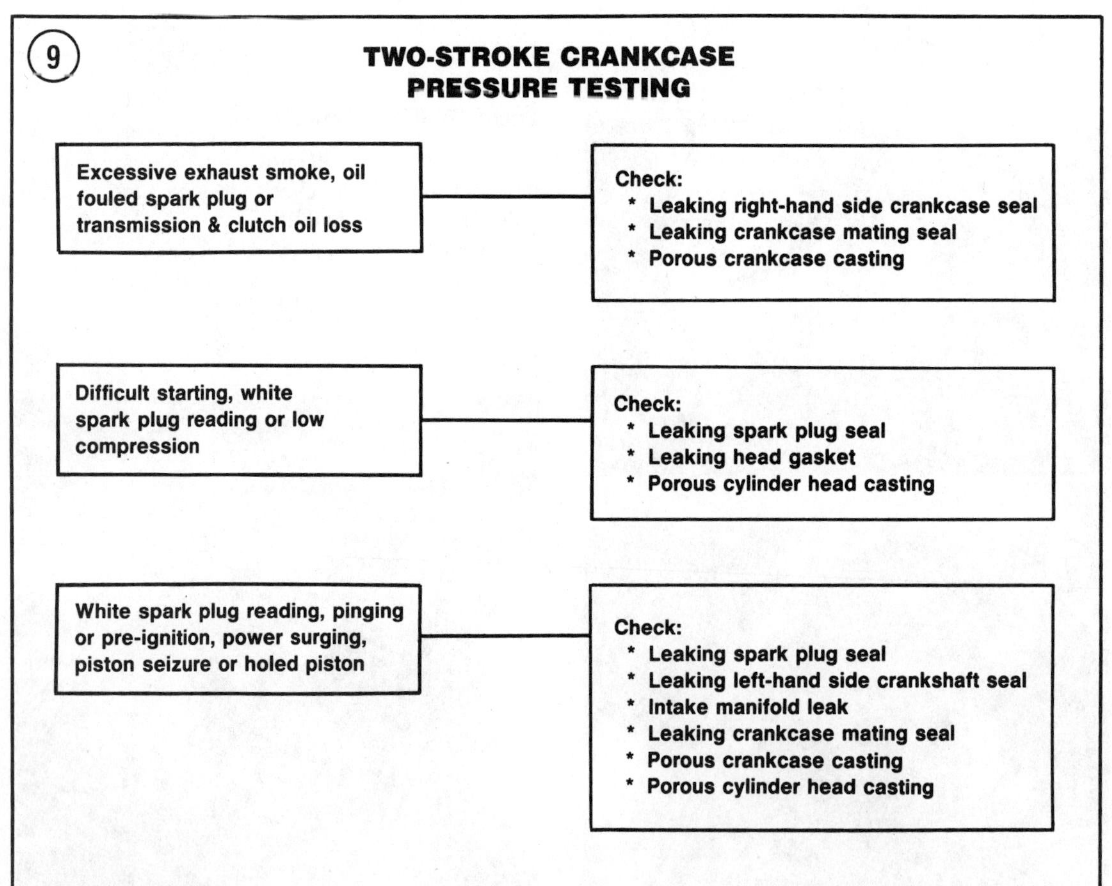

9
TWO-STROKE CRANKCASE PRESSURE TESTING
Excessive exhaust smoke, oil fouled spark plug or transmission & clutch oil loss
Check:
* Leaking right-hand side crankcase seal
* Leaking crankcase mating seal
* Porous crankcase casting
Difficult starting, white spark plug reading or low compression
Check:
* Leaking spark plug seal
* Leaking head gasket
* Porous cylinder head casting
White spark plug reading, pinging or pre-ignition, power surging, piston seizure or holed piston
Check:
* Leaking spark plug seal
* Leaking left-hand side crankshaft seal
* Intake manifold leak
* Leaking crankcase mating seal
* Porous crankcase casting
* Porous cylinder head casting

e. Water or other contaminants in fuel.
f. Clogged fuel line.
g. Excessive cylinder clearance.

Engine Loses Power

a. Carburetor incorrectly adjusted.
b. Engine overheating.
c. Ignition timing incorrect due to improper timing or defective ignition component(s).
d. Incorrectly gapped spark plug.
e. Obstructed muffler.
f. Dragging brake(s).

Engine Lacks Acceleration

a. Carburetor adjustment incorrect.
b. Clogged fuel line.
c. Ignition timing incorrect due to improper timing or faulty ignition component(s).
d. Dragging brake(s).

ENGINE NOISES

1. *Knocking or pinging during acceleration—* Caused by using a lower octane fuel than recommended. May also be caused by poor fuel available at some "discount" gasoline stations. Pinging can also be caused by a spark plug of the wrong heat range and incorrect carburetor jetting. Refer to *Correct Spark Plug Heat Range* in Chapter Three.
2. *Slapping or rattling noises at low speed or during acceleration—* May be caused by piston slap, i.e., excessive piston-cylinder wall clearance.
3. *Knocking or rapping while decelerating—* Usually caused by excessive rod bearing clearance.
4. *Persistent knocking and vibration—* Usually caused by worn main bearings.
5. *Rapid on-off squeal—* Compression leak around cylinder head gasket or spark plug.

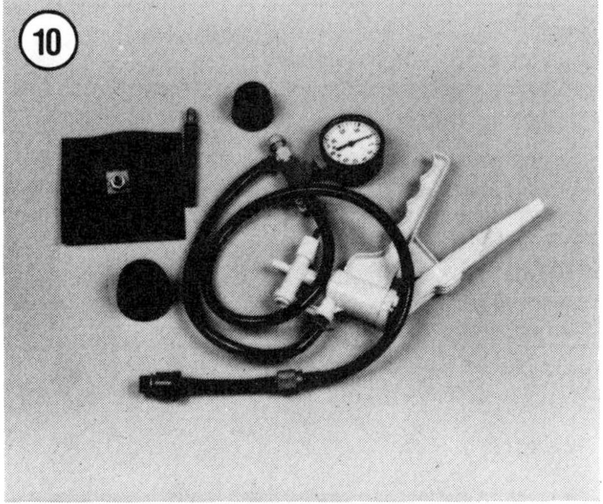

EXCESSIVE VIBRATION

Usually this is caused by loose engine or suspension mounting hardware. If not, it can be difficult to find without disassembling the engine.

TWO-STROKE PRESSURE TESTING

Many owners of 2-stroke bikes are plagued by hard starting and generally poor running, for which there seems to be no cause. Carburetion and ignition may be good, and compression tests may show that all is well in the engine's upper end.

What a compression test does not show is lack of primary compression. The crankcase in a 2-stroke engine must be alternately under pressure and vacuum. After the piston closes the intake port, further downward movement of the piston causes the entrapped mixture to be pressurized so that it can rush quickly into the cylinder when the scavenging ports are opened. Upward piston movement creates a slight vacuum in the crankcase, enabling the fuel/air mixture to be drawn in from the carburetor.

NOTE
*The operational sequence of a two-stroke engine is illustrated in **Chapter Four** under **Engine Principles**.*

If crankcase seals or cylinder gaskets leak, the crankcase cannot hold pressure or vacuum, and proper engine operation becomes impossible. Any other source of leakage such as a defective cylinder base gasket or porous or cracked crankcase castings will result in the same conditions. See **Figure 9**.

It is possible, however, to test for and isolate engine pressure leaks. The test is simple but requires special equipment. A typical two-stroke pressure test kit is shown in **Figure 10**. Briefly, what is done is to seal off all natural engine openings, then apply air pressure. If the engine does not hold air, a leak or leaks is indicated. Then it is only necessary to locate and repair all leaks.

The following procedure describes a typical pressure test.

1. Remove the carburetor.

NOTE
Do not remove the intake manifold. The manifold should remain on the engine during this test as it may be causing the leak.

2. Use a rubber plug and insert it tightly in the intake manifold.
3. Remove the exhaust pipe and block off the exhaust port, using suitable adapters and fittings.
4. Remove the spark plug and install the pressure gauge adaptor into the spark plug hole. Connect the pressurizing lever and gauge to the pressure fitting installed in the spark plug hole. Squeeze the lever until the gauge indicates approximately 6-8 psi.

CAUTION
Do not apply more than 8 psi. or the crankcase seals may be damaged.

5. Observe the pressure gauge. If the engine is in good condition, the pressure should hold for 3-5 minutes. If the pressure starts to immediately drop, there is a leak.

Before condemning the engine, first be sure that there are no leaks in the test equipment or sealing plugs. If the equipment shows no signs of leakage, go over the entire engine carefully. Large leaks can be heard; smaller ones can be found by going over every possible leakage source with a small brush and soap suds solution. Possible leakage points are listed in the following:

a. Crankshaft seals.
b. Spark plug.
c. Cylinder head joint.
d. Cylinder base joint.
e. Carburetor base joint.
f. Crankcase joint.
g. Porous crankcase, cylinder or cylinder head casting.

NOTE
To check the left-hand and right-hand crankcase seals, the clutch and magneto assemblies must be removed. Refer to Chapter Six and Chapter Nine for details.

CLUTCH

The three basic clutch troubles are:
a. Clutch noise.
b. Clutch slipping.
c. Improper clutch disengagement.

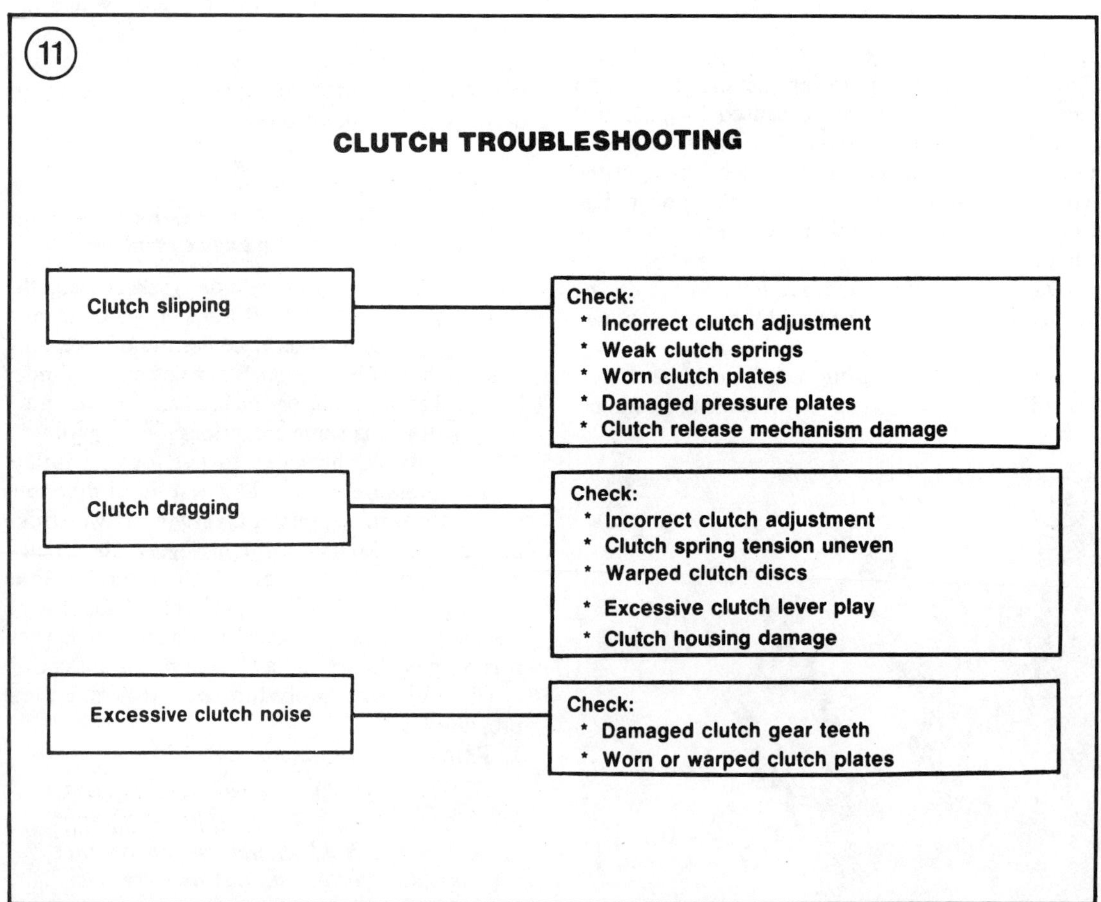

11
CLUTCH TROUBLESHOOTING
Clutch slipping
Check:
* Incorrect clutch adjustment
* Weak clutch springs
* Worn clutch plates
* Damaged pressure plates
* Clutch release mechanism damage
Clutch dragging
Check:
* Incorrect clutch adjustment
* Clutch spring tension uneven
* Warped clutch discs
* Excessive clutch lever play
* Clutch housing damage
Excessive clutch noise
Check:
* Damaged clutch gear teeth
* Worn or warped clutch plates

All clutch troubles, except adjustments, require partial engine disassembly to identify and cure the problem. Refer to Chapter Six for procedures.

The troubleshooting procedures outlined in **Figure 11** will help you solve the majority of clutch troubles in a systematic manner.

TRANSMISSION

The basic transmission troubles are:

a. Excessive gear noise.
b. Difficult shifting.
c. Gears pop out of mesh.
d. Incorrect shift lever operation.

Transmission symptoms are sometimes hard to distinguish from clutch symptoms. Be sure that the clutch is not causing the trouble before working on the transmission.

The troubleshooting procedures outlined in **Figure 12** will help you solve the majority of transmission troubles.

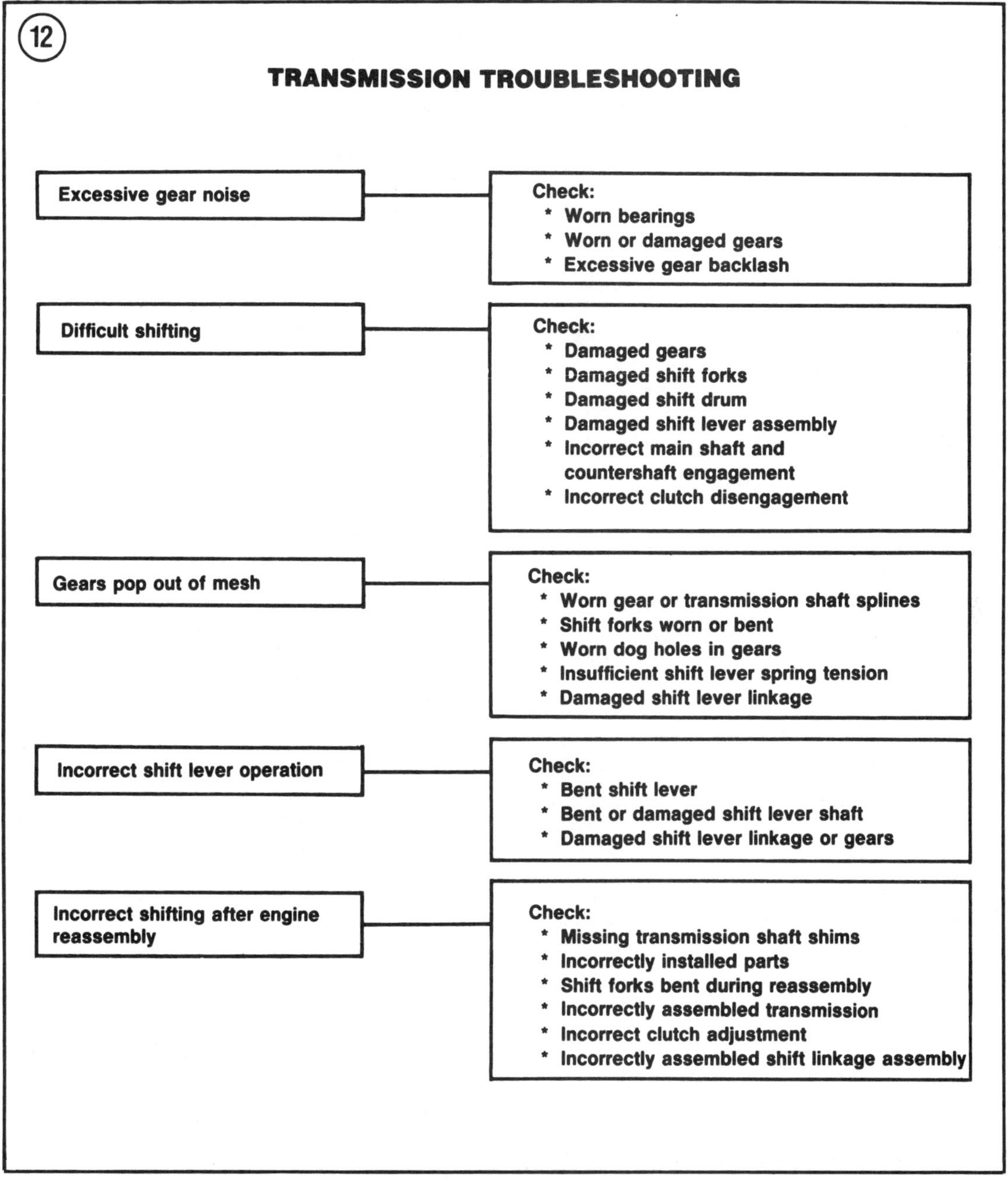

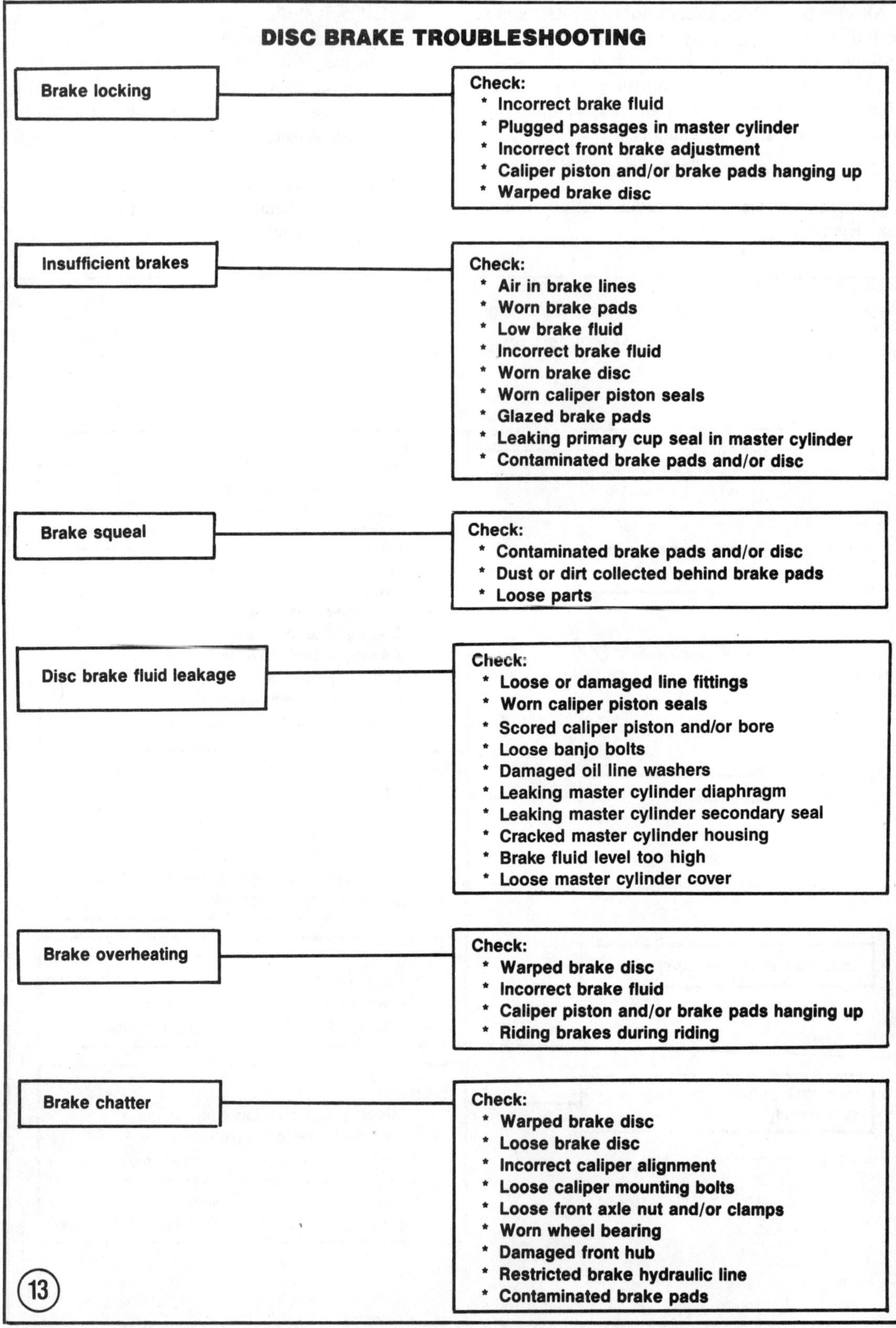
DISC BRAKE TROUBLESHOOTING
Brake locking
Check:
* Incorrect brake fluid
* Plugged passages in master cylinder
* Incorrect front brake adjustment
* Caliper piston and/or brake pads hanging up
* Warped brake disc
Insufficient brakes
Check:
* Air in brake lines
* Worn brake pads
* Low brake fluid
* Incorrect brake fluid
* Worn brake disc
* Worn caliper piston seals
* Glazed brake pads
* Leaking primary cup seal in master cylinder
* Contaminated brake pads and/or disc
Brake squeal
Check:
* Contaminated brake pads and/or disc
* Dust or dirt collected behind brake pads
* Loose parts
Disc brake fluid leakage
Check:
* Loose or damaged line fittings
* Worn caliper piston seals
* Scored caliper piston and/or bore
* Loose banjo bolts
* Damaged oil line washers
* Leaking master cylinder diaphragm
* Leaking master cylinder secondary seal
* Cracked master cylinder housing
* Brake fluid level too high
* Loose master cylinder cover
Brake overheating
Check:
* Warped brake disc
* Incorrect brake fluid
* Caliper piston and/or brake pads hanging up
* Riding brakes during riding
Brake chatter
Check:
* Warped brake disc
* Loose brake disc
* Incorrect caliper alignment
* Loose caliper mounting bolts
* Loose front axle nut and/or clamps
* Worn wheel bearing
* Damaged front hub
* Restricted brake hydraulic line
* Contaminated brake pads
13

BRAKES

Front Disc Brake (1986-on YZ80)

The front disc brake is critical to riding performance and safety. It should inspected frequently and any problems located and repaired immediately. When replacing or refilling the brake fluid, use only DOT 3 or DOT 4 brake fluid from a closed and sealed container. See Chapter Thirteen for additional information on brake fluid and disc brake service. The troubleshooting procedures in **Figure 13** will help you isolate the majority of front disc brake troubles.

Drum Brakes (1978-1985)

The front and rear drum brakes are relatively simple in design and operation. YZ brakes have always been one of the better brake units installed on production motocrossers. Yet, many riders do not get full stopping power because the shoes and drum are covered with residue. This residue buildup is due mainly from lack of maintenance. To work properly, the drum brakes must be cleaned and serviced weekly. Periodic maintenance will also allow inspection of parts so that they can be replaced before a part fails.

Refer to the troubleshooting chart in **Figure 14** for drum brake problems and checks to make.

FRONT SUSPENSION AND STEERING

Poor handling may be caused by improper front or rear tire pressure, a damaged or bent frame or front steering components, worn swing arm bushings, worn wheel bearings or dragging brakes.

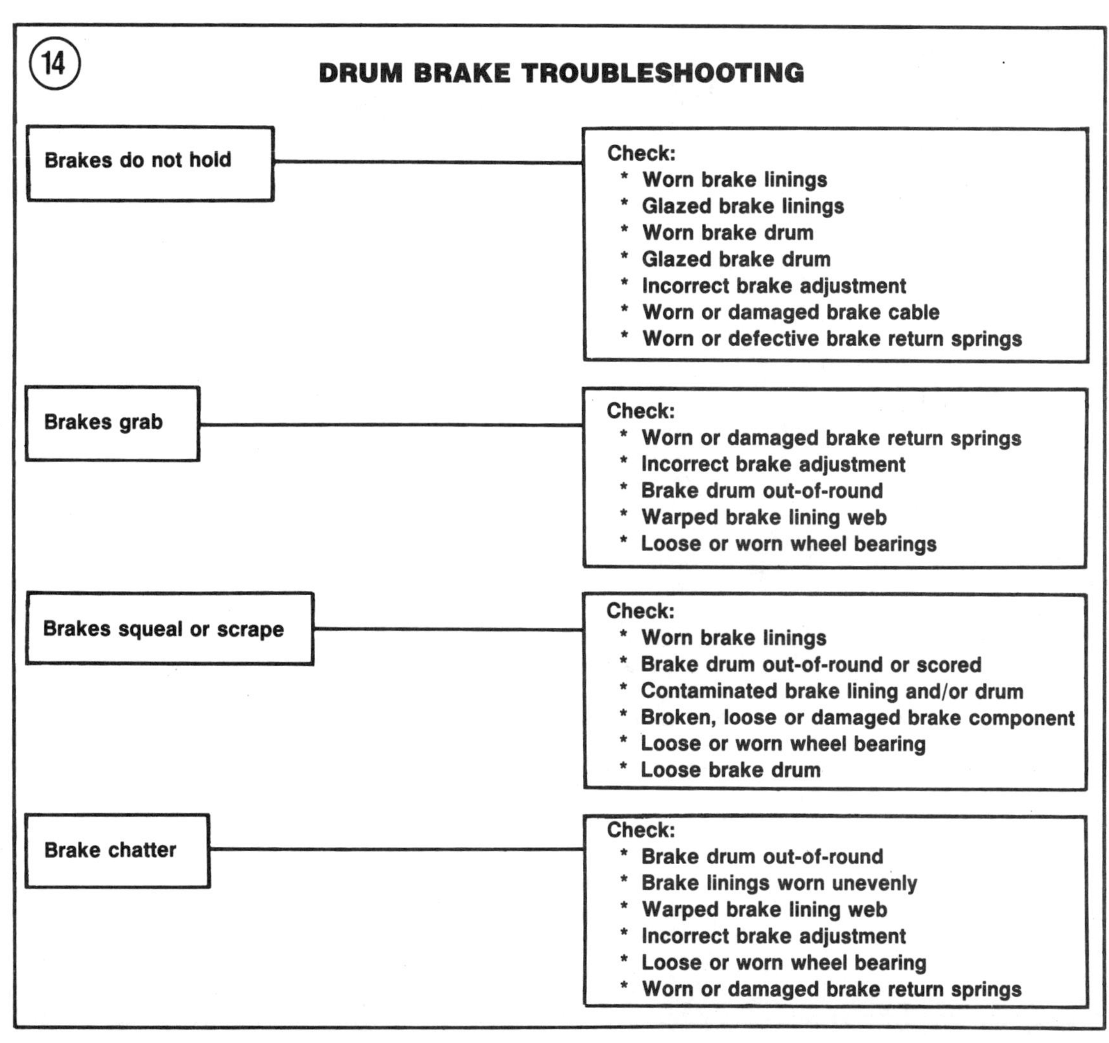

14
DRUM BRAKE TROUBLESHOOTING
Brakes do not hold
Check:
* Worn brake linings
* Glazed brake linings
* Worn brake drum
* Glazed brake drum
* Incorrect brake adjustment
* Worn or damaged brake cable
* Worn or defective brake return springs
Brakes grab
Check:
* Worn or damaged brake return springs
* Incorrect brake adjustment
* Brake drum out-of-round
* Warped brake lining web
* Loose or worn wheel bearings
Brakes squeal or scrape
Check:
* Worn brake linings
* Brake drum out-of-round or scored
* Contaminated brake lining and/or drum
* Broken, loose or damaged brake component
* Loose or worn wheel bearing
* Loose brake drum
Brake chatter
Check:
* Brake drum out-of-round
* Brake linings worn unevenly
* Warped brake lining web
* Incorrect brake adjustment
* Loose or worn wheel bearing
* Worn or damaged brake return springs

MAGNETO ASSEMBLY (OUTER ROTOR) MODEL YZ50

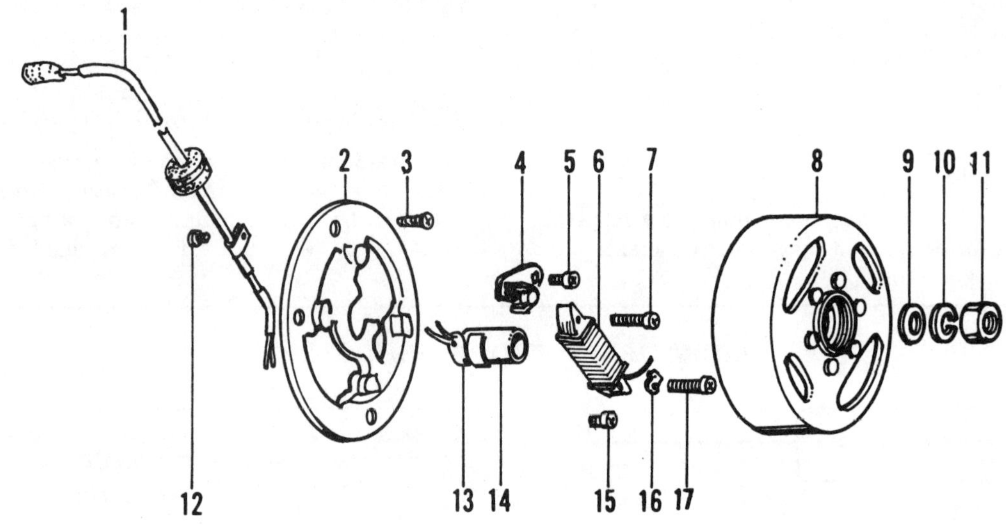

1. Electrical wire harness
2. Stator plate
3. Screw
4. Contact breaker point assembly
5. Phillips head screw
6. Source coil
7. Bolt
8. Rotor
9. Washer
10. Lockwasher
11. Nut
12. Clamp screw
13. Condenser clamp
14. Condenser
15. Screw
16. Timing plate
17. Screw

IGNITION SYSTEM (YZ50)

The YZ50 is equipped with a magneto ignition system. See **Figure 15** and **Figure 16**. The YZ50 magneto ignition system consists of the following components:

a. Magneto rotor.
b. Source coil.
c. Capacitor.
d. Contact breaker point assembly.
e. Engine stop switch.
f. Ignition coil (primary and secondary coil windings).
g. Contact point cam (magneto).

As the magneto rotor rotates, magnets located within it move past a stationary source coil in the stator, inducing a current in the coil. A contact breaker assembly controlled by a cam attached to the magneto rotor opens at the precise instant the piston reaches its firing position. The electrical energy produced in the source coil is then discharged to the primary side of the high-voltage ignition coil where it is increased, or stepped up, to a high enough voltage to jump the gap between the spark plug electrodes.

If you are experiencing a no spark or weak spark situation with your YZ50, check the following:

a. Point gap (Chapter Three).
b. Ignition timing (Chapter Three).
c. Breaker point contact surfaces (Chapter Three).
d. Source coil resistance (Chapter Nine).
e. Ignition coil primary resistance (Chapter Nine).
f. Ignition coil secondary resistance (Chapter Nine).
g. Kill switch for proper operation (Chapter Nine).

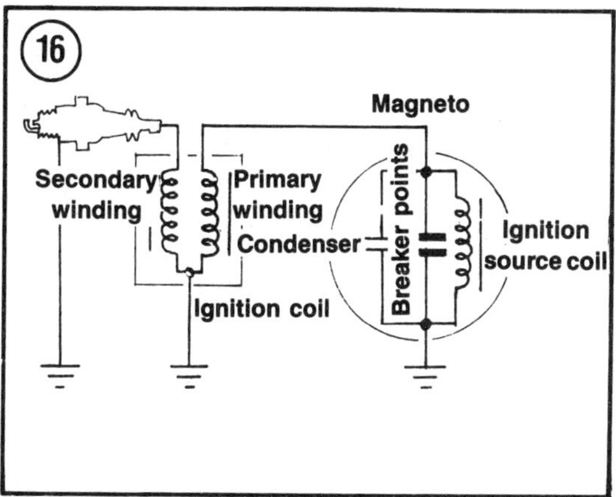

While the magneto ignition system is very simple in design, it is equipped with moving parts that wear during operation. Make sure to replace contact breaker points when worn. Also, make sure to keep the point contact area free of dirt and water. Always install the magneto cover with a gasket. Consider the following when troubleshooting the breaker points:

a. Low speed regular miss is normally caused by a bad condenser.
b. High speed regular miss is normally caused by a problem with the contact points.
c. Pitted points are caused by a condenser of the incorrect capacity. If you own a used YZ50, an incorrect condenser may have been installed by the previous owner.

IGNITION SYSTEM (YZ60 AND YZ80)

These models are equipped with a capacitor discharge ignition (CDI) system. This solid state system uses no contact breaker points or other moving parts. Because of the solid state design, problems with the capacitor discharge system are relatively few. However, when problems arise they typically have one of the following symptoms:

a. Weak spark.
b. No spark.

It is possible to check CDI systems that:

a. Do not spark.
b. Have broken or damaged wires.
c. Have a weak spark.

It is difficult to check CDI systems that malfunction due to:

a. Vibration problems.
b. Components that malfunction only when the engine is hot or under a load.

The troubleshooting procedures in **Figure 17** will help you isolate the ignition problem fast. When troubleshooting the ignition system, consider the following:

1. Disconnect the kill switch or kill button and see if the problem still exists.
2. Make sure that the stator plate screws are tight. If the screws are loose, recheck the ignition timing as described in Chapter Three.
3. Remove the fuel tank and untape all electrical connectors. Make sure the connectors are connected properly. If necessary, clean the connectors with aerosol electrical contact cleaner.
4. Check the left- and right-hand crankshaft bearings for excessive play. Remove the magneto rotor as described in Chapter Nine. Grab the end

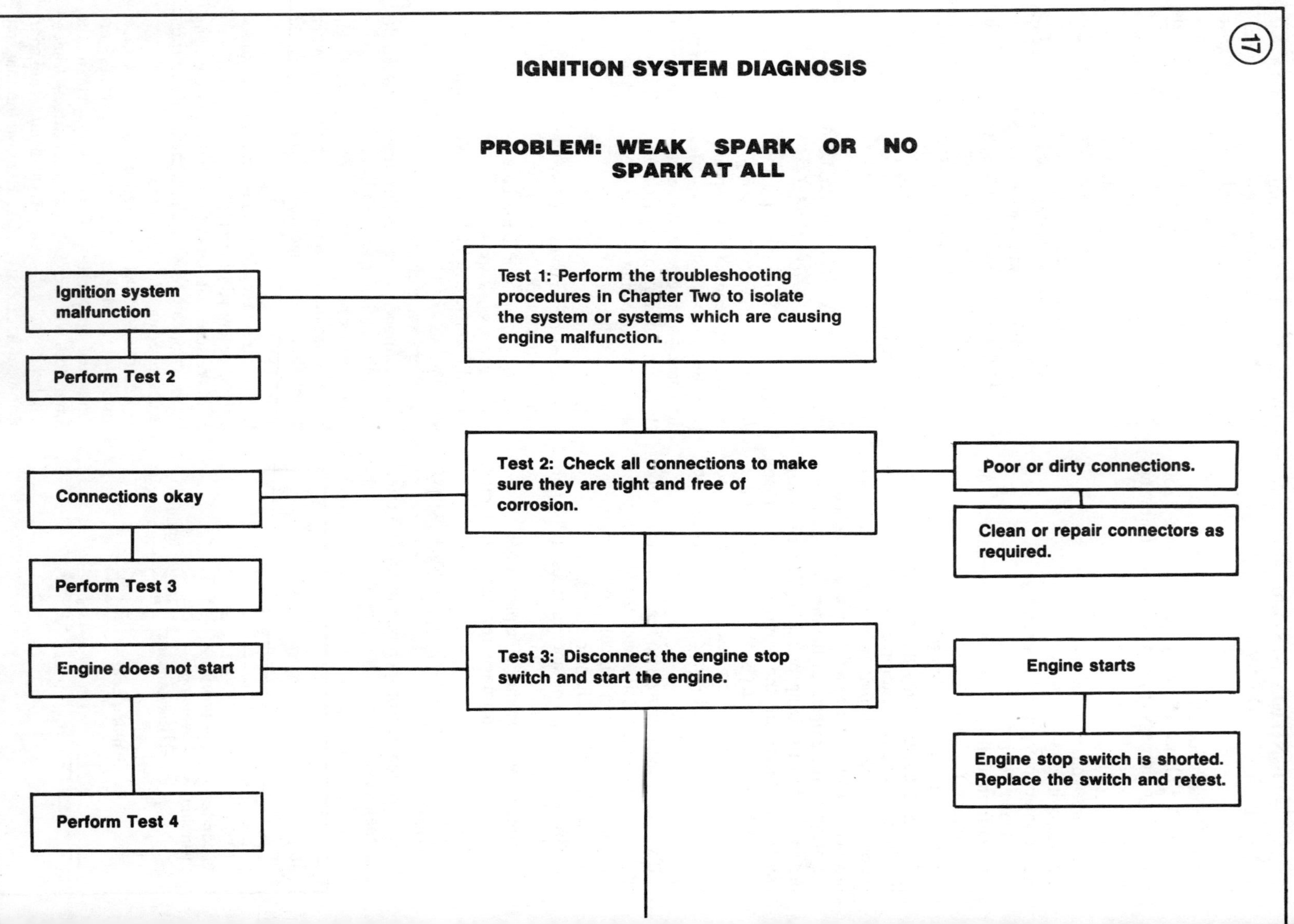
17
IGNITION SYSTEM DIAGNOSIS
PROBLEM: WEAK SPARK OR NO SPARK AT ALL
Test 1: Perform the troubleshooting procedures in Chapter Two to isolate the system or systems which are causing engine malfunction.
Ignition system malfunction
Perform Test 2
Test 2: Check all connections to make sure they are tight and free of corrosion.
Poor or dirty connections.
Clean or repair connectors as required.
Connections okay
Perform Test 3
Test 3: Disconnect the engine stop switch and start the engine.
Engine starts
Engine stop switch is shorted. Replace the switch and retest.
Engine does not start
Perform Test 4

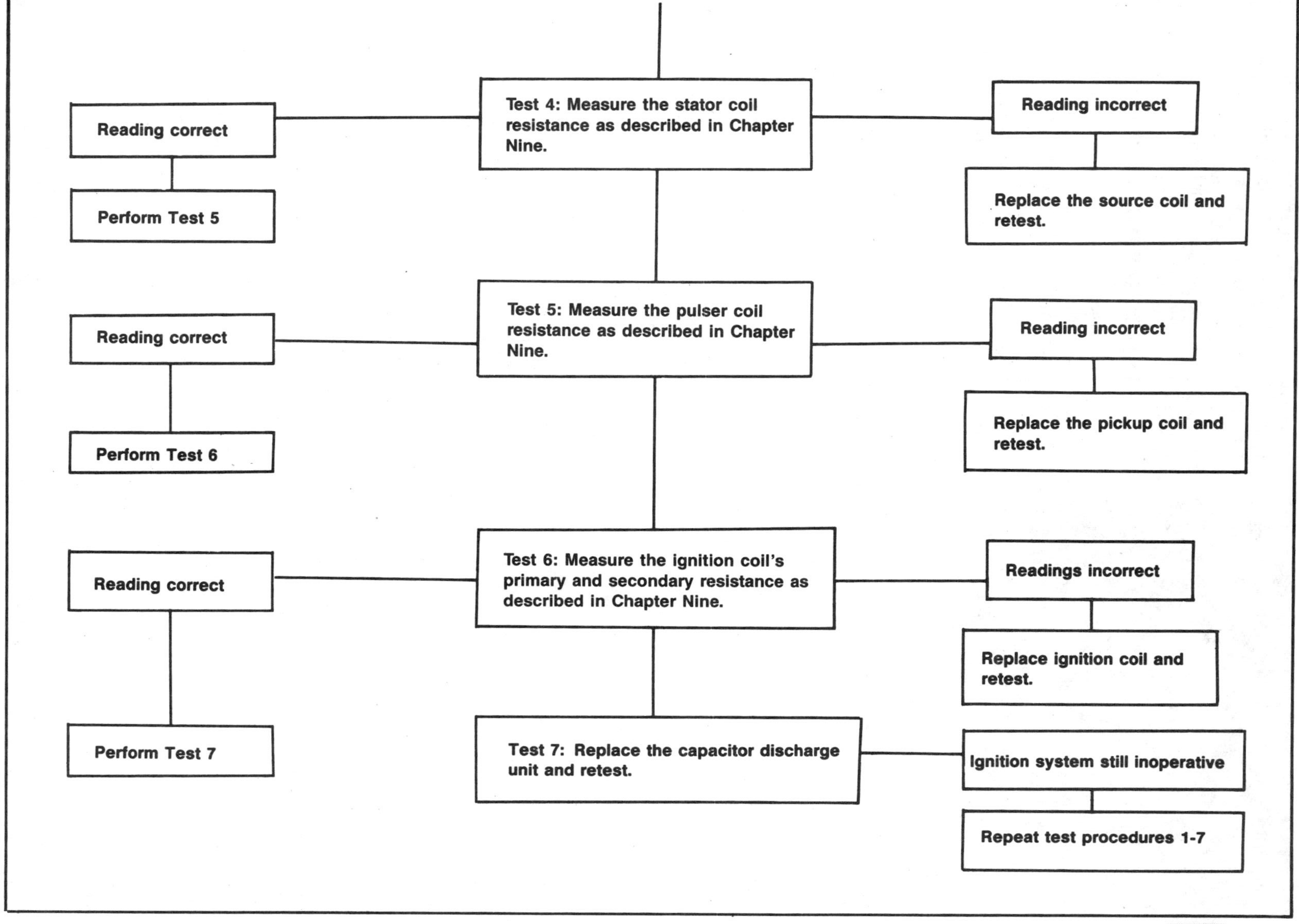
Test 4: Measure the stator coil resistance as described in Chapter Nine.
Reading correct
Perform Test 5
Reading incorrect
Replace the source coil and retest.
Test 5: Measure the pulser coil resistance as described in Chapter Nine.
Reading correct
Perform Test 6
Reading incorrect
Replace the pickup coil and retest.
Test 6: Measure the ignition coil's primary and secondary resistance as described in Chapter Nine.
Reading correct
Perform Test 7
Readings incorrect
Replace ignition coil and retest.
Test 7: Replace the capacitor discharge unit and retest.
Ignition system still inoperative
Repeat test procedures 1-7

2

of the crankshaft (A, **Figure 18**) and try to move it up and down. Any noticeable play indicates worn crankshaft bearings. Refer to Chapter Five.

5. Check the stator plate (B, **Figure 18**) for cracks or damage that would cause the pulser coil and magneto to be out of alignment.

LIQUID-COOLING SYSTEM

The water in the liquid-cooling system is used to conduct heat away from engine. If overheating problems are experienced, perform the checks listed under *Engine Performance, Engine Overheating* in this chapter. If those checks prove okay, refer to the troubleshooting procedures in **Figure 19**.

WATER COOLING SYSTEM TROUBLESHOOTING

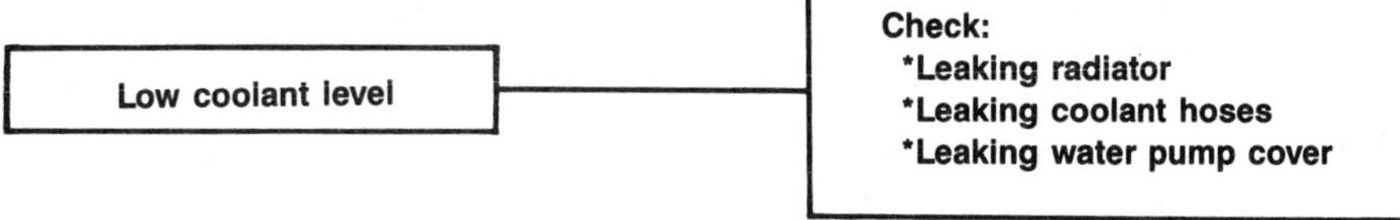

Overheating

Check:
*Low coolant level
*Faulty water pump
*Damaged radiator cap
*Clogged cooling passage(s)
*Incorrect coolant type
*Clogged radiator

CHAPTER THREE

LUBRICATION, MAINTENANCE AND TUNE-UP

DNF (did not finish) is a very unpopular, but nonetheless often repeated phrase, heard throughout race tracks worldwide. The cause of a rider's DNF is usually a mechanical breakdown or failure. This chapter covers all of the regular maintenance required to keep your YZ in top shape. Regular maintenance is something you can't afford to ignore, whether you are racing or just trail riding on the weekends. Because the Yamaha YZ model motorcycles are designed and built primarily for motocross competition, they are rugged and reliable and will handle difficult terrain at fast speeds. However, because competition motorcycles are subjected to tremendous heat, stress and vibration, they must be inspected and serviced at regular intervals.

When neglected, any bike becomes unreliable and actually dangerous to ride. By maintaining a routine service schedule as described in this chapter, costly mechanical problems and unexpected breakdowns (DNF's) can be prevented.

This chapter explains lubrication, maintenance and tune-up procedures required for 1978 and later Yamaha YZ50, YZ60 and YZ80 models. **Table 1** (1978-1981) and **Table 2** (1982-on) is a suggested maintenance schedule. **Tables 1-15** are at the end of the chapter.

NOTE

Due to the number of models and years covered in this book, be sure to follow the correct procedure and specifications for your specific model and year. Also use the correct quantity and type of fluid as indicated in the tables.

PRE-CHECKS

The following checks should be performed prior to each race or before the first ride of the day.

1. Inspect the fuel line and fittings for wetness.
2. Make sure the fuel tank is full and has the correct fuel/oil mixture. Refer to *Engine Lubrication* in this chapter.
3. Make sure the air cleaner is clean and that the cover is securely in place.
4. Check the clutch/transmission oil level.
5. Check the operation of the clutch and adjust if necessary.
6. Check that the clutch and brake levers operate properly with no binding.

CLYMER RACE TIP

*When checking the clutch and brake lever housings for tightness, do not tighten the lever housing screws (**Figure 1**) so tight that the lever assembly cannot be turned by hand. If the bike is dropped or if you crash, the lever housing will turn around the handlebar. If the housing is tight, the lever will probably bend or break.*

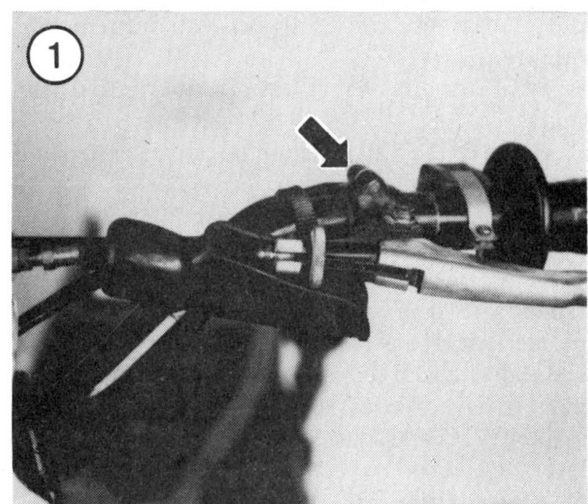

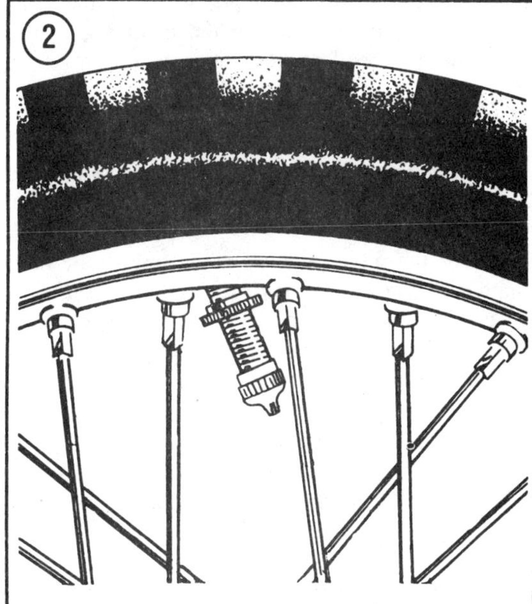

7. Inspect the condition of the front and rear suspension. Make sure it has a good solid feel with no looseness.
8. Check the drive chain for wear and correct tension.
9. Check tire pressure (**Table 3**).

NOTE
While checking tire pressure, also check the position of the valve stem. If the valve stem is cocked sideways like that shown in ***Figure 2****, your riding time could end quickly because of a flat tire. Refer to* ***Tires and Wheels*** *in this chapter.*

10. Check the exhaust system for damage.
11. Check the tightness of all fasteners, especially engine mounting hardware.
12. Check the rear sprocket and bolts as follows:
    a. Check the sprocket holes for signs of egg-shaping. If the sprocket is found in this condition, the sprocket bolts have loosened. Replace the sprocket before the hub is destroyed.
    b. Check the sprocket bolts for tightness. If countersunk bolts (**Figure 3**) are used on your model, always tighten the nut rather than the bolt. Also, check the surface between the countersunk bolt head and the machined countersink area in the hub. The bolt should sit flush in the countersunk area.
    c. Replace nuts that have started to round at their corners.

TIRES AND WHEELS

Tire Pressure

Tire pressure should be checked and adjusted to maintain good traction and handling. An accurate gauge should be carried in your tool box. The approximate tire inflation pressure specification for all models is listed in **Table 3**. When racing, track conditions usually dictate tire air pressure. Lower air pressures can be used for soft, smooth or muddy track conditions. If the track is rougher with a number of big jumps or rocks, you may need a higher air pressure.

Tire Inspection

The tires take a lot of punishment due to the variety of terrain they are subject to. Inspect them periodically for excessive wear, cuts, abrasions, etc. Sidewall tears are the most common cause of tire failure in motocross. This type of damage is usually caused by sharp rocks or other rider's footpegs. Often times, sidewall tears cannot be seen from the outside. If necessary, remove the tire from the rim as described in Chapter Eleven. Run your hand around the inside tire casing to feel for tears or sharp objects imbedded in the casing. The outside of the tire can be inspected visually.

CLYMER RACE TIP

If a regular standard inner tube is used, replace it every 10 races. A stronger heavy-duty tube will last longer and is not as easy to puncture. The stronger tube weighs more but it's a sacrifice that's easily offset by the increased durability.

While checking the tires, also check the position of the valve stem. If the valve stem is cocked sideways like that shown in **Figure 2**, your riding day could end because of a flat tire. Refer to *Valve Stem Alignment* in this chapter.

Wheel Spoke Tension

Tap each spoke with a wrench. The higher the pitch of sound it makes, the tighter the spoke. The lower the sound frequency, the looser the spoke. A "ping" is good, a "klunk" says the spoke is too loose.

If one or more spokes are loose, tighten them as described under *Wheels* in Chapter Eleven.

NOTE

Most spokes loosen as a group rather than individually. Extra-loose spokes should be tightened carefully. Over-tightening just a few spokes will put improper pressure across the wheel. Refer to ***Wheels*** *in Chapter Eleven.*

Rim Inspection

Frequently inspect the condition of the wheel rims. If a rim has been damaged it may be enough to cause excessive side-to-side play. Refer to *Wheels* in Chapter Eleven.

Tube Alignment

Before each riding day, check the tube's valve stem alignment. **Figure 2** shows a valve stem that has slipped. If the tube is not repositioned, the valve stem will eventually pull away from the tube, causing a flat. However, don't get your tire irons out yet, the tube can be aligned without removing the tire.

1. Wash the tire if it is very dirty or caked with mud.
2. Remove the valve stem core and release all air pressure from the tube.
3. Loosen the rim lock nut(s). See **Figure 4**.
4. With an assistant steadying the bike, squeeze the tire and break the tire-to-wheel seal all the way around the wheel. If the tire seal is very tight, it may be necessary to lay the bike on its side and break the tire seal with your foot or a rubber hammer. Use care though; have your assistant steady the bike so that it doesn't rock and damage the handlebars or a control lever.
5. After the tire seal is broken, put the bike on a stand so that the wheel clears the ground.
6. Apply a mixture of soap and water from a spray container (like that used when changing a tire) along the tire bead on both sides of the tire.
7. Have an assistant apply the rear brake "hard." If necessary, tighten the front or rear brake adjuster on drum brake models.
8. Using both of your hands, grab the tire and turn it (and the tube) until the valve stem is straight (90°). See **Figure 5**.
9. When the valve stem is straight, install the valve stem core and inflate the tire. If the soap and water solution has dried, reapply it to help the tire seat on the rim. Check the tire to make sure it seats all the way around the rim.

WARNING

Do not overinflate the tire and tube. If the tire will not seat properly remove the valve stem core and re-lubricate the tire.

10. Tighten the rim lock(s) securely.

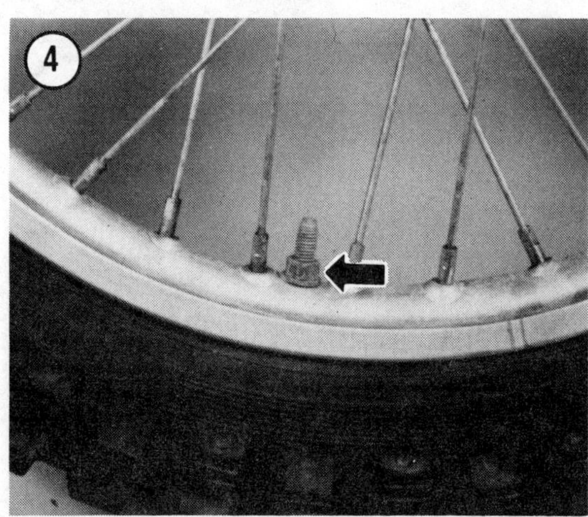

11. Adjust the tire pressure (**Table 3**). When installing the valve stem nut, do not tighten it against the rim. If the tube tire and tube slips again, the valve stem will pull away from the tube and cause a flat. Instead, tighten the nut against the valve cap as shown in **Figure 6**. This will allow the valve stem to slip without damage until you can reposition the tire and tube.

LUBRICANTS

Clutch/Transmission Oil

Oil is graded according to its viscosity, which is an indication of how thick it is. The Society of Automotive Engineers (SAE) system distinguishes oil viscosity by numbers, called "weights." Thick (heavy) oils have higher viscosity numbers than thin (light) oils. For example, a 5 weight (SAE 5) oil is a light oil while a 90 weight (SAE 90) oil is relatively heavy. The viscosity of the oil has nothing to do with its lubricating properties.

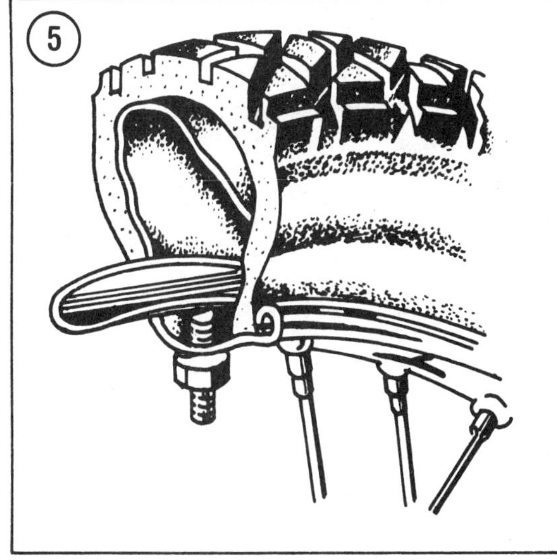

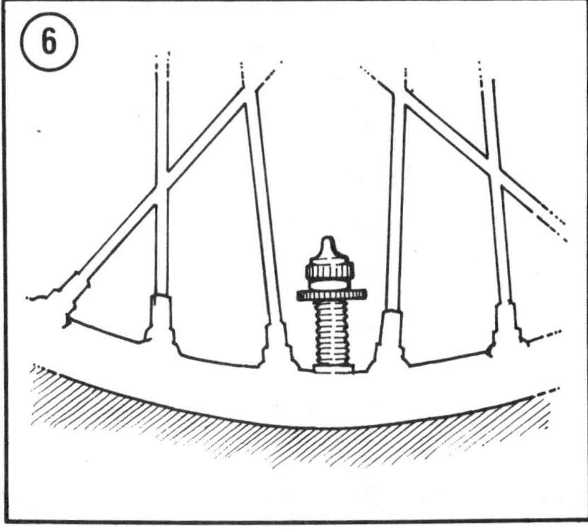

Grease

A good quality grease, preferably waterproof, should be used for many of the parts on the YZ. Water does not wash grease off parts as easily as it washes off oil. In addition, grease maintains its lubricating qualities better than oil on long and strenuous events.

CLEANING SOLVENT

A number of solvents can be used to remove old dirt, grease, and oil. Kerosene is readily available and comparatively inexpensive. Another inexpensive solvent similar to kerosene is ordinary diesel fuel. Both of these solvents have a very high temperature flash point and can be used safely in any adequately ventilated area away from open flames.

WARNING

Never use gasoline. *Gasoline is extremely volatile and contains tremendously destructive potential energy. The slightest spark from metal parts accidently hitting, or a tool slipping, could cause a fatal explosion.*

ENGINE LUBRICATION

WARNING

Serious fire hazards always exist around gasoline. Do not allow any smoking in areas where fuel is being mixed or while refueling your machine. Always have a fire extinguisher, rated for gasoline and electrical fires, within reach just to play it safe.

The engines in all YZ models are lubricated by oil mixed with gasoline. Refer to **Table 4** for recommended oils and fuel. Mix the oil and gasoline thoroughly in a separate clean, sealable container larger than the quantity being mixed to allow room for agitation. Always measure the quantities exactly. **Table 5** lists fuel/oil mixture ratios for all models. Fuel capacity for the various models is given in **Table 6**. Use a good grade of premium fuel rated at 90+ octane.

Use a discarded baby bottle with graduations in both cubic centimeters (cc) or fluid ounces (oz.) on the side. Pour the required amount of oil into the mixing container and add approximately 1/2 the required amount of gasoline. Agitate the mixture thoroughly, then add the remaining fuel and agitate again until all is mixed well.

NOTE
Always mix a fresh amount of fuel the morning of the race or ride; do not mix more than you will use that day. Do not keep any fuel overnight. Dispose of any excess properly.

To avoid any contaminants entering into the fuel system, use a funnel with a filter when pouring the fuel into the bike's tank.

CAUTION
Do not mix castor bean oils with petroleum lubricants. A gum may form and may cause serious engine damage.

PERIODIC LUBRICATION

Refer to **Figure 7** for lubrication points.

Clutch/Transmission Oil Checking and Changing

The oil lubricates both the transmission and the clutch. Proper operation and long service for the clutch and transmission require clean oil. Oil should be changed at the intervals indicated in **Table 1** or **Table 2**. Check the oil level frequently and add as necessary to maintain the correct level. Refer to **Table 7** for oil capacities for the various models.

Try to use the same brand of oil. Do not mix 2 brand types at the same time as they all vary slightly in their composition. Use of oil additives is not recommended as it may cause clutch slippage.

Checking

1. Start the engine and let it warm up approximately 2-3 minutes. Shut it off.
2. Place the bike in an upright position.

3A. *1978-1981:* Perform the following:
  a. Unscrew the oil fill cap (**Figure 8**) located just behind the kickstarter lever.
  b. Wipe the oil off the dipstick with a cloth.
  c. Insert the dipstick in the hole and remove it.
  d. The oil should just touch the bottom of the dipstick. If necessary add the recommended weight of oil to correct the level.
  d. Install the oil fill cap and tighten it securely.

3B. *1982-on:* Perform the following:
  a. Loosen and remove the Phillips oil check screw (A, **Figure 9**).

1. Front brake cam (drum brake models)
2. Steering head bearings
3. Control cables
4. Throttle grip
5. Front wheel bearings
6. Front fork oil
7. Clutch/transmission oil
8. Contact breaker point felt (Model YZ50 only)
9. Side stand pivot
10. Drive chain
11. Rear wheel bearings
12. Rear brake cam

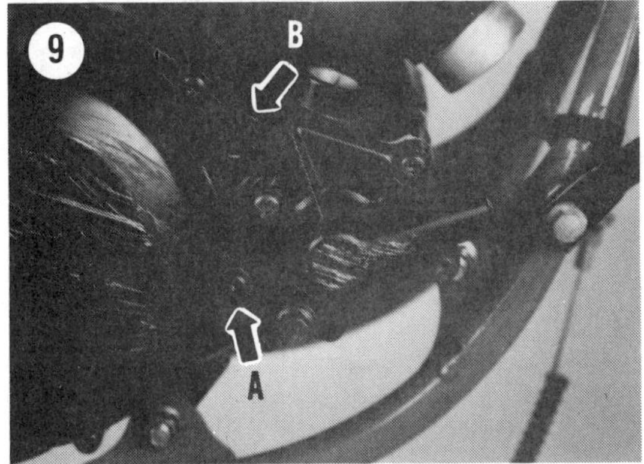

b. If oil flows out of the screw hole, the oil level is correct.

c. If the oil level is low, remove the oil fill cap (B, **Figure 9**). Add the recommended weight of oil until it just begins to flow out of the screw hole.

d. When oil stops flowing out of the screw hole, install the Phillips screw (A, **Figure 9**) and its gasket. Tighten the screw securely.

e. Install the oil fill cap (B, **Figure 9**) and tighten it securely.

Changing

To change the oil you will need the following:

a. Drain pan.

b. Funnel.

c. Can opener or pour spout.

d. 1 quart of oil.

NOTE

Never dispose of motor oil in the trash or pour it on the ground, or down a storm drain. Many service stations accept used motor oil. Many waste haulers provide curbside used motor oil collection. Do not combine other fluids with motor oil to be recycled. To find a recycling location contact the American Petroleum Institute (API) at www.recycleoil.org.

1. Start the engine and let it reach operating temperature.
2. Shut it off and place a drain pan under the engine.
3. Wipe all dirt and debris from around the drain plug. Then remove the drain plug (**Figure 10**). Remove the oil fill cap to help speed the flow of oil.
4. Let the oil drain completely.
5. Inspect the sealing washer on the drain plug. Replace if necessary.
6. Install the drain plug and tighten it securely.
7. Fill the transmission with the correct weight and quantity of oil. Refer to **Table 4** and **Table 7**.
8. Screw in the oil fill cap and start the engine. Let it idle for 2-3 minutes. Check for leaks.
9. Turn the engine off and check for correct oil level. Adjust as necessary.

Front Fork Oil Change (YZ50 and YZ60)

On YZ50 and YZ60 models, it is necessary to remove the front forks in order to drain the fork oil. These fork tubes are not fitted with drain screws.

1. Remove the front wheel as described under *Front Wheel Removal/Installation* in Chapter Eleven.
2. Remove the clamp (**Figure 11**) securing the front brake cable to the left-hand fork leg.

3. Loosen the upper fork bridge bolt (A, **Figure 12**). Then loosen but do not remove the fork cap (**Figure 13**).

NOTE

Prior to removing the fork, measure and write down on a piece of masking tape attached to the fork, the distance from the top of the fork tube to the top of the upper fork bridge. This will enable you to reinstall the fork tube in the same position.

4. Loosen the lower fork bridge bolt (B, **Figure 12**) and remove the fork assembly. If necessary, rotate the fork tube while removing it.

NOTE

To avoid intermixing of parts, remove and drain one fork leg at a time.

5. Remove the upper fork cap (**Figure 14**).
6. *YZ50 models:* Remove the spring collar (**Figure 15**) and the upper spring seat.
7. Remove the fork spring.
8. Turn the fork assembly upside down and drain out all fork oil. Never reuse the oil.

NOTE

Hold the fork assembly upside down and pump it a couple of times to expel any remaining oil trapped in the lower portion of the fork slider.

NOTE

Install the fork tubes in the same position as noted in Step 3.

9. Install the first fork assembly and repeat for the other fork assembly.
10. Install the last fork assembly. Tighten only the lower fork bridge bolts to the torque specifications in **Table 8**.
11. Fill each fork with the specified weight and quantity fork oil. Refer to **Table 4** and **Table 9**.

NOTE

The weight of the oil can vary according to your own preference and the conditions of the track (lighter weight for less damping and heavier for more damping action). Be sure to add the correct amount of oil as this specification should be followed.

NOTE

In order to measure the correct amount of fluid, use a discarded baby bottle. These have measurements in cubic centimeters (cc) and fluid ounces (oz.) on the side.

12. Install the fork spring.

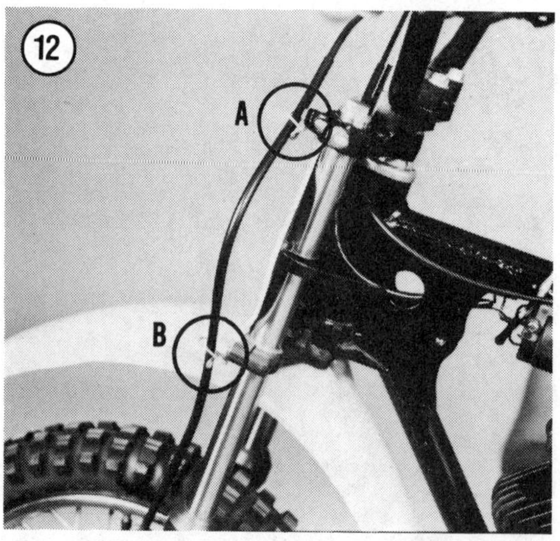

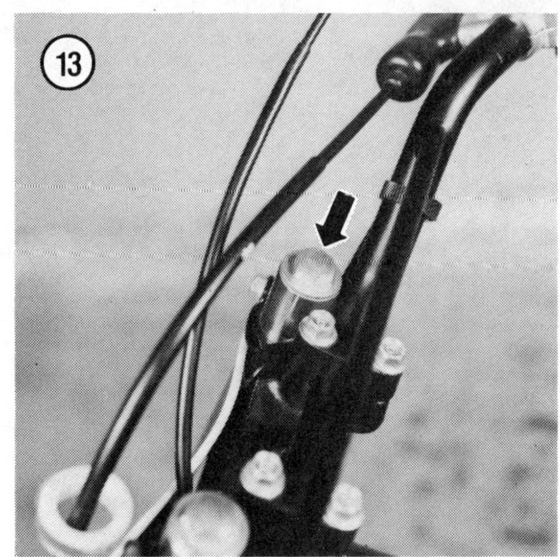

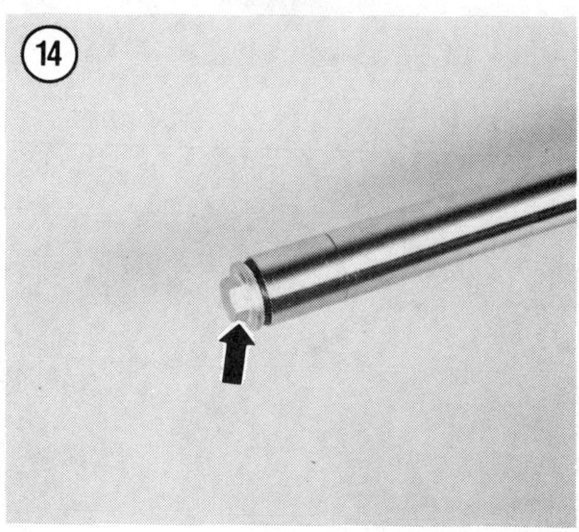

13. *YZ50 models:* Install the upper spring seat and the spring collar (**Figure 15**).
14. Inspect the O-ring seal on the upper fork cap (**Figure 16**) and replace if necessary.
15. Install the fork cap while pushing down on the spring. Start the fork cap slowly and don't cross-thread it. Tighten it securely.
16. Tighten the upper fork bridge bolt to the torque specification in **Table 8**. This bolt must be tightened after the fork cap has been installed and tightened.

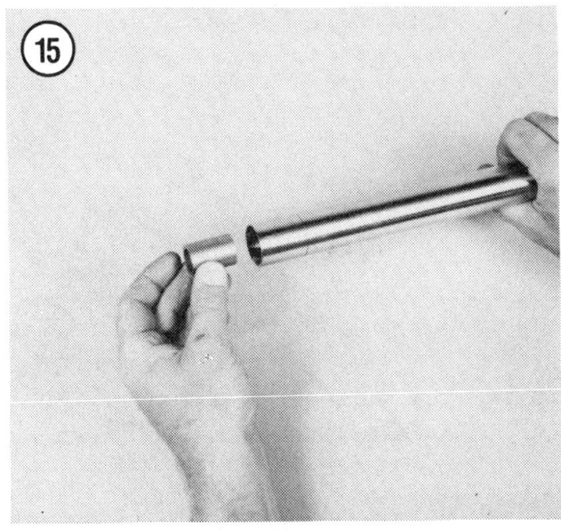

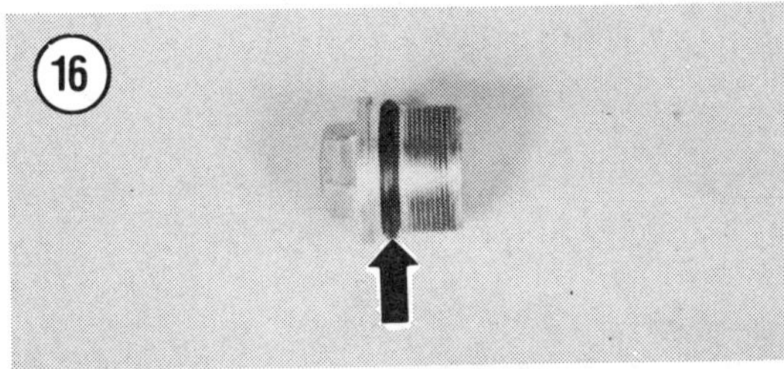

17. Install the front wheel as described under *Front Wheel Removal/Installation* in Chapter Eleven.
18. After installing each fork tube, slowly pump the forks several times to expel air from the upper and lower fork chambers and to distribute the oil.

Front Fork Oil Change (1978-1981 YZ80)

The fork oil should be changed at the interval listed in **Table 1**. If it becomes contaminated with dirt or water, change it immediately.

NOTE
These models were not equipped with factory installed air caps. However if air caps have been installed by yourself or a previous owner, depress the air valve to release all air pressure before performing the following procedure.

CAUTION
Release the air pressure gradually. If released too fast, oil may spurt out with the air. Protect your eyes accordingly.

1. Place a drain pan under the drain screw (**Figure 17**). Then remove the drain screw and allow the oil to drain. Never reuse the oil.

CAUTION
Do not allow the fork oil to come in contact with any of the brake components.

2. With both of the bike's wheels on the ground and the front brake applied, push down on the handlebar grips to work the forks up and down. Continue until all oil is expelled.
3. Inspect the gasket on the drain screw. Replace it if necessary. Install the drain screw.
4. Repeat for the other fork.
5. Place wood block(s) under the bike's frame to raise the front wheel off the ground.

NOTE
It is usually necessary to loosen the upper fork bridge bolt first as it is clamping the fork tube against the threads on the fork cap.

6A. On 1979 YZ80 models, loosen the upper fork bridge bolt then remove the fork cap, upper short fork spring, spring seat and lower long fork spring.
6B. On all other models, loosen the upper fork bridge bolt then remove the upper cap (**Figure 18**), spacer (1979 models) and the fork spring.
7. Fill each fork with the specified weight and quantity fork oil. See **Table 4** and **Table 9**.

NOTE
The weight of the oil can vary according to your own preference and the conditions of the track (lighter weight for less damping and heavier for more damping action). Be sure to add the correct amount of oil as this specification should be followed.

NOTE
In order to measure the correct amount of fluid, use a discarded baby bottle. These have measurements in cubic centimeters (cc) and fluid ounces (oz.) on the side.

8. Inspect the O-ring seal on the upper fork cap (**Figure 16**) and replace if necessary.
9. Install all fork spring components.
10. Install the fork top cap while pushing down on the spring. Start the fork cap slowly and don't cross-thread it. Tighten it securely.
11. Tighten the upper fork bridge bolt to the torque specification in **Table 8**.
12. After installing each fork tube, slowly pump the forks several times to expel air from the upper and lower fork chambers and to distribute the oil.
13. Ride the bike and check for leaks.

Front Fork Oil Change (1982-on YZ80)

The fork oil should be changed at the interval described in **Table 2**. If it becomes contaminated with dirt or water, change it immediately.
1. Support the motorcycle so that the front wheel clears the ground.

CAUTION
Release the air pressure gradually. If released too fast, oil may spurt out with the air. Protect your eyes accordingly.

2. Remove the fork tube air valve cap. Use a small screwdriver or punch and release all air pressure in the fork (A, **Figure 19**).

CAUTION
Do not allow the fork oil to contact any of the brake components or to run onto the front tire.

3. Place a drip pan underneath the drain screw (**Figure 20**). Remove the drain screw and seal and allow the oil to drain. Never reuse the oil.
4. Remove the stand or blocks from underneath the bike. With both of the bike's wheels on the ground, apply the front brake lever and push down on the handlebar. Repeat this action until all the oil is released from the fork tube.

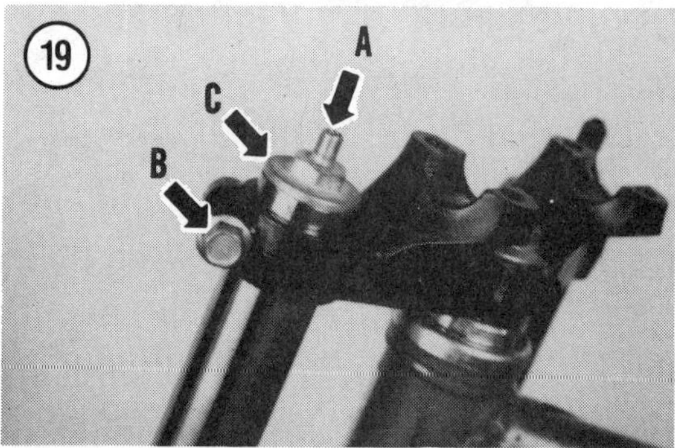

5. Check the drain screw seal. Replace it if worn or damaged.
6. Reinstall the drain screw and seal. Tighten it securely.
7. Repeat Steps 1-6 for the opposite fork.
8. Place the motorcycle on a stand so that the front wheel clears the ground.
9. If necessary, remove the handlebar holder bolts and lift the handlebar away from the triple clamp. Position the handlebar so that the control cables cannot be damaged.
10. Loosen the upper fork bridge bolts (B, **Figure 19**) and remove the fork cap (C, **Figure 19**).
11. *1983-on models:* Remove the spacer (**Figure 21**).
12. Remove the spring seat (**Figure 22**).
13. Remove the fork spring (**Figure 23**).
14. Repeat Steps 10-12 for the opposite fork.
15. Fill each fork with the specified weight and quantity fork oil. See **Table 4** and **Table 9**.
16. Allow the oil to settle for a few minutes. Then with an assistant's help, push the front wheel up and down to remove all air bubbles from the fork oil.
17. With an assistant's help, roll the bike off of the stand so that the forks are placed in a vertical position.
18. Using a fork oil level gauge (**Figure 24**) measure the distance from the top of the fork tube to the top of the oil (**Figure 25**). Refer to **Table 10** for the correct specifications. Repeat for the opposite fork. **Figure 26** shows a fork oil level gauge being used with the forks removed. If the oil level is too high, use the gauge to siphon some of the oil out of the fork tube. If the oil level is too low, pour some fork oil into the fork tube. Remeasure the fork oil level.

NOTE
*A tape measure or ruler (**Figure 27**) can be used to perform Step 18. However, to*

3

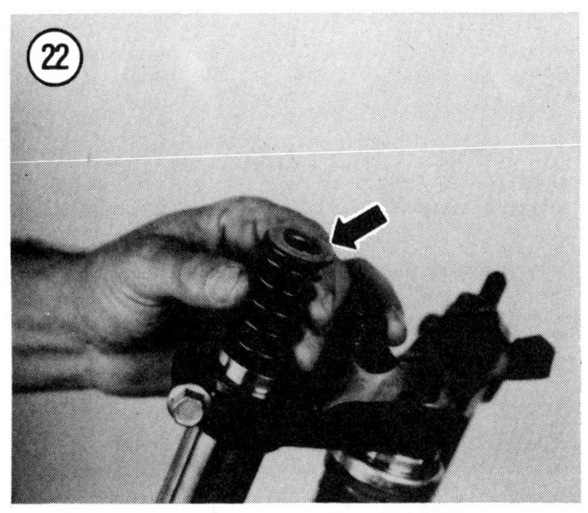

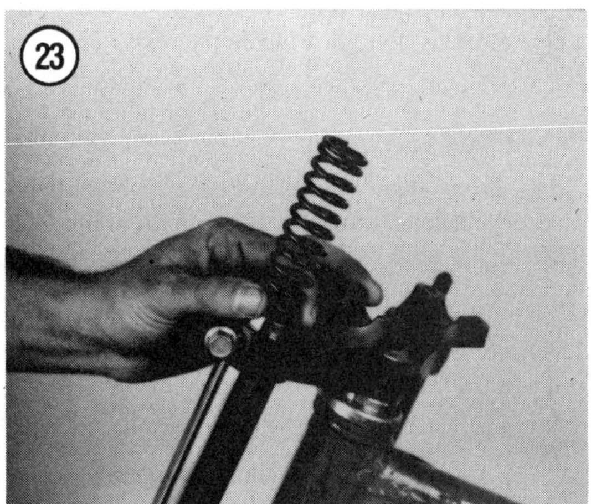

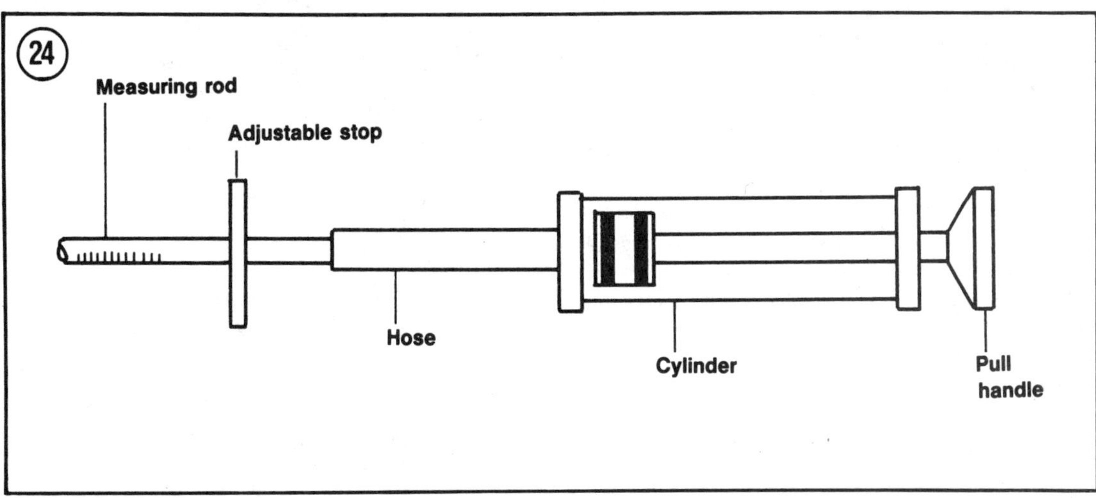

assure a precise oil level, you may want to invest in a fork oil level gauge offered by Yamaha or one of the numerous companies dealing in motocross accessories. This type of tool works well when you are trying to adjust the suspension at the race track.

19. Place the bike onto the stand so that the front wheel clears the ground. Push down on the front wheel so that the forks are completely extended.
20. Check the O-ring in the fork cap (**Figure 16**). Replace it if worn or damaged.
21. Install the fork spring (**Figure 23**), spring seat (**Figure 22**) and spacer (**Figure 21**) (1983-on).
22. Place the fork cap on the spring seat and push it down with a "T" handle or a speeder bar and socket. Install the fork cap by carefully threading it into the fork. Don't cross thread it. Tighten the fork cap securely.
23. If removed, install the handlebar assembly. Tighten the mounting bolt securely.
24. Inflate each fork tube to the correct amount of air pressure as described in Chapter Fourteen.

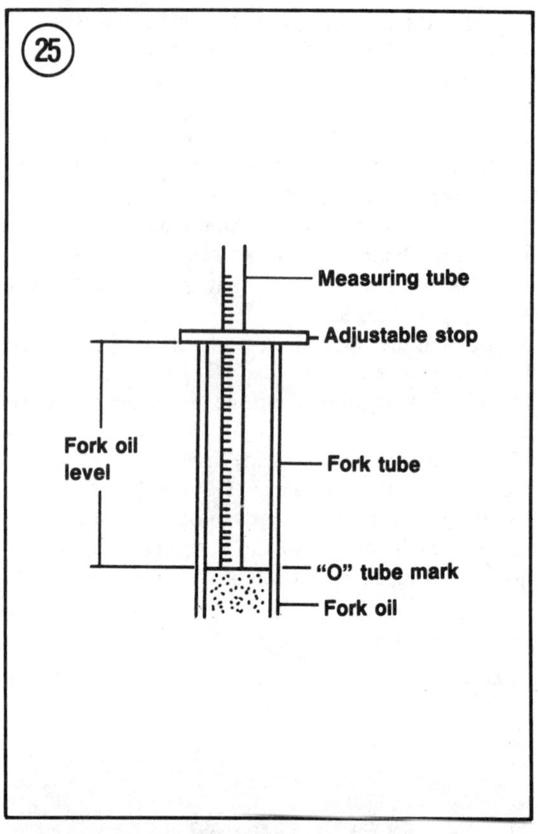

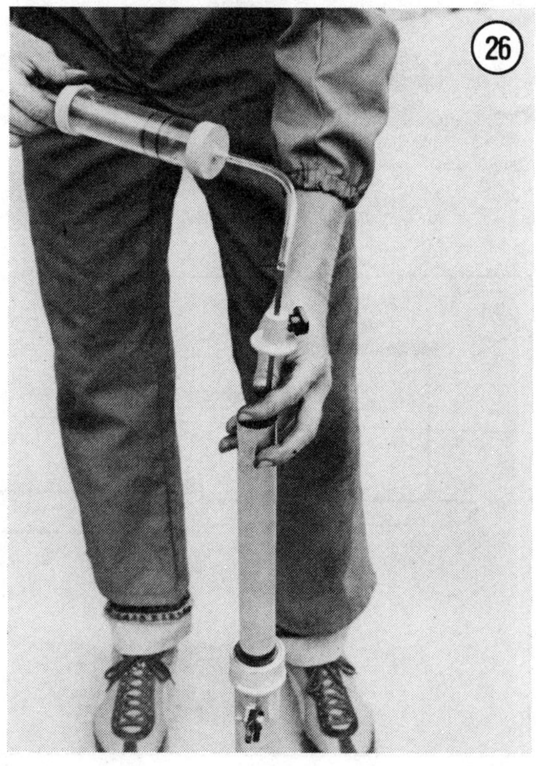

Drive Chain Lubrication

The drive chain should be cleaned after each race or weekend trail ride. The chain should be lubricated before each ride and during the day as required. A properly maintained chain will provide maximum service life and reliability.
1. Disconnect the master link (**Figure 28**) and remove the chain from the motorcycle.

CAUTION
*If a drive chain has been installed that is equipped with O-rings between the side plates (**Figure 29**), use only kerosene or diesel oil for cleaning. This is to prevent O-ring damage. Do not use gasoline or other solvents that will cause the O-rings to swell or deteriorate.*

2. Immerse the chain in a pan of cleaning solvent and allow it to soak for about half an hour. Move it around and flex it during this period so that the dirt between the pins and rollers may work its way out.
3. Scrub the rollers and side plates with a stiff brush and rinse away loosened dirt. Rinse it a couple of times to make sure all dirt and grit are washed out. Hang up the chain and allow it to thoroughly dry.

NOTE
If the chain is equipped with O-rings, use a chain lubricant specifically formulated

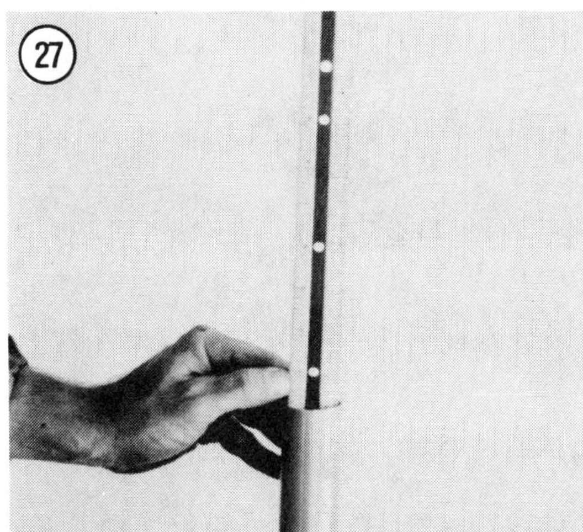

for O-ring chains or use SAE 80W-90 gear oil.

4. Lubricate the chain with a good grade of chain lubricant, carefully following the manufacturer's instructions.
5. Reinstall the chain on the motorcycle. Use a new master link clip and install it so that the closed end of the clip is facing the direction of chain travel (**Figure 30**).

WARNING
Always check the master link clip after the bike has been rolled backwards such as unloading from a truck or trailer. The master link clip may have snagged on the chain guide or tensioner and become disengaged. Losing a chain while riding can cause a serious spill not to mention the chain and engine damage which may occur.

Control Cables

The control cables should be lubricated at intervals as described in **Table 1** or **Table 2**. Also they should be inspected at this time for fraying

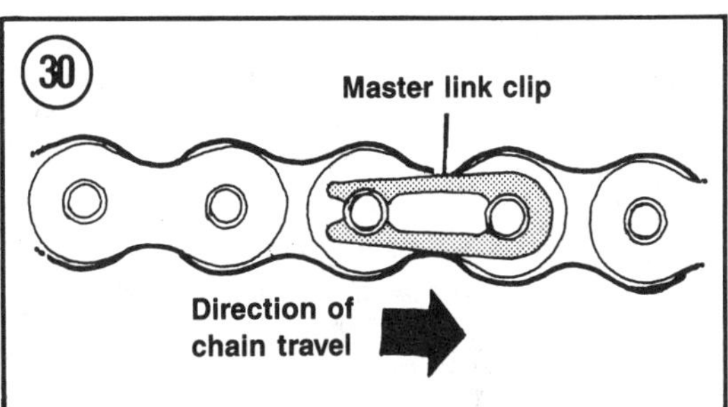

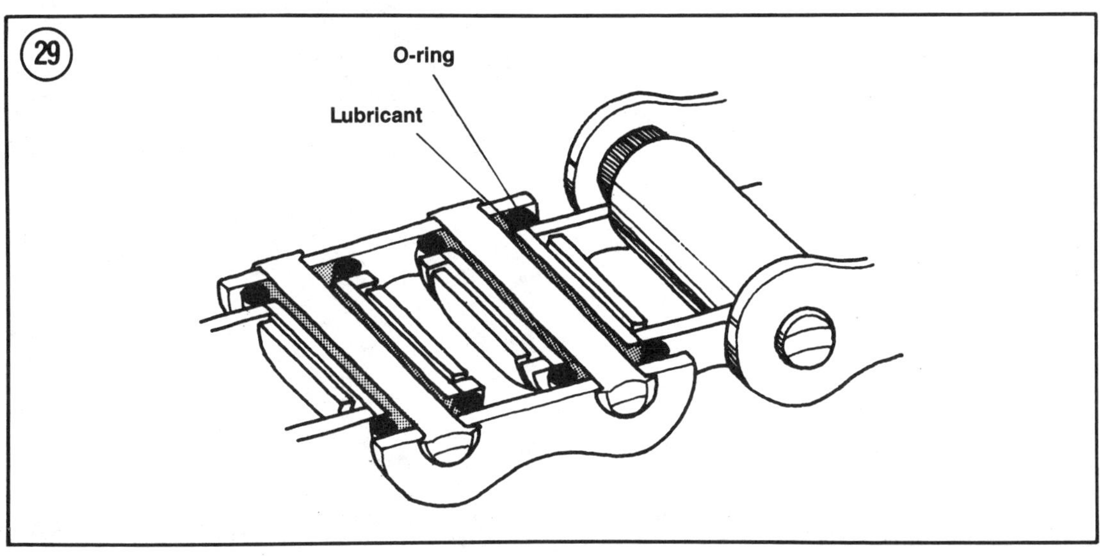

and the cable sheath should be checked for chafing. The cables are relatively inexpensive and should be replaced when found to be faulty.

A can of cable lube and a cable lubricator will be required for this procedure.

CAUTION

Never use a graphite cable lubricant on the throttle cable. The graphite will work its way through the cable and exit into the carburetor. The graphite can then cause excessive slide-to-carburetor bore wear. Replacement of the carburetor is then necessary. A graphite lubricant can be used on brake and clutch cables.

CLYMER RACE TIP

If you are having trouble with the stock cables you may want to install Teflon-lined cables, such as Terrycables. These cables are smoother than the stock cables and can be washed in warm soapy water. They don't require any oiling and will last longer than the standard cables.

1. Disconnect the cables from the clutch lever, front drum brake lever and the throttle grip assembly and from where they attach to the carburetor and clutch mechanism.
2. Attach a cable lubricator following the manufacturer's instructions (**Figure 31**).

NOTE

Place a shop cloth at the end of the cable to catch the oil as it runs out the end or place the end in an empty container. Discard this oil as it is dirty.

3. Insert the nozzle of the lubricant can in the lubricator, press the button on the can and hold down until the lubricant begins to flow out of the other end of the cable.
4. Remove the lubricator, reconnect the cable(s) and adjust the cable(s) as described in this chapter.

Contact Breaker Points Lubrication (YZ50)

The lubrication wick should be lubricated at the interval specified in **Table 1**.

1. Remove the gearshift lever and remove the left-hand crankcase cover (**Figure 32**).

NOTE

The clutch mechanism adjustment cover must be removed as the upper long screw is screwed into the crankcase.

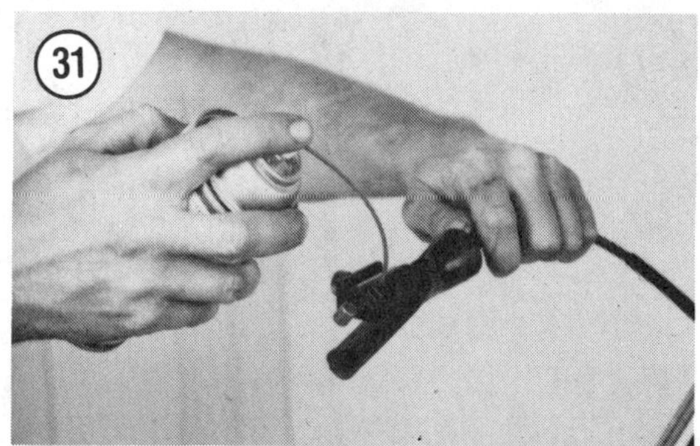

31

32

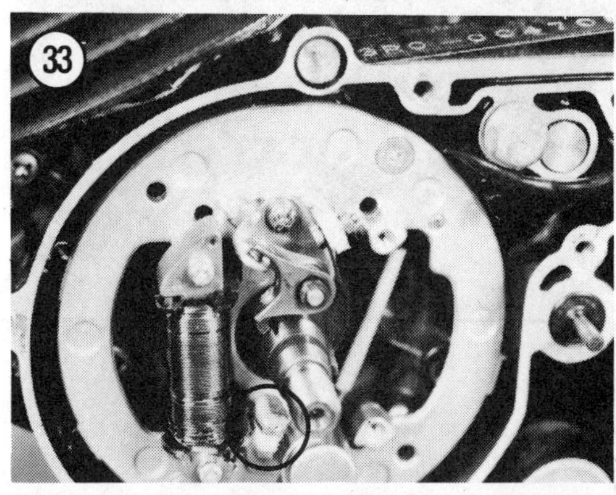

33

34

NOTE
***Figure 33** is shown with the magneto rotor removed for clarity.*

2. Apply 1 or 2 drops of light machine oil (3-in-1 Oil or equivalent) to the lubrication wick (**Figure 33**) that rubs against the breaker point cam on the magneto stator assembly. If you use too much oil, the cam will sling it out onto the points and foul them.
3. Install the left-hand crankcase cover, then the clutch adjustment cover with the long screw (**Figure 34**) on top. Tighten the screws securely. Install the shift lever.

35

36

37

Miscellaneous Lubrication Points

Lubricate the clutch lever, front brake lever, rear brake pedal pivot point and the sidestand pivot point.

PERIODIC MAINTENANCE

Drive Chain Adjustment

The drive chain should be checked and adjusted prior to each race or weekend ride. Note the following for your model before adjusting the chain. Drive chain free play is listed in **Table 11**.

a. On YZ50 models, drive chain slack is measured on the top chain run.
b. On YZ60 models, drive chain slack is measured on the bottom chain run with the chain resting against the front chain roller.
c. On 1978-1980 YZ80 models, drive chain slack is measured on the bottom chain run with the chain tensioner pulled down and not touching the chain.
d. On 1981 YZ80 models, drive chain slack is measured on the top chain run.
e. On 1982-1986 YZ80 models, drive chain slack is measured on the bottom chain run.
f. On 1987-on YZ80 models, drive chain slack is measured on the top chain run.

1. Place the bike on a work stand so that the rear wheel clears the ground. Spin the wheel and check the chain for tightness at several spots. Check and adjust the chain at its tightest point.
2. Lower the bike so that both wheels are on the ground. Support the bike by the sidestand. There should not be a rider on the bike when performing this adjustment.
3. Measure the drive chain slack for your model at a point midway between the 2 sprockets (**Figure 35**) with both wheels on the ground.
4. Compare the drive chain slack with the specifications for your model listed in **Table 11**. If necessary, adjust the drive chain as follows.
5. Remove the rear axle cotter pin (if so equipped). Discard the cotter pin. See **Figure 36**.
6. *YZ50 and YZ60 models:* On each side of the rear axle, turn the adjuster nut (**Figure 37**) in or out

as required in equal amounts. Be sure that the marks on both adjusters align with the same marks on each side of the swing arm (**Figure 38**).

7. *YZ80 models:* On each side of the rear axle, loosen the axle adjuster locknut (A, **Figure 39**) and turn the adjuster bolt (B, **Figure 39**). Turn the adjuster in or out as required in equal amounts. Be sure that the marks on both adjusters align with the same marks on each side of the swing arm (**Figure 38**).

8. Sight along the top of the drive chain from the rear sprocket to see that it is correctly aligned. It should leave the top of the rear sprocket in a straight line (A, **Figure 40**). If it is cocked to one side or the other (B or C, **Figure 40**) the wheel is incorrectly aligned and must be corrected. Refer to Step 6 or Step 7.

9. Tighten the rear axle nut to the tightening torque in **Table 8**.

10. If so equipped, install a new cotter pin and bend it over completely.

11. *YZ80 models:* Tighten the axle adjuster locknut on each side.

NOTE
Always install a new cotter pin. Never reuse an old one.

12. After the drive chain has been adjusted, the rear brake pedal free play has to be adjusted as described in this chapter.

Drive Chain Inspection

1. Adjust the drive chain as described in this chapter.

2. Prior to removing the drive chain from the bike, pull back on the chain with your fingers at the driven sprocket. If the chain can be pulled away from the sprocket by 1/2 the length of the sprocket teeth as shown in **Figure 41**, it has stretched excessively and must be be replaced.

38

39

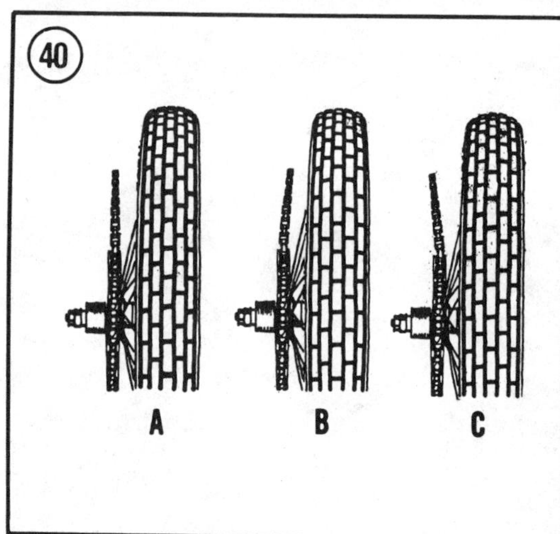
40

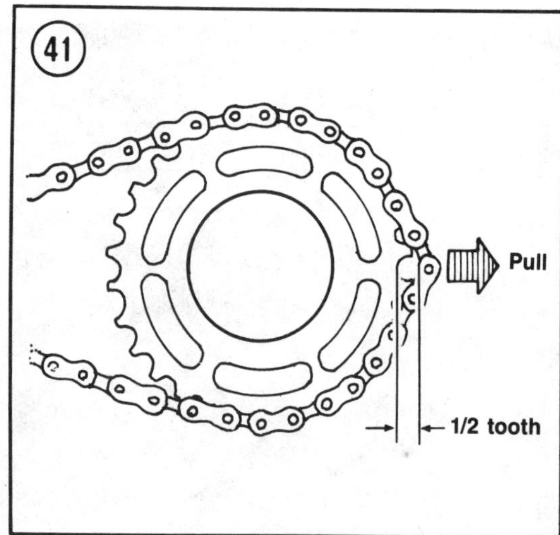
41

3. If the drive chain is worn as described in Step 2, replace it. If the drive chain is not worn severely, perform the following.
4. Remove the drive chain and clean it as described under *Drive Chain Lubrication* in this chapter.
5. After cleaning the chain, examine it carefully for wear or damage. If any signs are visible, replace the chain.

CAUTION
*Always check both sprockets (**Figure 42**) every time the chain is removed. If any wear is visible on the teeth, replace the sprocket(s). Never install a new chain over worn sprockets or a worn chain over new sprockets.*

6. Check the inner faces of the inner plates (**Figure 43**). They should be lightly polished on both sides. If they show considerable wear on both sides, the sprockets are not aligned. Adjust alignment as described under *Drive Chain Adjustment* in this chapter.
7. Lubricate the drive chain as described in this chapter.

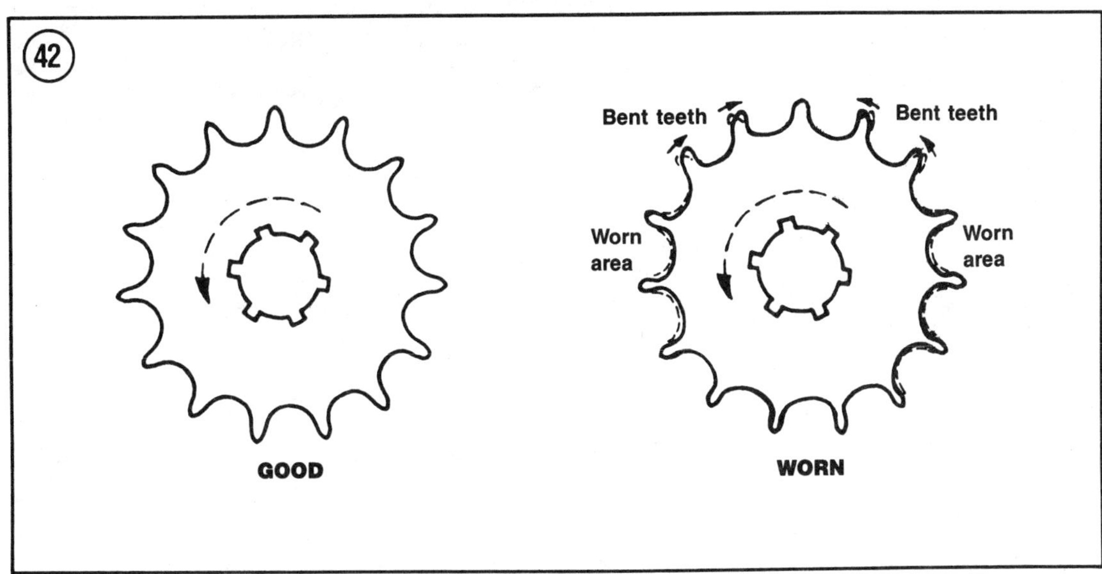

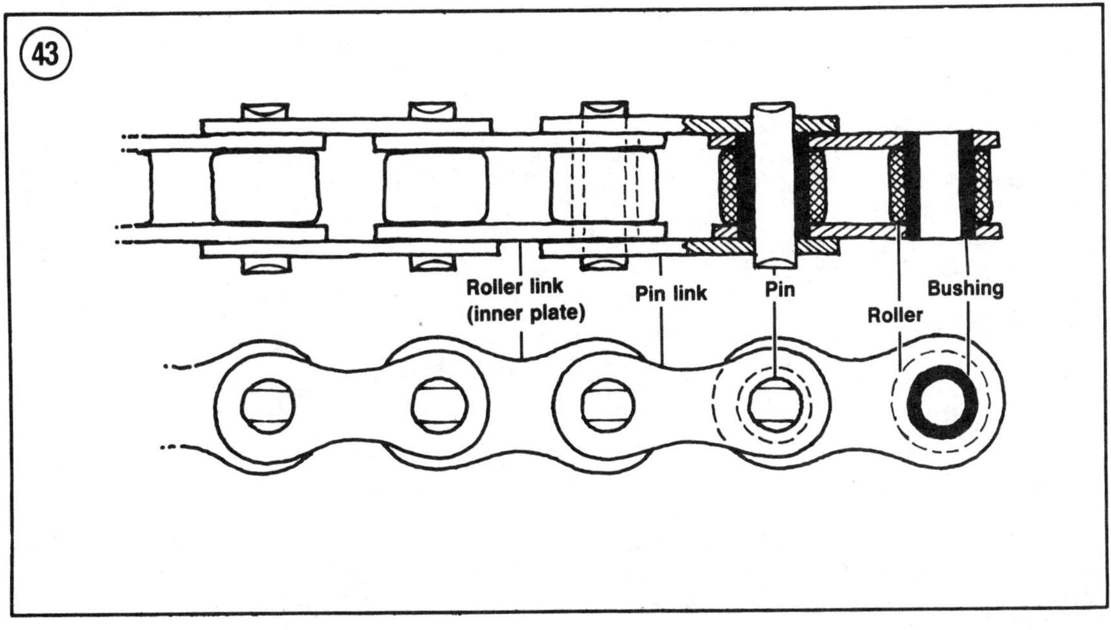

8. Reinstall the chain as described under *Drive Chain Lubrication* in this chapter.
9. Adjust the rear brake pedal free play as described in this chapter.

Drive Chain Guard and Rollers Replacement

The drive chain guard and rollers should be inspected and replaced as necessary. It is a good idea to inspect them prior to each race. A worn or damaged chain guard or roller can allow the drive chain to damage the swing arm.

If it is necessary to remove the swing arm to replace a guard or roller, refer to Chapter Twelve.

Front Brake Lever Adjustment (Drum Brakes)

The front brake lever should be adjusted to suit your own personal preference, but should maintain a minimum cable slack of 5-8 mm (3/16-5/16 in.). Refer to **Figure 44**. The brake lever should travel this amount before the brake shoes come in contact with the drum, but it must not be adjusted so closely that the brake shoes contact the drum with the lever relaxed. The primary adjustment should be made at the hand lever.

1. Slide back the rubber boot.
2. Loosen the locknut (A, **Figure 45**) and turn the adjusting barrel (B, **Figure 45**) in or out to achieve the correct amount of free play. Tighten the locknut.
3. Because of normal brake wear, this adjustment will eventually be "used up." It is then necessary to loosen the locknut (A) and screw the adjusting barrel (B) all the way in toward the hand grip. Tighten the locknut (B).
4. At the adjuster on the brake panel, loosen the locknut (C, **Figure 46**) and turn the adjuster nut (D, **Figure 46**) until the brake lever adjusting barrel can be used once again for the fine adjustment. Be sure to tighten the locknut (C).
5. Repeat Step 2.
6. If proper adjustment cannot be achieved by the use of these adjustment points the cable has stretched and must be replaced as described under *Front Brake Cable Replacement* in Chapter Thirteen, or the brake shoes are worn and must be replaced as described in Chapter Thirteen.

Front Brake Lever Adjustment (Disc Brake)

Brake pad wear in the caliper is automatically adjusted as the piston moves outward in the caliper. However, the front brake lever free play must be

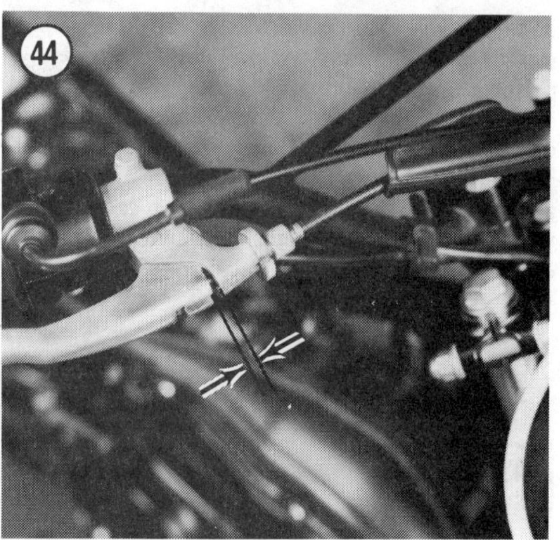

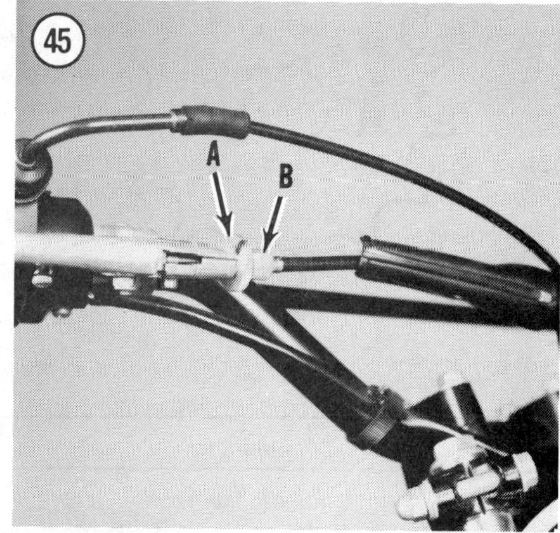

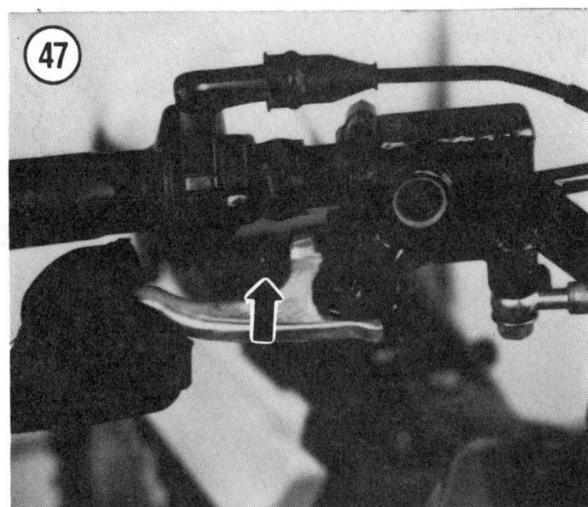

maintained to prevent excessive brake drag. This would cause premature brake pad wear.

1. Loosen the locknut and turn the adjuster bolt (**Figure 47**) in or out to achieve the following free play:
   a. 1986 YZ80 models: 5-8 mm (1/8-3/16 in.).
   b. 1987-1989 YZ80 models: 10-20 mm (13/32-25/32 in.).
   c. 1990 YZ80 models: 2-5 mm (5/64-3/16 in.).
2. Tighten the locknut and reposition the rubber boot.

Rear Brake Pedal Adjustment

Turn the adjustment nut on the end of the brake rod (**Figure 48**) until the pedal has 20-30 mm (25/32-1 3/16 in.) of free play (**Figure 49**). Free play is the distance the pedal travels from the at-rest position to the applied position when the pedal is lightly depressed by hand.

Rotate the rear wheel and check for brake drag. Also operate the pedal several times to make sure it returns to the at-rest position immediately after release.

Front Brake Fluid Level Check (1986-on)

The brake fluid level should be above the lower mark on the reservoir window (**Figure 50**). If the brake fluid reaches the lower mark, the fluid level must be corrected by adding fresh DOT 3 or DOT 4 brake fluid.

NOTE
If the brake fluid level lowers rapidly, check the disc brake line and fittings.

1. Place the bike on level ground and position the handlebar so the master cylinder reservoir is level.
2. Clean any dirt from the top cover prior to removing the cover.
3. Remove the top cover screws and remove the cover and diaphragm.

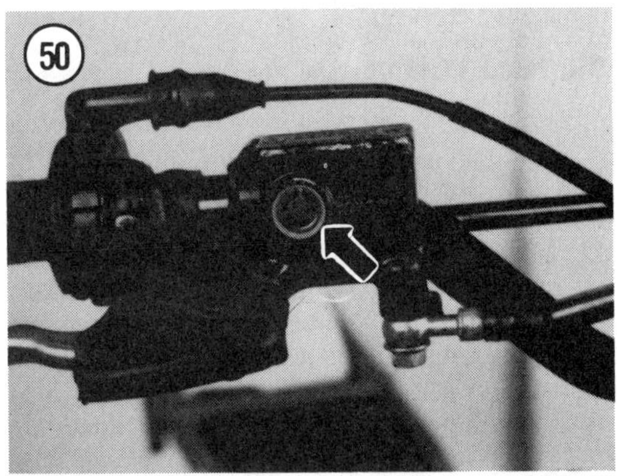

4. Add fresh brake fluid (DOT 3 or DOT 4) from a sealed container.

WARNING

Use brake fluid clearly marked DOT 3 or DOT 4 and specified for disc brakes. Others may vaporize and cause brake failure. Do not intermix different brands or types of brake fluid as they may not be compatible. Do not intermix a silicone based (DOT 5) brake fluid as it can cause brake component damage leading to brake system failure.

CAUTION

Be careful when handling brake fluid. Do not spill it on painted or plastic surfaces as it will destroy the surface. Wash the area immediately with soap and water and thoroughly rinse it off.

5. Reinstall the diaphragm and top cover. Install the screws and tighten securely.

Disc Brake Lines

Check the brake line between the master cylinder and the brake caliper. If there is any leakage, tighten the connections and bleed the brake as described in Chapter Thirteen. See **Figure 51** and **Figure 52**. If this does not stop the leak or if a brake line is obviously damaged, cracked or chafed, replace the brake line and bleed the system.

Disc Brake Pad Wear

Inspect brake pads for excessive or uneven wear, scoring and oil or grease on the friction surface.

1. Remove the rubber plug from the front caliper inspection hole (**Figure 53**).
2. Look through the inspection hole (**Figure 54**). If the pads are worn to the wear line, they must be replaced as a set.
3. If the pads are worn or if the pad material is contaminated, replace the brake pads as described in Chapter Thirteen.

Disc Brake Fluid Change

Every time the reservoir top cover is removed, a small amount of dirt and moisture enters the brake fluid. The same thing happens if a leak occurs or any part of the hydraulic system is loosened or disconnected. Dirt can clog the system and cause unnecessary wear. Water in the brake fluid vaporizes at high temperature, impairing the hydraulic action and reducing the brake's stopping ability.

To maintain peak performance, change the brake fluid once a year. To change brake fluid,

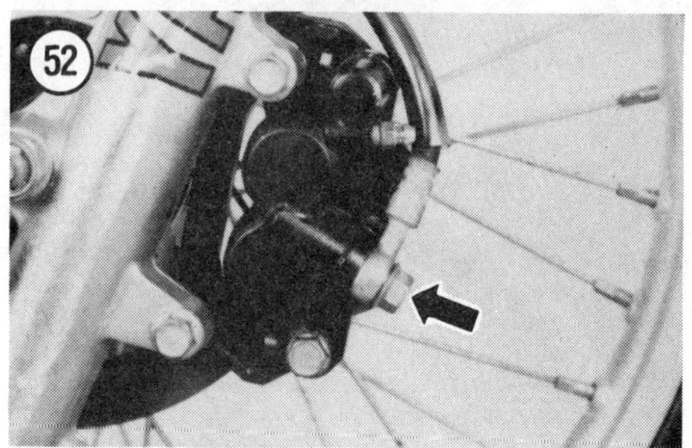

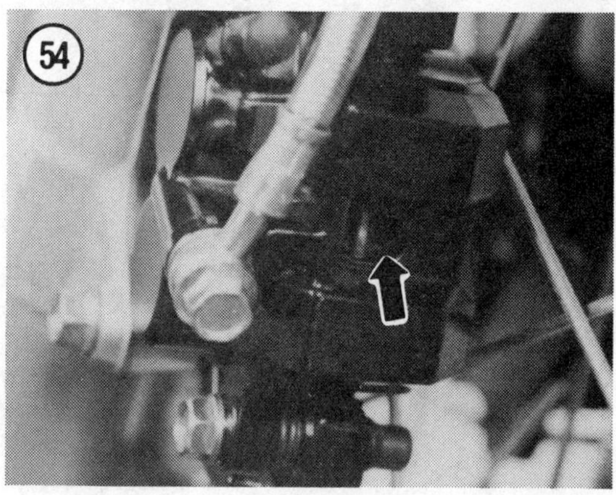

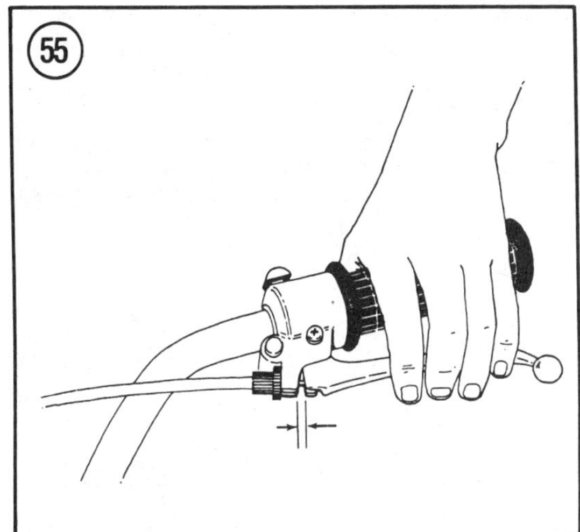
55

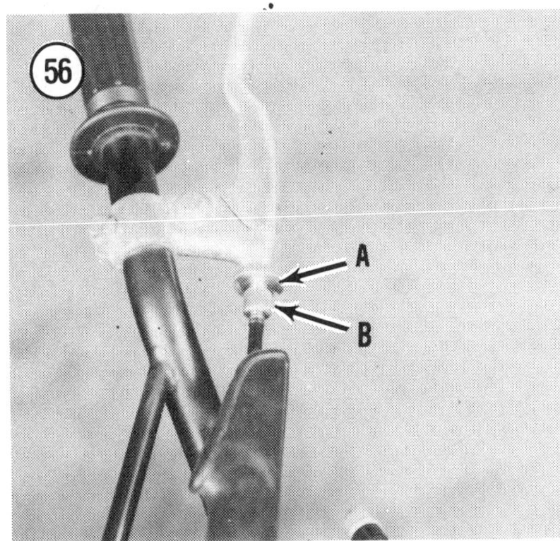

56

57

follow the *Bleeding the Brake System* procedure in Chapter Thirteen.

WARNING
Use brake fluid clearly marked DOT 3 or DOT 4 and specified for disc brakes. Others may vaporize and cause brake failure. Do not intermix different brands or types of brake fluid as they may not be compatible. Do not intermix a silicone based (DOT 5) brake fluid as it can cause brake component damage leading to brake system failure.

Clutch Adjustment (1978-1980)

Minor clutch adjustment on these models is made at the clutch lever. Major clutch adjustment is made at the clutch mechanism adjuster installed on the left-hand side cover. All initial clutch adjustments should be made at the clutch lever. If the clutch will not adjust correctly, adjust the mechanism adjuster.

Clutch lever free play adjustment

Clutch lever free play should be adjusted according to rider preference but a minimum cable slack 2-3 mm (3/32-1/8 in.) should be maintained. Refer to **Figure 55**.

1. See **Figure 56**. At the hand lever loosen the locknut (A) and turn the adjusting barrel (B) in or out to obtain the correct amount of free play. Tighten the locknut (A).
2. If the proper amount of free play cannot be achieved at this adjustment point, loosen the locknut and turn the adjusting barrel at the top of the left-hand side cover in or out. Tighten the locknut.
3. If the proper amount of clutch cable free play cannot be achieved using these adjustment points, adjust the clutch mechanism adjuster.

Clutch mechanism adjustment

1. See **Figure 56**. Loosen the hand lever locknut (A) and turn the adjusting barrel (B) all the way in toward the hand grip.

CAUTION
An impact driver with a Phillips bit (described in Chapter One) may be required to loosen the cover screws in Step 2. Attempting to loosen the screws with a Phillips screwdriver may ruin the screw heads.

2A. *YZ50 models:* Remove the small cover plate from the left-hand side cover (**Figure 57**).

3

2B. *YZ80 models:* Remove the left-hand side cover (**Figure 58**).

3. Loosen the locknut and turn the adjusting screw (**Figure 59**) in until resistance is felt, thus removing free play in the clutch pushrod. Back it off 1/4 turn and tighten the locknut securely.

NOTE

*On YZ50 models, make sure to install the long screw (**Figure 60**) in the top hole. The cover is made of a plastic material and the long screw is necessary to keep the cover from distorting when the clutch is operated. The clutch will not release properly if the correct length screw is not used.*

4. Install the side cover or small cover plate.

5. Adjust clutch lever free play as described in this chapter.

58

59

60

Clutch Adjustment (1981-on)

Continuous use of the clutch lever causes the clutch cable to stretch. For the clutch to operate correctly, the clutch cable free play (**Figure 55**) must be maintained at 2-3 mm (3/32-1/8 in.). If there is no clutch cable free play, the clutch cannot disengage completely. This would cause clutch slippage and rapid clutch plate wear.

1. Pull the clutch lever toward the handlebar. When cable resistance is felt, hold the lever and measure the gap shown in **Figure 55** with a ruler; this is clutch cable free play. If resistance was felt as soon as you pulled the clutch lever, there is no cable free play.

2. See **Figure 56**. At the hand lever loosen the locknut (A) and turn the adjusting barrel (B) in or out to obtain the correct amount of free play. Tighten the locknut (A).

3. If the proper amount of free play cannot be achieved at this adjustment point, loosen the cable's midline adjuster locknut and turn the adjusting barrel in or out (**Figure 61**). Tighten the locknut.

4. If the clutch cable free play cannot be achieved using these adjustment points, the clutch cable has stretched excessively and must be replaced as described under *Clutch Cable Replacement* in Chapter Six.

Throttle Cable Adjustment and Operation

For correct operation, the throttle cable should have 3-5 mm (1/8-3/16 in.) free play. In time, the throttle cable free play will become excessive from cable stretch. This will delay throttle response and

61

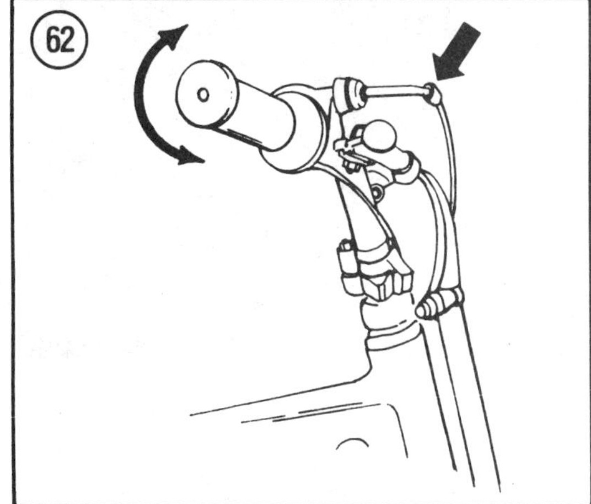
62

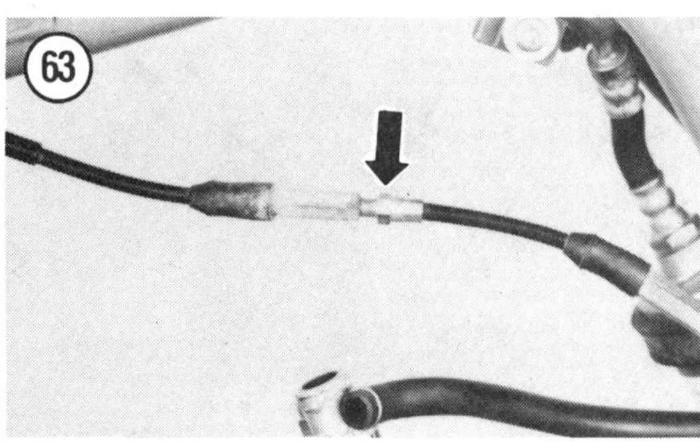
63

64

affect low speed operation. On the other hand, if there is no throttle cable free play, an excessively high idle can result.

1. Start the engine and allow it to idle.
2. With the engine at idle, twist the throttle (**Figure 62**) to raise engine speed.
3. Determine the amount of movement (free play) required to raise the engine speed from idle. If the free play is incorrect, perform the following.
4. Depending on the model year, throttle cable adjusters are found at the throttle grip (**Figure 62**), between the grip and carburetor (**Figure 63**) and at the top of the carburetor (**Figure 64**).
5. Loosen one of the adjuster locknuts and turn the adjuster in or out to achieve proper free play. Tighten the locknut securely.
6. Make sure the throttle grip rotates freely from a fully closed to fully open position.
7. Start the engine and allow it to idle. Turn the handlebar from side-to-side. If the idle increases, the throttle cable is routed incorrectly or there is not enough cable free play. Correct this problem immediately.

Throttle Grip

After each race, the throttle grip and throttle housing should be cleaned and serviced.

1. Remove the Phillips screws securing the throttle housing (**Figure 65**).
2. Separate the throttle housings.
3. Disconnect the throttle cable at the twist grip.
4. Clean the inner twist grip bore with aerosol electrical contact cleaner.
5. Clean the throttle housings thoroughly.
6. Check the end of the handlebar for burrs or other damage that would cause the twist grip to

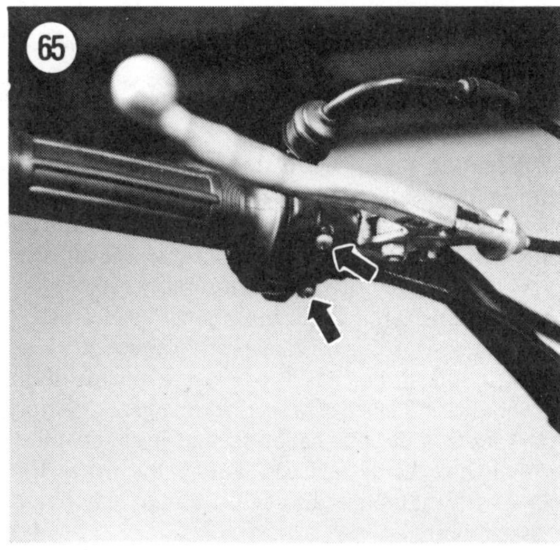
65

3

stick or operate sluggishly. If necessary, smooth the end of the handlebar with a file.

7. Install by reversing these steps. Make sure the throttle grip rotates freely from a fully closed to fully open position.

Air Cleaner Service

The air cleaner element should be removed, cleaned and re-oiled at intervals indicated in **Table 1** or **Table 2**.

The air cleaner removes dust and abrasive particles from the air before it enters the carburetor and engine. Very fine particles that may enter into the engine will cause rapid wear to the piston rings, cylinder and bearings and may clog small passages in the carburetor. Never run the YZ without the air cleaner element installed.

Proper air cleaner servicing can do more to insure long service from your engine than any other single item.

CLYMER RACE TIP

Keep 1 or 2 extra air cleaner elements on hand (already serviced) and stored in a plastic bag so that if race conditions are extremely dusty or muddy, the dirty element can be replaced after practice or between motos.

Foam filter cleaning

All models are equipped with foam air filter element. To work properly, the filter element must be properly cleaned then oiled with a foam air filter oil.

1. Remove the air filter element for your model as described in this chapter.
2. Stuff a clean shop rag into the carburetor opening.
3. Examine the inside of the air box. **Figure 66** shows the inside of a typical air box. There should be no signs of dust or dirt on the inside of the air box cover or sides. If dirt is noticeable, the air filter may be damaged or it was improperly serviced.
4. Clean the inside of the air box with a clean shop rag soaked in solvent or soap and water.
5. After the air box has dried, coat the inside of the air box with a layer of wheel bearing grease. Apply the grease with your hands so that it covers all of the air box inside surfaces. The grease works like an additional filter and will help to catch any passed dirt.
6. If necessary, remove the guide from inside the filter element.

CAUTION

Do not clean the air filter element with gasoline. Besides being a fire hazard, gasoline will break down your filter's seam glue and corrode the seam stitching.

7. Fill a clean pan with liquid cleaner and warm water. If you are using an accessory air filter, the manufacturer may sell a special air filter cleaner.

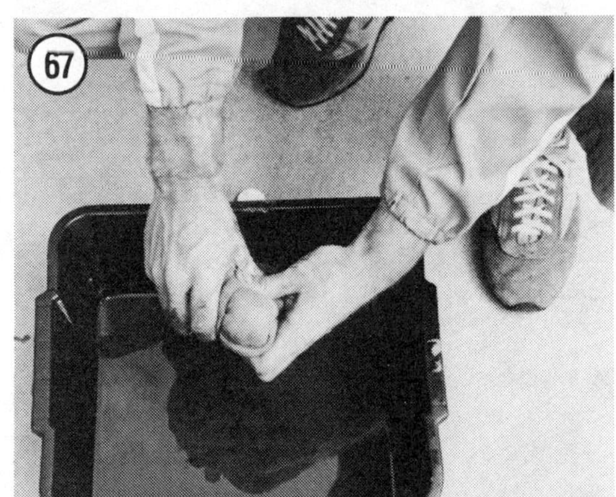

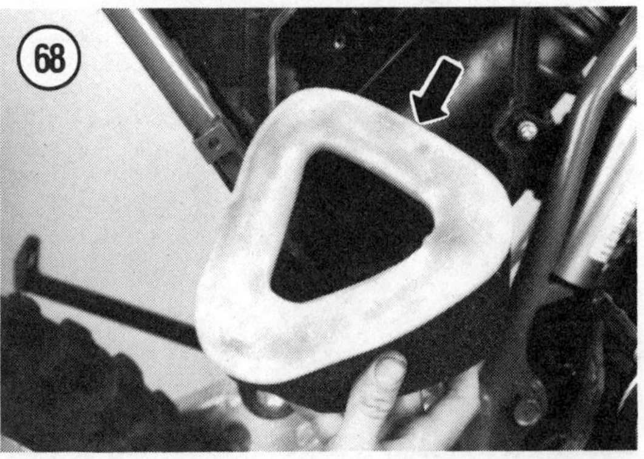

CAUTION
Do not wring or twist the filter when cleaning it. This harsh action could damage a filter pore or tear the filter loose at a seam. This would allow unfiltered air to enter the engine and cause severe and rapid wear.

8. Submerge the filter into the cleaning solution and gently work the cleaner into the filter pores. Soak and gently squeeze the filter to clean it. See **Figure 67**.
9. Rinse the filter under warm water while soaking and gently squeezing it.
10. Repeat Step 8 and Step 9 two or three times or until there are no signs of dirt being rinsed from the filter.

69

70

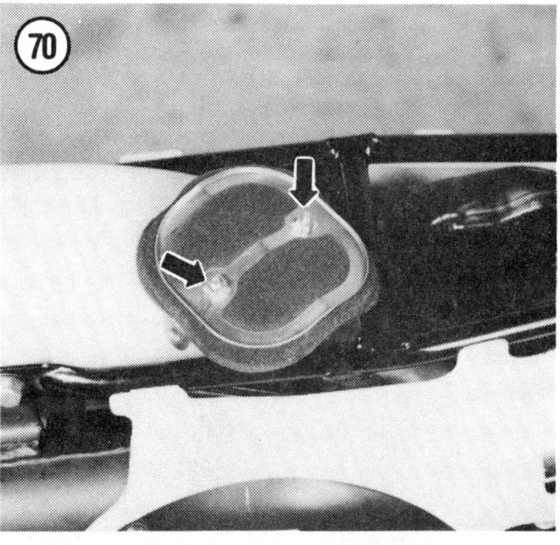

11. After cleaning the element, inspect it. If it is torn or broken in any area it should be replaced. Do not run with a damaged element as it may allow dirt to enter the engine and cause severe engine wear.
12. Set the filter aside and allow it to dry thoroughly.

CAUTION
A damp filter will not trap fine dust. Make sure the filter is completely dry before oiling it.

13. Properly oiling an air filter element is a messy job. You may want to wear a pair of disposable rubber gloves when performing this procedure. Oil the filter as follows:
   a. Purchase a box of gallon size reclosable storage bags. The bags can be used when cleaning the filter as well as for storing engine and carburetor parts during disassembly.
   b. Place the cleaned filter element into a storage bag.
   c. Pour foam air filter oil onto the filter to soak it.
   d. Gently squeeze and release the filter element to soak filter oil into the filter's pores. Repeat until all of the filter's pores are discolored with the oil.
   e. Remove the filter element from the bag and check the pores for uneven oiling. This is indicated by light or dark areas. If necessary soak the filter and squeeze it again.
   f. When the filter oiling is even, squeeze the filter element a final time.
14. Remove the filter element from the bag. Install the plastic filter support inside the filter, if so equipped.
15. On YZ80 models, apply a coat of thick wheel bearing grease to the filter's sealing surface (**Figure 68**).
16. Install the air filter for your model as described in this chapter.
17. Pour the left over filter oil from the bag back into the oil bottle for reuse.
18. Dispose of the plastic bag.

YZ50 air cleaner removal/installation

1. Remove the seat.
2. Remove the single screw (**Figure 69**) at the rear of the element and lift the element out of the air box.
3. Remove the screws (**Figure 70**) and separate the element from the holders.
4. Clean the element as described in this chapter.

5. Inspect all fittings, hoses and connections from the air box to the carburetor. Make sure that all are airtight and free of any damage.
6. Install the element into the holder. Apply a light coat of wheel bearing grease to the sealing edges of the element to provide a good airtight seal between the element and the air box.
7. Install the element assembly into the air box. Make sure it seats properly against the air box for an airtight seal. Tighten the screw securely.

CAUTION
An improperly installed air cleaner element will allow dirt and grit to enter the carburetor and engine, causing expensive engine damage.

8. Install the seat.

YZ60 air cleaner removal/installation

Refer to **Figure 71** for this procedure.
1. Remove the screws securing the side cover to the frame and remove the side cover.
2. Remove the screw securing the air filter cover to the housing and remove the cover.
3. Remove the screws securing the filter element and guide to the housing and remove the filter and guide. Separate the filter from the guide.
4. Clean the element as described in this chapter.
5. Inspect all fitting, hoses and connections from the air box to the carburetor. Make sure that all are airtight and that they will not let in any unfiltered air.
6. Position the guide at the front of the filter, making sure to align all sides evenly. Then insert the filter and guide assembly into the housing and secure with the attaching screws. Install the side cover and screws.

YZ80 air cleaner removal/installation

Due to the number of different YZ80 models covered in this manual, the following should be used as a basic guide for removal and installation.
1. Remove the left- or right-hand side cover.
2. Remove the air filter element mounting screw and remove the filter. See **Figure 72** or **Figure 73**. On some models, a mounting screw is not used. Pull the element out of the air box.

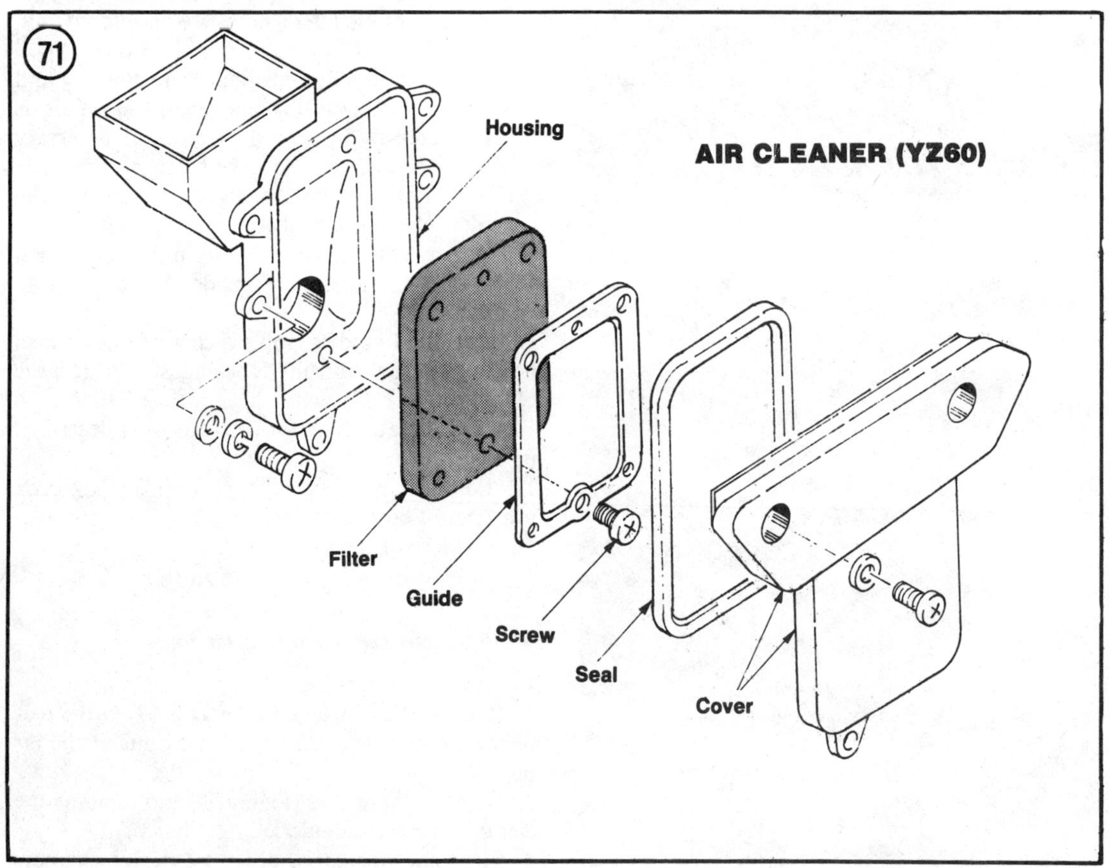

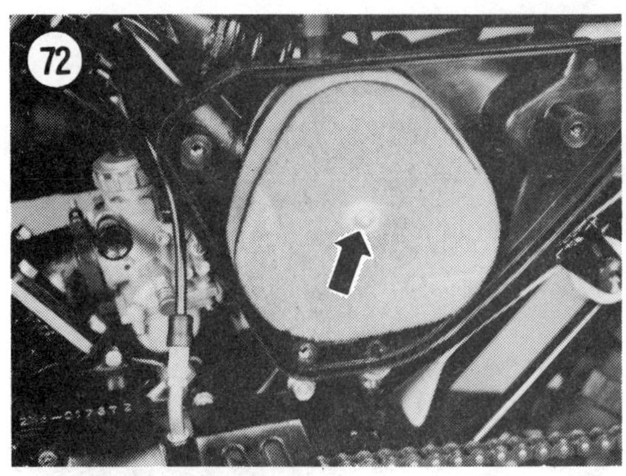

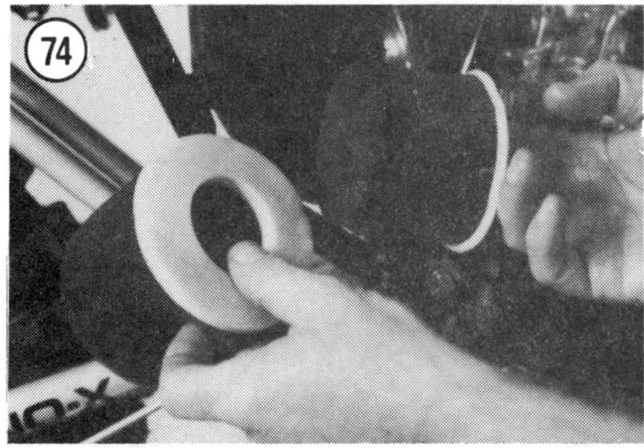

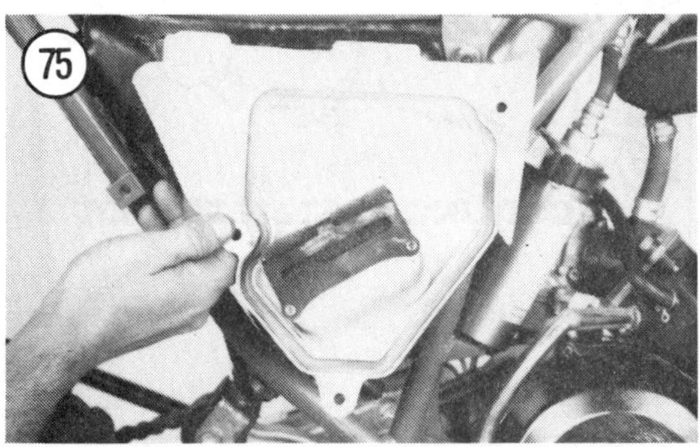

3. On models with dual elements, separate them before cleaning (**Figure 74**).
4. Inspect all fitting, hoses and connections from the air box to the carburetor. Make sure that all are airtight and that they will not let in any unfiltered air.
5. Clean the air filter element as described in this chapter.
6. Install the filter element by reversing these steps.
7. *1984-1986:* Remove and clean the element seal (**Figure 75**) on the side cover. Blow the seal dry and reinstall it. Do not oil the element seal.

Fuel Line Inspection

Inspect the fuel line from the fuel tank to the carburetor (**Figure 76**). If it is cracked or starting to deteriorate it must be replaced. Make sure the small hose clamps are in place and holding securely. Also make sure that the overflow and vent tubes are in place.

WARNING
A damaged or deteriorated fuel line presents a very dangerous fire hazard to both the rider and the machine if fuel should spill onto a hot engine or exhaust pipe.

CLYMER RACE TIP
If you have been experiencing fuel contamination that is plugging up the carburetor's jets (especially the pilot jet), install a fuel filter in the fuel line between the gas tank and the carburetor. Use the stock Yamaha fasteners to hold the line to the filter.

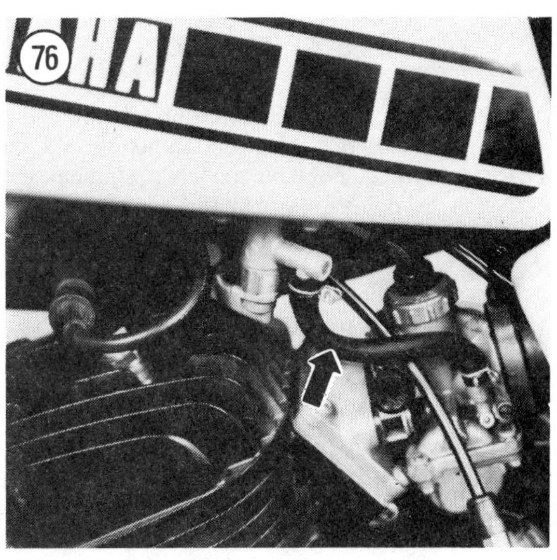

Wheel Bearings

The wheel bearings should be cleaned and repacked once a year or more often if the vehicle is operated often in water (especially salt water). The correct service procedures are covered in Chapter Eleven (front) or Chapter Twelve (rear).

Steering Head Adjustment Check

The steering head on 1978-1984 models consists of upper and lower bearings with loose ball bearings. On 1985 and later models, loose ball bearings are installed at the top of the steering stem and a tapered roller bearing installed at the lower end. Because the YZ models are subjected to rough terrain and conditions, bearing play should be checked and adjusted weekly. A loose bearing adjustment will hamper steering and cause premature bearing and race wear. In severe conditions, a loose bearing adjustment can cause loss of control.

1. Place the bike on a stand so that the front wheel clears the ground.
2. Hold the front fork tubes and gently rock the fork assembly back and forth. If you can feel looseness, adjust the steering head bearings as described in Chapter Eleven.

Cooling System Inspection (1982-on)

WARNING

When performing any service work to the engine or cooling system, never remove the radiator cap, coolant drain screws or disconnect any hose while the engine and radiator are hot. Scalding fluid and steam may be blown out under pressure and cause serious injury.

Once a year, or whenever troubleshooting the cooling system, the following items should be checked. If you do not have the test equipment, the tests can be done by a Yamaha dealer, radiator shop or service station.

1. Remove the radiator cap (**Figure 77**).
2. Check the rubber washers on the radiator cap (**Figure 78**). Replace the cap if the washers show signs of deterioration, cracking or other damage. If the radiator cap is okay, perform Step 3.
3. Have the radiator cap pressure tested (**Figure 79**). The specified radiator cap relief pressure is listed in **Table 12**. The cap must be able to sustain this pressure for 10 seconds. Replace the radiator cap if it does not hold pressure.

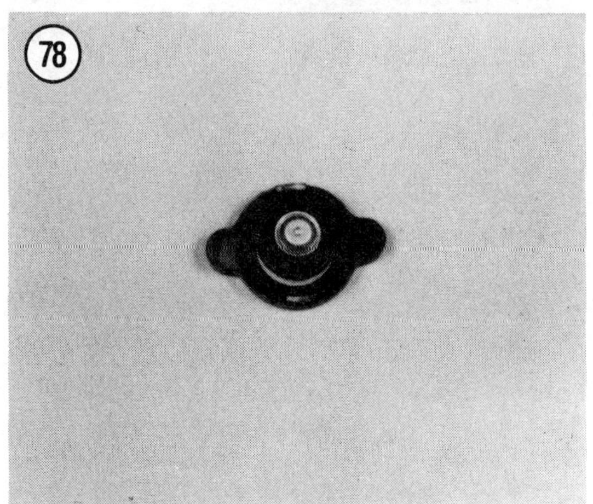

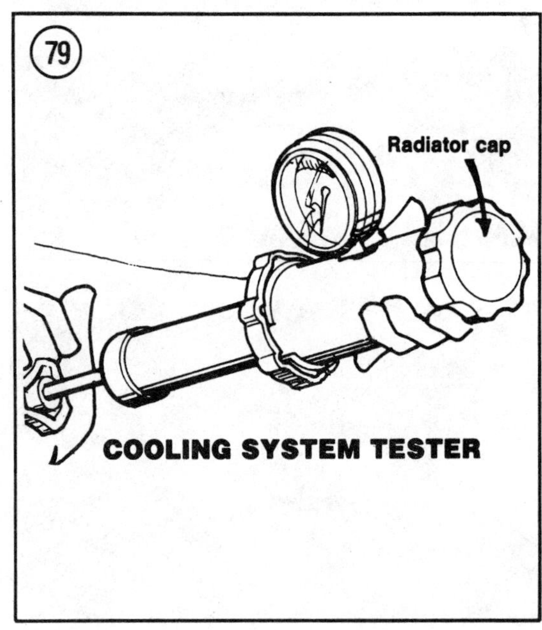

4. Leave the radiator cap off and have the entire cooling system pressure tested. The entire cooling system should be pressurized up to, but not exceeding the specifications in **Table 12**. The system must be able to hold this pressure for 10 seconds. Replace or repair any components that fail this test.
5. Check all cooling system hoses for damage or deterioration. Replace any hose that is questionable. Make sure all hose clamps are tight.
6. Carefully clean any dirt, mud, bugs, etc. from the radiator core. Use a whisk broom, compressed air or low-pressure water. If the radiator has been hit by a rock, *carefully* straighten out the fins with a screwdriver.

NOTE
If the radiator has been damaged across 15% or more of the frontal area, the radiator should be replaced.

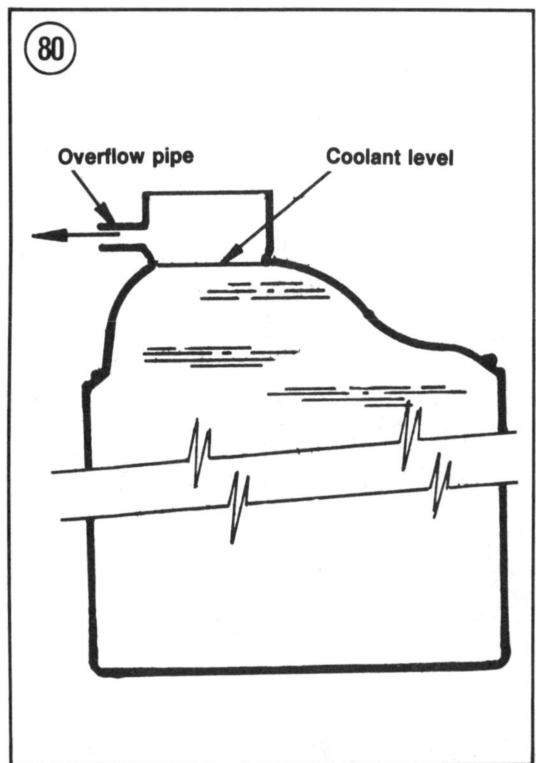

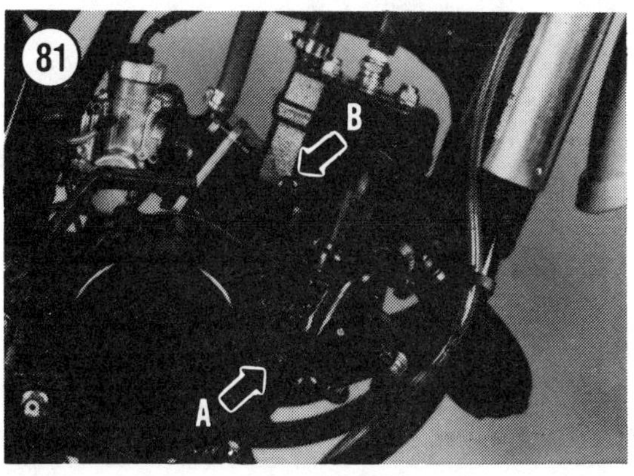

Coolant Check

WARNING
Do not remove the radiator cap when the engine is hot.

Before starting the bike, check the coolant level in the radiator. Remove the radiator cap (**Figure 77**) and make sure the level is just below the overflow pipe as indicated in **Figure 80**. If the level is low, add a sufficient amount of antifreeze and water (in a 50:50 ratio) as described under *Coolant* in this chapter.

Coolant

Only a high quality ethylene glycol-based coolant compounded for aluminum engines should be used. The coolant should be mixed with water in a 50:50 ratio. Coolant capacity is listed in **Table 12**. When mixing antifreeze with water, make sure to use only soft or distilled water. Never use tap or salt water as this will damage engine parts. Distilled water can be purchased at supermarkets in gallon containers.

Coolant Change

The cooling system should be completely drained and refilled at least once a year or whenever the top end is rebuilt.

CAUTION
Use only a high quality ethylene glycol antifreeze specifically labeled for use with aluminum engines. Do not use an alcohol-based antifreeze.

The following procedure must be performed when the engine is *cool*.

CAUTION
Be careful not to spill antifreeze on painted surfaces as it will stain or destroy the surface. Wash immediately with soapy water and rinse thoroughly with clean water.

1. Place a clean container under the water pump.
2. Remove the radiator cap (**Figure 77**). This will speed up the draining process.
3A. *1982-1985 models:* Remove the water pump drain bolt (A, **Figure 81**) and the cylinder drain bolt (B, **Figure 81**) and allow the coolant to drain.

3B. *1986-on models:* Remove the water pump drain bolt (**Figure 82**) and allow the coolant to drain.
4. Do not install the drain bolts.
5. Flush the cooling system with clean tap water directed through the radiator filler neck. Allow this water to drain completely.
6. Install the drain bolt(s).
7. Refill the radiator. Add the coolant through the radiator filler neck. Use a 50:50 mixture of antifreeze and distilled water. Radiator capacity for all models is listed in **Table 12**. Do not install the radiator cap at this time.
8. Start the engine and let it run at idle speed until the engine reaches normal operating temperature. Make sure there are no air bubbles in the coolant and that the coolant level stabilizes at the correct level (**Figure 80**). Add coolant as necessary.
9. Install the radiator cap and tighten securely.

Handlebars

Inspect the handlebars after each outing for any signs of damage. A bent or damaged handlebar should be replaced. The knurled section of the bars should be very rough. Keep the clamps clean with a wire brush. Any time that the bars slip in the clamps (like when you land flat and they move forward slightly) they should be removed and wire brushed clean. This will prevent small balls of aluminum from gathering in the clamps and reducing their gripping abilities.

CLYMER RACE TIP

Some riders find it preferable to "tune" the handlebar width by cutting up to 2 inches from each end. This will allow a smaller rider to more easily handle the machine. There are many excellent aftermarket handlebars available which come in a variety of sizes, shapes and colors. When looking for handlebars look for a comfortable bend and strong material, preferably chrome-moly, which is stronger than steel and won't bend easily. You also should purchase a cross bar pad to protect your face and teeth.

Nuts, Bolts, and Other Fasteners

Constant vibration can loosen many of the fasteners on the motorcycle. Check the tightness of all fasteners, especially those on:

a. Engine mounting hardware.
b. Engine crankcase covers.
c. Handlebar and front forks.
d. Gearshift lever.
e. Kickstarter lever.
f. Brake pedal and lever.
g. Exhaust system.

ENGINE TUNE-UP

The number of definitions of the term "tune-up" is probably equal to the number of people defining it. For the purposes of this book, a tune-up is general adjustment and maintenance to ensure peak engine performance.

The following paragraphs discuss each facet of a proper tune-up which should be performed in the order given. Unless otherwise specified, the engine should be thoroughly cool before starting any tune-up procedure.

Have the new parts on hand before you begin.

To perform a tune-up on your YZ, you will need the following tools and equipment:

a. 14 mm spark plug wrench.
b. Socket wrench and assorted sockets.

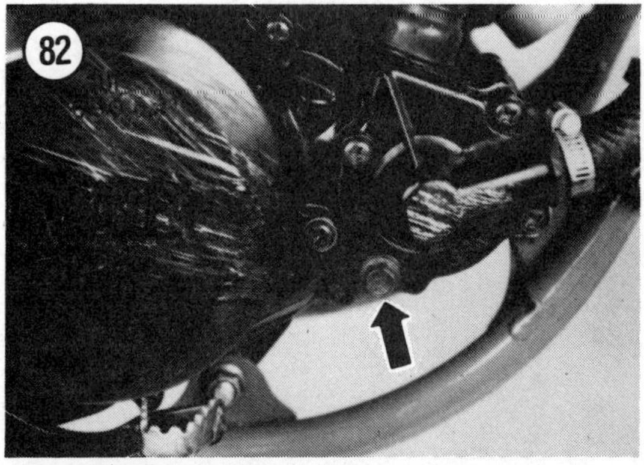

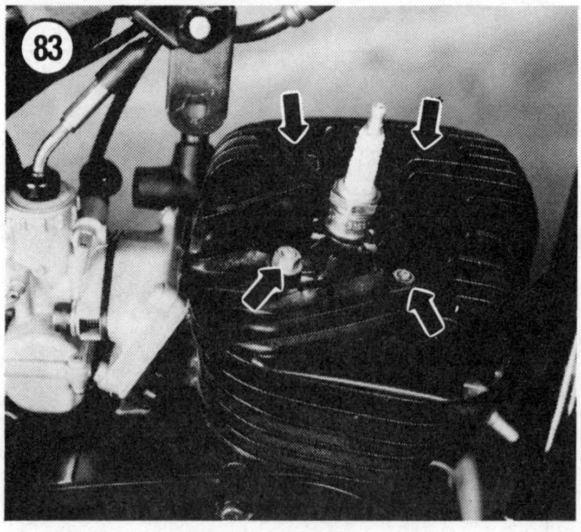

c. Phillips head screwdriver.
d. Spark plug wire feeler gauge and gapper tool.
e. Dial indicator.
f. Flywheel puller.
g. *YZ50 models:* Points checker, buzz box or ohmmeter.

Cylinder Head Nuts

The engine must be at room temperature for this procedure.

1. Place workstand under the frame to hold the bike securely.
2. Remove the seat.
3. Turn the fuel shutoff valve to the OFF position and remove the fuel line to the carburetor.
4. Remove the fuel tank.
5. Remove the exhaust system as described under *Exhaust System Removal/Installation* in Chapter Eight.
6. Tighten each nut (**Figure 83**) equally in a crisscross pattern to the tightening torque in **Table 8**.
7. Leave the seat and fuel tank off for the next procedures.

Correct Spark Plug Heat Range

Spark plugs are available in various heat ranges, hotter or colder than the plugs originally installed at the factory.

Select plugs of the heat range designed for the loads and conditions under which the YZ will be run. Use of incorrect heat ranges can cause a seized piston, scored cylinder wall or damaged piston crown.

In general, use a hot plug for low speeds and low temperatures. Use a cold plug for high speeds, high engine loads and high temperatures. The plug should operate hot enough to burn off unwanted deposits, but not so hot that they burn themselves or cause preignition. A spark plug of the correct heat range will show a light tan color on the portion of the insulator within the cylinder after the plug has been in service.

The reach (length) of a plug is also important. A longer than normal plug could interfere with the piston, causing permanent and severe damage. Refer to **Figure 84**.

The standard heat range spark plug for the various models is listed in **Table 13**.

Spark Plug Removal/Cleaning

1. Grasp the spark plug lead as near the plug as possible and pull it off the plug. If it is stuck to the plug, twist it slightly to break it loose.
2. Blow away any dirt that has accumulated in the spark plug well.

CAUTION
The dirt could fall into the cylinder when the plug is removed, causing serious engine damage.

3. Remove the spark plug with a 14 mm spark plug wrench.

NOTE
If the plug is difficult to remove, apply penetrating oil, like WD-40 or Liquid Wrench, around the base of the plug and let it soak about 10-20 minutes.

4. Inspect the plug carefully. Look for a broken center porcelain, excessively eroded electrodes and excessive carbon or oil fouling.

Gapping and Installing the Plug

A new spark plug should be carefully gapped to ensure a reliable, consistent spark. You must use a special spark plug gapping tool and a wire feeler gauge.

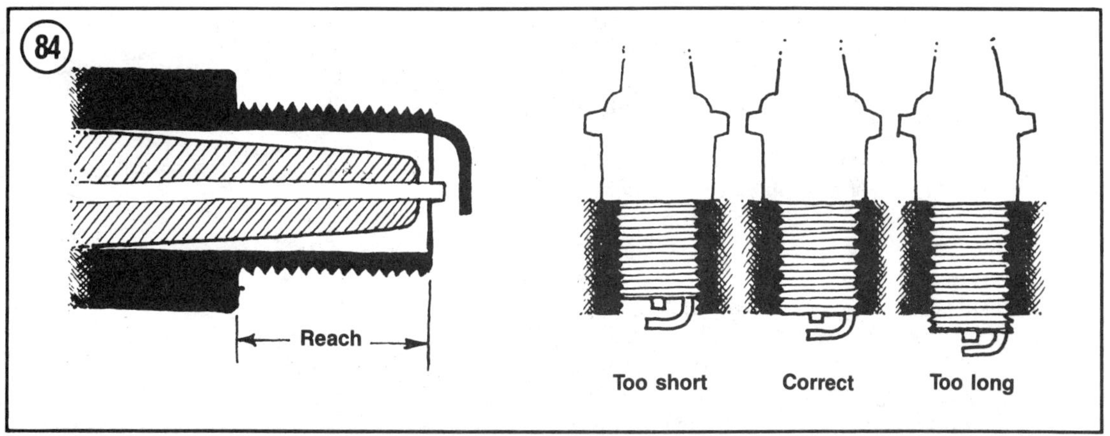

1. Remove the new spark plug from the box. Screw on the small piece that is loose in the box (**Figure 85**).
2. Insert a wire feeler gauge between the center and side electrode (**Figure 86**). The correct gap is listed in **Table 13**. If the gap is correct, you will feel a slight drag as you pull the wire through. If there is no drag, or the gauge won't pass through, bend the side electrode with a gapping tool (**Figure 87**) to set the proper gap.
3. Apply anti-seize to the plug threads before installing the spark plug.

NOTE
Anti-seize can be purchased at most automotive parts stores.

4. Screw the spark plug in by hand until it seats. Very little effort is required. If force is necessary, you have the plug cross-threaded. Unscrew it and try again.

NOTE
Do not overtighten. This will only squash the gasket and destroy its sealing ability.

5. Use a spark plug wrench and tighten the plug an additional 1/4 to 1/2 turn after the gasket has made contact with the head. If you are installing an old, regapped plug and reusing the old gasket, only tighten an additional 1/4 turn.
6. Install the spark plug wire. Make sure it is on tight.

CAUTION
Make sure the spark plug wire is pulled away from the exhaust pipe.

7. Reinstall the seat, fuel tank and exhaust system.

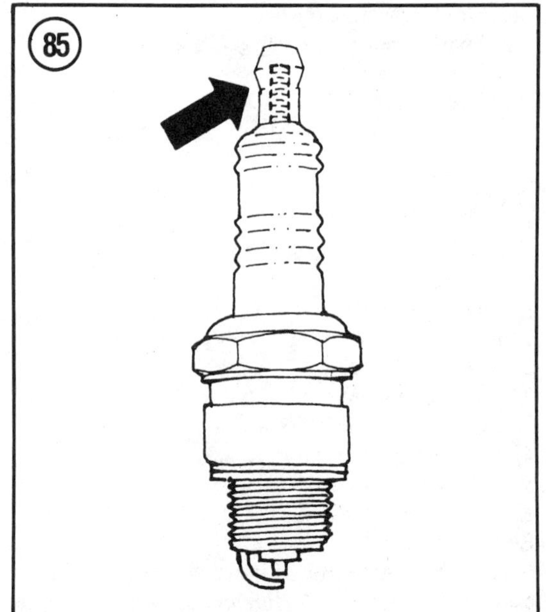
85

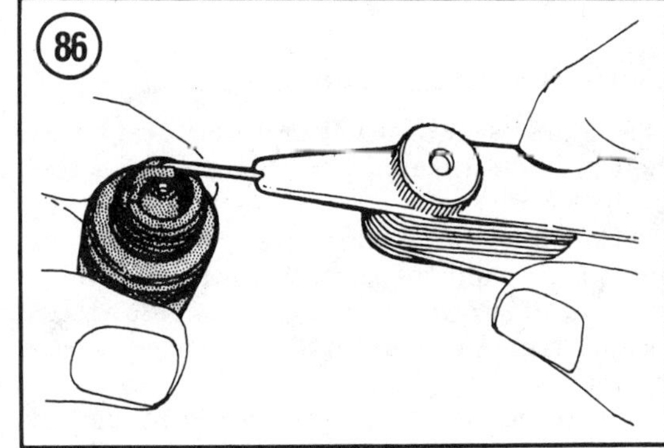
86

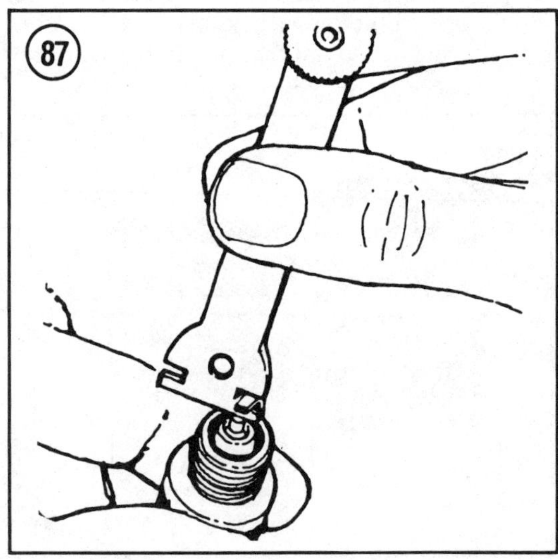
87

Reading Spark Plugs

Much information about engine and spark plug performance can be determined by careful examination of the spark plug. This information is only valid after performing the following steps.

1. Ride the bike a short distance at full throttle in any gear.
2. Push on the kill switch before closing the throttle and simultaneously pull in the clutch or shift to neutral; coast and brake to a stop.
3. Remove the spark plug and examine it. Compare it to **Figure 88**.

If the insulator is white or burned, the plug is too hot and should be replaced with a colder one.

A too-cold plug will have sooty or oily deposits.

If the plug has a light tan or gray colored deposit and no abnormal gap wear or electrode erosion is

SPARK PLUG CONDITIONS

NORMAL USE

OIL FOULED

CARBON FOULED

OVERHEATED

GAP BRIDGED

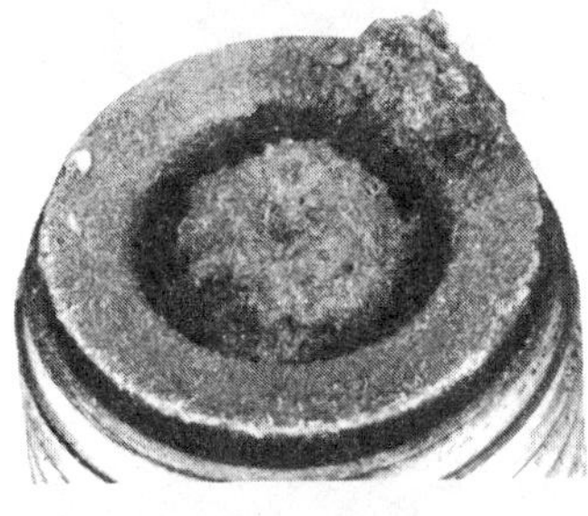

SUSTAINED PREIGNITION

WORN OUT

evident, the plug and the engine are running properly.

If the plug exhibits a black insulator tip, damp oily film over the firing end, and a carbon layer over the entire nose, it is oil fouled. An oil fouled plug can be cleaned, but it is better to replace it.

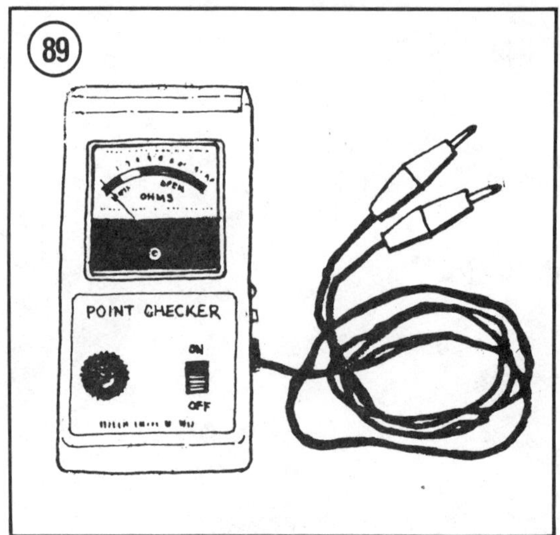

Ignition Timing

YZ50

The YZ50 is equipped with a contact breaker point ignition system. Unlike the CDI ignition system used on the YZ60 and YZ80 models, this system does have moving parts that wear and must be watched more carefully. Adjust the breaker points at the frequency indicated in **Table 1**. This procedure requires the use of an ohmmeter, test light, point checker unit **(Figure 89)**, or buzz box. The test light can be a homemade unit **(Figure 90)** that consists of 2 C or D size flashlight batteries and a light bulb, all mounted on a piece of wood, some light gauge electrical wire and alligator clips. These items can be purchased from most hardware stores.

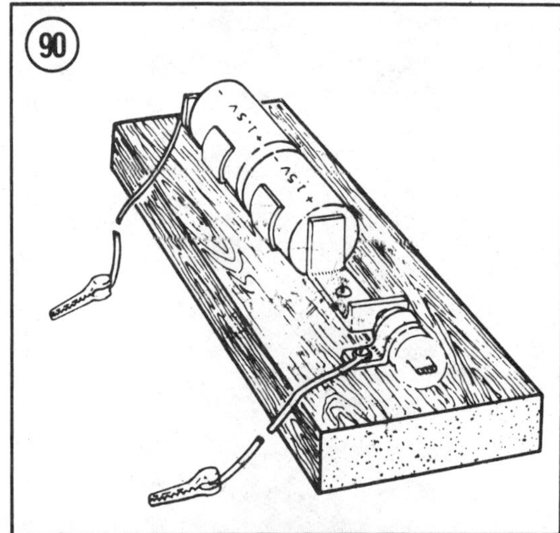

The following procedure is based on the test unit shown in **Figure 90**. If another type is used, follow the manufacturer's instructions.

1. Remove the shift lever.
2. Clean all dirt and residue from around the spark plug. Then twist the spark plug cap and pull it off of the spark plug. Remove the spark plug.
3. Remove the clutch adjustment cover **(Figure 91)** and the left-hand crankcase cover. The clutch adjustment cover must be removed first as the upper long cover bolt is screwed into the crankcase.

NOTE
Tie the left-hand crankcase cover to the frame to keep any strain off the clutch cable.

4. Disconnect the magneto electrical harness from the ignition coil **(Figure 92)**.

CAUTION
If piston top dead center (TDC) is not correctly determined as described in Step 5, the dial indicator will be damaged.

5. Locate piston top dead center (TDC) with a dial indicator as follows:
   a. Insert a long pencil or wooden dowel in the spark plug hole and rotate the crankshaft until the pencil rises to its highest point. This is approximately top dead center (TDC). Remove the pencil.

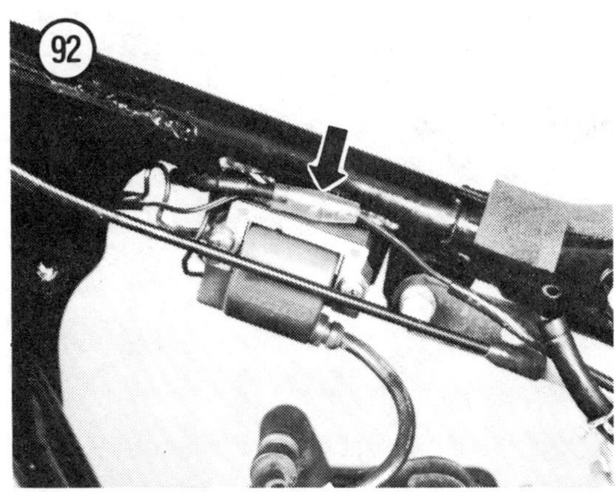

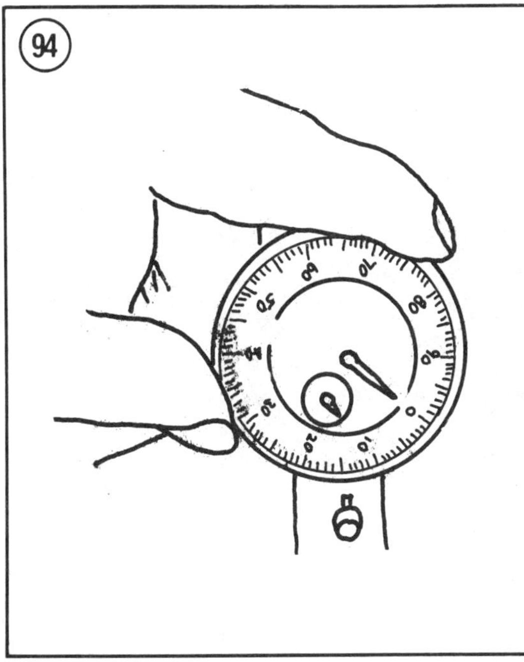

b. Screw the dial indicator holder into the cylinder head.

c. Install an extension rod onto the dial indicator.

d. Install the dial indicator (**Figure 93**) into the holder. Push the dial indicator in its holder until the gauge reads approximately 3 mm. Tighten the set screw. When the dial indicator is pushed into the holder, the extension arm on the dial indicator will compress against the piston crown.

e. Slowly rotate the magneto rotor *clockwise* as viewed from the left-hand side and watch the dial pointer. When the pointer stops and reverses direction, this is TDC. Zero the dial gauge by aligning the 0 with the dial pointer (**Figure 94**).

f. Rotate the magneto rotor one revolution and check TDC. Readjust if necessary.

NOTE

Prior to attaching the tester, check the condition of the batteries by touching the 2 test leads together. The light should be ON. If it is not, replace the batteries and/or check the connections and the light bulb on the tester. Be sure the tester is operating correctly before using it. Use this check procedure for any type of test equipment used for this procedure.

6. Connect one test lead of the test light to the black wire in the wire harness coming from the magneto and the other one to an unpainted surface of one of the cooling fins on the engine or to one of the crankcase bolts or screws. The test light should now be ON and bright, indicating the points are closed.

7. Starting at TDC rotate the magneto rotor *clockwise* until the dial needle turns approximately 3 complete turns before top dead center (BTDC).

8. Slowly turn the magneto rotor *counterclockwise* until the dial gauge reads within the dimension range listed in **Table 14**.

9. At this time the test light should still be on but DIM, indicating that the breaker points have just begun to open.

10. Repeat Steps 8-10 to verify that the points are opening at the specified time.

11. If timing is incorrect, loosen the Phillips head screw (**Figure 95**) and carefully rotate the contact breaker assembly with a common screwdriver. Move it a small amount at a time and repeat Steps 8-10 until the timing is correct. Tighten the Phillips head screw.

12. After the ignition timing is correct, check that the contact breaker point gap is within tolerance. Insert a flat feeler gauge (**Figure 96**). The opening should be within the following dimensions:

a. Normal: 0.35 mm (0.014 in.).
b. Minimum: 0.30 mm (0.012 in.).
c. Maximum: 0.40 mm (0.016 in.).

If the gap is greater, or over tolerance, the contact breaker point assembly must be replaced as described under *Contact Breaker Point Replacement* in this chapter.

NOTE

*Do not try to bend the fixed arm of the contact breaker point assembly to decrease the gap. This will only upset the alignment of the 2 point surfaces (**Figure 97**) which will result in premature component failure and a difficulty in trying to set the timing correctly.*

13. Remove the dial indicator, extension rod and indicator holder. Connect the magneto electrical harness and install the spark plug.
14. Install the left-hand crankcase cover and shift lever.

NOTE

Be sure to install the long bolt into the upper hole in the clutch adjustment cover. This is necessary for proper clutch operation.

Contact Breaker Point Replacement (YZ50)

1. Remove the shift lever (A, **Figure 98**).
2. Remove the screws securing the left-hand crankcase cover (B, **Figure 98**) and the clutch mechanism adjustment cover (C, **Figure 98**) and remove both covers.

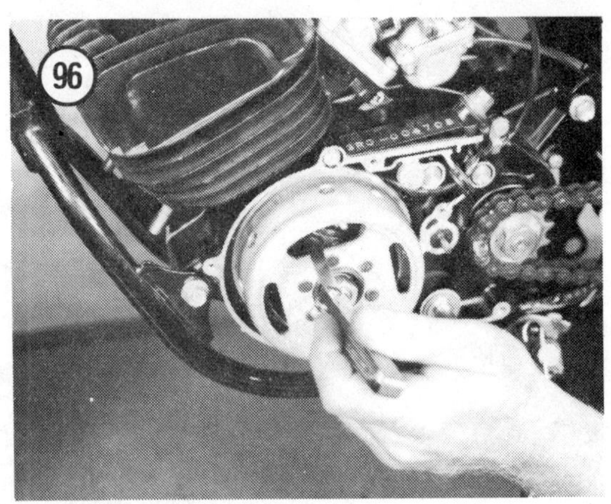

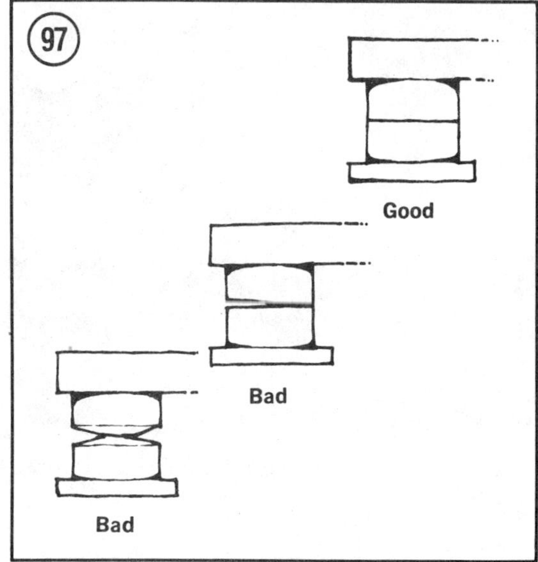

NOTE
Tie up the crankcase cover to the frame to keep the strain off the clutch cable.

3. Remove the magneto rotor as described under *Magneto Removal/Installation* in Chapter Nine.
4. Remove the screw (A, **Figure 99**) securing the contact breaker assembly to the stator backing plate. Remove the screw and nut (B, **Figure 99**) securing the electrical lead to the point assembly.
5. Install a new breaker point assembly, making sure all electrical connections are clean and tight.
6. Adjust the point gap as described under *Ignition Timing—YZ50* in this chapter.
7. Install the left-hand crankcase cover, making sure to install the long screw in the upper hole of the clutch adjustment cover (**Figure 100**). This is necessary for proper clutch operation.
8. Install the shift lever.

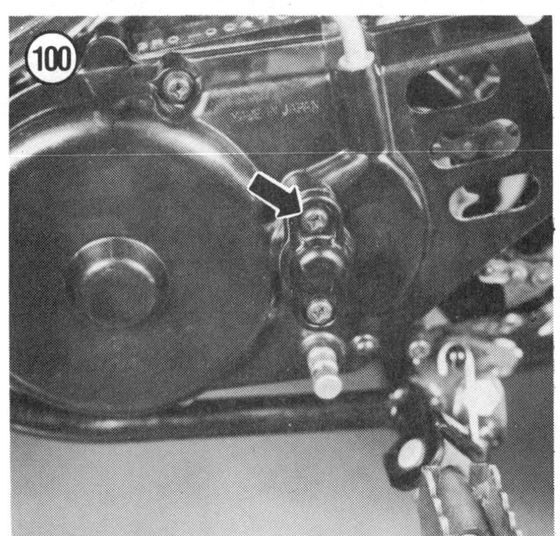

Ignition Timing (YZ60 and YZ80)

These models are equipped with a capacitor discharge ignition (CDI). This system uses no breaker points and greatly simplifies ignition timing and makes the ignition system much less susceptible to failures caused by dirt, moisture and wear.

Since there are no components to wear, adjusting the ignition timing is only necessary after the engine has been disassembled or if the stator base plate screws have worked loose.

1. Place the bike on the sidestand.
2. Remove the ignition cover (**Figure 101**).
3. Clean all dirt and residue from around the spark plug. Then twist the spark plug cap and pull it off of the spark plug. Remove the spark plug (**Figure 102**).

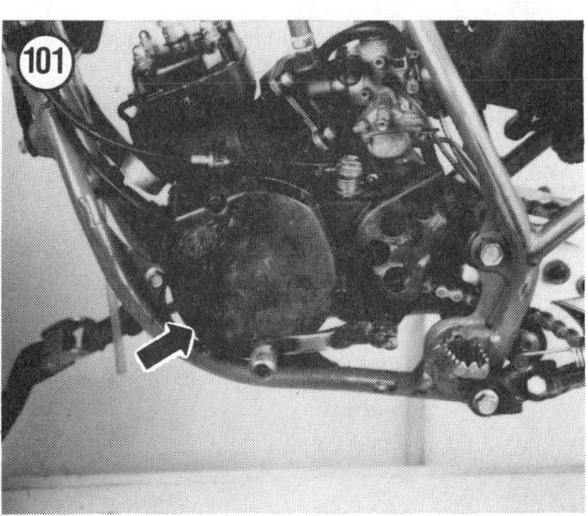

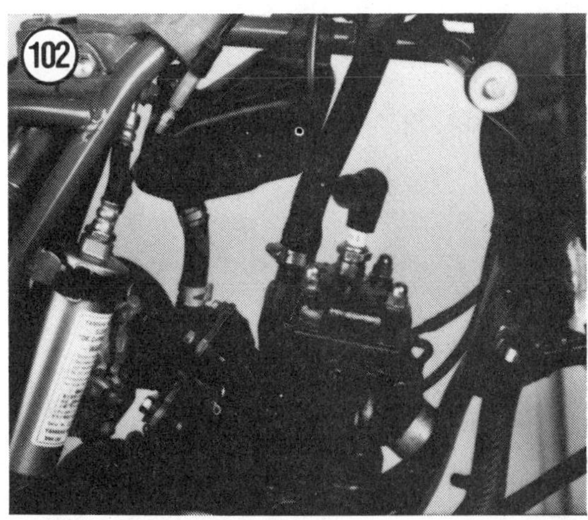

4. Remove the exhaust pipe, if necessary.

CAUTION
If piston top dead center (TDC) is not correctly determined as described in Step 5, the dial indicator will be damaged.

5. Locate piston top dead center (TDC) with a dial indicator as follows:
   a. Insert a long pencil or wooden dowel in the spark plug hole and rotate the crankshaft until the pencil rises to its highest point. This is approximately top dead center (TDC). Remove the pencil.
   b. Screw the dial indicator holder into the cylinder head.
   c. Install an extension rod onto the dial indicator.
   d. Install the dial indicator (**Figure 103**) into the holder. Push the dial indicator until the gauge reads approximately 3 mm. Tighten the set screw. When the dial indicator is pushed into the holder, the extension arm on the dial indicator will compress against the piston crown.
   e. Rotate the magneto rotor *clockwise* as viewed from the left-hand side and watch the dial pointer. When the pointer stops and reverses direction, this is TDC. Zero the dial gauge by aligning the 0 with the dial pointer (**Figure 94**).
   f. Rotate the magneto rotor one revolution and check TDC. Readjust if necessary.
6. From TDC, rotate the magneto rotor *clockwise* until the dial reads the dimension given in **Table 14**.
7. *YZ60 and 1978 YZ80:* Check and adjust ignition timing as follows:

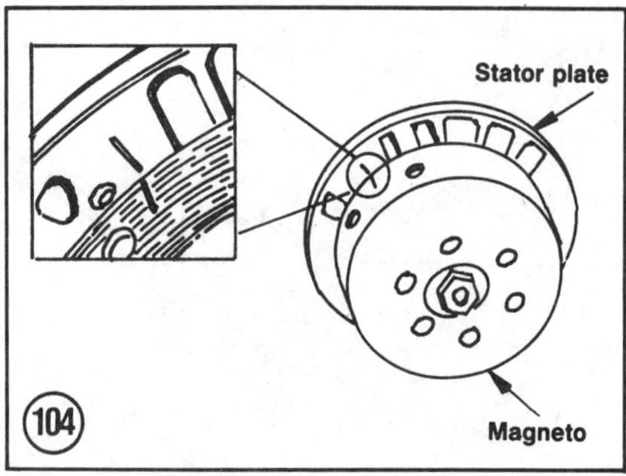

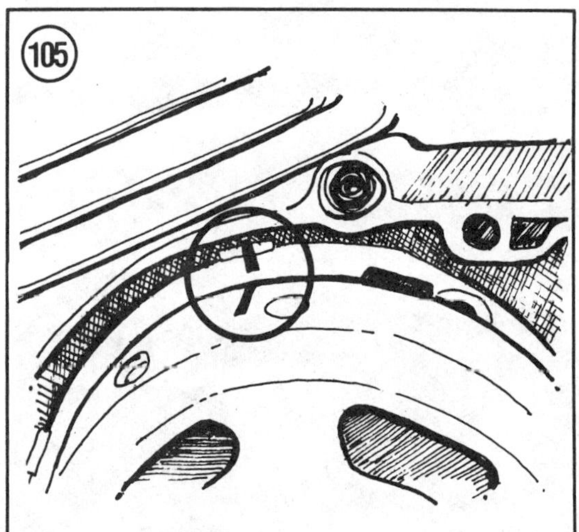

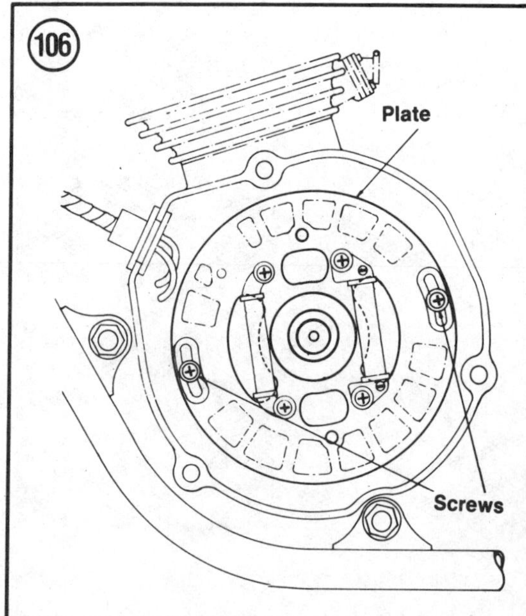

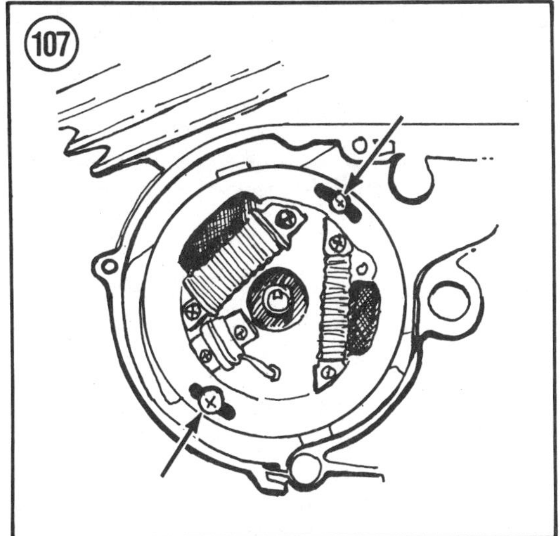

a. Check that the timing mark on the magneto is aligned with the crankcase mark. See **Figure 104** (YZ60) or **Figure 105** (YZ80). If the timing is incorrect, perform the following.
b. Remove the magneto rotor as described under *Magneto, Outer Rotor Type* in Chapter Nine.
c. See **Figure 106** (YZ60) or **Figure 107** (YZ80). Loosen the base plate until the stator base plate mark aligns with the fixed mark on the crankcase. Tighten the screws securely, making sure the stator base plate does not move. Recheck the timing.
d. Install the magneto rotor as described in Chapter Nine.

8. *1979-1983 YZ80:* Check and adjust ignition timing as follows:
a. Check that the timing marks on the inner rotor and the stator base plate align. See A, **Figure 108** (1979-1980) or A, **Figure 109** (1981-1983). If the timing is incorrect, perform the following.
b. Loosen the stator base plate screws (B). Then rotate the base plate and align the base plate timing mark with the mark on the rotor.
c. Tighten the base plate screws (B) securely.
d. Recheck the ignition timing.

9. *1984-on YZ80:* Check and adjust the ignition timing as follows:
a. Check that the timing mark on the magneto rotor aligns with the fixed mark on the stator plate (**Figure 110**). If the timing is incorrect, perform the following.
b. Punch a mark on the crankcase in line with the rotor mark if a mark is not already there.
c. Remove the magneto as described in Chapter Nine.
d. Loosen the two stator plate screws (A, **Figure 111**) and rotate the stator plate until the stator

plate mark aligns with the crankcase mark or the new mark made in sub-step b.

e. Tighten the stator plate screws and recheck the timing mark alignment.

10. Remove the dial indicator, extension and indicator holder.
11. Install the left-hand side cover. Tighten the screws securely.
12. Install the spark plug and spark plug cap.

Carburetor Idle Speed Adjustment

Proper idle speed is a balance between a low enough idle to give adequate compression braking and a high enough idle to prevent engine stalling (if desired). The idle air/fuel mixture affects transition from idle to part throttle openings.

1. Make sure that the throttle cable free play is correct; adjust if necessary.

CAUTION

Never turn the pilot air screw in tight. You'll damage the screw or the soft aluminum seat in the carburetor.

2. Turn the pilot air screw (A, **Figure 112**) in until it seats lightly, then back it out the number of turns specified in **Table 15**.
3. Warm up the engine completely. Then turn the idle speed screw (B, **Figure 112**) to set the idle as low as possible without stalling the engine.
4. Turn the pilot air screw (A, **Figure 112**) until the engine drops off quickly one way and then where the idle shoots up when its turned the other way. The midpoint between high and low engine idle is the correct pilot air screw adjustment.

NOTE

The pilot air screw should not be opened more than 3 turns or it may vibrate out. If you cannot get the bike to idle properly, check that the air cleaner is clean. If air cleaner is okay and other engine systems are operating correctly, the pilot jet size may be incorrect. Refer to Chapter Eight.

5. Reset the idle speed (B, **Figure 112**) as desired.

NOTE

After this adjustment is completed, test ride the bike. Throttle response from idle should be rapid and without any hesitation. If there is any hesitation, turn the pilot air screw in or out in 1/4 turn increments until this problem is solved.

WARNING

With the engine idling, move the handlebar from side to side. If idle speed increases during this movement, the throttle cable needs adjusting or it may be incorrectly routed through the frame. Correct this problem immediately. Do not ride the bike in this unsafe condition.

Decarbonizing

The carbon deposits should be removed from the piston, cylinder head, exhaust port and muffler as indicated in **Table 1** or **Table 2**. If it is not cleaned off it will cause reduced performance, preignition (ping) or overheating.

Engine decarbonizing

1. Remove the cylinder head and cylinder as described under *Cylinder Removal/Installation* in Chapter Four.

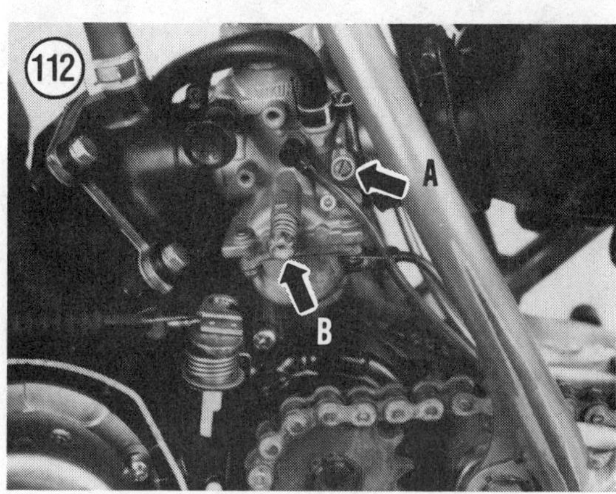

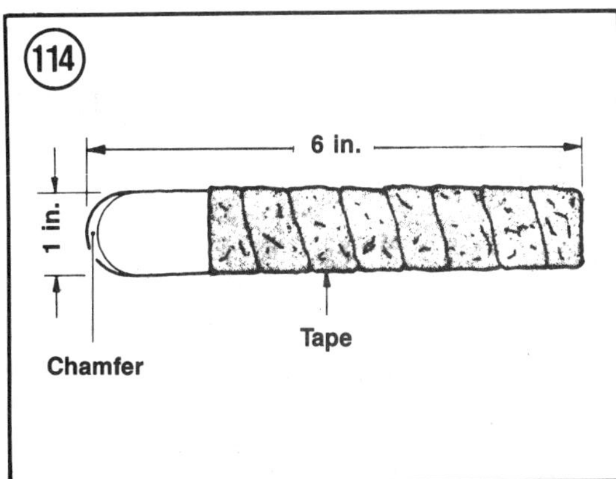

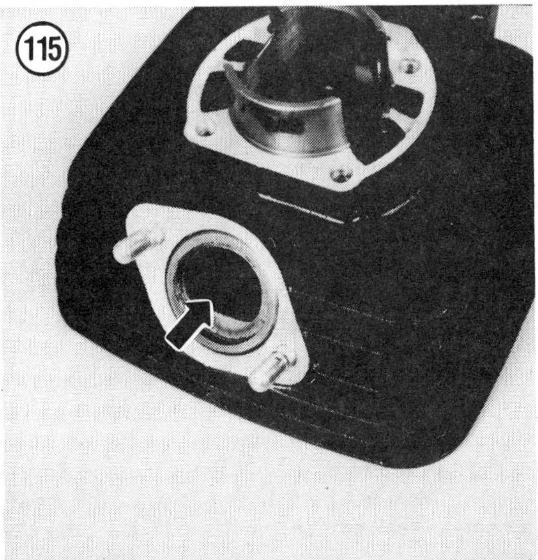

2. Gently scrape off carbon deposits from the top of the piston and cylinder head (**Figure 113**) with a dull screwdriver or end of a hacksaw blade (**Figure 114**). Do not scratch the surface. Stuff a shop cloth into the opening in the crankcase to keep any residue from entering into it.
3. Wipe the surfaces clean with a cloth dipped in cleaning solvent.
4. Scrape off the carbon in the exhaust port (**Figure 115**) with a dull screwdriver or end of a hacksaw blade. Do not scratch the surface.
5. Install the cylinder and cylinder head.

Exhaust system decarbonizing

1. Remove the exhaust pipe assembly as described under *Exhaust System Removal/Installation* in Chapter Eight.
2. Gently scrape off carbon deposits from the interior of the head pipe where it attaches to the cylinder.

WARNING
*If a length of cable is used in an electric drill to clean the inside of the exhaust pipe, do not start the drill **until** the cable is inserted into the exhaust pipe. Operating the drill with the cable out of the pipe could cause serious injury if the cable should whip against your face or body.*

3. Clean out the rest of the interior of the expansion chamber by running a piece of used motorcycle drive chain around in it. Another way is to chuck a length of wire cable, with one end frayed, in an electric drill. Run it around in the front portion a couple of times. Shake out all loose carbon. Also tap on the outer shell of the exhaust pipe assembly with a plastic mallet to break any additional carbon loose.
4. Blow out the expansion chamber with compressed air.
5. Clean out the interior of the silencer.
6. Visually inspect the entire exhaust pipe assembly, especially in the many areas of welds, for cracks or other damage. Replace if necessary, or repair as described in Chapter Eight.
7. Install the assembly.

STORAGE

Several months of inactivity can cause serious problems and a general deterioration of the YZ's condition. This is especially true in areas of weather extremes. During the winter months it is advisable to specially prepare the bike for lay-up.

Selecting a Storage Area

Most riders store their bikes in their home garages. If you do not have a home garage, facilities suitable for long-term motorcycle storage are readily available for rent or lease in most areas. In selecting a building, consider the following points.
1. The storage area must be dry, free from dampness and excessive humidity. Heating is not necessary, but the building should be well insulated to minimize extreme temperature variations.
2. Buildings with large window areas should be avoided, or such windows should be masked (also a good security measure) if direct sunlight can fall on the bike.
3. Buildings in industrial areas, where factories are liable to emit corrosive fumes, are not desirable, nor are facilities near bodies of salt water.
4. The area should be selected to minimize the possibility of loss from fire, theft or vandalism. The area should be fully insured, perhaps with a package covering fire, theft, vandalism, weather and liability. Talk this over with your insurance agent and get approval on these matters. The building should be fireproof and items such as the security of doors and windows, alarm facility and proximity of police should be considered.

Preparing Bike for Storage

Careful preparation will minimize deterioration and make it easier to restore the bike to service later. Use the following procedure.
1. Wash the bike completely. Make certain to remove all dirt in all the hard to reach parts like the cooling fins on the head and cylinder (on air cooled models). Completely dry all parts of the bike to remove all moisture. Wax all painted and polished surfaces, including any chromed areas.
2. Run the bike for about 20-30 minutes to warm up the oil in the clutch and transmission. Drain the oil, regardless of the time since the last oil change. Refill with the normal quantity and type of oil.
3. Drain all gasoline from the fuel tank, interconnecting hose and the carburetor. Leave the fuel shutoff valve in the ON position. As an alternative, a fuel preservative may be added to the fuel. This preservative is available from many motorcycle shops and marine equipment suppliers.
4. Lubricate the drive chain and control cables; refer to specific procedures in this chapter.
5. Remove the spark plug and add about one teaspoon of two-stroke engine oil into the cylinder. Reinstall the spark plug and turn the engine over to distribute the oil to the cylinder walls and piston. Depress the engine kill switch while doing this to prevent it from starting.
6. Tape or tie a plastic bag over the end of the silencer to prevent the entry of moisture.
7. Check the tire pressure, inflate to the correct pressure and move the bike to the storage area. Place it securely on wood block(s) with both wheels off the ground.
8. Cover the bike with a tarp, blanket or heavy plastic drop cloth. Place this cover over the bike mainly as a dust cover—do not wrap it tightly, especially any plastic material, as it may trap moisture causing condensation. Leave room for air to circulate around the bike.

Inspection During Storage

Try to inspect the bike weekly while in storage. Any deterioration should be corrected as soon as possible. For example, if corrosion of bright metal parts is observed, cover them with a light coat of grease or silicone spray after a thorough polishing.

Turn the engine over a couple of times. Don't start it; use the kickstarter and hold the kill switch on. Pump the front forks to keep the seals lubricated.

Restoring Bike to Service

A bike that has been properly prepared and stored in a suitable area requires only light maintenance to restore to service. It is advisable, however, to perform a spring tune-up.
1. Before removing the bike from the storage area, reinflate the tires to the correct pressures. Air loss during storage may have nearly flattened the tires, and moving the bike can cause damage to tires, tubes and rims.

WARNING
Place a metal container under the carburetor to catch all expelled fuel—this presents a real fire danger if allowed to drain onto the bike and the floor. Dispose of the fuel properly.

2. When the bike is brought to the work area, turn the fuel shutoff valve to the OFF position, and refill the fuel tank with the correct fuel/oil mixture. Remove the main jet cover on the base of the carburetor, turn the fuel shutoff valve to the ON position, and allow several cups of fuel to pass through the fuel system. Turn the fuel shutoff valve to the OFF position and install the main jet cover.
3. Remove the spark plug and squirt a small amount of fuel into the cylinder to help remove the oil coating.

4. Install a fresh spark plug and start up the engine.

NOTE

If you have a YZ50 and the engine will not start, remove the ignition cover and spray the contact breaker points with a good grade of aerosol electrical contact cleaner. This will help remove any oil residue or small amount of corrosion on the points.

5. Perform the standard tune-up as described in this chapter.

6. Check the operation of the engine kill switch. Oxidation of the switch contacts during storage may make it inoperative.

7. Clean and test ride the motorcycle.

WARNING

If any type of preservative (Armor All or equivalent) has been applied to the tire treads be sure the tires are well "scrubbed-in" prior to any fast riding or cornering on a hard surface. If not they will slip right out from under you.

Tables are on the following pages.

Table 1 MAINTENANCE SCHEDULE*

Item	Model YZ80 (1978-1981)	Model YZ50
Piston		
Clean and inspect	Every race	Every 80 hours
Replace	Every 5th race	As required
Piston rings		
Replace	Every 2nd race	Every 80 hours
Cylinder head		
Inspect	Every race	Every 40 hours
Clean and retighten	Every race	Every 40 hours
Cylinder		
Clean and inspect	Every race	Every 40 hours
Retighten	Every race	—
Crankshaft main bearing		
Inspect	Every 5th race	Every 80 hours
Replace	As required	As required
Piston wrist pin		
Inspect	Every 5th race	Every 80 hours
Replace	As required	As required
Magneto rotor nut		
Retighten	Every 5th race	Every 160 hours
Kickstarter idle gear		
Inspect and replace	As required	As required
Clutch		
Adjust	Every 3rd race	Every 40 hours
Inspect	Every race	Every 40 hours
Replace	As required	As required
Transmission		
Change oil	Every 5th race	Every 80 hours
Inspect gears and shift forks	As required	As required
Exhaust system		
Inspect	Every race	Every 40 hours
Decarbonize	Every 5th race	Every 80 hours
Carburetor		
Inspect and adjust	Every race	Every 80 hours
Clean and retighten	Every race	Every 160 hours
Fuel shutoff valve		
Clean	As required	Every 40 hours
Air filter		
Clean and oil	Every race	Every 40 hours
Replace	As required	As required
Spark plug		
Inspect and clean	Every race	Every 40 hours
Replace	As required	As required

(continued)

Table 1 MAINTENANCE SCHEDULE* (continued)

Item	Model YZ80 (1978-1981)	Model YZ50
Ignition timing	—	Every 80 hours
Contact breaker point lubrication wick		
Lubricate	—	Every 160 hours
Drive chain		
Clean and lubricate	Every race	Every 40 hours
Check tension and alignment	Every race	Every 40 hours
Replace	As required	As required
Chain guards and rollers		
Inspect and replace	As required	As required
Frame		
Clean and inspect	Every race	Every 40 hours
Front fork		
Change oil	After initial 5 races, every 10th race thereafter	Every 80 hours
Replace oil seal	As required	As required
Monoshock		
Inspect and adjust	Every race	Every 40 hours
Lubricate	Every race	Every 40 hours
Steering head		
Inspect adjustment	Every race	Every 40 hours
Clean and lubricate	Every 5th race	Every 160 hours
Replace bearings	As required	As required
Swing arm		
Inspect	Every race	Every 80 hours
Lubricate	Every race	Every 80 hours
Wheels and tires		
Check pressure, runout, and spoke tension	Every race	Every 40 hours
Inspect wheel bearings	Every race	Every 40 hours
Lubricate oil seals	Every race	Every 80 hours
Replace wheel bearings	As required	As required
Throttle control		
Lubricate	Every race	Every 80 hours
Control cables		
Check routing and connections	Every race	Every 40 hours
Inspect and lubricate	Every race	Every 80 hours
Clutch and brake hand lever pivot points		
Lubricate	Every race	Every 80 hours
Retighten	Every race	Every 80 hours
Brakes		
Clean, inspect, adjust	Every race	Every 40 hours
Lubricate pivots	Every race	Every 80 hours
Replace linings	As required	As required
Miscellaneous bolts and fasteners		
Inspect and tighten	Every race	Every 40 hours

*This Yamaha Factory maintenance schedule should be considered as a guide to general maintenance and lubrication intervals after the normal initial break-in maintenance has been performed. Harder than normal use and exposure to mud, water, sand, high humidity, etc. will naturally dictate more frequent attention to most maintenance items.

3

Table 2 MAINTENANCE SCHEDULE (YZ80 1982-ON)

Every race	• Clean and inspect piston • Inspect, clean and retighten cylinder head • Inspect exhaust system • Inspect, clean and adjust carburetor • Inspect YEIS • Clean air filter • Inspect spark plug • Clean, lubricate and adjust drive chain • Inspect cooling system; tighten connections • Clean and inspect frame • Inspect rear shock absorber • Lubricate rear pivot shaft • Check and adjust steering head free play • Inspect wheels and tires • Inspect wheel bearings • Inspect and lubricate throttle • Inspect and lubricate control cables • Lubricate and tighten clutch and brake levers • Lubricate relay arm* • Check brake fluid level** • Check front brake pad wear**
Every 2nd race	• Replace piston rings • Inspect clutch
Every 3rd race	• Adjust clutch • Lubricate wheel bearing seals
Every 5th race	• Replace piston • Change transmission oil • Inspect engine main bearings • Inspect connecting rod • Inspect piston pin • Tighten rotor nut • Clean exhaust system • Clean and lubricate steering head bearings • Lubricate swing arm pivot axle • Change fork oil***
As required** **	• Replace clutch plates • Inspect transmission • Replace connecting rod • Replace piston pin • Inspect kickstarter, replace parts as needed • Replace air filter • Replace spark plug • Replace drive chain • Replace coolant • Clean fuel tank • Replace fork seals • Adjust rear shock absorber • Replace steering head bearings • Replace drive chain guard • Replace wheel bearings • Replace brake linings • Replace brake fluid**

* 1984-on models.
** 1986 models.
*** Initially after 5 races, then every 10 races
**** Perform as indicated by inspection procedures.

Table 3 TIRE INFLATION PRESSURE

Front	1.0 kg/cm² (14 psi)
Rear	1.0 kg/cm² (14 psi)

Table 4 RECOMMENDED LUBRICANTS AND FUEL

Engine oil	Yamaha Yamalube "R", Castrol R
Transmission oil	SAE 10W/30 "SE" or "SF" motor oil
Front fork oil	
1978-1982	20 wt. fork oil
1983-on	10 wt. fork oil
Air filter	Foam air filter oil
Drive chain	Chain lube
Control cables	Cable lube
Control lever pivots	10W/30 motor oil
Swing arm assembly	Lithium soap base grease
Steering head, wheel bearings	Wheel bearing, waterproof type bearings
Fuel	Premium grade—research octane 90 or higher
Brake fluid	DOT 3 or DOT 4

Table 5 GAS/OIL PREMIX RATIO

Model	Premix ratio with Yamalube "R"	Premix ratio with Castrol R
YZ5	20:1	20:1
YZ60		
1981	16:1	20:1
1982	24:1	20:1
YZ80		
1978	20:1	20:1
1979-1980	32:1	20:1
1981	16:1	20:1
1982-on	24:1	20:1

RATIO 16:1

Gasoline U.S. gal.	Oil Oz.	Oil cc
	8	237
2	16	473
3	24	710
4	32	946
5	40	1183

RATIO 20:1

Gasoline U.S. gal.	Oil Oz.	Oil cc
1	6.4	190
2	12.8	380
3	19.2	570
4	25.6	760
5	32	945

(continued)

Table 5 GAS/OIL PREMIX RATIO (continued)

RATIO 24:1		
Gasoline	Oil	
U.S. gal.	Oz.	cc
1	5.3	157
2	10.7	316
3	16	473
4	21.2	627
5	26.6	786
RATIO 32:1		
Gasoline	Oil	
U.S. gal.	Oz.	cc
1	4	118
2	8	237
3	12	355
4	16	473
5	20	591

Table 6 FUEL TANK CAPACITY

Model	U.S. gal.	Liters
YZ50	0.8	3.0
YZ60		
1981	0.8	3.0
1982	0.9	3.3
YZ80		
1978-1981	1.2	4.6
1982	1.4	5.2
1983-on	1.3	5.0

Table 7 CLUTCH/TRANSMISSION OIL CAPACITY

Model	Drain/refill	Rebuild
YZ50	600-650 cc	650-700 cc
YZ60	650-700 cc	700-750 cc
YZ80		
1978	600-700 cc	650-700 cc
1979-1981	650-700 cc	700-750 cc
1982-1986	625-675 cc	675-725 cc
1987-on	650 cc	700 cc

Table 8 MAINTENANCE TORQUE SPECIFICATIONS

Item	N·m	ft.-lb.
Cylinder head nuts or bolts		
YZ50	10	7
YZ60	30	21
YZ80		
1978-1980	13-15	9-11
1981-1982	30	21
1983-on	25	18
Fork bridge bolts		
YZ50	15	11
YZ60	16	12
YZ80		
1978	24	17
1979-1979	23	16
1980-1981	15	11
1982	18	13
1983-1985	23	17
1985-on	18	13
Rear axle nut		
YZ50	40	29
YZ60	45	32
YZ80		
1978	70	49
1979-1980	75	54
1981	70	49
1982-on	85	61

Table 9 FRONT FORK OIL CAPACITY*

Model	cc	oz.
YZ50	75	2.5
YZ60	78	2.6
YZ80		
1978	83	2.8
1979-1980	150	5.07
1981-1982	188	6.4
1983	260	8.8
1984-on	272	9.2

* Each fork leg capacity.

Table 10 FORK OIL LEVEL (1982-ON)*

Model	Standard mm (in.)	Minimum mm (in.)	Maximum mm (in.)
YZ80 (1982)	160 (7.87)	**	**
YZ80 (1983)	173 (6.81)	**	**
YZ80 (1984-1987)	157 (6.18)	**	**
YZ80 (1988-on)	157 (6.18)	130 (5.12)	180 (7.09)

* Distance from top of fork tube.
** Not specified.

Table 11 DRIVE CHAIN SLACK

Model	mm	in.
YZ50	5-10	3/16-7/16
YZ60	5-10	3/16-7/16
YZ80		
1978	50-55	2-2 1/8
1979	45-50	1 25/32-2.0
1980	50-55	2-2 1/8
1981-1982	15-20	19/32-25/32
1983-1986	30-35	1 3/16-1 3/8
1987	15-20	19/32-25/32
1988-on	30-35	1 3/16-1 3/8

Table 12 COOLANT CAPACITY AND SPECIFICATIONS* (1982-ON YZ80)

Model	Liter	U.S. qt.
YZ80 (1982)	1.1	1.2
YZ80 (1983)	0.45	0.48
YZ80 (1984-1985)	0.38	0.40
YZ80 (1986)	**	**
YZ80 (1987-on)	0.49	0.52
Radiator cap pressure test	0.95-1.25 Kg/cm² (14-18 psi)	
Cooling system pressure test	1.1	Kg/cm² (16 psi)

* Coolant and water mix ratio: 1:1 (50% water; 50% coolant).
** Not specified by Yamaha.

Table 13 SPARK PLUG TYPE* AND GAP

Model	Type	Gap mm (in.)
YZ50	NGK B9ES	0.6-0.8 (0.024-0.031)
YZ60	Champion N-2	0.7-0.8 (0.028-0.031)
YZ80		
1978	NGK B8ES	0.5-0.6 (0.020-0.024)
1979-1982	NGK B8ES	0.7-0.8 (0.028-0.031)
1983-1985	Champion N-84	0.6-0.7 (0.024-0.028)
1986-1987	Champion N-84	0.5-0.6 (0.020-0.024)
1988-on	NGK B9EG	0.5-0.6 (0.020-0.024)

* Standard heat range spark plugs.

Table 14 IGNITION TIMING (WITH DIAL INDICATOR)*

Model	mm	in.
YZ50	1.65-1.95	0.065-0.077
YZ60	0.85-1.15	0.033-0.045
YZ80		
1978	2.0	0.08
1979	0.8	0.031
1980	1.0	0.039
1981-1983	0.8	0.031
1984	0.62	0.024
1985	0.8	0.031
1986-1987	1.16	0.046
1988-on	0.78	0.031

* All dimensions taken before top dead center (BTDC).

Table 15 CARBURETOR PILOT AIR SCREW ADJUSTMENT

Model	No. of turns
YZ50	1 1/2
YZ60	
1981	1 1/2
1982	1 1/4
YZ80	
1978-1979	1 1/2
1980-1981	1
1982-1983	1 1/2
1984-on	1 3/4

CHAPTER FOUR

ENGINE TOP END

This chapter covers information to service the cylinder head, cylinder, piston, piston rings and reed valve. Engine lower end service (crankshaft, transmission, shift drum and shift forks) is covered in Chapter Five. Clutch and kickstarter service is covered in Chapter Six.

Prior to removing and disassembling the engine top end, clean the entire engine and frame with a good grade commercial degreaser, like Gunk or Bel-Ray engine degreaser or equivalent. It is easier to work on a clean engine and you will do a better job.

Make certain that you have all the necessary tools available and purchase replacement parts prior to disassembly. Also make sure you have a clean place to work.

It is a good idea to identify and mark parts as they are removed so that errors will be avoided during assembly and installation. Clean all parts thoroughly upon removal, then place them in trays or boxes with their associated mounting hardware. Do not rely on memory alone as it may be days or weeks before you complete the job. In the text there is frequent mention of the left-hand and right-hand side of the engine. This refers to the engine as it sits in the bike's frame (from the rider's view) not as it sits on your workbench.

Engine specifications are listed in **Table 1** and **Table 2**. **Tables 1-4** are found at the end of the chapter.

ENGINE PRINCIPLES

Figure 1 explains how a typical two-stroke engine works. This will be helpful when troubleshooting or repairing the engine.

ENGINE LUBRICATION

Engine lubrication is provided by the fuel/oil mixture used to power the engine. There is no oil supply in the crankcase, as it would be drawn into the cylinder causing the spark plug to foul.

ENGINE COOLING

Air-cooled Engines (1978-1981)

Cooling is provided by air passing over the cooling fins on the engine cylinder head and cylinder. To prevent engine damage from overheating, it is important to keep these fins free from a buildup of dirt, oil, grease and other foreign matter. Brush out the fins with a whisk broom or small stiff paint brush.

CAUTION

Remember cooling fins are thin and may be damaged if struck too hard.

(1)

2-STROKE OPERATING PRINCIPLES

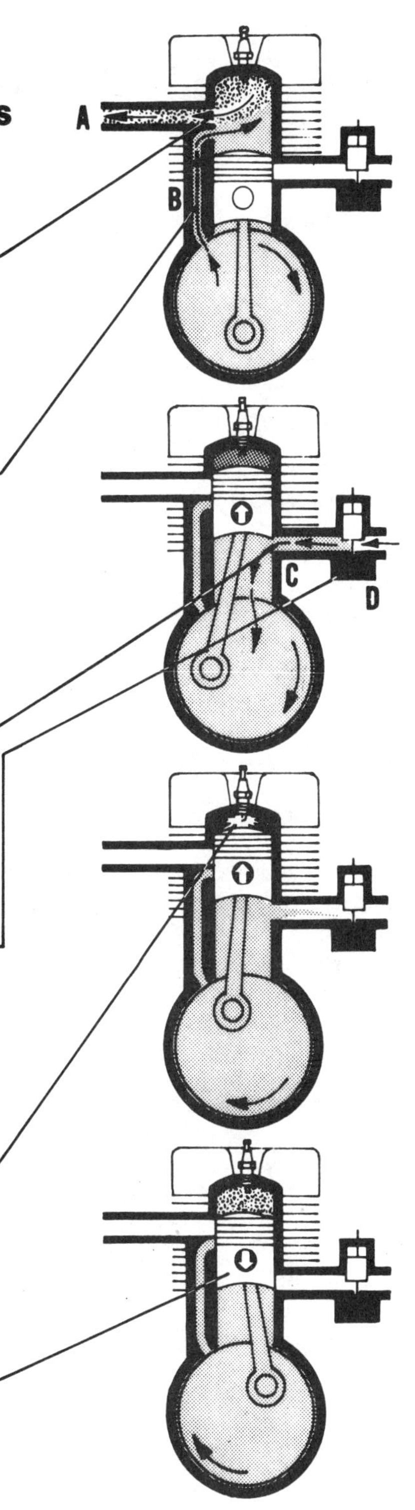

As the piston travels downward, it uncovers the exhaust port (A) allowing the exhaust gases, that are under pressure, to leave the cylinder. A fresh fuel/air charge, which has been compressed slightly, travels from the crankcase into the cylinder through the transfer port (B). Since this charge enters under pressure, it also helps to push out the exhaust gases.

While the crankshaft continues to rotate, the piston moves upward, covering the transfer (B) and exhaust (A) ports. The piston is now compressing the new fuel/air mixture and creating a low pressure area in the crankcase at the same time. As the piston continues to travel, it uncovers the intake port (C). A fresh fuel/air charge, from the carburetor (D), is drawn into the crankcase through the intake port, because of the low pressure within it.

Now, as the piston almost reaches the top of its travel, the spark plug fires, thus igniting the compressed fuel/air mixture. The piston continues to top dead center (TDC) and is pushed downward by the expanding gases.

As the piston travels down, the exhaust gases leave the cylinder and the complete cycle starts all over again.

4

Liquid-cooled Engines (1982-on)

The cylinder head and cylinder on these models is liquid cooled. A radiator is mounted at the front of the bike and a water pump is mounted behind the clutch cover. The cylinder head and cylinder are cast without cooling fins.

CLEANLINESS

Repairs go much faster and easier if your engine is clean before you begin work. This is especially important when servicing your engine's top end. If the top end is being serviced while the engine is installed in the frame, note that dirt trapped underneath the fuel tank or upper frame tube can fall into cylinder or crankcase opening. There are special cleaners for washing the motor and related parts. Just spray or brush on the cleaning solution, let it stand, then rinse it away with a garden hose. See Chapter One. If you are servicing the bike at a race track, you may not have access to soap and water to clean the bike. Instead, wrap a large clean cloth around the gas tank and upper frame tube. This will prevent dirt from falling into the engine with the top end removed.

SERVICING ENGINE IN FRAME

Some of the components can be serviced while the engine is mounted in the frame (the bike's frame is a great holding fixture—especially for breaking loose stubborn bolts and nuts):

a. Cylinder head.
b. Cylinder.
c. Piston.
d. Carburetor.
e. Magneto.
f. Clutch.
g. External shift mechanism.

CYLINDER HEAD

The cylinder head is bolted to the top of the cylinder with 4 nuts or bolts. A gasket separates the cylinder head and cylinder.

Removal/Installation (1978-1981 Air-cooled)

CAUTION
To prevent warpage and damage to any component, remove the cylinder head only when the engine is at room temperature.

1. Remove the seat, side covers and fuel tank.
2. Remove the exhaust system as described under *Exhaust System Removal/Installation* in Chapter Eight.
3. Disconnect the spark plug wire (A, **Figure 2**) and move it out of the way.

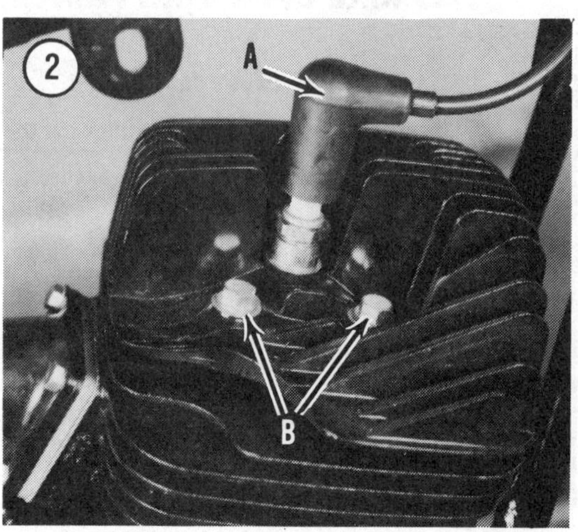

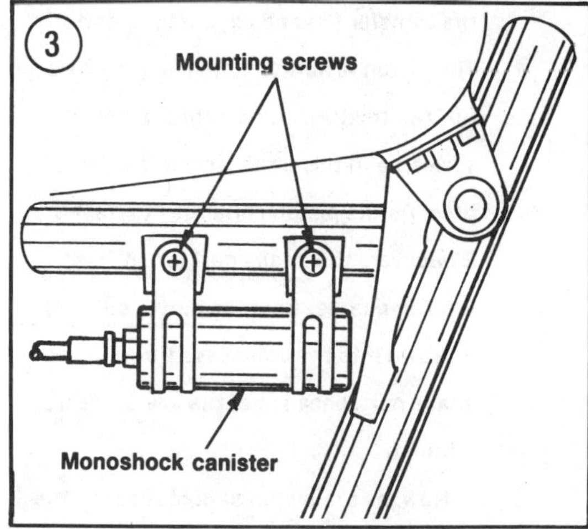

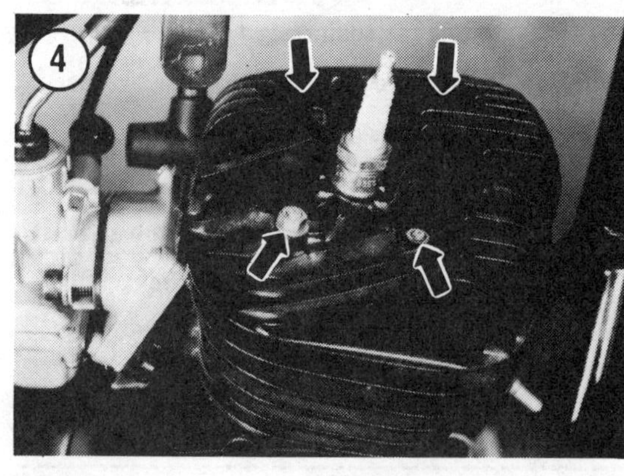

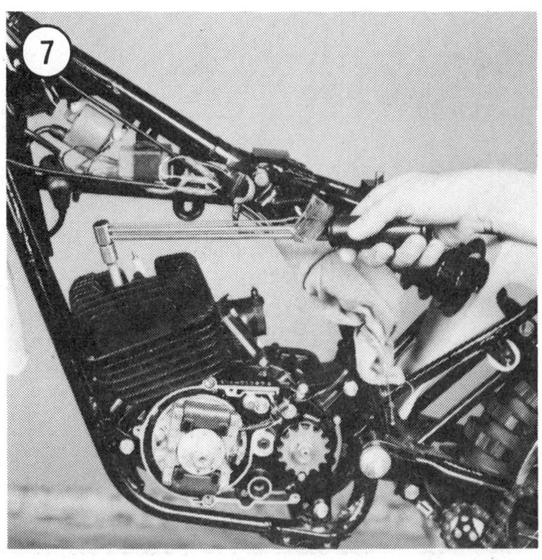

NOTE

If you think that it may be necessary to remove the spark plug later, loosen it now while the cylinder head is bolted down.

4A. *1981 YZ80H models:* Remove the monoshock auxiliary canister (**Figure 3**) from underneath the frame tube. Do not disconnect the high pressure hose from the canister. Secure the canister to take all pressure off the hose.
4B. *YZ50 models:* Remove the nuts and washers (**Figure 4**) in a crisscross pattern.
4C. *YZ60 and YZ80 models:* Remove the tube nuts (B, **Figure 2**) in a crisscross pattern.

CAUTION

Remember, the cooling fins are fragile and may be damaged if tapped or pried on too hard. Never use a metal hammer.

5. Loosen the head by tapping around the perimeter with a rubber or plastic mallet.

NOTE

Do not pry the head if it is stuck. Sometimes it is possible to loosen the head with engine compression. Rotate the engine with the kickstarter (with the spark plug installed). As the piston reaches TDC, it may pop the head loose.

6. Remove the cylinder head by pulling straight up and off the crankcase studs (**Figure 5**). Store the cylinder head with the gasket surface placed on a thick piece of cardboard.
7. Remove the cylinder head gasket and discard it.
8. Using the kickstarter, bring the piston to top dead center (TDC). Lay a rag over the cylinder to prevent dirt from falling into the cylinder.
9. Inspect the cylinder head as described in this chapter.
10. Install the cylinder head by reversing these steps. Note the following:
   a. Install the head gasket with the point or projection facing forward (**Figure 6**).

NOTE

On YZ50 models, don't forget to install the washers under the nuts.

   b. Install the cylinder head and screw on the special nuts only finger-tight.
   c. Tighten the nuts (**Figure 7**) in a crisscross pattern to the torque values in **Table 3** at the end of this chapter.
   d. Install all items removed.

4

Removal/Installation (1982-on YZ80)

Refer to **Figure 8** (1982) or **Figure 9** (1983-on) for this procedure.

1. Remove the seat, side covers and fuel tank.
2. Remove the exhaust system as described under *Exhaust System Removal/Installation* in Chapter Eight.

NOTE
If you think that it may be necessary to remove the spark plug later, loosen it now while the cylinder head is bolted down.

3. Disconnect the spark plug wire (A, **Figure 10**) and move it out of the way.
4. Drain the radiator as described in Chapter Three.
5. Disconnect the radiator hose at the cylinder head (B, **Figure 10**).
6. Remove the nuts (**Figure 11**) securing the cylinder head in a crisscross pattern.
7. Loosen the cylinder head by tapping around the perimeter with a rubber or plastic mallet. Never use a metal hammer.
8. Remove the cylinder head by pulling straight up and off the crankcase studs.

NOTE
*On 1982 YZ80 models, there are 4 O-rings on each of the cylinder head stud holes (**Figure 12**).*

9A. *1982 models:* There are 2 O-rings in the top of the cylinder. These can be removed and replaced at this time if required. See **Figure 13**.

9B. *1983-on models:* Remove the cylinder head gasket (**Figure 14**).

10. Installation is the reverse of these steps. Note the following.
11. *1982 models:* Check all cylinder head and cylinder O-rings and replace any that are worn or damaged.

12A. *1982 models:* Install the 2 O-rings in the top of the cylinder (**Figure 13**) and the 4 O-rings in the cylinder head (**Figure 12**).

12B. *1983-on models:* Install a new cylinder head gasket. Align the tab on the gasket with the notch on the front of the cylinder (**Figure 15**).

13. Place the cylinder head on the cylinder with the radiator hose coupling facing toward the rear (**Figure 16**). Screw on the cylinder head nuts or bolts finger-tight. Make sure to install a washer under each nut.
14. Tighten the nuts in a crisscross pattern to the torque specifications in **Table 3**.

CYLINDER HEAD (YZ80J) 1982

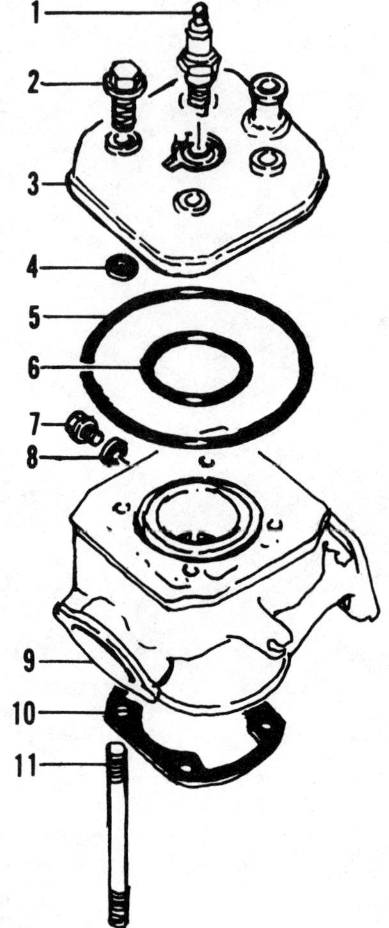

1. Spark plug
2. Bolt
3. Cylinder head
4. O-ring
5. O-ring
6. O-ring
7. Bolt
8. Gasket
9. Cylinder
10. Base gasket
11. Stud

4

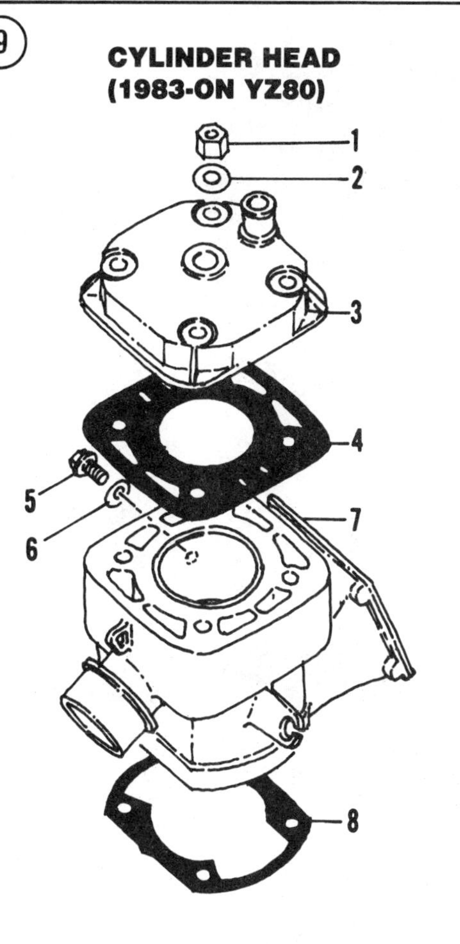
9
CYLINDER HEAD
(1983-ON YZ80)
1
2
3
4
5
6
7
8
1. Nut
2. Washer
3. Cylinder head
4. Head gasket
5. Coolant drain screw
6. Washer
7. Cylinder
8. Base gasket

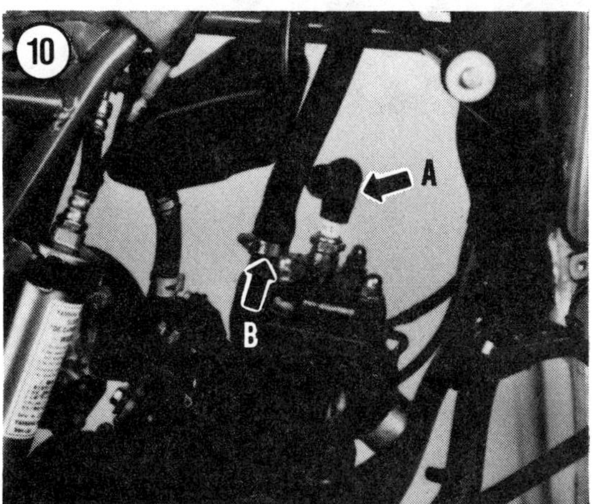
10
A
B

11

12

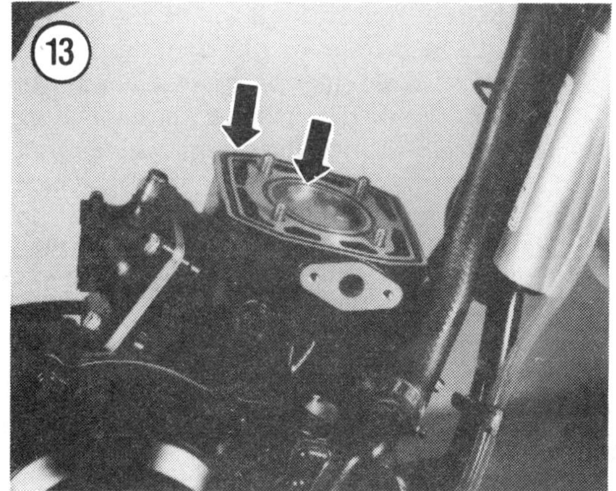
13

14

15. Reinstall the radiator hose at the cylinder head and tighten the hose clamp securely (**Figure 17**).
16. Fill the radiator as described in Chapter Three under *Coolant Change.*
17. Install the exhaust system, tighten the spark plug and install the spark plug wire, the seat, the side covers and fuel tank.

Inspection (All Models)

1. Clean the cylinder head as described under *Engine Decarbonizing* in Chapter Three.
2. Use a straightedge and feeler gauge and measure the flatness of the cylinder head. If the cylinder head warpage exceeds 0.03 mm (0.0012 in.), resurface the cylinder head as follows:
   a. Tape a piece of 400-600 grit wet emery sandpaper onto a piece of thick plate glass or surface plate.
   b. Slowly resurface the head by moving it in figure-eight patterns on the sandpaper.
   c. Rotate the head several times to avoid removing too much material from one side. Check progress often with the straightedge and feeler gauge.
   d. If the cylinder head warpage still exceeds the service limit excessively, it will be necessary to have the head resurfaced by a machine shop. Note that removing excessive amounts of material from the cylinder head mating surface will change the compression ratio. Consult with the machinist on how much material was removed; it may be necessary to use 2 cylinder head gaskets (except on 1982 YZ80 models which use O-rings to seal the cylinder head).

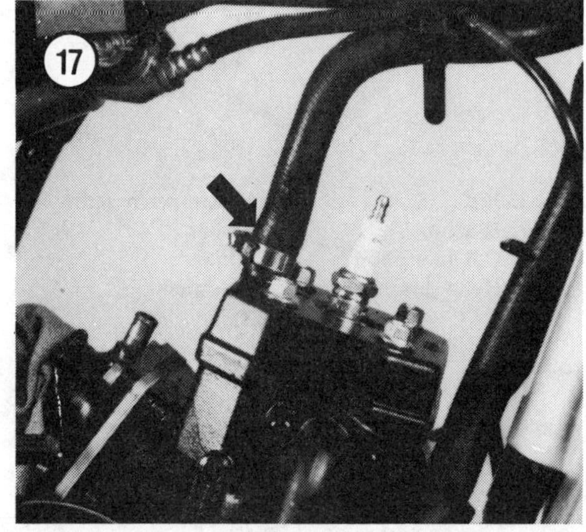

NOTE
Always use an aluminum thread fluid or Kerosene on the tap and threads when performing Step 3.

3. With the spark plug removed, check the end of the spark plug threads in the cylinder head (A, **Figure 18**) for any signs of carbon buildup or cracking. The carbon can be removed with a 14 mm spark plug tap.
4. Check the flatness of the 4 cylinder head nut or bolt surfaces (**Figure 19**). Remove any burrs with a file or sandpaper.
5. *Liquid-cooled engines:* Check the coolant passages in the head (B, **Figure 18**) for sludge buildup. Clean with a soft wood dowel.
6. Wash the cylinder head in hot soap and water and rinse thoroughly before installation.

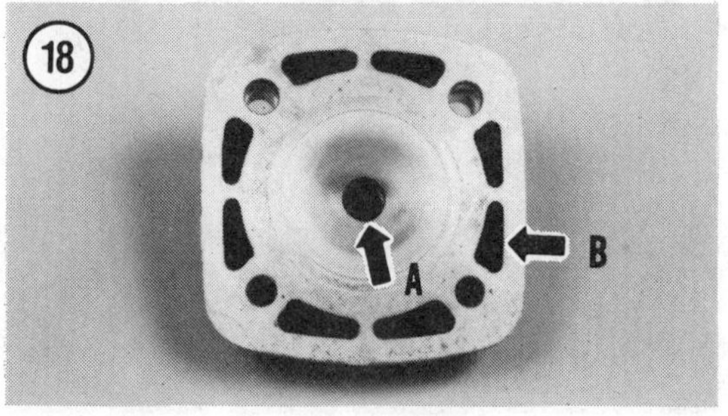

CYLINDER

Removal/Installation (Air-cooled Engines)

1. Remove the cylinder head as described under *Cylinder Head Removal/Installation* in this chapter.
2. Remove the carburetor as described under *Carburetor Removal/Installation* in Chapter Eight.

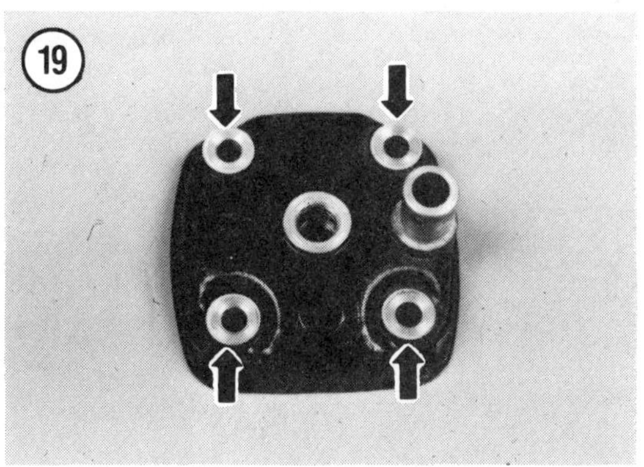
19

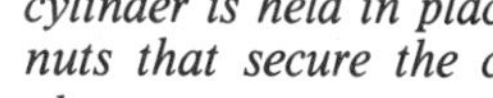

NOTE
There are no additional nuts or bolts to remove for cylinder removal. The cylinder is held in place with the same nuts that secure the cylinder head in place.

3. Loosen the cylinder by tapping around the perimeter with a rubber or plastic mallet.
4. Using the kickstarter, rotate the engine so the piston is at the bottom of its stroke. Pull the cylinder straight up and off the crankcase studs and piston. See **Figure 20**.

CAUTION
Remember the cooling fins are fragile and may be damaged if tapped or pried on too hard. Do not use a metal hammer.

5. Remove the cylinder base gasket and discard it. Install a piston holding fixture under the piston (**Figure 21**) to protect the piston skirt from damage. This fixture may be purchased or may be a homemade unit of wood. See **Figure 22**.

20

21

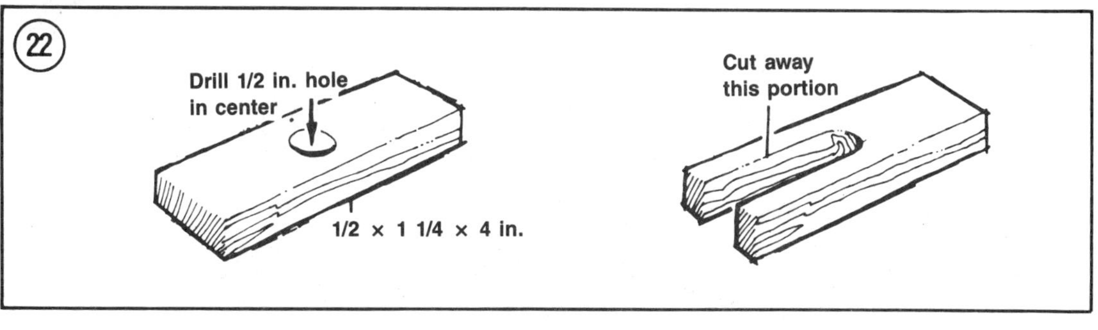

22

6. Place a clean shop cloth into the crankcase opening to prevent the entry of foreign material.
7. Install the cylinder as follows.
8. Clean the cylinder bore as described under *Inspection* in this chapter.
9. Check that the top surface of the crankcase and the bottom surface of the cylinder are clean prior to installation.
10. Install a new base gasket.
11. Make sure the end gaps of the piston rings are lined up with the locating pins in the ring grooves (A, **Figure 23**). Lightly oil the piston rings and the inside of the cylinder bore. Rotate the crankshaft to bring the piston in contact with the piston holding fixture (B, **Figure 23**).
12. Start the cylinder down over the piston with the exhaust port facing *forward.* See **Figure 20**.

NOTE
Make sure the rings are still properly aligned with the locating pins in the piston.

13. Compress each ring, with your fingers, as the cylinder starts to slide over it.
14. Slide the cylinder down until it bottoms on the piston holding fixture.
15. Remove the piston holding fixture and slide the cylinder into place on the crankcase.
16. Hold the cylinder in place with one hand and push the kickstarter lever down with the other hand. If the piston catches or stops in the cylinder, the piston rings were not lined up properly. The piston should move up and down the cylinder bore smoothly. If necessary, remove the cylinder and repeat Steps 11-16.
17. Install the cylinder head as described under *Cylinder Head Removal/Installation* in this chapter.
18. Install the carburetor as described under *Carburetor Removal/Installation* in Chapter Six.
19. Follow the *Break-in Procedure* in this chapter if the cylinder was rebored or honed.

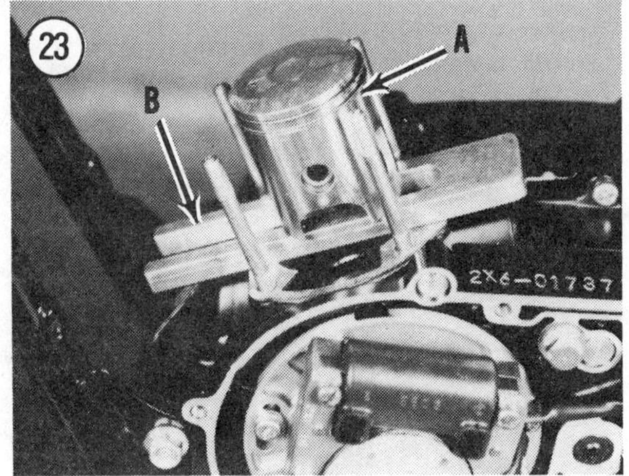

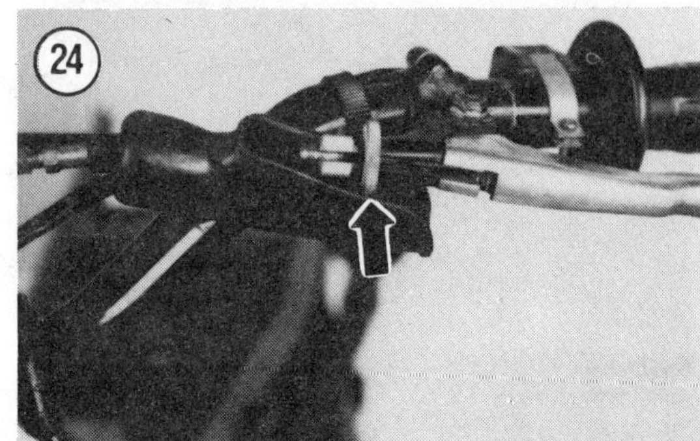

Removal/Installation (Liquid-cooled Engines)

Refer to **Figure 8** (1982) or **Figure 9** (1983-on) for this procedure.

1. See **Figure 24.** Loosen the clutch cable adjuster locknut and turn the adjuster all the way in to loosen the clutch cable. Then pull the cable out of its mounting bracked on the left side of the cylinder (**Figure 25**).
2. Disconnect the YEIS hose at the intake manifold (**Figure 26**).

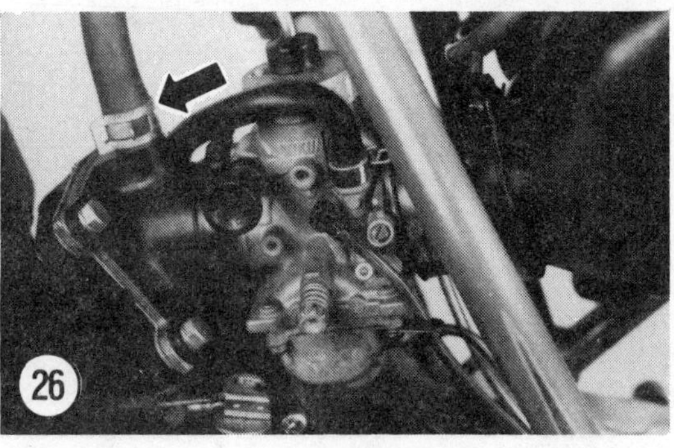

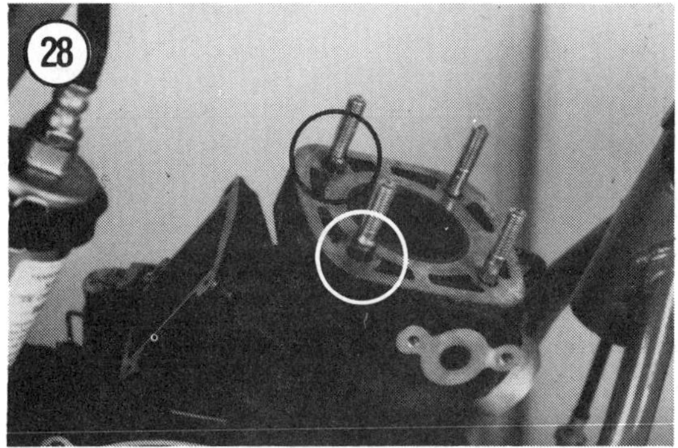

3. Drain the coolant as described under *Coolant Change* in Chapter Three.
4. Remove the screws securing the coolant pipe joint on the right side of the cylinder. Pull the coolant pipe joint (**Figure 27**) away from the cylinder and off the water pump and remove it.
5. Remove the cylinder head as described in this chapter.
6. *1986-on models:* Remove the 2 dowel pins (**Figure 28**).

NOTE
There are no additional nuts or bolts to remove for cylinder removal. The cylinder is held in place with the same nuts that secure the cylinder head in place.

7. Loosen the cylinder by tapping around the perimeter with a rubber or plastic mallet.
8. Using the kickstarter, rotate the engine so the piston is at the bottom of its stroke. Pull the cylinder (**Figure 29**) straight up and off the crankcase studs and piston.
9. Remove the cylinder base gasket and discard it. Install a piston holding fixture under the piston (**Figure 30**) to protect the piston skirt from damage. This fixture may be purchased or may be a homemade unit of wood. See **Figure 22**.
10. Place a clean shop cloth into the crankcase opening to prevent the entry of foreign material.
11. Install the cylinder as follows.
12. Clean the cylinder bore as described under *Inspection* in this chapter.
13. Check that the top surface of the crankcase and the bottom surface of the cylinder are clean prior to installation.
14. Install a new base gasket.
15. Make sure the end gaps of the piston ring(s) are lined up with the locating pins in the ring grooves (**Figure 31**).

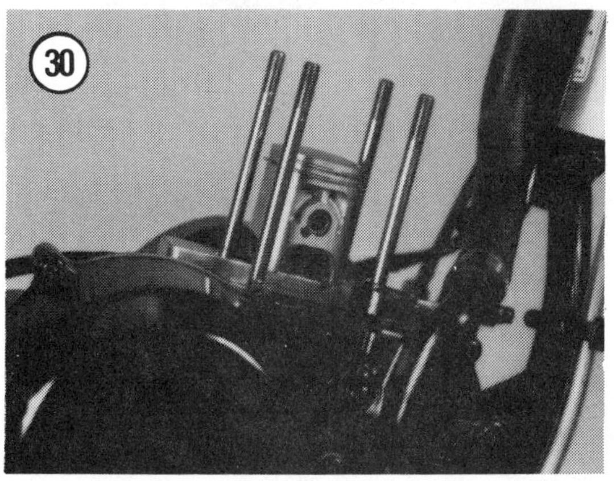

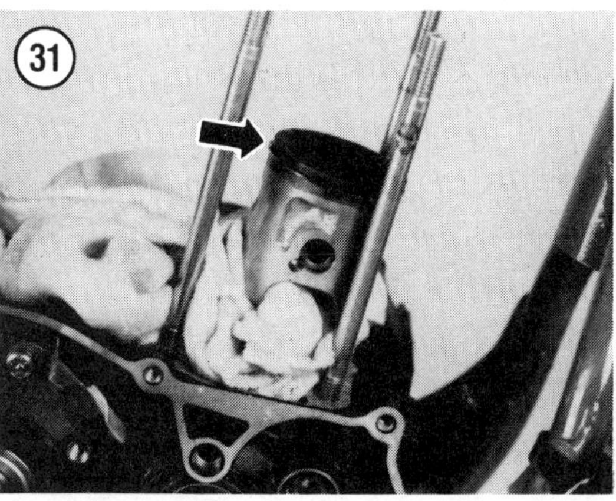

16. Lightly oil the piston rings and the inside of the cylinder bore. Rotate the crankshaft to bring the piston in contact with the piston holding fixture.
17. Start the cylinder down over the piston with the exhaust port facing *forward*. See **Figure 29**.

NOTE
Make sure the ring(s) are still properly aligned with the locating pin(s) in the piston.

18. Compress each ring, with your fingers, as the cylinder starts to slide over it.
19. Slide the cylinder down until it bottoms on the piston holding fixture.
20. Remove the piston holding fixture and slide the cylinder into place on the crankcase.
21. Hold the cylinder in place with one hand and push the kickstarter lever down with the other hand. If the piston catches or stops in the cylinder, the piston ring(s) were not lined up properly. The piston should move up and down the cylinder bore smoothly. If necessary, remove the cylinder and repeat Steps 15-19.
22. *1986-on models:* Install the 2 dowel pins.
23. Install the cylinder head as described under *Cylinder Head Removal/Installation* in this chapter.
24. Check the coolant pipe joint O-rings (**Figure 32**) for wear or damage. Replace if required.
25. Insert the lower end of the coolant pipe joint into the top of the water pump and secure the coolant pipe with the attaching screws. See **Figure 27**.

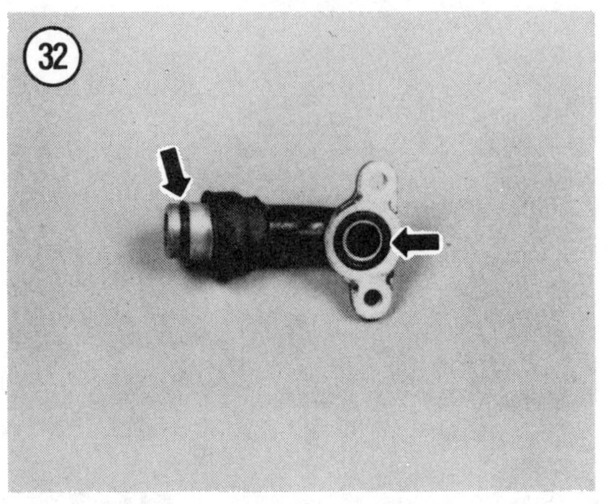

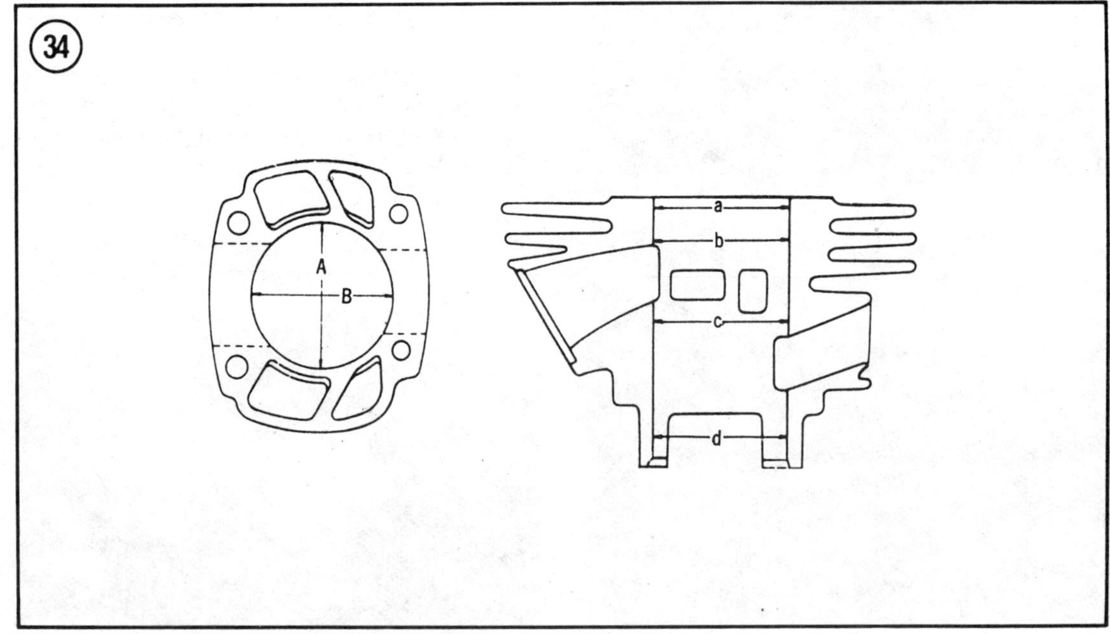

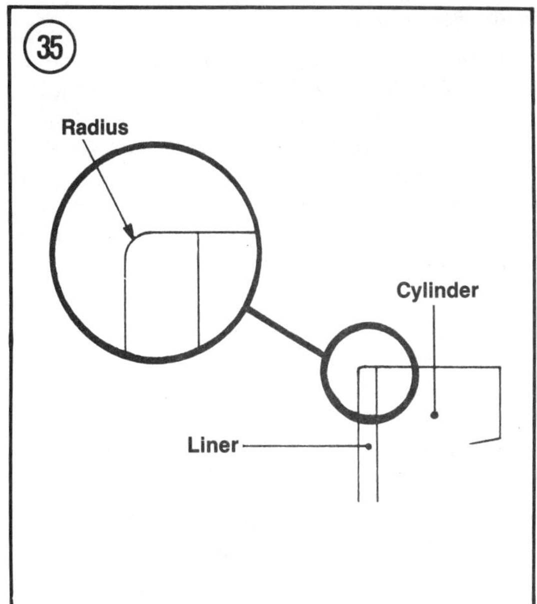

26. Install the carburetor as described under *Carburetor Removal/Installation* in Chapter Eight.
27. Attach the YEIS hose at the intake manifold (**Figure 26**).
28. Attach the clutch cable at the left side of the cylinder (**Figure 25**). Adjust the clutch as described in Chapter Three.
29. Follow the *Break-in Procedure* in this chapter if the cylinder was rebored or honed.

4

Inspection (All Models)

1. Remove and inspect the condition of the reed valve as described in this chapter.
2. *Liquid-cooled models:* Check inside the cylinder water jackets (**Figure 33**) for mineral sludge or rust. Remove with a blunt wooded scraper.

NOTE
The following procedure requires the use of highly specialized and expensive measuring tools. If such equipment is not readily available, have the measurements performed by a dealer or machine shop.

3. Measure the cylinder bore with a cylinder gauge or inside micrometer, at the points shown in **Figure 34**. Measure in 2 axes—in line with the wrist pin and at 90° to the pin. If the taper or out of round exceeds specifications in **Table 1** or **Table 2**, the cylinder must be rebored to the next oversize and a new piston and piston rings installed.

NOTE
*The new piston should be obtained first before the cylinder is bored so that the piston can be measured; slight manufacturing tolerances must be taken into account to determine the actual size and working clearance indicated in **Table 1** or **Table 2**.*

NOTE
If a non-factory Yamaha piston is being installed, refer to the piston manufacturer's clearance specifications and bore the cylinder to these specifications. Usually, this clearance is different from that specified by Yamaha.

4. After the cylinder has been bored, the edges of the ports must be radiused with a fine file or grinder to prevent them from snagging the rings (**Figure 35**).
5. Inspect the exhaust (**Figure 36**) and transfer (**Figure 37**) ports. Clean the exhaust port as described in Chapter Three.

6. Check the exhaust pipe studs for thread damage or looseness. If thread damage is minor, they may be cleaned up with a M8×1.25 metric die. If the studs are damaged or loose, replace them as follows:
   a. Thread two nuts onto the damaged cylinder stud as shown in **Figure 38**. Then tighten the 2 nuts against each other so that they are locked.
   b. Turn the bottom nut *counterclockwise* (**Figure 39**) and unscrew the stud.
   c. Clean the threads in the cylinder with solvent or electrical contact cleaner and allow to thoroughly dry.
   d. Install 2 nuts on the top half of the new stud as in sub-step a. Make sure they are locked securely.
   e. Coat the bottom half of a new stud with Loctite 271 (red).
   f. Turn the top nut *clockwise* and thread the new stud into the cylinder. Tighten to 15 N•m (11 ft.-lb.).
   g. Remove the nuts and repeat as required.
   h. Follow Loctite's directions on cure time before installing the cylinder head and cylinder head nuts.
7. If the cylinder requires boring, remove the dowel pins (if used) from the cylinder before dropping it off at the dealer or machine shop.

CAUTION
A combination of soap and water is the only solution that will completely clean the cylinder bore. Solvent and kerosene cannot wash the fine grit out of cylinder crevises. Grit left in the bore will act like a grinding compound and cause premature wear to the new piston and rings.

8. After the cylinder has been serviced, wash the bore in hot soapy water. This is the only way to clean the cylinder bore of the fine grit material left from the bore or honing job. After washing the cylinder, wipe the bore with a clean white cloth. The rag shouldn't show any traces of grit or debris. If the rag is dirty, the bore is not thoroughly clean and must be rewashed. When the cylinder bore is clean, lubricate it with clean two-cycle engine oil to prevent the liner from rusting.

PISTON, WRIST PIN, AND PISTON RINGS

The piston is made of an aluminum alloy. The wrist pin is a precision fit and is held in place by a clip at each end. A caged needle bearing is used on the small end of the connecting rod.

Piston Removal

1. Remove the cylinder head and cylinder as described under *Cylinder Removal* in this chapter.
2. Before removing the piston, hold the rod tightly and rock the piston as shown in **Figure 40**. Any rocking motion (do not confuse with the normal sliding motion) indicates wear on the wrist pin, needle bearing, wrist pin bore, or more likely a combination of all three.

NOTE
Wrap a clean shop cloth under the piston so that the clip will not fall into the crankcase.

WARNING
Safety glasses should be worn when performing Step 3.

3. Remove the clips from each side of the wrist pin bore (A, **Figure 41**) with a small screwdriver or

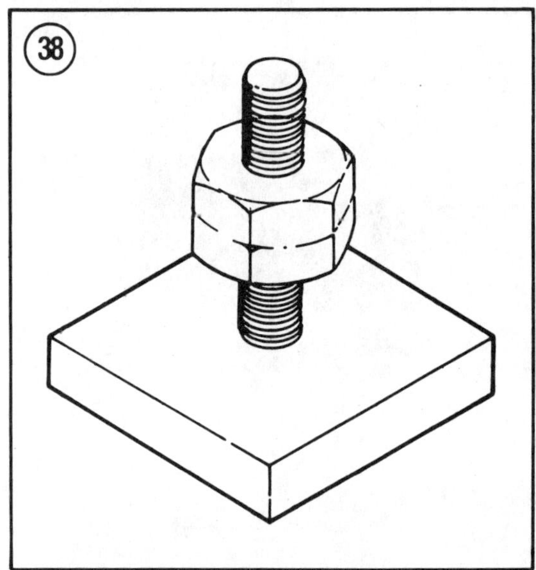

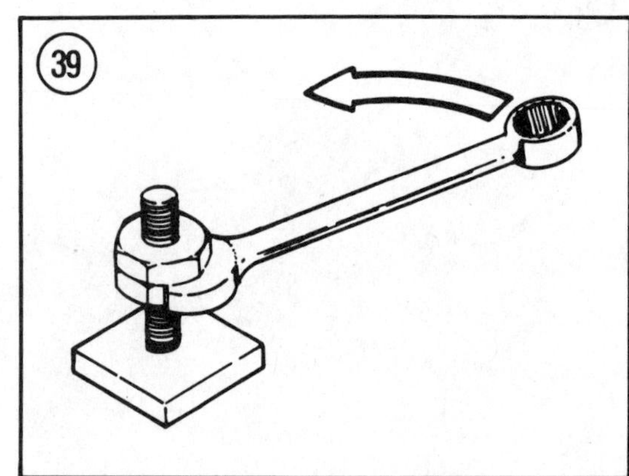

scribe. Hold your thumb over one edge of the clip when removing it to prevent it from springing out.
4. Use a proper size wooden dowel or socket extension and push out the wrist pin.

CAUTION

If the engine ran hot or seized, the wrist pin will probably be very difficult to remove. However, do not drive the wrist pin out of the piston. This will damage the piston, needle bearing and connecting rod. If the wrist pin will not push out by hand, remove it as described in Step 5.

5. If the wrist pin is tight, fabricate the tool shown in **Figure 42**. Assemble the tool onto the piston and pull the wrist pin out of the piston. Make sure to install a pad between the piston and piece of pipe to prevent from scoring the side of the piston.
6. Lift the piston (B, **Figure 41**) off the connecting rod.

40

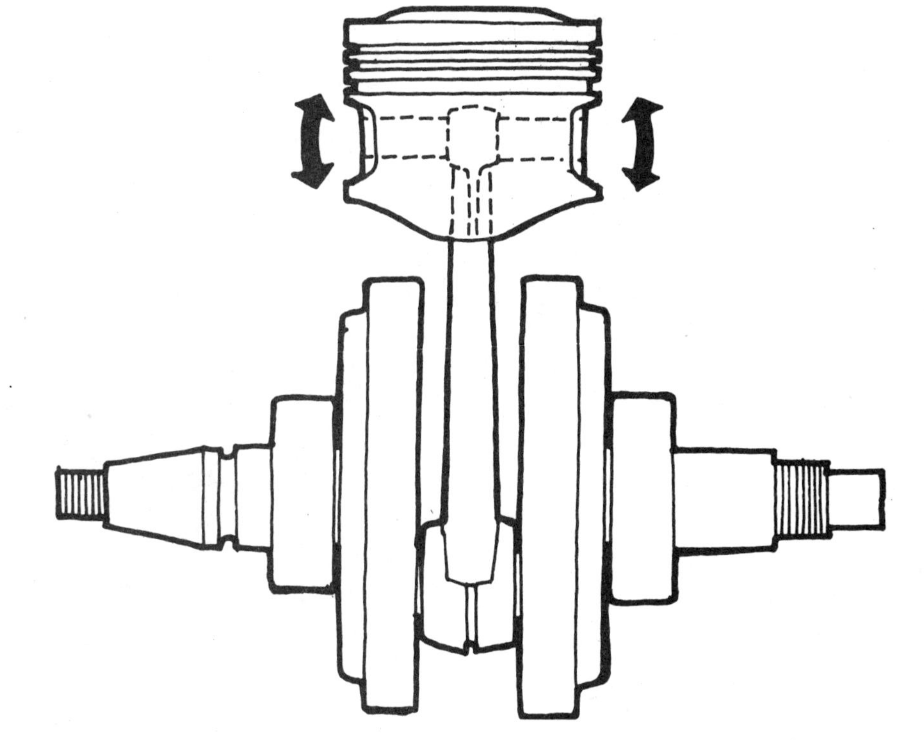

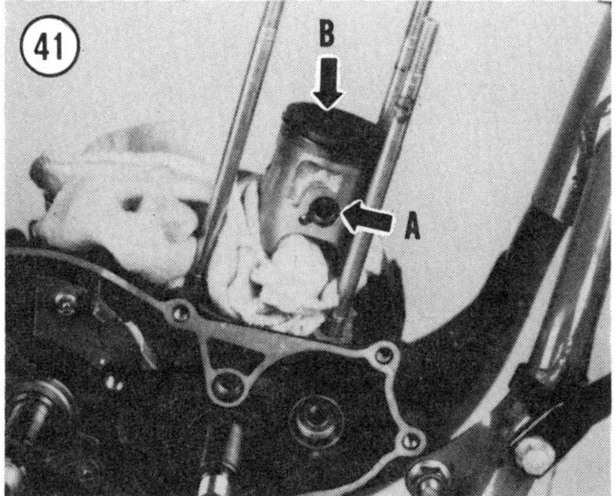

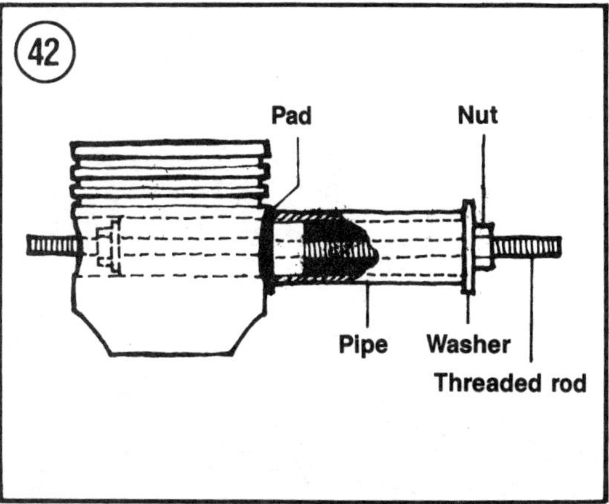

7. Remove the needle bearing from the connecting rod (**Figure 43**).
8. If the piston is going to be left off for some time, place a piece of foam insulation tube, or shop cloth, over the end of the rod to protect it.

NOTE
Models are equipped with either 1 or 2 pistons rings. Always remove the top piston ring first.

9. First remove the top ring by spreading the ends with your thumbs just enough to slide it up over the piston (**Figure 44**). Repeat for the other ring.

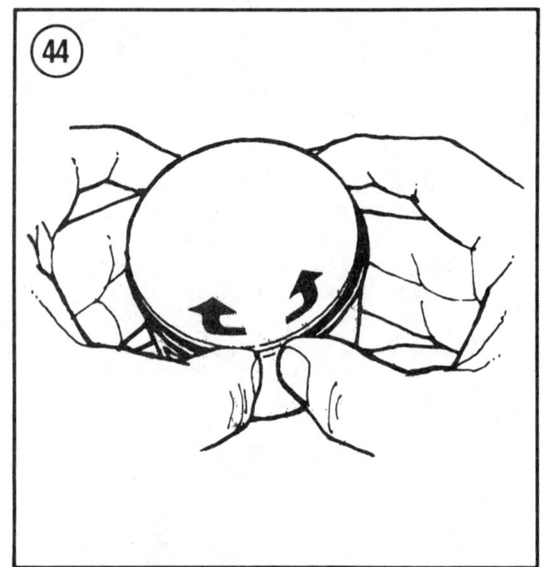

Inspection

1. Clean the needle bearing in solvent and dry it thoroughly. Use a magnifying glass and inspect the bearing cage for cracks at the corners of the needle slots (**Figure 45**) and inspect the needles themselves for cracking. If any cracks are found, the bearing must be replaced.
2. Wipe the wrist pin bore in the connecting rod with a clean rag and check it for galling, scratches, or any other signs of wear or damage. If any of these conditions exist, replace as described in Chapter Five.
3. Check the wrist pin (**Figure 46**) for severe wear, scoring or chrome flaking. Also check the wrist pin for cracks along the top and side. Replace the wrist pin if necessary.
4. Oil the needle bearing and pin and install them in the connecting rod. Slowly rotate the pin and check for radial play (**Figure 47**). If any play exists, the pin and bearing should be replaced, providing the rod bore is in good condition. If the condition

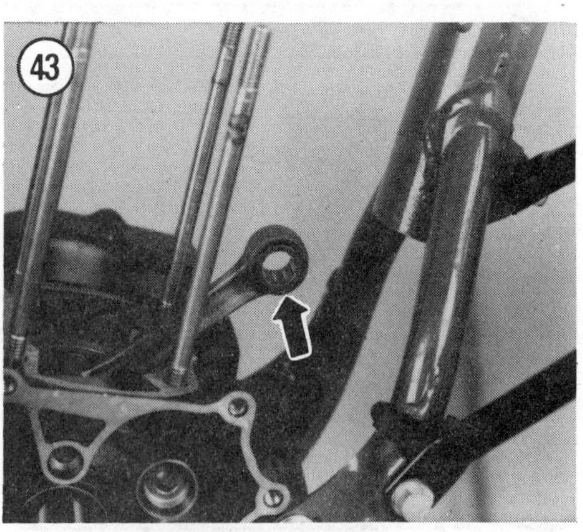

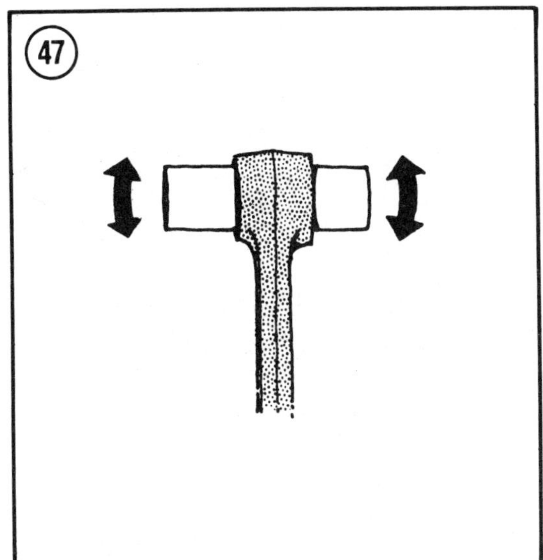

of the rod bore is in question, the old pin and bearing can be checked with a new connecting rod.

CAUTION
If there are signs of piston seizure or overheating, replace the wrist pin and bearing. These parts have been weakened from excessive heat and may fail after the engine is rebuilt.

5. Carefully check the piston for cracks at the top edge of the transfer cutaways (**Figure 48** and **Figure 49**) and replace if found. Check the piston skirt (**Figure 50**) for brown varnish buildup. More than a slight amount is an indication of worn or sticking rings which should be replaced.
6. Check the piston skirt for galling and abrasion which may have resulted from piston seizure. If light galling is present, smooth the affected area with No. 400 emery paper and oil or a fine oilstone. However if galling is severe or if the piston is deeply scored, replace it.
7. Check the piston ring locating pin(s) in the piston. The pin(s) should be tight and the pistons should show no signs of cracking around the pin. If any one locating pin is loose, replace the piston. A loose pin will eventually fall out and cause severe engine damage.

NOTE
Maintaining proper piston ring end gap helps to ensure peak engine performance. Excessive ring end gap reduces engine performance and can cause overheating. Insufficient ring end gap will cause the ring ends to butt together and cause the ring to break. This would cause severe engine damage. So that you don't have to wait

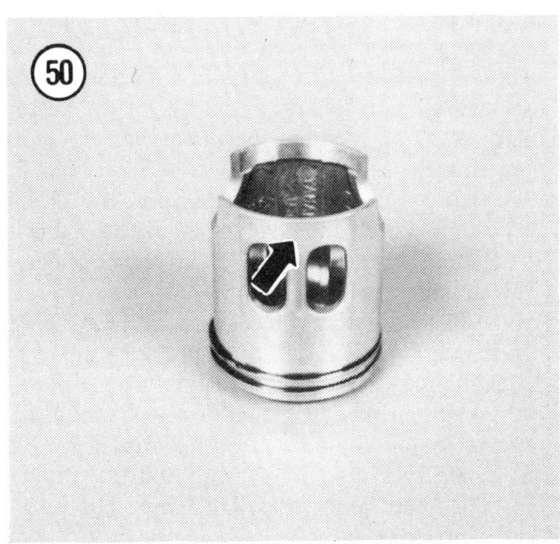

> *for parts, always order extra cylinder head and base gaskets to have on hand for routine top end inspection and maintenance.*

8. Measure piston ring end gap. Place a ring into the cylinder and push it in about 20 mm (3/4 in.) with the crown of the piston (**Figure 51**). This ensures that the ring is square in the cylinder bore. Measure the gap with a flat feeler gauge (**Figure 52**) and compare to specifications in **Table 1** or **Table 2**. If the gap is greater than specified, the ring(s) should be replaced.

> *NOTE*
> *When installing new rings, measure their end gap in the same manner as for old ones. If the gap is less than specified, carefully file the ends with a fine cut file until the gap is correct.*

9. Carefully remove all carbon buildup from the ring grooves with a broken ring (**Figure 53**). Inspect the grooves carefully for burrs, nicks, or broken and cracked lands. Recondition or replace the piston if necessary.

10. Measure the side clearance of each ring in its groove with a flat feeler gauge (**Figure 54**) and compare to dimensions given in **Table 1** or **Table 2**. If the clearance is greater than specified, the rings must be replaced, and if the clearance is still excessive with the new rings, the piston must also be replaced.

11A. *1978-1980 models:* Measure the outside diameter of the piston across the skirt (**Figure 55**) at right angles to the piston pin bore. Because of piston taper, it is important to measure the piston at a specified distance up from the bottom of the skirt (**Figure 56**); refer to **Table 4** for piston measuring height positions.

11B. *1981-on models:* All 1981 and later models use pistons with a large cutaway on the piston intake skirt. To measure the piston accurately on these models, perform the following:

a. Using a micrometer, measure across the piston skirt at the height specified in **Table 4**. Record this specification (which is considered the partial measurement).
b. Add to the partial measurement (sub-step a) the adjustment amount (determined by Yamaha) in **Table 4**. The total of the partial measurement and the adjustment amount is the piston diameter. For example, if your piston measures 41.970 mm and the **Table 4** adjustment amount is 0.025 mm, the piston diameter is 41.970 + 0.025 = 41.995 mm.

51

52

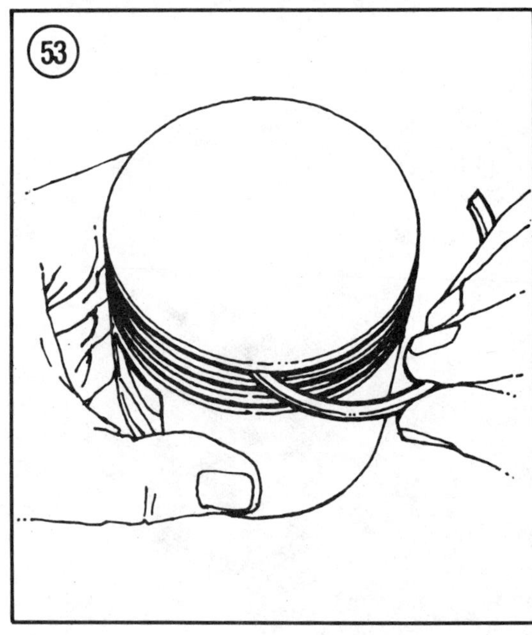
53

Thus, in this example, 41.995 mm is the piston diameter.

NOTE
The following procedure requires the use of highly specialized and expensive measuring tools. If such equipment is not readily available, have the measurements performed by a dealer or machine shop.

12. Measure the cylinder bore with a cylinder gauge or inside micrometer, at the points shown in **Figure 34**. Measure in 2 axes—in line with the wrist pin and at 90° to the pin. If the taper or out-of-round is 0.01 mm (0.04 in.) or greater, the cylinder must be rebored to the next oversize and a new piston and ring(s) installed.
13. Piston clearance is the difference between the maximum piston diameter and the minimum cylinder diameter. For a run-in (used) piston and cylinder, subtract the dimension of the piston from the cylinder dimension. If the clearance exceeds the dimension in **Table 1** or **Table 2**, the cylinder should be rebored to the next oversize and a new matched oversize piston and ring(s) installed.
14. To establish a final overbore dimension with a new piston, add the piston skirt measurement to the specified clearance. This will determine the dimension for the cylinder overbore size.

NOTE
If a non-factory Yamaha piston is being installed, refer to the piston manufacturer's clearance specifications and bore the cylinder to these specifications. Usually, this clearance is different from that specified by Yamaha.

Piston Installation

1. Apply assembly oil to the needle bearing and install it in the connecting rod (**Figure 43**).
2. Oil the wrist pin and install it in the piston until the end of it extends slightly beyond the inside of the boss (**Figure 57**).

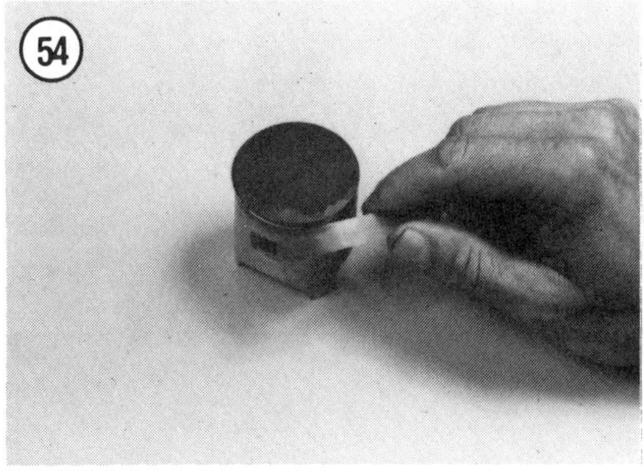

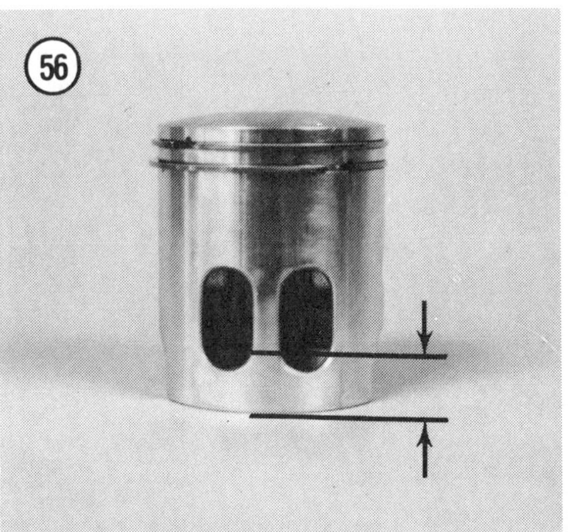

4

3. Place the piston over the connecting rod with the arrow on the piston crown pointing forward (**Figure 58**). Line up the pin with the bearing and push the pin into the piston until it is even with the wrist pin clip grooves.

CAUTION

*If the wrist pin will not slide in the piston smoothly, use the home-made tool described during **Piston Removal** to install the wrist pin (**Figure 42**). When using the home-made tool, the pipe and pad is not required. Instead, run the threaded rod through the wrist pin. Secure the end of the wrist pin next to the piston with the small washer and nut. Slide the large washer onto the threaded rod so that it is next to the wrist pin. Install the nut next to the large washer and tighten the nut to push the wrist pin into the piston.*

4. Install new wrist pin clips (A, **Figure 41**) in the ends of the pin boss. Make sure they are seated in the grooves.
5. Check the installation by rocking the piston back and forth around the pin axis and from side to side along the axis. It should rotate freely back and forth but not from side to side.
6. Install the piston rings—first the bottom one, then the top—by carefully spreading the ends of the ring with your thumbs and slipping the ring over the top of the piston. Make sure that the marks on the piston rings are toward the top of the piston.
7. Make sure the rings are seated completely in the grooves, all the way around the circumference, and that the ends are aligned with the locating pins.
8. Follow the *Break-in Procedure* in this chapter if new piston or ring(s) were installed.

BREAK-IN PROCEDURE

If the rings were replaced, a new piston installed or the cylinder rebored, the engine must be run in at moderate speeds and loads for no less than 2 hours. Don't exceed 75 percent of normal allowable rpm during run in. After the first half hour, remove the spark plug and check its condition. The electrode should be dry and clean and the color of the insulation should be light to medium tan. If the insulation is white (indicating a too lean fuel/air mixture) or if it is dark and oily (indicating a too rich fuel/air mixture ratio), correct the condition with a main jet change; both

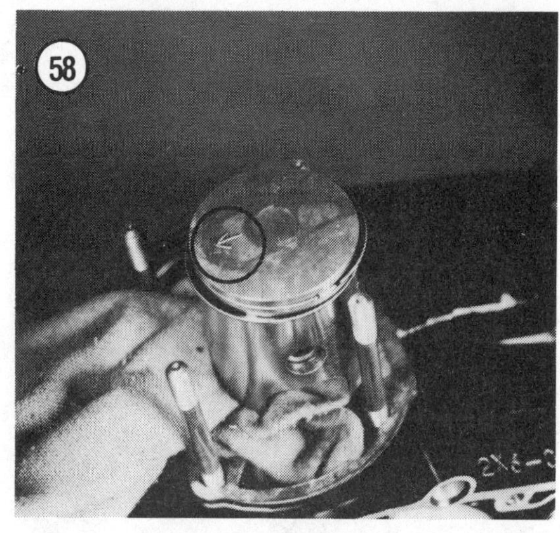

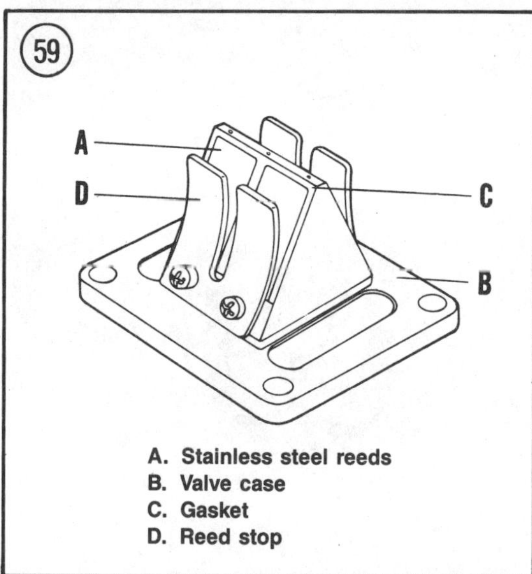

A. Stainless steel reeds
B. Valve case
C. Gasket
D. Reed stop

incorrect conditions produce excessive engine heat and can lead to damage to the rings, piston and cylinder before they have had a chance to seat in.

Refer to Chapter Three for further information on how to read a spark plug and to Chapter Eight for carburetor jet change.

REED VALVE ASSEMBLY

All models are equipped with a reed valve assembly (**Figure 59**) installed in the intake tract between the carburetor and crankcase. The reed is a thin flexible diaphragm made of stainless steel or fiber material. The reed valve regulates the air/fuel mixture drawn from the carburetor into the crankcase.

Particular care must be taken when handling and repairing the reed valve assembly.

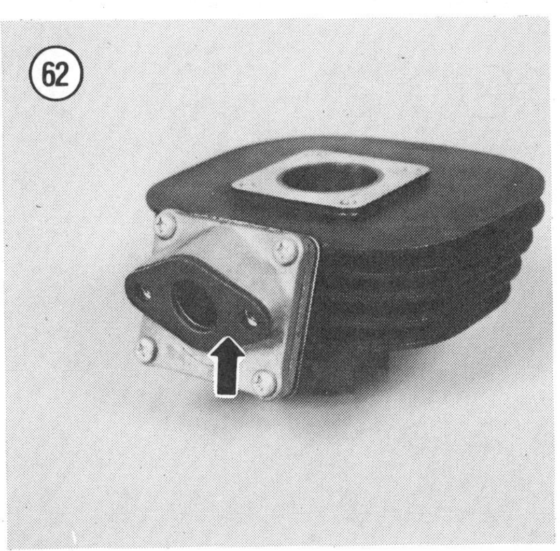

Removal/Installation

The reed valve can be removed with the cylinder removed or installed on the bike.

1. If the reed valve is going to be removed with the cylinder installed on the bike, note the following:
   a. Wash the bike thoroughly before disassembly.
   b. Remove the carburetor as described under *Carburetor Removal/Installation* in Chapter Eight.

2. Remove the bolts securing the intake manifold (**Figure 60**) to the cylinder.

3. Pull the reed cage assembly (**Figure 61**) out of the cylinder intake tract.

NOTE

Some mechanics choose to seal the reed cage against the cylinder with a chemical sealer. This is not necessary (unless mating surfaces are damaged) and it can make removal of the reed cage difficult. If the reed cage on your model is secured with a sealer, do not pry the cage off. Undoubtedly this will damage the mating surfaces and cause an air leak. Instead, tap the side (non-gasket area) of the cage with a rubber mallet or soft-faced drift until the cage breaks free of the sealer. Do not use a hard-faced drift or screwdriver to tap the reed cage off; this will flare the edge of the reed cage surface and cause an air leak. If you are working on a bike in which a sealer was used, check the reed cage carefully for pry marks or other damage.

4. Remove and discard the reed cage gasket. If a sealer was used, carefully scrape all gasket residue from the cylinder mating surface.

5. Inspect the reed valve assembly as described in this chapter.

6. Install a new gasket and insert the reed valve assembly into the cylinder (**Figure 61**). The assembly is not marked or indexed as to a top or bottom so it can be installed either way with no problems.

7. *YZ50 models:* Be sure to install the manifold gasket (**Figure 62**).

8. *YZ60 and YZ80 models:* Install the rubber intake manifold with the carburetor locating notch facing UP. See **Figure 60**.

9. Tighten the screws evenly in a crisscross pattern. Tighten the screws securely.

NOTE
*If you are concerned about an air leak at the reed cage, apply silicone sealant around the outside mating areas as shown in **Figure 63**. Fill the depression formed by edge of the cylinder, reed cage and manifold completely with sealant. Follow the manufacturer's sealant cure time recommendations before starting the engine.*

Inspection

Refer to **Figure 59** for basic reed valve construction. Reed valves (a) open and close the intake port in response to crankcase pressure changes allowing the fuel/air mixture to enter and then close off to allow the crankcase to pressurize. The reed stops (d) are limiters to prevent the reed valves from opening too far.

1. Carefully examine the reed valve assembly for visible signs of wear, distortion or damage.
2. Use vernier calipers and measure the distance from the reed stop to the surface of the reed (**Figure 64**). Both reed stops should be the same distance from the reed plate. The correct distance is listed in **Table 1** and **Table 2**.

If reed stops are not equally spaced from the reed plate, remove the reed stops. Then pad the jaws of a wide jaw pair of pliers and gently bend reed stops as necessary.

3. Use a flat feeler gauge and check the clearance between the reed plate and the gasket (**Figure 65**). Refer to the service limits in **Table 1** or **Table 2**. If the clearance exceeds this dimension the reed plate(s) must be replaced.
4. Remove the screws (A, **Figure 66**) securing the reed stop to the reed body. Be careful that the screwdriver does not slip off and damage the reed plate.
5. Carefully examine the reed plate, reed stop and gasket.

Check for signs of cracks, metal fatigue, distortion, or foreign matter damage. Pay particular attention to the rubber gasket seal. The reed stops and reed plates are available as replacement parts, but if the rubber gasket seal is damaged the entire assembly should be replaced.

6. Check the thread holes in the reed cage. If the threads are stripped, do not repair the threads. Instead, it will be safer to replace the reed cage. Loose screws can fall into the engine and cause expensive damage.
7. Reassemble the unit. Install the reed plate and reed stop with the cut off corner (B, **Figure 66**) in the lower right-hand corner. Apply Loctite 242 (blue) to the threads prior to installation and tighten securely.

NOTE
Make sure that all parts are clean and free of any small dirt particles or lint from a shop cloth as they may cause a small amount of distortion in the reed plate.

8. Reinstall the reed valve assembly as previously described.

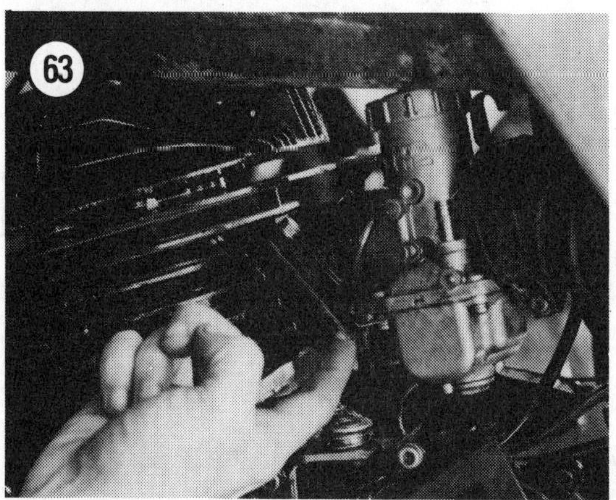

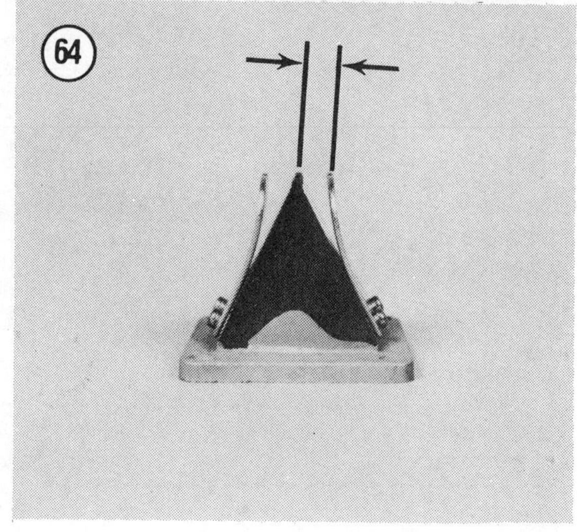

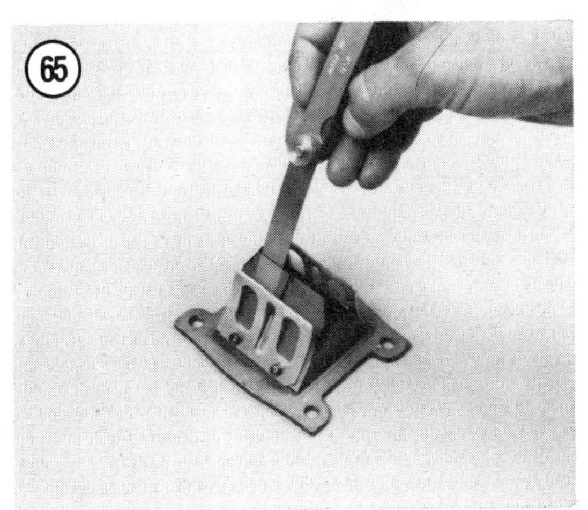

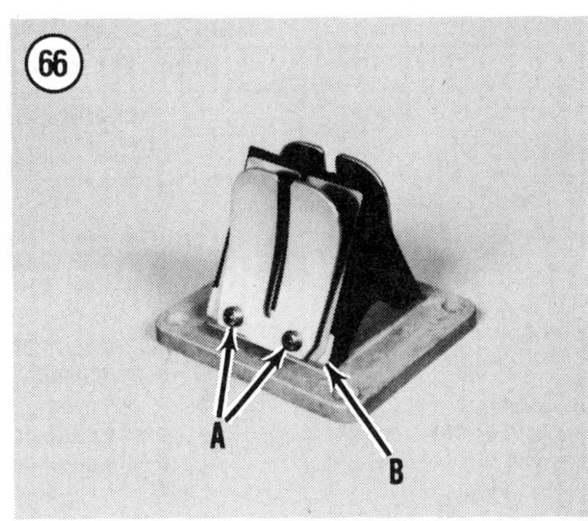

Table 1 ENGINE SPECIFICATIONS

(1978-1981 YZ80 AND ALL YZ50, YZ60)		
Item	**Specifications mm (in.)**	**Wear limit mm (in.)**
Cylinder		
Bore and stroke		
YZ50	40×39.7 (1.57×1.56)	—
YZ60	42×42 (1.65×1.65)	—
YZ80	49×42 (1.93×1.65)	—
Bore		
YZ50	40.0 (1.57)	40.02 (1.5708)
YZ60	42.0 (1.65)	42.02 (1.658)
YZ80	49.0 (1.93)	49.02 (1.9308)
Taper limit	—	0.05 (0.0020)
Out of round	—	0.01 (0.0004)
Piston		
Piston/cylinder clearance		
YZ50	0.035-0.040 (0.0014-0.0016)	—
YZ60		
1981	0.030-0.035 (0.0012-0.0014)	—
1982	0.055-0.060 (0.0022-0.0024)	—
YZ80		
1978-1980	0.035-0.040 (0.0014-0.0016)	—
1981	0.055-0.060 (0.0022-0.0024)	—
Piston measuring point		
YZ50	5 (0.2)	—
YZ60	20 (0.8)	—
YZ80		
1978-1980	5 (0.2)	—
1981	16 (0.6)	—
Piston rings		
Ring end gap		
YZ50	0.15-0.35 (0.006-0.014)	—
YZ60	0.15-0.35 (0.006-0.014)	—
YZ80		
1978-1980		
Nippon	0.4-0.5 (0.016-0.020)	—
Teikoku	0.2-0.5 (0.008-0.020)	—
1981	0.2-0.4 (0.008-0.016)	—

(continued)

Table 1 ENGINE SPECIFICATIONS (continued)

(1978-1981 YZ80 AND ALL YZ50, YZ60)		
Item	**Specifications mm (in.)**	**Wear limit mm (in.)**
Ring side clearance		
YZ50		
Top	0.04-0.08 (0.002-0.003)	—
Second	0.03-0.07 (0.0012-0.003)	—
YZ60		
Top	0.04-0.08 (0.002-0.003)	—
Second	0.02 (0.0008)	—
YZ80		
1978-1980	0.03-0.05 (0.0012-0.0020)	—
1981	0.04-0.08 (0.002-0.003)	—
Reed valve		
Stopper height		
YZ50	7 (0.28)	—
YZ60	9 (0.35)	—
YZ80		
1978	7 (0.28)	—
1979-1981	8.3 (0.32)	—
Reed valve bend limit		
All models	0.3 (0.012)	—

Table 2 ENGINE SPECIFICATIONS (1982-ON YZ80)

Item	Specifications mm (in.)	Wear limit mm (in.)
Cylinder		
Bore and stroke		
YZ80	—	
1982-1983	47×45.6 (1.85×1.80)	—
1984-on	48×45.6 (1.89×1.80)	—
Bore		
YZ80		
1982-1983	47 (1.850)	—
1984-on	48 (1.870)	48.1 (1.894)
Taper limit	—	0.05 (0.0020)
Out of round	—	0.01 (0.0004)
Piston		
Piston/cylinder clearance		
All models	0.060-0.065 (0.0024-0.0026)	0.1 (0.004)
Piston rings		
Ring end gap		
YZ80		
1982	0.2-0.4 (0.008-0.016)	—
1983-on	0.30-0.45 (0.012-0.018)	0.6 (0.024)

(continued)

Table 2 ENGINE SPECIFICATIONS (1982-ON YZ80) (continued)

Item	Specifications mm (in.)	Wear limit mm (in.)
Ring side clearance		
YZ80		
1982-1983	0.04-0.08 (0.002-0.003)	—
1984-on	0.03-0.07 (0.0012-0.0028)	0.10 (0.004)
Reed valve		
Stopper height		
YZ80		
1982	8.3 (0.32)	—
1983-1984	10.3 (0.41)	—
1985-on	8.5 (0.33)	—
Reed valve bend limit		
All models	0.3 (0.012)	—

4

Table 3 ENGINE TORQUE SPECIFICATIONS

Item	N•m	ft.-lb.
Cylinder head nuts		
YZ50	10	7
YZ60	30	21
YZ80		
1978-1980	13-15	9-11
1981-1982	30	21
1983-on	25	18
Clutch nut		
YZ50	60	43
YZ60	50	36
YZ80		
1978	60	43
1979	45	33
1980-1982	50	36
1983-on	55	40
Magneto or rotor		
YZ50	50	36
YZ60	40	28
YZ80		
1978	60	43
1979-1982	40	29
1983-on	35	25
Cylinder drain bolt		
YZ80		
1982-on	10	7.2
Water pump housing cover		
YZ80		
1982-on	10	7.2

Table 4 PISTON CUTAWAY/HEIGHT SPECIFICATIONS

Model	Measurement height* mm (in.)	Adjustment amount mm (in.)
YZ50	5 (0.2)	0
YZ60		
1981	19 (3/4)	0.025 (0.0010)
1982	19 (3/4)	0.040 (0.0016)
YZ80		
1978-1980	5 (0.2)	0
1981	16 (5/8)	0
1982	16 (5/8)	0.048 (0.0020)
1983	26.4 (1 1/32)	0.01 (0.0004)
1984-on	15 (19/32)	0

H

Intake skirt cutaway

CHAPTER FIVE

ENGINE LOWER END

5

This chapter describes service procedures for the following lower end components:

a. Crankcases.
b. Crankshaft.
c. Connecting rod.
d. Transmission (removal and installation).
e. Internal shift mechanism (removal and installation).

Prior to removing and disassembling the crankcase, clean the entire engine and frame with a good grade commercial degreaser, like Gunk or Bel-Ray engine degreaser or equivalent. It is easier to work on a clean engine and you will do a better job.

Make certain that you have all the necessary tools available, especially any special tool(s) and purchase replacement parts prior to disassembly. Also make sure you have a clean place to work.

It is a good idea to identify and mark parts as they are removed so that errors will be avoided during assembly and installation. Clean all parts thoroughly upon removal, then place them in trays or boxes with their associated mounting hardware. Do not rely on memory alone as it may be days or weeks before you complete the job. In the text there is frequent mention of the left-hand and right-hand side of the engine. This refers to the engine as it sits in the bike's frame, not as it sits on your workbench.

Crankshaft specifications are listed in **Table 1**. **Table 1** and **Table 2** are at the end of the chapter.

SERVICING ENGINE IN FRAME

Some of the components can be serviced while the engine is mounted in the frame (the bike's frame is a great holding fixture—especially for breaking loose stubborn bolts and nuts):

a. Cylinder head.
b. Cylinder.
c. Piston.
d. Carburetor.
e. Magneto.
f. Clutch.
g. External shift mechanism.

ENGINE

Removal/Installation

The engines covered in this manual are very compact and can be easily removed by an adult. If the engine is going to be removed for non-engine related service, engine disassembly is not required. Instead, remove the engine as a unit. If service requires crankcase disassembly, use the frame as a holding tool and remove all of the engine sub-assemblies while the engine is mounted in the frame. After the sub-assemblies are removed, the crankcase can be removed as a unit then serviced as required.

1. Place a wood block(s) under the frame to support the bike securely.

2. Remove the seat and both side covers.
3. Remove the fuel tank as described in Chapter Eight.
4. Remove the exhaust system as described under *Exhaust System Removal/Installation* in Chapter Eight.
5. Remove the carburetor as described under *Carburetor Removal/Installation* in Chapter Eight.
6. Remove the shift lever pinch bolt and slide the lever (**Figure 1**) off of the shift shaft. If the lever is tight, pry the lever slot open with a screwdriver and pull the lever off.

NOTE
An impact driver with a Phillips bit (described in Chapter One) will be necessary to loosen the left-hand side cover screws in Step 7. Attempting to loosen the screws with a Phillips screwdriver may ruin the screw heads.

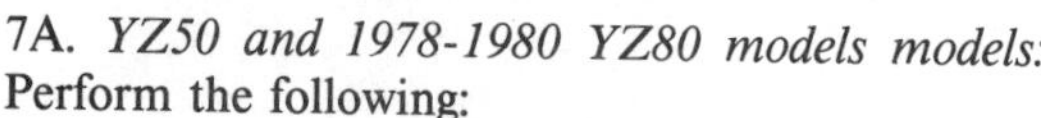

7A. *YZ50 and 1978-1980 YZ80 models models:* Perform the following:

a. On YZ50 models, remove the clutch mechanism adjustment cover and screws (**Figure 2**). The upper screw (long) is screwed into the crankcase (**Figure 3**).
b. Remove the screws securing the left-hand side cover and remove the cover and gasket.
c. Lay the side cover over the upper frame tube and out of the way. If it is necessary to remove the side cover from the bike, perform the following.
d. See **Figure 4**. Loosen the clutch cable adjuster locknut at the handlebar and turn the adjuster clockwise to loosen the clutch cable. Then disconnect the clutch cable from the side cover (**Figure 5**) and remove the cover.

7B. *YZ60 and 1981-on YZ80:* Perform the following:

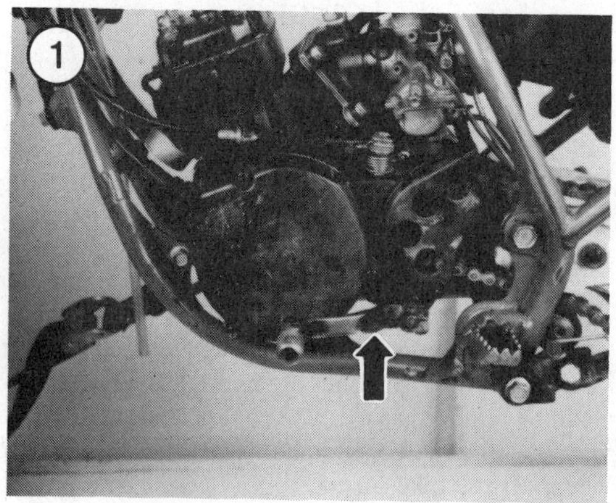

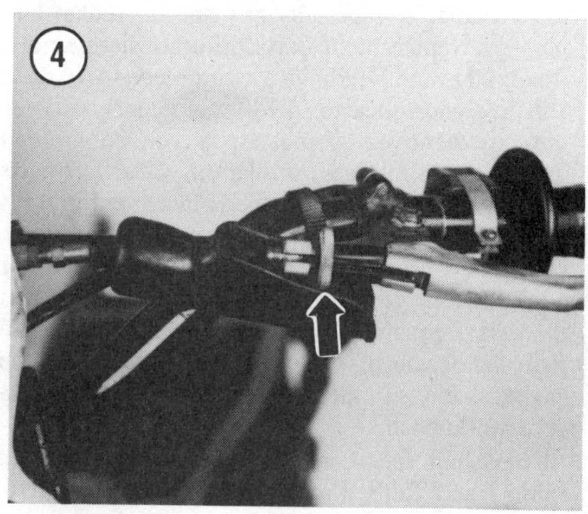

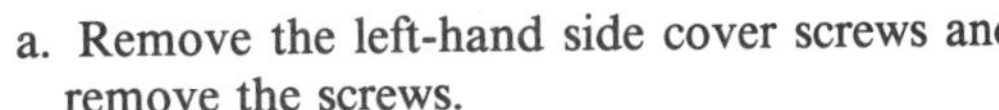

a. Remove the left-hand side cover screws and remove the screws.
b. See **Figure 4**. Loosen the clutch cable adjuster locknut at the handlebar and turn the adjuster clockwise to loosen the clutch cable.
c. See **Figure 6**. Pull the clutch cable out of the cylinder cable guide (A). Then disconnect the cable at the push lever (B).

8. On early YZ80 models, remove the right-hand footpeg assembly (A, **Figure 7**) and the rear brake pedal assembly (B, **Figure 7**).

9. Remove the master link on the drive chain (**Figure 8**). Then disconnect the drive chain and remove it.

10. *Liquid-cooled engines:* Perform the following:
   a. Drain the coolant as described under *Coolant Change* in Chapter Three.
   b. Disconnect the water hose at the cylinder head (**Figure 9**).

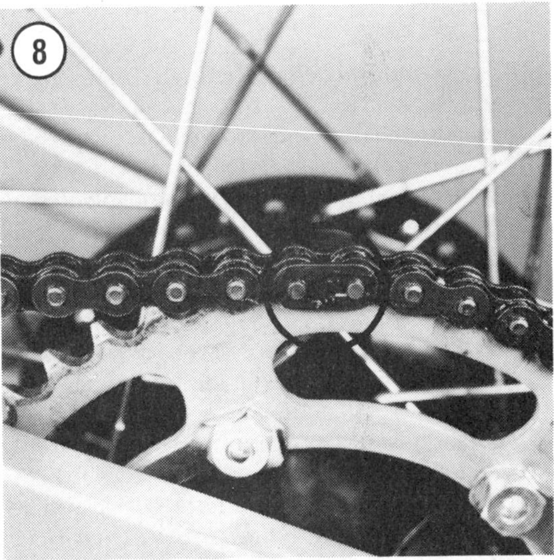

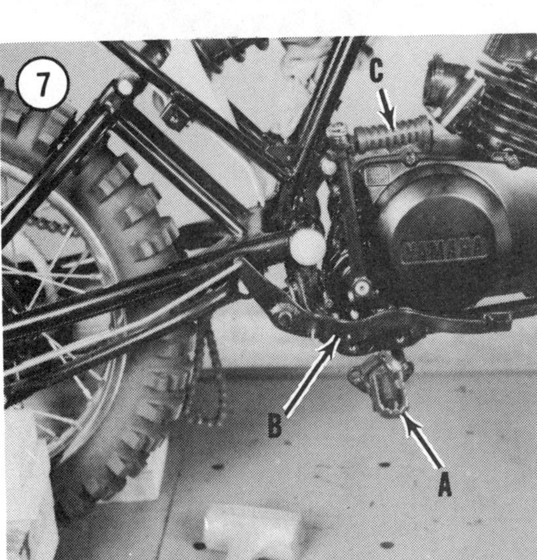

c. Disconnect the water hose at the water pump (**Figure 10**).

11. If you plan on disassembling the crankcases, remove the following engine sub-assemblies:
   a. Cylinder head (Chapter Four).
   b. Cylinder (Chapter Four).
   c. Piston (Chapter Four).
   d. Magneto (Chapter Nine).
   e. Clutch (Chapter Six).
   f. Kickstarter (Chapter Six).

12A. *1978-1981 models:* Remove the engine mounting bolts (**Figure 11**) and remove the engine assembly from the frame.

NOTE
On YZ50 models, the lower rear bolt is almost an interference fit with the left-hand foot peg. There is enough room though and it is not necessary to remove it to remove the bolt. Just carefully tap on the right-hand end of the bolt and it will pass by the footpeg assembly.

12B. *1982-on models:* Remove the engine assembly as follows:
   a. Remove the front and lower engine mount bolts (**Figure 12**).
   b. Remove the engine-to-swing arm pivot shaft (**Figure 13**) and withdraw the pivot shaft (**Figure 14**) from the right-hand side.
   c. Lift the engine (**Figure 15**) out of the frame.
   d. The swing arm is now loose from its mounting on the frame. If it is necessary to move the bike, align the swing arm with the frame and install the pivot shaft and nut.

13. Install by reversing these removal steps.

14. If the engine oil was drained, fill the clutch/transmission with the correct type and quantity oil as described under *Clutch/Transmission Oil* in Chapter Three.

15. *Liquid-cooled engines:* Refill the cooling system as described under *Coolant Change* in Chapter Three.

16. Reinstall the drive chain. Connect the master link so that the closed end of the chain faces the direction of chain travel (**Figure 16**).

17. Adjust the clutch, drive chain and rear brake pedal as described in Chapter Three.

18. Start the engine and check for leaks.

CRANKCASE AND CRANKSHAFT

Disassembly of the crankcase—splitting the cases—and removal of the crankshaft assembly require that the engine be removed from the frame. However, the cylinder head, cylinder and all other attached assemblies should be removed with the engine in the frame.

The crankcase is made in 2 halves of precision diecast aluminum alloy and is of the "thin-walled" type. To avoid damage to them do not hammer or

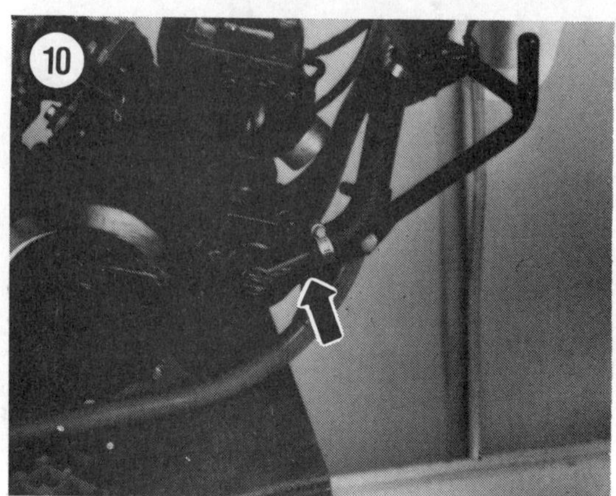

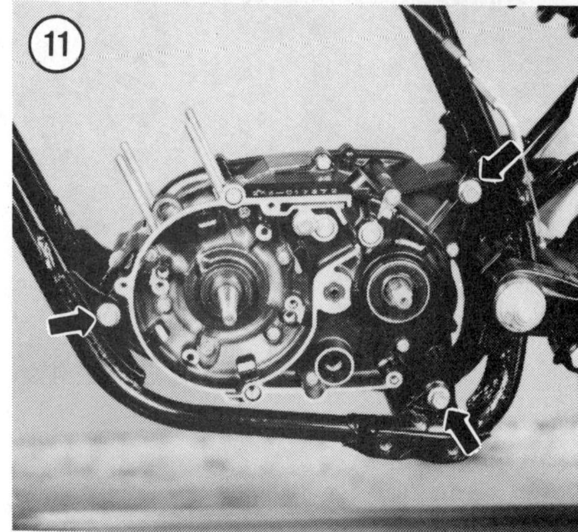

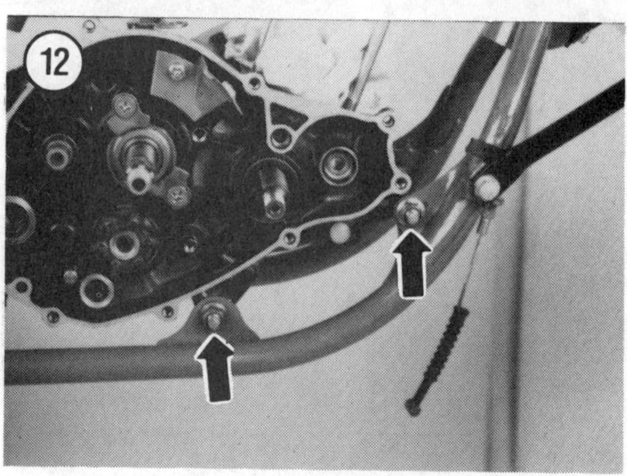

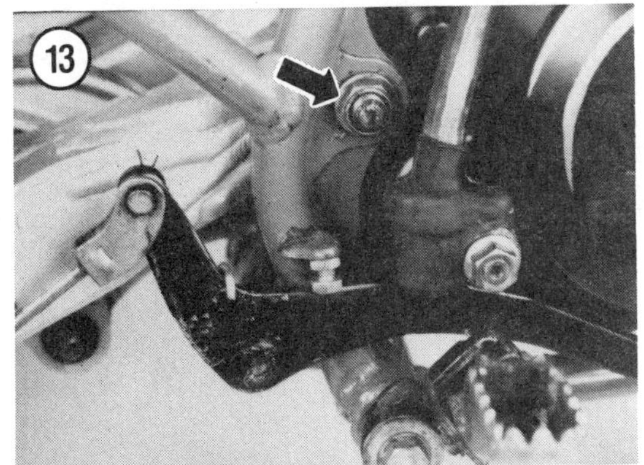

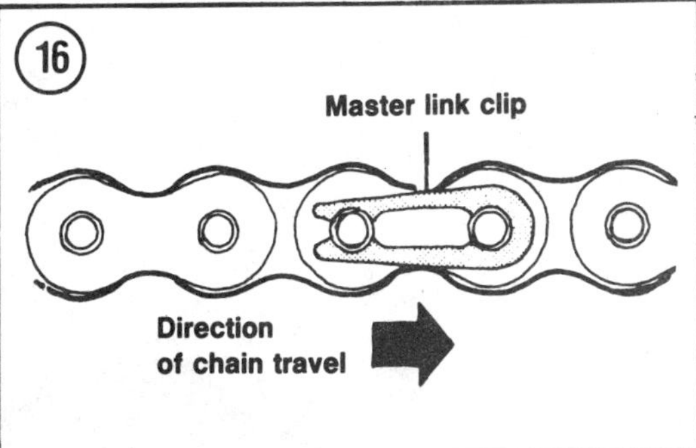

pry on any of the interior or exterior projected walls. These areas are easily damaged if stressed beyond what they are designed for. They are assembled without a gasket; only gasket sealer is used while dowel pins align the crankcase halves when they are bolted together.

The crankshaft assembly is made up of 2 full-circle flywheels pressed together on a hollow crankpin. The connecting rod big end bearing on the crankpin is a needle bearing assembly (**Figure 17**). The crankshaft assembly is supported by 2 ball bearings in the crankcase.

The procedure which follows is presented as a complete, step-by-step major lower end rebuild that should be followed if an engine is to be completely reconditioned.

Remember that the right- and left-hand side of the engine relates to the engine as it sits in the bike's frame, not as it sits on your workbench.

Special Tools

When splitting the crankcase assembly, a few special tools will be required. These tools allow easy disassembly and reassembly of the engine without prying or hammer use. Remember, the crankcase halves can be easily damaged by improper disassembly or reassembly techniques.

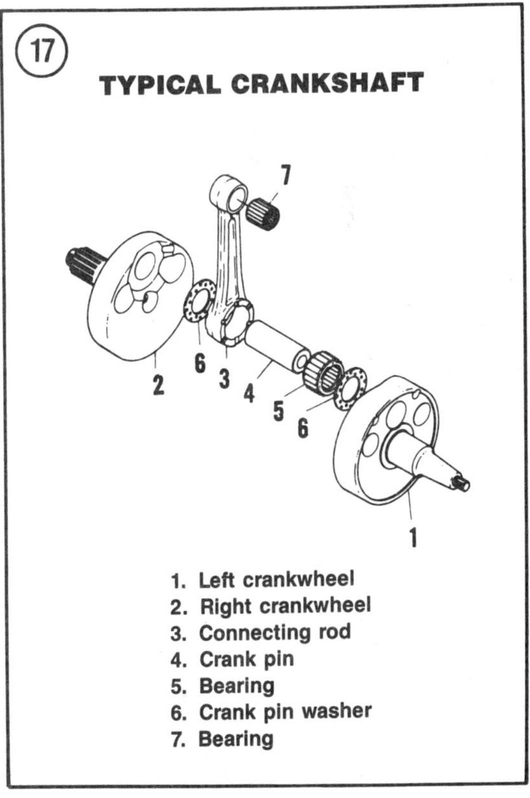

a. Yamaha crankcase separating tool (Part No. YU-01135) (**Figure 18**). This tool threads into the crankcase and is used to separate the crankcase halves and to press the crankshaft out of the crankcase. The tool is very simple in design and a similar type of tool can be substituted as long as the 2 bolts that thread into the crankcase have a M8×1.25 metric thread.
b. Yamaha crankshaft installing set (Part No. YU-90050) and adapter (Part No. YM-90062) (**Figure 19**). After the crankshaft is pressed out of the crankcase, it must be carefully pressed back in. The Yamaha tool allows the crankshaft to be pressed into the crankcase. The crankshaft is assembled to very close tolerances. Banging on the crankshaft during installation will knock it out of alignment.

Crankcase Disassembly (1978-1980)

This procedure describes disassembly of the crankcase halves and removal of the crankshaft, transmission and internal shift mechanism.

1. Remove all exterior engine assemblies as described in this chapter and other related chapters.

NOTE
Drain the clutch/transmission oil as described in Chapter Three. To avoid misplacing the drain bolt, reinstall it after the oil is completely drained.

2. To remove the drive sprocket; straighten the tab on the lockwasher (**Figure 20**).
3. Unscrew the locknut and remove it and the lockwasher (**Figure 21**).
4. Remove the drive sprocket (**Figure 22**) and collar (**Figure 23**).
5. Remove the shift drum neutral detent from the top of the crankcase (**Figure 24**).

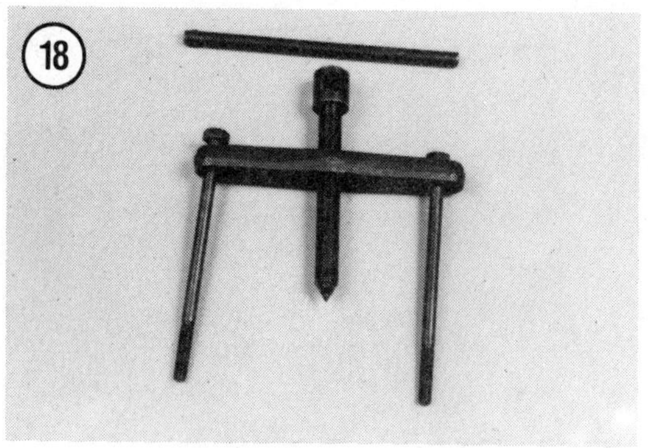
18

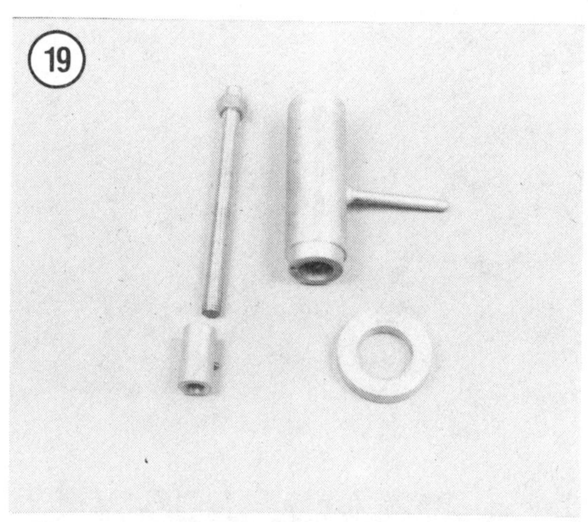
19

20

21

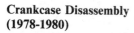

NOTE
*Be sure to remove all 3 parts—bolt, spring and detent (**Figure 25**).*

6. Remove the engine from the frame as described in this chapter.
7. Loosen all screws securing the crankcase halves together one-quarter turn. To prevent warpage, loosen them in a crisscross pattern.

NOTE
*Set the engine on two wood blocks or fabricate a holding fixture with 2×4 inch wood as shown in **Figure 26**.*

8. Remove all screws loosened in Step 7 (**Figure 27**). Be sure to remove all of them.

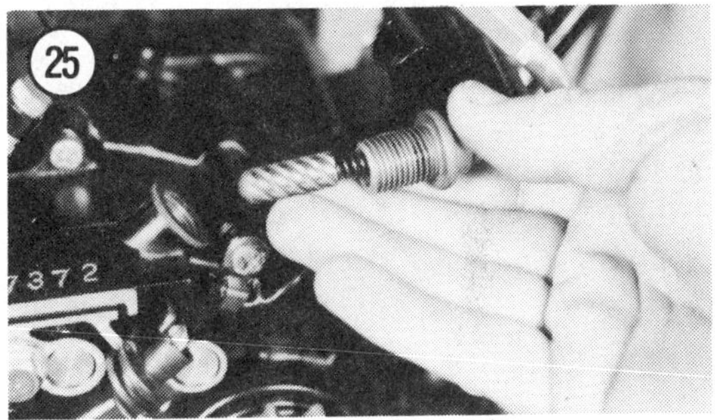

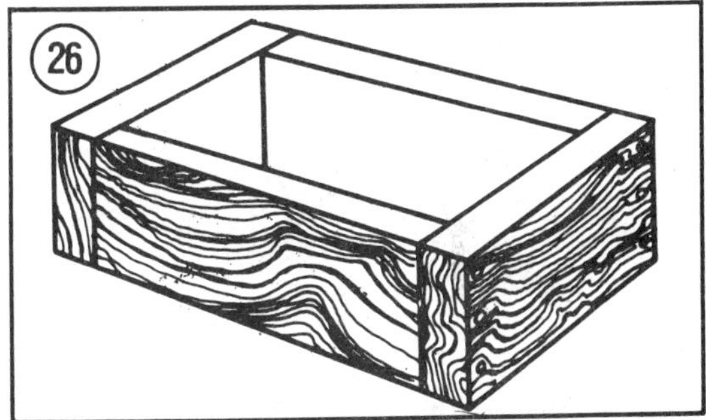

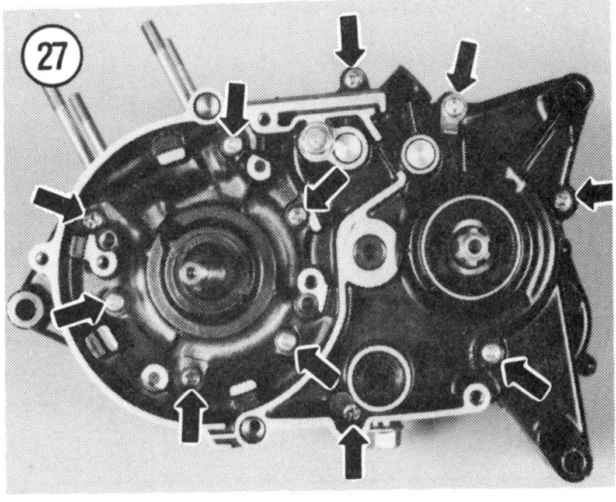

NOTE
*To prevent screw loss and to ensure proper location during assembly, draw the crankcase outline on cardboard (**Figure 28**), then punch holes to correspond with screw locations. Insert the screws in their appropriate locations. Also record the position of any clips that hold electrical wires or drain tubes.*

CAUTION
*Perform this operation over and close down to the work bench as the crankcase halves may easily separate. **Do not** hammer on the crankcase halves as they will be damaged.*

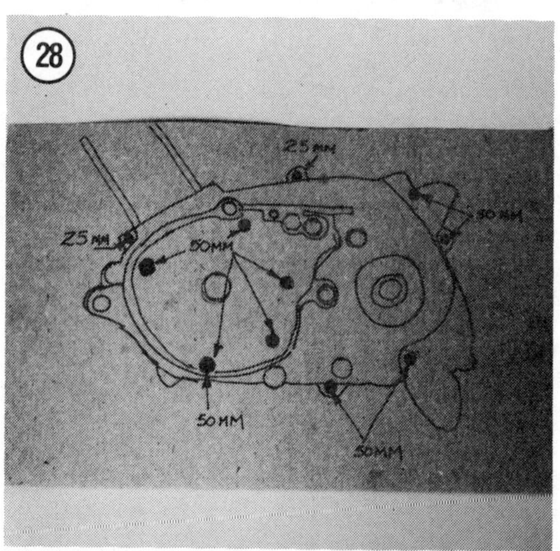

30

Keep parallel

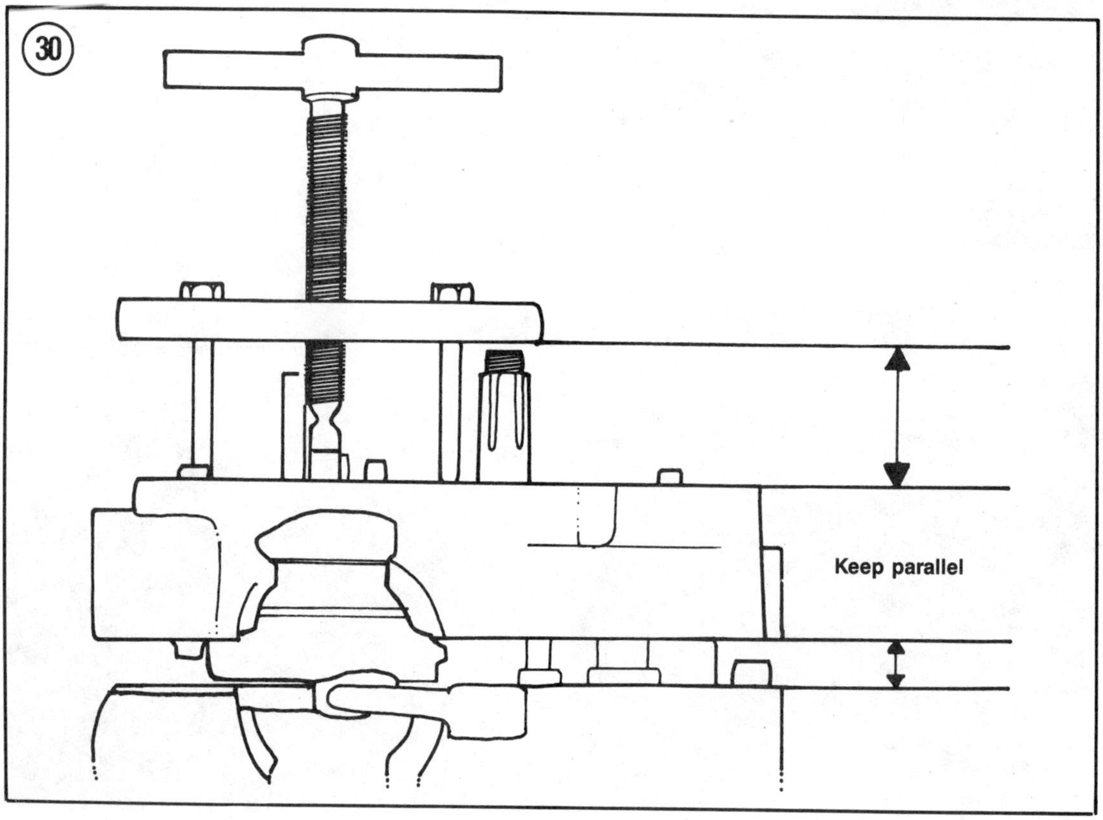

9. Install the crankcase separating tool (**Figure 18**) into the threaded holes (**Figure 29**) on the right-hand crankcase. Center the center threaded bolt on the end of the crankshaft. Tighten the securing bolts into the crankcase, making sure the tool body is parallel with the crankcase. If necessary, back out one of the separating tool bolts.
10. See **Figure 30**. Screw the puller *clockwise* until both cases begin to separate.

CAUTION
*While tightening the puller make sure the body is kept parallel to the crankcase surface during this operation (**Figure 30**). Otherwise it will put an uneven stress on the case halves and may damage them.*

11. Use a plastic or rubber mallet and tap the crankcase half and transmission shaft to help during separation.

CAUTION
*Crankcase separation requires only hand pressure on the puller screw. If extreme pressure seems to be needed, or if both halves will not remain parallel, **stop immediately**. Relieve the pressure immediately. Check for crankcase screws not removed, or any part that is still attached, or transmission shafts hung up in a bearing.*

CAUTION
Never pry between case halves. Doing so may result in oil leaks, requiring replacement of the case halves.

12. Don't lose the 2 locating dowels.
13. Unscrew the crankcase separator tool.
14. The transmission assemblies and the crankshaft assemblies will usually stay in the left-hand case half.
15. Lift up and carefully remove the transmission and shift drum assemblies (**Figure 31**).

NOTE
*Step 16 describes crankshaft removal. As explained under **Special Tools** in this chapter, the Yamaha crankcase separating tool will be required to remove the crankshaft and the Yamaha crankshaft installing set will be required to install it. If you do not have the Yamaha crankshaft installing set, remove the crankshaft with the separating tool. This will allow you to perform all crankshaft inspection procedures and to replace crankcase bearings and seals as required. When you are ready to assemble the engine, take the crankshaft and the left-hand crankcase to your Yamaha dealer and have the crankshaft installed. The labor cost required to install the crankshaft will be small compared to the purchase of the special tool for one time use.*

16. Remove the crankshaft from the left-hand crankcase as follows. The Yamaha crankcase separating tool will be required to remove the crankshaft. See *Special Tools* in this chapter.
   a. Install the left-hand crankcase/crankshaft assembly on wood blocks.
   b. Assemble the crankcase separating tool onto the crankcase and align the pressure bolt with the end of the crankshaft (**Figure 32**). Make sure to thread the 2 bolts all the way into the crankcase.
   c. Hold the connecting rod at top dead center (TDC) and turn the pressure bolt with the handle clockwise and press the crankshaft out

of the crankcase. Make sure the separating tool is held parallel to the crankcase when removing the crankshaft. If necessary, loosen one of the bolts to align the tool.

17. Inspect the crankcase halves and crankshaft as described under *Crankcase and Crankshaft Inspection—All Models* later in this chapter.

Crankcase Assembly (1978-1980)

1. Pack all of the crankcase oil seals with grease.
2. Install the crankshaft into the left-hand crankcase as follows. The Yamaha crankshaft installing tool will be required to install the crankshaft. See *Special Tools* in this chapter.
   a. Align the crankshaft with the left-hand crankcase main bearing.
   b. Lay the large spacer from the installing tool onto the left-hand crankcase (A, **Figure 33**).
   c. Thread the adapter onto the end of the crankshaft (B, **Figure 33**).
   d. Thread the large threaded rod into the adapter (C, **Figure 33**).
   e. Align the pot (**Figure 34**) with the threaded rod and install the large nut on the threaded rod. Tighten the nut and pull the crankshaft into the bearing. Hold the connecting rod at top dead center (TDC) to prevent it from contacting the crankcase when installing the crankshaft.
   f. Remove the crankshaft tool.

CAUTION
If you do not have access to the special tool, have the crankshaft installed by a Yamaha dealer. Do not drive the crankshaft into the bearing.

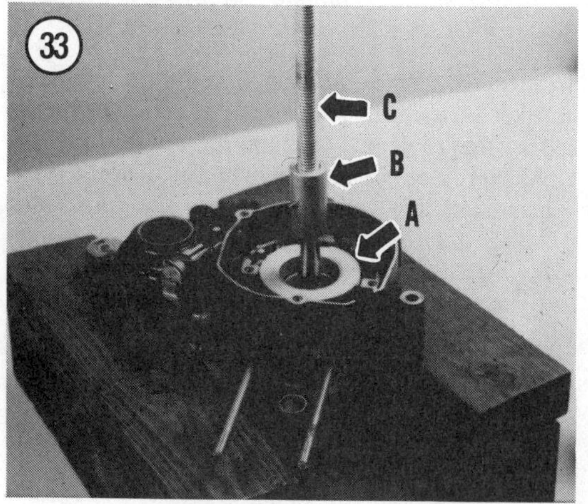

3. Apply assembly oil to the inner race of all bearings (**Figure 35**) in the right-hand crankcase half.
4. Install the transmission as follows:
   a. Coat all sliding surfaces with assembly oil.

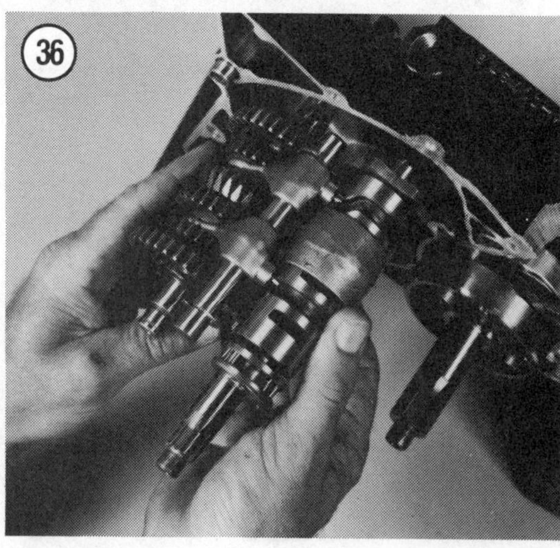

37

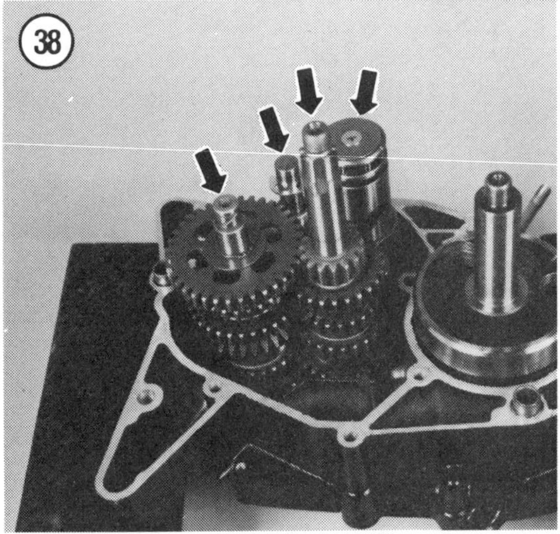
38

39

b. Mesh the 2 transmission assemblies, shift drum and shift fork assembly together in their proper relationship to each other (**Figure 36**).

c. Install the assembly into the left-hand crankcase. See **Figure 37** (5-speed) or **Figure 38** (6-speed).

d. After installing the transmission assembly, tap on the end of both transmission shafts to make sure they are completely seated in the crankcase bearings.

e. Make sure all cam pin followers are in mesh with the shift drum grooves. See **Figure 39** (5-speed) or **Figure 40** (6-speed).

NOTE

This procedure is best done with the aid of a helper as the gear assemblies tend to bind when unsupported. Have the helper spin the transmission shaft while you turn the shift drum through all the gears.

f. Spin the transmission shafts and shift through the gears using the shift drum. Make sure you can shift into all gears. This is the time to find that something may be installed incorrectly—not after the crankcase is completely assembled.

NOTE

***Do not** install the shift drum neutral detent at this time. The spring pressure will push the shift drum over just enough to misalign the free end with the bearing in the right-hand crankcase during assembly.*

5. Set the crankcase assembly on 2 wood blocks or a wood holding fixture shown in the disassembly procedure.

40

5

6. Install the 2 locating dowels (**Figure 41**).
7. Apply a light coat of *non-hardening liquid gasket* (**Figure 42**) such as Yamabond No. 4, 4-Three Bond or equivalent to the mating surfaces of both crankcase halves.

NOTE
Make sure the mating surfaces are clean and free of all old gasket material. This is to make sure you get a leak free seal.

8. Set the upper crankcase half over the one on the blocks. Push it down squarely into place until it reaches the crankshaft bearing (**Figure 43**), usually with about 1/2 inch left to go.
9. Lightly tap the case halves together with a plastic or rubber mallet (**Figure 44**) until they seat. After the cases are assembled make sure each shaft rotates smoothly.

CAUTION
Crankcase halves should fit together without force. If the crankcase halves do

41

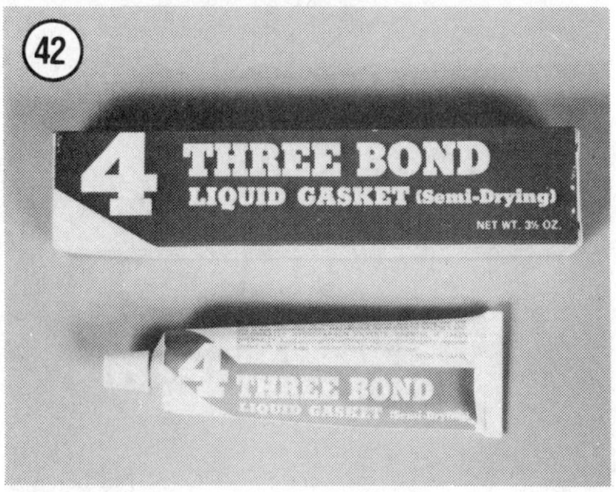

42

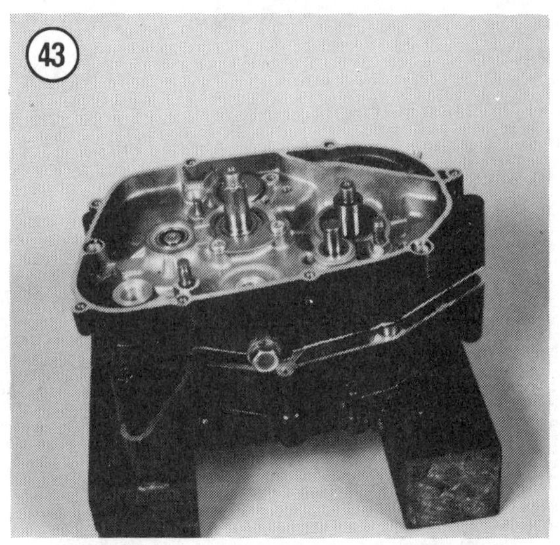
43

44

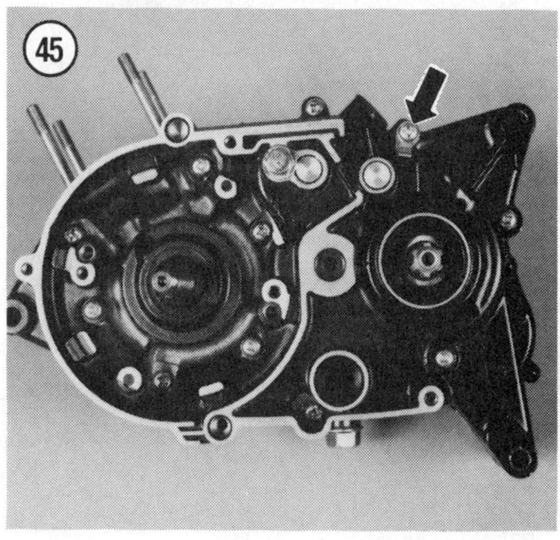
45

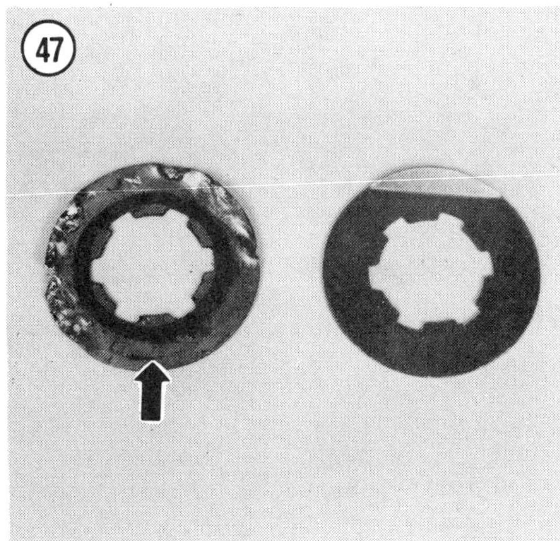

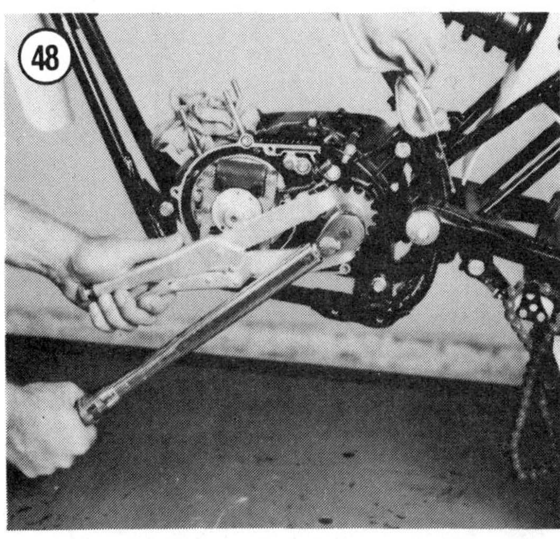

not fit together completely, do not attempt to pull them together with the crankcase screws. Separate the crankcase halves and investigate the cause of the interference. If the transmission shafts were disassembled, recheck to make sure that a gear is not installed backwards. Also check that the shift drum neutral detent is not installed—it must be removed during this procedure. Crankcase halves are a matched set and are very expensive. Do not risk damage by trying to force the crankcases together.

10. Place any clips (**Figure 45**) under the screws in the locations recorded during disassembly. Install all the crankcase screws and tighten only finger-tight at first.
11. Securely tighten the screws in 2 stages in a crisscross pattern until they are firmly hand-tight.
12. After the crankcase halves are completely assembled, rotate the crankshaft and transmission shafts to make sure there is no binding. If any is present, disassemble the crankcase and correct the problem.
13. Install the engine in the frame and tighten the mounting bolts and nuts securely.
14. Install the shift drum neutral detent (**Figure 46**).

NOTE
When installing the shift drum neutral detent, the plunger may slide out of the hollow bolt. If this happens the plunger may hang up on the end of the bolt making it impossible to start screwing in the bolt. Just wiggle the end of the shift drum on the opposite end of the detent and this will usually move the plunger around enough to align them properly for installation.

CAUTION
*If the previously mentioned problem happens, **do not** try to force the parts together as they will be damaged along with the threads in the crankcase. Remove all parts and reinstall them correctly.*

15. Install the collar, drive sprocket and a new lockwasher. Install a new lockwasher after the second removal or when the lockwasher begins to look like the one on the left in **Figure 47**.
16. Attach a "Grabbit" to the drive sprocket (**Figure 48**) and tighten the nut to the torque specification in **Table 2**.

17. Bend over the tab on the lockwasher (**Figure 49**).
18. Install all exterior engine assemblies as described in this chapter and other related chapters.

Crankcase Disassembly (1981-on)

This procedure describes disassembly of the crankcase halves and removal of the crankshaft, transmission and internal shift mechanism.

1. Remove all exterior engine assemblies as described in this chapter and other related chapters.

NOTE

Drain the clutch/transmission oil as described in Chapter Three. To avoid misplacing the drain bolt, reinstall it after the oil is completely drained.

2. Remove the circlip and slide the drive sprocket and drive chain (**Figure 50**) off of the countershaft.
3. Remove the engine from the frame as described in this chapter.

NOTE

An impact driver with a Phillips bit (described in Chapter One) will be necessary to loosen many of the Phillips screws in the following procedures. Attempting to loosen the screws with a Phillips screwdriver may ruin the screw heads.

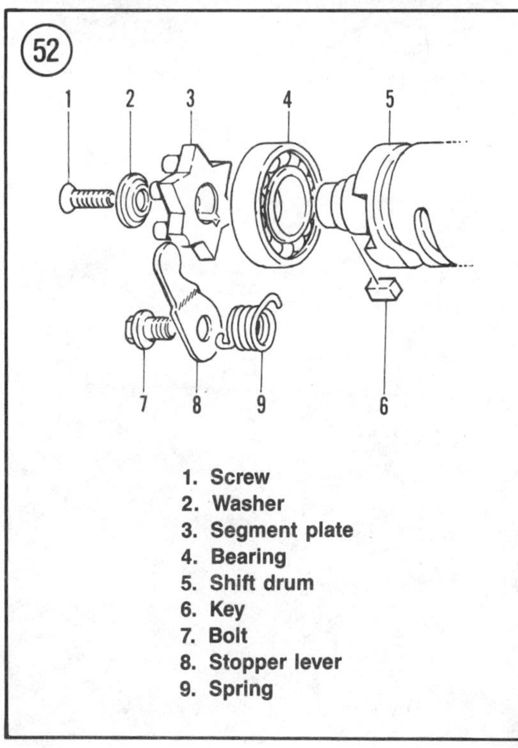

1. Screw
2. Washer
3. Segment plate
4. Bearing
5. Shift drum
6. Key
7. Bolt
8. Stopper lever
9. Spring

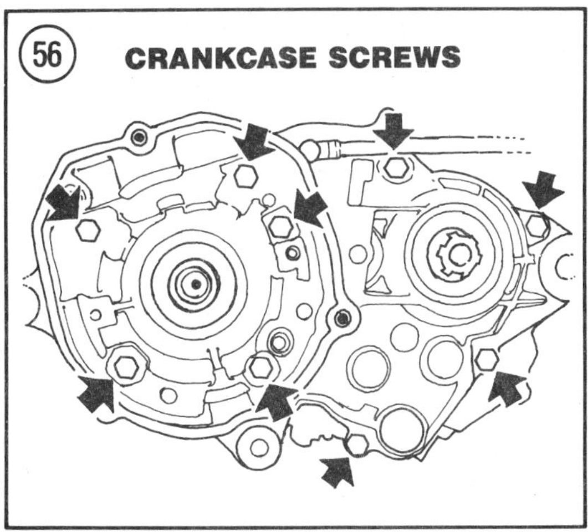

4. *1981-1982 models:* Perform the following:
   a. Remove the bolt and remove the stopper lever and spring (**Figure 51**).
   b. Remove the segment plate Phillips screw (**Figure 52**). Then remove the washer and segment plate (**Figure 52**).
5. *1983-on models models:* Remove the bolt and remove the stopper lever (**Figure 53**) and spring (**Figure 54**).
6. Loosen and remove the 2 bearing holder Phillips screws (**Figure 55**). Then remove the bearing holders.
7. Loosen all screws securing the crankcase halves together one-quarter turn (**Figure 56**). To prevent warpage, loosen them in a crisscross pattern.

NOTE

Set the engine on 2 wood blocks or fabricate a holding fixture with 2×4 inch wood as shown in ***Figure 57****.*

8. Remove all screws loosened in Step 7 (**Figure 56**). Be sure to remove all of them.

NOTE

To prevent loss and to ensure proper location during assembly, draw the crankcase outline on cardboard, then punch holes to correspond with screw locations. Insert the screws in their appropriate locations. Also record the position of any clips that hold electrical wires or drain tubes.

CAUTION

Perform this operation over and close down to the work bench as the crankcase halves may easily separate. ***Do not*** *hammer on the crankcase halves as they will be damaged.*

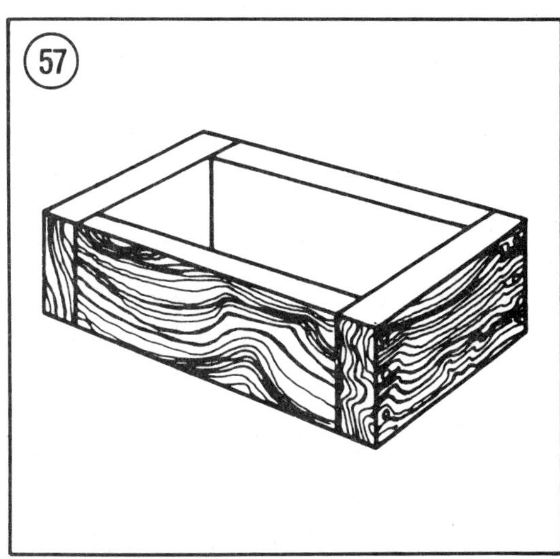

9. *1983-on:* Align the shift cam segment with the slots in the right-hand crankcase (**Figure 58**) so that the cam segments will not catch on the crankcase during engine disassembly.

10. Remove the plug (**Figure 59**) from the right-hand crankcase. The plug covers one of the separating tool thread holes.

11. Install the crankcase separating tool (**Figure 60**) into the threaded holes on the right-hand crankcase. Center the pressure bolt on the end of the crankshaft. Tighten the securing bolts into the crankcase, making sure the tool body is parallel

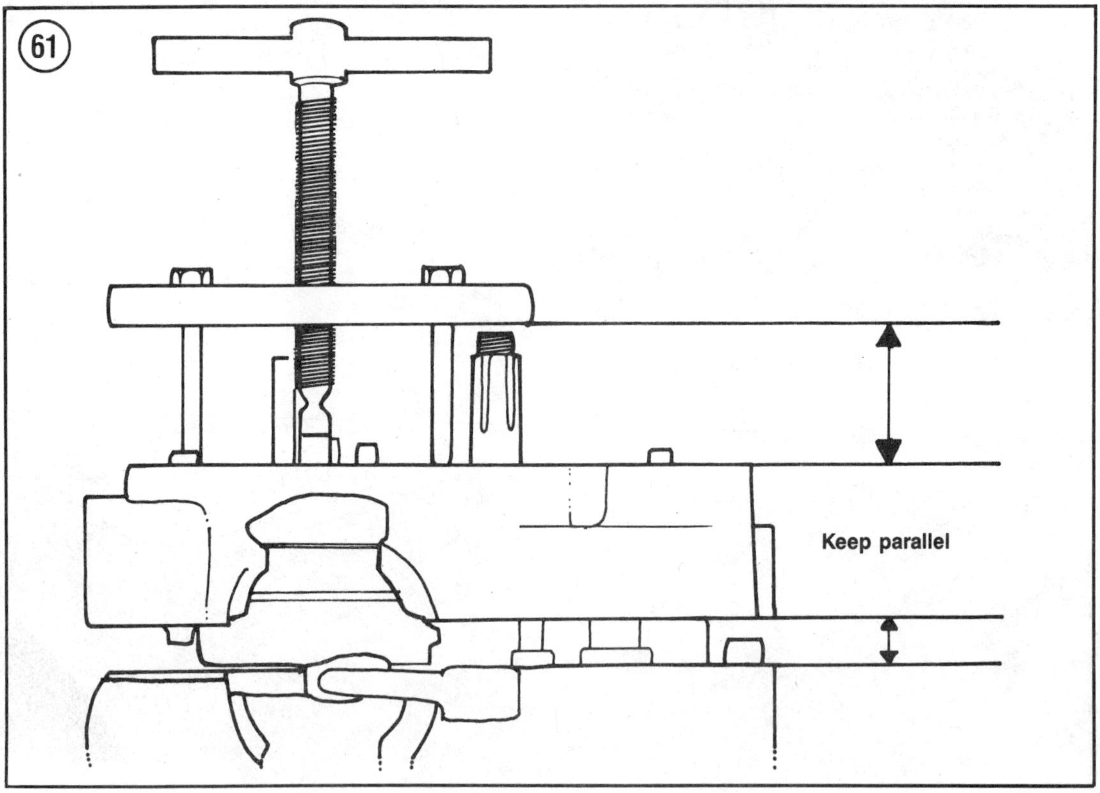

with the crankcase. If necessary, back out one of the separating tool bolts.

12. Screw the puller *clockwise* until both cases begin to separate.

CAUTION

*While tightening the puller make sure the body is kept parallel to the crankcase surface during this operation (**Figure 61**). Otherwise it will put an uneven stress on the case halves and may damage them.*

13. Use a plastic or rubber mallet and tap the crankcase half and transmission shaft to help during separation.

CAUTION

*Crankcase separation requires only hand pressure on the puller screw. If extreme pressure seems to be needed, or if both halves will not remain parallel, **stop immediately**. Relieve puller pressure immediately. Check for crankcase screws not removed, or any part that is still attached, or transmission shafts hung up in a bearing.*

CAUTION

Never pry between case halves. Doing so may result in oil leaks, requiring replacement of the case halves.

14. Remove the 2 dowel pins (**Figure 62**).
15. Unscrew the crankcase separator tool.
16. The transmission assemblies and the crankshaft assemblies will usually stay in the left-hand case half (**Figure 63**).
17. Remove the transmission assembly as follows:
    a. Remove the shift fork shafts. See **Figure 64** and **Figure 65**.
    b. Remove the No. 1 shift fork (**Figure 66**).

c. Remove the shift drum (A, **Figure 67**).
d. Remove the No. 2 shift fork (B, **Figure 67**).
e. Remove the No. 3 shift fork (C, **Figure 67**).
f. Remove the transmission shafts (**Figure 68**).

NOTE
*Each shift fork is equipped with a cam follower pin (**Figure 69**). Don't lose the pins while the engine is disassembled (**Figure 70**).*

NOTE
*Step 18 describes crankshaft removal. As explained under **Special Tools** in this chapter, the Yamaha crankcase separating tool will be required to remove the crankshaft and the Yamaha crankshaft installing set will be required to install it. If you do not have the Yamaha crankshaft installing set, remove the crankshaft with the separating tool. This will allow you to perform all crankshaft inspection procedures and to replace crankcase bearings and seals as required. When you are ready to assemble the engine, take the crankshaft and the left-hand crankcase to your Yamaha dealer and have the crankshaft installed. The labor cost required to install the crankshaft will be small compared to the purchase of the special tool for one time use.*

18. Remove the crankshaft from the left-hand crankcase as follows. The Yamaha crankcase separating tool will be required to remove the crankshaft. See *Special Tools* in this chapter.
a. Install the left-hand crankcase/crankshaft assembly on wood blocks.
b. Assemble the crankcase separating tool onto the crankcase and align the pressure bolt with

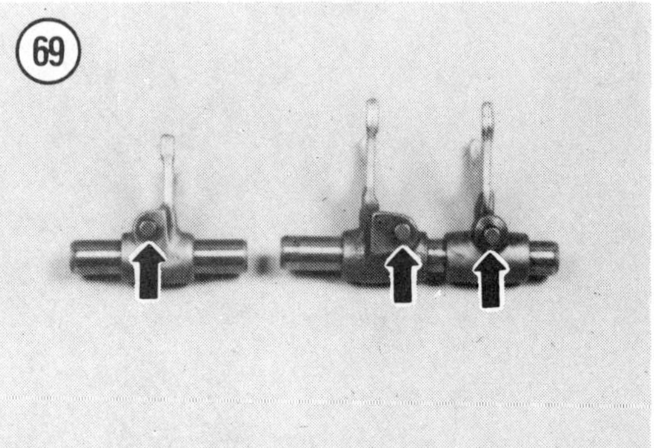

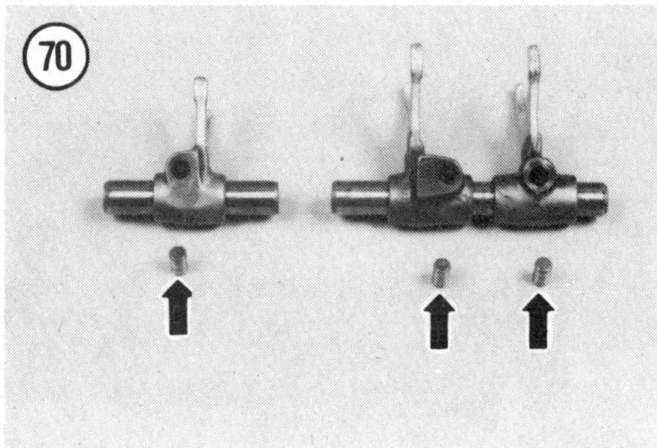

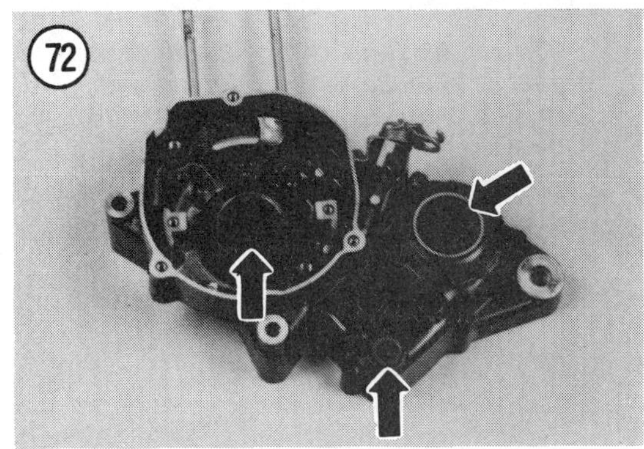

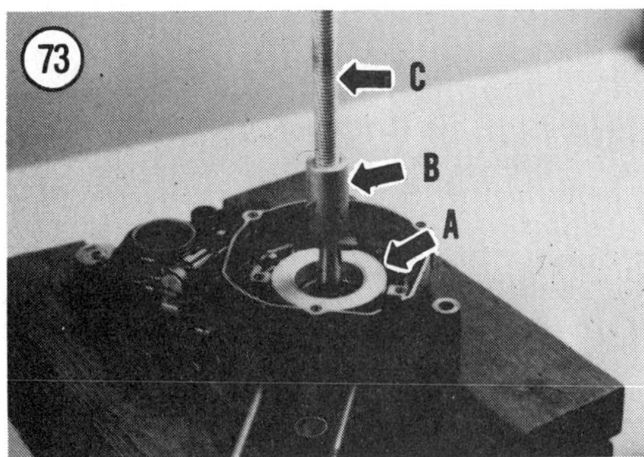

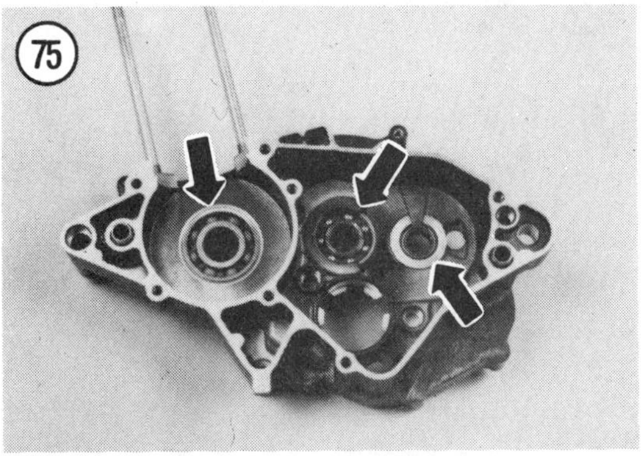

the end of the crankshaft (**Figure 71**). Make sure to thread the 2 bolts all the way into the crankcase.

c. Hold the connecting rod at top dead center (TDC) and turn the pressure bolt with the handle clockwise and press the crankshaft out of the crankcase. Make sure the separating tool is held parallel to the crankcase when removing the crankshaft. If necessary, loosen one of the bolts to align the tool.

19. Inspect the crankcase halves and crankshaft as described under *Crankcase and Crankshaft Inspection—All Models* later in this chapter.

5

Crankcase Assembly (1981-on)

1. Pack all of the crankcase oil seals (**Figure 72**) with grease.
2. Install the crankshaft into the left-hand crankcase as follows. The Yamaha crankshaft installing tool will be required to install the crankshaft. See *Special Tools* in this chapter.
   a. Align the crankshaft with the left-hand crankcase main bearing.
   b. Lay the large spacer from the installing tool onto the left-hand crankcase (A, **Figure 73**).
   c. Thread the adapter onto the end of the crankshaft (B, **Figure 73**).
   d. Thread the large threaded rod into the adapter (C, **Figure 73**).
   e. Align the pot (**Figure 74**) with the threaded rod and install the large nut on the threaded rod. Tighten the nut and pull the crankshaft into the bearing. Hold the connecting rod at top dead center (TDC) to prevent it from contacting the crankcase when installing the crankshaft.
   f. Remove the crankshaft tool.

CAUTION
If you do not have access to the special tool, have the crankshaft installed by a Yamaha dealer. Do not drive the crankshaft into the bearing.

3. Apply assembly oil to the inner race of all bearings (**Figure 75**) in the right-hand crankcase half.
4. Install the transmission as follows:

NOTE
On these models, the transmission is installed in sequence instead as a

*complete assembly. **Figure 76** shows the transmission shafts meshed together illustrating shift fork alignment.*

a. Coat all sliding surfaces with assembly oil.
b. Install the transmission shafts (**Figure 68**) into the left-hand crankcase.

NOTE
The shift forks are numbered 1, 2 or 3 representing position. When installing the shift forks, the numbered side must face toward the left-hand side of the engine.

c. Install the No. 3 shift fork (C, **Figure 67**).
d. Install the No. 2 shift fork (B, **Figure 67**).
e. Install the shift drum (B, **Figure 67**). Engage the shift fork cam pin follower into the correct shift drum machined slot.
f. Install the No. 1 shift fork (**Figure 66**) and engage the cam pin follower into the middle shift drum groove.
g. Install the shift fork shafts. See **Figure 65** and **Figure 64**. Make sure the shafts engage the shaft holes in the left-hand crankcase.
h. Make sure all cam pin followers mesh with the shift drum grooves. See **Figure 63**.
i. Spin the transmission shafts and shift through the gears using the shift drum. Make sure you can shift into all gears. This is the time to find that something may be installed incorrectly—not after the crankcase is completely assembled.

NOTE
This procedure is best done with the aid of a helper as the gear assemblies tend to bind when unsupported. Have the helper spin the transmission shaft while you turn the shift drum through all the gears.

5. Set the crankcase assembly on 2 wood blocks or a wood holding fixture shown in the disassembly procedure.
6. Install the 2 locating dowels (A, **Figure 77**).
7. Apply a light coat of *non-hardening liquid gasket* (**Figure 42**) such as Yamabond No. 4, 4-Three Bond or equivalent to the mating surfaces of both crankcase halves.

NOTE
Make sure the mating surfaces are clean and free of all old gasket material. This is to make sure you get a leak free seal.

NOTE
*When installing the right-hand crankcase, make sure to align the shift drum segment arms (**Figure 78**) with the slots in the case hole (B, **Figure 77**) so that they don't hit together.*

8. Set the upper crankcase half over the one on the blocks. Push it down squarely into place until it reaches the crankshaft bearing, usually with about 1/2 inch left to go.
9. Lightly tap the case halves together with a plastic or rubber mallet until they seat. After the cases are assembled make sure each shaft rotates smoothly.

CAUTION
Crankcase halves should fit together without force. If the crankcase halves do not fit together completely, do not attempt to pull them together with the crankcase screws. Separate the crankcase halves and investigate the cause of the interference. If the transmission shafts were disassembled,

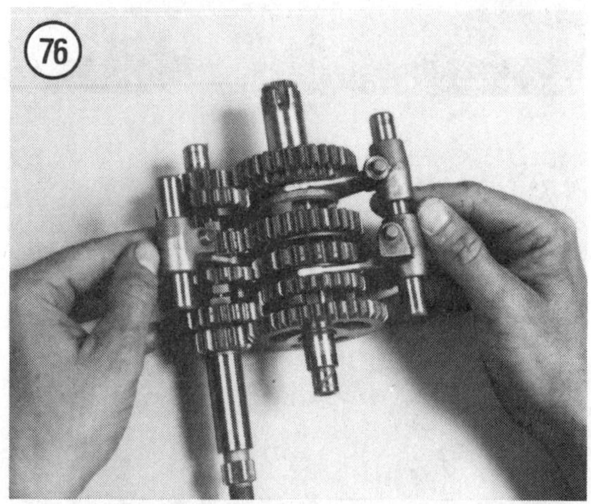

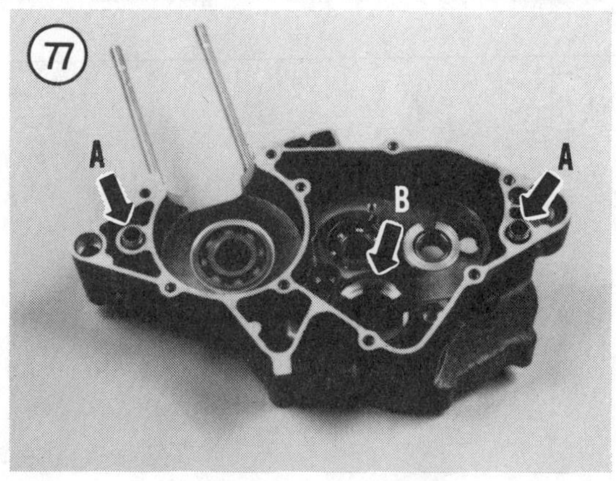

recheck to make sure that a gear is not installed backwards. Also check that the shift drum neutral detent is not installed—it must be removed during this procedure. Crankcase halves are a matched set and are very expensive. Do not risk damage by trying to force the cases together.

10. Place any clips under the screws in the locations recorded during disassembly. Install all the crankcase screws (**Figure 56**) and tighten only finger-tight at first.

11. Securely tighten the screws in 2 stages in a crisscross pattern until they are firmly hand-tight.

12. After the crankcase halves are completely assembled, rotate the crankshaft and transmission shafts to make sure there is no binding. If any is present, disassemble the crankcase and correct the problem.

13. Install the 2 bearing holders and the Phillips screws (**Figure 55**). Apply Loctite 242 (blue) onto the screws before assembly.

14. *1981-1982 models:* Perform the following:
   a. Install the segment plate and washer (**Figure 52**). Apply Loctite 242 (blue) onto the Phillips screw thread and install the screw. Tighten the screw securely.
   b. Remove the stopper lever spring and lever (**Figure 52**). Apply Loctite 242 (blue) onto the bolt threads and install the bolt. Tighten the bolt securely.

15. *1983-on models:* Install the spring (**Figure 54**) and stoppper lever (**Figure 53**). Apply Loctite 242 (blue) onto the bolt thread and install the bolt. Tighten the bolt securely.

16. Install the engine in the frame and tighten the mounting bolts and nuts securely.

17. Install the drive sprocket and drive chain onto the countershaft. Secure it with the circlip (**Figure 50**).

18. Install all exterior engine assemblies as described in this chapter and other related chapters.

78

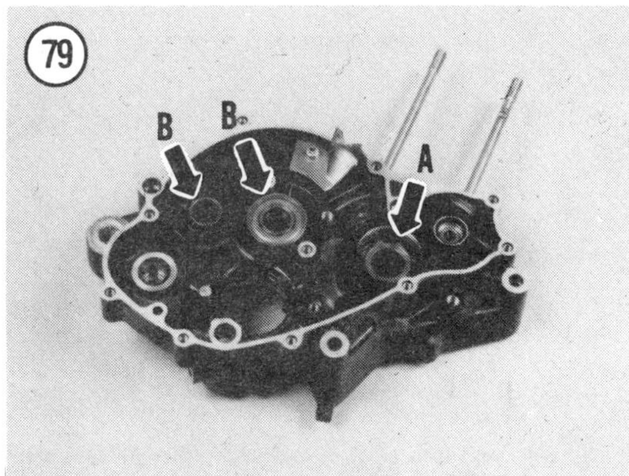

79

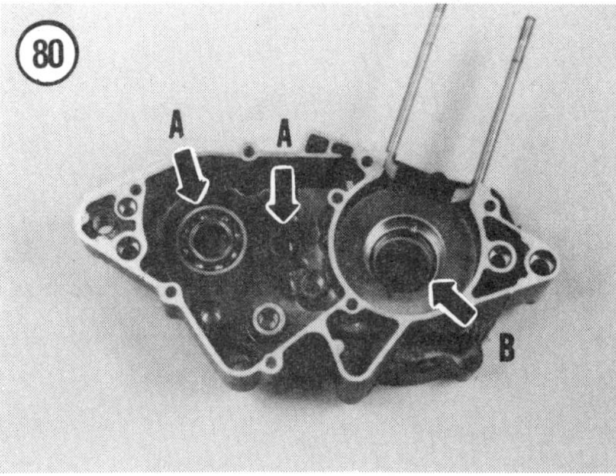

80

Crankcase Inspection

1. Remove the crankcase oil seals as described under *Bearing and Oil Seal Replacement* in this chapter.

2. Clean both crankcase halves inside and out with cleaning solvent. Thoroughly dry with compressed air and wipe off with a clean shop cloth. Be sure to remove all traces of old gasket sealer from all mating surfaces.

3. Oil the bearings with clean two-stroke engine oil before checking the bearings in Steps 4 and 5.

4. Check the crankshaft main bearings (A, **Figure 79**) for roughness, pitting, galling, and play by rotating them slowly by hand. If any roughness or play can be felt in the bearing it must be replaced.

NOTE
Always replace both crankcase main bearings as a set.

5. Inspect the other bearings as described in the previous step. See B, **Figure 79** and A, **Figure 80**.

5

6. Replace any worn or damaged bearings as described under *Bearing and Oil Seal Replacement* in this chapter.
7. Carefully inspect the cases for cracks and fractures, especially in the lower areas where they are vulnerable to rock damage. Also check the areas around the stiffening ribs, around bearing bosses and threaded holes. If any cracks are found, have them repaired by a shop specializing in the repair of precision aluminum castings or replace them.

Bearing and Oil Seal Replacement

1. Pry out the oil seals (B, **Figure 80**) with a screwdriver. Place a rag or wood block underneath the screwdriver to prevent damaging the crankcase. See **Figure 81**. If the seals are old and difficult to remove, heat the cases as described later and use an awl and punch a small hole in the steel backing of the seal. Install a small sheet metal screw into the seal and pull the seal out with a pair of pliers.

CAUTION
Do not install the screw too deep or it may contact and damage the bearing behind it.

NOTE
An impact driver with a Phillips bit (described in Chapter One) will be required to loosen the bearing retainer screws in step 2. Attempting to loosen the screws with a Phillips screwdriver may ruin the screw heads.

2. Remove the bearing retainer Phillips screws and remove the bearing retainer (**Figure 82**).

CAUTION
Before heating the crankcases in this procedure to remove the bearings, wash the cases thoroughly with detergent and water. Rinse and rewash the cases as required to remove all traces of coolant and oil residue.

3. The bearings are installed with a slight interference fit. The crankcase must be heated to a temperature of about 212° F (100° C) in an oven or on a hot plate. An easy way to check to see that it is at the proper temperature is to drop tiny drops of water on the case; if they sizzle and evaporate immediately, the temperature is correct. Heat only one case at a time.

CAUTION
Do not heat the cases with a torch (propane or acetylene)—never bring a flame into contact with the bearing or case. The direct heat will destroy the case hardening of the bearing and will likely warp the case half.

4. Remove the case from the oven or hot plate and hold onto the 2 crankcase studs with a kitchen pot holder, heavy gloves, or heavy shop cloths—*it is hot.*
5. Remove the oil seals if not already removed.

NOTE
*A suitable size socket and extension (**Figure 83**) works well for removing and installing bearings.*

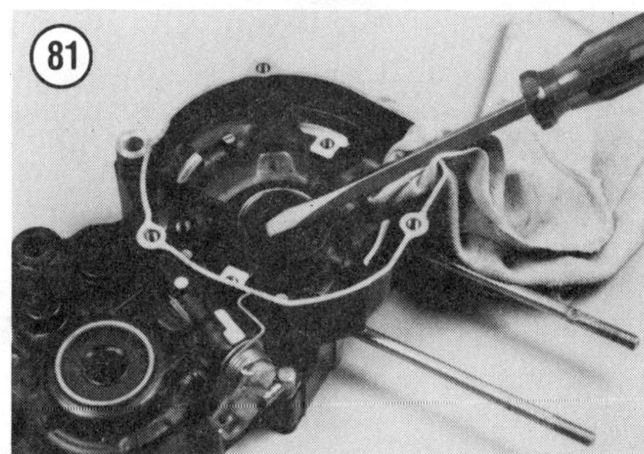
81

82

83

6. Hold the crankcase with the bearing side down and tap the bearing out (**Figure 84**). Repeat for all bearings in that case half.

7. While heating up the crankcase halves, place the new bearings in a freezer if possible. Chilling them will slightly reduce their overall diameter while the hot crankcase is slightly larger due to heat expansion. This will make installation much easier.

84

85

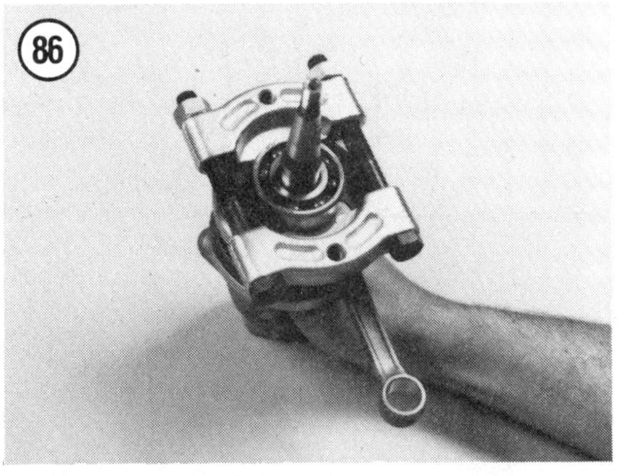

86

NOTE

Prior to installing new bearing(s) or oil seal(s) apply a light coat of lithium based grease to the inside and outside to aid in installation. Be sure to apply the same grease to the lips of new grease seals.

8. While the crankcase is still hot, press the new bearing(s) into place in the crankcase by hand until it seats completely. Do not hammer it in. If the bearing will not seat, remove it and cool it again. Reheat the crankcase and install the bearing again.

NOTE

Always install bearings with the manufacturer's mark or number facing outward or so that after the crankcase is assembled you can still see these marks.

9. Oil seals can be installed with a suitable size socket and extension (**Figure 83**). When installing oil seals, it is important to drive the seal in squarely. See **Figure 85**. Drive the seals in until they are flush with the case.

10. Align the bearing retainers (**Figure 82**) with the crankcase. Apply Loctite 242 (blue) to the retainer screws and tighten them securely.

NOTE

*Sometimes a main bearing will come off with the crankshaft instead of staying in the crankcase. If it is necessary to replace a bearing mounted on the crankshaft, a bearing adapter (**Figure 86**) and a hydraulic press will be required.*

Crankshaft Inspection

1. Clean the crankshaft thoroughly with solvent. Dry the crankshaft thoroughly. Then lubricate all bearing surfaces with a light coat of Two-cycle engine oil.

2. Check the crankshaft journals and crankpin for scratches, heat discoloration or other defects.

3. Check flywheel taper, threads and keyway for damage. If one crankshaft half is damaged, the crankshaft can be disassembled and the damaged part replaced as described in this chapter.

4. Check crankshaft oil seal surfaces for grooving, pitting or scratches.

5. Check crankshaft bearing surfaces for chatter marks and excessive or uneven wear. Minor cases of chatter mark may be cleaned up with 320 grit carborundum cloth. If 320 cloth is used, clean crankshaft in solvent and check surfaces. If they

5

did not clean up properly, disassemble the crankshaft and replace the damaged part.

6. Slide the connecting rod to one side and check the connecting rod to crankshaft side clearance with a flat feeler gauge (**Figure 87**). Compare to dimensions given in **Table 1** at the end of this chapter. If the clearance is greater than specified the crankshaft assembly must be disassembled and the connecting rod replaced.

7. Check crankshaft runout with a dial indicator and V-blocks as shown in **Figure 88**. Retrue the crankshaft if the runout exceeds the wear limit in **Table 1**.

8. Check crankshaft small end free play. Slide the connecting rod to one side and hold it firmly against the crankshaft. Attempt to rock the upper connecting rod end (**Figure 89**) from side to side. This is small end free play. If any perceptible radial play is felt, the crankshaft must be disassembled and the crankshaft rebuilt. Do not mistake side play in the lower end for play at the upper end.

9. If necessary, overhaul the crankshaft as described in this chapter.

Crankshaft Overhaul

Crankshaft overhaul requires a hydraulic press of 10 to 12 tons (9,000-11,000 kg) capacity, holding jigs, crankshaft alignment jig and dial indicators. For this reason, crankshaft overhaul is not practical for home mechanics. The procedure is described here to familiarize you with what a dealer or machine shop will do. A typical crankshaft is shown in **Figure 90.**

1. Measure the crank wheel width at the machined edge with a micrometer or vernier caliper (**Figure 91**). Record the measurement and compare to specifications in **Table 1**. This measurement will be used when reassembling the crankshaft.

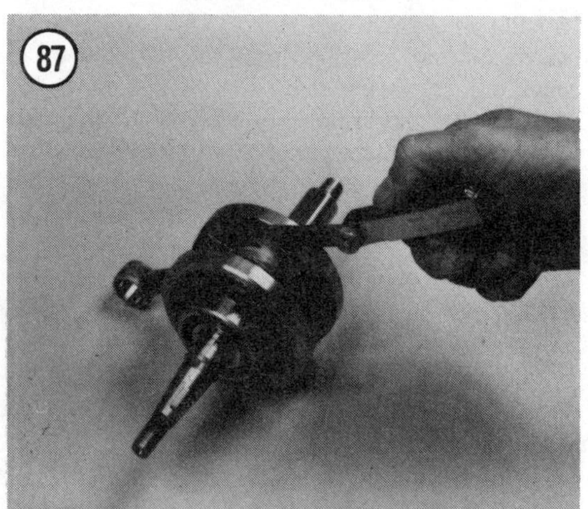

2. Place the crankshaft assembly in a suitable jig. Then press out the crankpin from one crank wheel. Use an adapter between the press and crankpin. See **Figure 92**. Make sure to hold onto the lower crank wheel half and catch the crankpin assembly.

3. Remove the spacers, connecting rod and lower end bearing (**Figure 93**).

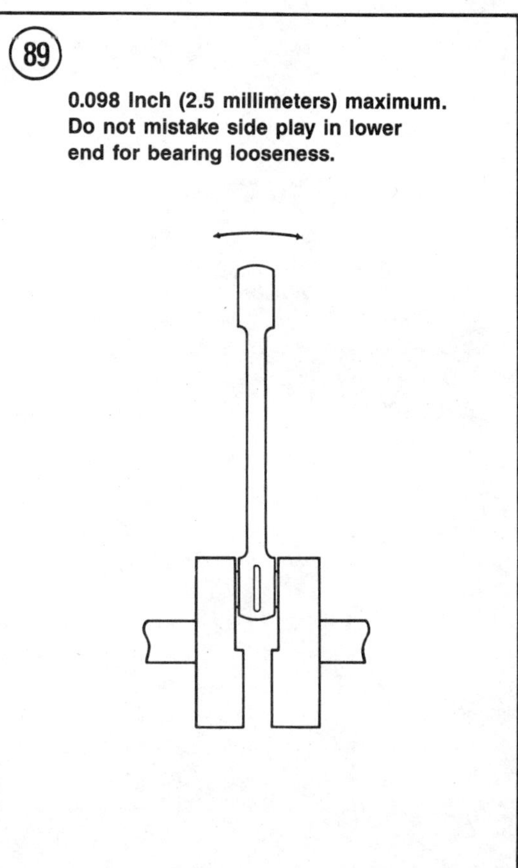

89
0.098 inch (2.5 millimeters) maximum.
Do not mistake side play in lower
end for bearing looseness.

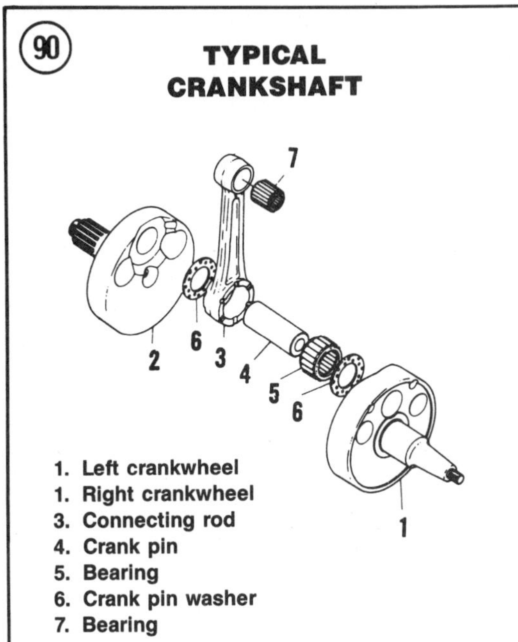

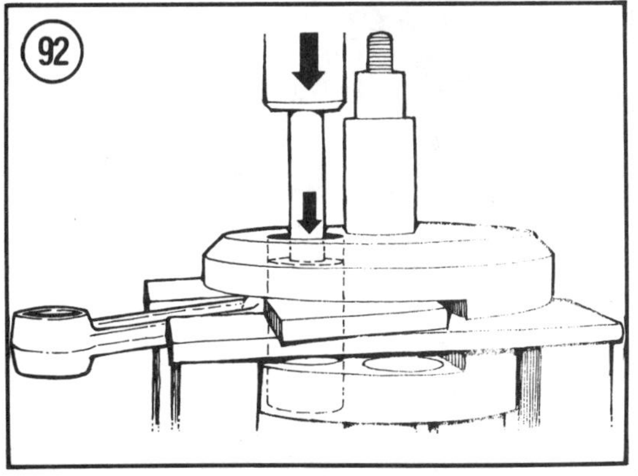

4. Press out the crankpin (**Figure 94**) from the opposite crank wheel.

5. Wash the crank halves thoroughly in solvent.

6. Using a suitable alignment fixture, press the replacement crankpin into one crank wheel half (**Figure 95**) until the crankpin is flush with the outside of the crank wheel half.

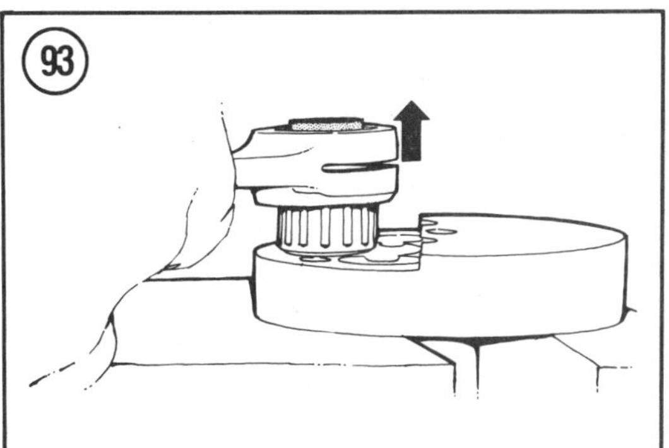

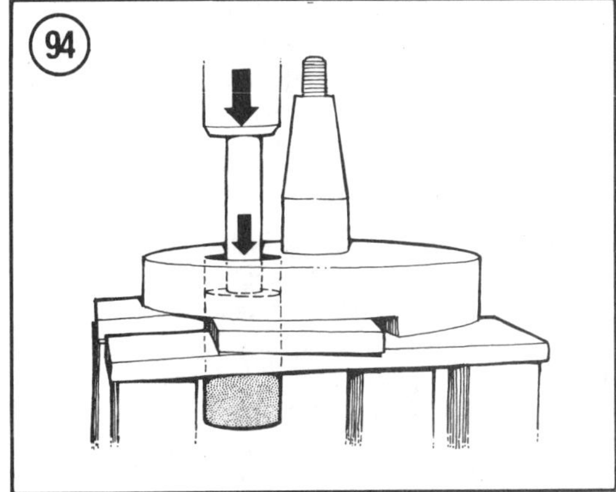

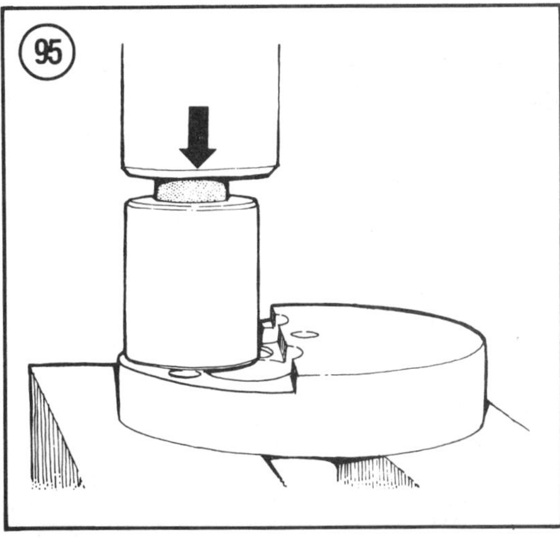

5

7. Install a spacer and the needle bearing over the crankpin (**Figure 96**).
8. Install the connecting rod (**Figure 97**) and the remaining spacer. There is no front or back to the connecting rod; it fits either way.
9. Using a small square for initial alignment (**Figure 98**), start pressing the crank wheel half onto the crankpin assembly.
10. Insert a suitable size feeler gauge between the upper thrust washer and the crank wheel half (**Figure 99**). Then continue pressing the crank wheel half onto the crankpin until the feeler gauge fits tightly. Refer to crankshaft big end side clearance in **Table 1** for clearance.
11. Release all pressure from the press. The feeler gauge will then slip out easily.
12. Measure crank wheel width (**Figure 91**) and compare to the specifications in **Table 1**.
13. Check and adjust crankshaft alignment as described in this chapter.

Crankshaft Alignment

After overhauling the crankshaft or when disassembling the engine, it is important to check crankshaft alignment and adjust as required so that both crank halves and the shafts extending from them all rotate on a common center line. The crankshaft should be checked for runout and wheel deflection as follows.

Mount the assembled crankshaft in a suitable fixture or on V-blocks using 2 dial indicators. Slowly rotate the crankshaft through one or more complete turns and observe both dial indicators. One of several conditions will be observed.

1. *Runout:* Neither dial indicator needle begins its swing at the same time, and the needles will move in opposite directions during part of the crankshaft rotation cycle. Each needle will probably indicate a different amount of total travel.

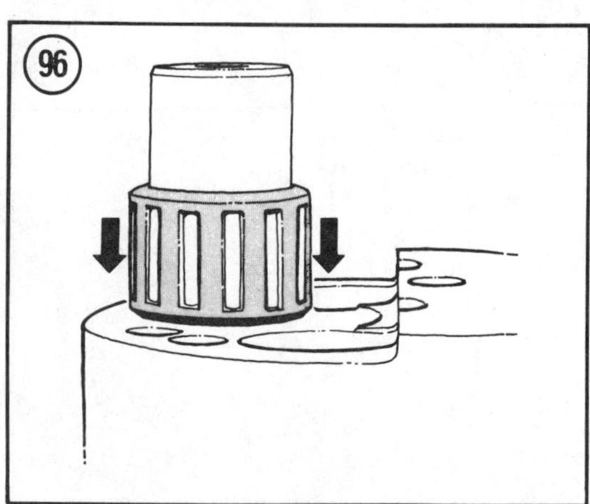

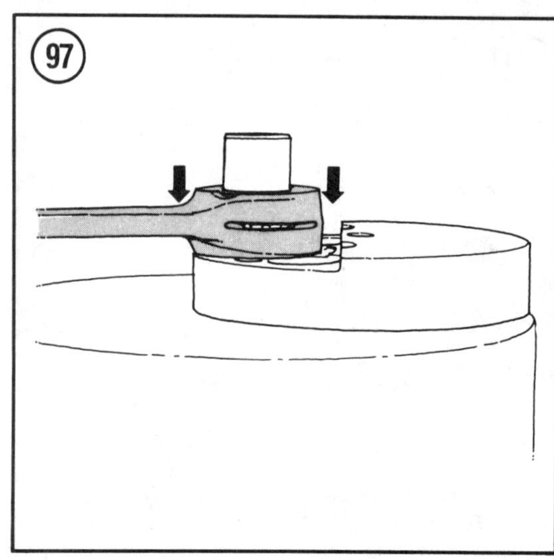

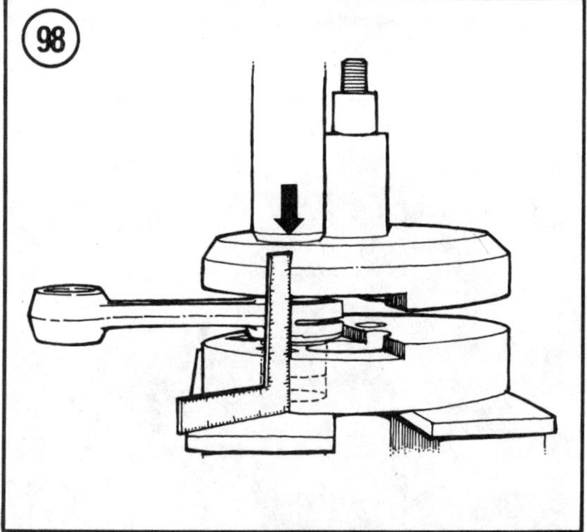

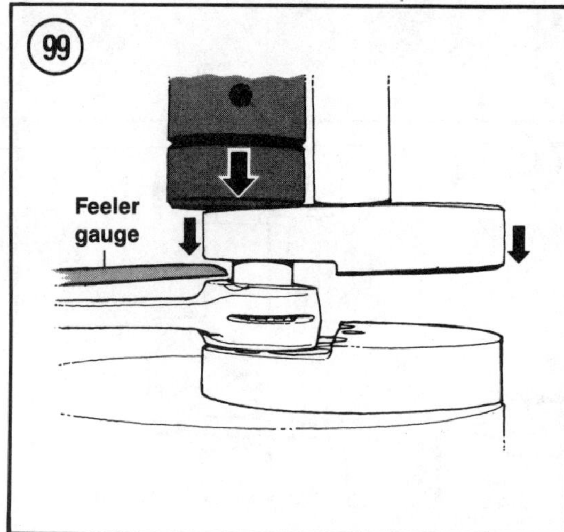

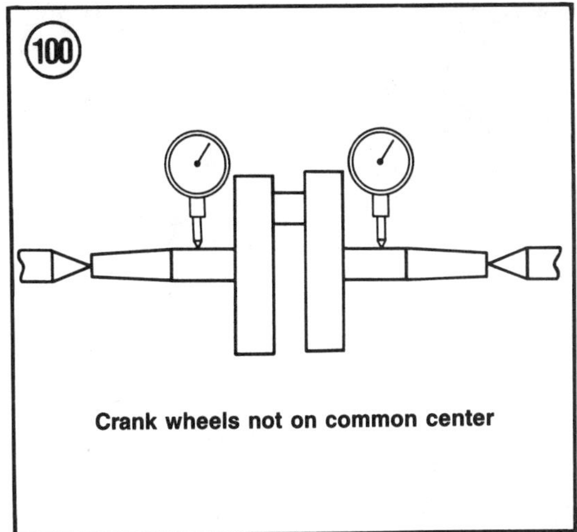
Crank wheels not on common center

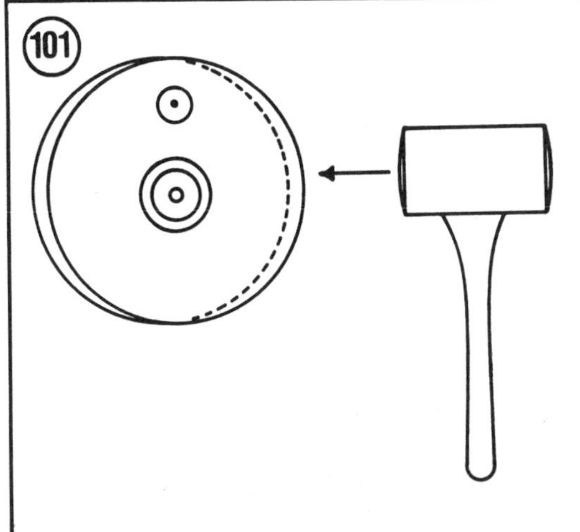

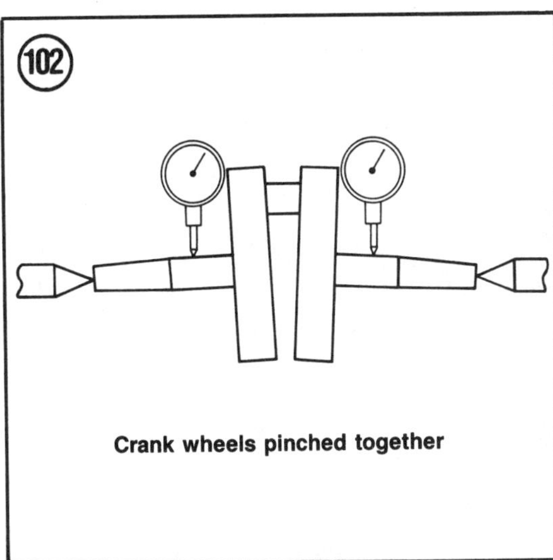
Crank wheels pinched together

This condition is caused by eccentricity (both crank wheels not being on the same center line), as shown in **Figure 100**. To correct, slowly rotate the crankshaft assembly until the drive side dial gauge indicates its maximum. Mark the rim of the drive side crank wheel at the point in line with the plungers on both dial indicators.

Remove the crankshaft assembly. Then, while holding one side of the crankshaft, strike the mark a sharp blow with a brass hammer (**Figure 101**). Recheck alignment after each blow and continue this procedure until both dial gauges begin and end their swings at the same time.

CAUTION
Make sure that only a brass faced hammer is used to strike the crankshaft wheels. A lead hammer will damage the crankshaft wheels, requiring replacement.

2. *Wheel deflection:* The crank wheels can become pinched or spread. This conditioned can be checked by measuring crank wheel width (**Figure 91**) at various spots or by checking runout with 2 dial indicators (**Figure 102** and **Figure 103**). When checking in an alignment jig, both dial indicators will indicate maximum travel when the crankpin is toward the dial gauges if the crank wheels are pinched. Correct the condition by removing the crankshaft assembly from the fixture. Then drive a wedge or chisel between the two crank wheels at a point opposite maximum dial gauge indication. Recheck alignment after each adjustment. Continue until the dial gauges indicate no more than 0.01 mm (0.0004 in.) runout.

If the dial gauges indicated their maximum when the crankpin was on the side of the alignment jig away from the dial gauges, the crank wheels are spread. Correct this condition by tapping the outside of one of the wheels toward the other with

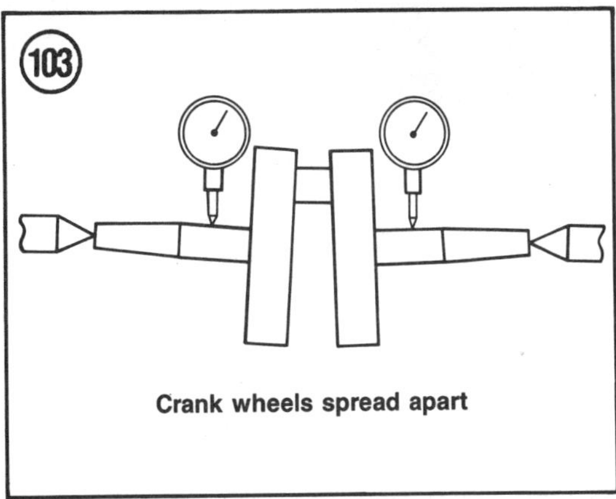
Crank wheels spread apart

5

a brass mallet. Recheck alignment after each blow. Continue adjustment until runout is within 0.01 mm (0.0004 in.) runout.

NOTE
When adjusting wheel deflection, it will be necessary to recheck and readjust runout as required.

Crankcase Stud Replacement

Damaged cylinder studs (**Figure 104**) can cause loss of engine performance and eventual engine damage from compression loss. The crankcase studs can be replaced with 2 wrenches, 2 nuts and a tube of Loctite 271 (red). See **Figure 105**.

1. Measure the distance from the crankcase to the top of the stud. The new studs should be installed to this length.
2. Thread 2 nuts onto the stud being removed (**Figure 106**).
3. Tighten the 2 nuts together as shown in **Figure 107**.
4. Using a wrench on the inner nut (**Figure 108**), turn the nut *counterclockwise* and remove the stud from the crankcase.

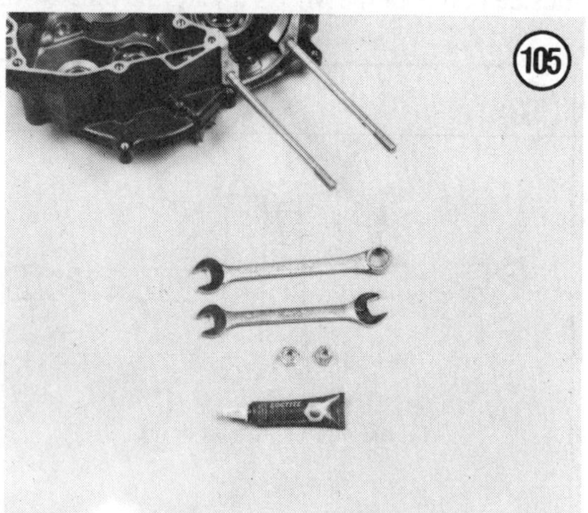

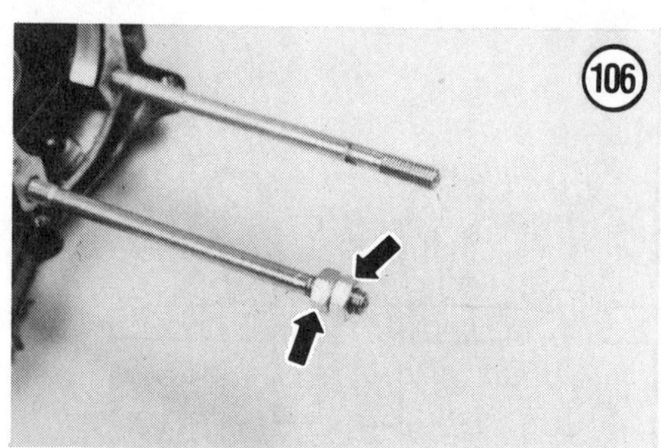

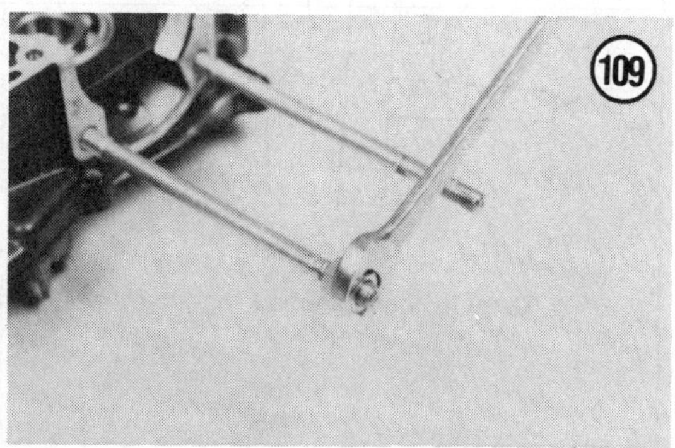

5. Remove the 2 nuts from the old stud.

6. Use a bottom tap and chase the stud hole in the crankcase. Then clean the threads with solvent and dry thoroughly.

7. Thread the 2 nuts onto the upper end of the new stud and tighten together.

8. Apply Loctite 271 (red) to the stud lower end threads and install the stud into the crankcase.

9. Tighten the stud *clockwise* with a wrench placed on the outer nut (**Figure 109**). Tighten the stud until its installed height is the same as that recorded in Step 1.

10. Loosen and remove the 2 nuts.

Table 1 CRANKSHAFT/CONNECTING ROD WEAR LIMIT SPECIFICATIONS

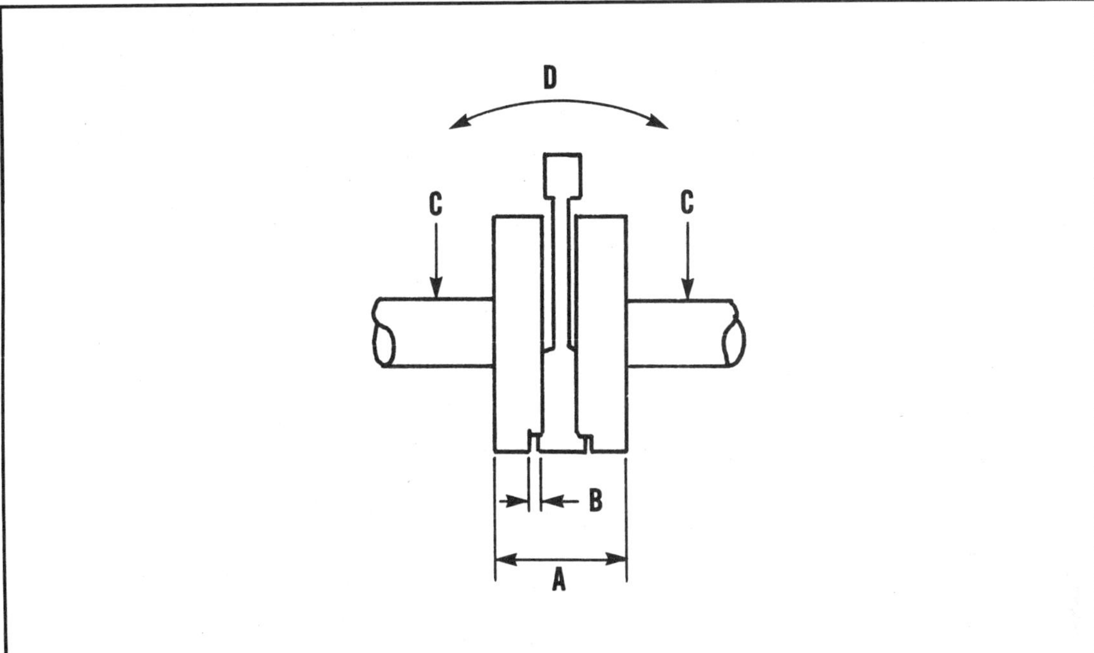

Item	mm	in.
Crankshaft assembly width (A)		
YZ50	37.9-37.95	1.492-1.494
YZ60	44.9-44.95	1.767-1.770
YZ80		
1978	*	*
1979-1980	42.9-42.95	1.689-1.691
1981-on	44.9-44.95	1.767-1.770
Big end side clearance (B)	0.2-0.7	0.008-0.028
Runout limit (C)	0.03	0.0012
Small end deflection (D)		
YZ50	0.3-1.1	0.01-0.04
YZ60	0.5-1.2	0.019-0.047
YZ80		
1978	0.2-0.7	0.008-0.027
1979	0.8-2.0	0.03-0.08
1980	1.0-2.0	0.04-0.08
1981-on	0.5-1.2	0.019-0.047

Table 2 DRIVE SPROCKET NUT TIGHTENING TORQUES

	N•m	ft.-lb.
YZ50	60	43
YZ60	60	43
YZ80		
1978	60	43
1979-1980	55	40
1981-on	*	*

* A circlip is used to secure the drive sprocket on these models.

CHAPTER SIX

CLUTCH, EXTERNAL SHIFT MECHANISM AND KICKSTARTER

6

This chapter contains removal, inspection and installation of the clutch, external shift mechanism and kickstarter. These sub-assemblies can be removed with the engine in the frame. **Table 1** (specifications) and **Table 2** (tightening torques) are found at the end of the chapter.

CLUTCH COVER

Removal/Installation

1. Place a workstand under the frame to support the bike securely.

2. Drain the clutch/transmission oil as described in Chapter Three.
3. *Liquid-cooled models:* Perform the following:
   a. Drain the coolant as described under *Coolant Change* in Chapter Three.
   b. Disconnect the water hose at the water pump **(Figure 1)**.
4. Remove the right-hand footpeg assembly. See A, **Figure 2** (early models) or A, **Figure 3** (late models).
5. Remove the rear brake pedal assembly. See B, **Figure 2** (early models) or B, **Figure 3** (late models).

6A. *Early models:* Loosen the bolt securing the kickstarter lever **(Figure 4)** and remove the lever.

6B. *Late models:* Remove the nut securing the kickstarter lever **(Figure 5)** and remove the lever.

NOTE

The kickstarter lever on late models can be difficult to remove if rust forms between the lever and the kickstarter shaft. If the kickstarter lever is tight, use a 2-jaw puller to remove it.

7. At the handlebar, loosen the clutch cable adjuster locknut **(Figure 6)** and loosen the adjuster to reduce clutch cable tension.

NOTE
An impact driver with a Phillips bit (described in Chapter One) will be required to loosen the clutch cover screws in Step 8. Attempting to loosen the screws with a Phillips screwdriver may damage the screw heads.

8A. *1978-1980 models:* Remove the screws (**Figure 7**) securing the clutch cover and remove it and the gasket. Don't lose the 2 dowel pins or the oil baffle (**Figure 8**) on the inside of the cover.

8B. *1981-on models:* Remove the screws securing the clutch cover (**Figure 9**) and the 2 water pump screws (**Figure 10**). Remove the clutch cover and the 2 dowel pins (**Figure 11**).

9. Check the clutch cover oil seal (**Figure 12**) for damage. If necessary, replace the seal by prying it out of the cover with a screwdriver. Install the new seal by driving it into the cover with a suitable size socket. Install the seal so that it is flush with the cover.

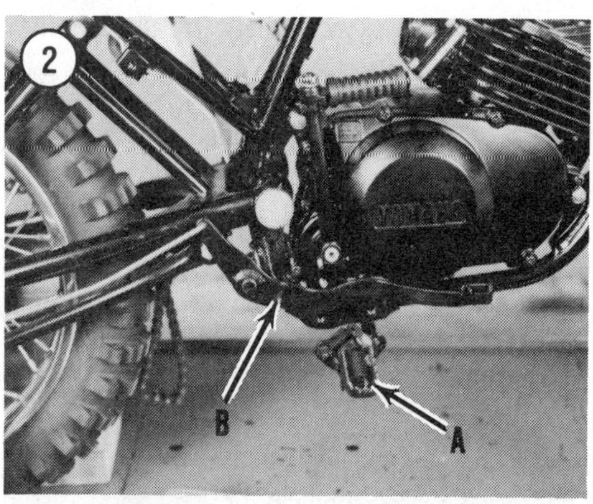

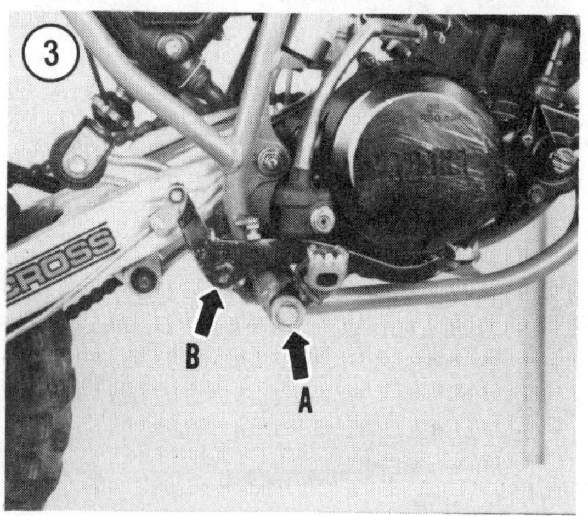

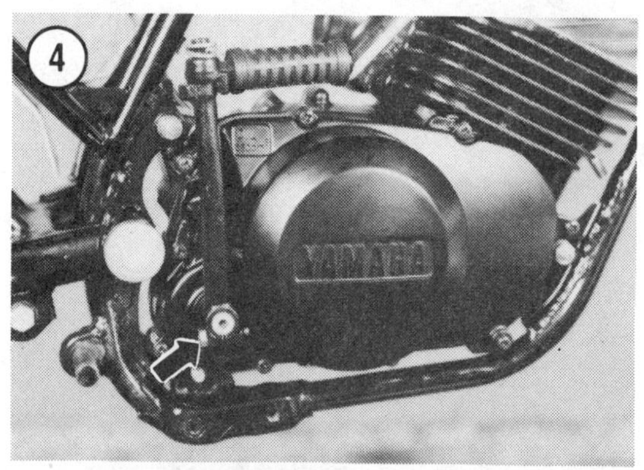

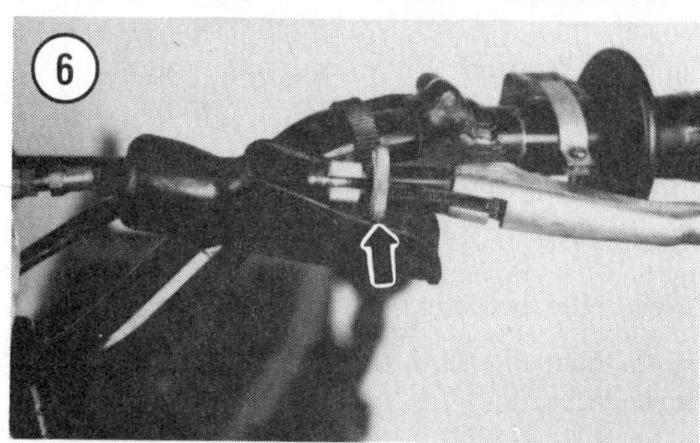

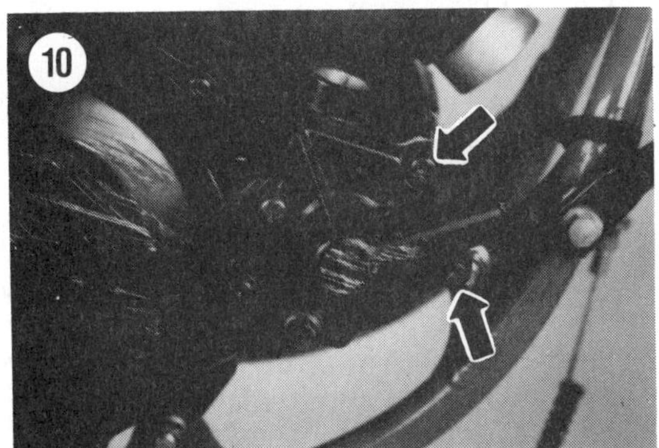

10. *Liquid-cooled models:* Check the water pump gear (**Figure 13**) for wear or damage. Also make sure the circlip is installed on the gear shaft completely. If the gear is damaged or if it does not turn smoothly, refer to Chapter Ten.
11. Make sure the water pipe joint O-rings are in place (**Figure 14**). Replace the O-rings if necessary.
12. Installation is the reverse of these steps. Note the following.
13. Make sure to install the 2 dowel pins and a new cover gasket.
14. *Liquid-cooled models:* Refill the cooling system as described in Chapter Three.
15. Refill the clutch/transmission oil as described in Chapter Three.
16. Adjust the clutch as described in Chapter Three.

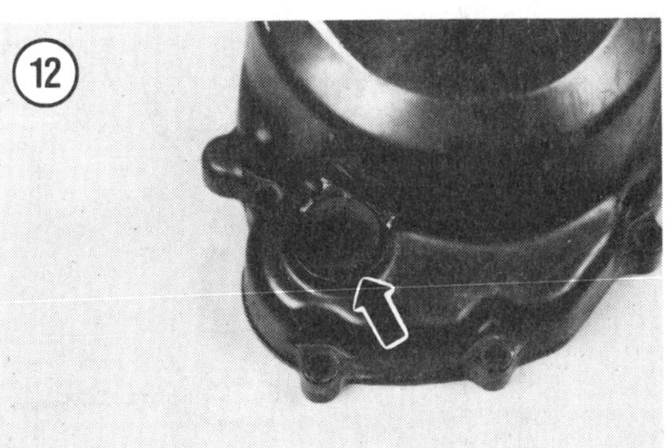

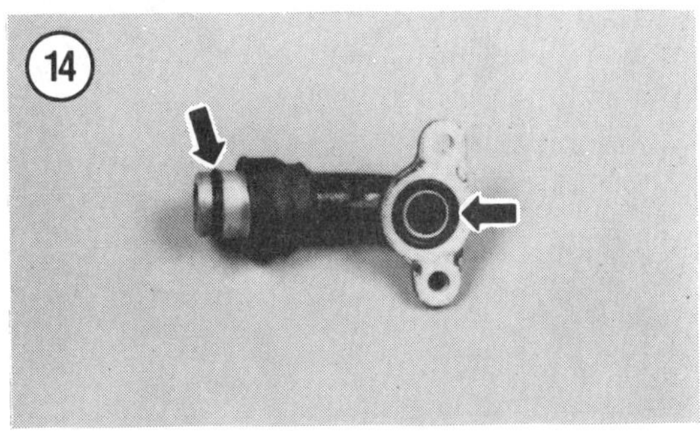

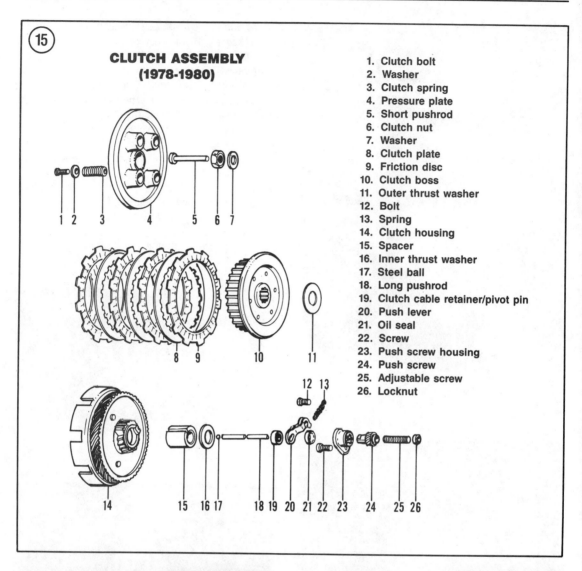

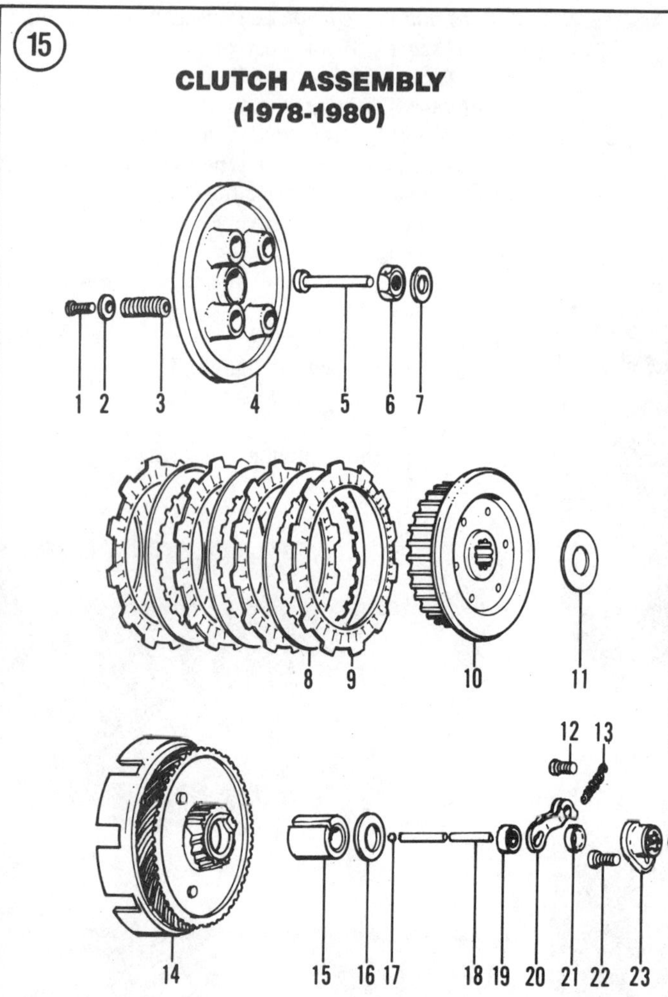

15

CLUTCH ASSEMBLY (1978-1980)

1. Clutch bolt
2. Washer
3. Clutch spring
4. Pressure plate
5. Short pushrod
6. Clutch nut
7. Washer
8. Clutch plate
9. Friction disc
10. Clutch boss
11. Outer thrust washer
12. Bolt
13. Spring
14. Clutch housing
15. Spacer
16. Inner thrust washer
17. Steel ball
18. Long pushrod
19. Clutch cable retainer/pivot pin
20. Push lever
21. Oil seal
22. Screw
23. Push screw housing
24. Push screw
25. Adjustable screw
26. Locknut

CLUTCH

The clutch is a wet multiplate type which operates immersed in the oil supply it shares with the transmission. The clutch boss is splined to the transmission mainshaft and the clutch housing can rotate freely on the main shaft. The clutch housing is geared to the primary drive gear attached to the crankshaft.

The clutch release mechanism is mounted within the left-hand crankcase cover on the opposite side of the clutch mechanism.

The clutch can be removed with the engine in the frame.

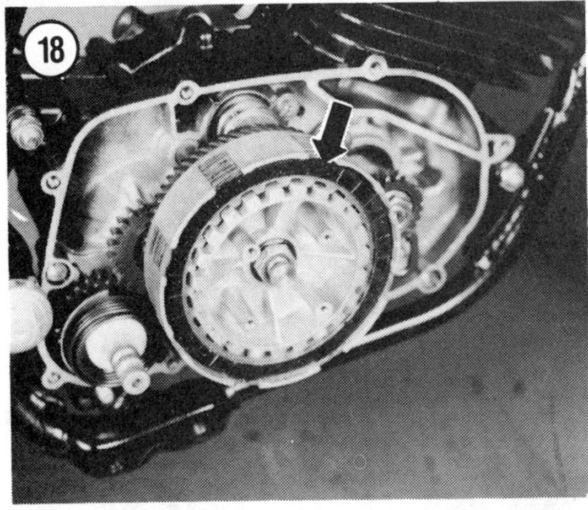

Removal (1978-1980)

Refer to **Figure 15**.

1. Remove the clutch cover as described in this chapter.
2. Loosen the pressure plate bolts (**Figure 16**) in a crisscross pattern. Remove the bolts and clutch springs.
3. Remove the pressure plate (**Figure 17**).
4. Remove all the clutch plates and friction discs (**Figure 18**).
5. Remove the short pushrod (**Figure 19**).

CAUTION
Do not insert a screwdriver or pry bar between the clutch housing and the clutch boss to secure the clutch boss. The fingers on the clutch housing are fragile and can be broken very easily.

6. Secure the clutch boss with a holding tool such as the "Grabbit" and remove the clutch nut (**Figure 20**).
7. See **Figure 21**. Remove the lockwasher (A) and clutch boss (B).
8. Remove the steel ball and long pushrod.

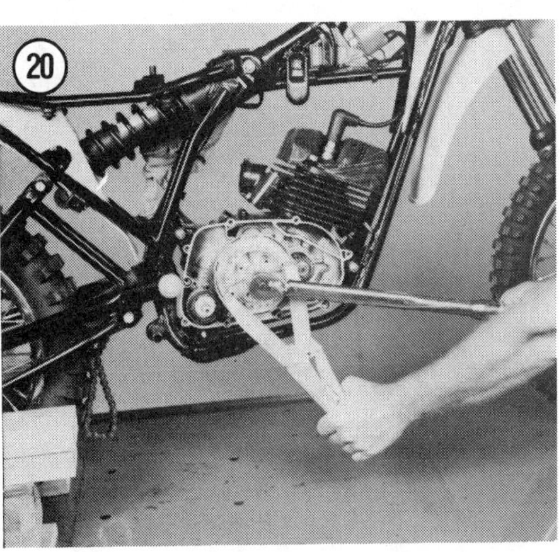

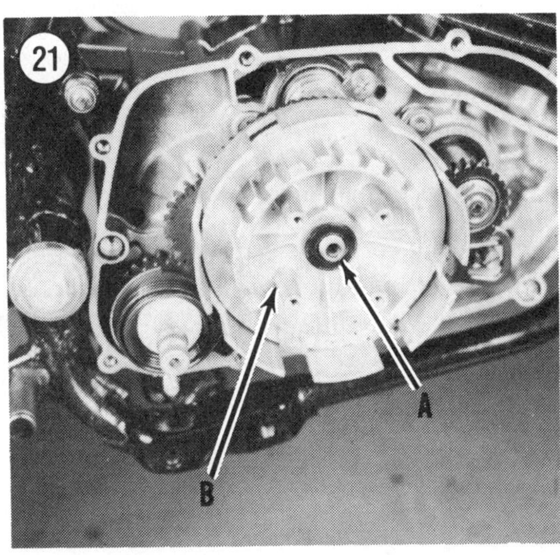

9. Remove the outer thrust washer (A, **Figure 22**) and the clutch housing (B, **Figure 22**).
10. Remove the spacer and inner thrust washer (**Figure 23**).
11. Inspect the clutch components as described under *Inspection (All Models)* in this chapter.

Assembly (1978-1980)

1. Coat all clutch parts with transmission oil before reassembly.

NOTE
Install the lockwasher with the convex (dished) side facing outward.

2. Install the clutch inner thrust washer and spacer (**Figure 23**).
3. See **Figure 22**. Slide on the clutch housing (B) and install the outer thrust washer (A).

NOTE
Install the lockwasher with the convex (dished) side facing outward.

4. See **Figure 21**. Slide on the clutch boss (B) and lockwasher (A).
5. Install the clutch nut and secure the clutch boss with the same tool used during removal. Tighten the clutch nut to the torque specification in **Table 2**.
6. Apply a light coat of grease to the long pushrod prior to installation. Install the long clutch pushrod (**Figure 24**).
7. Apply a light coat of grease to the ball and install it (**Figure 25**). Make sure it does not roll out.
8. Install the short pushrod (**Figure 19**).

CAUTION
If either or both friction discs and/or clutch plates have been replaced with new ones or if they were cleaned, apply new clutch/transmission oil to all surfaces to avoid clutch plate wear.

9. Install a friction disc first (**Figure 26**) and then a clutch plate. Continue to install a friction disc, then a clutch plate until all are installed. The last item installed is a friction disc.
10. Install the clutch pressure plate. See **Figure 17**.
11. Install the clutch springs and bolts (**Figure 16**). Tighten the bolts securely in a crisscross pattern in 2-3 stages.
12. Install the clutch cover as described in this chapter.

Removal (1981-on)

Refer to **Figure 27** for this procedure.

(27) CLUTCH ASSEMBLY (1981-ON)

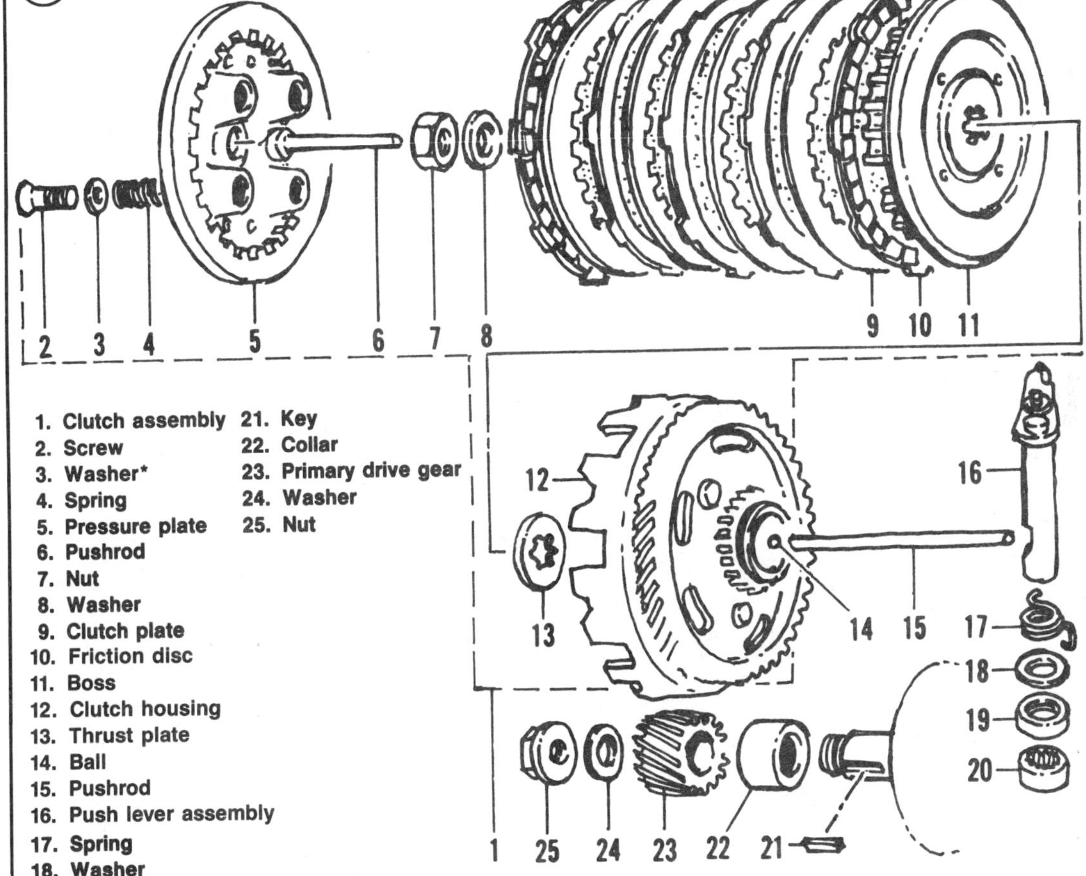

1. Clutch assembly
2. Screw
3. Washer*
4. Spring
5. Pressure plate
6. Pushrod
7. Nut
8. Washer
9. Clutch plate
10. Friction disc
11. Boss
12. Clutch housing
13. Thrust plate
14. Ball
15. Pushrod
16. Push lever assembly
17. Spring
18. Washer
19. Oil seal
20. Bearing
21. Key
22. Collar
23. Primary drive gear
24. Washer
25. Nut

* Not used on 1986 models.

1. Remove the clutch cover as described in this chapter.
2. Loosen the pressure plate bolts (A, **Figure 28**) in a crisscross pattern.

NOTE
*Don't lose the water pump shaft washer (B, **Figure 28**).*

3. Remove the bolts, washers (1981-1985) and springs.
4. Remove the pressure plate (**Figure 29**).
5. Remove the clutch plates and friction discs (**Figure 30**).
6. Remove the short pushrod (**Figure 31**).
7. Remove the clutch ball (**Figure 32**).
8. Remove the long pushrod (**Figure 33**).

CAUTION
Do not insert a screwdriver or pry bar between the clutch housing and the clutch boss to secure the clutch boss. The fingers on the clutch housing are fragile and can be broken very easily.

9. Secure the clutch boss with a holding tool such as the "Grabbit" and remove the clutch nut (**Figure 34**).
10. Remove the lockwasher (**Figure 35**).

11. Remove the clutch boss (**Figure 36**).
12. Remove the washer (**Figure 37**).
13. Remove the clutch housing (**Figure 38**).
14. Inspect the clutch components as described under *Inspection* in this chapter.

Assembly (1981-on)

1. Coat all clutch parts with transmission oil before reassembly.
2. Install the clutch housing (**Figure 38**).
3. Install the washer (**Figure 37**).
4. Install the clutch boss (**Figure 36**).

NOTE
Install the lockwasher with the convex (dished) side facing outward.

5. Install the washer (**Figure 35**).
6. Install the clutch nut and secure the clutch boss with the same tool used during removal. Tighten the clutch nut (**Figure 39**) to the torque specification in **Table 2**.

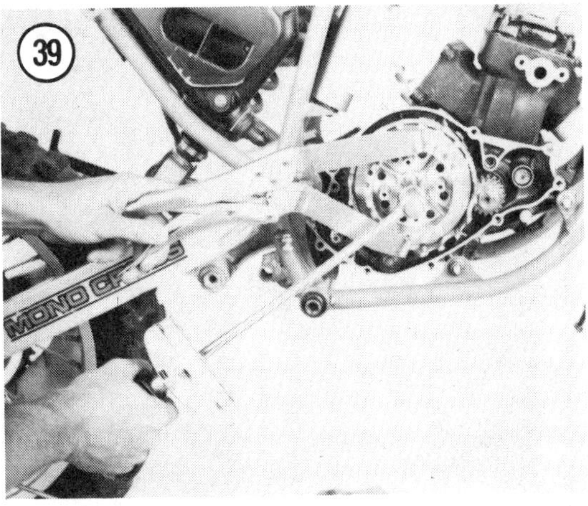

7. Apply a light coat of grease to the pushrod prior to installation. Install the long clutch pushrod (**Figure 33**).
8. Apply a light coat of grease to the ball and install it (**Figure 32**). Make sure it does not roll out.
9. Install the short pushrod (**Figure 31**).

CAUTION
If either or both friction discs and/or clutch plates have been replaced with new ones or if they were cleaned, apply new clutch/transmission oil to all surfaces to avoid having the clutch lock up when used for the first time.

10. Install a friction disc first (**Figure 30**) and then a clutch plate (**Figure 40**). Continue to install a friction disc, then a clutch plate until all are installed. The last item installed is a friction disc.
11. Install the clutch pressure plate (**Figure 29**). Align the mark on the clutch boss with the arrow on the pressure plate during installation (**Figure 41**).
12. Install the clutch springs.
13. *1981-1985:* Install the washers.
14. Install the bolts (A, **Figure 28**). Tighten the bolts securely in a crisscross pattern in 2-3 stages.
15. Make sure the washer (B, **Figure 28**) is installed in the water pump shaft pivot hole.
16. Install the clutch cover as described in this chapter.

Inspection (All Models)

Clutch service specifications and wear limits are listed in **Table 1**.

1. Clean all parts in a petroleum based solvent such as kerosene and thoroughly dry with compressed air.
2. Measure the free length of each clutch spring (**Figure 42**) with a vernier caliper. Replace any springs that are too short.

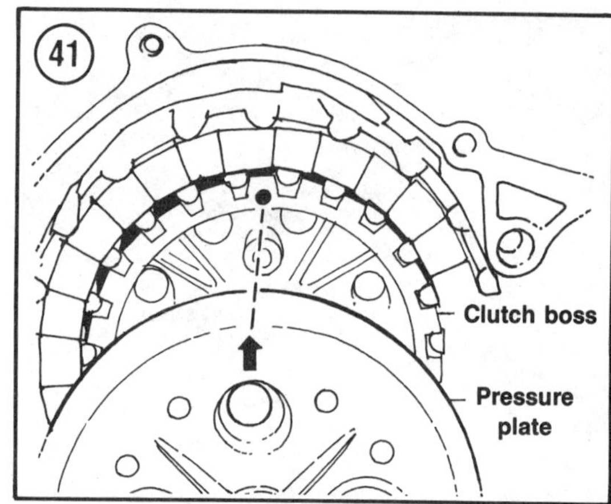

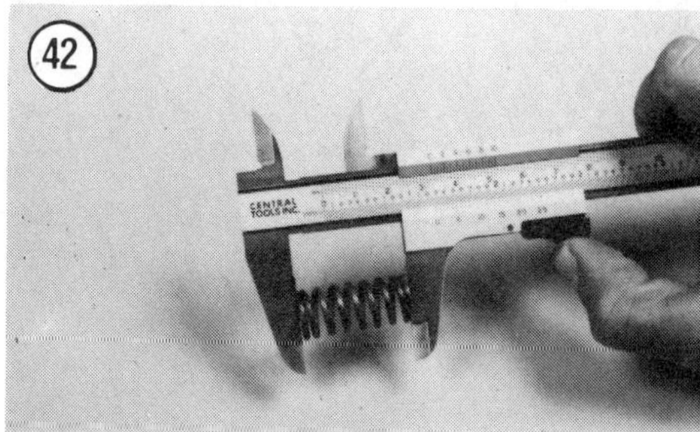

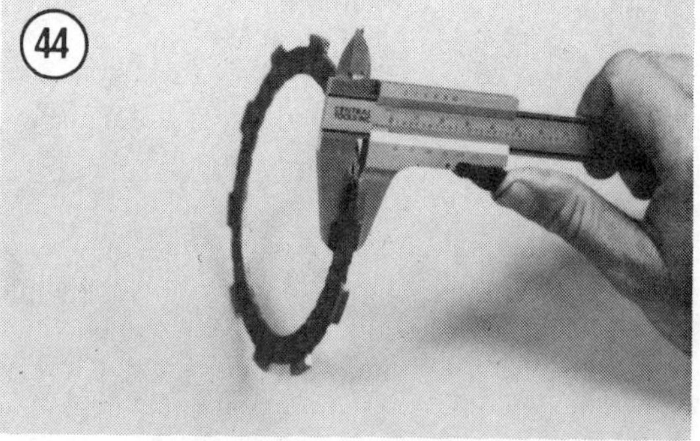

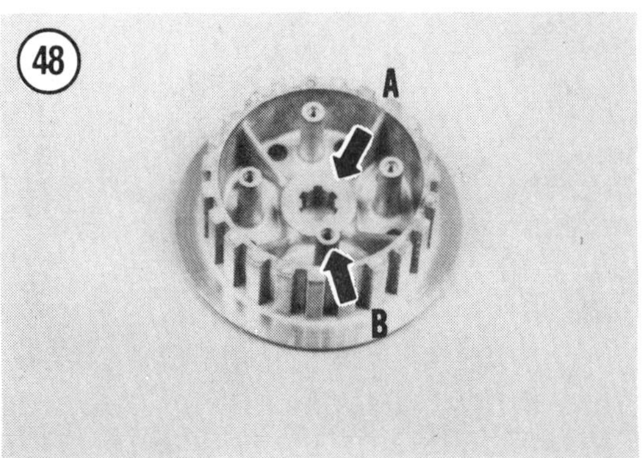

3. **Table 1** lists the number of stock friction discs (**Figure 43**) used in each model. The friction material is made of cork that is bonded onto an aluminum plate for warp resistance and durability. Measure the thickness of each friction plate at several places around the disc (**Figure 44**) with a vernier caliper. Replace all friction plates if any one is found too thin. Do not replace only 1 or 2 plates.

4. **Table 1** lists the number of stock clutch metal plates (**Figure 45**) used in each model. Place each clutch metal plate on a surface plate or a thick piece of glass and check for warpage with a feeler gauge (**Figure 46**). If any plate is warped more than specified, replace the entire set of plates. Do not replace only 1 or 2 plates.

5. The clutch metal plate inner teeth (**Figure 45**) mesh with the clutch boss splines (**Figure 47**). Check the splines for cracks or galling. They must be smooth for chatter-free clutch operation. If the clutch boss splines are worn, check the clutch metal plate teeth for wear or damage.

6. Inspect the shaft splines (A, **Figure 48**) in the clutch boss assembly. If damage is only a slight amount, remove any small burrs with a fine cut file. If damage is severe, replace the assembly.

7. Inspect the clutch boss bolt studs (B, **Figure 48**) for thread damage or cracks at the base of the studs. Thread damage may be repaired with a M6×1 metric tap. Use kerosene on the tap threads. If a bolt stud is cracked, the clutch boss must be replaced.

8. Inspect the pressure plate (**Figure 49**) for signs of damage or warpage (A). Check the spring towers (B) for cracks or damage. Check the pressure plate teeth (C) where they engage the clutch boss for cracks or damage. Replace the pressure plate if necessary.

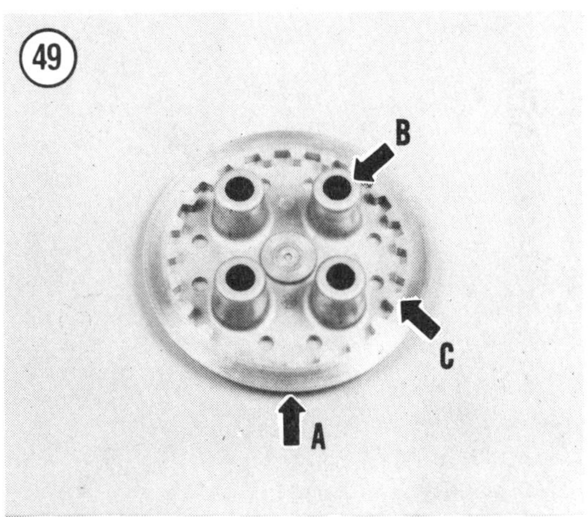

9. The friction plates (**Figure 43**) have tabs that slide in the clutch housing grooves (**Figure 50**). Inspect the tabs for cracks or galling in the grooves. They must be smooth for chatter-free clutch operation. Light damage can be repaired with an oilstone. Replace the clutch housing if damaged is severe.
10. Check the clutch housing bearing bore (A, **Figure 51**) for cracks, deep scoring, excessive wear or heat discoloration. If the bearing bore is damaged, also check the transmission mainshaft for damage. Replace worn or damaged parts.
11. Check the clutch housing gear teeth (B, **Figure 51**) for tooth wear, damage or cracks. Replace the clutch housing if necessary.

NOTE
If the clutch housing gear teeth are damaged, the gear teeth on the primary drive gear and the kickstarter idler gear may also be damaged. Inspect both of these gears also.

12. Check the ends of the pushrod for wear or damage. Also roll the pushrod on a surface plate or thick piece of glass and check for bending. A bent pushrod may bind inside the transmission mainshaft when under load. Replace if necessary.

PRIMARY DRIVE PINION GEAR

The primary drive pinion gear is part of the primary drive gear system where power flows from the crankshaft to the transmission. On YZ models, the primary drive pinion gear is fixed onto the right-hand side of the crankshaft with a straight key and secured with a nut and a special concave washer. The pinion gear meshes with the clutch housing drive gear. On liquid-cooled models, a special two sided pinion gear is used; the opposite half of the gear meshes with the water pump drive gear.

Removal/Installation

Removal of the primary drive pinion gear is not required except for replacement, crankcase disassembly or when checking the right-hand crankshaft oil seal during a pressure test.
1. Remove the clutch cover as described in this chapter.

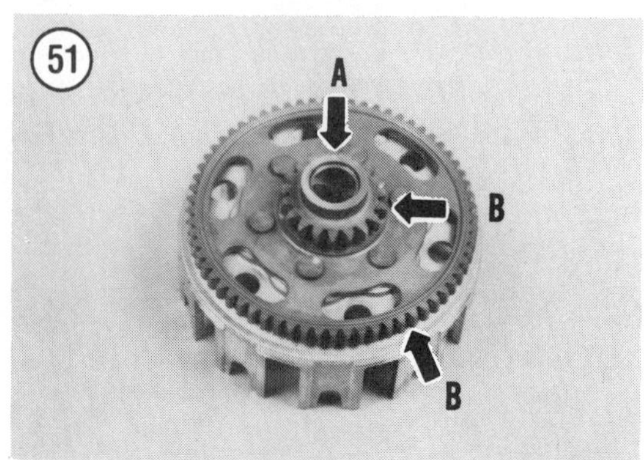

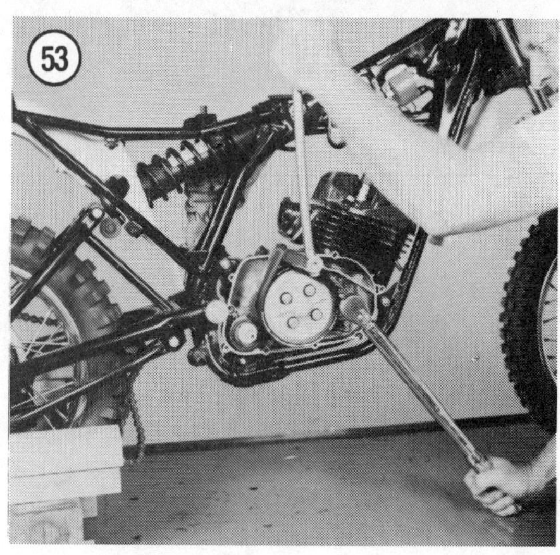

2. Place a piece of copper between the pinion gear and the clutch housing drive gear (A, **Figure 52**).

NOTE

*A strap wrench can be used to secure the clutch housing (**Figure 53**) when removing the pinion gear nut. If a strap wrench is used, make sure the clutch plates are installed in the clutch housing and that the webbing is centered on the housing to avoid any damage to the housing.*

3. Loosen the pinion gear nut (B, **Figure 52**).
4. Remove the clutch housing as described in this chapter.

5A. *1978-1980 models:* Perform the following:
   a. Remove the washer and pinion gear (**Figure 54**).
   b. Remove the straight key (**Figure 55**).
   c. Remove the spacer (**Figure 56**).

5B. *1981-on models models:* Perform the following:
   a. Remove the washer (**Figure 57**).
   b. Remove the pinion gear (**Figure 58**).

6

c. Remove the straight key (**Figure 59**).
d. Remove the spacer (**Figure 60**).

6. Installation is the reverse of these steps. Note the following:
   a. Reverse step 5 to install the pinion gear.
   b. Do not attempt to tighten the pinion gear nut until the clutch is installed.
   c. Use the same tool to lock the clutch housing when tightening the pinion gear nut. If you are using a piece of copper to lock the gears, place it underneath the gears at the point indicated in **Figure 61**.
   d. Tighten the pinion gear nut to the tightening torque in **Table 2**.
   e. Install the clutch cover as described in this chapter.

CLUTCH CABLE

Replacement

In time the clutch cable will stretch to the point that it is no longer useful and will have to be replaced.

1. Remove the fuel tank.

NOTE
Some of the following figures are shown with the engine partially disassembled for clarity. It is not necessary to remove these components for cable replacement.

2. Pull the protective boot away from the clutch lever and loosen the locknut (A, **Figure 62**) and adjusting barrel (B, **Figure 62**).
3. Slip the cable end out of the hand lever.

4A. *1978-1980 models:* Perform the following:
   a. Remove the shift lever (A, **Figure 63**) and left-hand crankcase cover (B, **Figure 63**). On

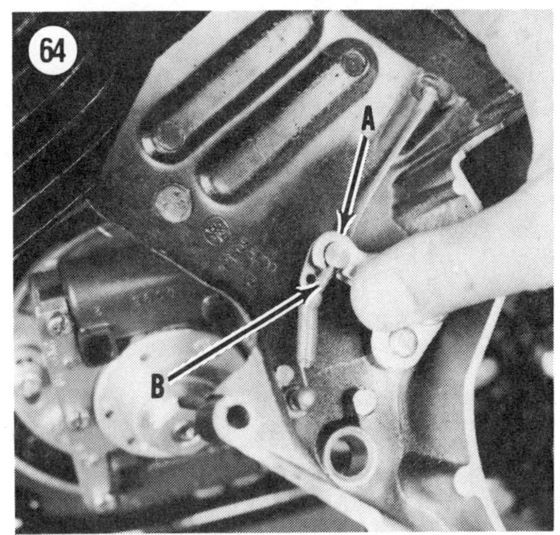

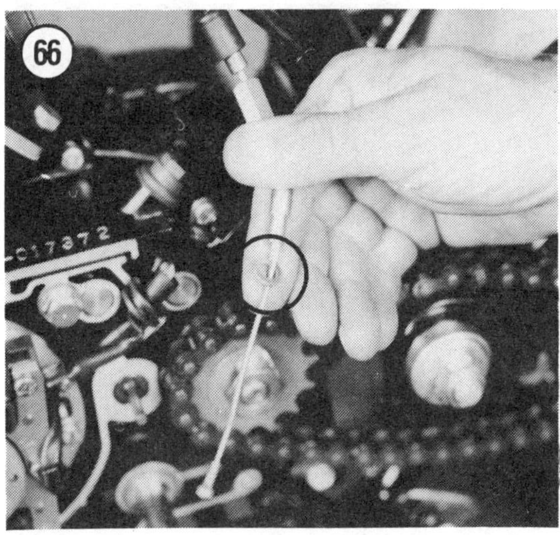

YZ50 models, remove both screws securing the clutch mechanism cover (C, **Figure 63**). This is necessary because the upper bolt (long) screws into the crankcase.

b. Inside the crankcase cover, push up on the push lever (A, **Figure 64**) until the cable tip is exposed and remove the cable retainer/pivot pin (B, **Figure 64**).
c. This will free the cable end (**Figure 65**).
d. Withdraw the cable and lower adjuster from the crankcase cover; don't lose the small flat washer (**Figure 66**).

4B. *1981-on models:* See **Figure 67**. Pull the clutch cable out of the cylinder cable mount (A) and disconnect the clutch cable at the clutch release mechanism (B).

NOTE
Prior to removing the cable make a drawing (or take a Polaroid picture) of the cable routing through the frame. It is very easy to forget its routing after it has been removed. Replace the cable exactly as it was, avoiding any sharp turns.

5. Pull the cable out of any retaining clips on the frame.
6. Remove the cable and replace it with a new one.
7. Install by reversing these removal steps. Make sure it is correctly routed with no sharp turns. Adjust the clutch cable as described in Chapter Three.

CLUTCH RELEASE MECHANISM

Removal/Installation (1978-1980)

1. Perform Step 2 and Step 4 under *Clutch Cable, Replacement* in this chapter.

2. Remove the locknut, unscrew the adjustment screw, and remove the push lever and spring (A, **Figure 68**).
3. Remove the Phillips head screw (B, **Figure 68**) and remove the push screw housing and push screw (C, **Figure 68**).
4. Inspect the splines in the push screw and push screw housing. If they are worn or damaged in any way replace either or both worn parts.
5. Install by reversing the removal steps.
6. Install the clutch cable by reversing Step 4 and Step 2 under *Clutch Cable, Replacement* in this chapter.

NOTE
On YZ50 models the left-hand crankcase cover is made of a nylon-reinforced plastic material. Carefully inspect the area around the clutch release mechanism cover for cracks or damage. If for some reason the clutch has been operated without the long upper bolt installed on the cover plate, there will have been unnecessary stress placed on the cover. This may lead to cracks or fractures and if damage is apparent, replace the crankcase cover as clutch release operation may be erratic or nonexistent.

Removal/Installation (1981-on)

1. Pull the protective boot away from the clutch lever and loosen the locknut (A, **Figure 62**) and adjusting barrel (B, **Figure 62**).
2. See **Figure 67**. Pull the clutch cable out of the cylinder cable mount (A) and disconnect the clutch cable at the clutch release mechanism (B).
3. Remove the release mechanism lever assembly (B, **Figure 67**) from the crankcase, together with its spring and washer.
4. Examine the lever for damage, especially at the cam portion which operates against the pushrod (**Figure 69**). If it is worn or damaged, the release mechanism lever should be replaced.
5. Examine the release mechanism lever oil seal in the left-hand crankcase. If damaged, replace the seal by prying it out of the crankcase with a small screwdriver, making sure not to gouge the crankcase. Install a new seal by tapping it in with a suitable size socket.
6. Install the spring and washer onto the end of the lever. Attach one end of the spring onto the lever.
7. Insert the release mechanism lever into the crankcase with the cam portion facing toward the clutch. Attach the spring to the crankcase.
8. Adjust the clutch as described in Chapter Three.

EXTERNAL SHIFT MECHANISM

The external shift mechanism is located on the same side of the crankcase as the clutch assembly

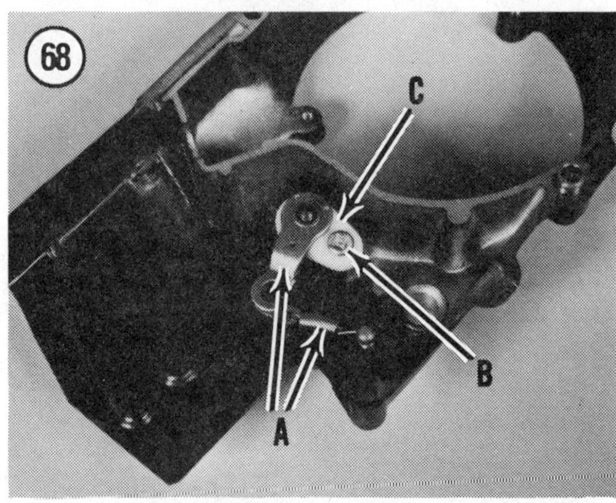

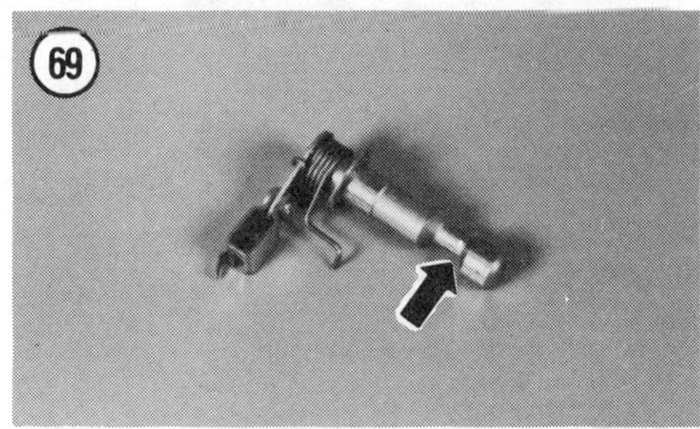

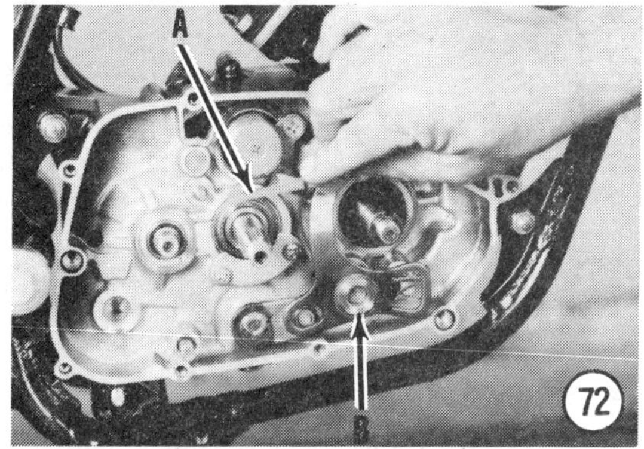

and can be removed with the engine in the frame. To remove the shift drum and shift forks it is necessary to remove the engine and split the crankcases.

NOTE

The gearshift lever is subject to a lot of abuse under race conditions. If the motorcycle has been in a hard spill, the gearshift lever may have been hit and the shaft may have been bent. If the shaft is bent, it is very hard to straighten without subjecting the crankcase to abnormal stress where the shaft enters the case. If the shaft is bent enough to prevent it from being withdrawn from the crankcase, there is little recourse but to cut the shaft off with a hacksaw very close to the crankcase. It is much cheaper in the long run to replace the shaft than risk damaging a set of expensive crankcases. After cutting off the end of the shaft, use a file or rotary grinder to remove all burrs from the shaft before removing it.

Removal/Installation (1978-1980)

1. Remove the clutch assembly as described in this chapter.
2. On the left-hand side, remove the E-clip (**Figure 70**) and flat washer (**Figure 71**) from the shift lever.
3. Push down on the upper shift arm to disengage it from the shift drum (A, **Figure 72**) and withdraw the gearshift lever assembly (B, **Figure 72**).
4. Remove the small bushing (**Figure 73**) from the shift lever shaft.
5. Withdraw the shift lever shaft (**Figure 74**). See NOTE in the introduction to this procedure regarding a bent shaft if the assembly is difficult to remove.
6. Inspect both springs (**Figure 75**). If broken or weak they must be replaced.

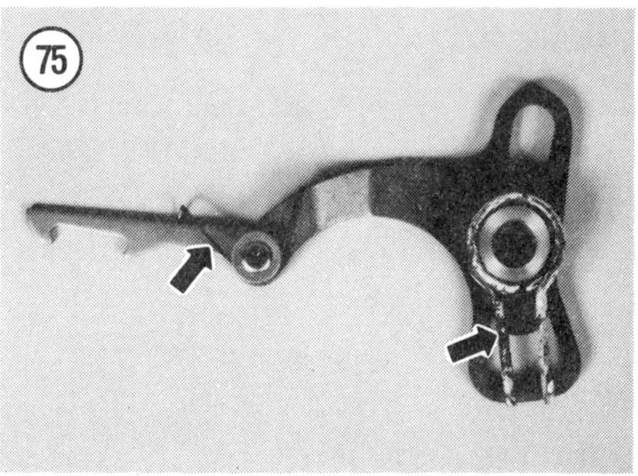

7. Inspect the gearshift lever assembly shaft for bending, wear or other damage; replace if necessary.
8. Install the shift lever shaft and small bushing (**Figure 73**).
9. Install the gearshift lever assembly. Tap it into place with a plastic mallet or soft-faced hammer (**Figure 76**) until it is completely seated. Make sure the return spring is correctly positioned onto the stopper plate bolt (A, **Figure 77**) and that it is positioned correctly on the small bushing (B, **Figure 77**).
10. Shift the transmission into 2nd gear. Make sure the index marks on the shift cam and the upper shift arm align (**Figure 78**). On 1978 YZ80 models, there should be the same amount of free play between the engagement tangs on the upper shift arm and the shift drum pins within this engagement area.

NOTE
These 2 marks must align for a proper shift progression from gear to gear.

11. If they do not align, loosen the locknut with a wrench and turn the eccentric screw with a screwdriver (**Figure 79**) in or out for proper alignment. After alignment is correct tighten the locknut securely.
12. Install the clutch assembly as described in this chapter.

Removal/Installation (1981-on)

Refer to **Figure 80** for this procedure.

1. Remove the pinch bolt and remove the shift lever (**Figure 81**) from the left-hand side.

77

78

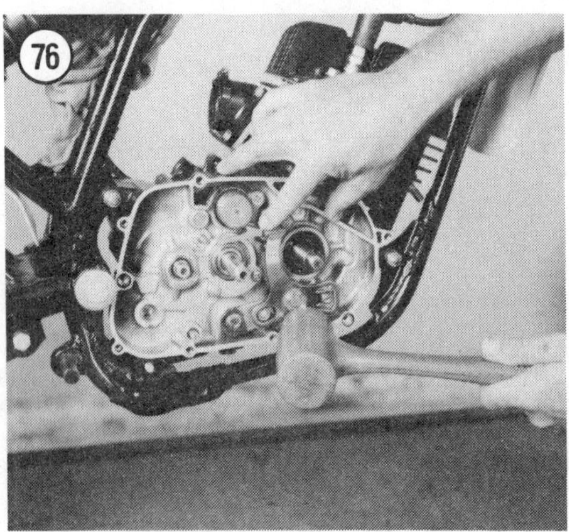
76

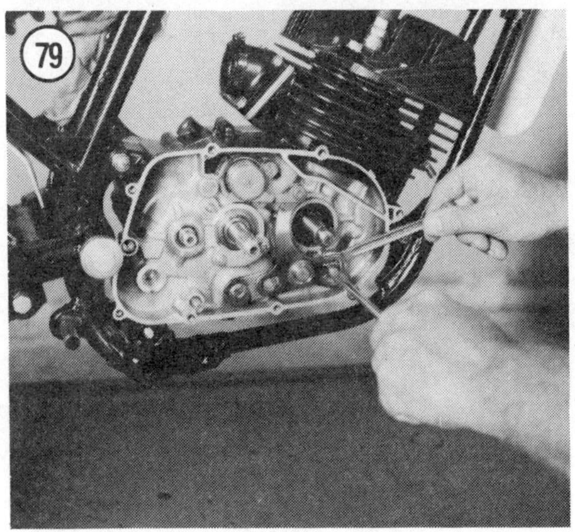
79

2. Remove the clutch assembly as described in this chapter.

3. Shift the transmission into 2nd gear.

4. Remove the shift lever shaft (**Figure 82**). See NOTE in the introduction to this procedure regarding a bent shaft if the assembly is difficult to remove.

5. Remove the stopper lever (A, **Figure 83**) as follows:

   a. Remove the stopper lever bolt (B) and remove the stopper lever (A).
   b. Remove the spring (**Figure 84**).

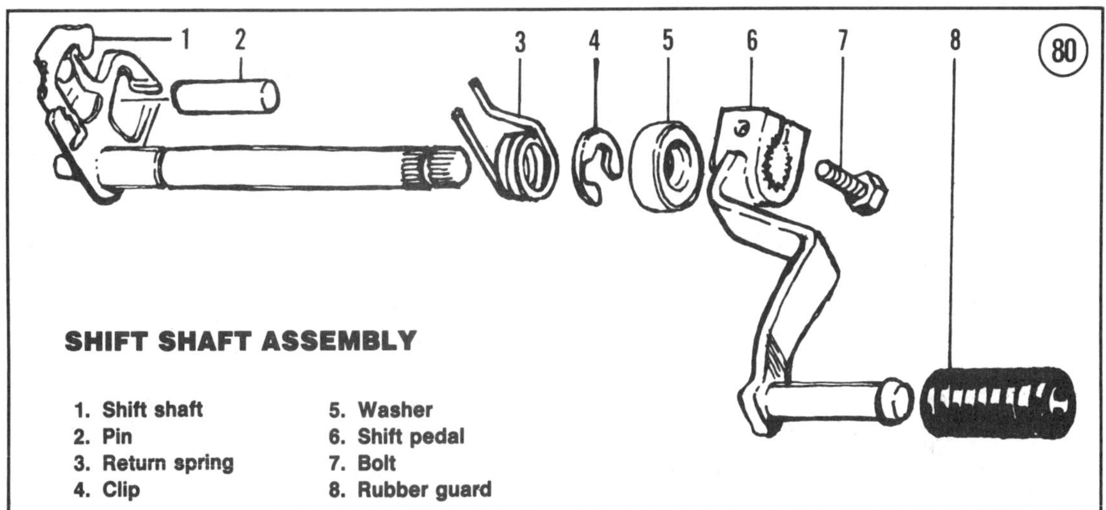

SHIFT SHAFT ASSEMBLY

1. Shift shaft
2. Pin
3. Return spring
4. Clip
5. Washer
6. Shift pedal
7. Bolt
8. Rubber guard

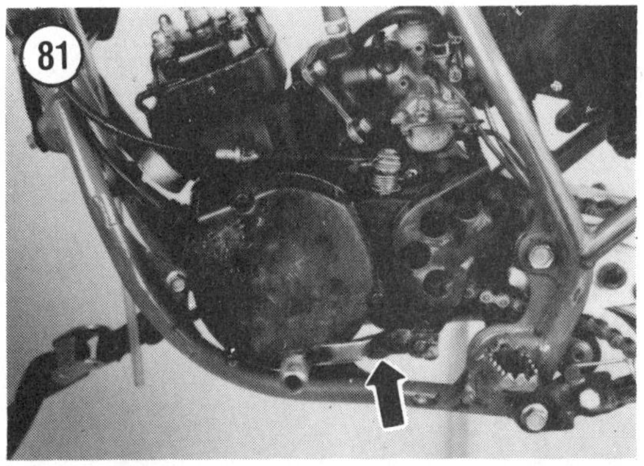

6

6. Inspect the external shift mechanism assembly as follows. Replace worn or damaged parts.
   a. Check the shift shaft (A, **Figure 85**) for cracks or bending. Check the splines (B, **Figure 85**) on the end of the shaft for damage.
   b. Check the circlip (**Figure 86**) on the shaft. Make sure it seats in the groove completely.
   c. Check the return spring (A, **Figure 87**). The return spring arms should be installed on the shaft arm as shown in A, **Figure 87**. Replace the return spring if it shows signs of fatigue or if it is cracked. To replace the spring, remove the circlip (**Figure 86**) and remove the spring. Install the new spring and secure it with the circlip.
   d. Check the engagement arms (B, **Figure 87**) on the shift pawl for wear or damage. Damage or severe wear will cause shifting problems.
7. Install the stopper lever (A, **Figure 83**) as follows:
   a. Install the spring into the crankcase (**Figure 84**).
   b. Install the stopper lever and engage it with the spring as shown in A, **Figure 83**.
   c. Apply Loctite 242 (blue) onto the mounting bolt threads. Install the bolt and tighten it securely.
   d. Engage the wheel on the stopper lever with shift cam. See **Figure 83**.
8. Install the shift lever assembly (**Figure 82**). Make sure that the return spring on the shift lever shaft is positioned correctly on the locating pin (**Figure 82**). Make sure the shift pawl arms engage with the shift cam pins.
9. Install the clutch assembly as described in this chapter.
10. Install the shift lever. Install the pinch bolt and tighten securely.

KICKSTARTER (1978-1980)

Figure 88 is an exploded view drawing of the kickstarter mechanism for the YZ50 and YZ80 models. Minor variations exist between the various models so pay particular attention to the location of shims and circlips as this will make assembly easier.

Removal

NOTE

This procedure is shown on a 1979 YZ80. Service procedures are basically the same for all 1978-1980 models; where differences occur, they will be noted in the text.

1. Remove the clutch assembly as described in this chapter.

WARNING

The spring is under pressure during this part of the procedure; protect yourself accordingly.

2. Using Vise Grips, remove the kickstarter return spring from the pin (**Figure 89**) and pull the assembly (**Figure 90**) from the crankcase.

85

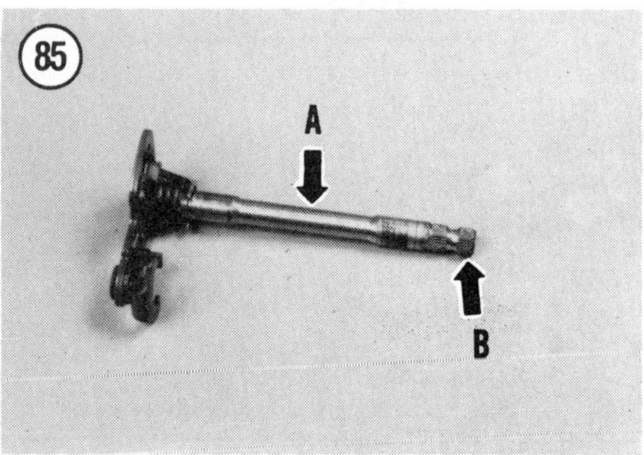

86

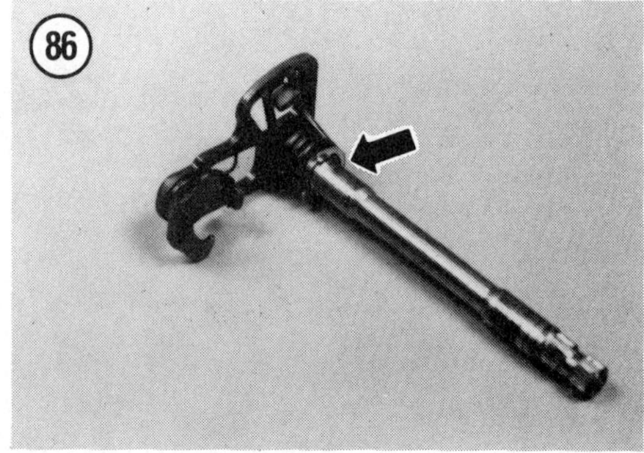

87

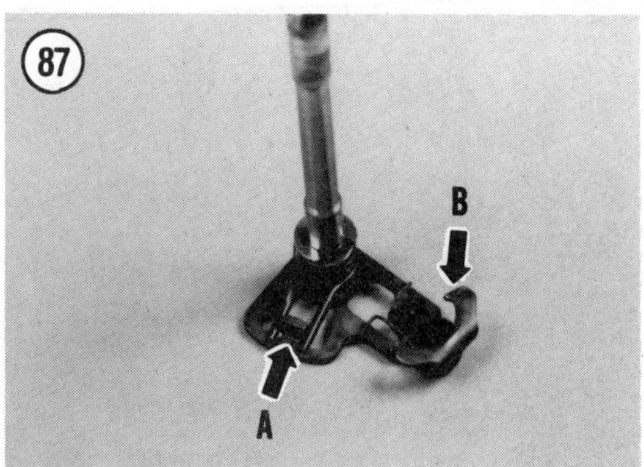

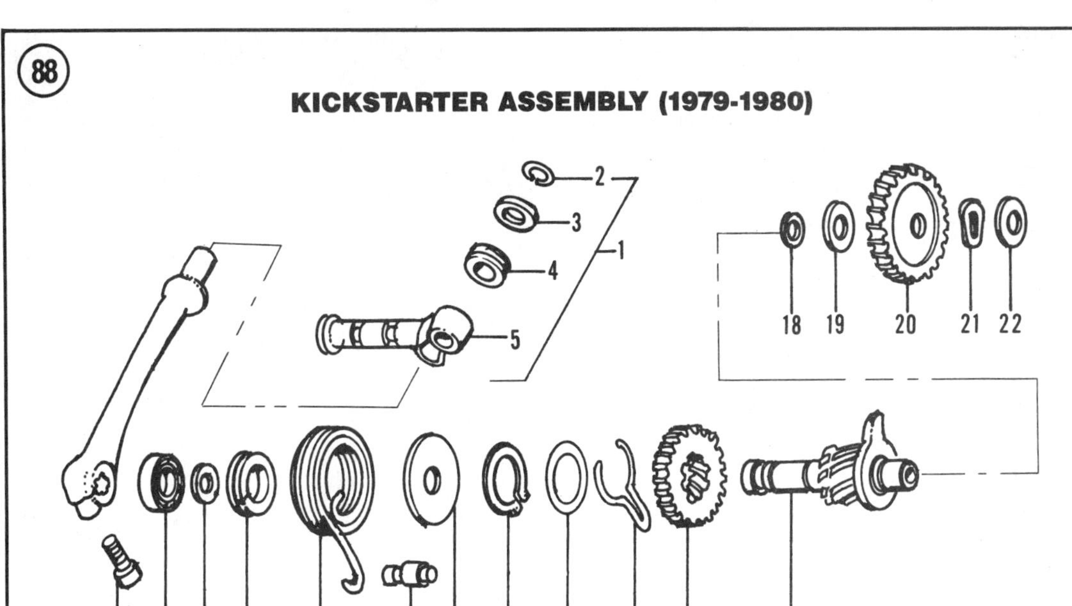

1. Kick crank assembly
2. Circlip
3. Washer
4. Spring
5. Lever
6. Bolt
7. Oil seal
8. Circlip*
9. Collar
10. Kickstarter return spring
11. Stopper pin (on crankcase)
12. Spring cover
13. Circlip*
14. Shim*
15. Spring clip
16. Kickstarter gear
17. Shaft
18. Circlip
19. Outer shim
20. Idle gear
21. Spring washer*
22. Inner shim*

* Parts used on Model YZ50 only

3. Remove the circlip and outer shim (A, **Figure 91**) securing the kickstarter idle gear and remove the gear (B, **Figure 91**).
4. *YZ50 models:* Remove the spring washer and inner shim behind the gear on the transmission shaft (A, **Figure 92**).

Disassembly/Inspection/Assembly

Refer to **Figure 88** for this procedure.

NOTE
This procedure is shown on a 1980 YZ50. As previously mentioned there are differences between the different models.

1. *YZ50 models:* Remove the circlip (**Figure 93**) securing the collar.
2. On all models, remove the collar (A, **Figure 94**), kickstarter return spring (B, **Figure 94**) and the spring cover (C, **Figure 94**).
3. *YZ50 models:* Remove the circlip and shim (**Figure 95**).
4. Slide off the kickstarter ratchet gear and spring clip assembly (**Figure 96**).
5. Check for broken, chipped, or missing teeth on the gear; replace as necessary.
6. Make sure the ratchet gear operates properly and smoothly on the shaft and that the splines are not damaged (**Figure 97**).
7. Check all parts for uneven wear. Replace any that are questionable.
8. Apply assembly oil to the sliding surfaces of all parts.
9. Slide on the ratchet gear and spring clip assembly. On YZ50 models, install the shim and circlip.

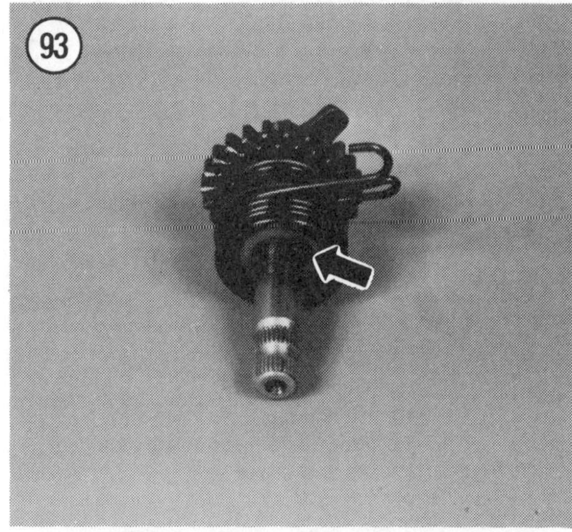

95

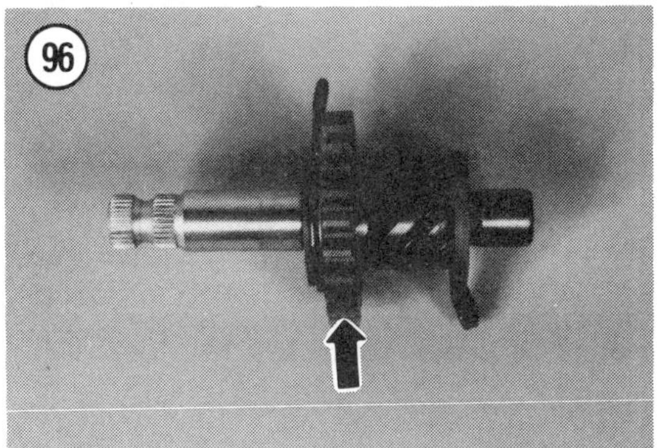
96

97

98

10. Install the spring cover and kickstarter return spring. Insert the end of the spring into the hole in the shaft (**Figure 98**).
11. Install the collar, aligning the notch in it with the spring end that is inserted into the shaft.
12. *YZ50 models:* Install the circlip. Make sure it seats in the groove completely.

NOTE
*Prior to installing the assembled unit in the crankcase, check **Figure 99** for correct placement of all components.*

Installation

1. *YZ50 models:* Install the inner shim and spring washer on the transmission shaft (A, **Figure 92**).
2. Install the kickstarter idle gear (**Figure 100**) and outer shim and circlip (A, **Figure 91**).

6

99

100

3. Install the assembled kickstarter unit into the crankcase (**Figure 90**).

NOTE

*Make sure the flat surface on the kickstarter ratchet is positioned onto the recessed flat surface of the crankcase (B, **Figure 92**).*

WARNING

The spring is under pressure during this part of the procedure; protect yourself accordingly in this next step.

4. Pull the return spring into position with Vise Grips and place it on the stopper (**Figure 89**).
5. Install the clutch assembly as described in this chapter.

KICKSTARTER (1981-ON)

Refer to **Figure 101** when servicing the kickstarter assembly.

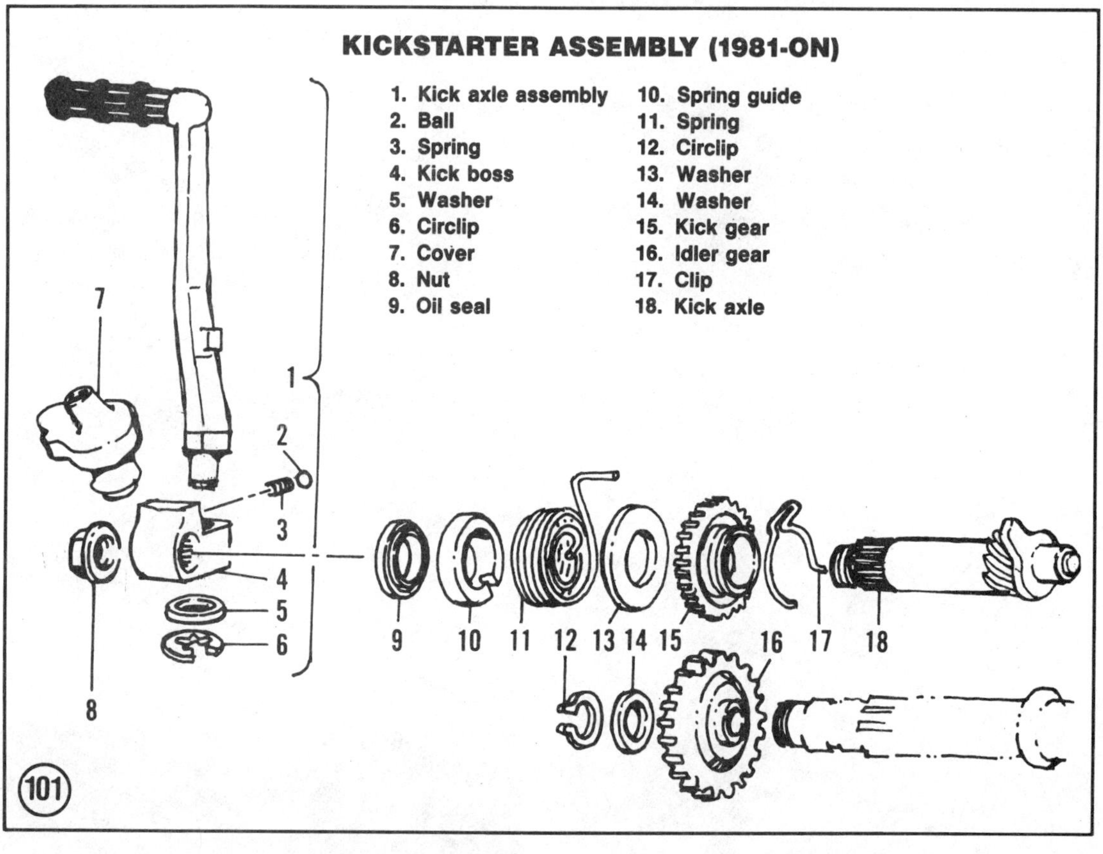

KICKSTARTER ASSEMBLY (1981-ON)

1. Kick axle assembly
2. Ball
3. Spring
4. Kick boss
5. Washer
6. Circlip
7. Cover
8. Nut
9. Oil seal
10. Spring guide
11. Spring
12. Circlip
13. Washer
14. Washer
15. Kick gear
16. Idler gear
17. Clip
18. Kick axle

101

Removal

1. Remove the clutch assembly as described in this chapter.
2. Remove the idler gear as follows:
   a. Remove the circlip (**Figure 102**).
   b. Remove the washer (**Figure 103**).
   c. Remove the idler gear (**Figure 104**).

WARNING
The spring is under pressure during this part of the procedure; protect yourself accordingly.

3. Using a pair of needlenose pliers, remove the kickstarter return spring from its hole in the crankcase (A, **Figure 105**). Release the spring and allow it to unwind. Then rotate the kickstarter (B, **Figure 105**) assembly *counterclockwise* by hand and remove it from the crankcase.

6

Disassembly/Inspection/Assembly

Refer to **Figure 101**.

1. Remove the plastic spring guide (A, **Figure 106**).
2. Remove the return spring (**Figure 107**).
3. Remove the washer (**Figure 108**).
4. Remove the kick gear and spring (**Figure 109**).

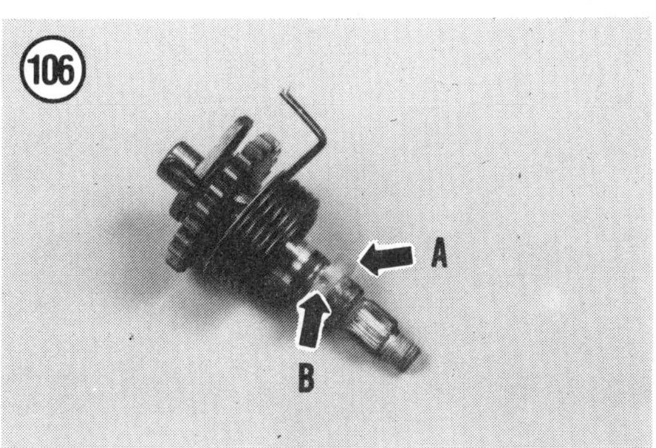

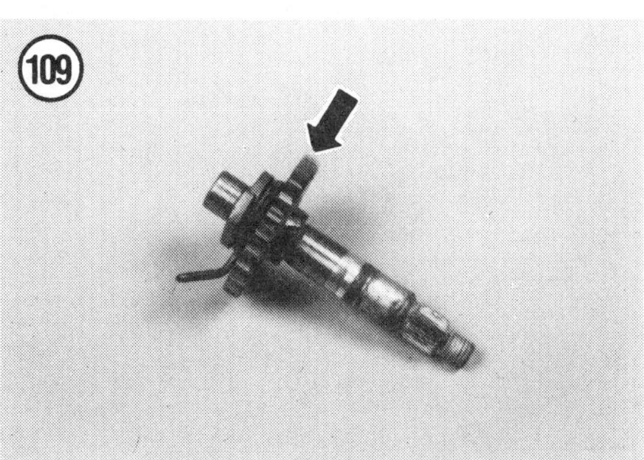

5. Wash all parts thoroughly in solvent (**Figure 110**).
6. Check for broken, chipped, or missing teeth on the gears (A, **Figure 111**). Replace as necessary.
7. Check the kickstarter shaft (**Figure 112**) as follows:
   a. Check the kickstarter lever splines (A) for damage that would allow the lever to slip when the kickstarter is used.
   b. Check the shaft surface (B) for cracks, deep scoring or other damage.
   c. Check the return spring hole (C) in the shaft for cracks, wallowing or other conditions that would allow the spring to slip out when using the kickstarter.
   d. Install the kick gear onto the shaft and check that the gear operates smoothly on the shaft. Check the shaft splines (D) for cracks or other damage.
   e. Replace the kickstarter shaft if necessary.
8. Check the return spring (**Figure 113**) for cracks, breakage or other damage. Replace if necessary.

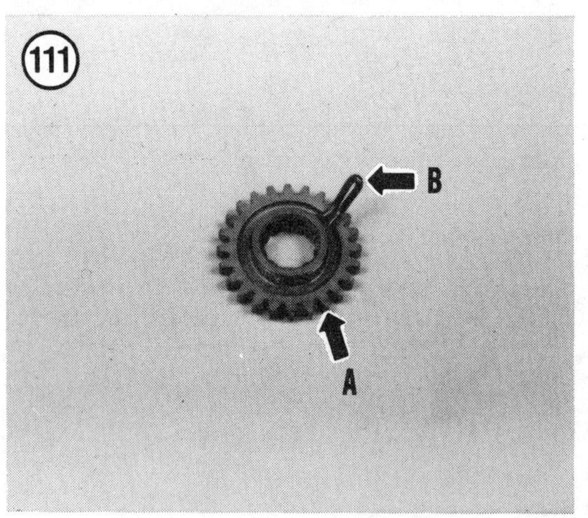

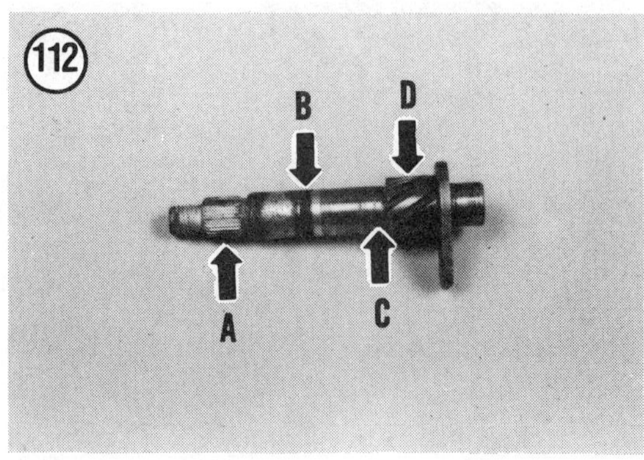

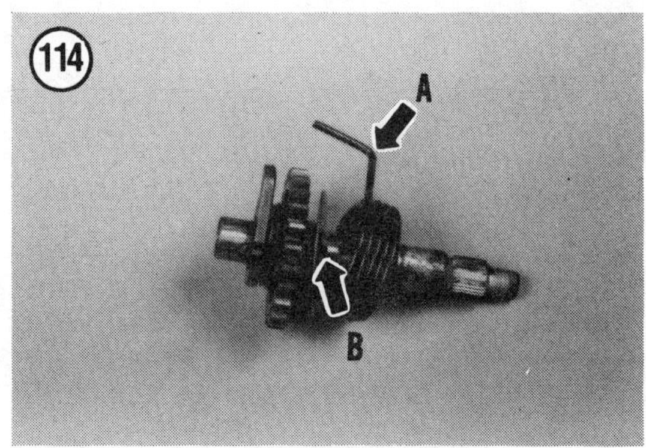

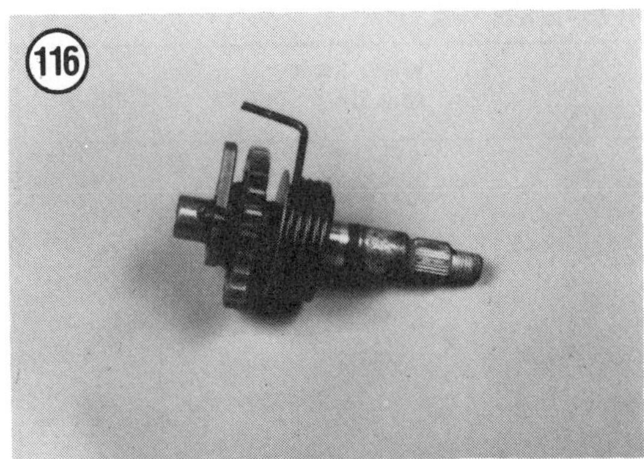

9. Check the clip (B, **Figure 111**) on the kick gear for cracks or other damage. Replace if necessary.
10. Apply assembly oil to the sliding surfaces of all parts.
11. Install the kick gear and clip (**Figure 109**) onto the kickstarter shaft.
12. Install the washer (**Figure 108**).
13. Install the return spring onto the kickstarter shaft in the direction shown in A, **Figure 114**. Insert the end of the spring into the hole (B, **Figure 114**) in the shaft.
14. Install the spring guide (A, **Figure 106**) as follows:
   a. Align the notch in the spring guide (B, **Figure 106**) with the portion of the return spring that fits into the shaft and install the spring guide.
   b. The spring guide has 2 dots (**Figure 115**) on its face that should be aligned with the spring if the guide is properly installed.

NOTE
*Prior to installing the assembled unit in the crankcase, check with **Figure 116** for the correct placement of all components.*

Installation

1. With the kickstarter stopper positioned at the top (**Figure 117**), align the spring clip with the crankcase slot (A, **Figure 118**) and insert the kickstarter into the crankcase.
2. Using needlenose pliers, hook the return spring into the hole in the crankcase (B, **Figure 118**).

NOTE
*Make sure the kickstarter stopper is positioned into the recessed flat surface in the crankcase (**Figure 117**).*

3. Install the idler gear as follows:
   a. Install the idler gear (**Figure 104**).
   b. Install the washer (**Figure 103**).
   c. Install the circlip (**Figure 102**). Make sure the circlip seats in the groove completely.
4. Install the clutch cover as described in this chapter.

6

Tables are on the following pages.

Table 1 CLUTCH SPECIFICATIONS

Item	Standard mm (in.)	Wear limit mm (in.)
Friction disc thickness		
YZ50	3.5 (0.14)	3.2 (0.13)
YZ60	3.0 (0.12)	2.7 (0.11)
YZ80	3.0 (0.12)	2.7 (0.11)
Clutch plate thickness		
YZ50	1.6 (0.06)	—
YZ60	1.2 (0.05)	—
YZ80		
1978-1980	1.6 (0.06)	—
1981-1986	1.2 (0.05)	—
1987-on	1.6 (0.06)	—
Clutch plate warpage	—	0.05 (0.002)
Clutch spring free length		
YZ50	31.5 (1.24)	30.5 (1.20)
YZ60	30.1 (1.19)	29.1 (1.15)
YZ80		
1978-1980	34.0 (1.34)	33.0 (1.30)
1981-1982	31.5 (1.24)	30.5 (1.20)
1983-1986	32.0 (1.26)	31.0 (1.22)
1987-on	33.0 (1.30)	31.0 (1.22)
Number of friction discs		
YZ50	3	
YZ60	4	
YZ80		
1978-1980	4	
1981-1985	5	
1986-on	6	
Number of metal clutch plates		
YZ50	2	
YZ60	3	
YZ80		
1978-1980	3	
1981-1985	4	
1986-on	5	
Clutch pushrod bend	—	0.15 (0.006)

Table 2 CLUTCH TIGHTENING TORQUES

Item	N•m	ft.-lb.
Clutch nut		
YZ50	60	43
YZ60	50	36
YZ80		
1978	60	43
1979	45	33
1980-1982	50	36
1983-on	55	40
Clutch cover screws	10	7.2
Clutch pressure plate	10	7.2
Pinion gear nut		
YZ50	65	47
YZ60	65	47
YZ80		
1978	65	47
1979	60	43
1980-1981	65	47
1982-on	68	49
Kickstarter lever		
YZ50	12	8.5
YZ60	12	8.5
YZ80		
1978	*	*
1979	12	8.5
1980	10	7
1981	12	8.5
1982-on	35	25

*Not specified by Yamaha.

6

CHAPTER SEVEN

TRANSMISSION AND INTERNAL SHIFT MECHANISM

The transmission and internal shift mechanism (shift drum and forks) are all basically the same. The transmission is either a 5-speed or 6-speed unit depending on the model. To gain access to the transmission and internal shift mechanism it is necessary to remove the engine and split the crankcase (Chapter Five). Once the crankcase has been split, removal of the transmission and shift drum and forks is a simple task of pulling the assemblies up and out of the crankcase. Installation is more complicated and is covered more completely than the removal sequence.

Because of the differences between models pay particular attention to the location of spacers, washers and bearings during disassembly. Write down the order in which parts were removed to simplify assembly and ensure the correct placement of all parts.

Transmision troubleshooting is covered in Chapter Two.

NOTE

If disassembling a used, well run-in engine for the first time by yourself, pay particular attention to any additional shims that may have been added by a previous owner. These may have been added to take up the tolerance of worn components and must be reinstalled in the same position since the shims have developed a wear pattern. If new parts are going to be installed these shims may be eliminated. This is something you will have to determine upon reassembly.

TRANSMISSION OPERATION

The transmission has either 5 or 6 pairs of constantly meshed gears (**Figure 1**) on the mainshaft (A) and countershaft (B). Each pair of meshed gears gives one gear ratio. In each pair, one of the gears is locked to its shaft and always turns with it. The other gear is not locked to its shaft and can spin freely on it. Next to each free spinning gear is a third gear which is splined to the same shaft, always turning with it. This third gear can slide from side to side along the shaft splines. The side of the sliding gear and the free spinning gear have mating "dogs" and "slots." When the sliding gear moves up against the free spinning gear, the 2 gears are locked together, locking the free spinning gear to its shaft. Since both meshed mainshaft and countershaft gears are now locked to their shafts, power is transmitted at that gear ratio.

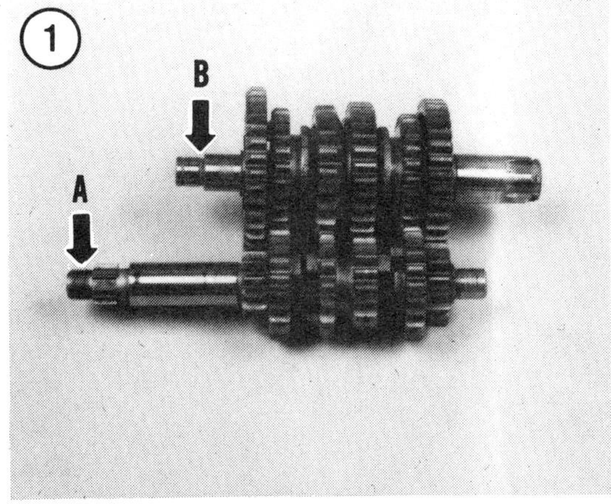

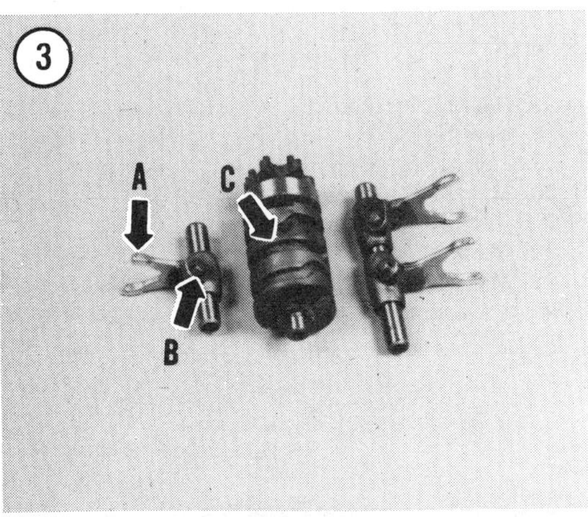

Shift Drum and Forks

Each sliding gear has a deep groove machined around its outside (**Figure 2**). The curved shift fork arm rides in this groove, controlling the side-to-side sliding of the gear, and therefore the selection of different gear ratios. Each shift fork (A, **Figure 3**) slides back and forth on a guide shaft, and has a peg (B, **Figure 3**) that rides in a groove machined in the shift drum (C, **Figure 3**). When the shift linkage rotates the shift drum, the zigzag grooves move the shift forks and sliding gears back and forth thus shifting from one gear to another.

TRANSMISSION OVERHAUL (5-SPEED)

A 5-speed transmission is used on all YZ50 models and 1978 YZ80 models.

Removal/Installation

Remove and install the transmission and internal shift mechanism as described under *Crankcase Disassembly/Reassembly* in Chapter Five.

Mainshaft Disassembly/Assembly

Refer to **Figure 4** and **Figure 5** for this procedure.

1. Place the assembled shaft into a large can or plastic bucket and thoroughly clean with solvent and stiff brush. Dry with compressed air or let sit on rags to drip dry.

NOTE

*A helpful "tool" that should be used for transmission disassembly is a large egg flat (the type that restaurants get their eggs in). As you remove a part from the shaft set it in one of the depressions in the exact same position from which it was removed (**Figure 6**). This is an easy way to remember the correct relationship of all parts.*

2. A hydraulic press is required to remove fifth gear from the mainshaft. Before disassembly, measure the assembled gear length with a vernier caliper (**Figure 7**) and record the measurement for reassembly. Press off fifth gear.
3. Remove second gear.
4. Remove third gear.
5. Remove the circlip and slide off fourth gear.
6. Inspect the countershaft assembly as described under *Transmission Inspection* in this chapter.
7. Slide on fourth gear and install the circlip.

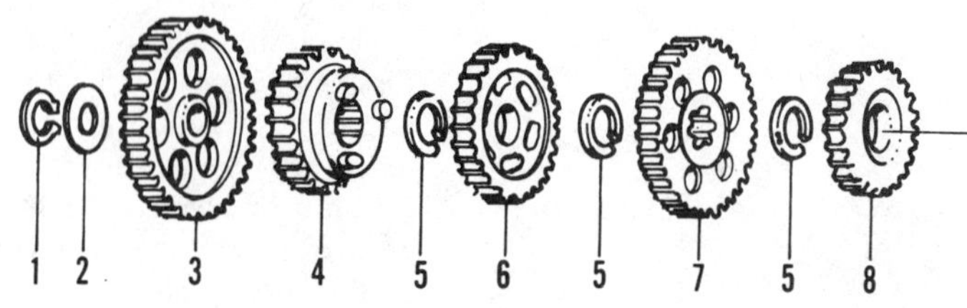

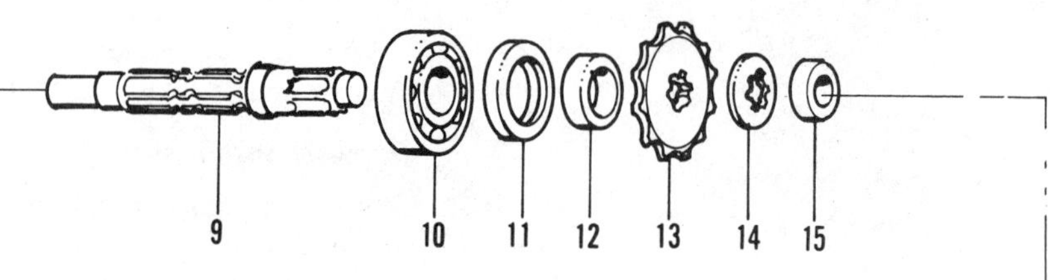

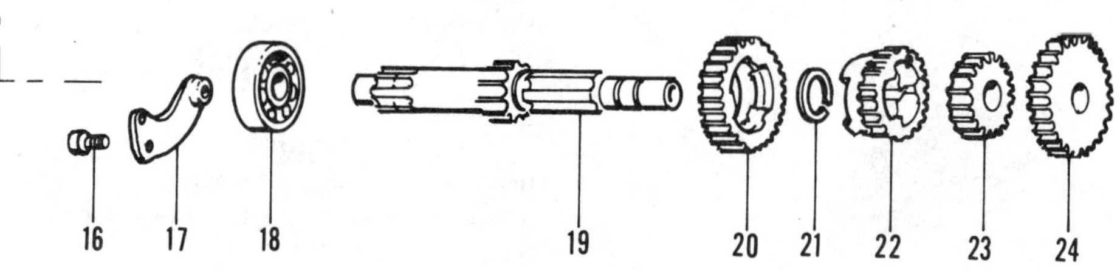

TRANSMISSION ASSEMBLY (5-SPEED)

1. Circlip
2. Thrust washer
3. Countershaft 1st gear
4. Countershaft 4th gear
5. Circlip
6. Countershaft 3rd gear
7. Countershaft 2nd gear
8. Countershaft 5th gear
9. Countershaft
10. Bearing
11. Oil seal
12. Collar
13. Drive sprocket
14. Lockwasher
15. Nut
16. Bolt
17. Bearing retainer
18. Bearing
19. Mainshaft/1st gear
20. Mainshaft 4th gear
21. Circlip
22. Mainshaft 3rd gear
23. Mainshaft 2nd gear
24. Mainshaft 5th gear

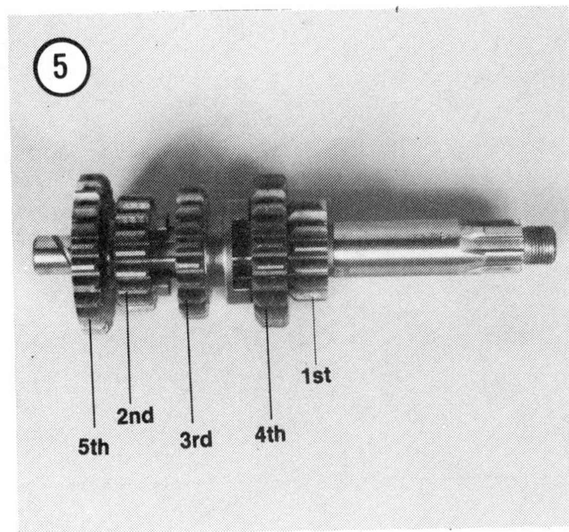

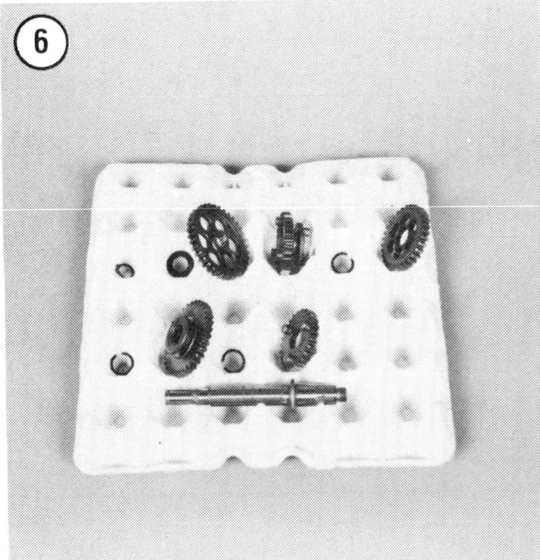

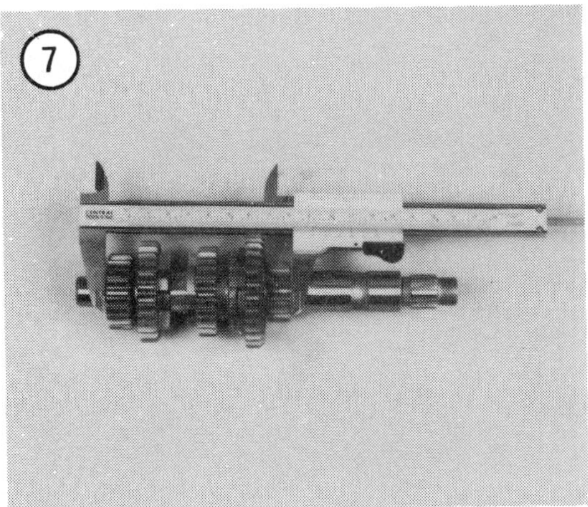

8. Slide on third gear.
9. Slide on second gear.
10. Before pressing on fifth gear, refer to **Figure 5** for the correct placement of all gears. Make sure all circlips are seated correctly in the mainshaft grooves.
11. Press fifth gear onto the mainshaft. Install fifth gear to the dimensions recorded in Step 2.

Countershaft Disassembly/Assembly

Refer to **Figure 4** for this procedure.

1. Place the assembled shaft into a large can or plastic bucket and thoroughly clean with solvent and a stiff brush. Dry with compressed air or let sit on rags to drip dry.
2. Remove the circlip and washer and slide off the first and fourth gears.
3. Remove the circlip and slide off third gear.
4. Remove the circlip and second gear.
5. Remove the circlip and fifth gear.
6. Inspect the mainshaft assembly as described under *Transmission Inspection* in this chapter.
7. Slide on fifth gear and install the circlip (**Figure 8**).
8. Slide on second gear and install the circlip (**Figure 9**).

7

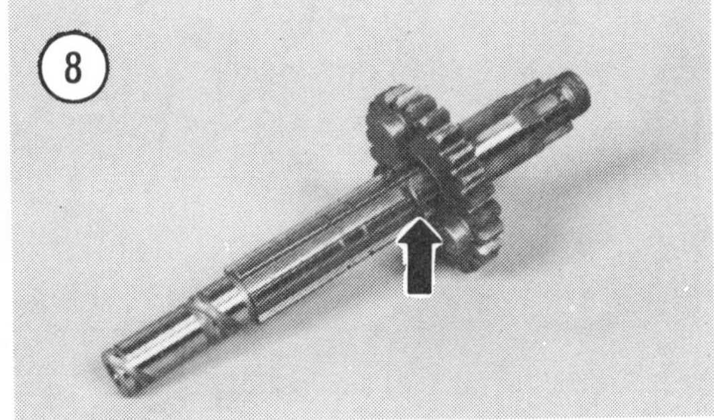

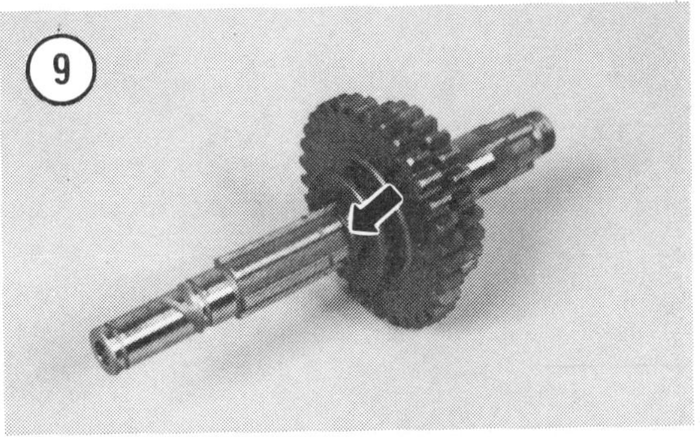

9. Slide on third gear and install the circlip (**Figure 10**).
10. Slide on fourth gear (**Figure 11**).
11. Slide on first gear (A, **Figure 12**) and install the washer and circlip (B, **Figure 12**).
12. After the countershaft is assembled, refer to **Figure 13** for the correct placement of all gears. Make sure all circlips are seated correctly in the countershaft grooves.
13. After the transmission shaft has been assembled, mesh both shaft assemblies together in the correct position (**Figure 14**). Check that all gears meet correctly. This is your last check prior to installing the assemblies into the crankcase to make sure they are correctly assembled.

Transmission Inspection

1. Check each gear for excessive wear, burrs, pitting, or chipped or missing teeth.
2. Make sure the lugs (dogs) on the gears are in good condition. See **Figure 15**.

NOTE
Defective gears should be replaced, and it is a good idea to replace the mating gear even though it may not show as much wear or damage.

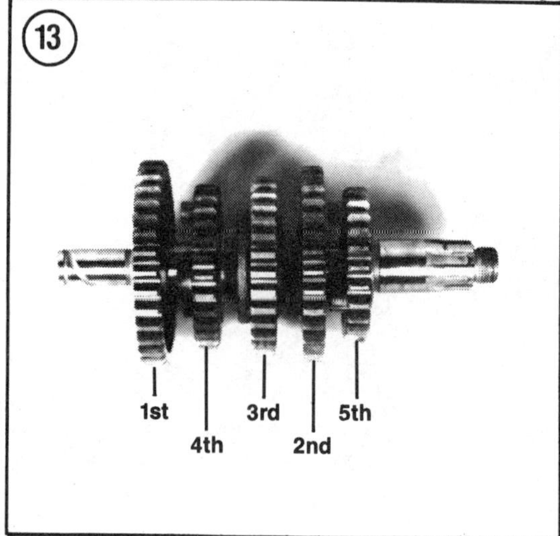

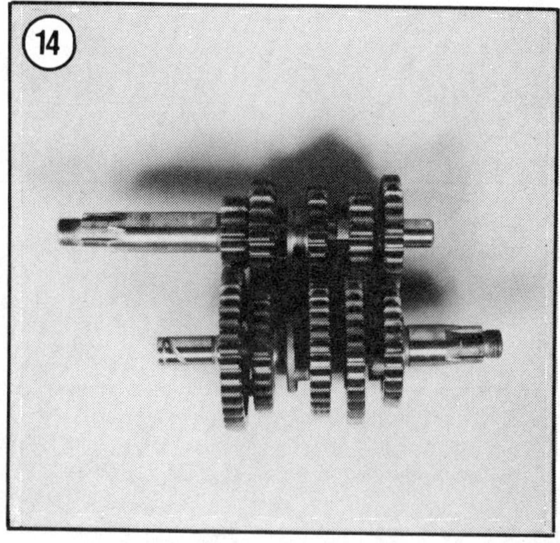

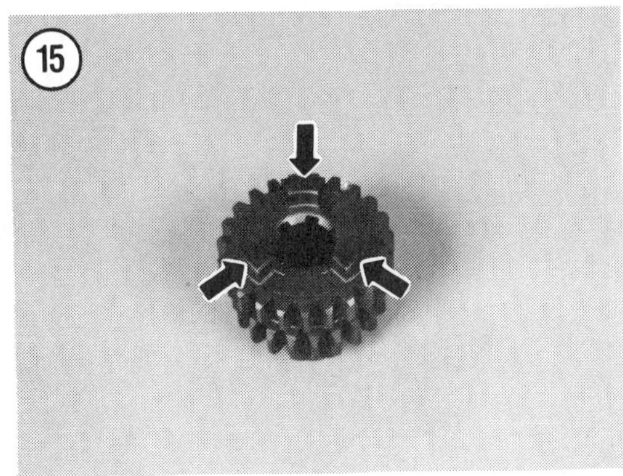

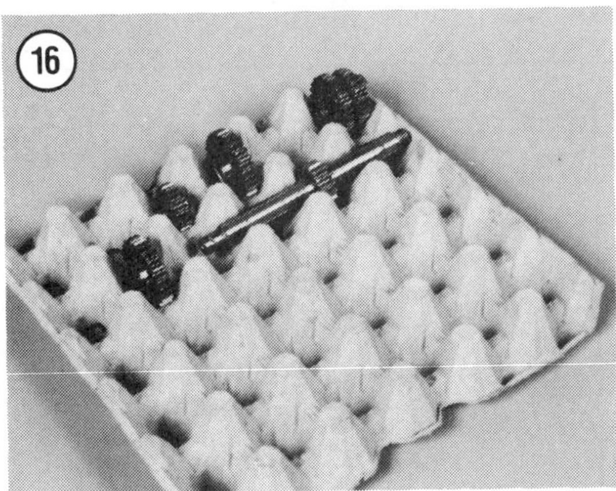

3. Make sure that all gears slide on their respective shafts smoothly.
4. Replace all circlips during reassembly. In addition, check the washers for burn marks, scoring or cracks. Replace if necessary.

TRANSMISSION OVERHAUL (1979-1980 6-SPEED)

A 6-speed transmission is used on all 1979-1980 YZ80 models.

Removal/Installation

Remove and install the transmission and internal shift mechanism as described under *Crankcase Disassembly/Reassembly* in Chapter Five.

NOTE
*A helpful "tool" that should be used for transmission disassembly is a large egg flat (the type that restaurants get their eggs in). As you remove a part from the shaft set it in one of the depressions in the exact same position from which it was removed (**Figure 16**). This is an easy way to remember the correct relationship of all parts.*

Mainshaft Disassembly/Assembly

Refer to **Figure 17** for this procedure.

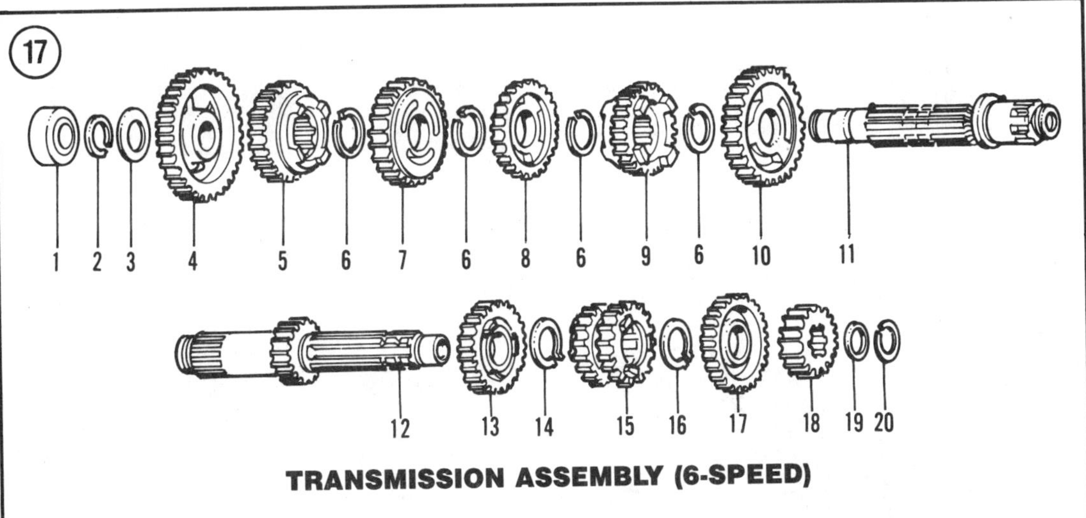

TRANSMISSION ASSEMBLY (6-SPEED)

1. Bearing
2. Circlip
3. Thrust washer
4. Countershaft 1st gear
5. Countershaft 5th gear
6. Circlip
7. Countershaft 3rd gear
8. Countershaft 4th gear
9. Countershaft 6th gear
10. Countershaft 2nd gear
11. Countershaft
12. Mainshaft 1st gear
13. Mainshaft 5th gear
14. Circlip
15. Mainshaft 3rd/4th gear
16. Circlip
17. Mainshaft 6th gear
18. Mainshaft 2nd gear
19. Washer
20. Circlip

1. Place the assembled shaft into a large can or plastic bucket and thoroughly clean with solvent and stiff brush. Dry with compressed air or place on rags to drip dry.
2. Remove the circlip and washer and slide off second and sixth gears.
3. Remove the circlip and the third/fourth combination gear.
4. Remove the circlip and fifth gear.
5. Inspect the mainshaft assembly as described under *Transmission Inspection* in this chapter.
6. Slide on the fifth gear and install the circlip (A, **Figure 18**).

NOTE
Install the third/fourth combination gear with the smaller diameter gear (third gear) on first toward fifth gear.

7. Slide on the third/fourth combination gear (B, **Figure 18**).
8. Install the circlip (A, **Figure 19**).
9. Slide on sixth gear (B, **Figure 19**).
10. Slide on second gear (A, **Figure 20**) and install the washer and circlip (B, **Figure 20**).
11. After assembly is complete refer to **Figure 21** for the correct placement of all gears.

Countershaft Disassembly/Assembly

Refer to **Figure 17** for this procedure.
1. Place the assembled shaft into a large can or plastic bucket and thoroughly clean with solvent and stiff brush. Dry with compressed air or place on rags to drip dry.
2. Remove the circlip and washer and slide off the first and fifth gears.

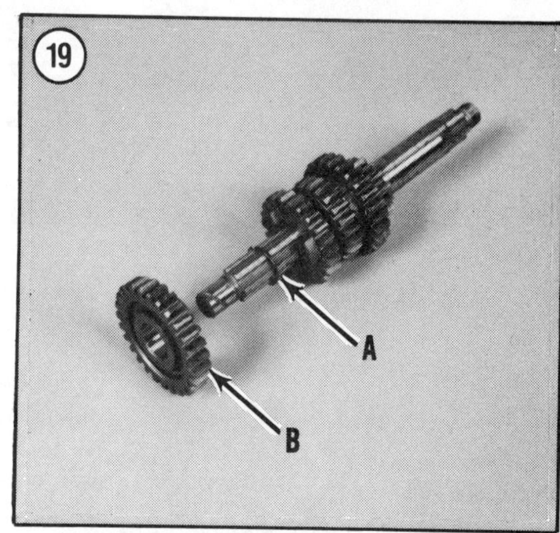

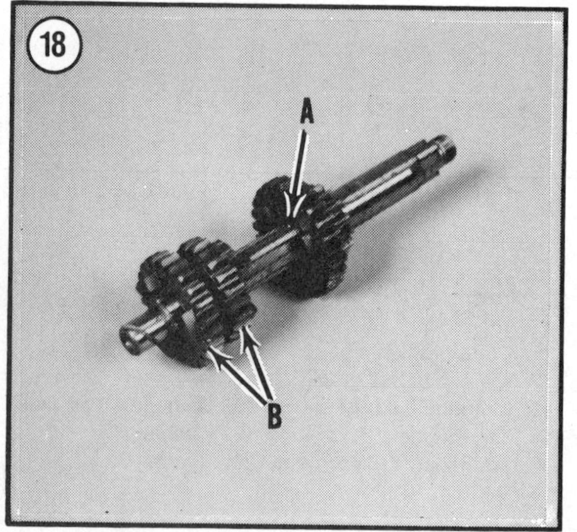

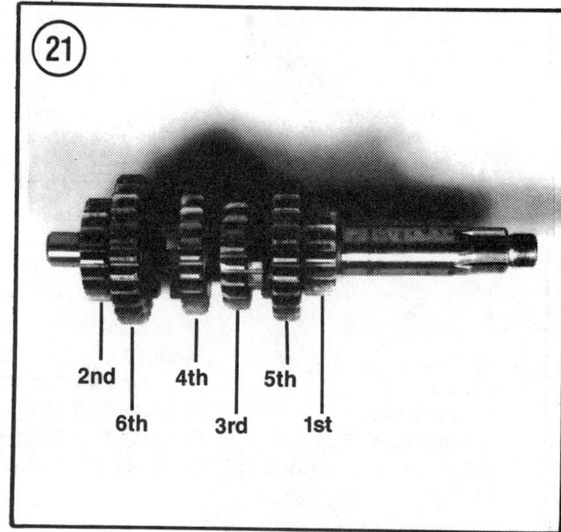

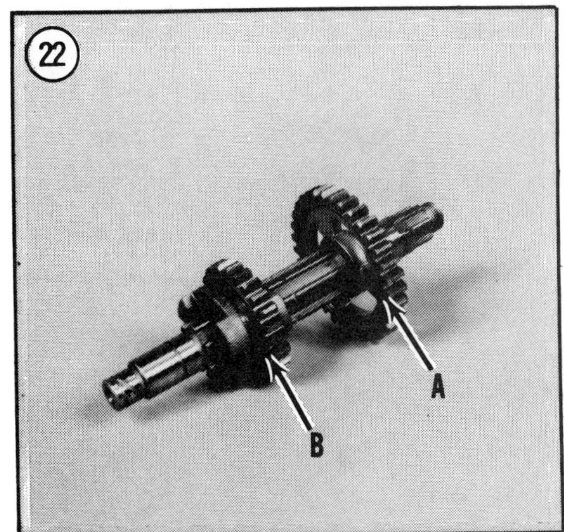

3. Remove the circlip and slide off third gear.
4. Remove the circlip and slide off fourth gear.
5. Remove the circlip and slide off sixth gear.
6. Remove the circlip and slide off second gear.
7. Inspect the countershaft assembly as described under *Transmission Inspection* in this chapter.
8. Slide on second gear (A, **Figure 22**) and install the circlip.
9. Slide on sixth gear (B, **Figure 22**).
10. Install the circlip (A, **Figure 23**) and slide on fourth gear (B, **Figure 23**) with the beveled side on last.
11. Install the circlip in the recess in fourth gear (A, **Figure 24**).
12. Install third gear (B, **Figure 24**)—flush side on first—and install the circlip.
13. Slide on fifth gear (**Figure 25**).
14. Slide on first gear (A, **Figure 26**)—flush side out—and install the washer and circlip (B, **Figure 26**).

7

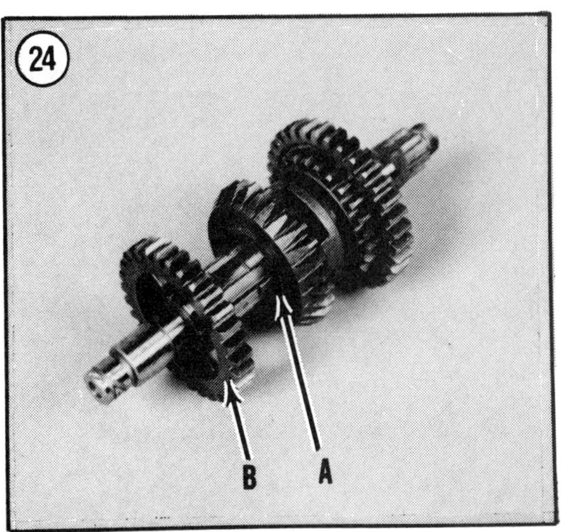

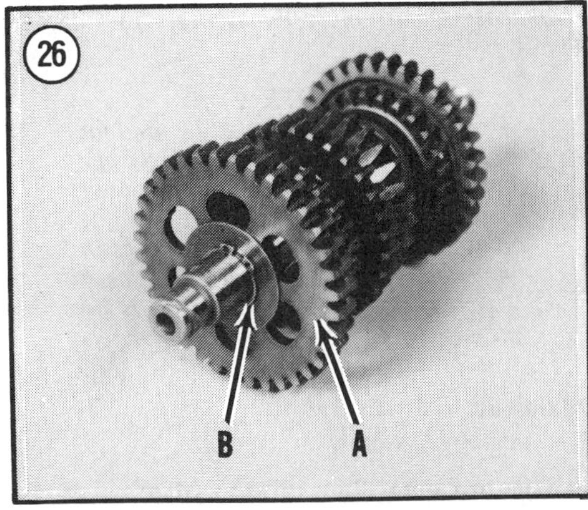

15. After assembly is complete refer to **Figure 27** for the correct placement of all gears. Make sure all circlips are seated correctly in the countershaft grooves.

NOTE
*After both transmission shafts have been assembled, mesh the 2 assemblies together in the correct position (**Figure 28**). Check that all gears meet correctly. This is your last check prior to installing the assemblies into the crankcase to make sure they are correctly assembled.*

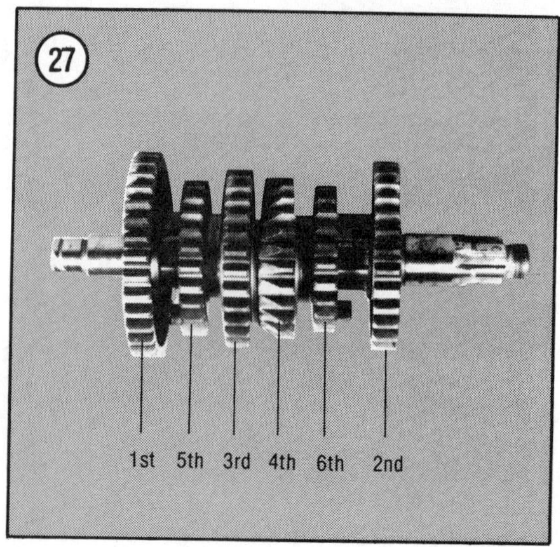

Transmission Inspection

1. Check each gear for excessive wear, burrs, pitting, or chipped or missing teeth.
2. Make sure the lugs (dogs) on the gears are in good condition. See **Figure 15**.

NOTE
Defective gears should be replaced, and it is a good idea to replace the mating gear even though it may not show as much wear or damage.

3. Make sure that all gears slide on their respective shafts smoothly.
4. Replace all circlips during reassembly. In addition, check the washers for burn marks, scoring or cracks. Replace if necessary.

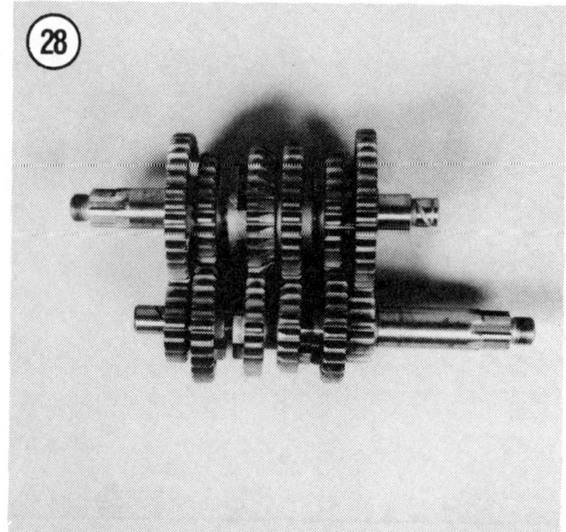

TRANSMISSION OVERHAUL (1981-ON 6-SPEED)

A 6-speed transmission is used on all 1981 and later YZ60 and YZ80 models.

Removal/Installation

Remove and install the transmission and internal shift mechanism as described under *Crankcase Disassembly/Reassembly* in Chapter Five.

NOTE
*A helpful "tool" that should be used for transmission disassembly is a large egg flat (the type that restaurants get their eggs in). As you remove a part from the shaft set it in one of the depressions in the exact same position from which it was removed (**Figure 29**). This is an easy way to remember the correct relationship of all parts.*

Mainshaft Disassembly/Assembly

Refer to **Figure 30** for this procedure.

30

TRANSMISSION ASSEMBLY (6-SPEED, 1981-ON YZ60 AND YZ80)

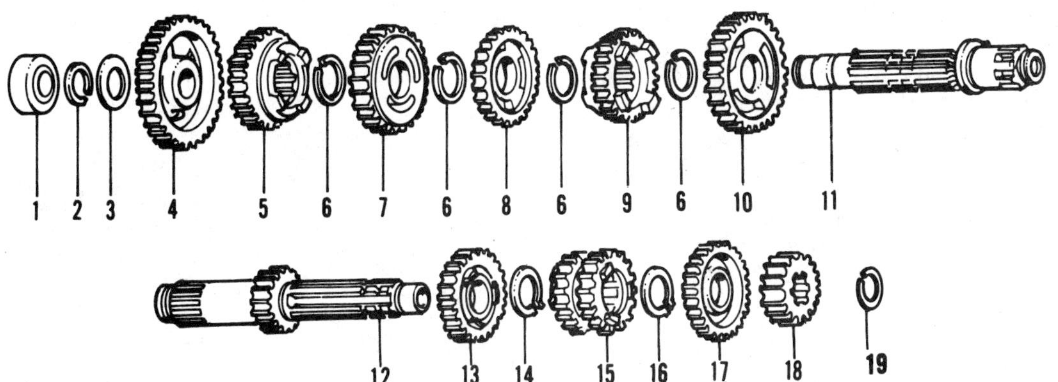

1. Bearing
2. Circlip
3. Thrust washer
4. Countershaft 1st gear
5. Countershaft 5th gear
6. Circlip
7. Countershaft 3rd gear
8. Countershaft 4th gear
9. Countershaft 6th gear
10. Countershaft 2nd gear
11. Countershaft
12. Mainshaft 1st gear
13. Mainshaft 5th gear
14. Circlip
15. Mainshaft 3rd/4th gear
16. Circlip
17. Mainshaft 6th gear
18. Mainshaft 2nd gear
19. Circlip

1. Place the assembled shaft into a large can or plastic bucket and thoroughly clean with solvent and stiff brush. Dry with compressed air or let sit on rags to drip dry.
2. Remove the circlip (**Figure 31**) and remove second gear (**Figure 32**).
3. Remove sixth gear (**Figure 33**).
4. Remove the circlip (**Figure 34**) and remove the third/fourth combination gear (**Figure 35**).
5. Remove the circlip (**Figure 36**) and remove fifth gear (**Figure 37**).
6. Inspect the mainshaft assembly as described under *Transmission Inspection* in this chapter.
7. Slide on fifth gear (**Figure 37**) and install the circlip (**Figure 36**).

NOTE
Install the third/fourth combination gear with the larger diameter gear (third) on first toward fifth gear.

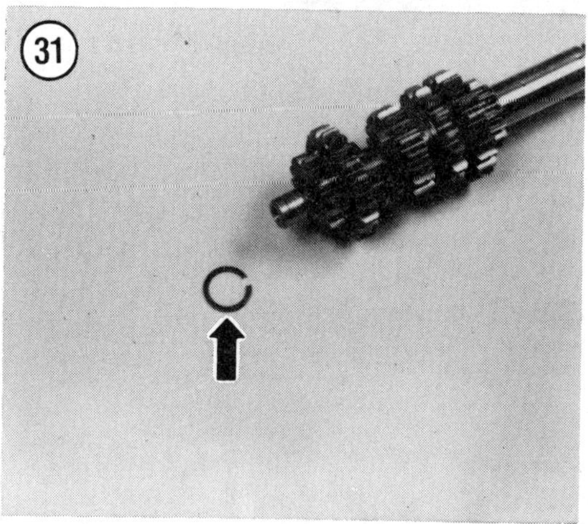

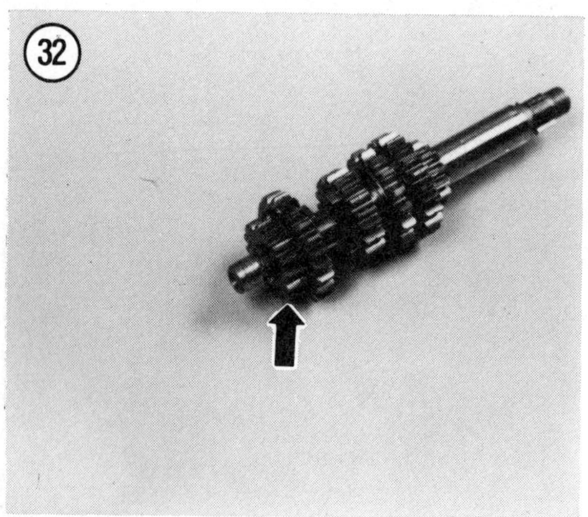

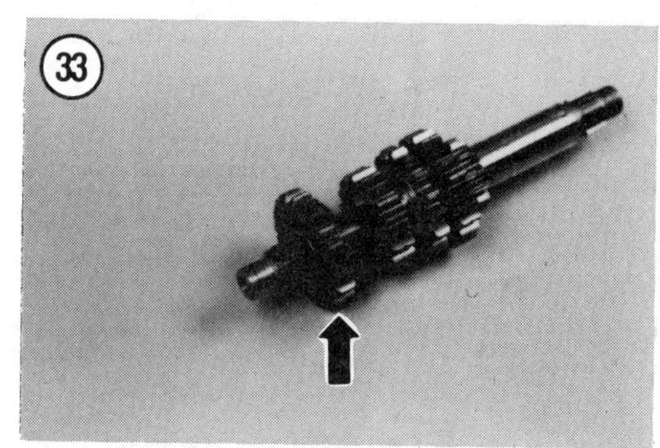

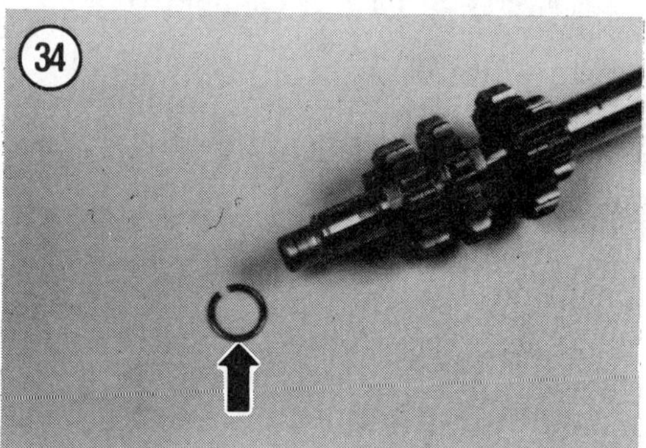

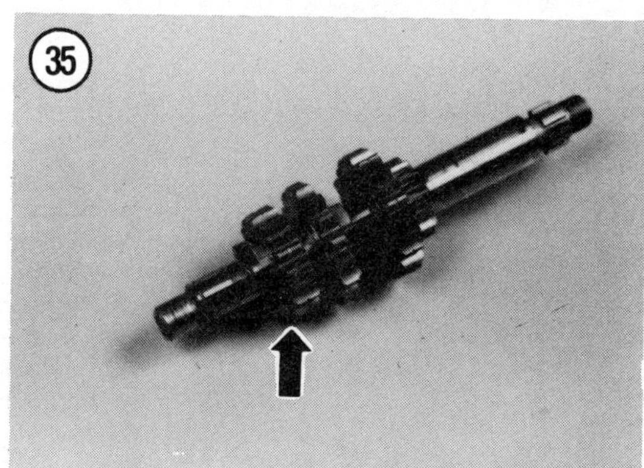

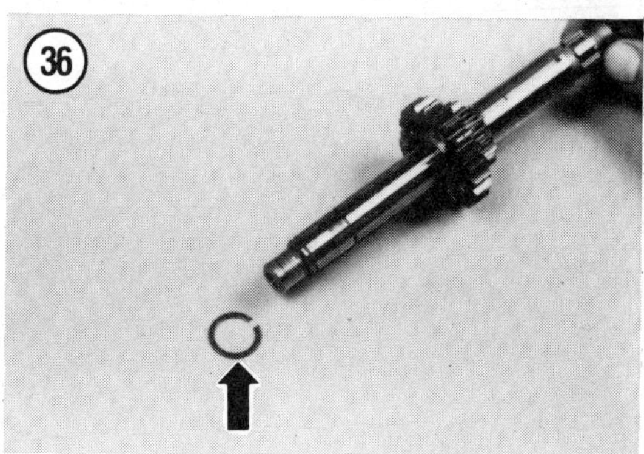

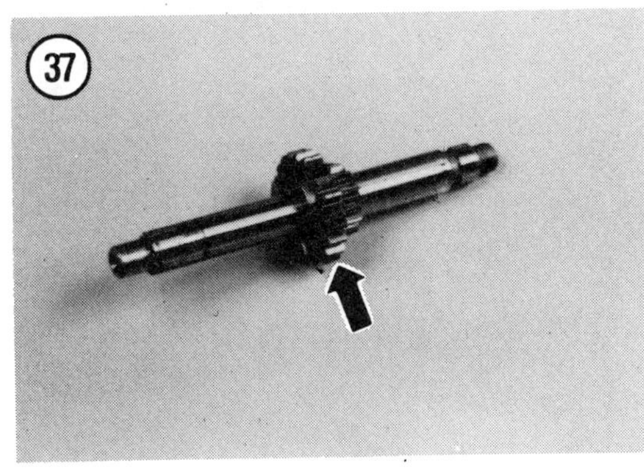

37

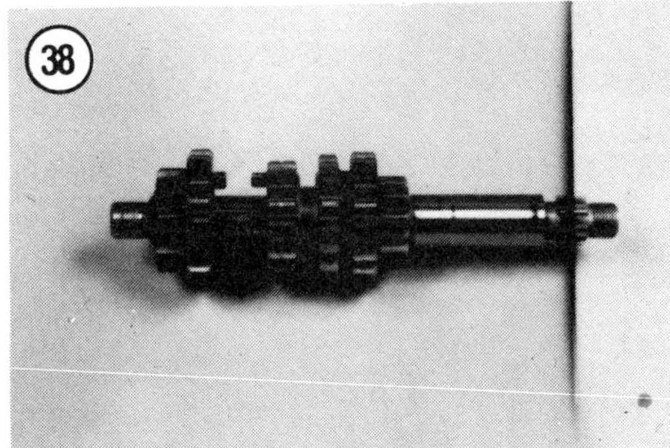

38

39

40

8. Install the third/fourth combination gear (**Figure 35**) and install the circlip (**Figure 34**).
9. Install sixth gear (**Figure 33**).
10. Install second gear (**Figure 32**) and install the circlip.
11. After assembly is complete refer to **Figure 38** for the correct placement of all gears.

Countershaft Disassembly/Assembly

Refer to **Figure 30** for this procedure.

1. Place the assembled shaft into a large can or plastic bucket and thoroughly clean with solvent and stiff brush. Dry with compressed air or let it sit on rags to drip dry.
2. Remove the circlip (**Figure 39**) and washer (**Figure 40**).
3. Remove first gear (**Figure 41**).
4. Remove fifth gear (**Figure 42**).

41

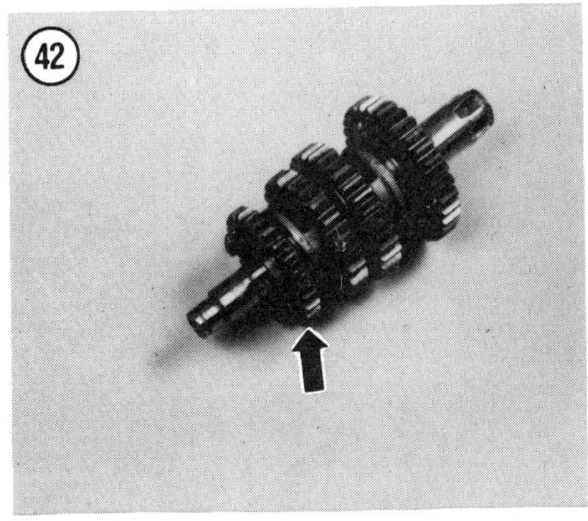

42

5. Remove the circlip (**Figure 43**) and remove third gear (**Figure 44**).
6. Remove the circlip (**Figure 45**) and remove fourth gear (**Figure 46**).
7. Remove the circlip (**Figure 47**) and remove sixth gear (**Figure 48**).
8. Remove the circlip (**Figure 49**) and remove second gear (**Figure 50**).
9. Inspect the countershaft assembly as described under *Transmission Inspection* in this chapter.
10. Install second gear onto the countershaft so that the flat side faces against the shaft stop (**Figure 51**).
11. Install the circlip (**Figure 49**).
12. Install sixth gear (**Figure 48**) and install the circlip (**Figure 47**).

43

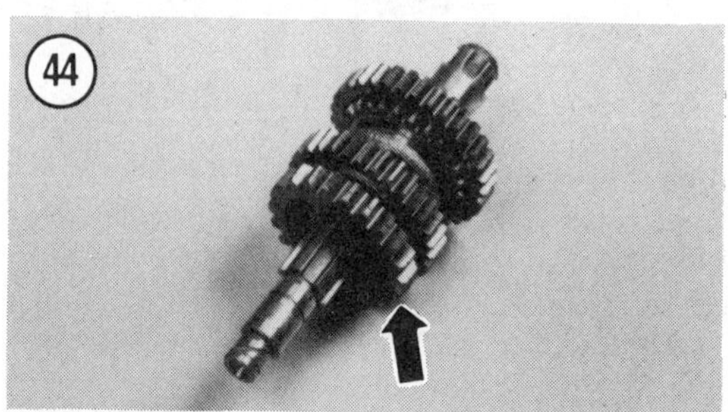
44

45

46

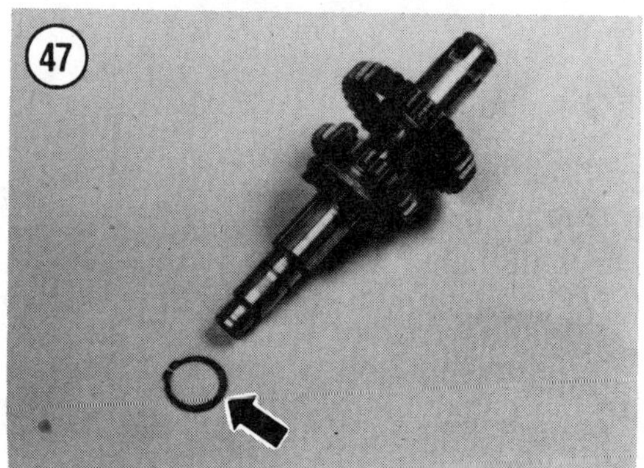
47

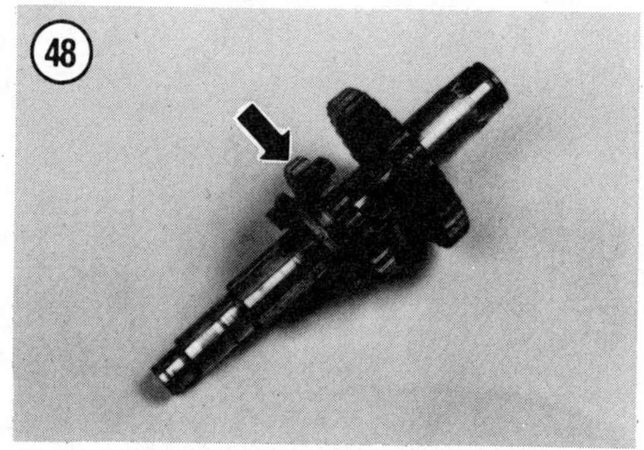
48

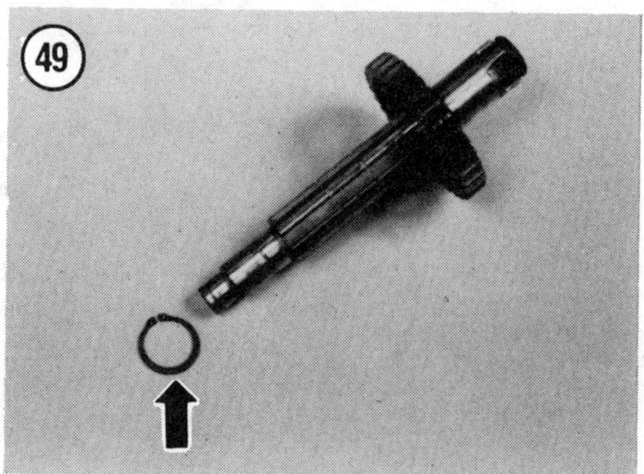
49

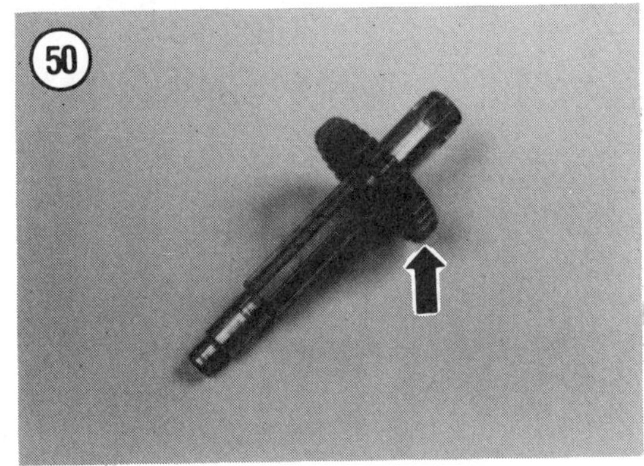

50

13. Install fourth gear (**Figure 46**) and install the circlip (**Figure 45**).
14. Install third gear (**Figure 44**) and install the circlip (**Figure 43**).
15. Install fifth gear (**Figure 42**).
16. Install first gear (**Figure 41**).
17. Install the washer (**Figure 40**) and the circlip (**Figure 39**).
18. After assembly is complete refer to **Figure 52** for the correct placement of all gears. Make sure all circlips are seated correctly in the countershaft grooves.

NOTE
*After both transmission shafts have been assembled, mesh the 2 assemblies together in the correct position (**Figure 53**). Check that all gears meet correctly. This is your last check prior to installing the assemblies into the crankcase to make sure they are correctly assembled.*

51

Transmission Inspection

1. Check each gear (**Figure 54**) for excessive wear, burrs, pitting, or chipped or missing teeth.
2. Make sure the lugs (dogs) on the gears are in good condition. See **Figure 55**.

52

54

53

55

NOTE
Defective gears should be replaced, and it is a good idea to replace the mating gear even though it may not show as much wear or damage.

3. Make sure that all gears slide on their respective shafts smoothly.
4. See **Figure 56**. Replace all circlips during reassembly. In addition, check the washers for burn marks, scoring or cracks. Replace if necessary.
5. Check all transmission splines for wear, cracks or other damage.

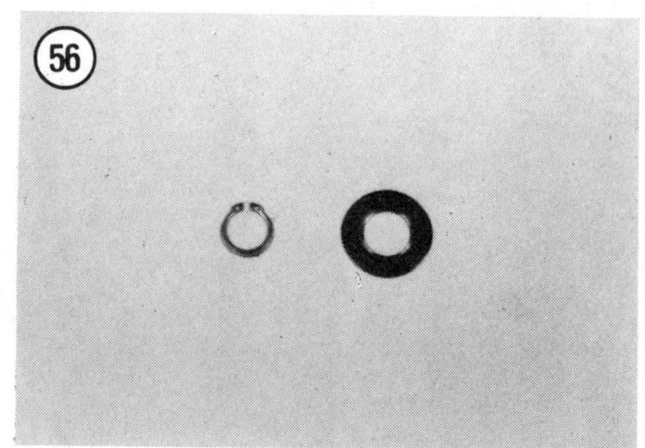
56

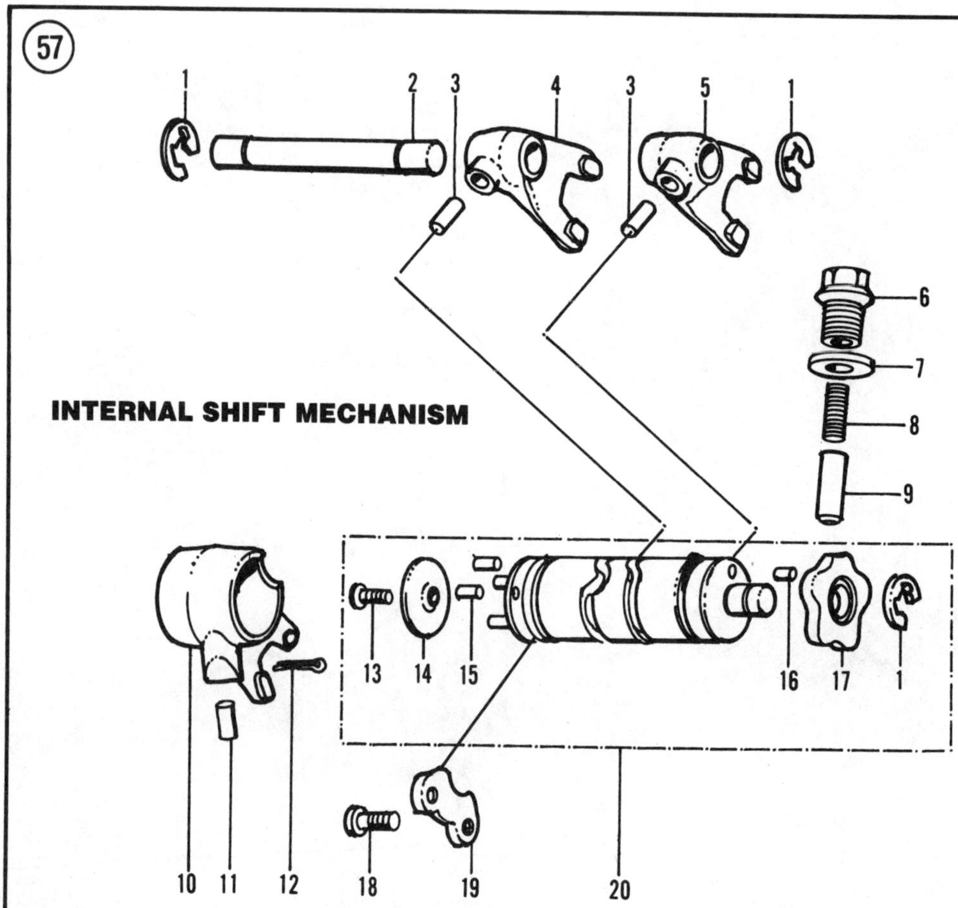

57

INTERNAL SHIFT MECHANISM

1. E-clip
2. Shift fork shaft
3. Cam pin follower
4. Shift fork
5. Shift fork
6. Bolt
7. Gasket
8. Spring
9. Stopper pin
10. Shift fork
11. Dowel pin
12. Cotter pin
13. Flat head screw
14. Side plate
15. Dowel pin
16. Dowel pin
17. Stopper plate
18. Bolt
19. Retainer plate
20. Shift drum assembly

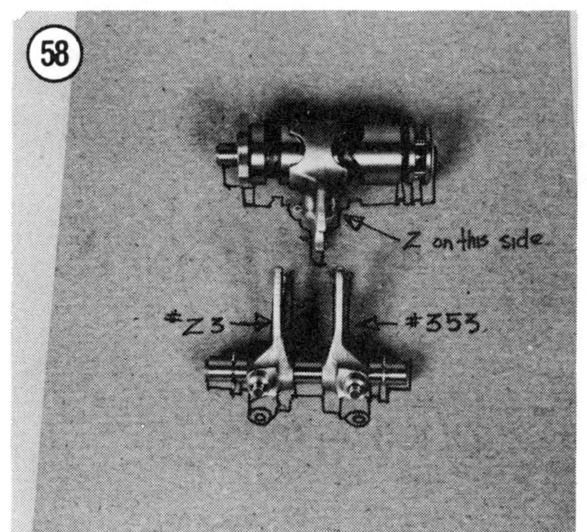

59

INTERNAL SHIFT MECHANISM (1978-1980)

Inspection

Refer to **Figure 57** for this procedure.

NOTE

*To assure the correct assembly of all components prior to removal or disassembly of any of the components, lay both shift fork and shift drum assemblies down on a piece of paper or cardboard and carefully trace around them (**Figure 58**). Also write down the identifying marks or numbers next to the item. Also mark where circlips are located. This will take a little extra time now but it may save some frustrating time during assembly.*

1. Disassemble the shift fork from the shift drum. Remove the cotter pin (**Figure 59**), remove the pin follower (A, **Figure 60**), and slide off the shift fork (B, **Figure 60**).

NOTE

Discard the cotter pin—never reuse an old cotter pin.

2. Inspect each shift fork for signs of wear or cracking.
Check for bending and make sure each fork slides smoothly on its respective shaft.

NOTE

*Check for any arc-shaped wear or burn marks (**Figure 61**) on the shift forks. If this is apparent, the shift fork has come in contact with the gear, indicating that the fingers are worn beyond use and the fork must be replaced.*

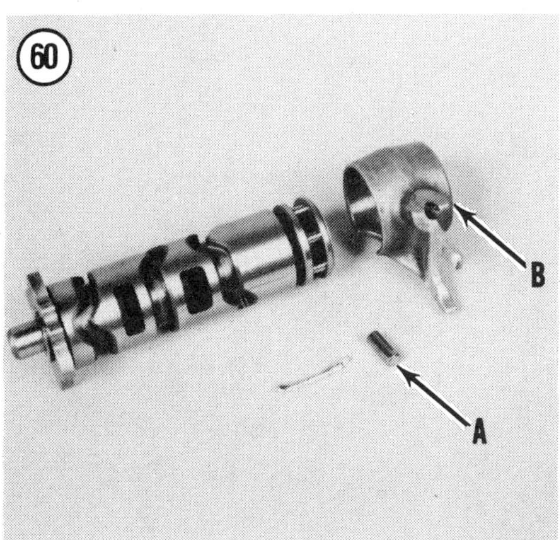

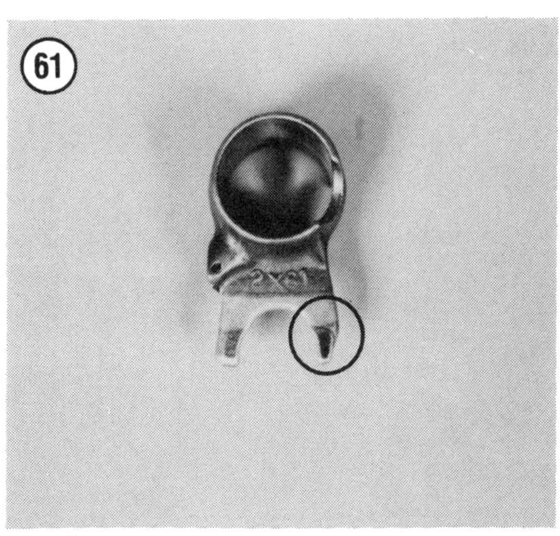

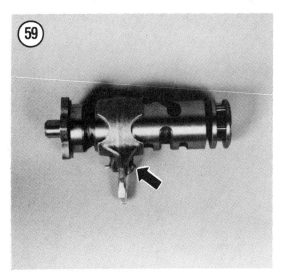

3. Roll the shift fork shaft on a flat surface (a piece of plate glass) and check for any bending. If the shaft is bent, replace it.
4. Check the grooves (A, **Figure 62**) in the shift drum for wear or roughness. If any of the groove profiles have excessive wear or damage, replace the shift drum.
5. Check the shift cam dowel pins (B, **Figure 62**) and side plate for wear, looseness, or damage; replace any defective parts.
6. Check the cam pin followers (**Figure 63**) in each shift fork. They should fit snug but not too tight. Check the end that rides in the shift drum for wear or burrs. Replace as necessary.
7. Inspect the ramps on the stopper plate (**Figure 64**) for wear or roughness. Also check the tightness of the E-clip securing the stopper plate. If it is loose, replace it with a new one.
8. If shift fork assemblies have been disassembled, apply a light coat of oil to the shafts and inside bores of the fingers prior to installation.
9. Assemble the shift fork onto the shift drum so that the cam pin follower hole (A, **Figure 65**) aligns with the middle or second groove over from the stopper plate (B, **Figure 65**). Install the cam pin follower (C, **Figure 65**) and install a *new* cotter pin (**Figure 59**).

NOTE
*Make sure to install the shift fork onto the shift drum as shown in **Figure 59**.*

INTERNAL SHIFT MECHANISM (1981-ON)

Inspection

Refer to **Figure 66** (1981-1982) or **Figure 67** (1983-on) for this procedure.

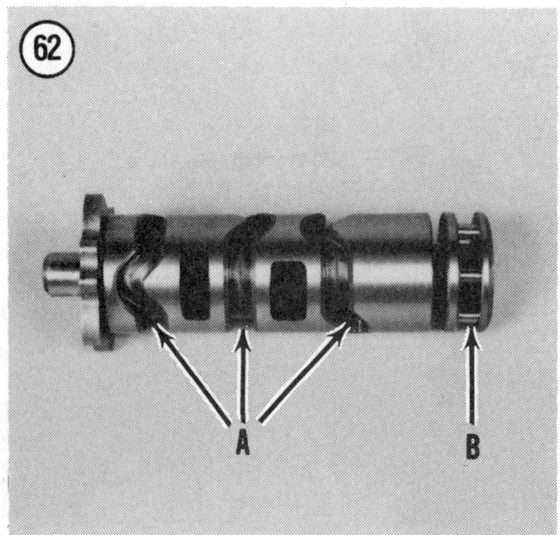

1. Inspect each shift fork (A, **Figure 68**) for signs of wear or cracking. Examine the shift forks at the points where they contact the slider gear (B, **Figure 68**). This surface should be smooth with no signs of wear or damage. Make sure the forks slide

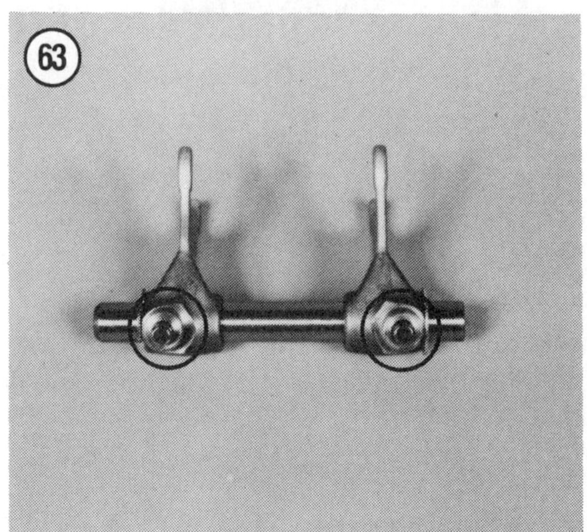

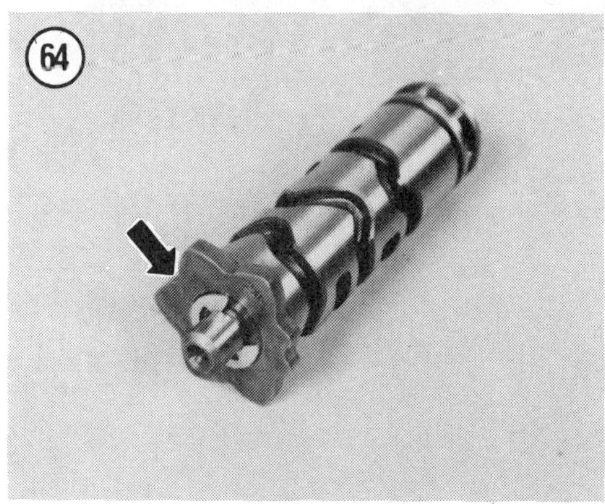

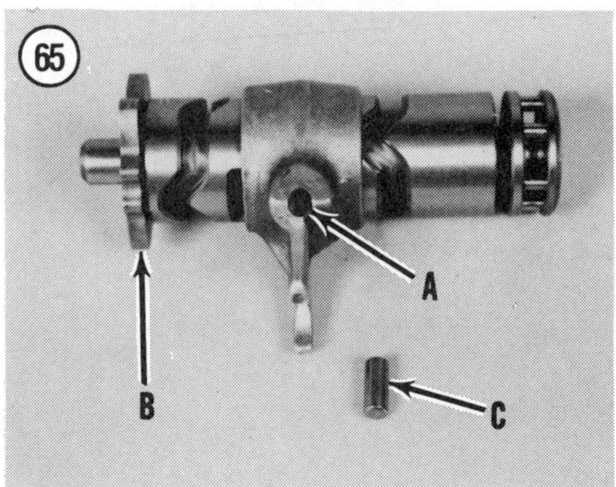

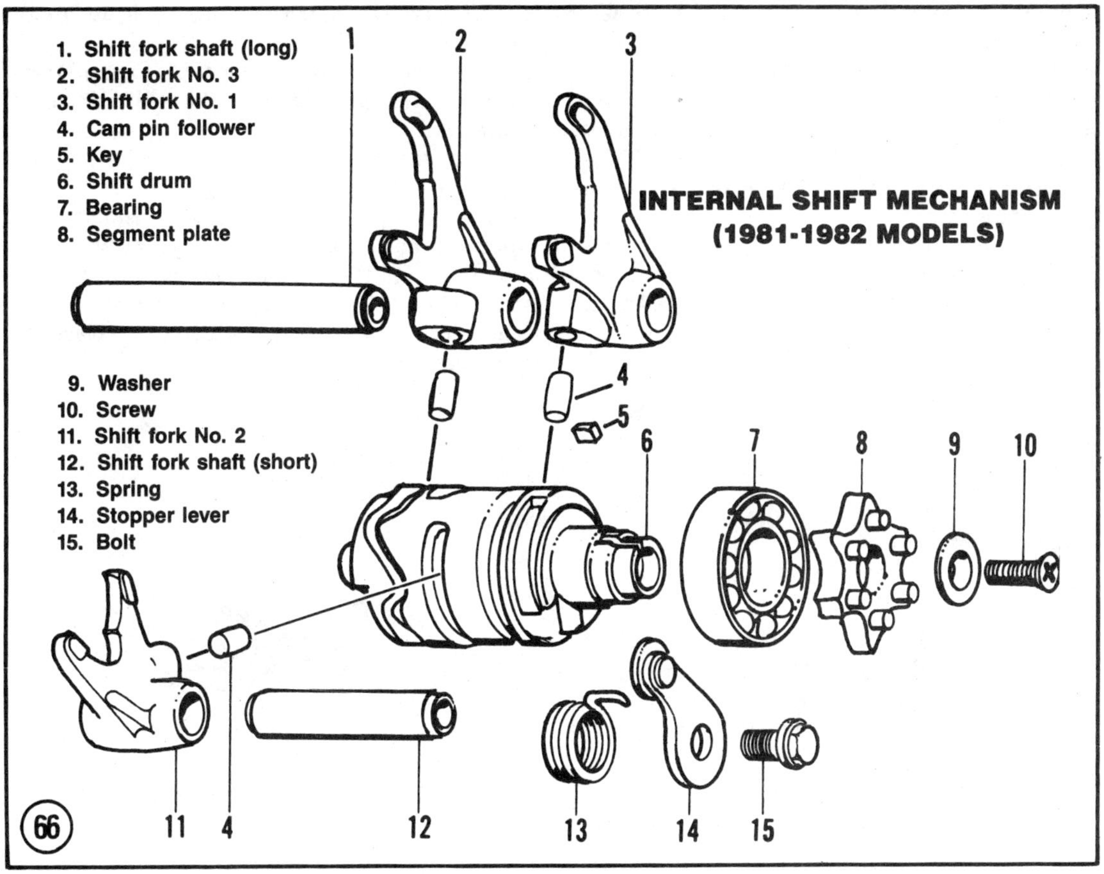

66
INTERNAL SHIFT MECHANISM
(1981-1982 MODELS)
1. Shift fork shaft (long)
2. Shift fork No. 3
3. Shift fork No. 1
4. Cam pin follower
5. Key
6. Shift drum
7. Bearing
8. Segment plate
9. Washer
10. Screw
11. Shift fork No. 2
12. Shift fork shaft (short)
13. Spring
14. Stopper lever
15. Bolt

67
SHIFT DRUM
(1983-ON YZ80)
1. Shift fork shaft (long)
2. Shift fork No. 3
3. Shift fork No. 1
4. Cam pin follower
5. Shift drum
6. Bolt
7. Shift cam stopper
8. Return spring
9. Shift fork No. 2
10. Shift fork shaft (short)

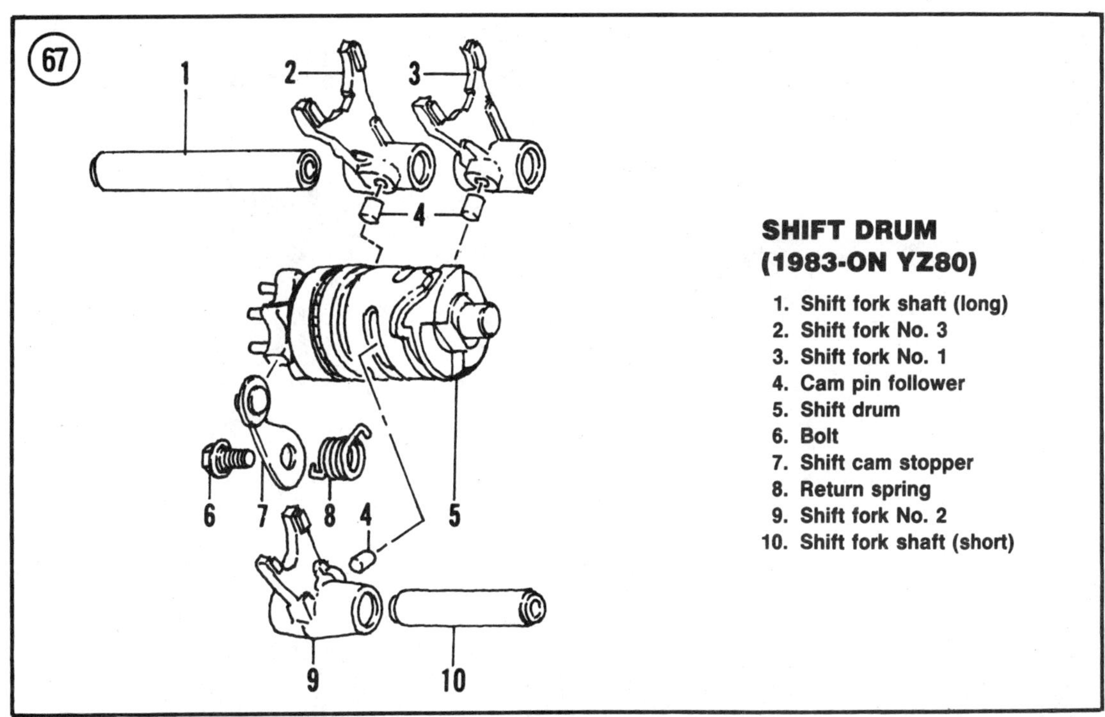

smoothly on their respective shaft (**Figure 69**). Make sure the shaft is not bent. This can be checked by removing the shift forks from the shaft and rolling the shaft on a piece of glass. Any clicking noise detected indicates that the shaft is bent.

2. Check the shift fork pins (C, **Figure 68**) for wear or looseness.
3. Check for any arc-shaped wear or burn marks on the shift forks. This indicates that the shift fork has come in contact with the gear. The fork fingers have become excessively worn and the fork must be replaced.
4. Check grooves in the shift drum (**Figure 70**) for wear or roughness.
5. Check the shift drum segment (A, **Figure 71**) for wear or damage. Replace the shift drum if damaged.
6. Check the shift drum bearing (B, **Figure 71**) for any signs of wear or damage. On 1981-1982 models, the shift drum can be disassembled and worn or damaged parts replaced separately. During assembly, apply Loctite 242 (blue) onto the Phillips screw. On 1983 and later models, the shift drum cannot be disassembled; if necessary, replace the shift drum assembly.

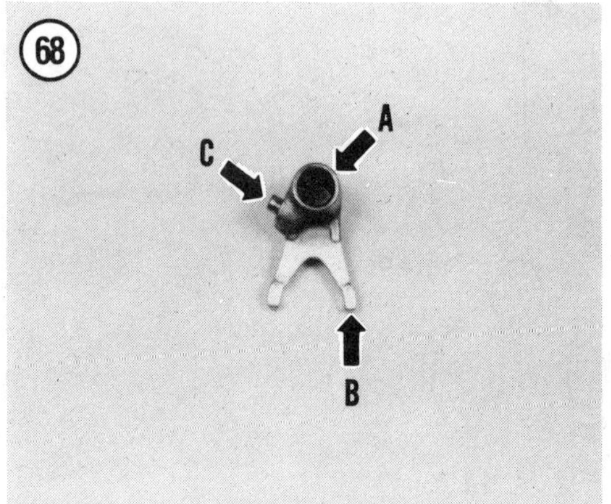

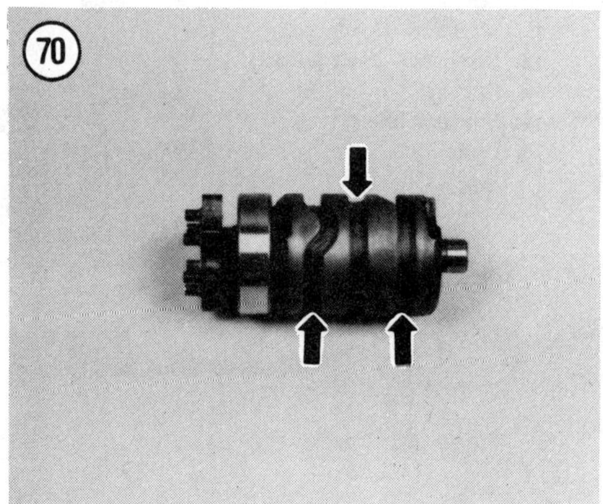

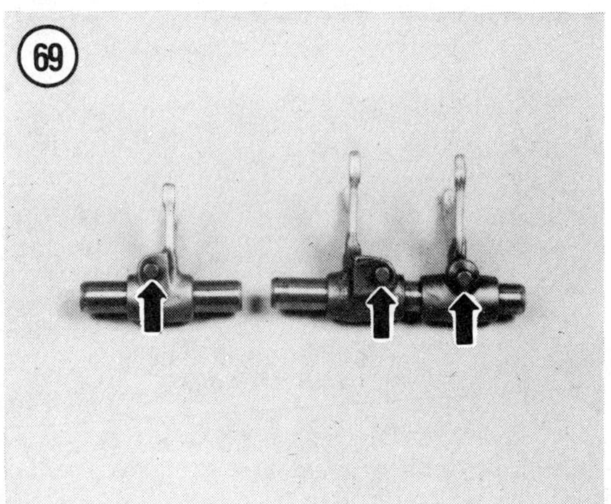

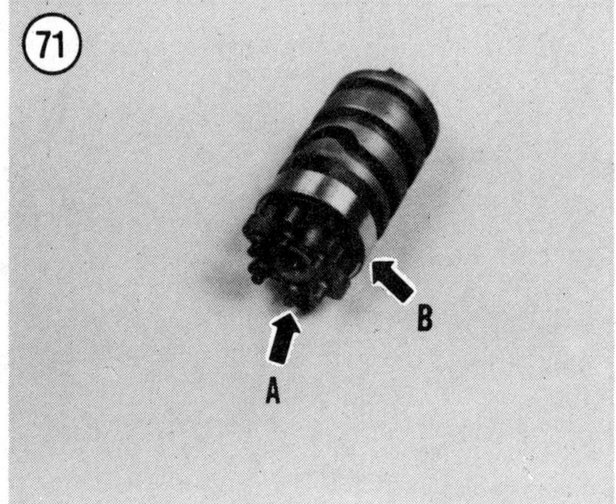

CHAPTER EIGHT

FUEL AND EXHAUST SYSTEMS

The fuel system consists of the fuel tank, shutoff valve and a single Mikuni carburetor and air cleaner. There are slight differences among the various models and they are noted in the various procedures.

The exhaust system consists of an exhaust pipe assembly and a silencer.

This chapter includes service procedures for all parts of the fuel system and exhaust system.

Carburetor specifications are listed in **Table 1** (end of chapter).

The air cleaner must be cleaned frequently. Refer to Chapter Three for specific procedures and service intervals.

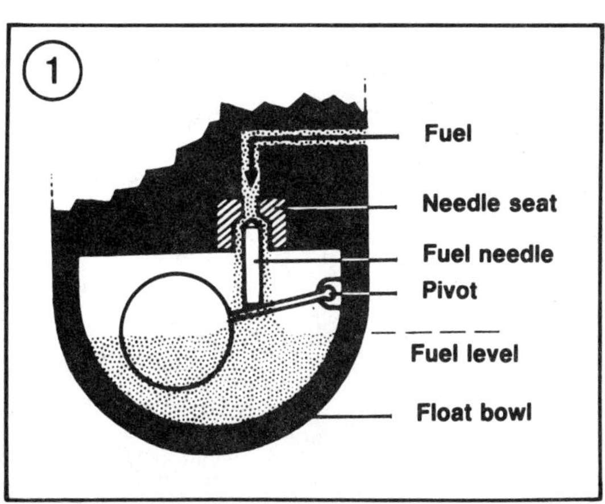

CARBURETOR OPERATION

For proper operation, a gasoline engine must be supplied with fuel and air mixed in proper proportions by weight. A mixture in which there is an excess of fuel is said to be rich. A lean mixture is one which contains insufficient fuel. A properly adjusted carburetor supplies the proper mixture to the engine under all operating conditions.

Mikuni carburetors consist of several major systems. A float and float valve mechanism maintain a constant fuel level in the float bowl. The pilot system supplies fuel at low speeds. The main fuel system supplies fuel at medium and high speeds. Finally a starter (choke) system supplies a rich mixture needed to start a cold engine.

Float Mechanism

To assure a steady supply of fuel, the carburetor is equipped with a float valve through which fuel flows by gravity from the gas tank into the float bowl (**Figure 1**). Inside the bowl is a combined float assembly that moves up and down with the fuel level. Resting on the float arm is a float needle, which rides inside the float valve. The float valve regulates fuel flow into the float bowl. The float needle and float valve contact surfaces are machined very accurately to insure correct fuel flow calibration. As the float rises, the float needle rises inside the float valve and blocks it, so that when the fuel has reached the required level in the float bowl, no more fuel can enter.

Pilot and Main Fuel Systems

The carburetor's purpose is to supply and atomize fuel and mix it in correct proportions with air that is drawn in through the air intake. At primary throttle openings (from idle to 1/8 throttle) a small amount of fuel is siphoned through the pilot jet by suction from the incoming air (**Figure 2**). As the throttle is opened further, the air stream begins to siphon fuel through the main jet and needle jet. The tapered needle increases the effective flow capacity of the needle jet as it rises with the throttle slide, in that it occupies progressivly less of the area of the needle jet (**Figure 3**). In addition, the amount of cutaway in the leading edge of the throttle slide aids in controlling the fuel/air mixture during partial throttle openings.

At full throttle, the carburetor venturi is fully open and the needle is lifted far enough to permit the main jet to flow at full capacity. See **Figure 4** and **Figure 5**.

Starting System

The starting system consists of a starter plunger, mixing tube, starter jet and air passage (**Figure 6**). When the plunger valve is lifted, it opens the air passage permitting air to flow through the passage where it siphons fuel through the starter jet, into the mixing tube and then into the air passage where it is mixed (fuel-rich) and discharged into the throttle bore.

CARBURETOR SERVICE (1978-1982)

Major carburetor service (removal and cleaning) should be performed after every race on competition bikes. On a bike that is used for fun on weekends, it should be performed whenever the engine is decarbonized or when poor engine performance, hesitation, and little or no response to mixture adjustment is observed. The service interval time will become natural to you after owning and running the bike for a period of time.

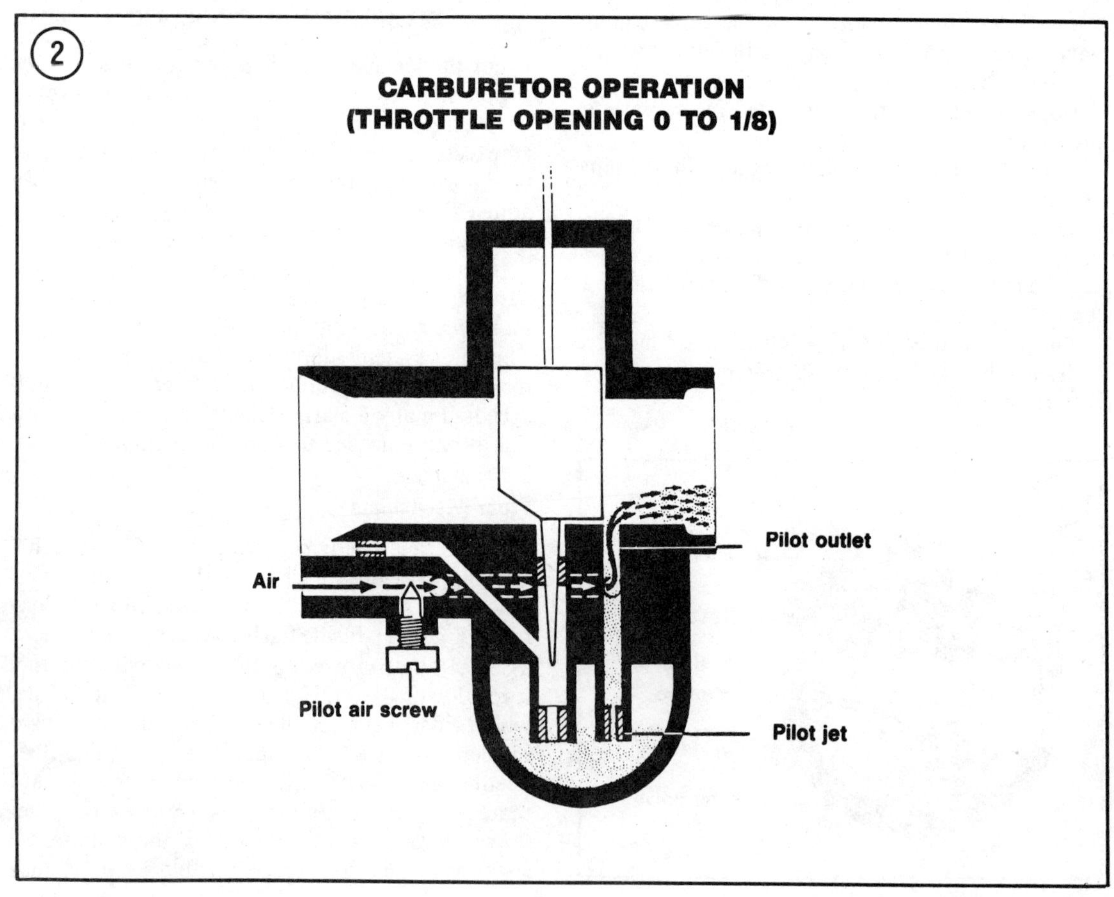

(3)

CARBURETOR OPERATION (THROTTLE OPENING 1/8 to 1/4)

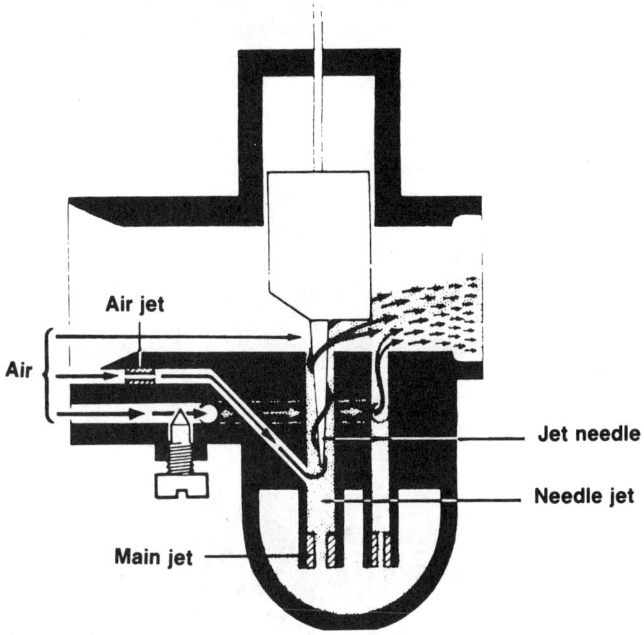

(4)

CARBURETOR OPERATION (THROTTLE OPENING 1/4 to 3/4)

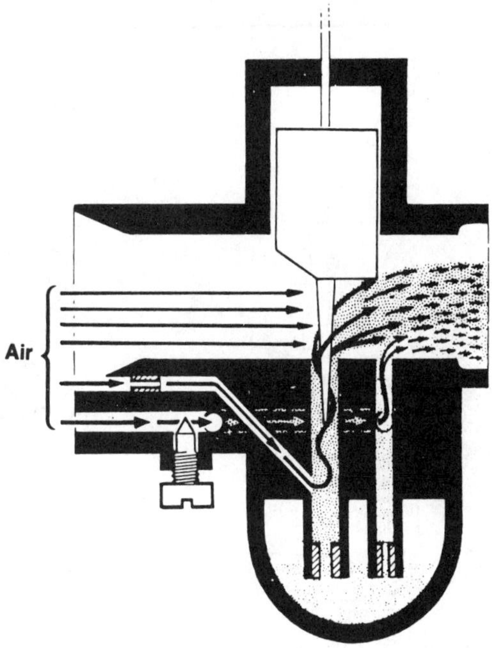

Carburetor Identification

The Mikuni carburetor used on the YZ80 differs slightly from the one used on YZ50 and YZ60 models, so it is important to pay particular attention to the location and order of parts during disassembly.

Refer to **Table 1** at the end of this chapter for carburetor specifications.

Removal/Installation

1. Place a workstand under the frame to support the motorcycle securely.
2. Turn the fuel shutoff valve to the OFF position (**Figure 7**) and remove the fuel line to the carburetor.
3. If necessary, remove the fuel tank as described in this chapter.

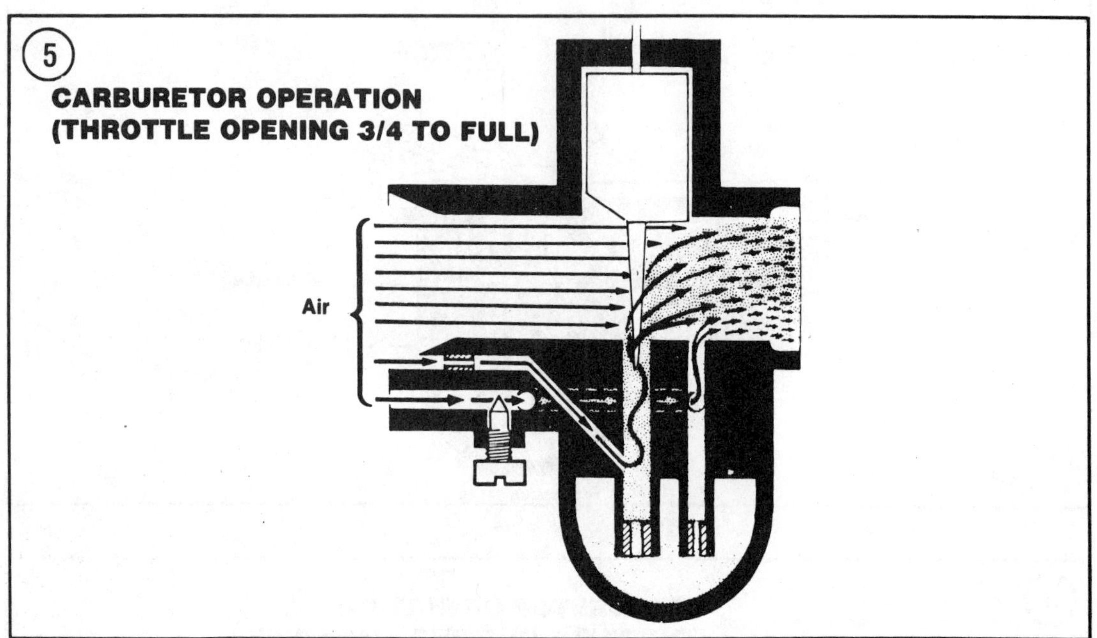

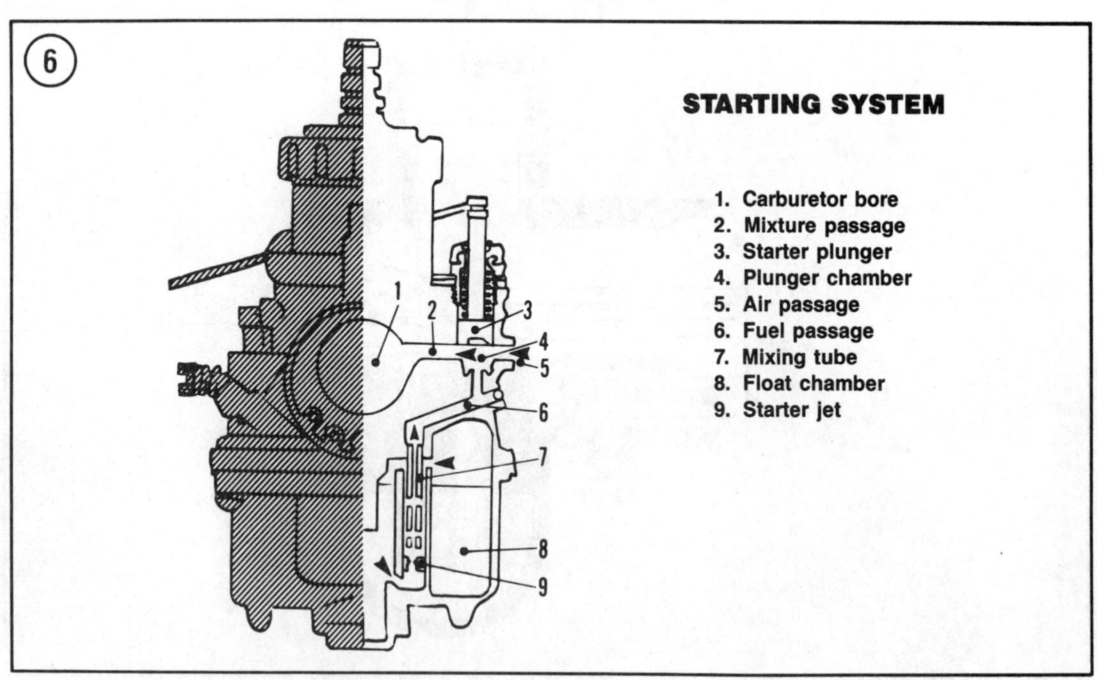

NOTE
Before removing the top cap, thoroughly clean the area around it so no dirt will fall into the carburetor.

4. Unscrew the carburetor top cap (A, **Figure 8**) and pull the throttle valve assembly up and out of the carburetor.

NOTE
If the top cover and slide assembly are not going to be removed for cleaning, wrap them in a clean shop cloth or place them in a plastic bag to help keep them clean.

5. *YZ50 models:* Remove the Allen bolts (**Figure 9**) securing the front of the carburetor and loosen the screws on the rear clamp. Slide the clamp off of the carburetor.

6. *YZ60 and YZ80 models:* Loosen the screws on both clamps (B, **Figure 8**) on the rubber boots. Slide the clamps away from the carburetor.

7. Make sure all overflow and drain tubes are free (**Figure 10**).

8. Carefully work the carburetor free from the rubber boots and remove it.

9. Take the carburetor to a workbench for disassembly and cleaning.

10. Install by reversing these removal steps, noting the following.

11. *YZ60 and YZ80 models:* When installing the carburetor onto the engine side be sure to align the

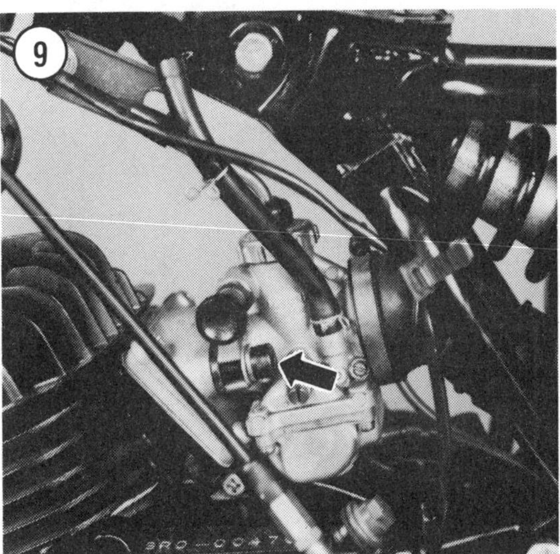

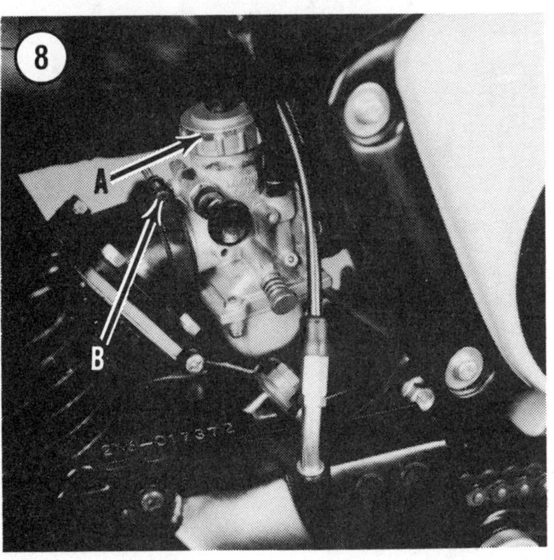

boss on the carburetor with the groove in the rubber boot (**Figure 11**).

12. *YZ60 and YZ80:* When installing the throttle valve assembly, make sure the groove in the slide aligns with the pin in the front of the carburetor body.

NOTE
YZ50 models do not have a groove in the throttle valve slide.

Disassembly/Assembly (1978-1982)

Refer to **Figure 12** (YZ50), **Figure 13** (YZ60) or **Figure 14** (YZ80) for this procedure.

The carburetors are basically the same even though minor variations exist between different models. Where differences occur they are identified.

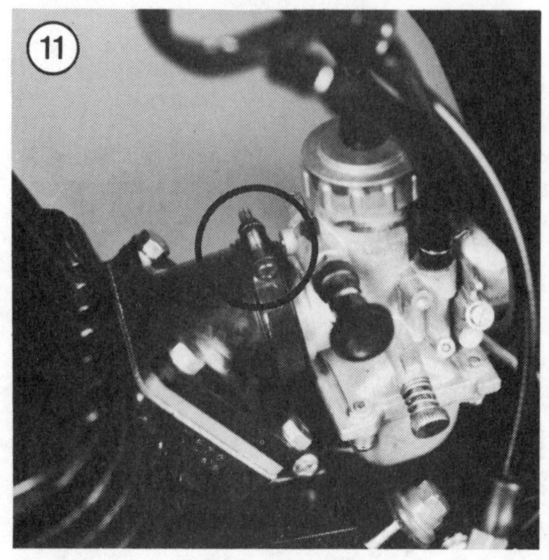
11

13

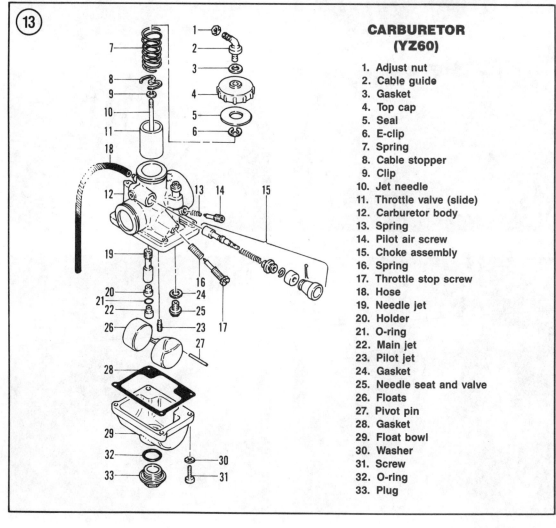

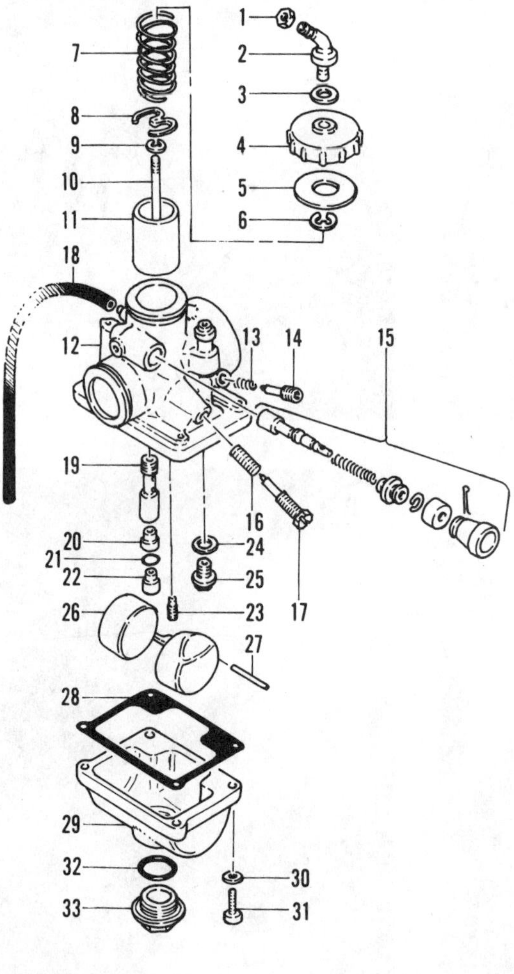

CARBURETOR (YZ60)

1. Adjust nut
2. Cable guide
3. Gasket
4. Top cap
5. Seal
6. E-clip
7. Spring
8. Cable stopper
9. Clip
10. Jet needle
11. Throttle valve (slide)
12. Carburetor body
13. Spring
14. Pilot air screw
15. Choke assembly
16. Spring
17. Throttle stop screw
18. Hose
19. Needle jet
20. Holder
21. O-ring
22. Main jet
23. Pilot jet
24. Gasket
25. Needle seat and valve
26. Floats
27. Pivot pin
28. Gasket
29. Float bowl
30. Washer
31. Screw
32. O-ring
33. Plug

(12)

CARBURETOR ASSEMBLY (YZ50)

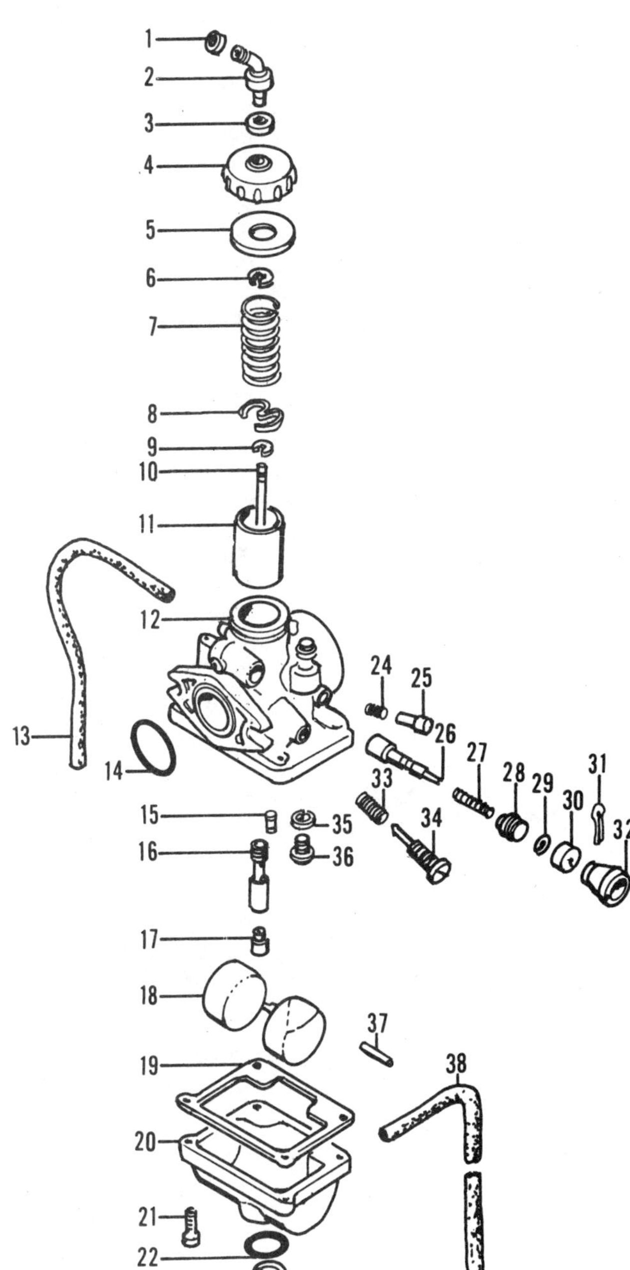

1. Adjust nut
2. Cable guide
3. O-ring
4. Top cap
5. Seal
6. E-clip
7. Throttle valve spring
8. Cable stopper
9. Clip
10. Jet needle
11. Throttle valve (slide)
12. Carburetor body
13. Vent tube
14. O-ring
15. Pilot jet
16. Needle jet
17. Main jet
18. Float
19. Gasket
20. Float bowl
21. Screw
22. O-ring seal
23. Drain plug
24. Spring
25. Pilot air screw
26. Plunger
27. Spring
28. Plunger cap
29. Plunger clip
30. Plunger cap cover
31. Cotter pin
32. Holder
33. Spring
34. Throttle stop screw
35. Valve seat washer
36. Valve seat assembly
37. Float pivot pin
38. Overflow tube

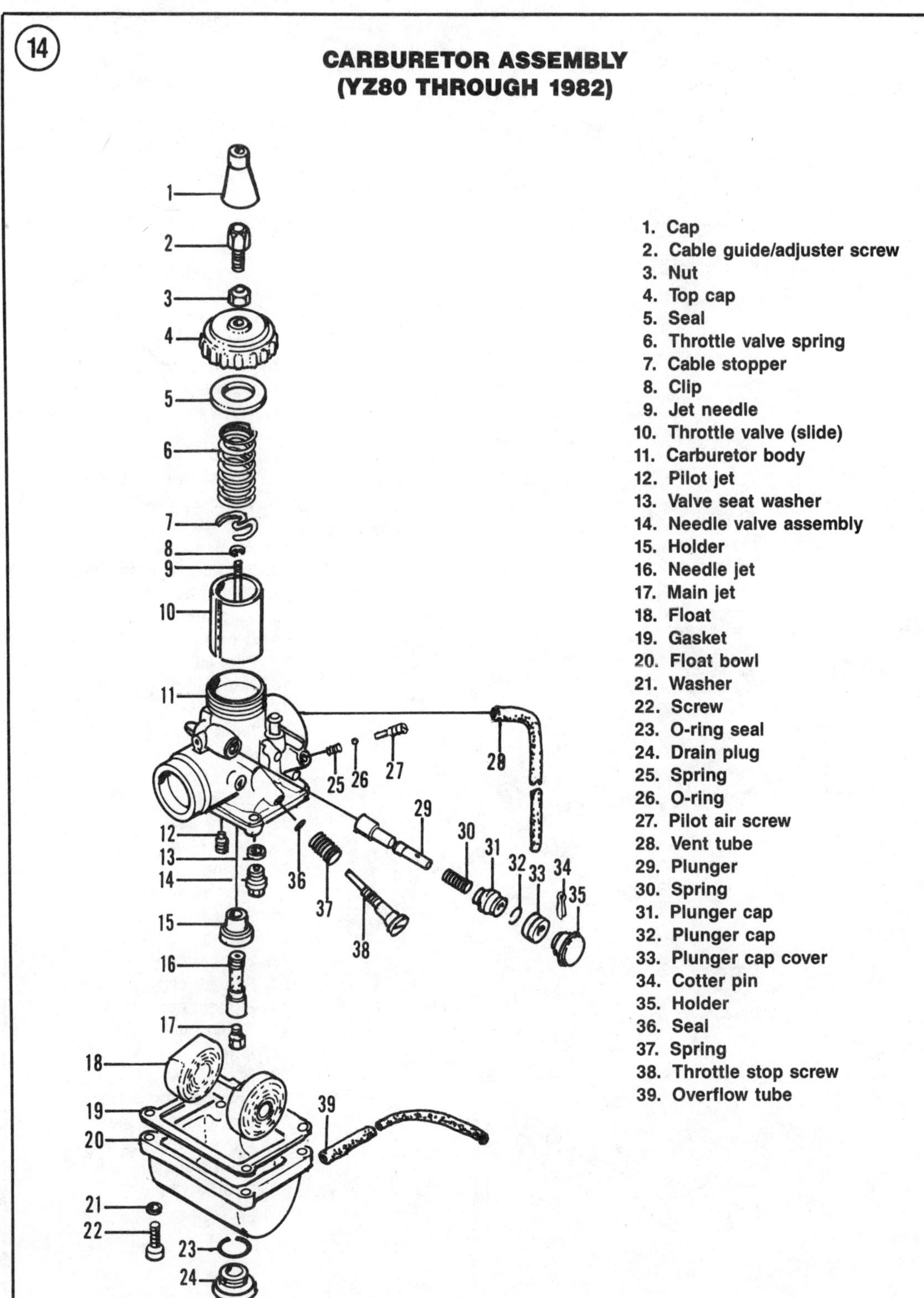
14
CARBURETOR ASSEMBLY
(YZ80 THROUGH 1982)
1
2
3
4
5
6
7
8
9
10
11
12
13
14
15
16
17
18
19
20
21
22
23
24
25
26
27
28
29
30
31
32
33
34
35
36
37
38
39
1. Cap
2. Cable guide/adjuster screw
3. Nut
4. Top cap
5. Seal
6. Throttle valve spring
7. Cable stopper
8. Clip
9. Jet needle
10. Throttle valve (slide)
11. Carburetor body
12. Pilot jet
13. Valve seat washer
14. Needle valve assembly
15. Holder
16. Needle jet
17. Main jet
18. Float
19. Gasket
20. Float bowl
21. Washer
22. Screw
23. O-ring seal
24. Drain plug
25. Spring
26. O-ring
27. Pilot air screw
28. Vent tube
29. Plunger
30. Spring
31. Plunger cap
32. Plunger cap
33. Plunger cap cover
34. Cotter pin
35. Holder
36. Seal
37. Spring
38. Throttle stop screw
39. Overflow tube

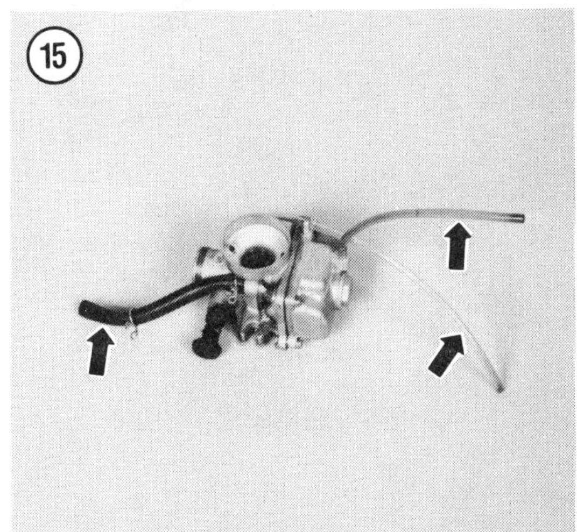

1. Remove the fuel line and all drain and overflow tubes (**Figure 15**).
2. Remove the screws (A, **Figure 16**) securing the float bowl and remove it. Unscrew the bowl plug (B, **Figure 16**) and O-ring seal.
3. Remove the float pin (**Figure 17**) and float assembly.
4. Remove the float valve needle, seat and washer (**Figure 18**).
5. Remove the main jet (**Figure 19**).
6. Remove the main jet holder/washer (**Figure 20**).

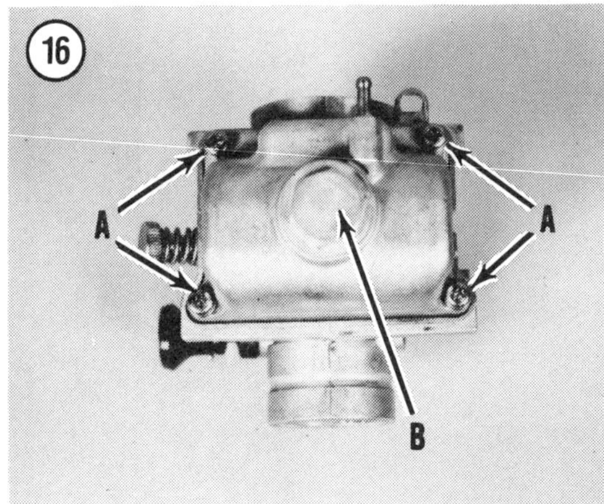

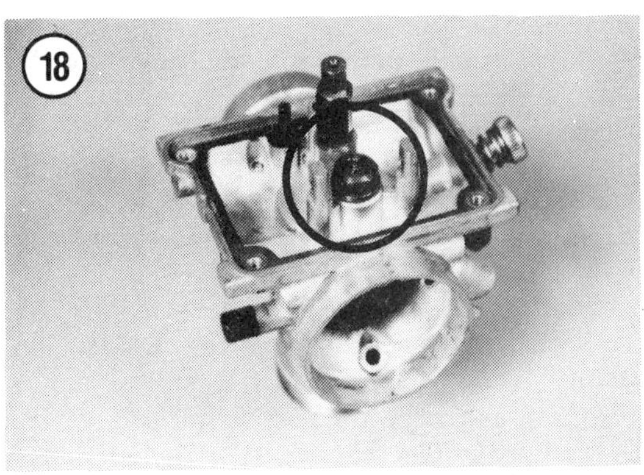

8

NOTE
*On YZ60 models, do not lose the O-ring installed between the main jet and holder (**Figure 13**).*

7. Unscrew the pilot jet (**Figure 21**).
8. Remove the float bowl gasket (**Figure 22**) if it is attached to the carburetor body.
9. Remove the pilot air screw (A, **Figure 23**).
10. Remove the throttle adjust screw and spring (B, **Figure 23**).
11. Remove the choke assembly (C, **Figure 23**).
12. Remove the float bowl gasket if it is attached to the float bowl.
13. *YZ50 models:* Remove the rubber O-ring seal from the carburetor air horn facing toward the reed valve assembly.
14. At the end of the throttle cable, compress the throttle valve (slide) spring (**Figure 24**).
15. Move the throttle cable end over to the larger hole in the throttle valve (**Figure 25**) and withdraw the cable out through the top and remove it (**Figure 26**).
16. Remove the jet needle from the throttle valve assembly (**Figure 27**).
17. Clean and inspect the carburetor components as described in this chapter.
18. After all parts have been cleaned and dried, reverse these steps to assemble thc carburetor. Note the following.
19. Make sure to install the gasket under the float needle seat (**Figure 28**).
20. *YZ60 models:* Make sure to install the O-ring between the main jet and holder (**Figure 13**).
21. Install the jet needle clip in the correct groove. The standard groove is listed in **Table 1**.
22. Check the float height and adjust if necessary. Refer to *Float Adjustment* in this chapter.
23. After the carburetor has been assembled adjust the pilot screw and the idle speed. Refer to *Pilot Screw and Idle Speed Adjustment* in Chapter Three.

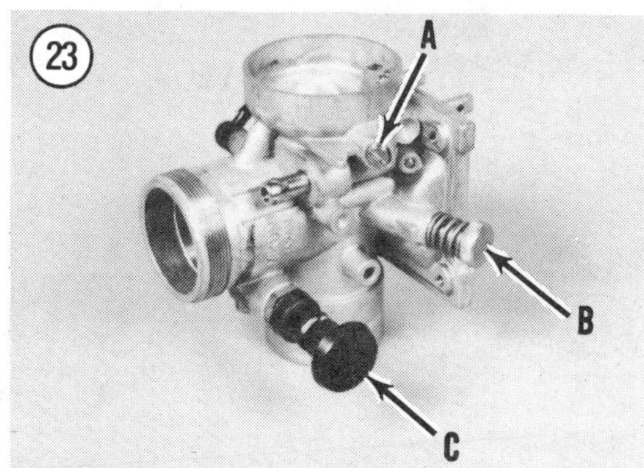

Disassembly/Reassembly (1983-on)

Refer to **Figure 29** for this procedure.

1. Remove the pilot screw and spring (A, **Figure 30**).
2. Remove the throttle stop screw and spring (B, **Figure 30**).
3. Remove the fuel line and all drain and overflow tubes (A, **Figure 31**).
4. Remove the screws securing the float bowl (B, **Figure 31**) and remove it. Unscrew the bowl plug (C, **Figure 31**) and O-ring seal.

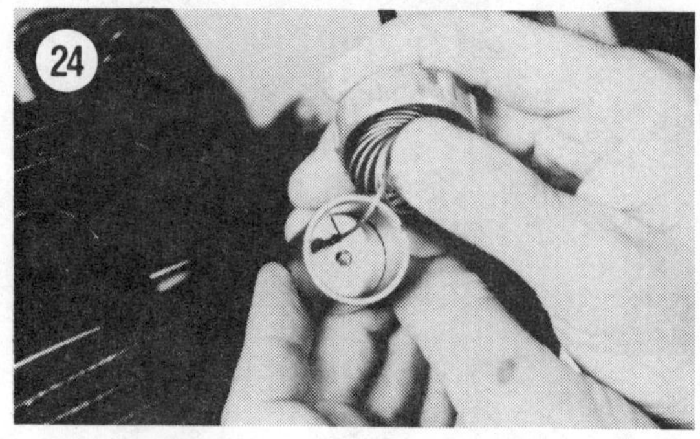

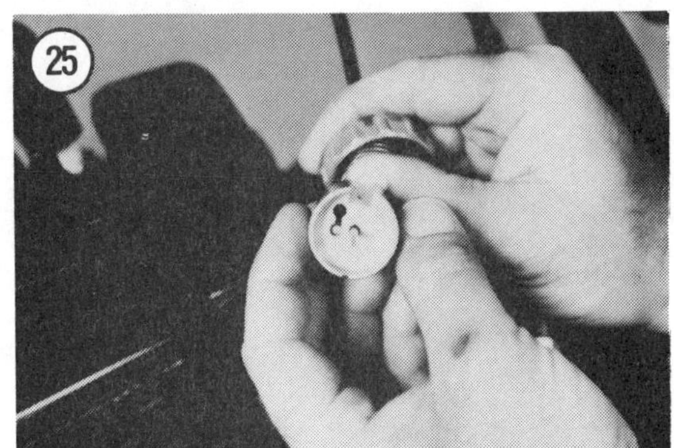

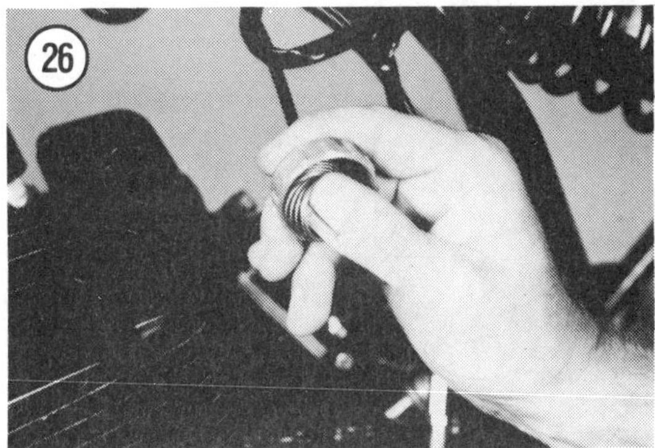

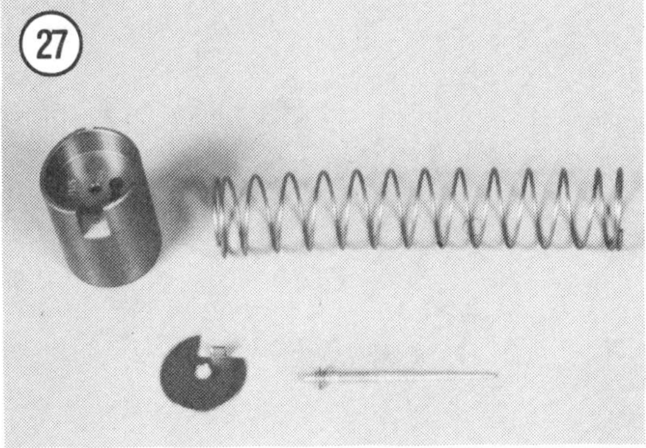

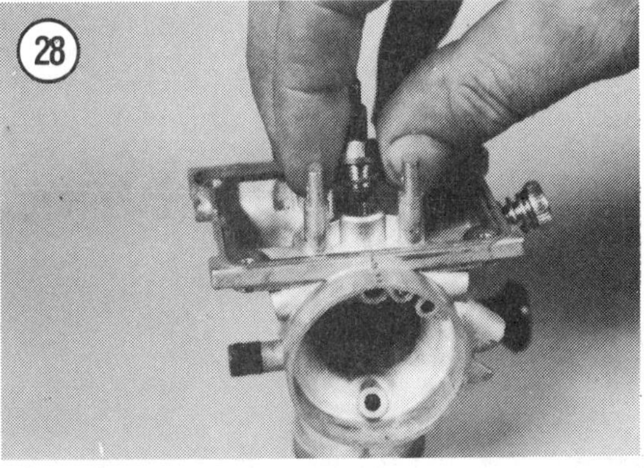

29

CARBURETOR (1983-ON YZ80)

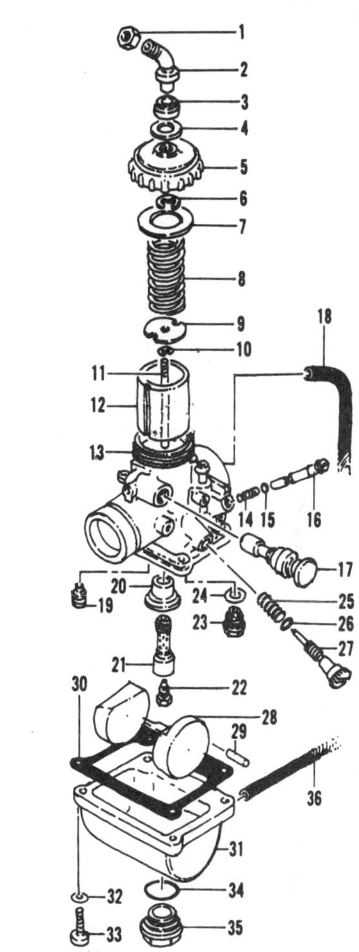

1. Nut	19. Pilot jet
2. Cable guide	20. Washer
3. Grommet	21. Needle jet
4. Washer	22. Main jet
5. Top cap	23. Valve seat
6. Circlip	24. Washer
7. Rubber washer	25. Spring
8. Spring	26. O-ring
9. Spring seat	27. Throttle stop screw
10. Circlip	28. Floats
11. Jet needle	29. Float pivot pin
12. Throttle valve (slide)	30. Gasket
13. Carburetor body	31. Float bowl
14. Spring	32. Lockwasher
15. O-ring	33. Screw
16. Pilot screw	34. O-ring
17. Choke	35. Drain plug
18. Hose	36. Hose

5. Remove the main jet (**Figure 32**).
6. See **Figure 33**. Remove the needle jet (A) and the plastic washer (B).
7. Unscrew and remove the pilot jet (**Figure 34**).
8. Remove the float pin (**Figure 35**) and float assembly.
9. Remove the float valve needle (**Figure 36**), seat and washer (**Figure 37**).
10. Unscrew the choke (**Figure 38**) and remove it. See **Figure 39**.
11. Remove the float bowl gasket (**Figure 40**).
12. At the end of the throttle cable, compress the throttle valve (slide) spring (**Figure 24**).
13. Move the throttle cable end over to the larger hole in the throttle valve (**Figure 25**) and withdraw the cable out through the top and remove it (**Figure 26**).
14. Remove the jet needle from the throttle valve assembly (**Figure 27**).
15. Clean and inspect the carburetor components as described in this chapter.
16. After all parts have been cleaned and dried, reverse these steps to assemble the carburetor. Note the following.
17. Make sure to install the gasket under the float needle seat (**Figure 28**).
18. Install the jet needle clip in the correct groove. The standard groove is listed in **Table 1**.
19. Check the float height and adjust if necessary. Refer to *Float Adjustment* in this chapter.

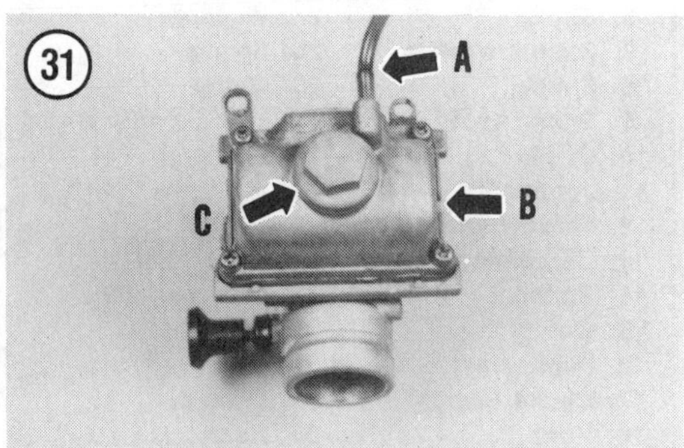

20. After the carburetor has been disassembled adjust the pilot screw and the idle speed. Refer to *Pilot Screw and Idle Speed Adjustment* in Chapter Three.

Cleaning/Inspection (All Models)

1. Clean all parts, except rubber or plastic parts, in spray carburetor cleaner.
2. Remove all parts from the cleaner and wash thoroughly in soap and water. Rinse with clean water and dry thoroughly.
3. Blow out the jets with compressed air. *Do not* use a piece of wire to clean them as minor gouges in the jet can alter flow rate and upset the fuel/air mixture. If compressed air is not available, use a piece of straw from a broom to clean the jets.
4. Be sure to clean out the float bowl overflow tube from both ends.
5. Inspect the tip of the float valve (**Figure 41**) for wear or damage. Replace the valve and seat as a set.

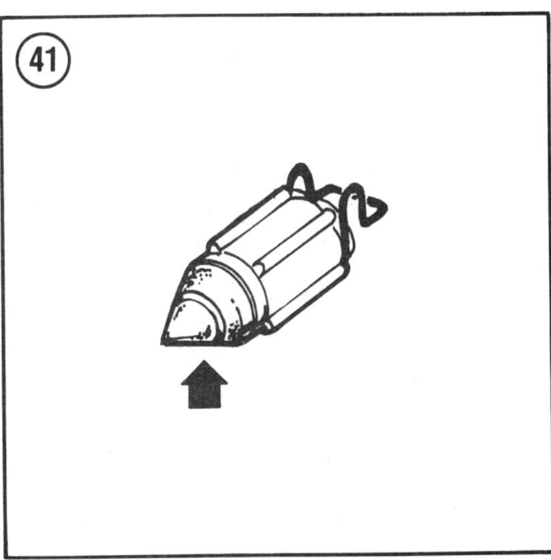

6. O-ring seals tend to become hardened after prolonged use and heat and therefore lose their ability to seal properly. Inspect all O-rings and replace if necessary.
7. Check the float assembly (**Figure 42**) for leaks. Place the floats in a container of water and push them down. There should be no signs of bubbles. Replace the floats if they leak.
8. Check the pilot air screw (A, **Figure 43**) tip for scratches, wear or damage. Replace the screw and/or spring as required.
9. Check the idle stop screw (B, **Figure 43**) for tip wear or thread damage. Replace the screw and/or spring as required.

CARBURETOR ADJUSTMENTS

Float Adjustment

The carburetor assembly has to be removed and partially disassembled for this adjustment.

NOTE
*Before performing this adjustment, remove the float assembly and check the condition of the float valve and valve seat (**Figure 44**). It they are worn this adjustment will be incorrect. Replace the valve and seat as an assembly.*

1. Remove the carburetor as described under *Carburetor Removal/Installation* in this chapter.
2. Remove the float bowl (B, **Figure 31**) from the main body.
3. Remove the float bowl gasket.
4. Measure the height of the float above the carburetor body (**Figure 45**). Use a float level gauge (**Figure 46**) or vernier caliper. Hold the carburetor so the float tang is just touching the float needle—not pushing it down. The correct level is listed in **Table 1**.
5. Adjust by carefully bending the tang on the float arm with a small screwdriver (**Figure 47**).

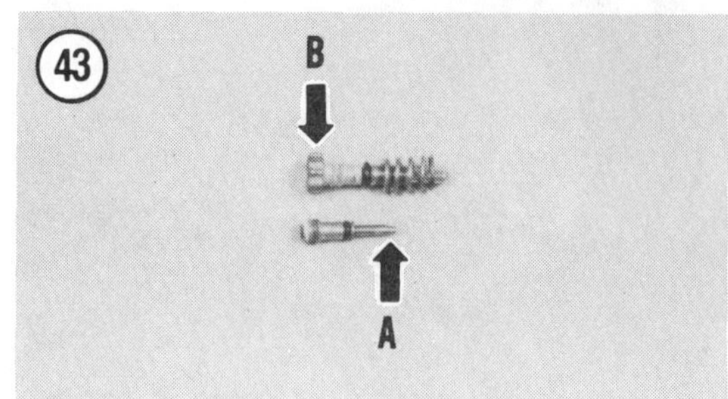

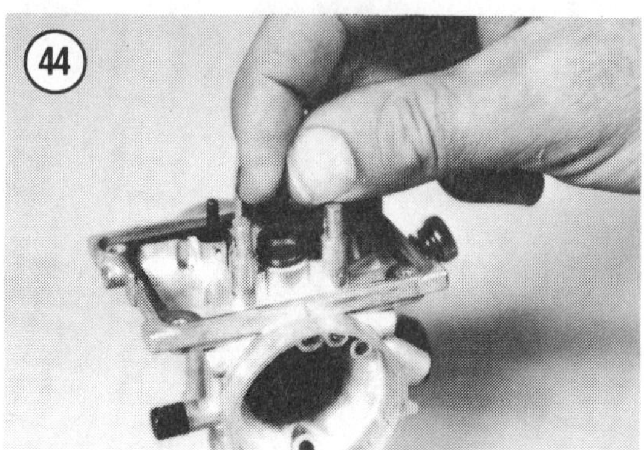

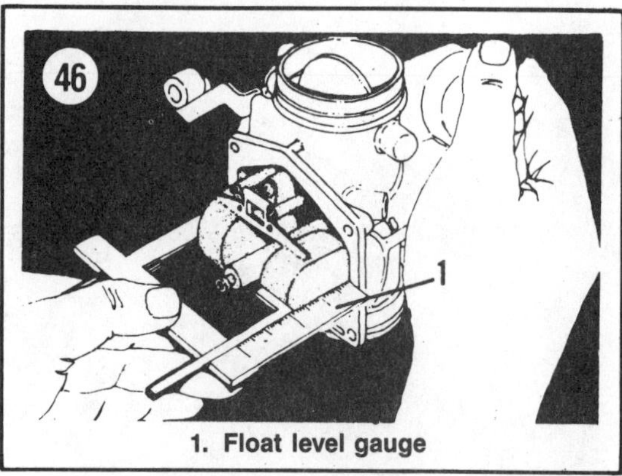

1. Float level gauge

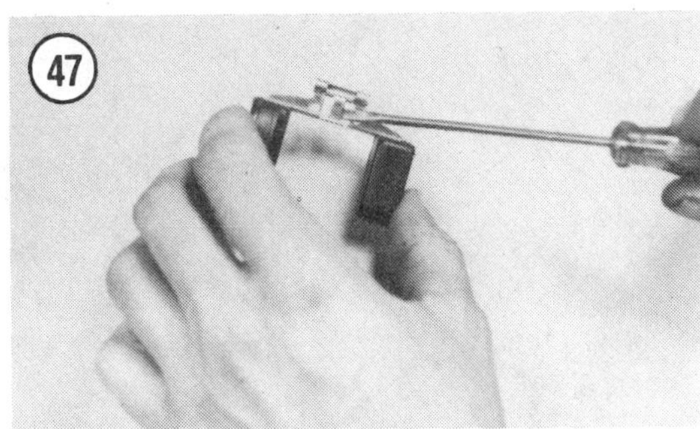

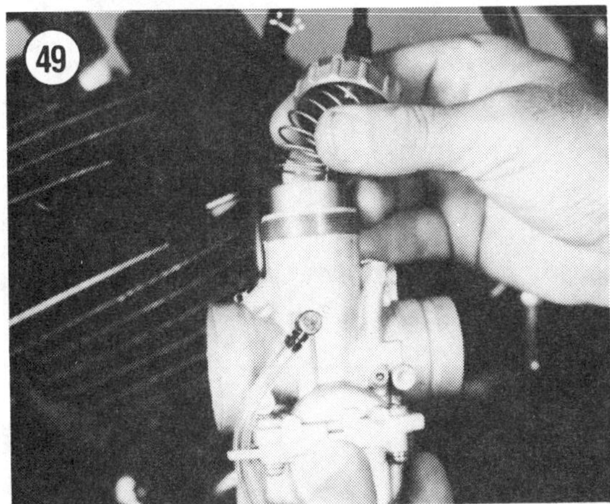

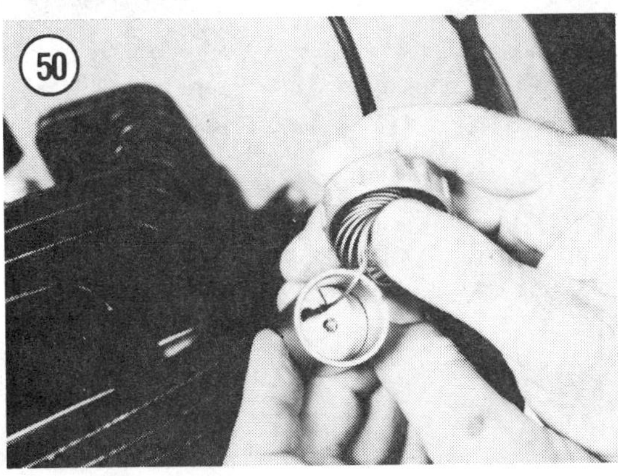

NOTE

Both float chambers must be at the same height.

6. If the float level is set too high, the result will be a rich fuel/air mixture. If it is set too low the mixture will be too lean.
7. Reassemble and install the carburetor.

Needle Jet Adjustment

The position of the needle jet can be adjusted to affect the fuel/air mixture for medium throttle openings.

The top of the carburetor must be removed for this adjustment. It is easier to perform this procedure with the fuel tank removed but it can be accomplished with it in place.

1.Turn the fuel shutoff valve to the OFF position and disconnect the fuel line from the carburetor.

NOTE

Before removing the top cap, thoroughly clean the area around it so no dirt will fall into the carburetor.

2A. *YZ50 models:* It is necessary to remove the carburetor as it cannot be pivoted. Refer to *Carburetor Removal/Installation* in this chapter.
2B. *YZ60 and YZ80:* Loosen the 2 screws on the clamping bands (**Figure 48**) on each side of the carburetor and pivot the carburetor to one side.
3. Unscrew the carburetor top cap (**Figure 49**) and pull the throttle valve assembly up and out of the carburetor.
4.. At the end of the throttle cable, compress the throttle valve (slide) spring (**Figure 50**).
5. Move the throttle cable end over to the larger hole in the throttle valve (**Figure 51**) and withdraw

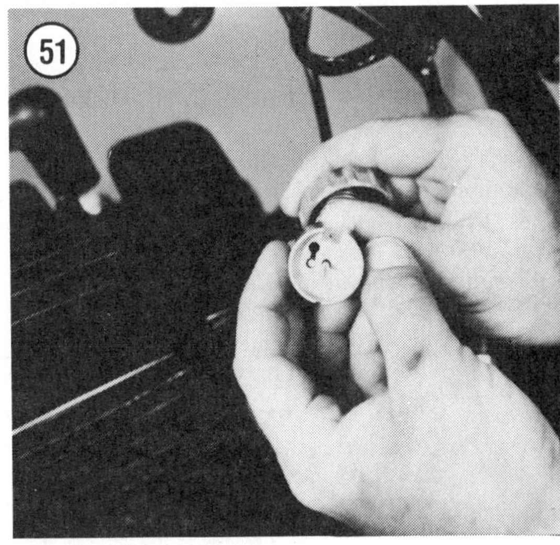

the cable out through the top and remove it (**Figure 52**).
6. Remove the needle jet from the throttle valve assembly.
7. Slide the needle jet out of the connector and note the position of the clip. Raising the needle (lowering the clip) will enrich the mixture during mid-throttle opening, while lowering it (raising the clip) will lean the mixture. Refer to **Figure 53**.
8. Refer to **Table 1** at the end of the chapter for standard clip position for all models.
9. Reassemble and install the top cap (**Figure 54**).

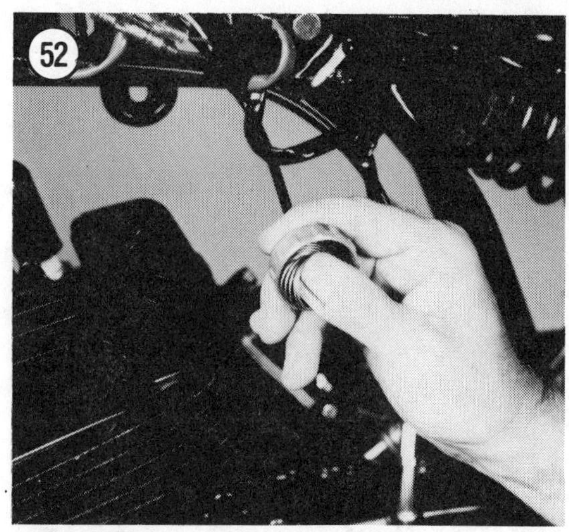
52

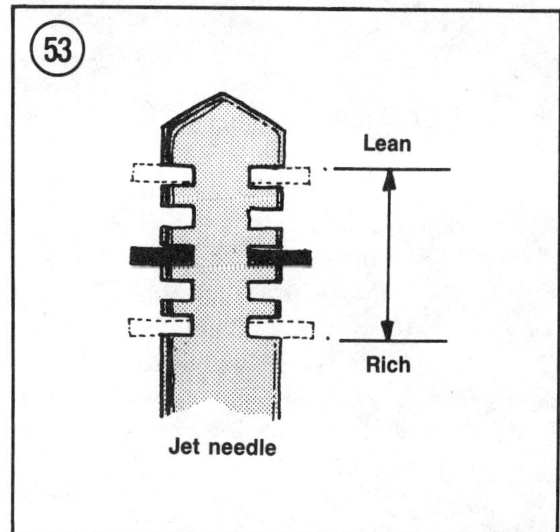

Pilot Screw and Idle Speed Adjustment

Refer to Chapter Three.

High Altitude Adjustment (Main Jet Replacement)

If the bike is going to be raced or ridden for any sustained period of time in high elevations (above 5,000 ft.; 1,500 m), the main jet should be changed to a one-step smaller jet; never change the jet by more than one size at a time without test riding the bike and running a spark plug test. Refer to *Reading Spark Plugs* in Chapter Three.

The carburetor is set with thc standard jet for normal sea level conditions. But if the bike is run at higher altitudes or under heavy load—deep sand or mud—the main jet should be replaced or it will run too rich and carbon up quickly.

CAUTION
If the bike has been rejetted for high altitude operation (smaller jet), it must be changed back to the standard main jet if ridden at altitudes below 5,000 ft. (1,500 m). Engine overheating and piston seizure will occur if the engine runs too lean with the smaller jet.

Refer to **Table 1**, at the end of this chapter, for standard main jet size.
1. Turn the fuel shutoff valve to the OFF position and disconnect the fuel line from the carburetor.
2A. *YZ50 models:* It is necessary to remove the carburetor as it cannot be pivoted. Refer to *Carburetor Removal/Installation* in this chapter.
2B. *YZ60 and YZ80 models:* Loosen the 2 screws on the clamping bands (**Figure 48**) on each side of the carburetor and pivot the carburetor to one side.

WARNING
Place a metal container under the cover to catch the fuel that will flow out. Do not let it drain out onto the engine or the bike's frame as it presents a real fire

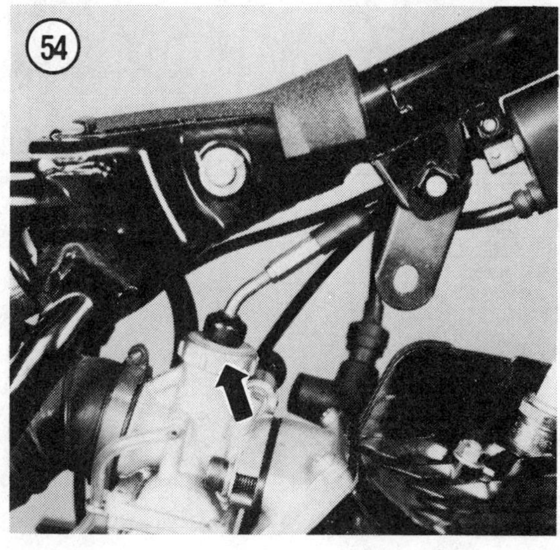
54

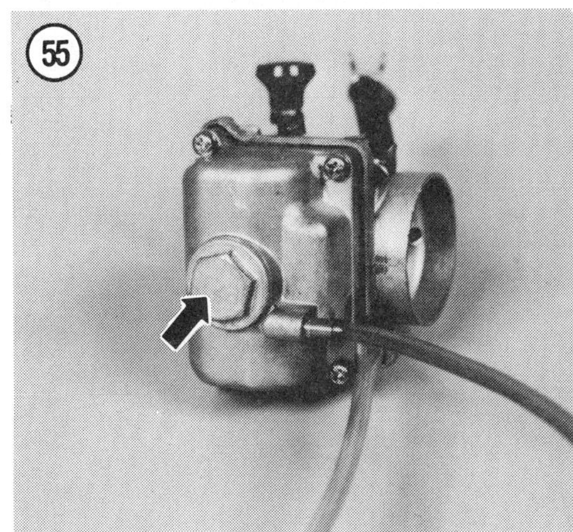

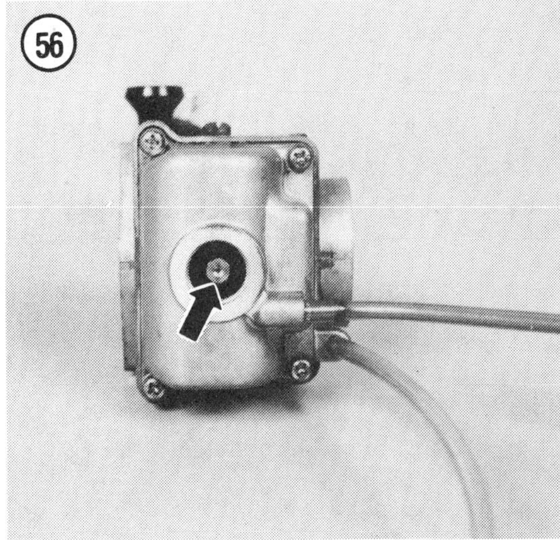

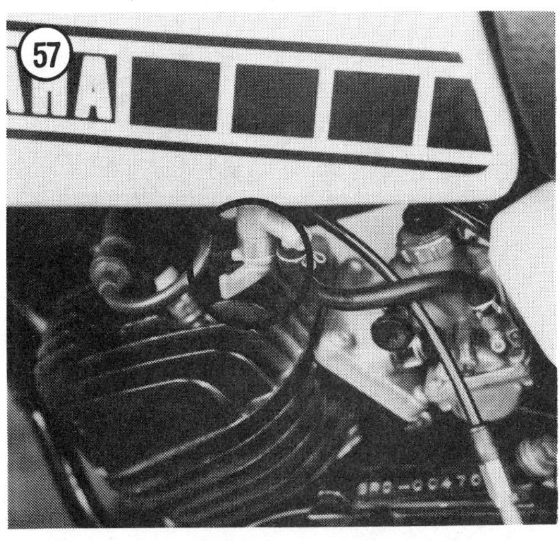

danger. ***Do not perform this procedure with a hot engine.*** *Dispose of the fuel properly; wipe up any that may have spilled on the bike and the floor.*

3. *YZ60 and YZ80 models:* Loosen the main jet cover (float bowl plug) and drain out all fuel in the bowl.
4. On all models remove the bowl plug **(Figure 55)** and O-ring seal.
5. The main jet (**Figure 56**) is directly under the cover. Remove it and replace it with one which is one size smaller; for example, 170 to 160. Remember, change only one jet size at a time, then retest.
6. Install the main jet cover; tighten it securely.
7. *YZ50 models:* Install the carburetor as described under *Carburetor Removal/Installation* in this chapter.
8. *YZ60 and YZ80 models:* Pivot the carburetor back to its original position; make sure it indexes into the slot in the rubber intake tube. Tighten the clamping band screws and reinstall the carburetor fuel line.

FUEL SHUTOFF VALVE

Removal/Installation

1. Remove the fuel tank as described in this chapter.
2. Drain the fuel into a fuel storage container.
3. Remove the screws or nut and remove the fuel shutoff valve.
4. Remove the screw above the handle or on the handle and disassemble the valve. Clean all parts in solvent with a medium soft toothbrush, then dry. Check the small O-ring within the valve and the O-ring gasket; replace if they are starting to deteriorate or get hard. Make sure the spring is not broken or getting soft; replace if necessary.
5. Reassemble the valve and install it on the tank. Don't forget the O-ring gasket between the valve and the tank.

FUEL TANK

Removal/Installation

1. Place a workstand under the frame to support the motorcycle securely.
2. Turn the fuel shutoff valve to the OFF position (**Figure 57**) and remove the fuel line to the carburetor.
3. Remove the seat.
4. Pull the fuel fill cap vent tube free from the steering head area.

5. Remove the bolts and strap securing the fuel tank and remove it.
6. Install by reversing these removal steps. Check for fuel leaks.

FUEL FILTER

The fuel shutoff valve is equipped with a small fuel filter. Due to dirt and residue that is found in gasoline it is a good idea to install an additional inline fuel filter to help keep the carburetor clean. A good quality inline fuel filter (**Figure 58**) is available at most auto and/or motorcycle supply stores. Just cut the flexible fuel line from the fuel tank to the carburetor and install it. You may have to cut out a section of the fuel line the length of the filter, so the fuel line does not get kinked and restrict fuel flow.

YAMAHA ENERGY INDUCTION SYSTEM (YEIS)

Starting in 1982, all YZ80 models are equipped with the Yamaha Energy Induction System (YEIS). See **Figure 59**. The YEIS system reduces airspeed fluctuations through the intake tract. To remove the YEIS chamber, disconnect the hose at the intake manifold (**Figure 60**) and its mounting strap under the fuel tank (**Figure 61**) and remove the YEIS unit. Reverse to install.

CAUTION
Do not attempt to alter or disassemble the YEIS chamber. The chamber is a sealed unit and any tampering will destroy its tuning effect on the engine.

EXHAUST SYSTEM

The exhaust system expansion chamber on a 2-stroke motorcycle engine is much more than a means of routing the exhaust gases to the rear of the bike. It's a vital performance component and frequently, because of its design, it is a vulnerable piece of equipment. Check the exhaust system for deep dents and fractures and repair them as described under *Exhaust System Repairs* at the end of this chapter. Check the expansion chamber frame mounting flanges for fractures and loose bolts and bushings. Check the cylinder mounting flange or collar for tightness. A loose headpipe connection will not only rob the engine of power, it could also damage the piston and cylinder.

The exhaust system consists of an exhaust pipe assembly (head pipe and expansion chamber) and a silencer. This system varies slightly with different models and years. All attachments are basically the same but they all vary a little.

Removal/Installation

1. Remove the seat, fuel tank and both side cover/number plates.
2. Place the bike on a workstand to support it securely.
3. To remove the silencer, loosen the clamping screws (A, **Figure 62**) securing the silencer to the exhaust pipe assembly.

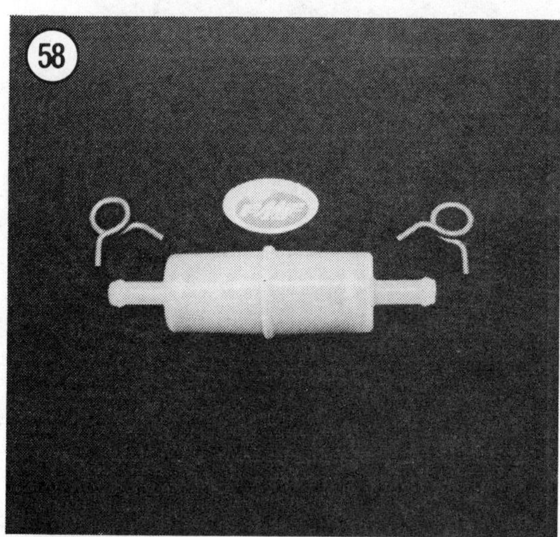
58

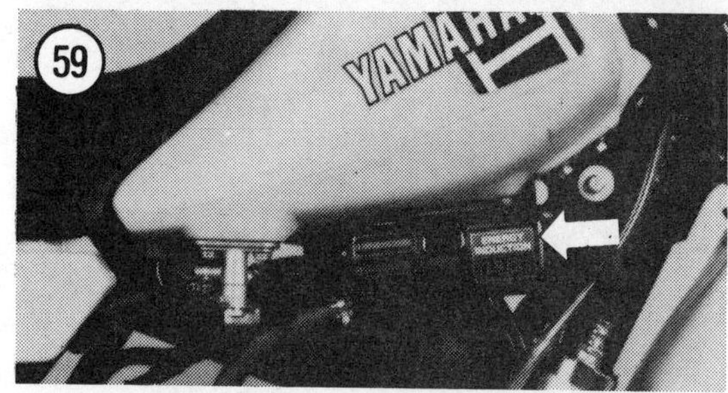

59

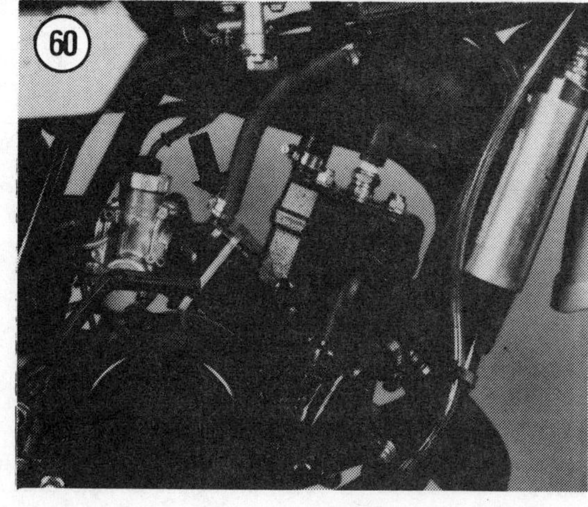
60

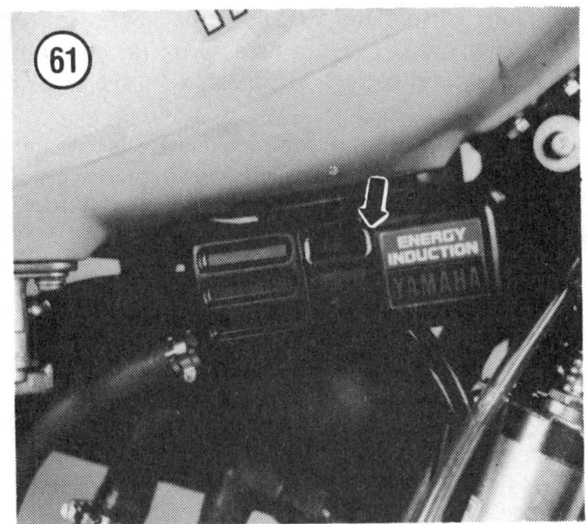

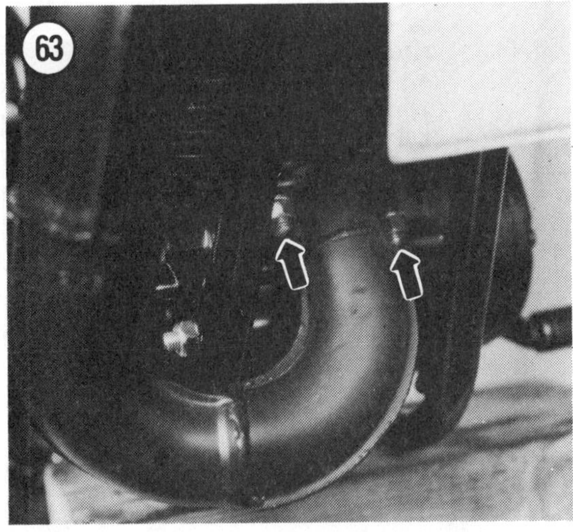

4. Remove the bolt and washer (B, **Figure 62**) securing the silencer to the frame and remove the silencer.
5. Loosen, but do not remove, the bolt and washers (C, **Figure 62**) securing the expansion chamber to the frame.
6. Remove the nuts and washers (**Figure 63**) securing the head pipe to the cylinder exhaust port.
7. Remove the nut and washers loosened in Step 5 and remove the exhaust pipe assembly.
8. Inspect the gaskets at all joints; replace as necessary.
9. Install the exhaust pipe assembly into position and install the frame bolt and washers only finger-tight at this time until the head pipe nuts and washers are installed. This will minimize an exhaust leak at the cylinder.
10. Inspect the head pipe gasket for wear or deterioration. Replace, if necessary.
11. Install the head pipe gasket and install the nuts and washers. Tighten the nuts securely.
12. Tighten the frame bolt securely.
13. Install the silencer and tighten the clamp securely. Tighten the frame bolt securely.
14. Install the fuel tank, seat and side cover/number plates.
15. After installation is complete, make sure there are no exhaust leaks.

EXHAUST SYSTEM REPAIR

A dent in the headpipe or expansion chamber of a 2-stroke exhaust system will alter the system's flow characteristics and degrade performance. Minor damage can be easily repaired if you have welding equipment, some simple body tools and a bodyman's slide hammer.

Small Dents

1. Drill a small hole in the center of the dent. Screw the end of the slide hammer into the hole.
2. Heat the area around the dent evenly with a torch.
3. When the dent is heated to a uniform orange-red color, operate the slide hammer to raise the dent.
4. When the dent is removed, unscrew the slide hammer and weld or braze the drilled hole closed.

Large Dents

Large dents that are not crimped can be removed with heat and a slide hammer as previously described. However, several holes must be drilled along the center of the dent so that it can be pulled out evenly.

If the dent is sharply crimped along the edges, the affected section should be cut out with a hacksaw, straightened with a body dolly and hammer and welded back into place.

Before cutting the exhaust pipe apart, scribe alignment marks over the area where the cuts will be made to aid correct alignment when the pipe is rewelded.

After the welding is completed, wire brush and clean up all welds. Paint the entire pipe with a high-temperature paint to prevent rusting.

Table 1 CARBURETOR SPECIFICATIONS

	YZ50	YZ60H	YZ60J	YZ80E
Model No.	VM20SH	VM24SS	VM24SS	VM26SS
I.D. mark	3R00	4V000	5X100	2J500
Main jet	170	200	200	170
Needle jet	N-8	0-4	0-4	0-0
Pilot jet	27.5	30	30	35
Jet needle	4J13	4G6	4K4	4J13
Clip position	3	3	3	3
Float level	26 mm (1.02 in.)	26 mm (1.02 in.)	21 mm (0.83 in.)	24 mm (0.94 in.)
	YZ80F	**YZ80G**	**YZ80H**	**YZ80J**
Model No.	VM26SS	VM26SS	VM24SS	VM26SS
I.D. mark	2X6-60	3R100	4V100	5X200
Main jet	190	210	190	210
Needle jet	0-0	0-0	0-0	0-0
Pilot jet	35	35	35	30
Jet needle	4J13	4J13	4H16	4J13
Clip position	4	3	4	3
Float level	24 mm (0.94 in.)	26 mm (1.02 in.)	26 mm (1.02 in.)	21 mm (0.83 in.)
	YZ80K	**YZ80L**	**YZ80N**	**YZ80S, T, U, W, A**
Model No.	VM26SS	VM26SS	VM26SS	VM26SS
I.D. mark	22W00	39K00	58T00	1LR00
Main jet	250	240	270	280
Needle jet	0-6	P-4	Q-2	Q-2
Pilot jet	45	35	35	35
Jet needle	4H16	4H16	5H22	5H22
Clip position	4	4	3	3
Float level	21 mm (0.83 in.)	21 mm (0.83 in.)	21 mm (0.83 in.)	21 mm (0.83 in.)

CHAPTER NINE

IGNITION SYSTEM

A breaker point ignition system is used on YZ50 models. A capacitor discharge ignition system is used on YZ60 and YZ80 models.

Electrical system specifications are found in **Tables 1-4** (end of chapter).

CONTACT BREAKER POINT IGNITION (YZ50)

The YZ50 is equipped with a magneto ignition system. See **Figure 1**. The YZ50 magneto ignition system consists of the following components:

a. Magneto rotor.
b. Source coil.
c. Capacitor.
d. Contact breaker point assembly.
e. Engine stop switch.

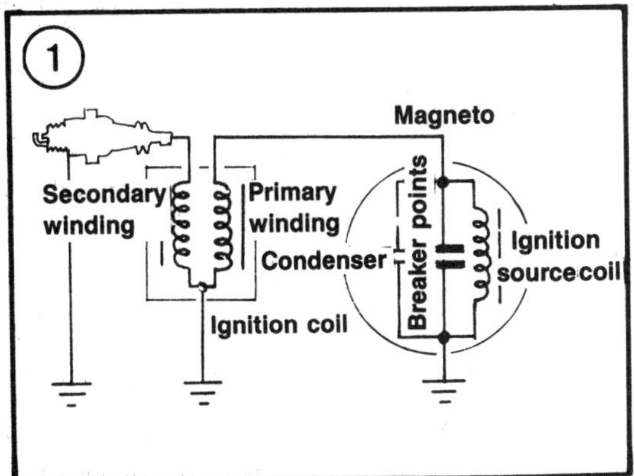

f. Ignition coil (primary and secondary coil windings).
g. Contact point cam (crankshaft).

As the magneto rotor turns, magnets located within it move past a stationary source coil in the stator, inducing a current in the coil. A contact breaker assembly controlled by a cam attached to the magneto rotor opens at the precise instant the piston reaches its firing position. The electrical energy produced in the source coil is then discharged to the primary side of the high-voltage ignition coil where it is increased, or stepped up, to a high enough voltage to jump the gap between the spark plug electrodes.

While the magneto ignition system is very simple in design, it is equipped with moving parts that wear during operation. Make sure to replace contact breaker points when worn. Also, make sure to keep the point contact area free of dirt and water. Always install the magneto cover with a gasket.

CAPACITOR DISCHARGE IGNITION

All YZ60 AND YZ80 models are equipped with a capacitor discharge ignition (CDI) system. This solid state system, unlike conventional ignition systems, uses no contact breaker points or other moving parts.

Alternating current from the magneto is rectified and used to charge the capacitor. As the piston approaches the firing position, a pulse from the pulser coil is rectified, shaped and then used to trigger the silicone controlled rectifier. This in turn allows the capacitor to discharge quickly into the primary side of the high-voltage ignition coil where it is increased, or stepped up, to a high enough voltage to jump the gap between the spark plug electrodes.

CDI Precautions

Certain measures must be taken to protect the capacitor discharge system. Damage to the semiconductors in the system may occur if the following is not observed.

1. Keep all connections between the various units clean and tight. Be sure that the wiring connectors are pushed together firmly.
2. Never disconnect any of the electrical connections while the engine is running.
3. Do not substitute another type of ignition coil.
4. The CDI unit is mounted on a rubber vibration isolator. Always be sure that the CDI unit is mounted correctly.

CDI Troubleshooting

Problems with the capacitor discharge system usually consists of production of a weak spark or no

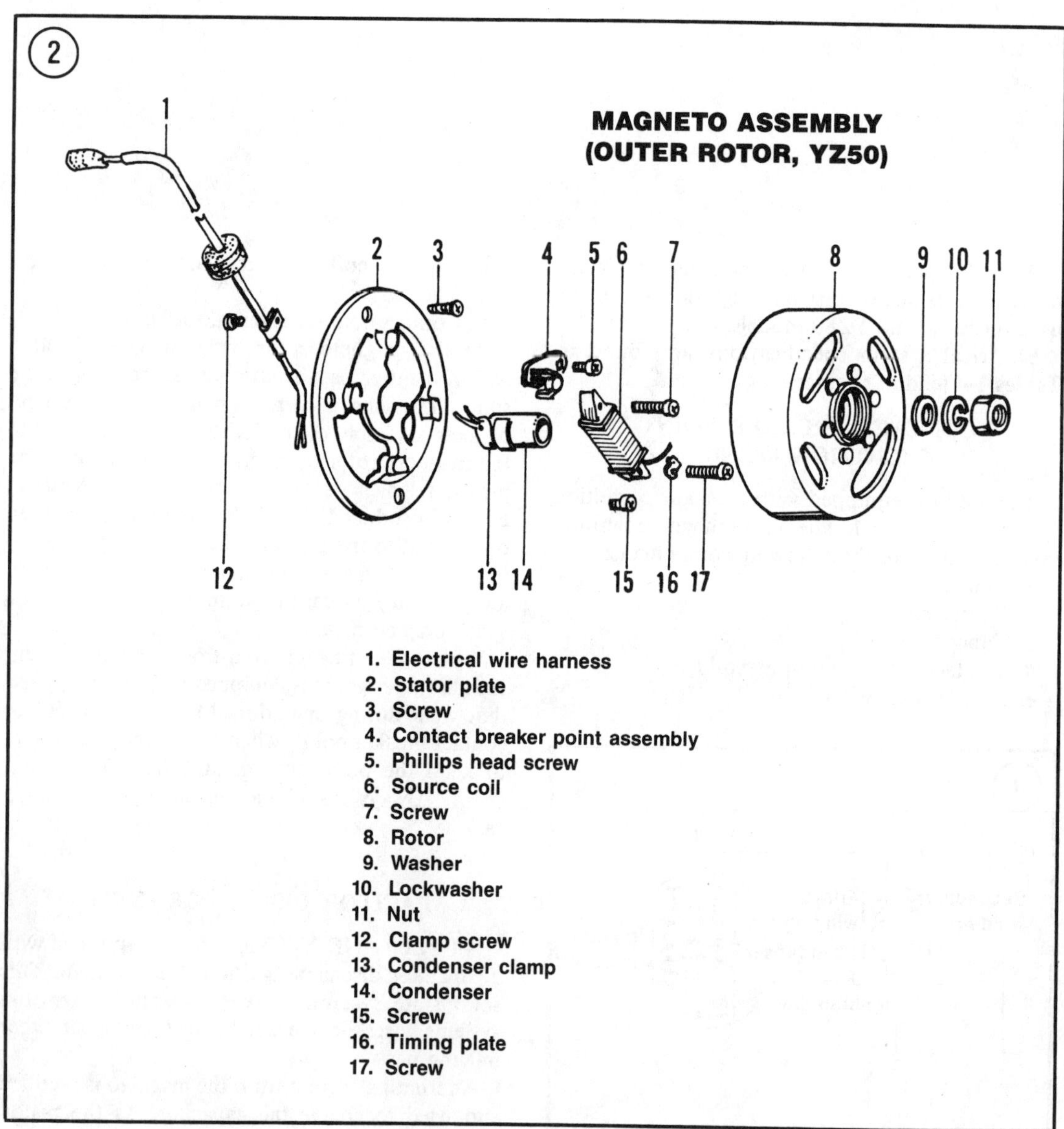

spark at all. Test procedures for troubleshooting the ignition system are found in Chapter Two.

1. Untape the electrical connectors and check for moisture and dirt buildup. Clean the connectors with aerosol electrical contact cleaner and reconnect. Retape the connectors with electrical tape.

2. Disconnect the kill switch and try to restart the engine. Refer to *Engine Kill Switch* in this chapter.

NOTE
If the engine starts with the kill switch disconnected, pull the choke all the way out to turn the engine off.

3. Check to see that the ignition coil high tension wire is connected securely to the ignition coil and spark plug cap.

4. Make sure that all stator plate screws are tight. If not, retighten the screws and retime the ignition as described in Chapter Three.

5. Check the crankshaft bearings for excessive wear as this could cause ignition problems. Refer to *Crankcase* in Chapter Five for details.

MAGNETO (OUTER ROTOR TYPE)

Rotor Removal/Installation

Refer to the following when performing this procedure:

a. **Figure 2** (YZ50).
b. **Figure 3** (YZ60).
c. **Figure 4** (1978 YZ80).
d. **Figure 5** (1984-on YZ80).

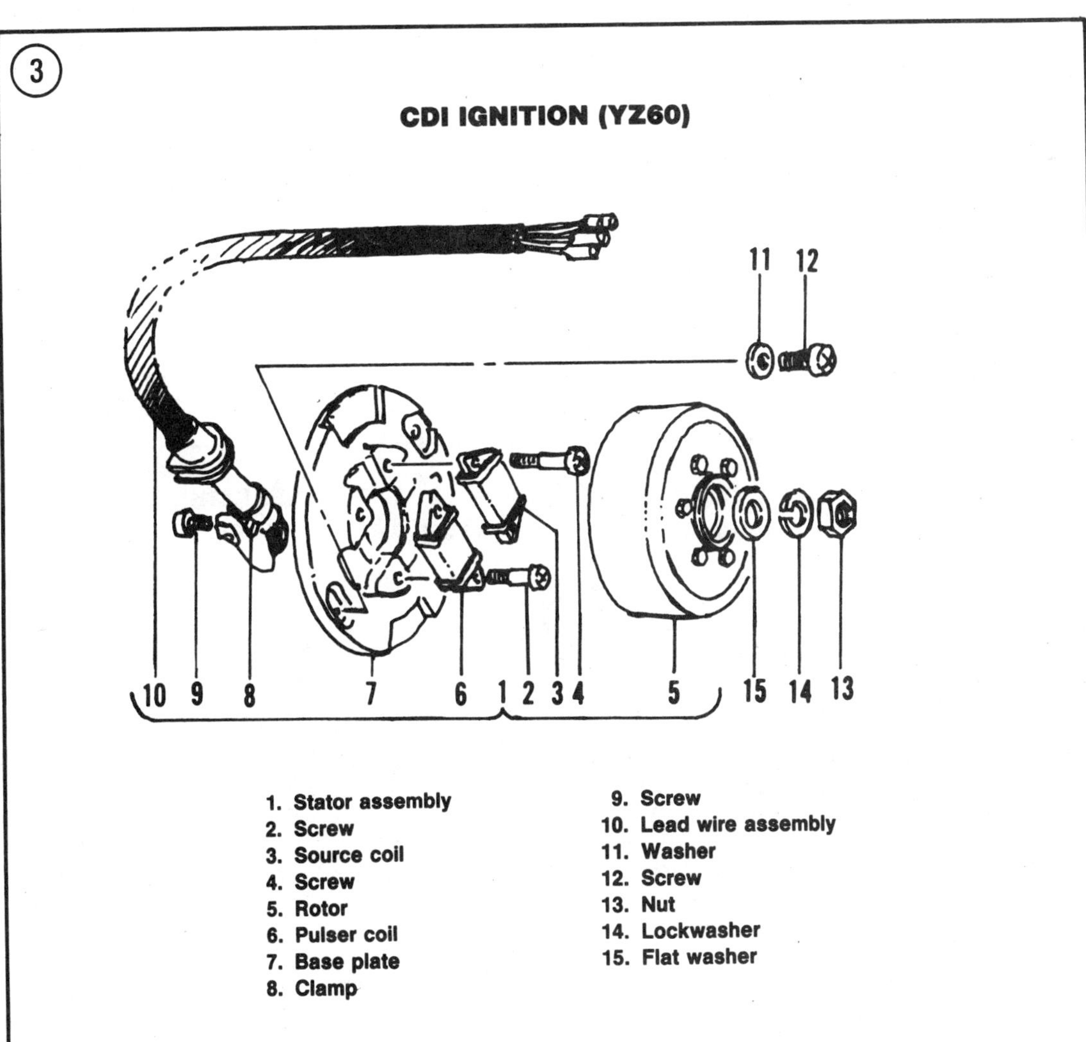

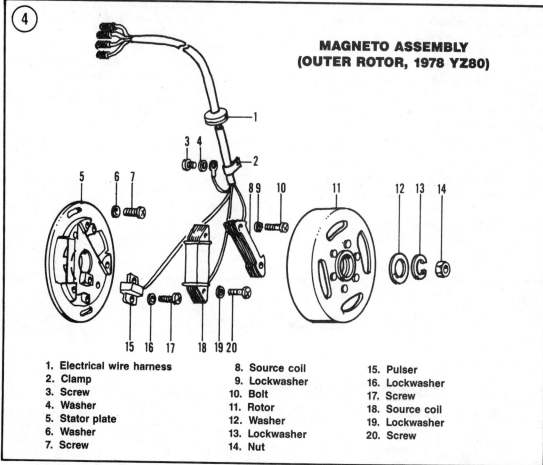

4

MAGNETO ASSEMBLY (OUTER ROTOR, 1978 YZ80)

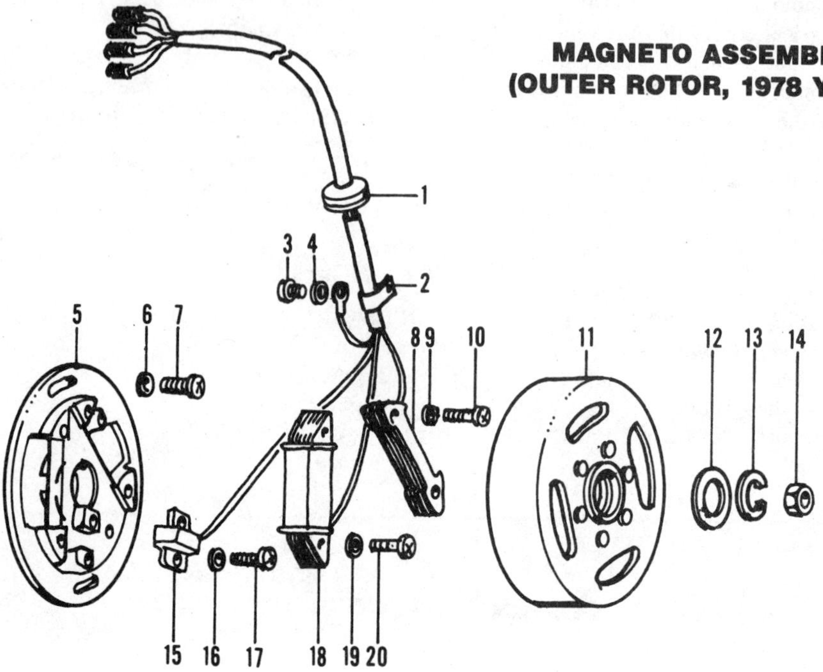

1. Electrical wire harness
2. Clamp
3. Screw
4. Washer
5. Stator plate
6. Washer
7. Screw
8. Source coil
9. Lockwasher
10. Bolt
11. Rotor
12. Washer
13. Lockwasher
14. Nut
15. Pulser
16. Lockwasher
17. Screw
18. Source coil
19. Lockwasher
20. Screw

5

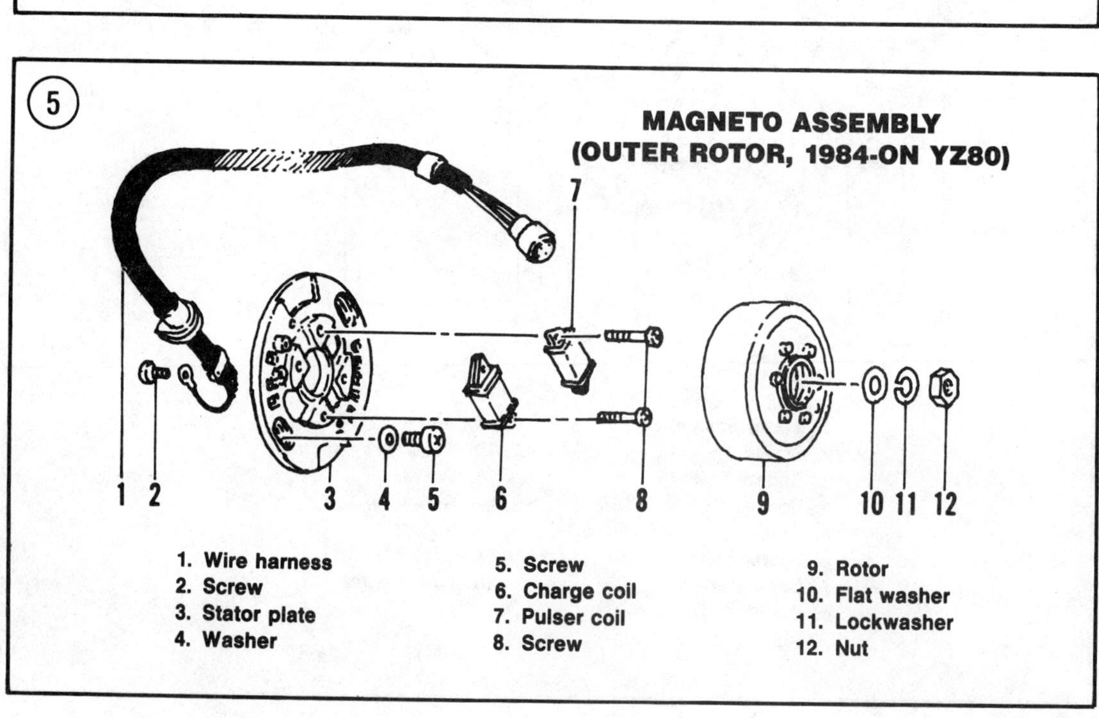

1. Wire harness
2. Screw
3. Stator plate
4. Washer
5. Screw
6. Charge coil
7. Pulser coil
8. Screw
9. Rotor
10. Flat washer
11. Lockwasher
12. Nut

1. Place the bike on a stand to support it securely.
2. Remove the shift lever (A, **Figure 6**).
3A. *YZ50 models:* Remove the clutch adjustment cover (**Figure 7**). Then remove the left-hand side cover (B, **Figure 6**).
3B. *YZ60 and YZ80 models:* Remove the left-hand side cover (**Figure 8**).

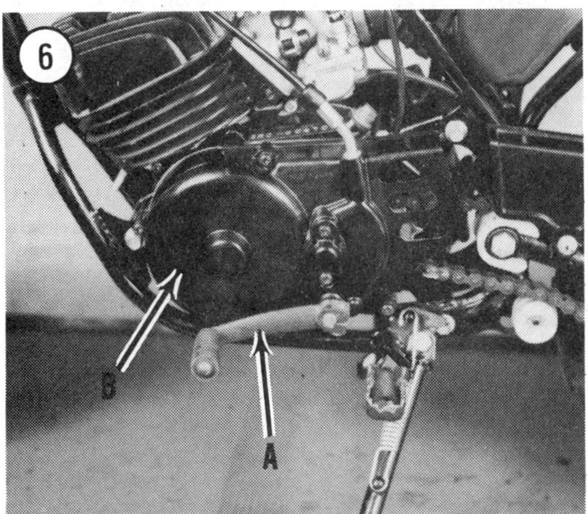

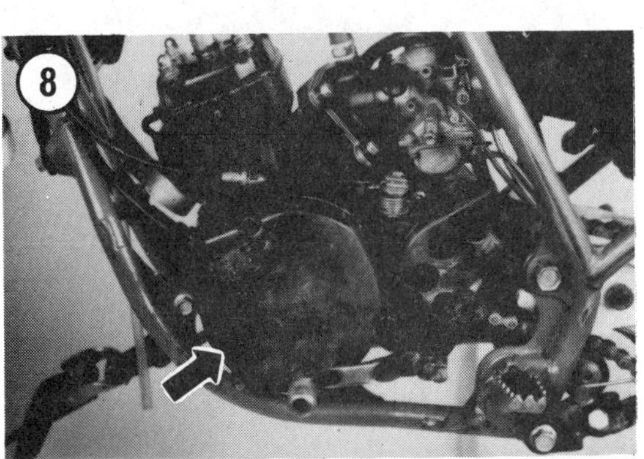

NOTE
*On early models, the side cover contains the clutch release mechanism and must be handled carefully. Either disconnect the clutch cable (**Figure 9**) from the mechanism or tie the cover up to the frame to keep any strain off the cable.*

4. Using a universal magneto holding tool (**Figure 10**) to secure the magneto, loosen the magneto rotor nut (**Figure 11**).

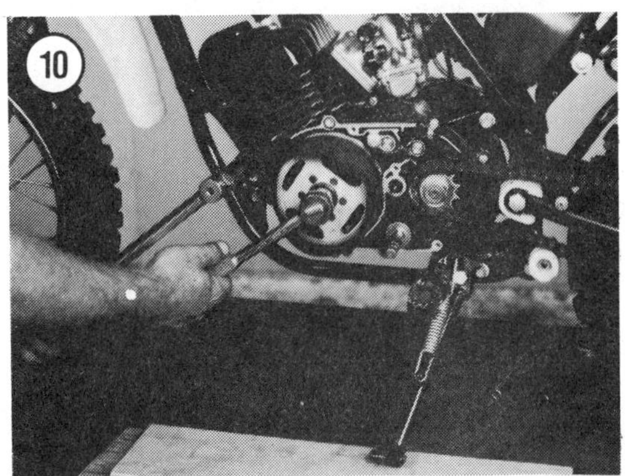

5. Remove the nut and plain washer. On some models, a lockwasher (**Figure 12**) is installed between the nut and plain washer.

NOTE
*A rotor puller (**Figure 13**) is required to remove the rotor. These can be purchased from your Yamaha dealer.*

6. Screw in a rotor puller (**Figure 14**) until it stops.

CAUTION
Don't try to remove the rotor without a puller; any attempt to do so will ultimately lead to some form of damage to the engine and/or rotor. Many aftermarket types of pullers are available from most motorcycle dealers or mail order houses. The cost of one of these pullers is about $10 and it makes an excellent addition to any mechanic's tool box. If you can't buy or borrow one, have a dealer remove the rotor.

7. Hold the puller with a wrench and gradually tighten the center bolt until the rotor disengages from the crankshaft. See **Figure 15**.

NOTE
If the rotor is difficult to remove, strike the puller's center bolt with a brass hammer a few times. This will usually break it loose.

CAUTION
If normal rotor removal attempts fail, do not force the puller as the threads may be stripped out of the rotor causing expensive damage. Take it to a dealer and have them remove it.

8. Remove the rotor and puller. Don't lose the Woodruff key (**Figure 16**) on the crankshaft.

CAUTION
*Carefully inspect the inside of the rotor (**Figure 17**) for small bolts, washers or other metal "trash" that may have been picked up by the magnets. These small metal bits can cause severe damage to the magneto stator plate components.*

9. Install by reversing these removal steps, noting the following:
   a. Make sure the Woodruff key (**Figure 16**) is in place on the crankshaft and align the keyway in the rotor with the key when installing the rotor.
   b. Be sure to install the washer(s) prior to installing the rotor nut. If a lockwasher is used (**Figure 12**), install it between the rotor nut and plain washer.

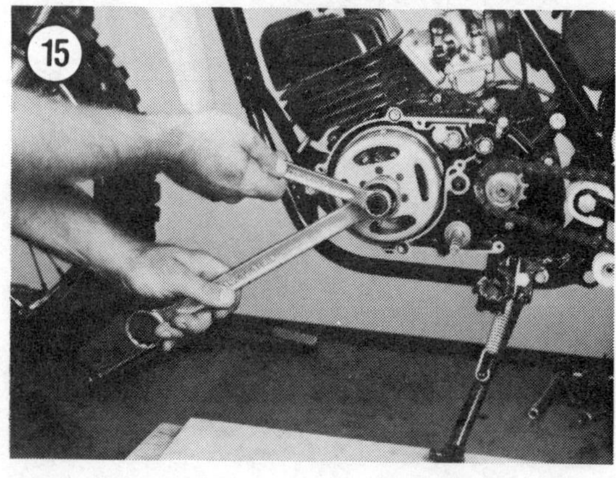

16

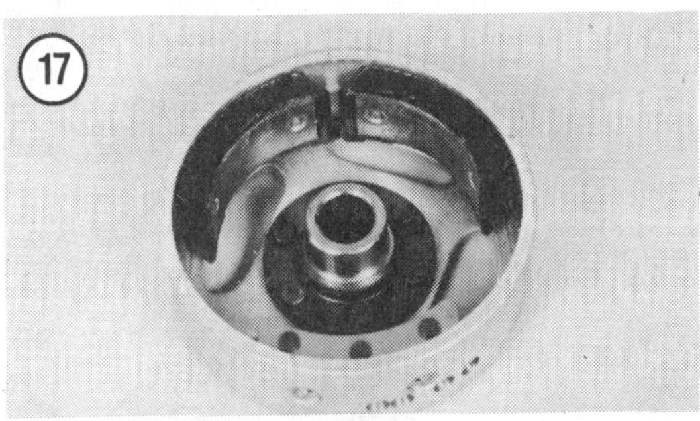
17

18

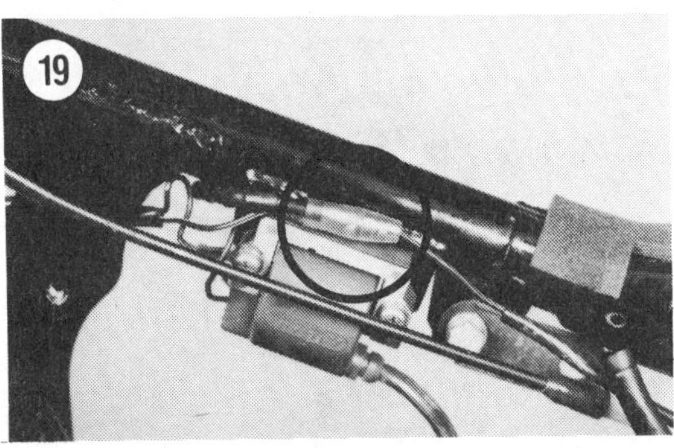
19

c. Install and tighten the rotor nut to the torque specification in **Table 1**. To keep the rotor from turning, hold it with the same tool used during removal.

NOTE

*On YZ50 models, make sure to install the long bolt (**Figure 18**) in the top hole. The cover is made of plastic material and the long bolt is necessary to keep the cover from distorting when the clutch is operated. The clutch will not release properly if this length bolt is not used.*

Stator Assembly Removal/Installation

1. Remove the magneto rotor as described under *Rotor Removal/Installation* in this chapter.
2. Remove the fuel tank as described in Chapter Eight.
3A. *YZ50 models:* Disconnect the electrical wire connectors from the ignition coil (**Figure 19**).
3B. *YZ60 and YZ80 models:* Disconnect the electrical wire connectors from the magneto to the CDI unit. See **Figure 20** or **Figure 21**.

20

21

4. *YZ60 and YZ80 models:* Note the timing marks on the stator plate and on the crankcase. These must be realigned during installation. If necessary, make a mark on the stator plate at the centerline of one attachment screw (**Figure 22**).

NOTE
On YZ50 models, this is not necessary as the stator plate can only be installed in one position.

5. Remove the screws securing the stator plate. See **Figure 23** (YZ50) or **Figure 24** (typical for YZ60 and YZ80).
6. Carefully pull the electrical harness out along with the rubber grommet from the crankcase and any holding clips on the engine.
7. Remove the stator assembly.
8. Install by reversing these removal steps, noting the following.
9. Route the electrical wires in the same way it was. Make sure to keep it away from the exhaust system.
10. Realign the stator plate and crankcase timing marks for preliminary ignition timing.
11. Check and adjust the ignition timing as described in Chapter Three.

Stator Plate Coil Replacement

When replacing an individual coil, it will be necessary to heat the wire connection at the bad coil with a soldering iron before disconnecting the wire. When the solder has melted, pull the wire away from the connection. This step will give you enough wire to work with when resoldering. If the wire is cut at the connection, it would cause the wire to fall short when resoldering the new coil.

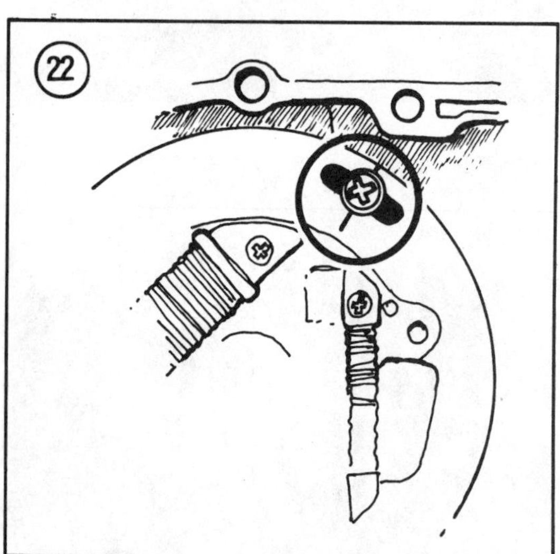

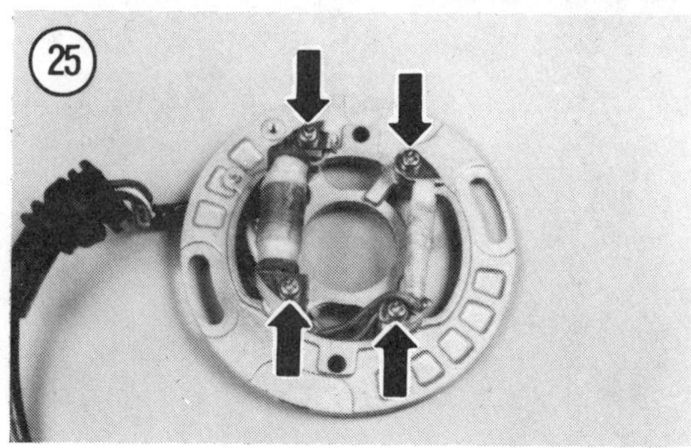

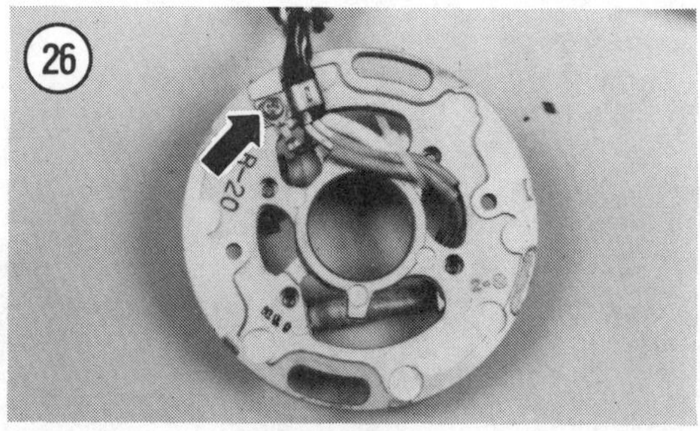

During reassembly, rosin core solder must be used—never use acid core solder on electrical connections—to reconnect the wire.

1. Remove the magneto stator assembly as previously described.
2. Remove the screws (**Figure 25**) securing the coil(s) to the stator plate.
3. Turn the stator plate over and disconnect the screw securing the clip and the ground connector (**Figure 26**).
4. Carefully unsolder the wire from the bad coil.
5. Install by reversing these removal steps.
6. Make sure all electrical connections are tight and free from corrosion.

MAGNETO (INNER ROTOR TYPE)

The inner rotor magneto (**Figure 27**) is found on 1979-1983 YZ80 models.

Rotor Removal/Installation

1. Place the bike on a stand to support it securely.
2. Shift the transmission into second gear.

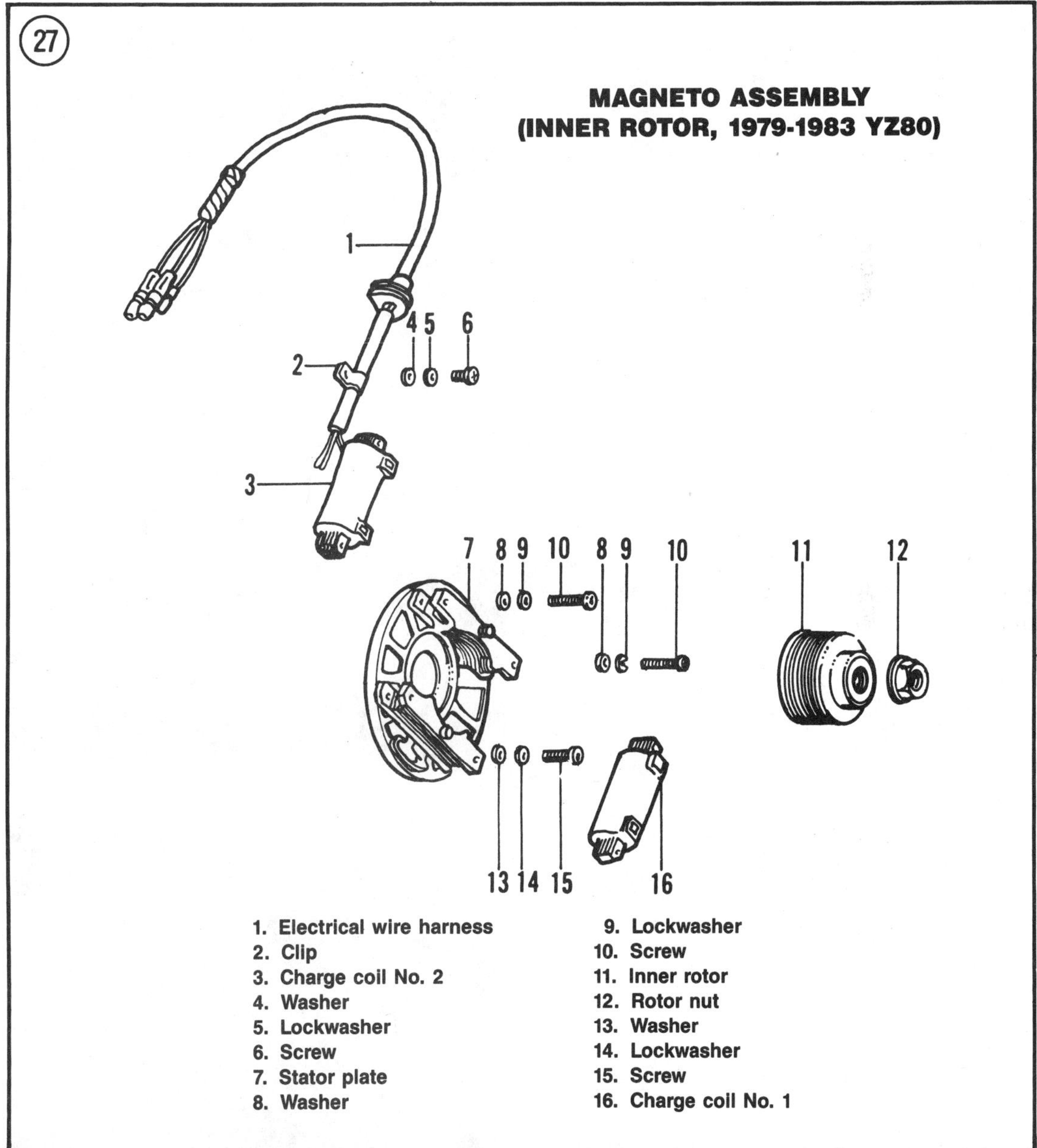

3A. *1979-1980 models:* Remove the shift lever (A, **Figure 28**) and the left-hand side cover (B, **Figure 28**).

NOTE
*On 1979-1980 models, the side cover contains the clutch release mechanism and must be handled carefully. Either disconnect the clutch cable (**Figure 29**) from the mechanism or tie the cover up to the frame to prevent cable damage.*

3B. *1981-1983 models:* Remove the shift lever and the left-hand side cover.
4. Have an assistant apply the rear brake. Then at the same time remove the inner rotor securing nut (**Figure 30**) with a wrench or socket.
5. Remove the lockwasher (if so equipped).

NOTE
A rotor puller is required to remove the rotor. These can be purchased from your Yamaha dealer.

6. Screw in a rotor puller (**Figure 31**) until it stops.

CAUTION
Don't try to remove the rotor without a puller; any attempt to do so will ultimately lead to some form of damage to the engine and/or rotor. Many aftermarket types of pullers are available from most motorcycle dealers or mail order houses. The cost of one of these pullers is about $10 and it makes an excellent addition to any mechanic's tool box. If you can't buy or borrow one, have a dealer remove the rotor.

7. Have an assistant apply the rear brake. Then gradually tighten the puller until the rotor (**Figure 32**) disengages from the crankshaft.

NOTE
If the rotor is difficult to remove, strike the puller with a brass hammer a few times. This will usually break it loose.

CAUTION
If normal rotor removal attempts fail, do not force the puller as the threads may be stripped out of the rotor causing expensive damage. Take it to a dealer and have them remove it.

8. Remove the rotor and puller. Don't lose the Woodruff key on the crankshaft (**Figure 33**).

CAUTION
Carefully inspect the outside of the rotor for small bolts, washers or other metal "trash" that may have been picked up by the magnets. These small

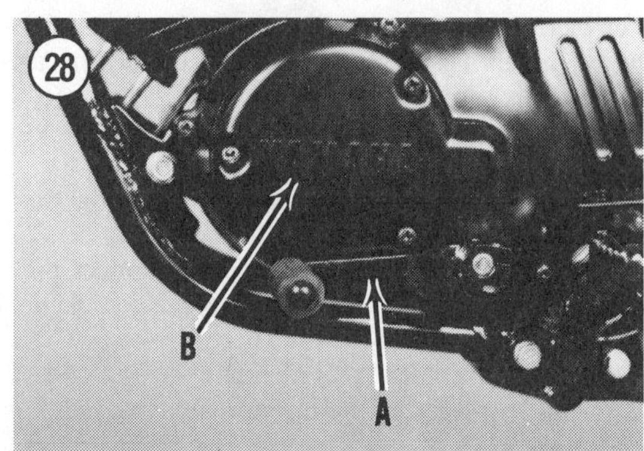

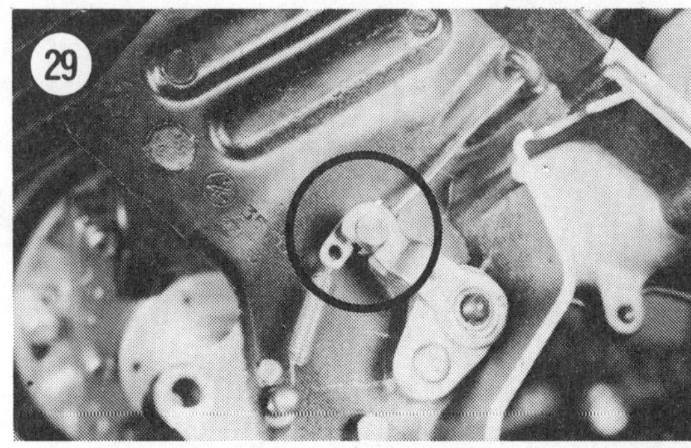

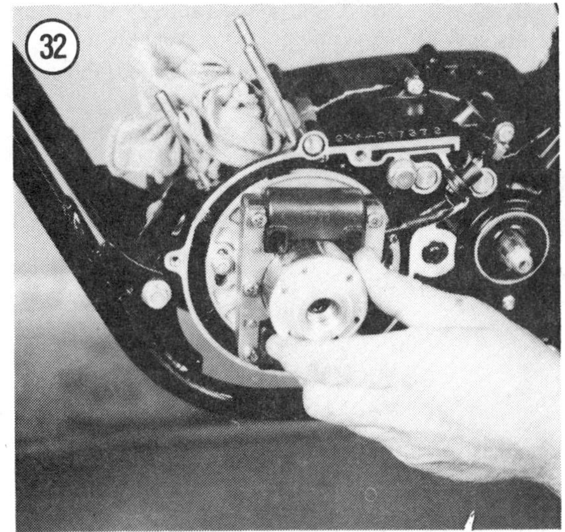

metal bits can cause severe damage to the magneto stator plate components.

9. Install by reversing these removal steps, noting the following:
   a. Make sure the Woodruff key is in place on the crankshaft (**Figure 33**) and align the keyway in the rotor with the key when installing the rotor.
   b. Be sure to install the lockwasher (if so equipped) prior to installing the rotor nut.
   c. Install and tighten the rotor nut to specifications in **Table 1**. To keep the rotor from turning, place the transmission in second gear and apply the rear brake.

Stator Assembly Removal/Installation

1. Remove the magneto rotor as described in this chapter.
2. Disconnect the electrical wire connectors from the magneto to the CDI unit. See **Figure 34**.
3. Note the timing marks on the stator plate and on the crankcase. These must be realigned during installation. If necessary, make a mark on the stator plate that lines up with the centerline of one mounting screw.
4. Remove the screws securing the stator plate (A, **Figure 35**).
5. Carefully pull the electrical harness out along with the rubber grommet (B, **Figure 35**) from the crankcase and any holding clips (C, **Figure 35**) on the engine.
6. Remove the stator assembly.
7. Install by reversing these removal steps, noting the following.

9

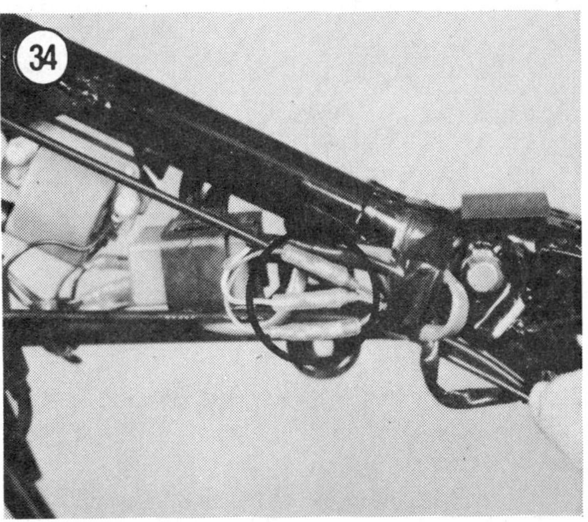

8. Route the electrical wires in the same way it was. Make sure to keep it away from the exhaust system.
9. Realign the stator plate and crankcase timing marks for preliminary ignition timing.
10. Check and adjust the ignition timing as described in Chapter Three.

Coil Replacement

1. Remove the magneto stator assembly as previously described.
2. Remove the screws (A, **Figure 36**) securing the coils to the stator plate.
3. Remove the screw (B, **Figure 36**) securing the clip.
4. Carefully remove the coils and wire harness.
5. Install by reversing these removal steps.
6. Make sure all electrical connections are tight and free from corrosion. This is absolutely necessary with a CDI ignition system.

STATOR COIL TESTING (ALL MODELS)

An ohmmeter is required for this procedure.

It is not necessary to remove the stator plate to perform the following tests.

In order to get accurate resistance measurements the stator assembly and coil must be warm (minimum temperature is 68° F [20° C]).

1. Remove the fuel tank as described in Chapter Eight.
2. Remove the left-hand side cover as described under *Magneto* in this chapter.
3. Locate the coil wire connectors at the upper frame rail. **Table 2** and **Table 3** list wire color codes for the individual coils. Disconnect the electrical connector (**Figure 37**) by pulling on the connector housings. Do not pull on the wires.

NOTE
The color wiring diagrams at the end of the book can also be used to determine individual coil wire colors.

4. Set the ohmmeter to the proper scale. This will depend on the ohm reading listed in **Table 2** or **Table 3** for your model. For example, if **Table 2** or **Table 3** specifies a coil resistance reading at 410-590 ohms, set the ohmmeter to the R×100 scale.
5. Touch the ohmmeter leads together and turn the ohmmeter calibration knob until the dial needle lines up with zero.
6. Using the ohmmeter leads, measure the resistance at the specified connector wires leading from the coil. See **Table 2** or **Table 3**. Interpret results as follows:
   a. If the specified resistance is obtained, the coil is good.
   b. If the resistance is less or more than specified, the coil is bad and must be replaced.
   c. Replace the bad coil(s) as described under *Magneto* for your model in this chapter.
7. Reconnect the electrical connector(s) and install the fuel tank. Install the left-hand side cover.

CAPACITOR DISCHARGE IGNITION UNIT

Removal/Installation

1. Support the bike on the sidestand.
2. Remove the seat and fuel tank.
3. Disconnect the CDI electrical connector (**Figure 37**).

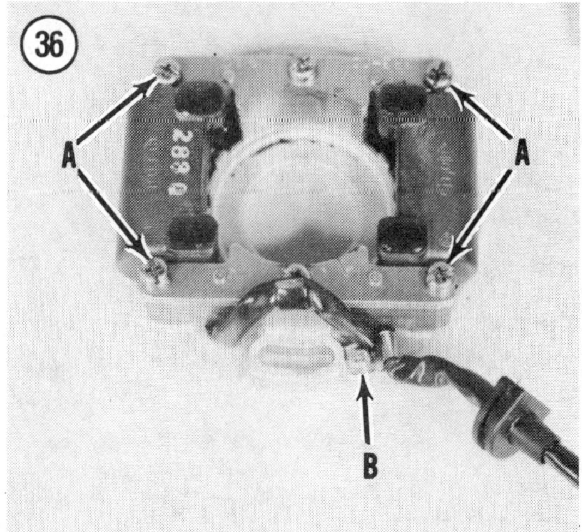

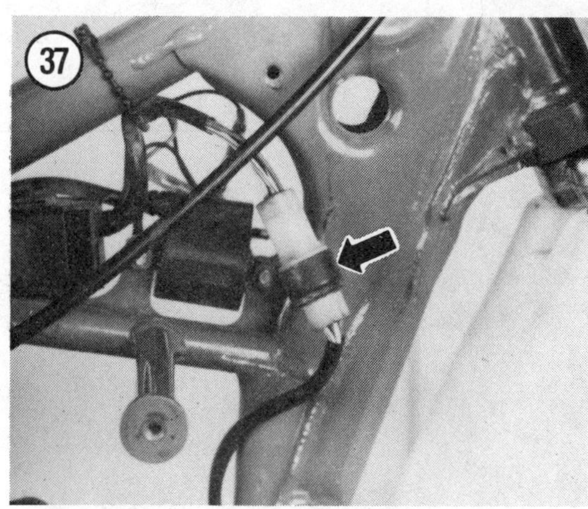

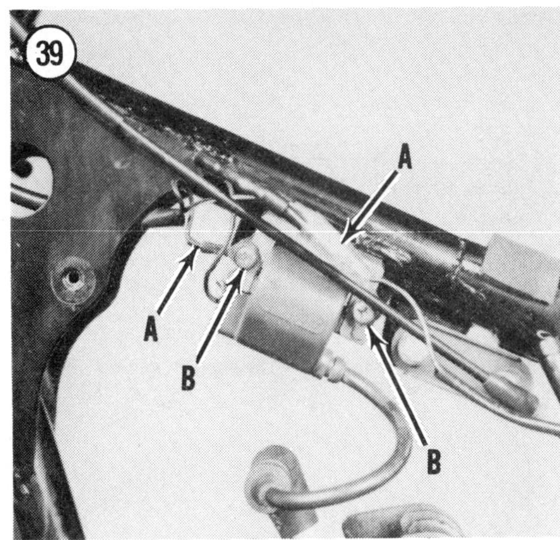

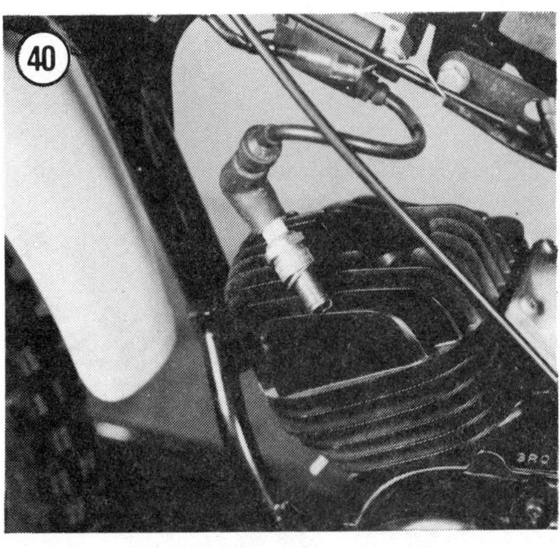

4. Slide the CDI unit out of the frame and remove it. See **Figure 38** (typical).
5. Install by reversing these removal steps. Make sure all electrical connectors are tight and free of corrosion.

Testing

The capacitor discharge ignition unit can only be tested with special electrical equipment. Refer all testing to a Yamaha dealer.

IGNITION COIL

Removal/Installation

1. Support the bike on the sidestand.
2. Remove the seat and fuel tank.
3. Disconnect the electrical wires to the ignition coil. See A, **Figure 39**.
4. Remove the screws (B, **Figure 39**) securing the ignition coil to the frame and remove it.
5. Install by reversing these removal steps. Make sure all electrical connectors are tight and free of corrosion. Make sure the ground wire is secured tightly.

Testing

The ignition coil is a form of transformer which develops the high voltage required to jump the spark plug gap. The only maintenance required is that of keeping the electrical connections clean and tight, and occasionally checking to see that the coil is mounted securely.

If the coil condition is doubtful, there are several checks which may be made.

First, as a quick check of coil condition, disconnect the high voltage lead from the spark plug. Then remove the spark plug and reconnect it to the high voltage lead. Lay the spark plug across the cylinder head (to ground the plug) **(Figure 40)**. Operate the kickstarter to turn the engine over. If a fat, blue spark occurs the coil is in good condition; if not, proceed as follows.

WARNING

Do not hold the spark plug wire when performing the previous test procedure as the high voltage generated by the ignition system could produce a serious fatal shock.

NOTE

The spark plug must be in good condition when performing the previous procedure. See Chapter Three for details if you are unsure.

Refer to **Figure 41** for this procedure.

1. Disconnect the coil wires before testing.
2. Measure the coil primary resistance, using an ohmmeter (set on ohms×1), between both coil primary terminals (**Figure 41**). Resistance is specified in **Table 4**.
3. Measure the coil secondary resistance (set on ohms×100) between either primary lead and the high voltage cable (**Figure 41**). Resistance is specified in **Table 4**.
4. Replace the coil if the spark plug lead exhibits visible damage or if they do not test within the specifications in Step 2 or Step 3.

SPARK PLUG

The spark plugs recommended by the factory are usually the most suitable for your machine. If riding conditions are mild, it may be advisable to go to spark plugs one step hotter than normal. Unusually severe riding conditions may require slightly colder plugs. See Chapter Three for details.

ENGINE KILL SWITCH

Testing and Replacement

1. Remove the fuel tank as described in Chapter Eight.

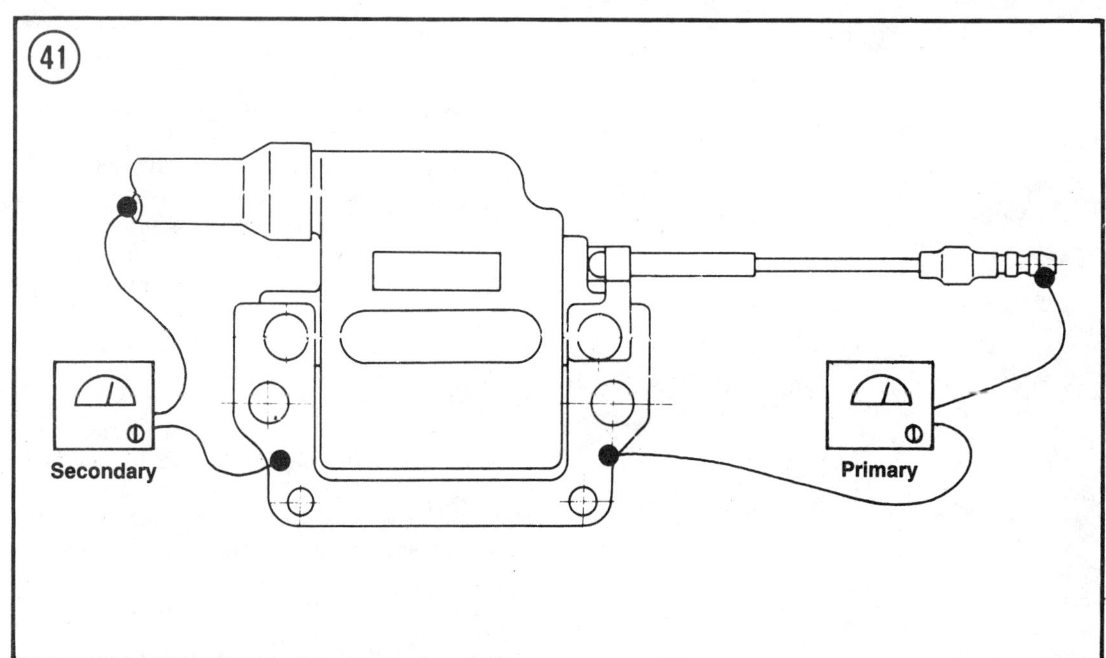

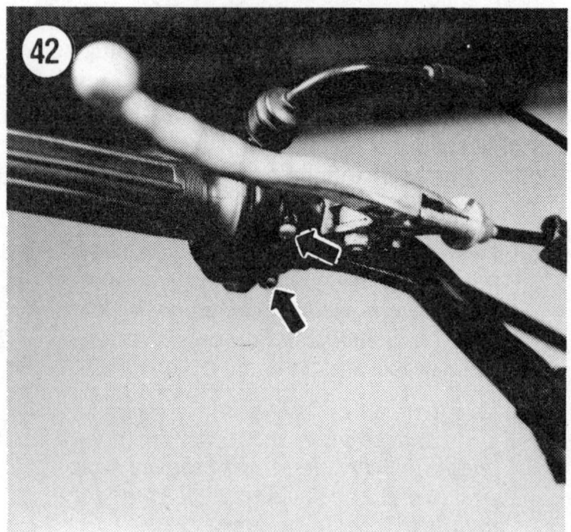

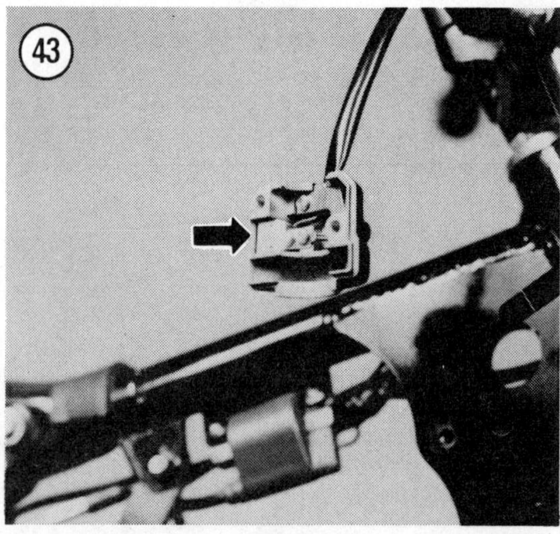

2. Disconnect the black kill switch connector at the ignition coil (YZ50) or CDI unit (YZ60 and YZ80).
3. Use an ohmmeter set at R×1 and connect the 2 leads of the ohmmeter to the 2 electrical wires of the switch.

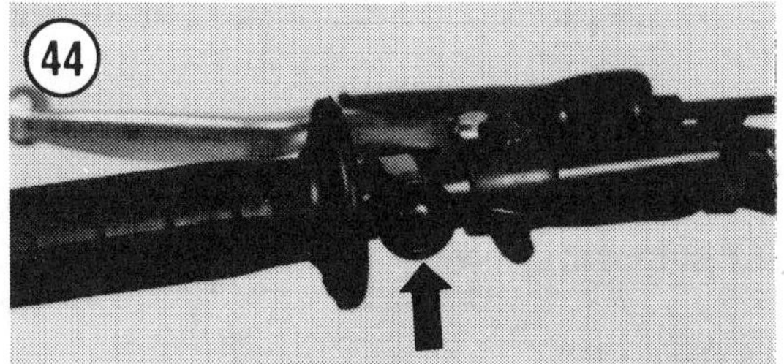

4. Push the kill switch button—if the switch is good there will be continuity (resistance).
5. If the needle does not move (no continuity) the switch is faulty and must be replaced.
6A. *Right-hand switch:* Remove the screws (**Figure 42**) securing the switch (**Figure 43**) and remove it. Reverse to install a new switch.
6B. *Left-hand switch:* Remove the screw securing the switch (**Figure 44**) and remove it. Reverse to install a new switch.
7. Reconnect the black kill switch connector. Make sure it is tight and free of corrosion.

WIRING DIAGRAMS

Wiring diagrams for all models are located at the end of this book.

Table 1 IGNITION SYSTEM TORQUE SPECIFICATIONS

Item	N•m	ft.-lb.
Magneto or rotor nut		
YZ50	50	36
YZ60	40	28
YZ80		
1978	60	43
1979-1982	40	28
1983-on	35	25

Table 2 STATOR COIL TEST SPECIFICATIONS (1978-1986)*

Item/model	Ohm reading**	Wire colors
Source coil		
YZ50	1.12	***
Charge coil		
YZ60	420 ±10%	Brown to black
YZ80		
1978	***	***
1979-1983	1437	Brown to red
1984	505	Brown to red
1985-1986	505	Black to brown
Pulser coil		
YZ60	12 ±10%	White/red to black
YZ80		
1978	***	***
1979-1983	500	Red to white/red
1984	10.4	Red to white/red
1985-1986	10.4	White/green to white/red

* Tests made @ a minimum temperature of 68° F (20° C).
** Test specifications within ±10%.
*** Test specifications not listed by Yamaha.

Table 3 STATOR COIL TEST SPECIFICATIONS (1987-ON)*

Item/model	Ohm reading*	Wire colors
Pulser coil	9.4-11.5	White/red to White/green
Stator coil	454.5-555.5	Brown to black

* Tests made @ a minimum temperature of 68° F (20° C).

Table 4 IGNITION COIL TEST SPECIFICATIONS*

Primary resistance	
YZ50	1.0 ohms ±15%
YZ60	1.0 ohms ±10%
YZ80	
1978	1.0 ohms ±15%
1979	0.60 ohms
1981-1982	1.0 ohms ±10%
1983	0.22 ohms ±10%
1984-1986	0.29 ohms ±15%
1987-on	0.2-0.3 ohms
Secondary resistance	
YZ50	5.9 K ohms ±15%
YZ60	5.9 K ohms ±20%
YZ80	
1978	5.9 K ohms ±15%
1979	6.2 K ohms
1981-1982	5.9 K ohms ±20%
1983	4.4 K ohms ±20%
1984-1986	4.0 K ohms ±15%
1987-on	3.4-4.6 K ohms

* Test made @ a minimum temperature of 68° F (20° C).

CHAPTER TEN

LIQUID COOLING SYSTEM

The liquid cooling system (1982-on YZ80) consists of a radiator, water pump, radiator cap and hoses. During operation, the coolant heats up and expands, thus pressuring the system. The radiator cap is used to seal the system. Water cooled in the radiator is pumped down through the radiator and into the cylinder head where it passes through the cylinder water passages and back into the radiator at the top. The water then drains down through the radiator where it is cooled and the cycle is repeated.

This chapter describes repair and replacement of the cooling system components.

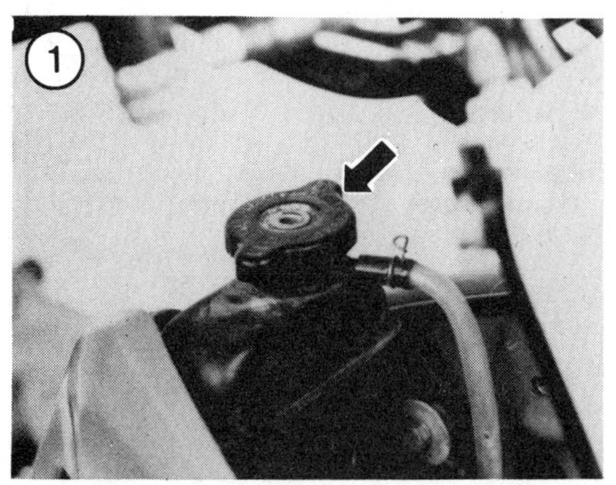
1

WARNING
*Do not remove the radiator cap (**Figure 1**) when the engine is hot. The coolant is very hot and is under pressure. Severe scalding could result if the coolant comes in contact with your skin.*

The cooling system must be cooled prior to removing any component of the system.

COOLING SYSTEM INSPECTION

1. Check the radiator for clogged or damaged fins. If more than 15% of the radiator fin area is damaged, repair or replace the radiator.
2. To clean a clogged radiator, blow compressed air from the rear (engine side).
3. Check all coolant hoses for cracks or damage. Replace all questionable parts. Make sure the hose clamps are tight, but not so tight that they cut the hoses.
4. Pressure test the cooling system as described in Chapter Three.

RADIATOR

Removal/Installation

Refer to **Figure 2** (1982 YZ80), **Figure 3** (1983-1985 YZ80) or **Figure 4** (1986-on YZ80).

10

(2)

RADIATOR ASSEMBLY (1982 YZ80)

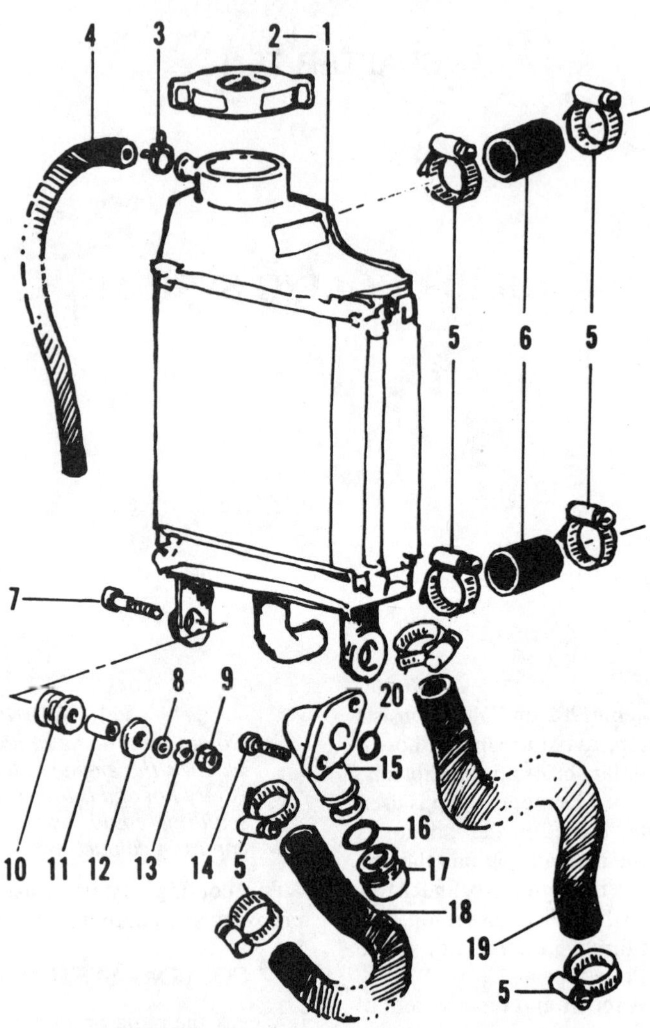

1. Radiator
2. Radiator cap
3. Clip
4. Overflow hose
5. Hose clamp
6. Hose
7. Bolt
8. Washer
9. Nut
10. Grommet
11. Collar
12. Washer
13. Spring washer
14. Bolt
15. Joint
16. O-ring
17. Pipe seal
18. Hose
19. Hose
20. O-ring

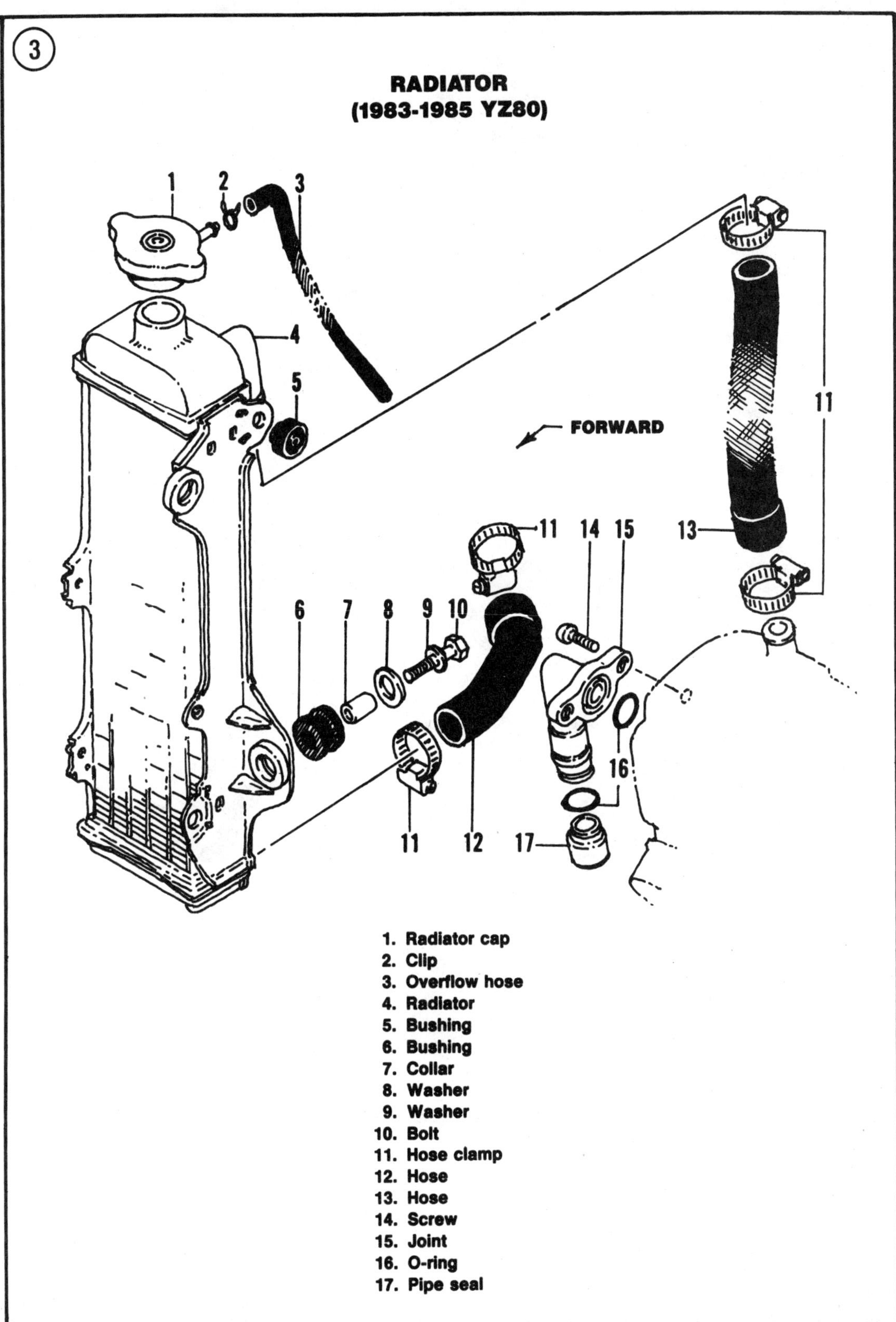

1. Radiator cap
2. Clip
3. Overflow hose
4. Radiator
5. Bushing
6. Bushing
7. Collar
8. Washer
9. Washer
10. Bolt
11. Hose clamp
12. Hose
13. Hose
14. Screw
15. Joint
16. O-ring
17. Pipe seal

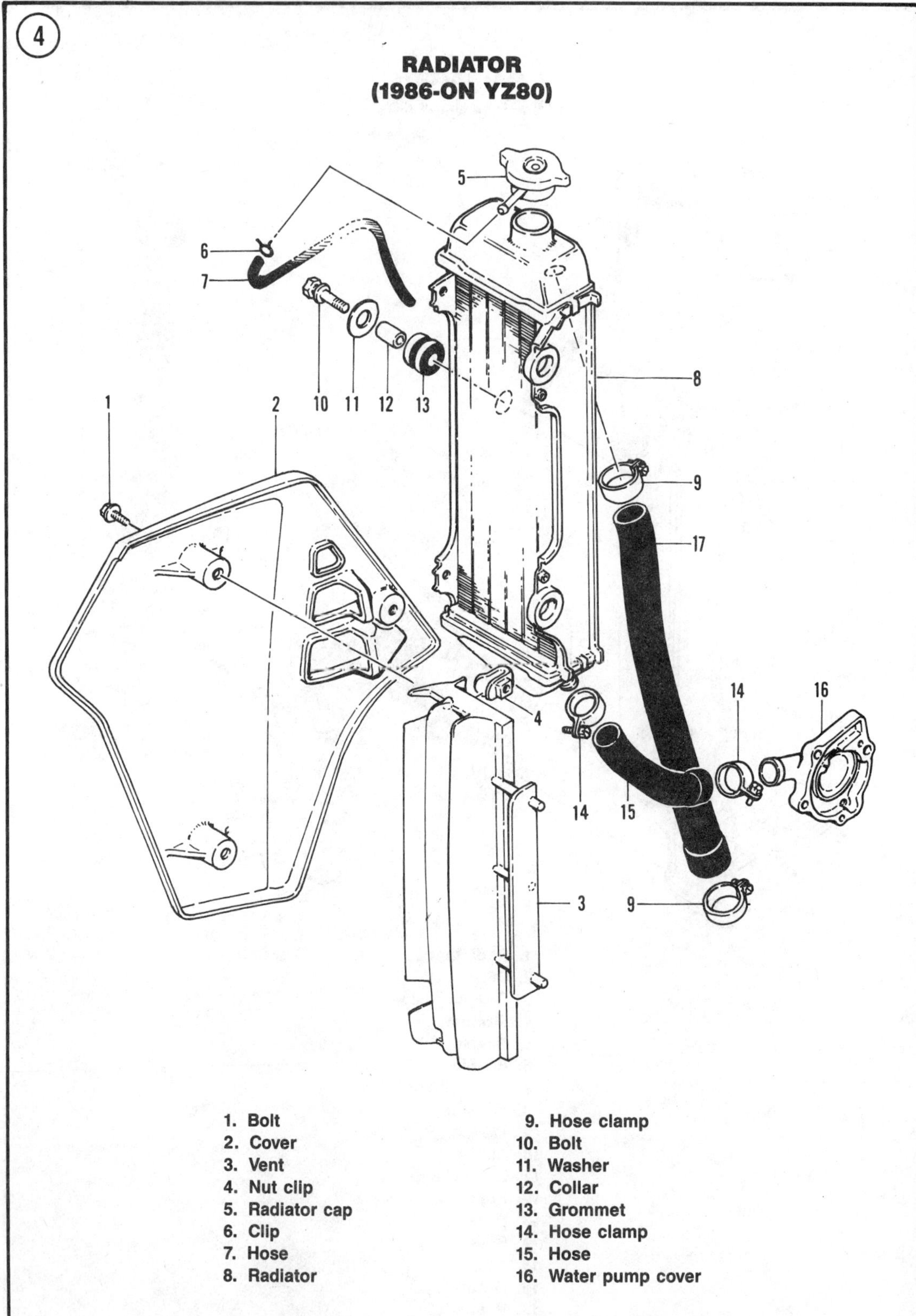
4
RADIATOR
(1986-ON YZ80)
5
6
7
8
1
2
10
11
12
13
9
17
4
14
16
14
15
3
9
1. Bolt
2. Cover
3. Vent
4. Nut clip
5. Radiator cap
6. Clip
7. Hose
8. Radiator
9. Hose clamp
10. Bolt
11. Washer
12. Collar
13. Grommet
14. Hose clamp
15. Hose
16. Water pump cover

1. Place the bike on a workstand to secure it.
2. Remove the fuel tank.
3. Drain the cooling system as described in Chapter Three.

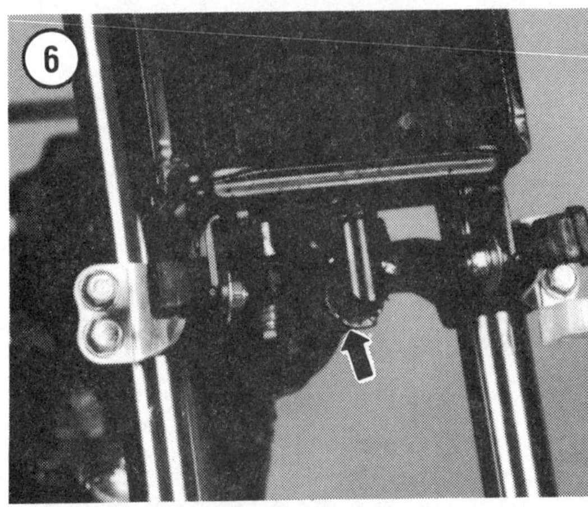

4A. *1982 YZ80 models:* Perform the following:
  a. Remove the number plate (**Figure 5**).
  b. Remove the screws securing the front fender to the lower steering crown and remove the fender.
  c. Disconnect the radiator upper and lower coolant hoses (**Figure 6**) where the hoses attach to the steering crown.
  d. Remove the lower radiator mounting bolts (**Figure 7**) and remove the radiator.

4B. *1983-on YZ80 models:* Perform the following:
  a. Remove the radiator cover (**Figure 8**) and deflector panel from the side of the radiator.
  b. Disconnect the radiator coolant hoses at the cylinder head (**Figure 9**) and water pump (**Figure 10**).

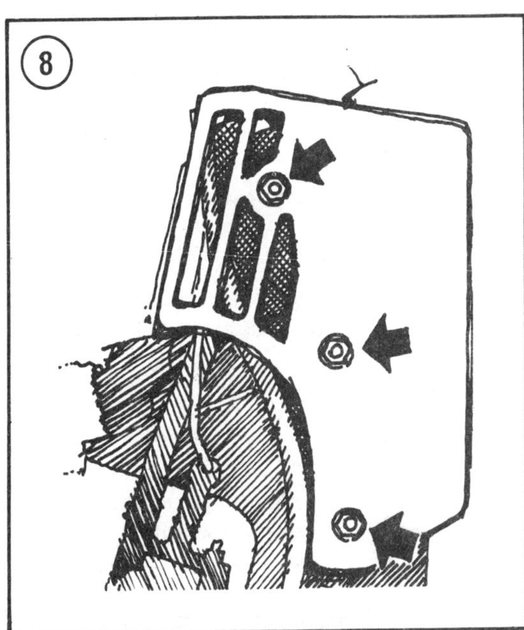

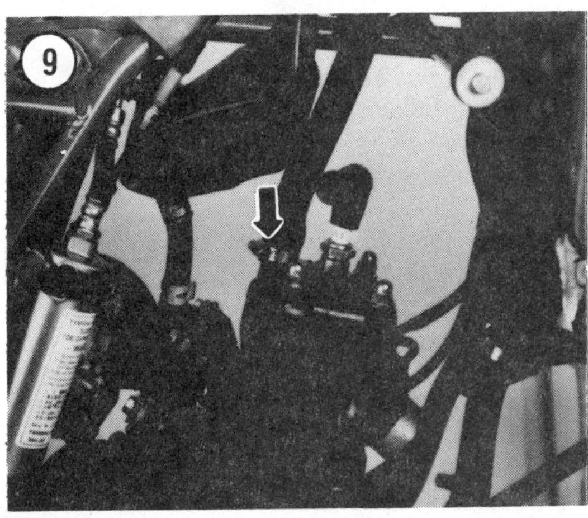

10

c. Remove the radiator mounting bolts and remove the radiator (**Figure 11**).

NOTE
Don't lose the clip-on nuts on the radiator.

5. Installation is the reverse of these steps.
6. Refill the coolant as described in Chapter Three.

Inspection

1. Examine the radiator cooling surface for damage. Also check along the sides at the lower mounting bushings (**Figure 12**). If the radiator is damaged, refer repair to a radiator repair shop. If damage is severe, replace the radiator.
2. *1982 YZ80 models:* Check the coolant hose mountings on the steering head for damage or coolant residue buildup; clean or replace as required (**Figure 13**).

NOTE
The steering head on 1982 YZ80 models is part of the cooling system. If coolant leaks from the steering head, refer to ***Steering Head (1982 YZ80)*** *in Chapter Eleven.*

3. Check the radiator coolant hoses and hose clamps for damage; replace if required.

WATER PUMP

The water pump is mounted in the clutch cover on all models. Under normal operating conditions, disassembly of the water pump should not be necessary. However, if the engine overheats or if the coolant level changes, the water pump should be removed and examined.

Disassembly

Refer to **Figure 14** for this procedure.

1. Drain the cooling system as described under *Coolant Change* in Chapter Three.
2. Remove the water pipe joint (**Figure 15**) at the cylinder.
3. Remove the screws securing the water pump cover (**Figure 16**) to the clutch cover and remove it. Remove the locating pin (**Figure 17**) and gasket from the cover.
4. Remove the clutch cover as described under *Clutch Cover Removal/Installation* in Chapter Six.
5. From the backside of the clutch cover, remove the circlip securing the impeller shaft gear to the impeller shaft (**Figure 18**).

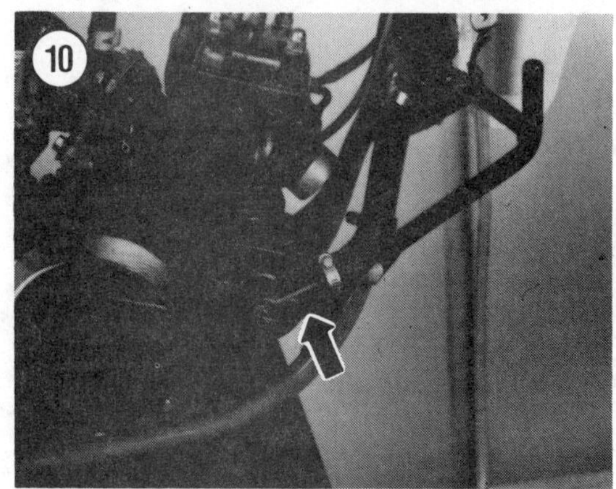
10

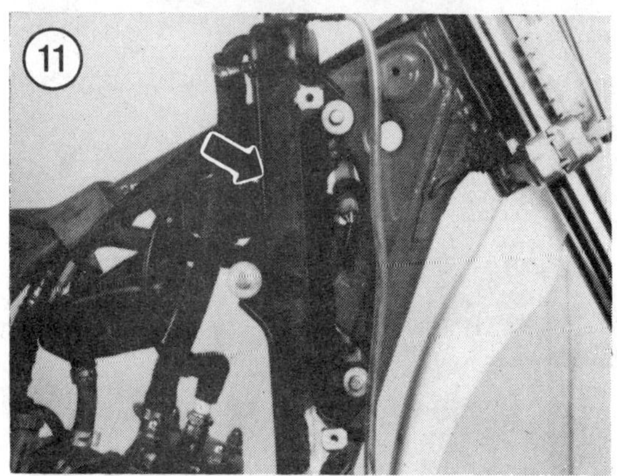
11

12

13

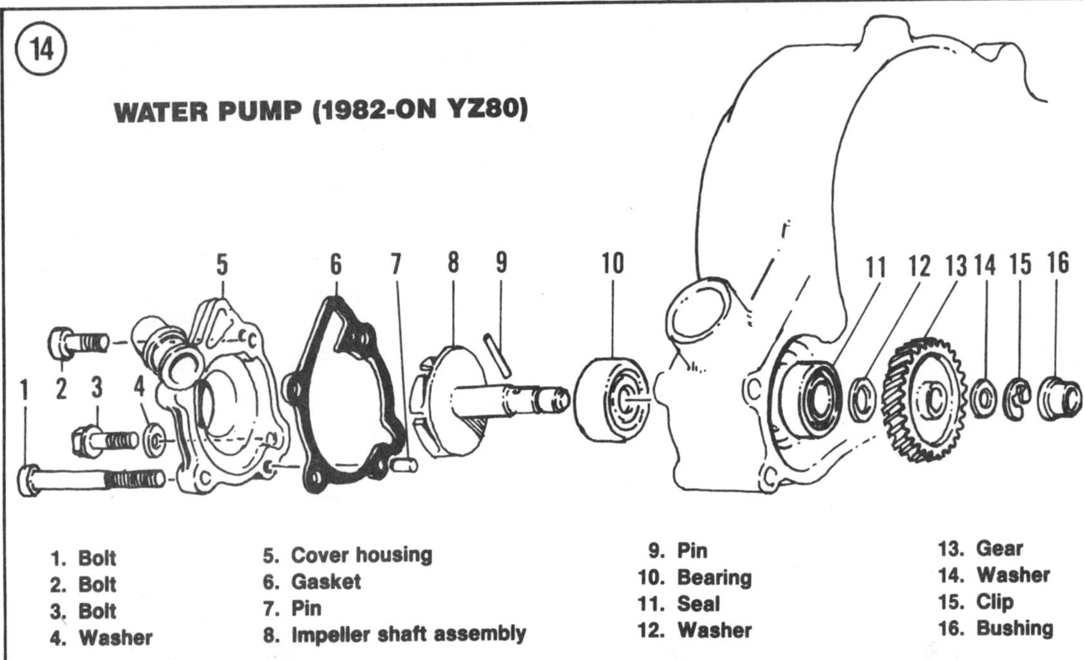
14
WATER PUMP (1982-ON YZ80)
1 2 3 4 5 6 7 8 9 10 11 12 13 14 15 16
1. Bolt
2. Bolt
3. Bolt
4. Washer
5. Cover housing
6. Gasket
7. Pin
8. Impeller shaft assembly
9. Pin
10. Bearing
11. Seal
12. Washer
13. Gear
14. Washer
15. Clip
16. Bushing

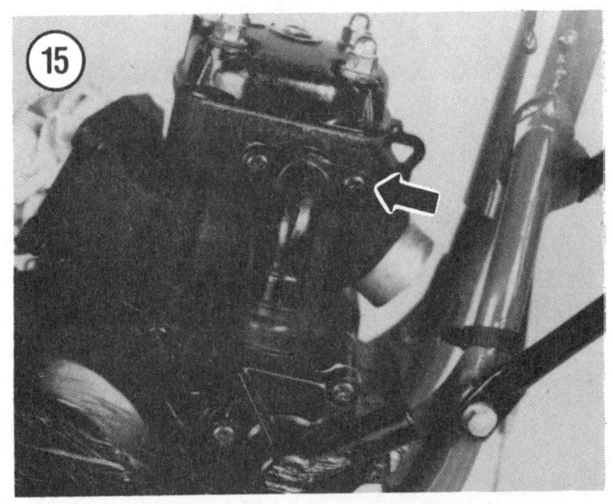
15

17

10

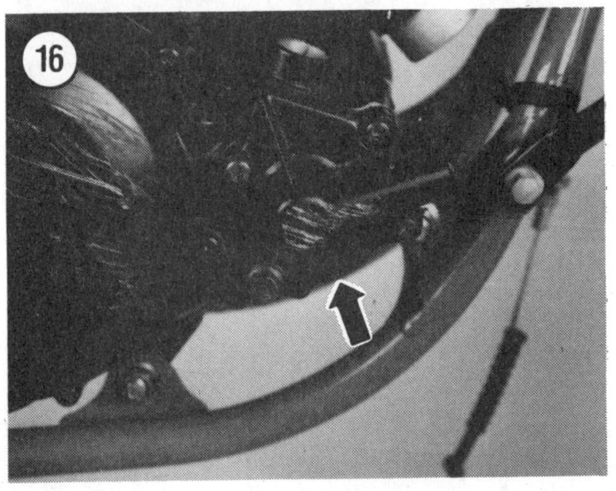
16

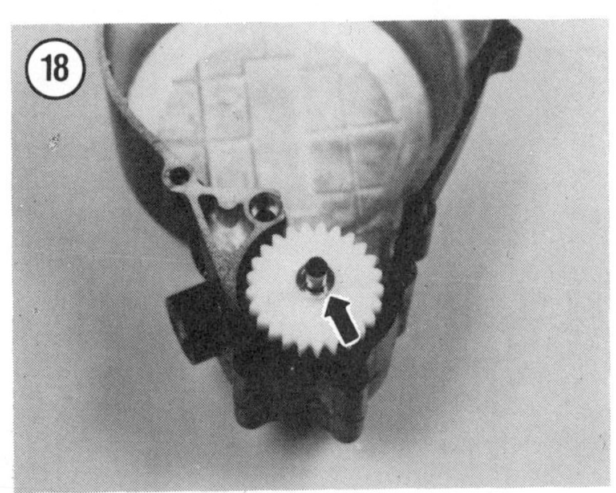
18

6. Remove the washer (**Figure 19**).
7. Slide the impeller gear off the shaft (**Figure 20**).
8. Remove the pin (**Figure 21**).
9. Remove the washer (**Figure 22**).
10. Remove the impeller shaft assembly from the front side of the clutch cover (**Figure 23**).

Inspection

1. Lay out the impeller shaft assembly parts as shown in **Figure 24** and examine each for wear or damage.
2. Check the impeller shaft (**Figure 25**).
   a. Check the impeller (A) for coolant crust and clean if necessary.
   b. Check the pin hole in the shaft (B) for wear or damage.
   c. Replace the impeller shaft if necessary.
3. Check the water pump seal (**Figure 26**) for wear or damage. On 1982 models, check the bearing (**Figure 27**) for wear or damage. If necessary, replace as described under *Bearing and Oil Seal Replacement* in Chapter Five.
4. Check the water passages in the water pump cover (**Figure 28**) for crust build up. Clean thoroughly.

19

20

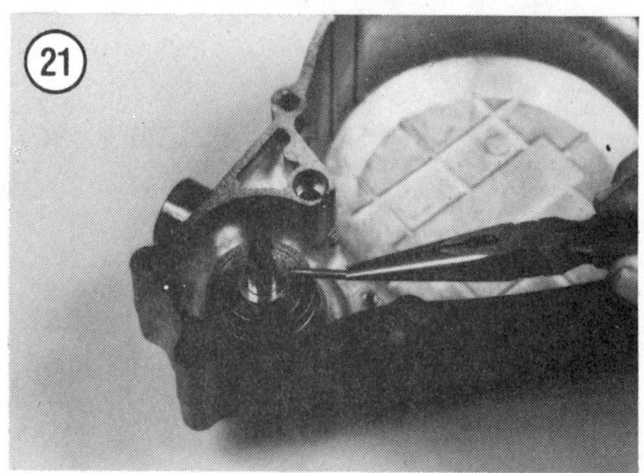
21

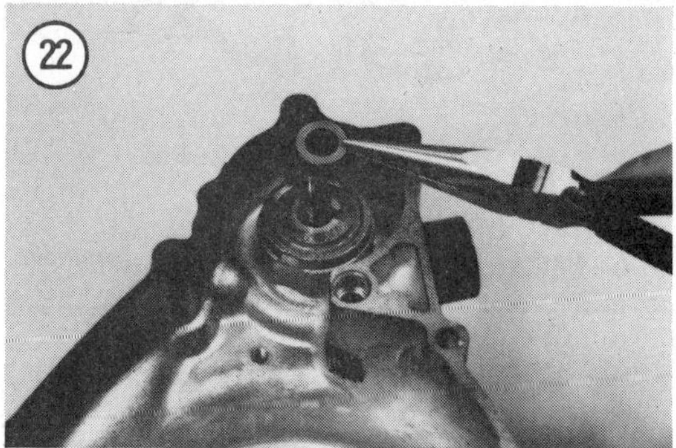
22

23

24

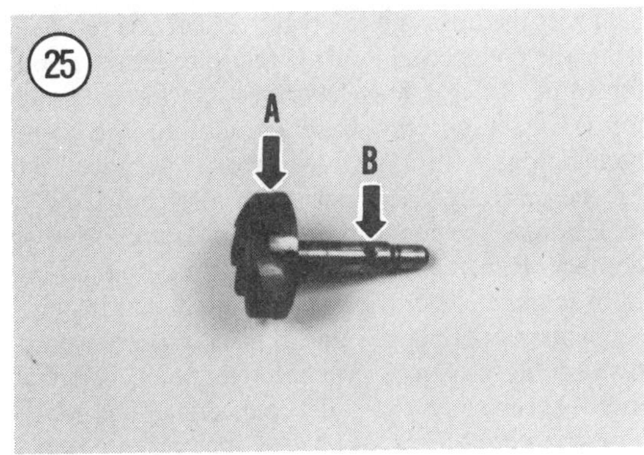

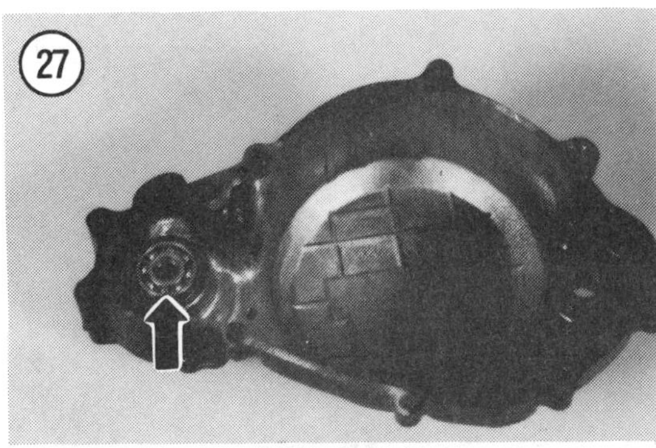

5. Check the water pump driven gear for wear or damage. Check the pin slots in the gear **(Figure 29)** for cracks or damage. Replace the gear if necessary.
6. Check the impeller shaft bearing surface in the right-hand crankcase (**Figure 30**). Remove any small burrs with fine grit sandpaper.

Assembly

1. Lightly grease the impeller shaft (**Figure 25**) and insert through the cover (**Figure 23**).
2. Install the washer (**Figure 22**).
3. Insert the pin through the shaft hole (**Figure 21**).
4. Align the slots in the gear (**Figure 31**) with the pin (**Figure 32**) and install the gear. See **Figure 20**.

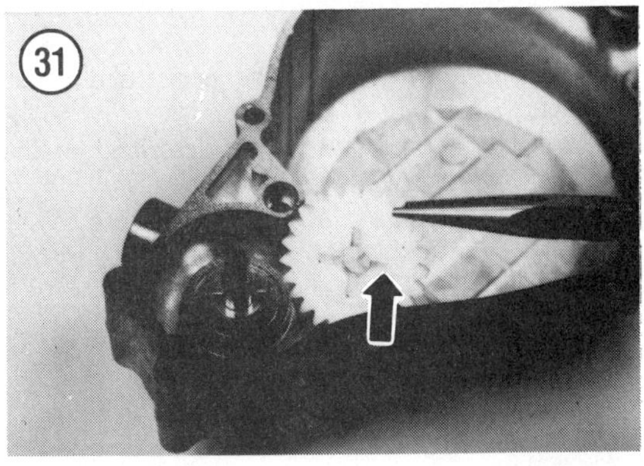

5. Install the washer (**Figure 19**).
6. Install the clip (**Figure 18**). Make sure it seats in the shaft groove completely.
7. Spin the gear by hand. It should turn freely. If the gear is tight, disassemble the impeller shaft assembly and check all parts.
8. Install the clutch cover as described under *Clutch Cover Removal/Installation* in Chapter Six.
9. Install a new water pump cover gasket. Insert the locating pin (**Figure 17**) into the pump cover.
10. Install the water pump cover (**Figure 16**). Tighten the attaching bolts securely.
11. Check the water pipe joint O-rings (**Figure 33**). Replace if necessary.
12. Install the water pipe joint (**Figure 15**). Tighten the screw securely.
13. Refill the cooling system as described under *Coolant Change* in Chapter Three.

HOSES

Hoses deteriorate with age and should be replaced periodically or whenever they show signs of cracking or leakage. To be safe, replace the hoses every 2 years. The spray of hot coolant from a cracked hose can cause rider injury. Loss of coolant will also cause the engine to overheat and result in severe damage.

Whenever any component of the cooling system is removed, inspect the hoses(s) and determine if replacement is necessary.

Inspection

1. With the engine cool, check the cooling hoses for brittleness or hardness. A hose in this condition will usually show cracks and must be replaced.
2. With the engine hot, examine the hoses for swelling along the entire hose length. Eventually a hose will rupture at this point.
3. Check area around hose clamps. Signs of rust around clamps indicate possible hose leakage.

Replacement

Hose replacement should be performed when the engine is cool.

1. Drain the cooling system as described under *Coolant Change* in Chapter Three.
2. Loosen the hose clamps from the hose to be replaced. Slide the clamps along the hose and out of the way.

CAUTION
Excessive force applied to the hose during removal could damage the connecting joint.

3. Twist the hose end to break the seal and remove from the connecting joint. If the hose has been on for some time, it may have become fused to the joint. If so, cut the hose parallel to the joint connections with a knife or razor. The hose then can be carefully pried loose with a screwdriver.
4. Examine the connecting joint for cracks or other damage. Repair or replace parts as required. If the joint is okay, clean it of any rust with sandpaper.
5. Inspect hose clamps and replace as necessary.
6. Slide hose clamps over the outside of hose and install hose to inlet and outlet connecting joint. Make sure the hose clears all obstructions and is routed properly.

NOTE
If it is difficult to install a hose on a joint, soak the end of the hose in hot water for approximately 2 minutes. This will soften the hose and ease installation.

7. With the hose positioned correctly on joint, position clamps back away from end of hose slightly. Tighten clamps securely, but not so much that hose is damaged.
8. Refill cooling system as described under *Coolant Change* in Chapter Three. Start the engine and check for leaks. Retighten hose clamps as necessary.

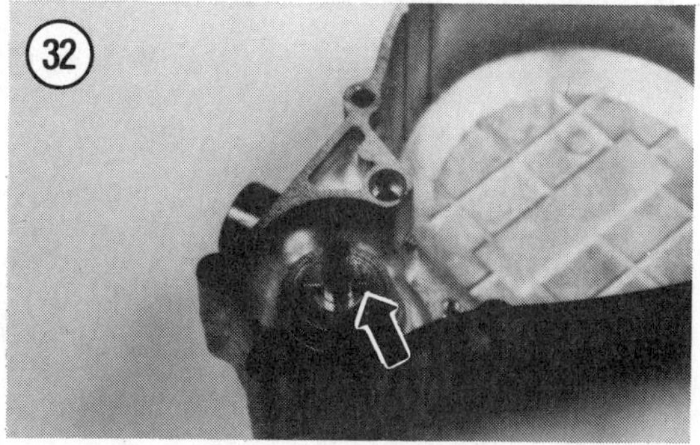

CHAPTER ELEVEN

FRONT SUSPENSION AND STEERING

This chapter describes repair and maintenance on the front wheel, forks and steering components.

Front fork specifications are listed in **Table 1**. **Table 1** and **Table 2** are at the end of the chapter.

FRONT WHEEL

Removal (1978-1981)

1. Place a workstand under the frame to support it securely with the front wheel off the ground.
2. Slacken the brake cable at the hand lever (**Figure 1**).
3. Remove the cotter pin and axle nut (**Figure 2**).
4. Remove the front axle from the right-hand side. Twist the axle while pulling it out.
5. Carefully pull the wheel down to disengage the brake panel from the boss on the front fork.
6. Pull the brake panel out of the front wheel. Support the brake panel with a Bungee cord to prevent front brake cable damage.
7. Remove the right-hand axle spacer (**Figure 3**).
8. Install the axle spacer and axle nut on the axle to prevent their loss when servicing the wheel.
9. Check the front wheel and axle as described under *Inspection (All Models)* in this chapter.

Installation (1978-1981)

1. Make sure the axle bearing surfaces of the fork sliders and the axle are free from burrs and nicks.
2. Clean the axle and the axle holes with solvent and thoroughly dry. Make sure all axle surface contact areas are free from dirt prior to installation.
3. Apply a light coat of grease to the axle, bearings and grease seals.
4. Insert the brake panel into the front wheel brake drum.
5. Install the right-hand axle spacer (**Figure 3**).
6. Position the wheel into place and insert the front axle from the right-hand side.

NOTE

*Make sure the boss on the left-hand fork slider is properly engaged in the groove in the brake panel (**Figure 4**). This is necessary for proper brake operation.*

7. Tighten the axle nut to the torque specification listed in **Table 2**.
8. Install a new cotter pin and bend it over completely. Never reuse an old cotter pin as it may break and fall out.

9. Adjust the brake as described under *Front Brake Adjustment* in Chapter Three.
10. After the wheel is installed, completely rotate it. Apply the brake several times to make sure it rotates freely and that the brake is operating correctly.
11. Remove the wood blocks from under the frame.

Removal (1982-on)

1. Place wood block(s) under the crankcase to support it securely with the front wheel off the ground.
2. Loosen and remove the front axle nut (**Figure 5**) and washer.
3. Slide the axle (**Figure 6**) out from the right-hand side and remove the front wheel.

NOTE
There is a washer installed on the right-hand side of the axle.

NOTE
*After removing the front wheel, insert a piece of wood or hose in the caliper between the brake pads (**Figure** 7). That way, if the brake lever is accidently squeezed, the piston will not be forced out of the brake caliper cylinder. If the brake lever is squeezed and the piston comes out, the caliper might have to be disassembled to reseat the piston and the system will have to be bled.*

4. Remove the left (**Figure 8**) and right (**Figure 9**) side axle spacers.

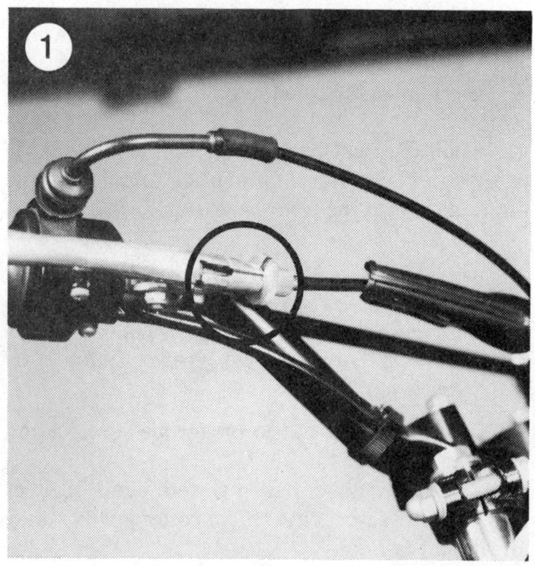

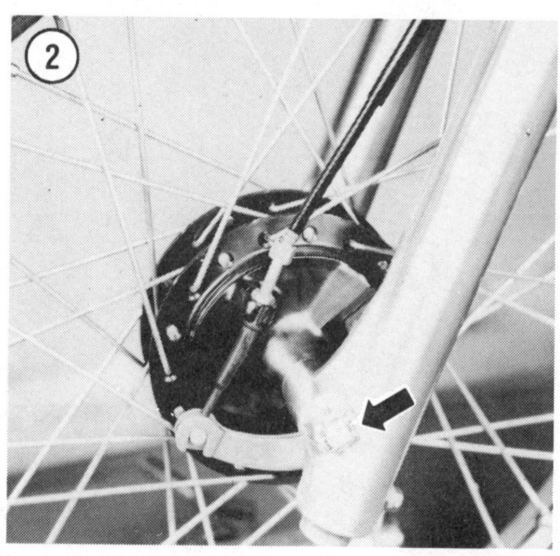

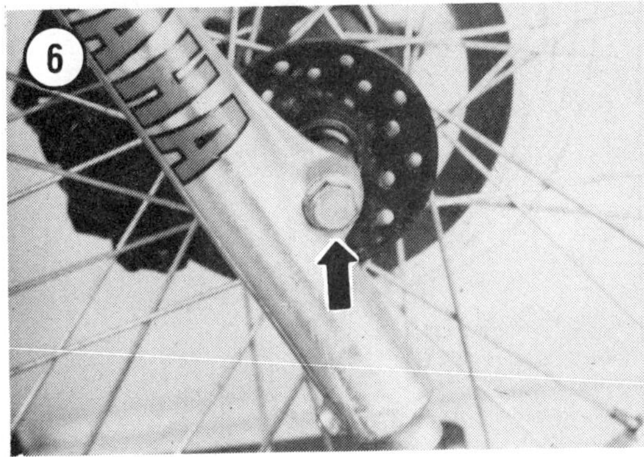

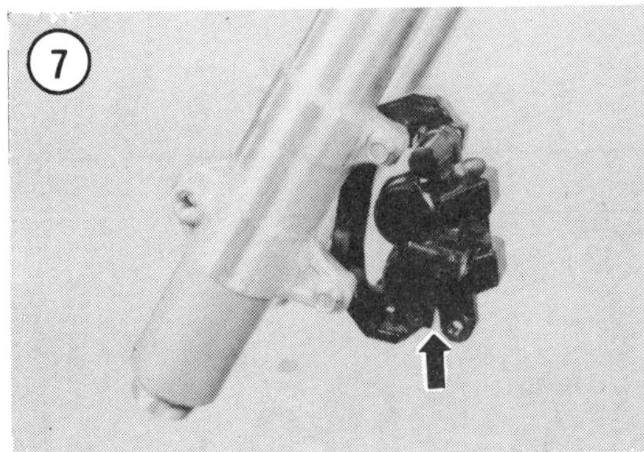

5. Install the axle spacers, washers and axle nut on the axle to prevent their loss when servicing the wheel. See **Figure 10**.

6. Check the front wheel and axle as described under *Inspection (All Models)* in this chapter.

Installation (1982-on)

1. Clean the axle and axle spacers in solvent and thoroughly dry. Make sure all axle contact surfaces are clean and free of dirt and old grease prior to installation. If these surfaces are not cleaned, the axle may be difficult to remove later on.

2. Apply a light coat of grease to the axle, bearings and grease seals.

3. Install the left (**Figure 8**) and right (**Figure 9**) side axle spacers.

4. Carefully insert the disc between the brake pads when installing the wheel.

NOTE

Don't forget to install a washer onto the axle before installing the axle in Step 5.

5. Install the axle from the right-hand side through the wheel hub (**Figure 6**).

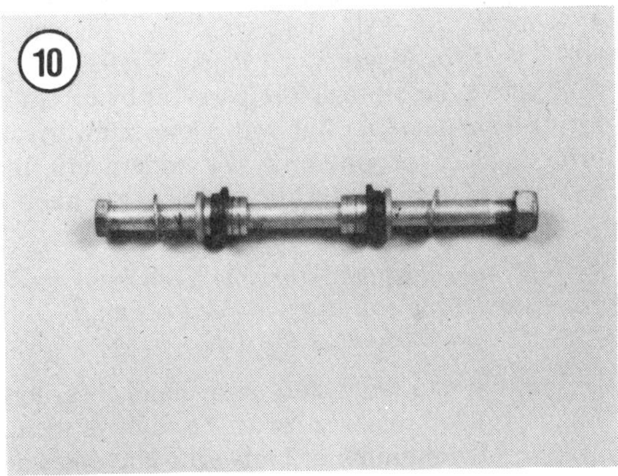

11

6. Install the washer and axle nut (**Figure 5**). Tighten the axle nut to the torque specification in **Table 2**.
7. After the wheel is completely installed, rotate the front wheel and apply the brake. Do this a couple of times to make sure the front wheel and brake are operating correctly.

Inspection (All Models)

The easiest way to check wheel rim straightness is with a truing stand (**Figure 11**). If a stand isn't available, you can make one yourself with some 2×4 wood scraps and 16 penny nails.

After mounting the wheel in a suitable stand, fix a pointer so that you can check radial (up and down) and axial (side-to-side) play (**Figure 12**).

Spin the wheel and check radial (up and down) and axial (side-to-side) play. When determining wheel play, it is more important to clean up the axial play. Since the wheel is bouncing up and down on a motocross track, radial play isn't as critical. It's more important for the wheel be vertically straight, so it isn't wobbling around between the fork legs.

Tighten or replace any bent or loose spokes. Refer to *Spoke Adjustment* or *Spoke Inspection and Replacement* in this chapter.

Check the axle runout as described under *Front Hub Inspection* in this chapter.

FRONT HUB

Refer to **Figure 13** (1978-1981) or **Figure 14** (1982-on) for this procedure.

Disassembly

1. Remove the front wheel as described under *Front Wheel Removal* in this chapter.
2. *1978-1981 models:* If still installed, pull the brake assembly straight up and out of the hub.
3. Remove the axle spacer(s). See **Figure 3** (1978-1981) or **Figure 8** and **Figure 9** (1982-on).
4. Remove the oil seal(s) (**Figure 15**) by carefully prying them out of the hub with a long screwdriver. Prop a piece of wood or rag underneath the screwdriver to prevent from damaging the hub.

NOTE
If the seal is tight, work the screwdriver around the seal every few degrees until the seal pops out of the hub.

5. Remove the left- and right-hand bearings (**Figure 16**) and distance collar. To remove them, insert a soft aluminum or brass drift into one side

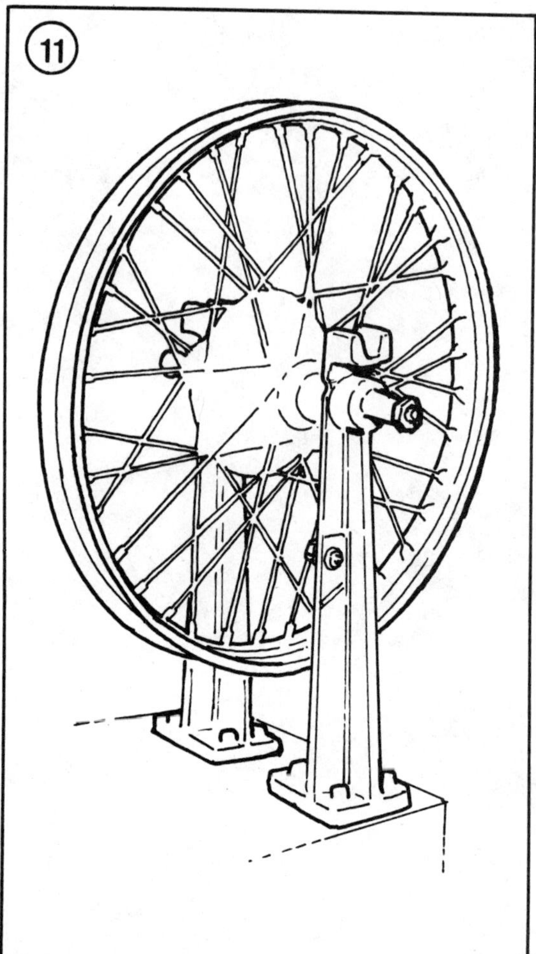

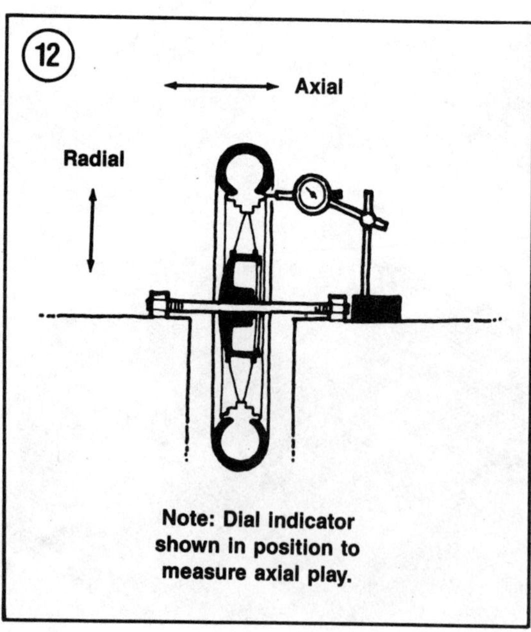

Note: Dial indicator shown in position to measure axial play.

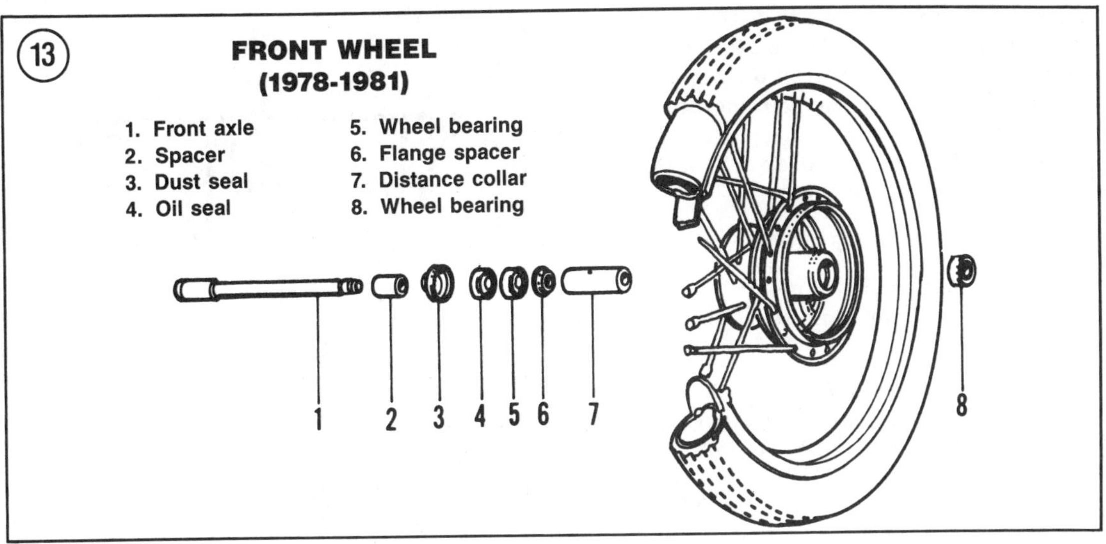
13
FRONT WHEEL
(1978-1981)
1. Front axle
2. Spacer
3. Dust seal
4. Oil seal
5. Wheel bearing
6. Flange spacer
7. Distance collar
8. Wheel bearing
1 2 3 4 5 6 7 8

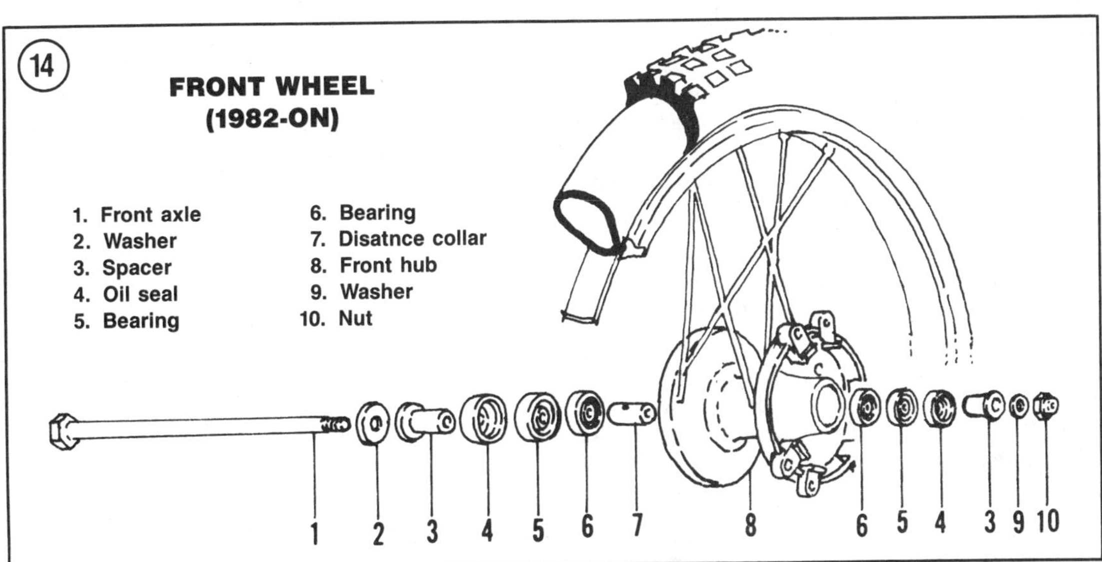
14
FRONT WHEEL
(1982-ON)
1. Front axle
2. Washer
3. Spacer
4. Oil seal
5. Bearing
6. Bearing
7. Disatnce collar
8. Front hub
9. Washer
10. Nut
1 2 3 4 5 6 7 8 6 5 4 3 9 10

11

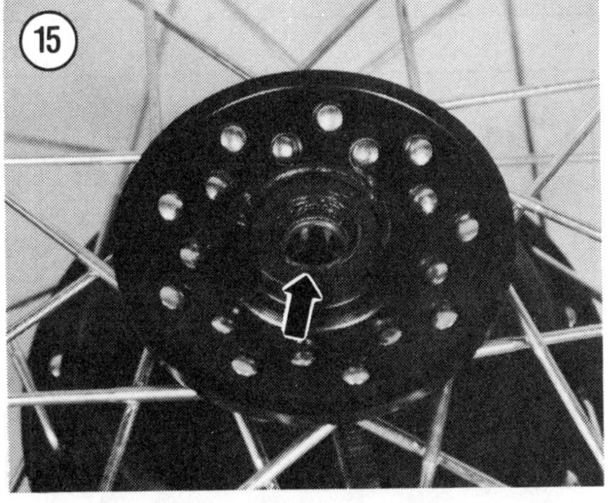
15

16

of the hub. Push the distance collar over to one side and place the drift on the inner race of the lower bearing (**Figure 17**). Tap the bearing out of the hub with a hammer, working around the perimeter of the inner race.

6. Remove the distance collar and tap out the opposite bearing.

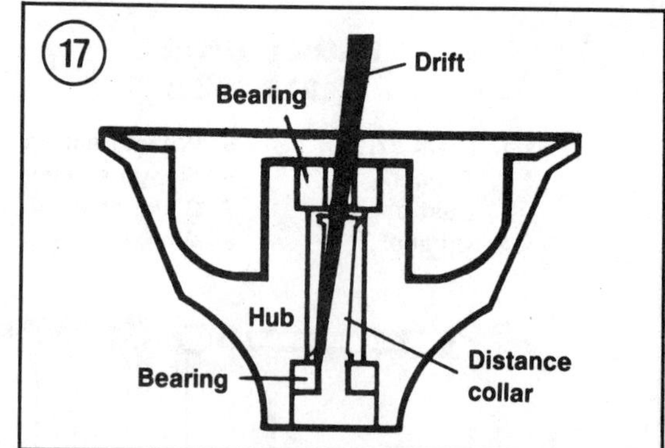

Inspection

1. Thoroughly clean out the inside of the hub with solvent and dry with compressed air or a shop cloth.

NOTE
Avoid getting any greasy solvent residue on the brake drum during this procedure. If this happens, clean it off with a shop cloth and lacquer thinner.

2. Do not clean sealed bearings in solvent as this will liquefy the bearing grease and cause bearing failure. Clean sealed bearing by wiping them off with a lint-free cloth. If non-sealed bearings are installed, clean them in solvent and thoroughly dry with compressed air. Do not let the bearing spin while drying.

3. Turn each bearing by hand (**Figure 18**). Make sure the bearings turn smoothly.

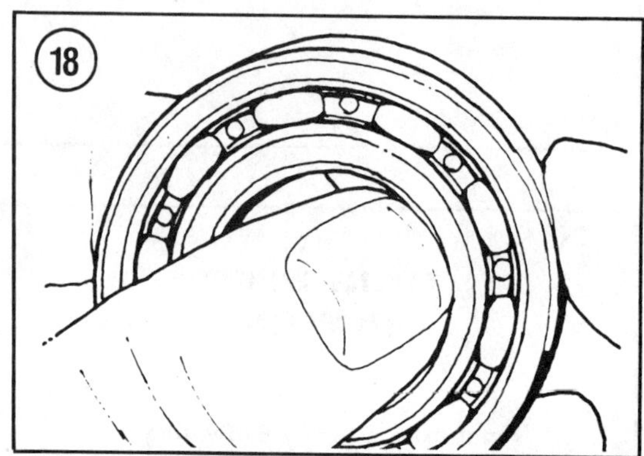

NOTE
Some axial play is normal, but radial play should be negligible. The bearing should turn smoothly.

4. On non-sealed bearings, check the balls for evidence of wear, pitting, or excessive heat (bluish tint). Replace bearing if necessary; always replace as a complete set.

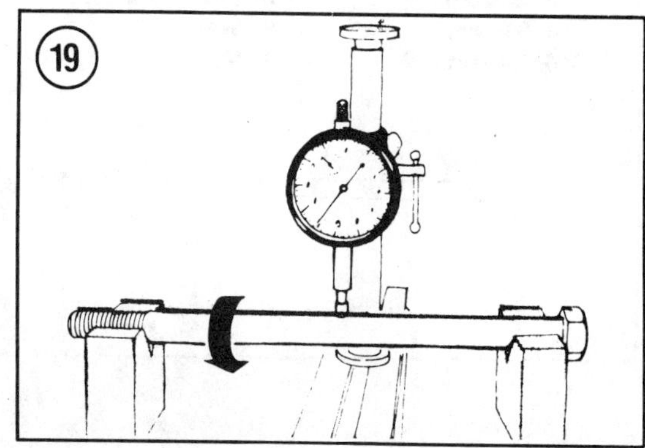

NOTE
Fully sealed bearings are available from many good bearing specialty shops. Fully sealed bearings provide better protection from dirt and moisture that may get into the hub.

5. Check the axle for wear and straightness. Use V-blocks and a dial indicator as shown in **Figure 19**. If the runout is 0.2 mm (0.008 in.) or greater, the axle should be replaced.

Assembly

1. Pack non-sealed bearings with good quality bearing grease. Work the grease in between the balls thoroughly. Turn the bearing by hand a couple of times to make sure the grease is distributed evenly inside the bearing.

2. Pack the wheel hub and distance collar with multipurpose grease.

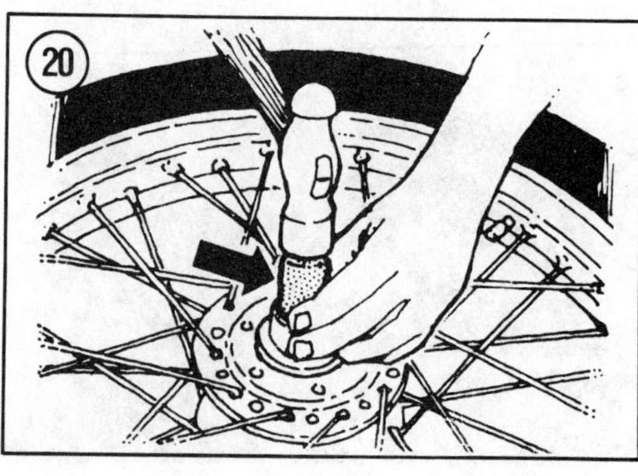

NOTE
*Install the wheel bearings with the sealed side facing out (**Figure 16**).*

CAUTION
*When installing the bearings in the following procedures, tap the bearings squarely into place and tap on the outer race only. Use a socket (**Figure 20**) that matches the outer race diameter. Do not tap on the inner race or the bearing might be damaged. Be sure that the bearings are completely seated.*

21

YAMAHA "Z" SPOKE TIGHTENING SEQUENCE

Valve stem

22

3. Install the left-hand bearing.
4. Install in the distance collar.
5. Install the right-hand bearing.
6. Install a new grease seal(s). Lubricate it with multipurpose grease and tap it squarely into the hub. Install the oil seal until it is at least flush with the hub. Install the dust seal and spacer(s).
7. Install the front wheel as described under *Front Wheel Installation* in this chapter.

WHEELS

The tire and wheel assemblies on any dirt bike take a lot of abuse and should be inspected prior to each race or weekend ride.

Spoke Inspection and Replacement

Spokes loosen with use and should be checked prior to each race or a weekend ride. The "tuning fork" method for checking spoke tightness is simple and works well. Tap each spoke with a spoke wrench or the shank of a screwdriver and listen for a tone.

A tightened spoke will emit a clear, ringing tone, and a loose spoke will sound flat. All the spokes in a correctly tightened wheel will emit tones of similar pitch but not necessarily the same precise tone.

Bent, stripped or broken (**Figure 21**) spokes should be replaced as soon as they are detected, as they can cause the destruction of an expensive rim and hub. Unscrew the nipple from the spoke. Remove the damaged spoke from the hub and use it to match a new spoke of identical length. If necessary, trim the new spoke to match the original and dress the end of the thread with a thread die. Install the new spoke in the hub and screw on the nipple; tighten it until the spoke's tone is similar to the tone of the other spokes in the wheel. Periodically check the new spoke; it will stretch and must be retightened several times before it takes its final set.

Spoke Adjustment

On 1978-1983 models, if all spokes appear loose, tighten the spokes on one side of the hub, then tighten all spokes on the other side. One-half to one turn should be sufficient; do not overtighten.

Starting in 1984, all YZ80 models are equipped with special "Z" spokes that require different tightening procedures. If the spokes appear loose, tighten every 3rd spoke in the sequence shown in **Figure 22**. After tightening spoke No. 32, you will have tightened each spoke once. After tightening each spoke, check spoke adjustment once again. If there are still loose spokes, repeat the procedure.

While tightening the spokes, check rim runout with a dial indicator to be sure you aren't pulling the rim out of shape.

Refer to *Inspection* in this chapter and **Figures 11** and **12**.

Spin the wheel and check radial and axial play. When determining wheel play, it is more important to clean up the axial play. Since the wheel is bouncing up and down on a motocross track, radial play isn't as critical. It's more important for the wheel be vertically straight, so it isn't wobbling around between the fork legs.

To pull the rim out, tighten spokes which terminate on the same side of the hub and loosen spokes which terminate on the opposite side of the hub (**Figure 23**).

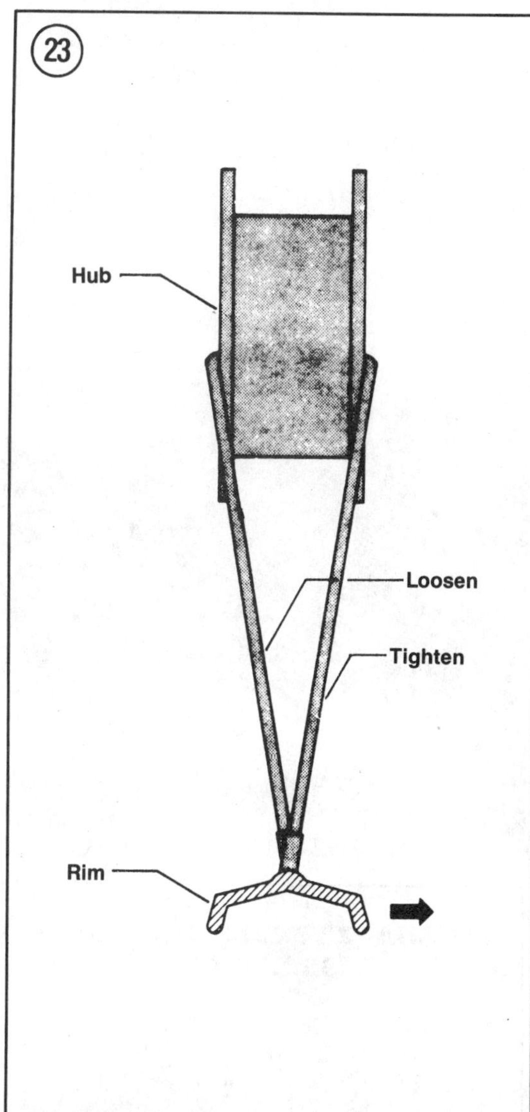

TIRE CHANGING

Removal

1. Remove the valve core and deflate the tire.
2. Loosen the rim lock nuts (**Figure 24**).
3. Press the entire bead on both sides of the tire into the center of the rim.
4. Lubricate the beads with soapy water.

NOTE
*Use only quality tire irons without sharp edges (**Figure 25**). If necessary, file the ends of the tire irons to remove rough edges.*

5. Insert the tire iron under the bead next to the valve (**Figure 26**). Force the bead on the opposite side of tire into the center of the rim and pry the bead over the rim with the tire iron.
6. Insert a second tire iron next to the first to hold the bead over the rim. Then work around the tire with the first tire iron, prying the bead over the rim. Be careful not to pinch the inner tube with the tire irons.
7. Remove the valve from the hole in the rim and remove the tube from the tire.

NOTE
Step 8 is required only if it is necessary to completely remove the tire from the rim, such as for tire replacement.

8. Stand the tire upright. Insert the tire iron between the second bead and the side of the rim that the first bead was pried over (**Figure 27**). Force the bead on the opposite side from the tire iron into the center of the rim. Pry the second bead off of the rim, working around as with the first.

Installation

1. Carefully check the tire for any damage, especially inside. Check the sidewall as it is very vulnerable to damage from rocks, motocross course stakes and other riders' footpegs.

2. Check that the spoke ends do not protrude through the nipples into the center of the rim to puncture the tube. File off any protruding spoke ends.

NOTE

If you are having trouble with water and dirt entering the wheel, remove and discard the rubber rim band. Then wrap the rim center with 2 separate revolutions of duct tape. Punch holes through the tape at the rim lock and valve stem mounting areas.

3. Install the rim lock if removed.
4. If you are using the rubber rim band, be sure the band is in place with the rough side toward the rim. Align the holes in the band with the holes in the rim.
5. Liberally sprinkle the inside tire casing with baby talcum powder. This helps to minimize tube pinching because the powder reduces chafing between the tire and tube.
6. If the tire was removed, lubricate one bead with soapy water. Then align the tire with the rim and push the tire onto the rim (**Figure 28**). Work around the tire in both directions (**Figure 29**).

25

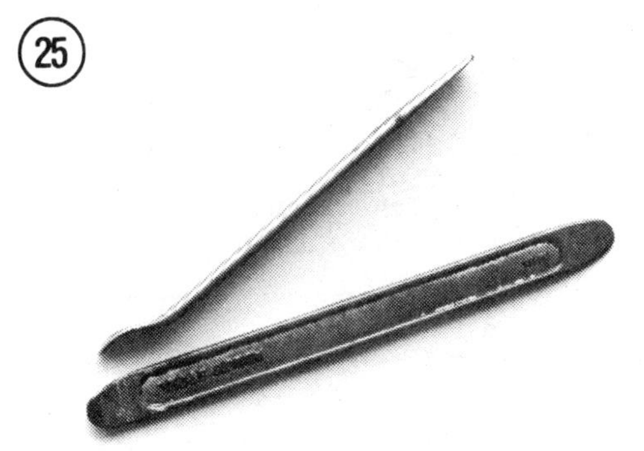

26

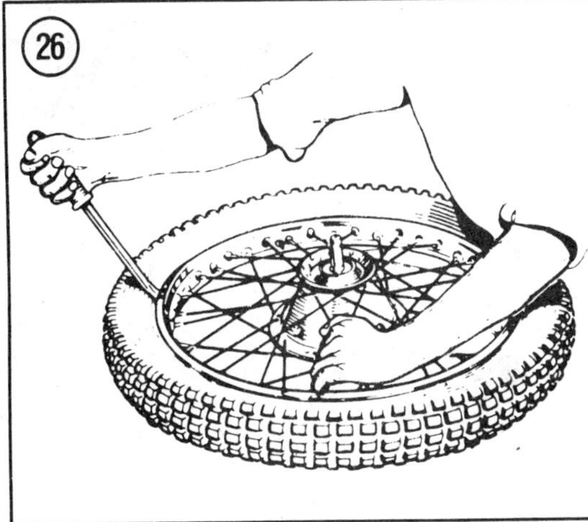

27

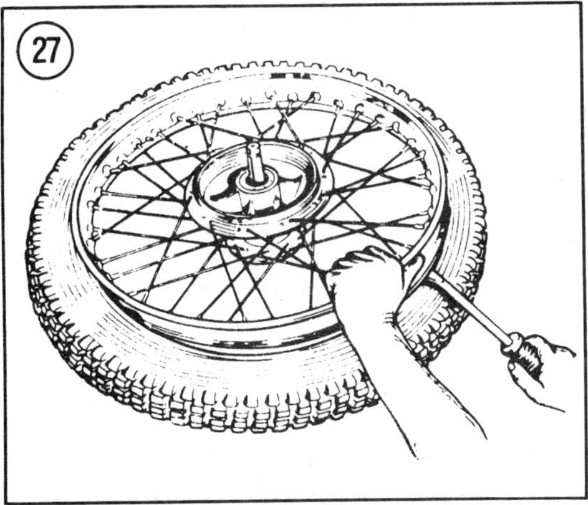

28

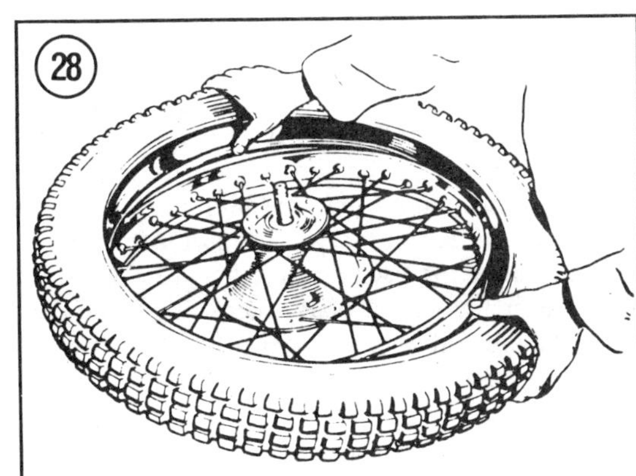

29

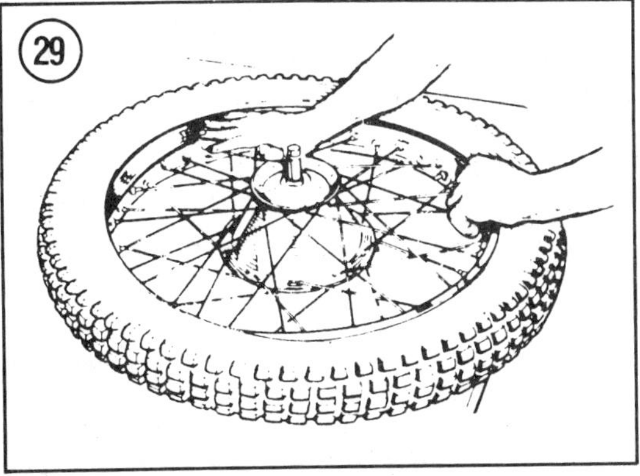

7. Install the core into the inner tube valve. Put the tube in the tire and insert the valve stem through the hole in the rim. Inflate just enough to round it out. Too much air will make installing it in the tire difficult, and too little will increase the chances of pinching the tube with the tire irons.
8. Lubricate the upper tire bead and rim with soapy water.
9. Press the upper bead into the rim opposite the valve. Pry the bead into the rim on both sides of the initial point with your hands and work around the rim to the valve. If the tire wants to pull up on one side, either use a tire iron or one of your knees to hold the tire in place. The last few inches are usually the toughest to install and is also where most pinched tubes occur. If you can, continue to push the tire into the rim with your hands. Relubricate the bead if necessary. If the tire bead wants to pull out from under the rim use both of your knees to hold the tire in place. If necessary, use a tire iron for the last few inches (**Figure 30**).
10. Wiggle the valve to be sure the tube is not trapped under the bead. Set the valve squarely in its hole before screwing on the valve nut.

NOTE
*Make sure the valve stem is not cocked in the rim as shown in **Figure 31**.*

11. Check the bead on both sides of the tire for even fit around the rim. Inflate the tire to approximately 25-30 psi to insure the tire bead is seated properly on the rim. If the tire is hard to seat, relubricate both sides of the tire and reinflate.
12. Tighten the rim lock nut (**Figure 24**).
13. Bleed the tire back down to between 10 and 14 psi. Never tighten the valve stem nut against the rim. It should always be installed finger-tight, near the valve stem cap rather than flush against the rim (**Figure 32**).

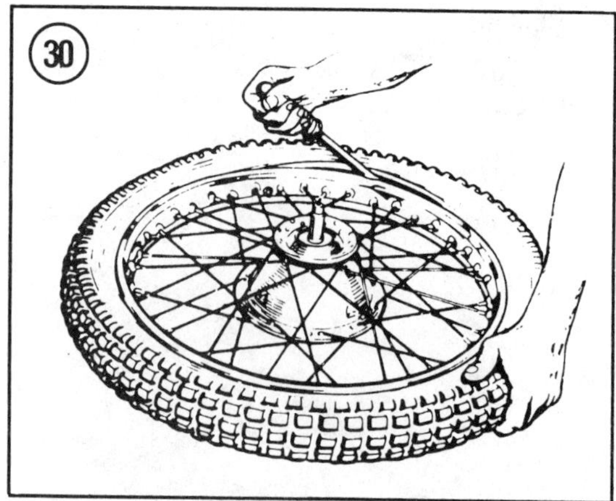
30

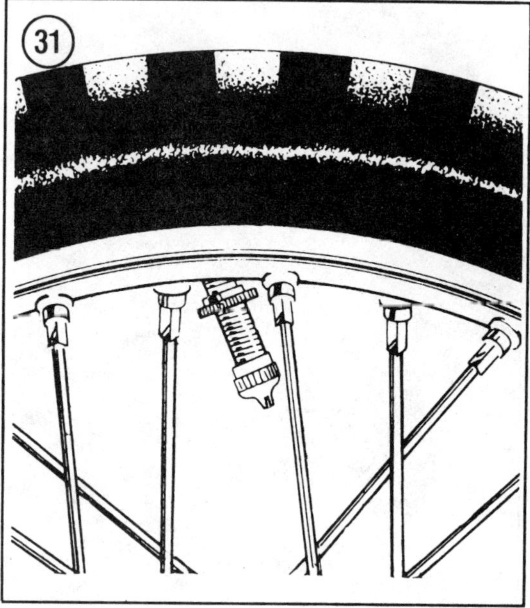
31

32

TIRE REPAIRS

Every dirt rider eventually experiences trouble with a tire or tube. Repairs and replacement are fairly simple and every rider should know how to patch a tube.

Patching a motorcycle tube is only a temporary fix, especially on a dirt bike. The tire flexes too much and the patch could rub right off.

CLYMER RACE TIP
If a regular standard inner tube is used replace it every 10 races. A stronger heavy-duty tube will last longer and is not as easy to puncture. The stronger tube weighs more where you least need

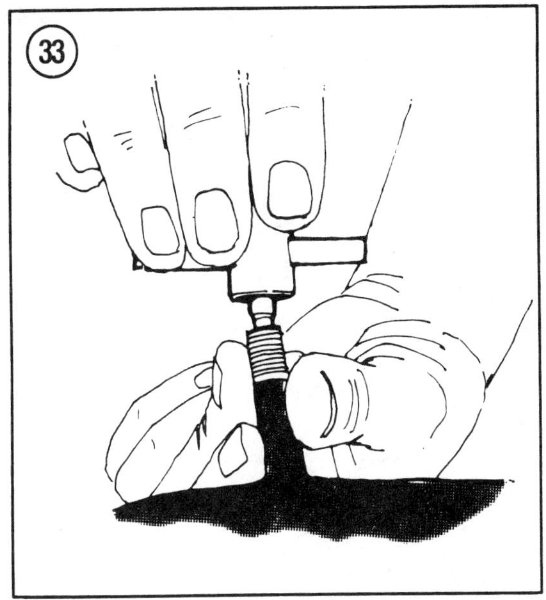

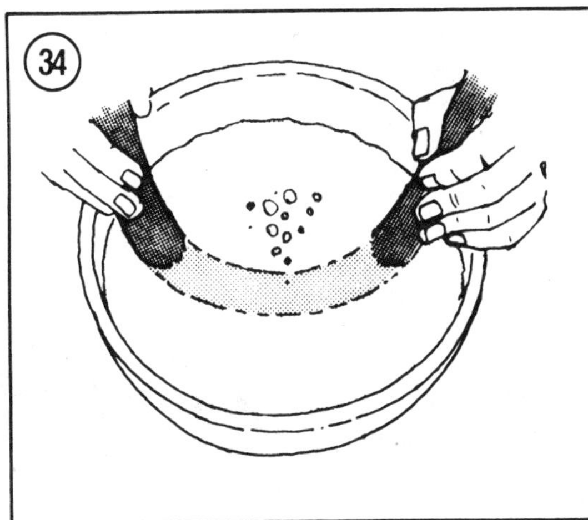

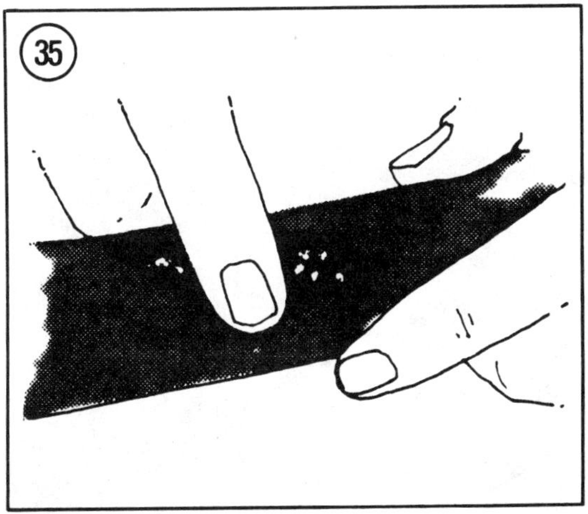

it (unsprung weight) but it's a small sacrifice that's offset by the increased durability.

Tire Repair Kits

Tire repair kits can be purchased from motorcycle dealers and some auto supply stores. When buying, specify that the kit you want is for motorcycles.

There are 2 types of tire repair kits:

a. Hot patch.

b. Cold patch.

Hot patches are stronger because they actually vulcanize to the tube, becoming part of it. However, they are far too bulky to carry for trail repairs and the strength is unnecessary for a temporary repair.

Cold patches are not vulcanized to the tube; they are simply glued to it. Though not as strong as hot patches, cold patches are still very durable. Cold patch kits are less bulky than hot and more easily applied out on a dusty trail or in the pits. A cold patch kit contains everything necessary and tucks easily in with your emergency tool kit.

Tube Inspection

1. Remove the tube as described under *Tire Changing* in this chapter.
2. Install the valve core into the valve stem (**Figure 33**) and inflate the tube slightly. Do not overinflate.
3. Immerse the tube in water a section at a time (**Figure 34**). Look carefully for bubbles indicating a hole. Mark each hole and continue checking until you are certain that all holes are discovered and marked. Also make sure that the valve core is not leaking. Tighten it if necessary.

NOTE

*If you do not have enough water to immerse sections of the tube, try running your hand over the tube slowly and very close to the surface. If your hand is damp, it works even better. If you suspect a hole anywhere, apply some saliva to the area to verify it (**Figure 35**).*

4. Apply a cold patch using the techniques described under *Cold Patch Repair,* following this procedure.
5. Dust the patch area with talcum powder to prevent it from sticking to the tire.
6. Carefully check the inside of the tire casing for small rocks, sand or twigs which may have damaged the tube. If the inside of the tire is split, apply a patch to the area to prevent it from pinching and damaging the tube again.

7. Check the inside of the rim. Make sure the rubber rim band is in place, with no spoke ends protruding, which could puncture the tube.
8. Deflate the tube prior to installation in the tire.

Cold Patch Repairs

1. Remove the tube from the tire as previously described.
2. Roughen an area around the hole slightly larger than the patch, using a cap from the tire repair kit or a pocket knife. Do not scrape too vigorously or you may cause additional damage.
3. Apply a small amount of the special cement from the kit to the puncture and spread it evenly with your finger (**Figure 36**).
4. Allow the cement to dry until tacky—usually 30 seconds or so is sufficient.
5. Remove the backing from the patch.

CAUTION
Do not touch the newly exposed rubber with your fingers or the patch will not stick firmly.

6. Center the patch over the hole. Hold patch firmly in place for about 30 seconds to allow the cement to set (**Figure 37**).
7. Dust the patched area with talcum powder to prevent sticking.
8. Install the tube as previously described.

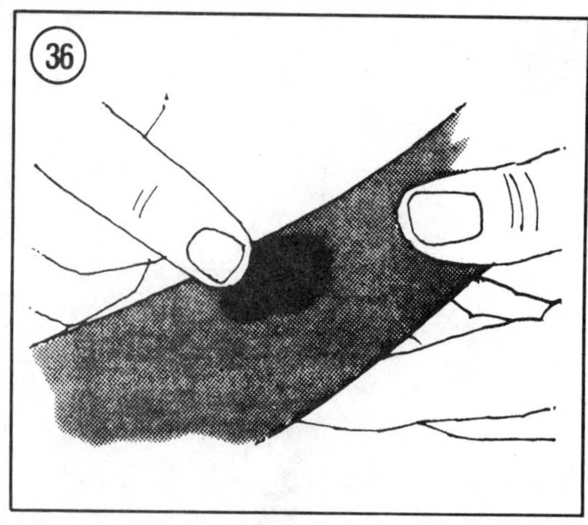

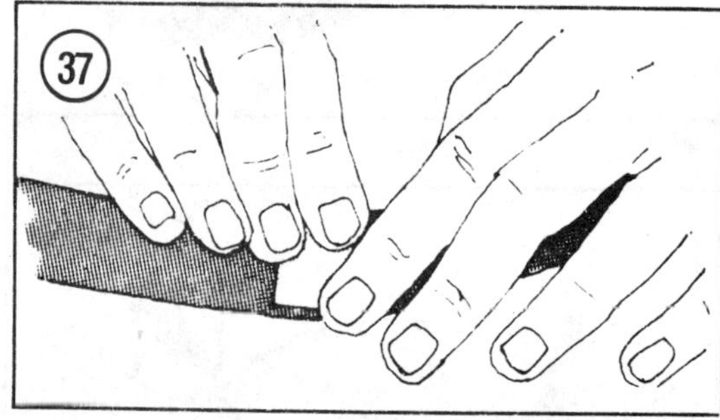

HANDLEBAR

Removal/Installation

1. Remove the plastic straps on the engine kill switch wire.

NOTE
Step 2 describes disassembly and removal of the throttle assembly. If it is not necessary to disassemble the throttle assembly when removing the handlebar, loosen the throttle screws only. Then when the handlebar bolts and handlebar are removed from the steering stem, slide the throttle assembly off the handlebar.

2A. *1978-1980 models:* Remove the screws securing the engine kill switch and throttle assembly and remove them.
2B. *1981-on models:* Perform the following:
  a. Remove the screw securing the kill switch (**Figure 38**) and remove it from the handlebar.
  b. Remove the screws securing the throttle assembly (A, **Figure 39**) and remove it.

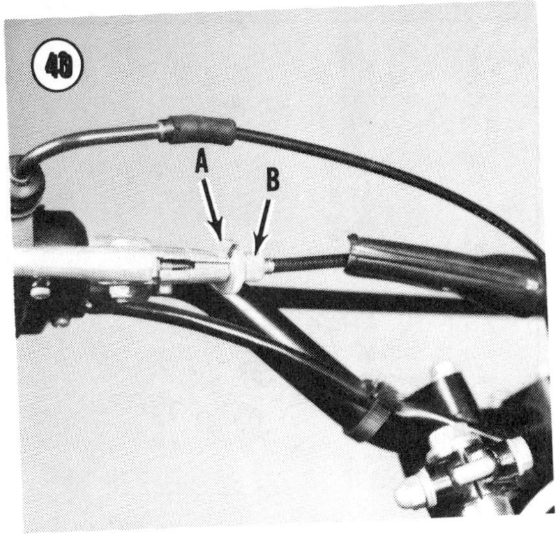

40

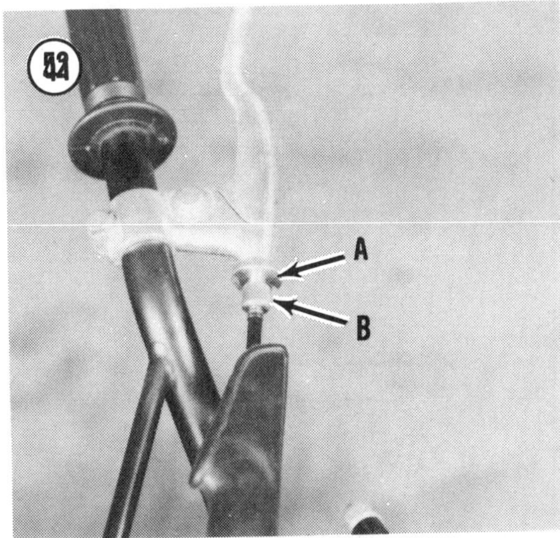

41

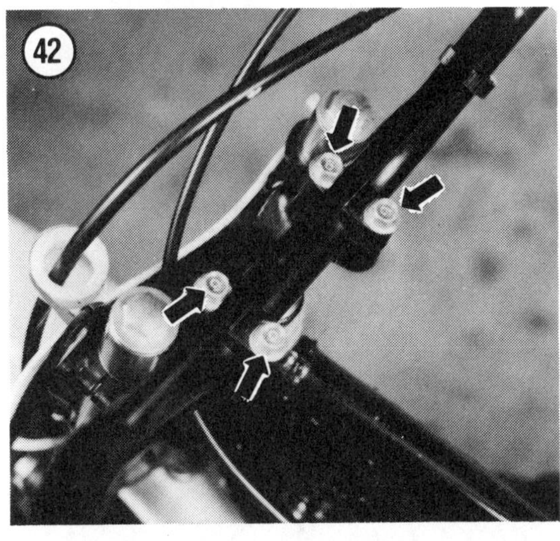

42

NOTE
Carefully lay the throttle assembly and cable over the front fender, or back over the frame, so the cable does not get crimped or damaged.

3. Disconnect the front brake cable (1978-1981) and clutch cable as follows. See **Figure 40** and **Figure 41**:
   a. Loosen the cable locknut (A) and screw the adjuster (B) all the way in towards the lever.
   b. Align the slot in the locknut and adjuster so that the cable can be removed.
   c. Grab the cable near the adjuster. Then pull the cable out of the adjuster.
   d. Disconnect the end of the cable from the hole in the lever.
4. *Disc brake models:* Remove the bolts securing the master cylinder to the handlebar and remove the master cylinder (B, **Figure 39**). Support the master cylinder upright and so that it does not hang by the hydraulic hose.

NOTE
If the master cylinder is allowed to hang too low, air may enter the brake line. Try to keep it near handlebar level.

5. Remove the bolts (**Figure 42**) securing the handlebar holders and remove the holders.
6. Remove the handlebar.
7. Install by reversing these removal steps noting the following.
8. To maintain a good grip in the handlebar and to prevent them from slipping down, clean the knurled section of the handlebar with a wire brush. It should be kept rough so it will be held securely by the holders. The holders should also be kept clean and free of any metal that may have been gouged loose by handlebar slippage.
9. Tighten the bolts securing the handlebar to the torque specifications listed in **Table 2**.
10. Apply a light coat of silicone spray to the throttle grip area on the handlebar prior to installation.

WARNING
After installation is completed, make sure the brake lever does not come in contact with the throttle grip assembly when it is pulled on fully.

11. Adjust the front drum brake (1978-1981) and clutch as described in Chapter Three.

WARNING
Make sure the front brake and clutch operate properly before riding the bike.

STEERING HEAD AND STEM (1978-1981 AND 1983)

The steering head on these models uses loose ball bearings. Refer to **Figure 43** (1978-1981) or **Figure 44** (1983) for this procedure.

Disassembly

1. Remove the front wheel as described under *Front Wheel Removal* in this chapter.
2. Remove the front fender.
3. Remove the handlebar as described under *Handlebar Removal/Installation* in this chapter.
4. Loosen but do not remove the steering bolt. See 5, **Figure 43** or 2, **Figure 44**.

NOTE
*Before removing the fork, measure and write down on a piece of paper, the distance from the top of the fork tube to the top of the upper fork bridge (**Figure 45**). This will enable the fork to be reinstalled in the same position.*

5. Remove the front forks as described under *Front Fork Removal/Installation* in this chapter.
6. Remove the steering bolt.
7. Remove the upper fork bridge assembly.
8. Remove the steering head adjusting nut (**Figure 46**). Use a spanner wrench (**Figure 47**), or channel-lock pliers.

NOTE
Have an assistant hold a large pan under the steering stem to catch the loose ball bearings and carefully lower the steering stem.

9. Lower the steering stem assembly down out of the steering head (**Figure 48**).
10. Do not intermix the balls as they are different sizes and quantity. The upper bearing has 3/16 in. balls (quantity—22) and the lower has 1/4 in. balls (quantity—19).
11. Remove the upper bearing race cover.
12. Remove the upper ball bearings (**Figure 49**).
13. Remove the lower ball bearings from the steering stem.

Inspection

1. Clean the bearing races in the steering head, the steering stem races and the ball bearings with solvent.
2. Check the welds around the steering head for cracks and fractures. If any are found, have them repaired by a competent frame shop or welding service.

(43)

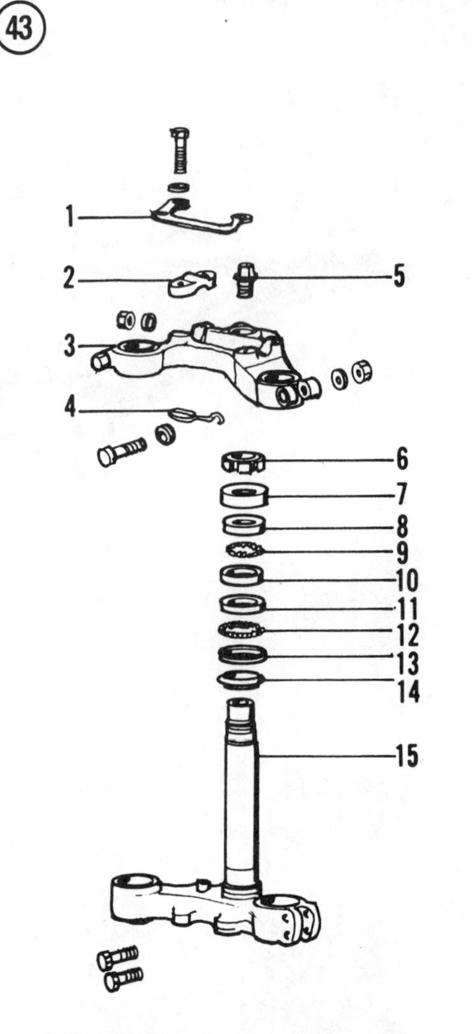

STEERING STEM ASSEMBLY (1978-1981)

1. Wire guide
2. Handlebar holder
3. Upper fork bridge
4. Cable holder/clip
5. Steering bolt
6. Steering stem adjusting nut
7. Upper ball race cover
8. Outer ball race (upper)
9. Upper balls-3/16 in. (22 total)
10. Inner ball race (upper)
11. Outer ball race (lower)
12. Lower balls-1/4 in (19 total)
13. Inner ball race (lower)
14. Dust seal
15. Steering stem

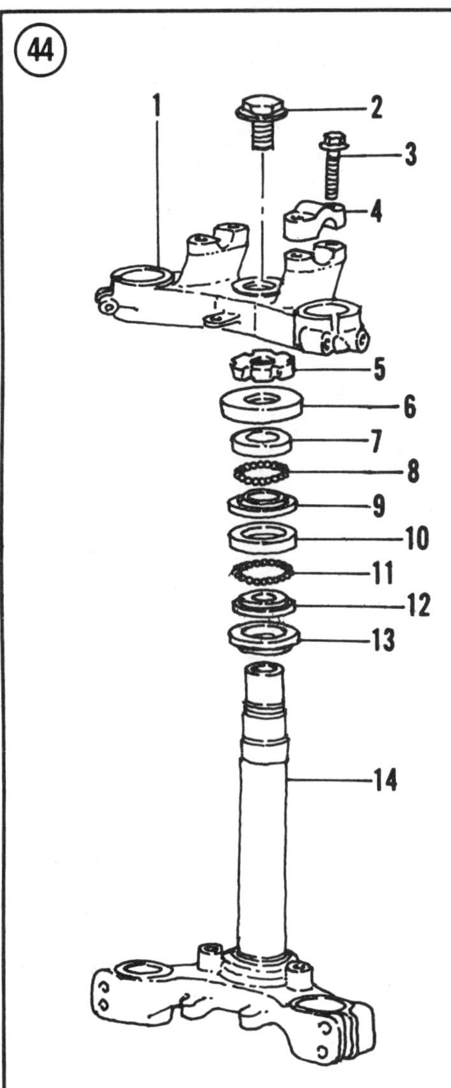

STEERING STEM ASSEMBLY (1983 YZ80)

1. Upper fork bridge
2. Steering bolt
3. Bolt
4. Handlebar holder
5. Steering stem adjusting nut
6. Upper ball race cover
7. Outer ball race (upper)
8. Upper balls (22 total)
9. Inner ball race (upper)
10. Outer ball race (lower)
11. Lower balls (19 total)
12. Inner ball race (lower)
13. Dust seal
14. Steering stem

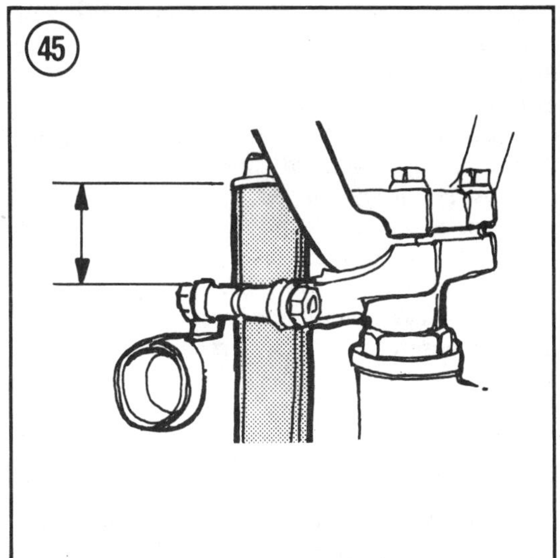

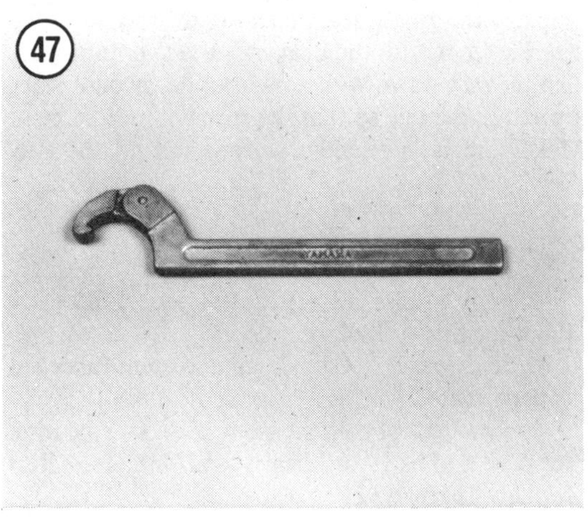

3. Check the balls for pitting, scratches, or discoloration indicating wear or corrosion. Replace them in sets if any are bad.
4. Check the races for pitting or galling and corrosion. If any of these conditions exist, replace the races as described under *Bearing Race Replacement* in this chapter.
5. Check the steering stem for cracks and check its race for damage or wear. If this race or any race is damaged, they should be replaced as a complete bearing set. Take the old races and bearings to your dealer to ensure accurate replacement.

Headset Race Replacement

To remove the headset race, insert a hardwood stick or soft punch into the head tube (**Figure 50**) and carefully tap the race out from the inside. After it is started, tap around the race so that neither the race nor the head tube is damaged.

NOTE
The upper and lower bearings and races are not the same size. Be sure that you install them at the proper ends of the head tube.

To install the headset race, tap it in slowly with a block of wood or suitable size socket or piece of pipe (**Figure 51**). Make sure they are squarely seated in the race bores before tapping them in. Tap them in until they are flush with the steering head.

Steering Stem Race and Grease Seal Replacement

To remove the steering stem race, try twisting and pulling it up by hand. If it will not come off, carefully pry it up with a screwdriver, while working around in a circle, prying a little at a time. Remove the race and the grease seal.

Install the grease seal and slide the race over the steering stem with the bearing surface pointing up. Tap the race down with a piece of hardwood; work around in a circle so that the race will not be bent. Make sure it is seated squarely and all the way down.

Steering Head Assembly

Refer to **Figure 43** (1978-1981) or **Figure 44** (1983) for this procedure.
1. Make sure the steering head and stem races are properly seated.
2. Apply a coat of cold grease to the lower bearing race cone and fit 19 ball bearings (1/4 in. diameter) around it (**Figure 52**).

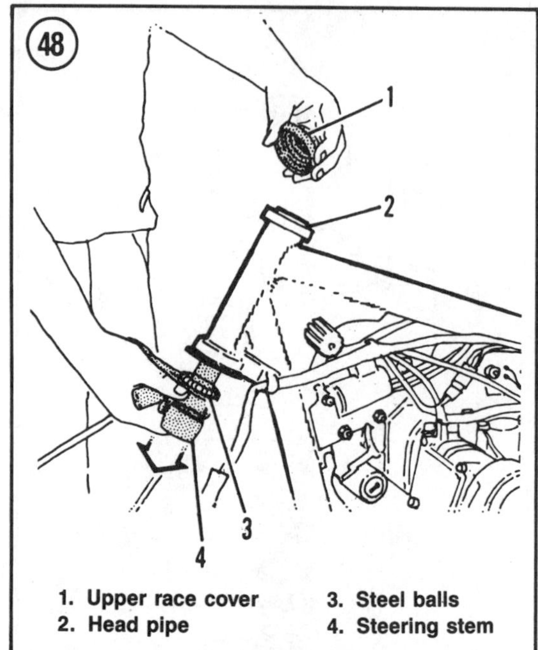

1. Upper race cover
2. Head pipe
3. Steel balls
4. Steering stem

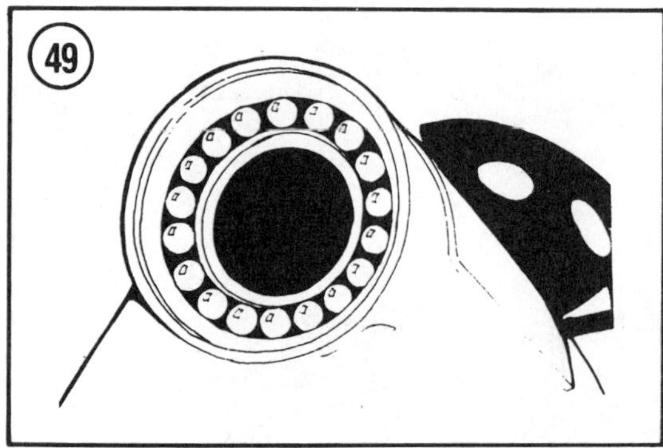

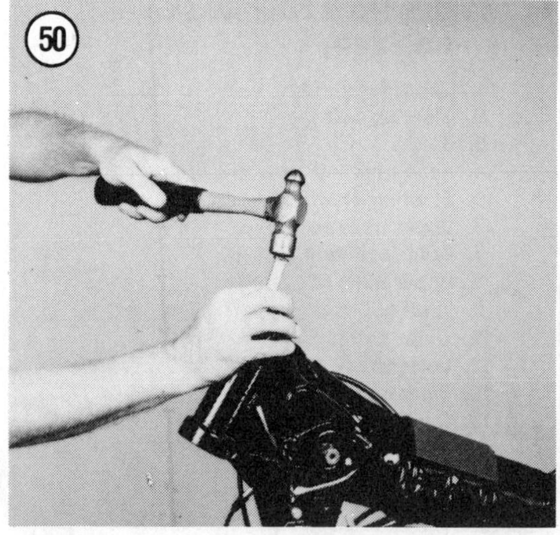

3. Apply a coat of cold grease to the upper bearing race cone and fit 22 ball bearings (3/16 in. diameter) around it (**Figure 49**).
4. Install the steering stem into the head tube and hold it firmly in place.

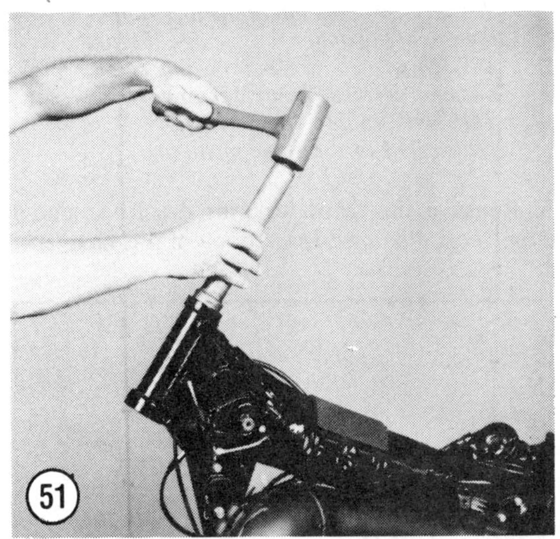

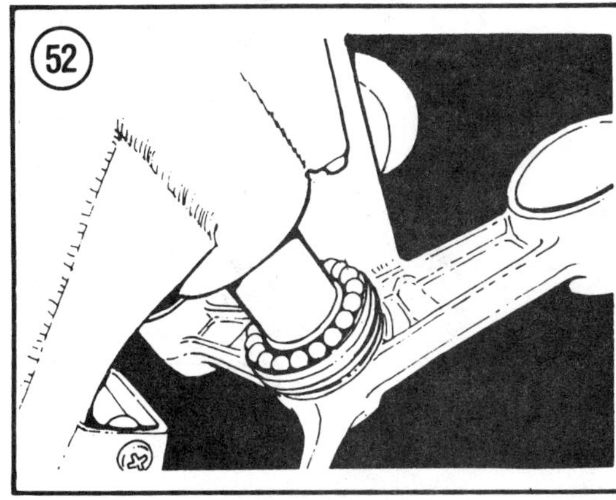

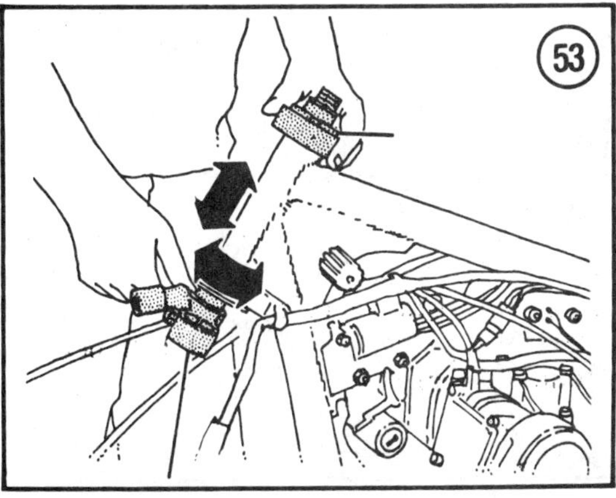

5. Install the upper bearing race cover.
6. Install the steering stem adjusting nut (**Figure 46**) and tighten it until it is snug against the upper race, then back it off 1/8 turn.

NOTE
*The adjusting nut should be just tight enough to remove play, both horizontal and vertical (**Figure 53**), yet loose enough so that the assembly will turn to both lock positions under its own weight after being pushed past the center point.*

7. Install the upper fork bridge and steering bolt—only finger-tight at this time.

NOTE
Steps 8-10 must be performed in this order to assure proper upper and lower fork bridge to fork alignment.

NOTE
*Install the fork tube the same distance up from the top of the upper fork bridge; see NOTE after Step 4, **Disassembly**.*

8. Slide both fork tubes into position and tighten the lower fork bridge bolts to the torque specification in **Table 2**.
9. Tighten the steering bolt to the torque specification in **Table 2**.
10. Tighten the upper fork bridge bolts to the torque specification in **Table 2**.
11. Continue assembly by reversing Steps 1-4, *Steering Stem Disassembly*.
12. After a few hours of riding the bearings have had a chance to seat; readjust the free play in the steering stem with the steering stem adjusting nut (**Figure 54**). Refer to Step 6.

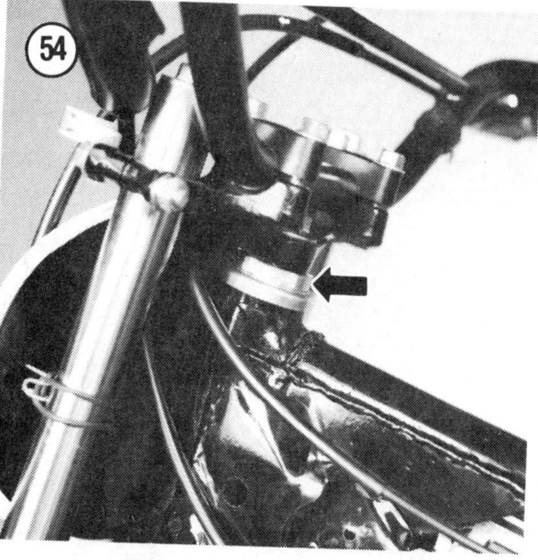

STEERING HEAD AND STEM (1982 YZ80)

The steering stem has been redesigned to accommodate the mounting and operation of the radiator. The steering stem assembly is shown in **Figure 55** and **Figure 56**.

Removal

1. Remove the front wheel as described under *Front Wheel Removal* in this chapter.
2. Remove the front fender.
3. Remove the handlebar as described under *Handlebar Removal/Installation* in this chapter.
4. Loosen but do not remove the steering nut (6, **Figure 55**).

NOTE
*Prior to removing the fork, measure and write down on a piece of paper, the distance from the top of the fork tube to the top of the upper fork bridge (**Figure 45**). This is not a standard dimension, but one derived from rider preference. This will enable the fork tube to be reinstalled in the same position.*

5. Remove the front forks as described under *Front Fork Removal/Installation* in this chapter.

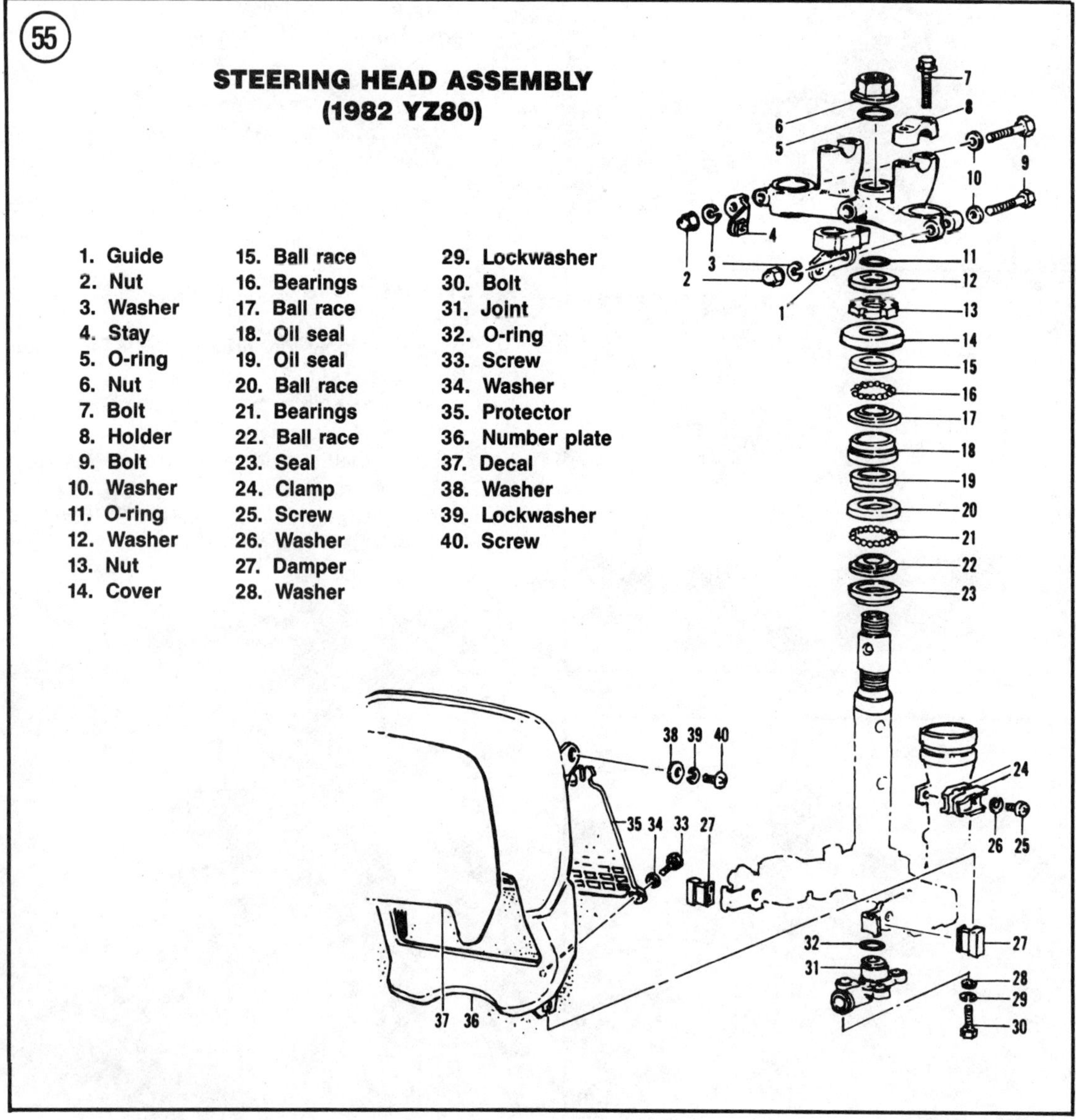

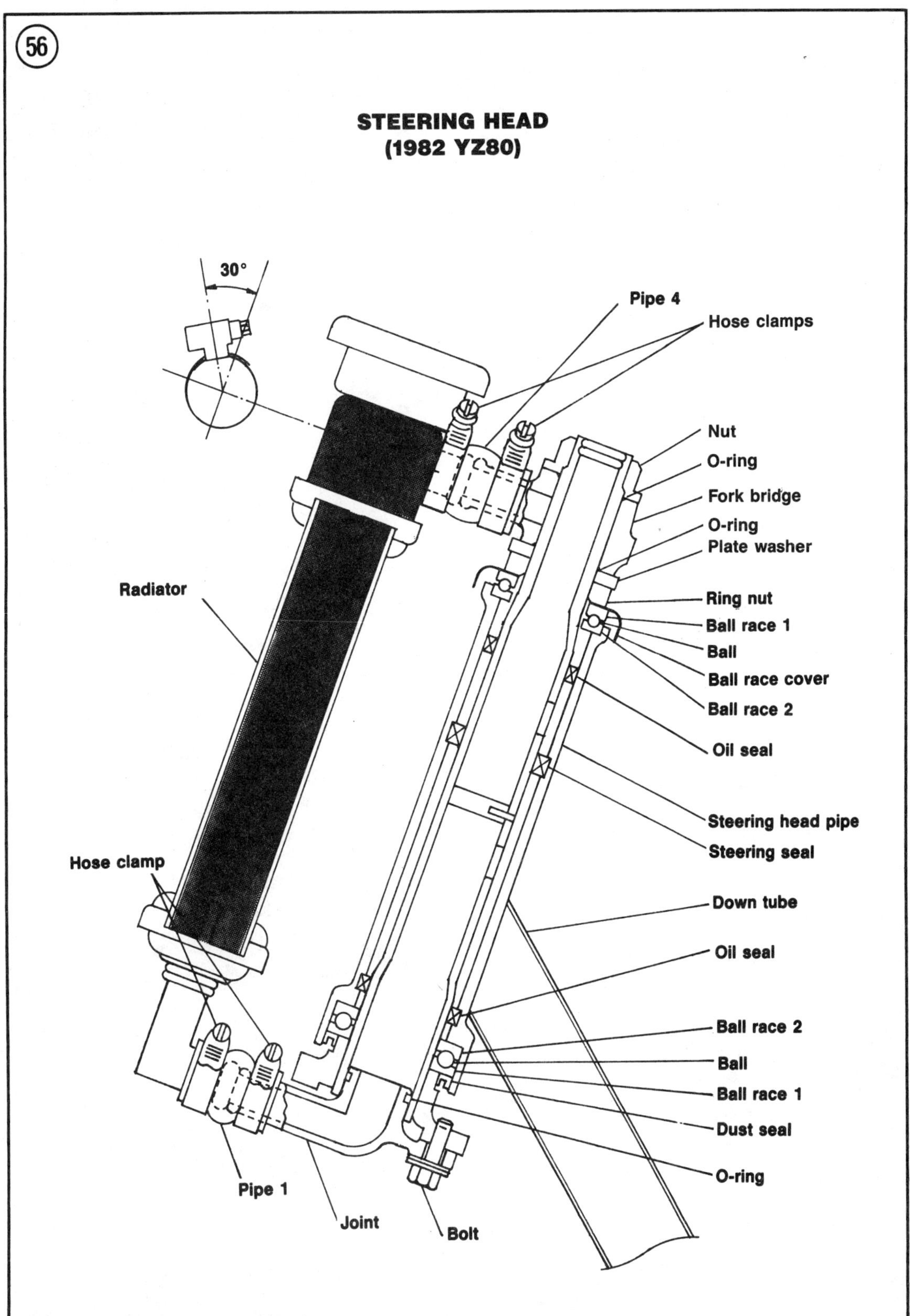
56
STEERING HEAD
(1982 YZ80)
30°
Pipe 4
Hose clamps
Nut
O-ring
Fork bridge
O-ring
Plate washer
Radiator
Ring nut
Ball race 1
Ball
Ball race cover
Ball race 2
Oil seal
Steering head pipe
Steering seal
Hose clamp
Down tube
Oil seal
Ball race 2
Ball
Ball race 1
Dust seal
O-ring
Pipe 1
Joint
Bolt

6. Remove the radiator as described in Chapter Ten.
7. Remove the radiator-to-steering stem coolant joint at the bottom of the steering stem (**Figure 57**).
8. Remove the steering stem flange nut (**Figure 58**) and O-ring (**Figure 59**). Then slip the upper fork bridge off the steering stem (**Figure 60**).
9. Slide the second O-ring off the steering stem (**Figure 61**). Then remove the plate washer (**Figure 62**) and the steering head adjusting nut (**Figure 63**). The steering head nut can be removed using a large drift and hammer or with a spanner wrench (**Figure 64**).

NOTE
Have an assistant hold a large pan under the steering stem to catch the loose ball bearings before performing Step 10.

10. Remove the upper bearing cap (**Figure 65**) and lower the steering stem assembly down and out of the steering head (**Figure 66**).
11. Do not intermix the balls. The upper bearing has 3/16 in. balls (quantity—22) and the lower has 1/4 in. balls (quantity—19).
12. Remove the upper ball bearings.
13. Remove the lower ball bearings from the steering stem.

Inspection

The steering stem (**Figure 67**) is designed to provide a path for coolant flow. During engine operation, the coolant travels through the radiator and steering stem to the engine and returns through the steering stem and back into the radiator. Because the coolant actually travels through the steering stem assembly, 3 special seals are press fitted into the steering head (**Figure 56**) to control coolant flow. The top seal prevents coolant from

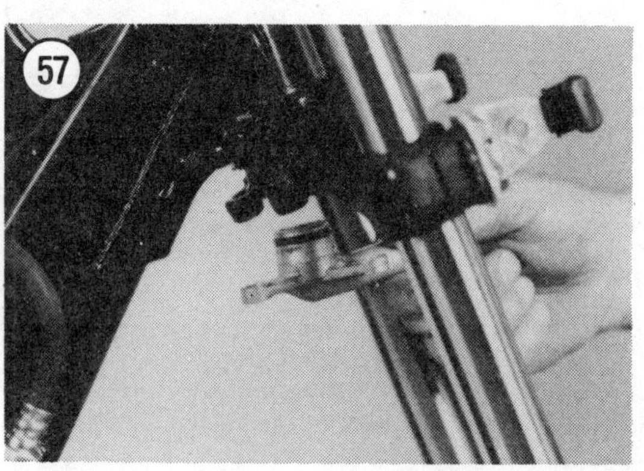
57

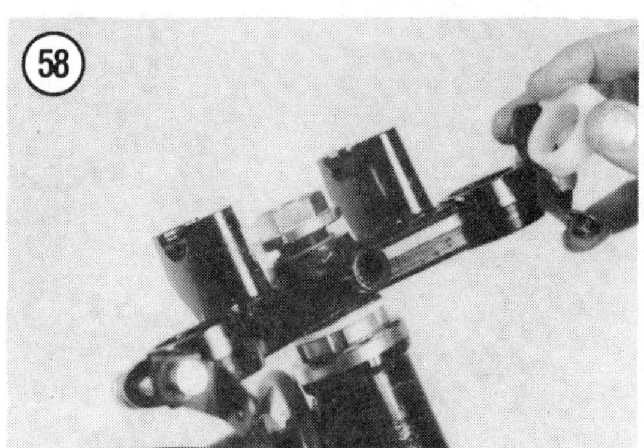
58

59

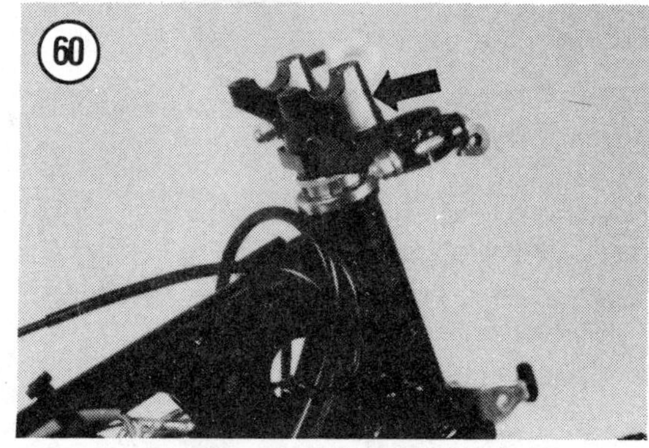
60

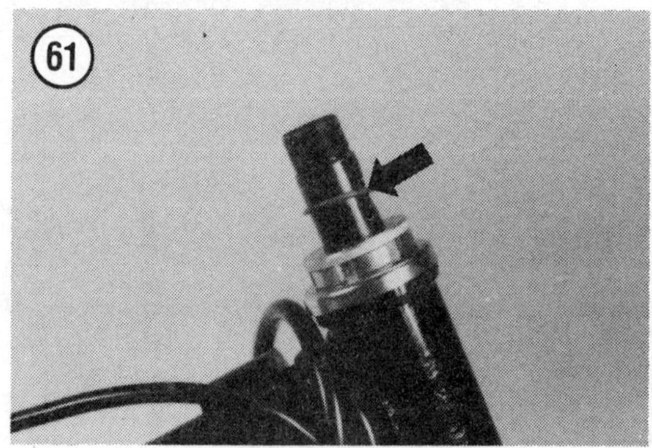
61

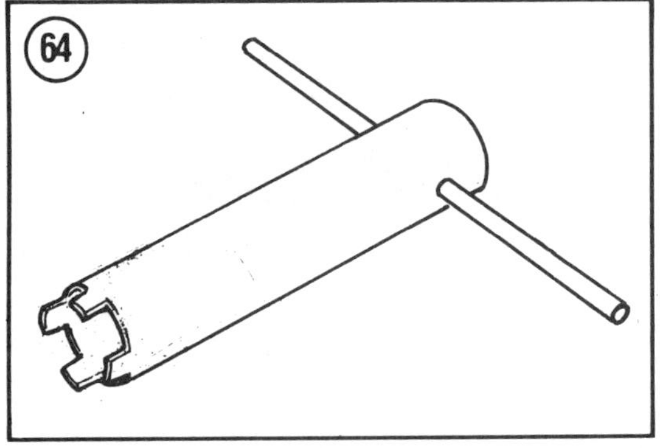

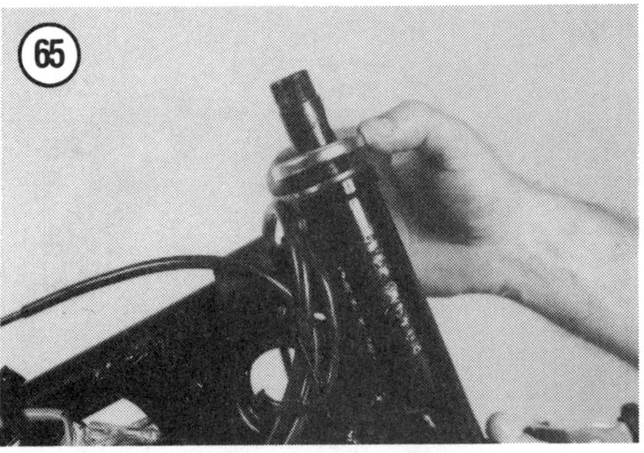

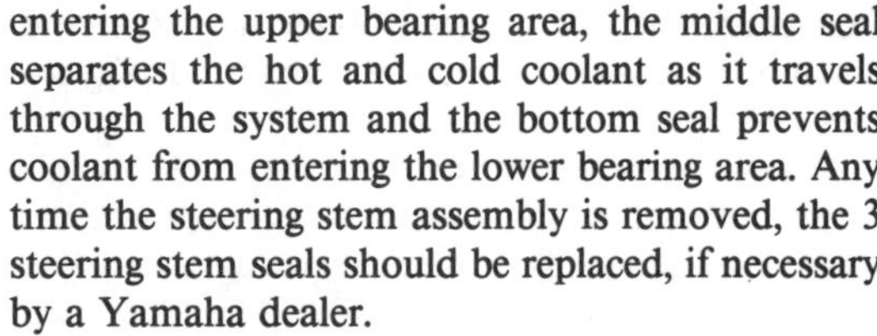

entering the upper bearing area, the middle seal separates the hot and cold coolant as it travels through the system and the bottom seal prevents coolant from entering the lower bearing area. Any time the steering stem assembly is removed, the 3 steering stem seals should be replaced, if necessary by a Yamaha dealer.

1. Clean the bearing races in the steering head, the steering stem races and the ball bearings with solvent.

2. Check the welds around the steering head for cracks and fractures. If any are found, have them repaired by a competent frame shop or welding service.

3. Check the balls for pitting, scratches, or discoloration indicating wear or corrosion. Replace them in sets if any are bad.

4. Check the races for pitting or galling and corrosion. If any of these conditions exist, replace the races as described under *Bearing Race Replacement* in this chapter.

5. Check the steering stem for cracks and check its race for damage or wear. If this race or any race is damaged, they should be replaced as a complete bearing set. Take the old races and bearings to your dealer to ensure accurate replacement.

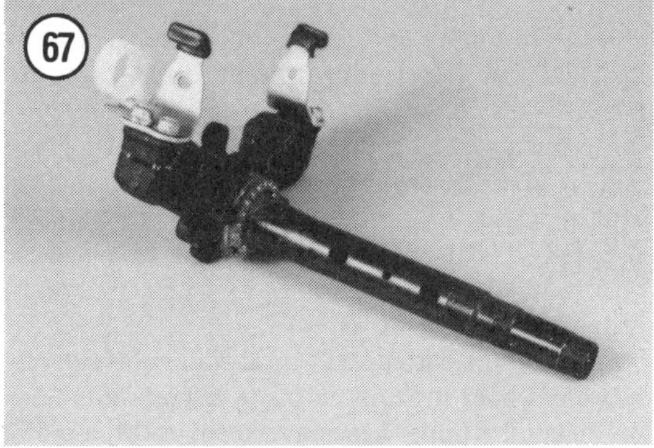

6. Examine the steering stem-to-radiator joint and O-ring for damage and replace if required (**Figure 68**).
7. Inspect upper (**Figure 69**) and lower (**Figure 70**) O-ring sealing areas on the fork bridge. Replace the upper fork bridge if these areas are damaged or worn.

Headset Race Replacement

To remove the headset race, insert a hardwood stick or soft punch into the head tube (**Figure 50**) and carefully tap the race out from the inside. After it is started, tap around the race so that neither the race nor the head tube is damaged.

To install the headset race, tap it in slowly with a block of wood or suitable size socket or piece of pipe (**Figure 51**). Make sure they are squarely seated in the race bores before tapping them in. Tap them in until they are flush with the steering head.

NOTE
The upper and lower bearings and races are not the same size. Be sure that you install them at the proper ends of the head tube.

Steering Stem Race and Grease Seal Replacement

To remove the steering stem race, try twisting and pulling it up by hand. If it will not come off, carefully pry it up with a screwdriver, while working around in a circle, prying a little at a time. Remove the race and the grease seal.

Install the grease seal and slide the race over the steering stem with the bearing surface pointing up. Tap the race down with a piece of hardwood; work around in a circle so that the race will not be bent. Make sure it is seated squarely and is all the way down.

Assembly

Refer to **Figure 55** for this procedure.

1. Make sure the steering head and stem races are properly seated.
2. Apply a coat of grease to the lower bearing race cone and fit 19 ball bearings (1/4 in. diameter) around it. See **Figure 52**.
3. Apply a coat of grease to the upper bearing race cone and fit 22 ball bearings (3/16 in. diameter) around it. See **Figure 71**.
4. Insert the steering stem up through the steering head and hold it firmly in place (**Figure 66**).
5. Install the upper bearing race cover (**Figure 65**).

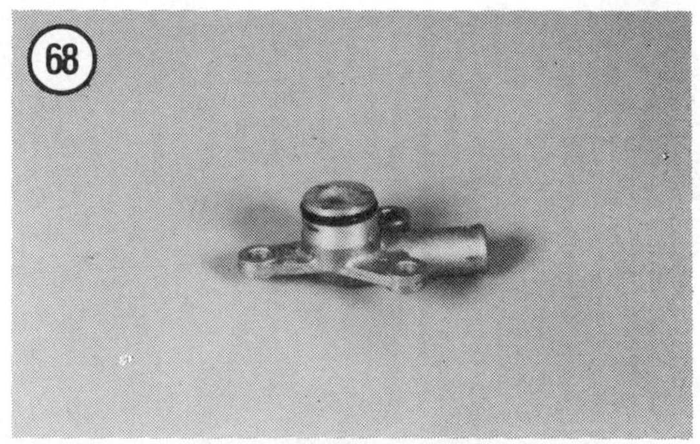
68

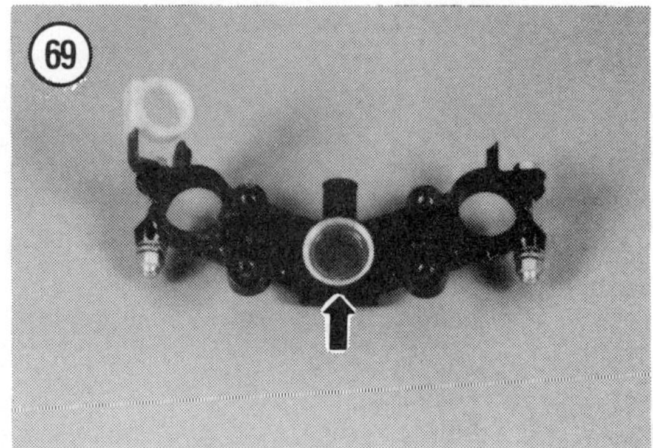
69

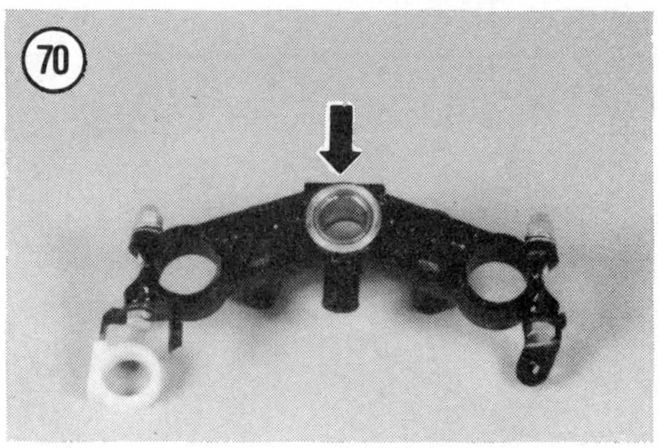
70

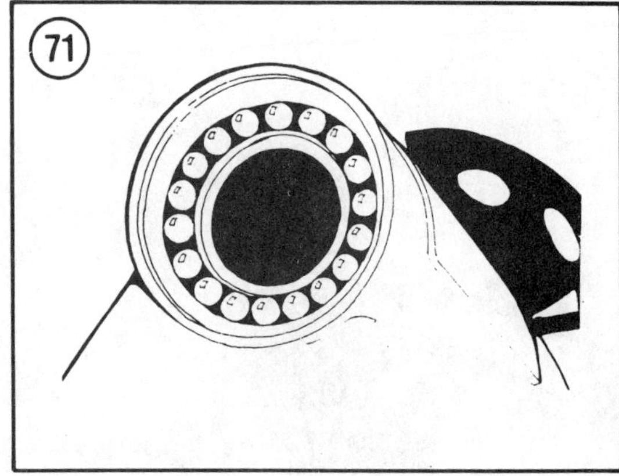
71

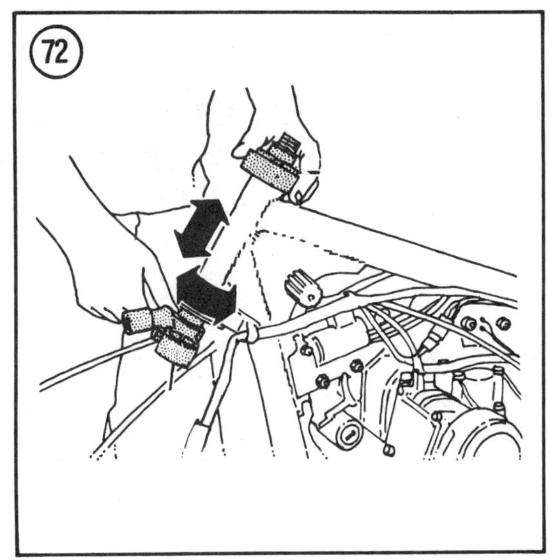

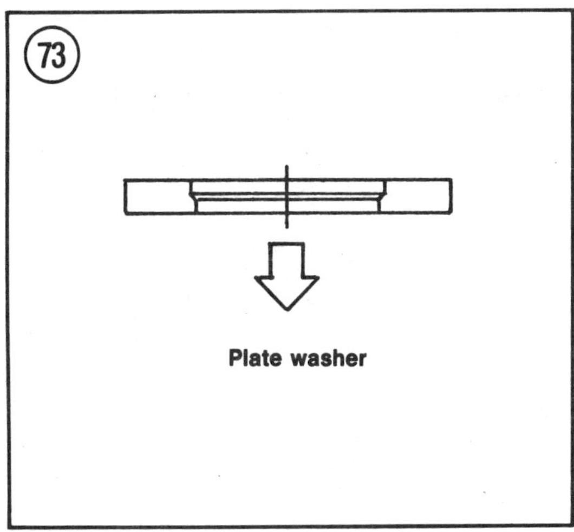

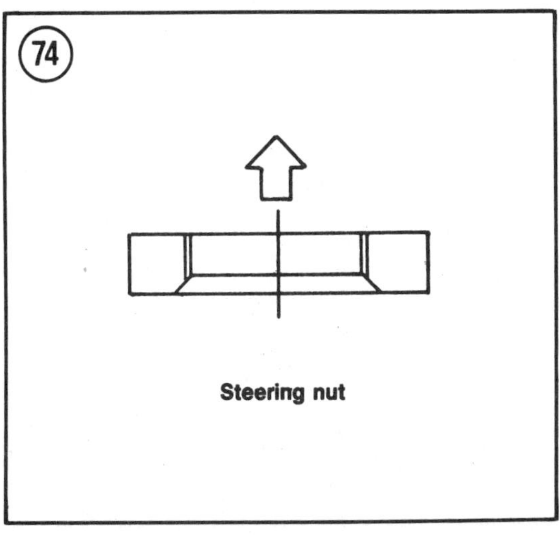

6. Install the steering stem adjusting nut (**Figure 63**) and tighten it until it is snug against the upper race, then back it off 1/8 turn.

NOTE
*The adjusting nut should be just tight enough to remove play, both horizontal and vertical (**Figure 72**), yet loose enough so that the assembly will turn to both lock positions under its own weight after being pushed past the center point.*

7. Install the plate washer (**Figure 62**). Then install the top O-ring (**Figure 61**).

NOTE
*Make sure to install the plate washer as shown in **Figure 73** so that it seats around the O-ring correctly.*

8. Install the upper fork bridge (**Figure 60**). Then install the top O-ring (**Figure 59**) and slide it down and into the recess in the steering crown.
9. Install the steering nut (**Figure 58**) finger-tight at this time.

NOTE
*Make sure to install the steering nut as shown in **Figure 74** so that it seats around the O-ring correctly.*

10. Push the steering stem-to-radiator coolant joint into the lower steering stem crown (**Figure 57**) and secure with the attaching bolt.

NOTE
Steps 11-13 must be performed in this order to assure proper upper and lower steering bracket-to-fork alignment.

NOTE
*Install the fork tube the same distance up from the top of the upper fork bridge; see NOTE after Step 4, **Disassembly**.*

11. Slide both fork tubes into position and tighten the lower fork bridge bolts to the torque specification in **Table 2**.
12. Tighten the steering stem flange nut to the torque specification in **Table 2**.
13. Tighten the upper fork bridge bolts to the torque specification in **Table 2**.
14. Install the radiator as described in Chapter Ten.
15. Install the handlebar and front wheel as described in this chapter.
16. After a few hours of riding, the bearings have had a chance to seat. Readjust the free play in the steering stem with the steering stem adjusting nut as described in Step 6.

STEERING HEAD AND STEM (1984-ON)

The steering head on these models uses loose ball bearings at the top and a tapered roller bearing at the bottom position. Refer to **Figure 75** for this procedure.

Disassembly

1. Remove the front wheel as described under *Front Wheel Removal* in this chapter.
2. Remove the front fender.
3. Remove the handlebar as described under *Handlebar Removal/Installation* in this chapter.
4. Loosen but do not remove the steering bolt (2, **Figure 75**).

NOTE
*Before removing the fork, measure and write down on a piece of masking tape attached to the fork, the distance from the top of the fork tube to the top of the upper fork bridge (**Figure 76**). This will enable the fork tube to be reinstalled in the same position.*

5. Remove the front forks (**Figure 77**) as described under *Front Fork Removal/Installation* in this chapter.
6. Remove the steering bolt (**Figure 78**).
7. Remove the upper fork bridge (**Figure 79**).
8. Remove the steering head adjusting nut (**Figure 80**). Use a large drift and hammer or a spanner wrench (**Figure 81**).
9. Remove the upper ball race cover (**Figure 82**).
10. Remove the outer ball race (**Figure 83**).

NOTE
Have an assistant hold a large pan under the steering stem to catch the loose ball bearings from the upper race and carefully lower the steering stem.

11. Lower the steering stem assembly down out of the steering head (**Figure 84**).
12. Remove the 22 upper ball bearings (3/16 in. diameter). See **Figure 85**.

Inspection

1. Clean the bearing races in the steering head, the steering stem races, ball bearings and the tapered roller bearing with solvent.
2. Check the welds around the steering head for cracks and fractures. If any are found, have them repaired by a competent frame shop or welding service.

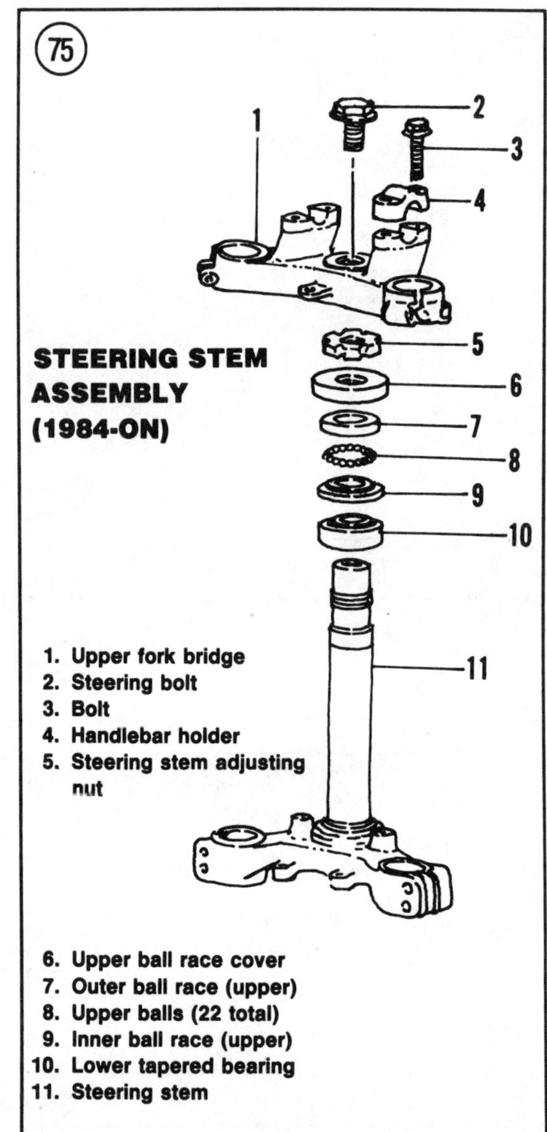

STEERING STEM ASSEMBLY (1984-ON)

1. Upper fork bridge
2. Steering bolt
3. Bolt
4. Handlebar holder
5. Steering stem adjusting nut
6. Upper ball race cover
7. Outer ball race (upper)
8. Upper balls (22 total)
9. Inner ball race (upper)
10. Lower tapered bearing
11. Steering stem

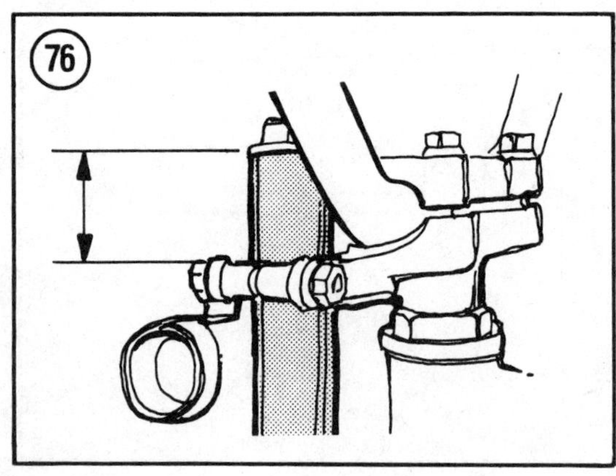

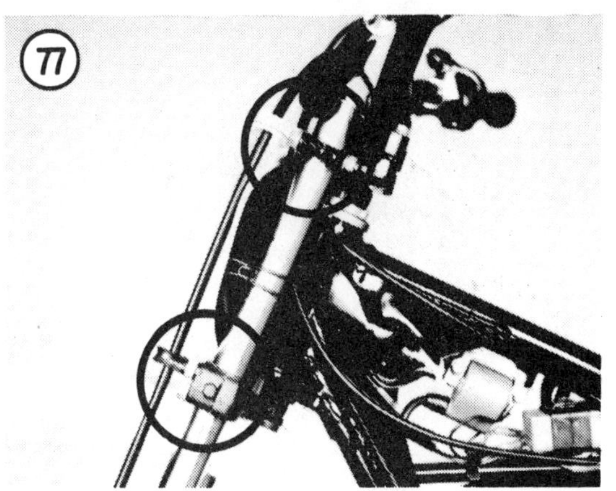
77

78

79

80

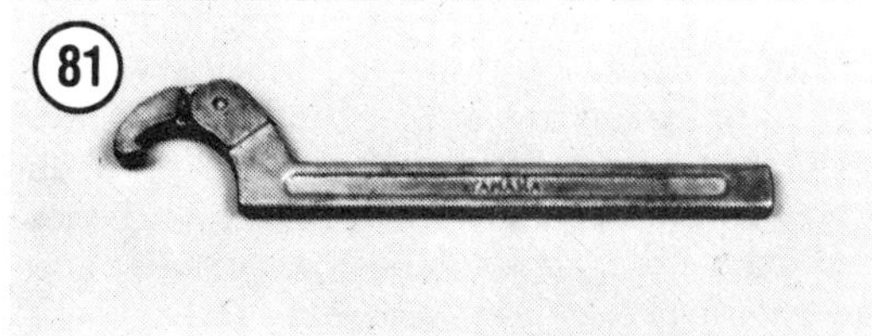
81

82

83

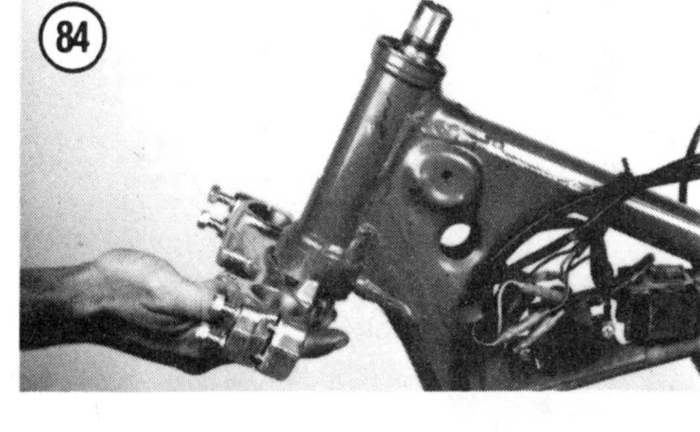
84

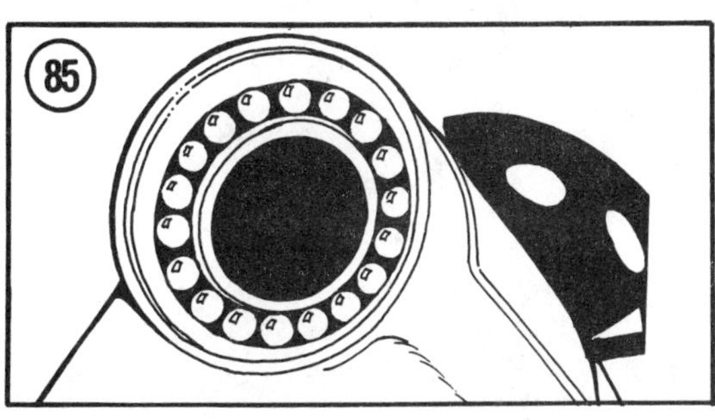
85

3. Check the balls for pitting, scratches, or discoloration indicating wear or corrosion. Replace them in sets if any are bad.
4. Check the races (**Figure 86** and **Figure 87**) for pitting or galling and corrosion. If any of these conditions exist, replace the races as described under *Bearing Race Replacement* in this chapter.
5. See **Figure 88**. Check the upper ball race cover (A) and the steering stem adjusting nut (B) for cracks or damage. Replace if necessary.
6. Check the steering stem (**Figure 89**) for cracks and damage.
7. Check the tapered roller bearing (**Figure 90**) for pitting, scratches or discoloration indicating wear or corrosion. If necessary, replace the bearing as follows:
   a. Install a bearing puller onto the steering stem and bearing.
   b. Pull the bearing off of the steering stem.
   c. Clean the steering stem thoroughly in solvent.
   d. Slide a new bearing onto the steering stem until it stops.
   e. Align the bearing with the machined portion of the shaft and slide a long hollow pipe over the steering stem (**Figure 91**) until it seats against the inner bearing race. Drive the bearing onto the shaft until it bottoms.

Headset Race Replacement

To remove the headset race, insert a hardwood stick or soft punch into the head tube (**Figure 92**) and carefully tap the race out from the inside. After it is started, tap around the race so that neither the race nor the head tube is damaged.

NOTE
The upper and lower bearings and races are not the same size. Be sure that you install them at the proper ends of the head tube.

To install the headset race, tap it in slowly with a block of wood or suitable size socket or piece of

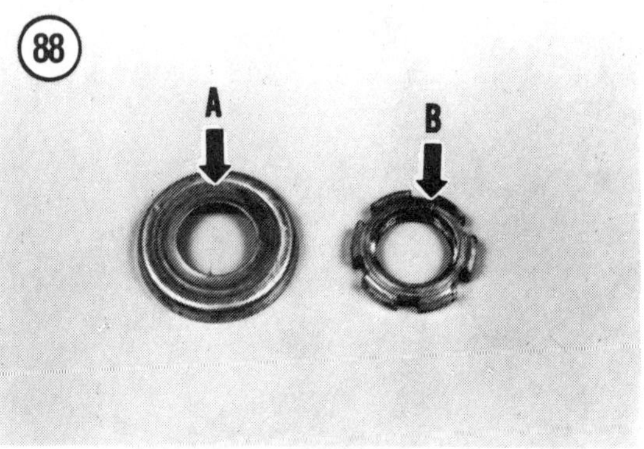

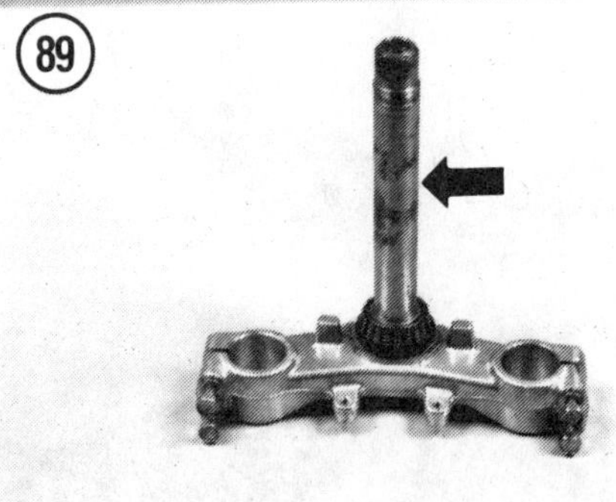

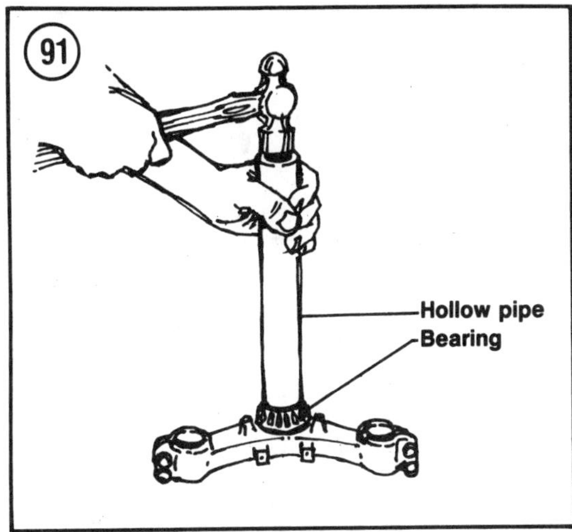

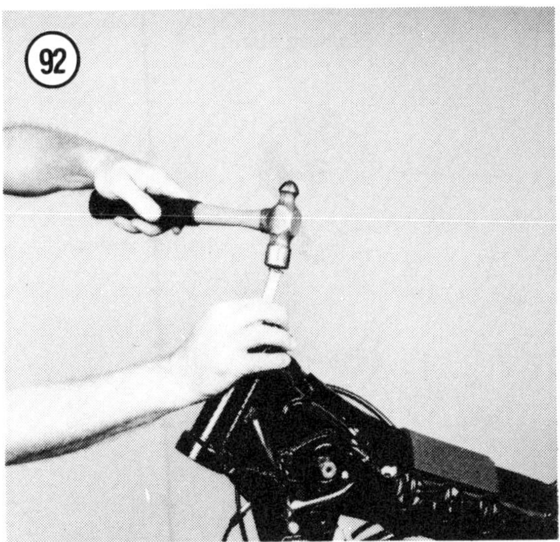

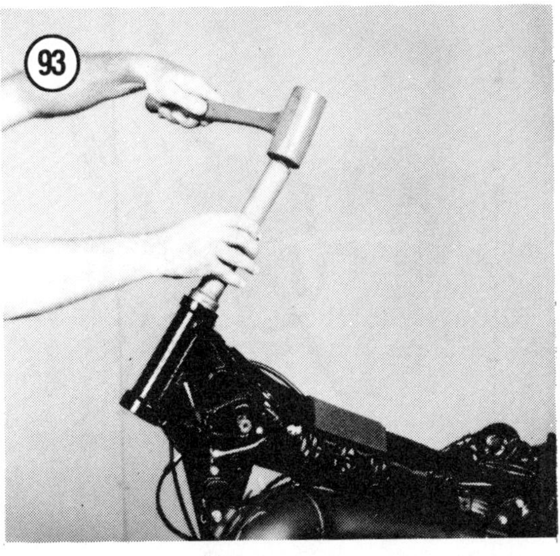

pipe (**Figure 93**). Make sure they are squarely seated in the race bores before tapping them in. Tap them in until they are flush with the steering head.

Steering Head Assembly

Refer to **Figure 75** for this procedure.

1. Make sure the steering head and stem races are properly seated.
2. Apply a coat of bearing grease to the tapered roller bearing on the steering stem (**Figure 90**). Carefully work the grease into the rollers.
3. Apply a coat of bearing grease to the upper bearing race cone and fit 22 ball bearings (3/16 in. diameter) around it (**Figure 85**).
4. Install the steering stem (**Figure 84**) into the head tube and hold it firmly in place. Check that the ball bearings are still in position around the inner race (**Figure 94**).
5. Install the outer ball race (**Figure 83**).
6. Install the upper bearing race cover (**Figure 82**).
7. Install and tighten the steering stem adjusting nut as follows:
   a. Install the steering stem adjusting nut (**Figure 80**).
   b. Tighten the adjusting nut securely (**Figure 95**) to seat the bearings.

11

NOTE
*The adjusting nut should be tightened to an initial torque of 37 N•m (27 ft.-lb.) to seat the bearings. To prevent from overtightening the adjusting nut, use the Yamaha ring nut wrench (part No. YU-33975) (**Figure 96**) and a torque wrench. Engage the ring nut wrench with the adjusting nut. Attach a torque wrench onto the end of the ring nut wrench so that both wrenches form a right angle (**Figure 97**). Tighten the adjusting nut to 37 N•m (27 ft.-lb.).*

c. Loosen the adjusting nut one turn. Then tighten the adjusting nut to approximately 10 N•m (7.2 ft.-lb.). Check the bearing play. The adjusting nut should be just tight enough to remove play, both horizontal and vertical yet loose enough so that the assembly will turn to both lock positions under its own weight after an assist.

8. Install the upper fork bridge (**Figure 79**).
9. Install the steering bolt (**Figure 78**) finger-tight at this time.

NOTE
Steps 10-12 must be performed in this order to assure proper upper and lower fork bridge to fork alignment.

NOTE
*Install the fork tube the same distance up from the top of the upper fork bridge; see NOTE after Step 4, **Disassembly**.*

10. Slide both fork tubes into position and tighten the lower fork bridge bolts to the torque specification in **Table 2**.
11. Tighten the steering bolt to the torque specification in **Table 2**.
12. Tighten the upper fork bridge bolts to the torque specification in **Table 2**.
13. Continue assembly by reversing Steps 1-3, *Disassembly*.
14. After a few hours of riding, the bearings have had a chance to seat; readjust the free play in the steering stem with the steering stem adjusting nut.

FRONT FORK (YZ50, YZ60 AND 1978-1982 YZ80)

To simplify fork service and to prevent the mixing of parts, the fork tubes should be removed, serviced and installed individually.

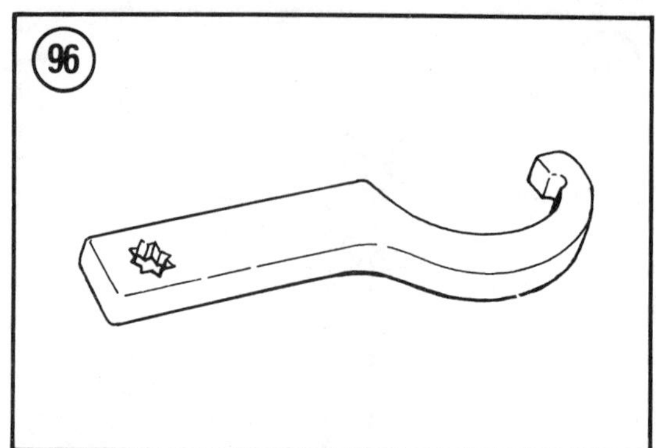

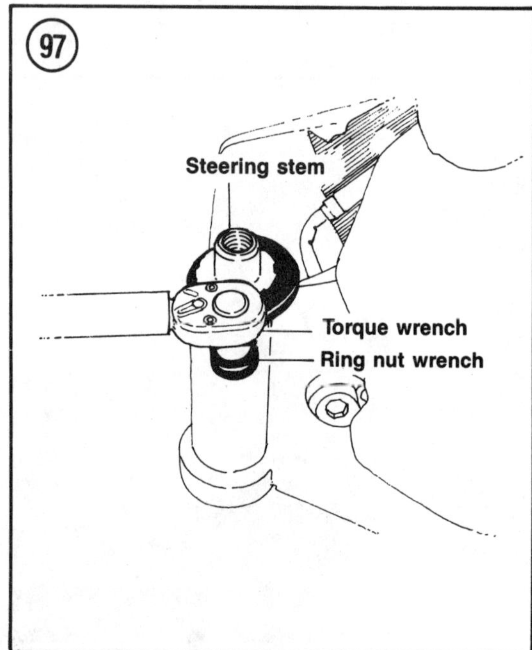

Removal/Installation

1. Remove the strap securing the front brake cable (**Figure 98**) to the left-hand fork.
2. Remove the front wheel as described under *Front Wheel Removal/Installation* in this chapter.
3. Remove the bolts (**Figure 99**) securing the front fender and remove it.

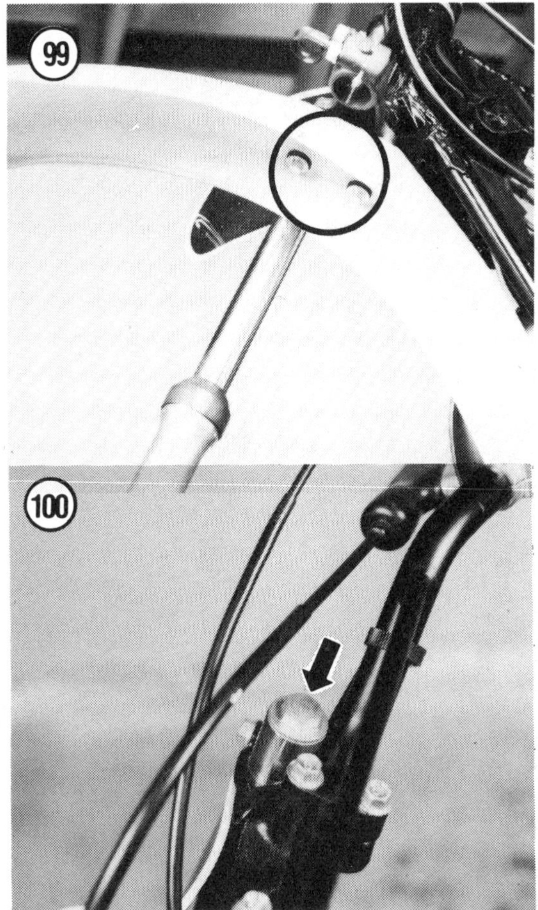

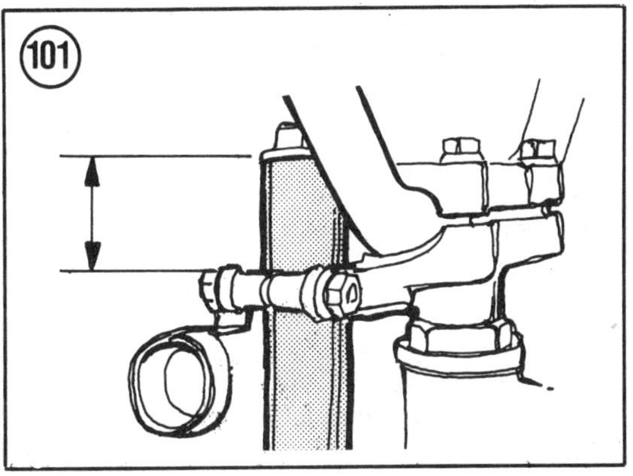

4. *Air-assist fork tubes:* Depress the fork tube air stem and release air from the fork tube. Repeat for the opposite side.
5. Loosen the top cap bolt (**Figure 100**) prior to removing the fork tube.

NOTE
*Prior to removing the fork, measure and write down on a piece of paper, the distance (**Figure 101**) from the top of the fork tube to the top of the upper fork bridge. This will enable the fork tube to be reinstalled in the same position.*

6. Loosen the upper and lower fork bridge bolts (**Figure 102**).
7. Twist the fork tube and slide it out of the fork bridge assembly.
8. Install by reversing these removal steps.
9. Install the fork tubes in the same position as noted in *Removal*, Step 6.
10. Tighten the fork bridge bolts to the torque specification in **Table 2.**

Disassembly

Refer to the front fork illustration for your model when servicing the front fork:

a. YZ50: **Figure 103**.
b. YZ60: **Figure 104**.
c. 1978 and 1980 YZ80: **Figure 105**.
d. 1979 YZ80: **Figure 106**.
e. 1981-1982 YZ80: **Figure 107**.

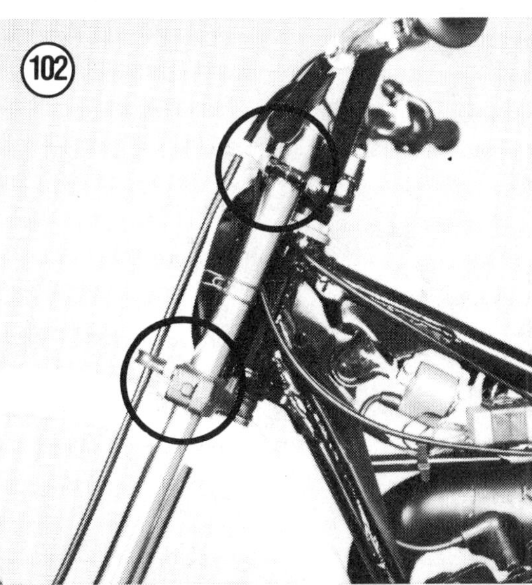

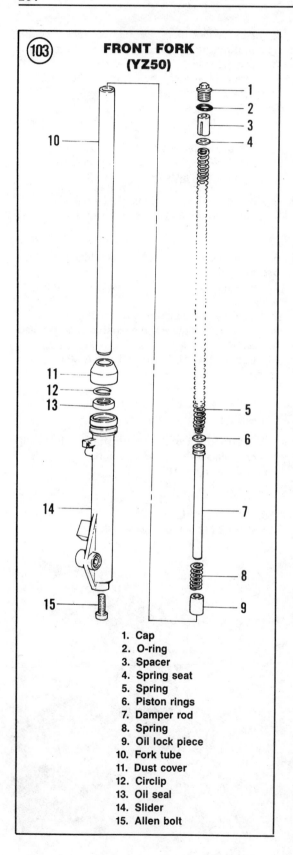

(103)

FRONT FORK (YZ50)

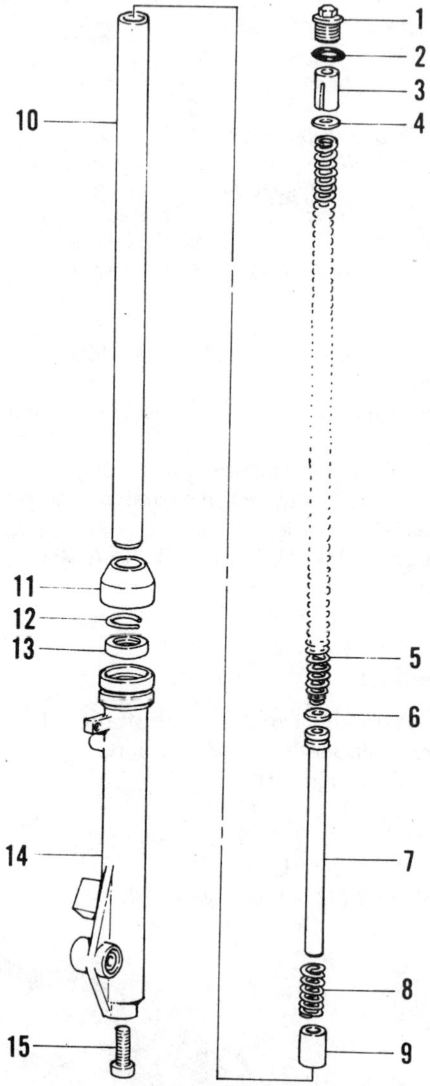

1. Cap
2. O-ring
3. Spacer
4. Spring seat
5. Spring
6. Piston rings
7. Damper rod
8. Spring
9. Oil lock piece
10. Fork tube
11. Dust cover
12. Circlip
13. Oil seal
14. Slider
15. Allen bolt

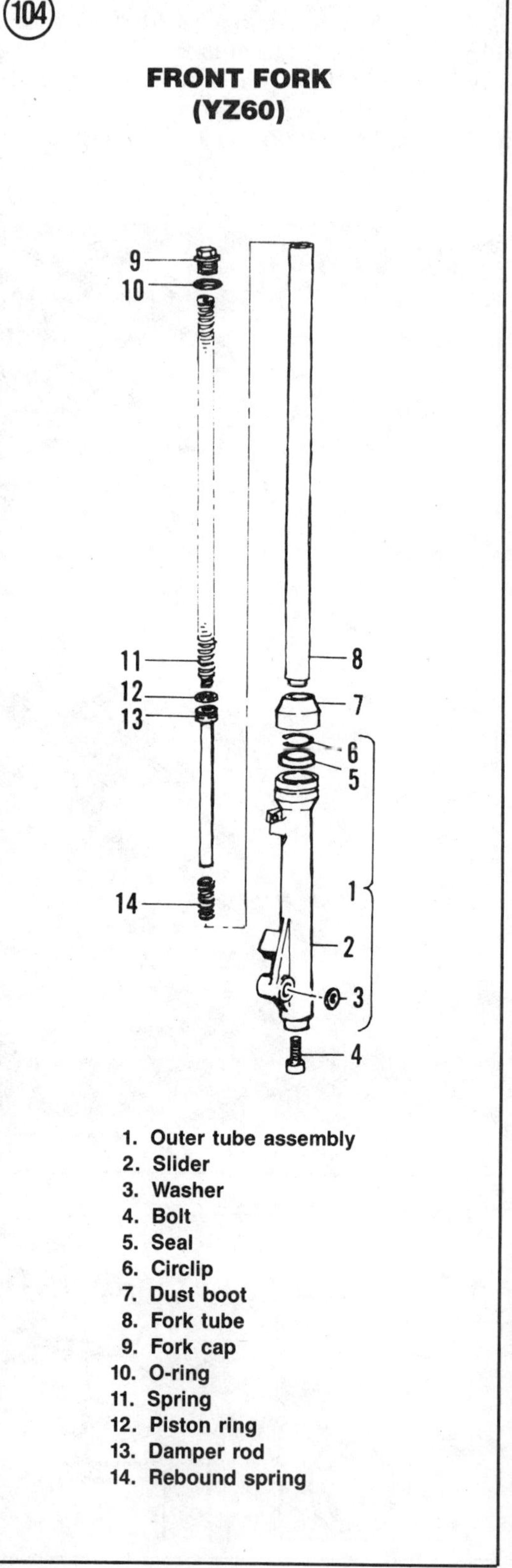

1. Outer tube assembly
2. Slider
3. Washer
4. Bolt
5. Seal
6. Circlip
7. Dust boot
8. Fork tube
9. Fork cap
10. O-ring
11. Spring
12. Piston ring
13. Damper rod
14. Rebound spring

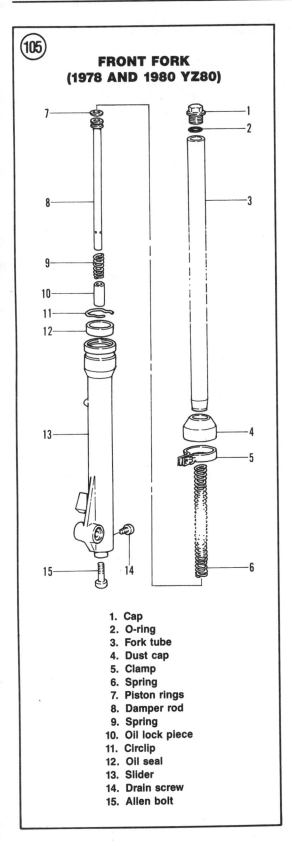

(105)

FRONT FORK
(1978 AND 1980 YZ80)

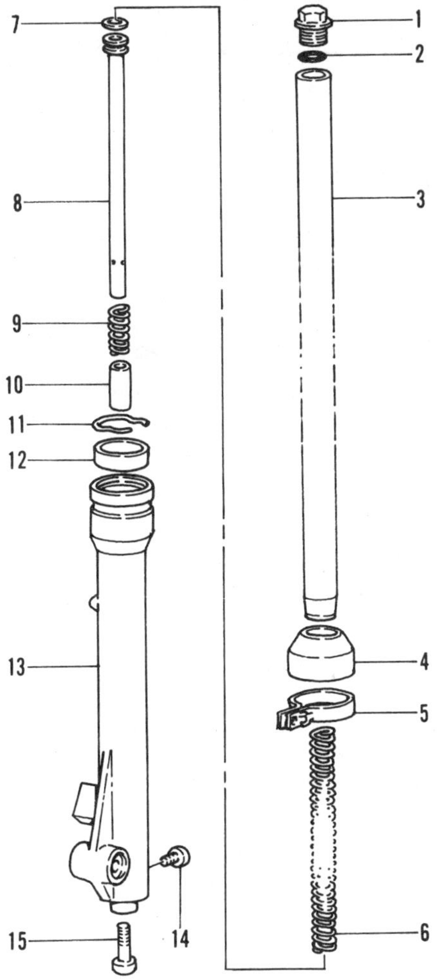

1. Cap
2. O-ring
3. Fork tube
4. Dust cap
5. Clamp
6. Spring
7. Piston rings
8. Damper rod
9. Spring
10. Oil lock piece
11. Circlip
12. Oil seal
13. Slider
14. Drain screw
15. Allen bolt

(106)

FRONT FORK
(1979 YZ80)

1. Cap
2. O-ring
3. Spacer
4. Upper spring
5. Spring seat
6. Lower spring
7. Fork tube
8. Dust cap
9. Clamp
10. Piston rings
11. Damper rod
12. Spring
13. Oil lock piece
14. Circlip
15. Oil seal
16. Slider
17. Drain screw
18. Allen bolt

11

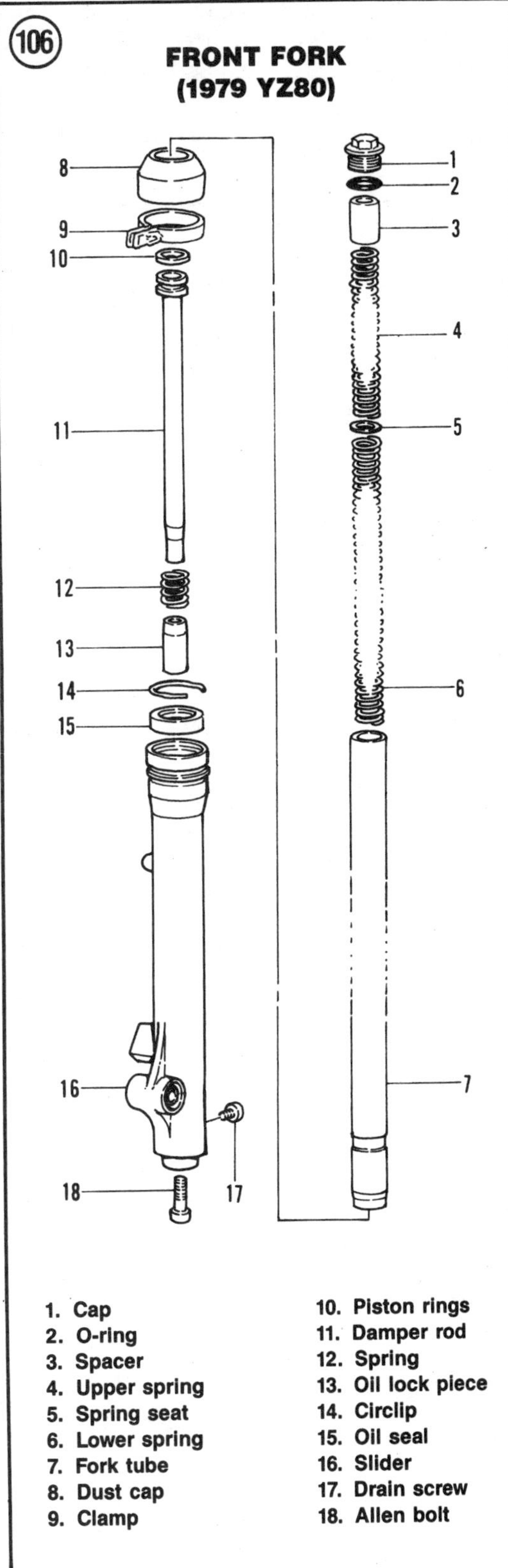

Pay particular attention to the location and positioning of spacers, washers, and springs to make sure they are assembled in the correct location.

1. Remove the dust seal cover.

2. Before removing the fork spring, loosen but do not remove the slider Allen bolt.

NOTE
The slider Allen bolt has been secured with a locking agent and can be very dif-

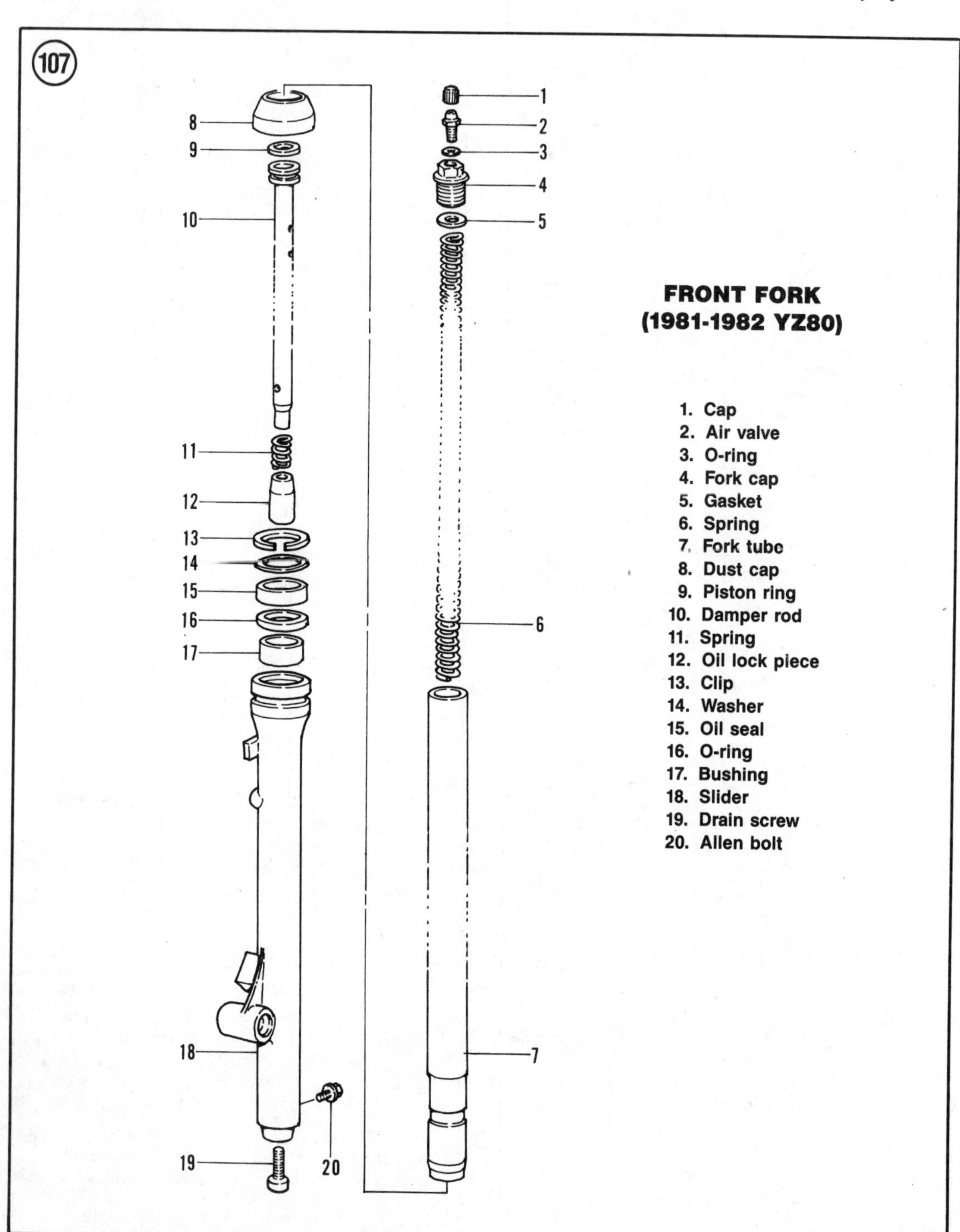

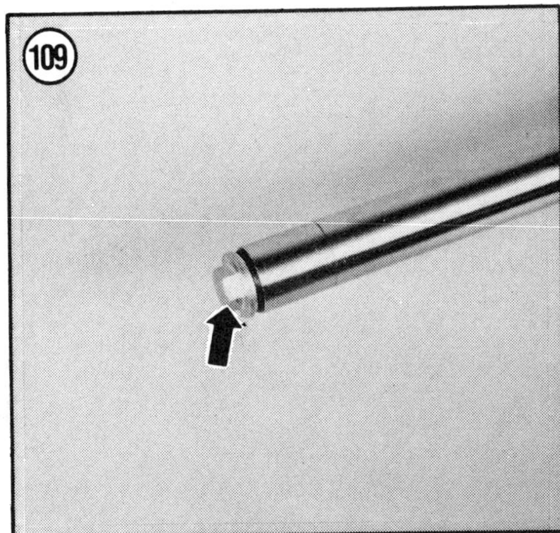

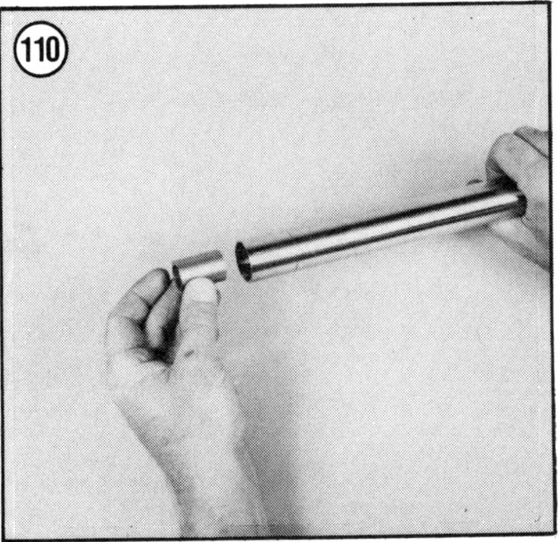

ficult to remove. If the fork spring is removed, the damper rod will turn inside the slider. If you are unable to remove it, take the fork tubes to a dealer and have them remove the bolts.

3. Hold the fork tube in a vise with soft jaws (**Figure 108**). Remove the fork cap (**Figure 109**).

4A. *YZ50 models:* Remove the spacer, washer and fork spring.

4B. *YZ60 models:* Remove the fork spring.

4C. *1978 and 1980 YZ80 models:* Remove the fork spring.

4D. *1979 YZ80 models:* Remove the following parts in order:

a. Remove the spacer (**Figure 110**).
b. Remove the upper short spring (**Figure 111**).
c. Remove the spring seat (**Figure 112**).
d. Remove the lower long spring (**Figure 112**).

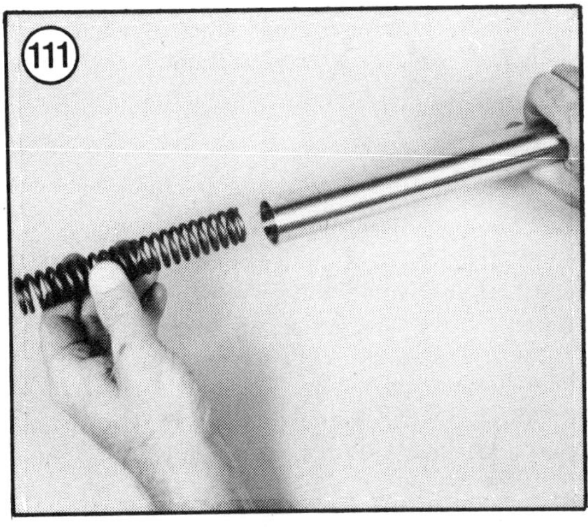

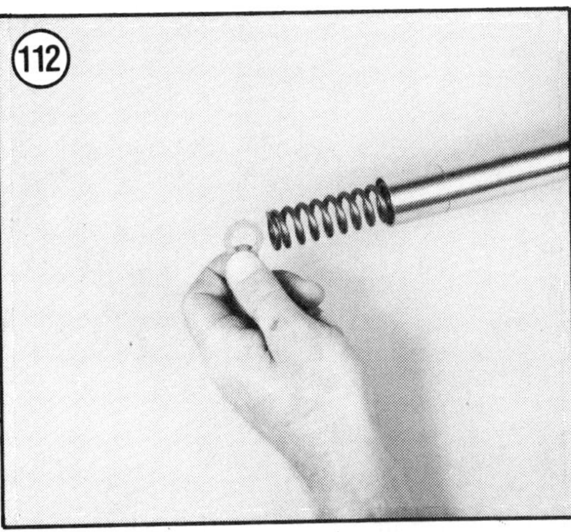

4E. *1981-1982 YZ80 models:* Remove the spring seat and spring.

5. Remove the fork from the vise and pour the fork oil out and discard it. Pump the fork several times by hand to expel most of the remaining oil.

6. Clamp the slider in a vise with soft jaws.

7. Remove the Allen bolt and gasket from the bottom of the slider (**Figure 113**).

8. Pull the fork tube out of the slider (**Figure 114**).

9. Remove the oil lock piece (**Figure 115**) from the end of the damper rod.

10. Slide the damper rod and spring (**Figure 116**) out of the fork tube.

11. If the oil seal (**Figure 117**) is damaged or leaking, remove it as follows:

   a. Remove the circlip from the top of the fork seal.
   b. *1981-1982 YZ80 models:* Remove the washer.
   c. Referring to **Figure 118**, pry the oil seal out of the slider. Do not damage the outer edge or inner slider surface. If necessary, pad the slider with a shop rag or small block of wood.
   d. *1981-1982 YZ80 models:* Remove the O-ring.

Inspection

1. Thoroughly clean all parts in solvent and dry. Check the fork tube for signs of wear or scratches.

2. Check the damper rod for straightness by rolling it on a surface plate or thick piece of glass. The rod should roll straight. Any clicking noise indicates a bent damper rod.

3. Carefully check the damper rod valve and piston (**Figure 119**) for wear or damage.

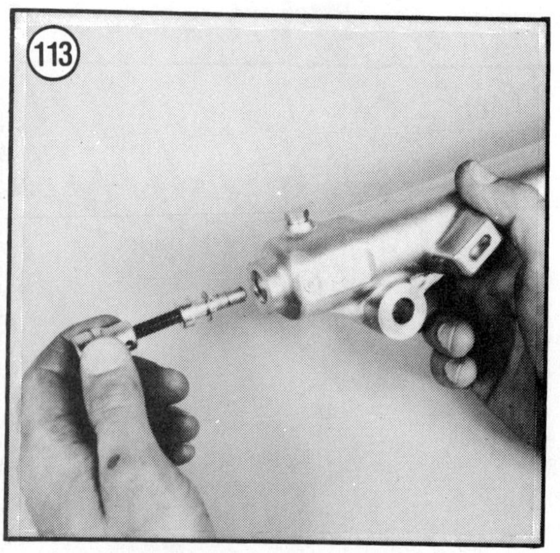

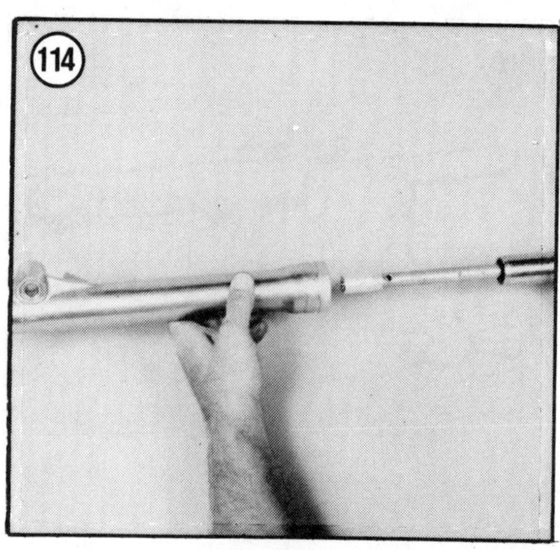

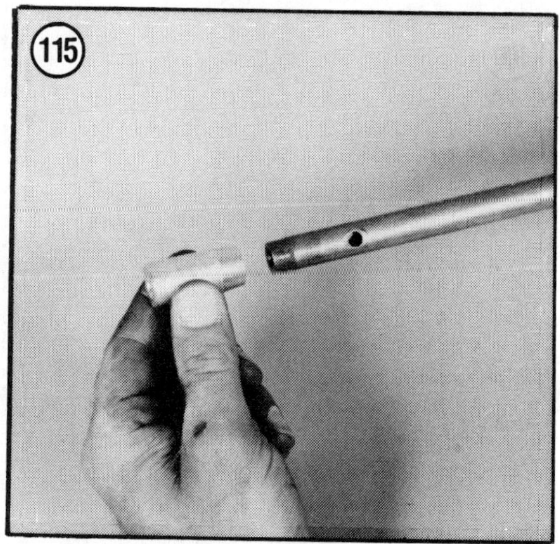

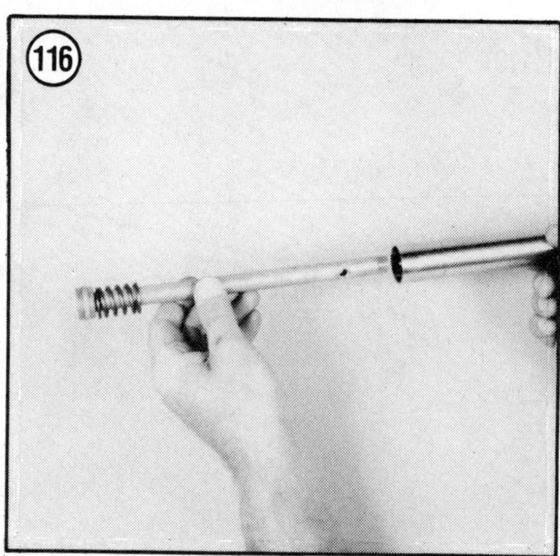

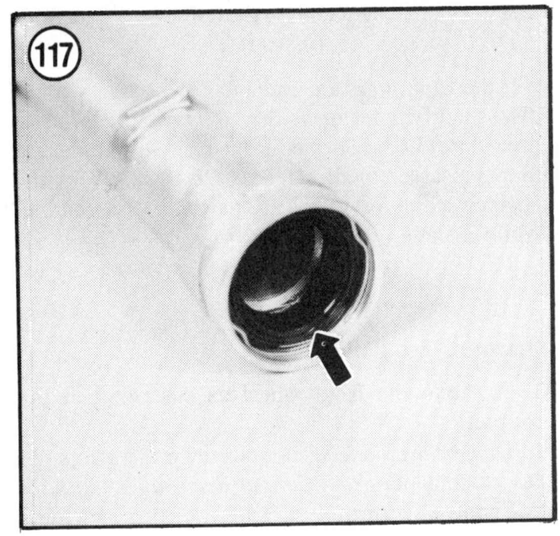

117

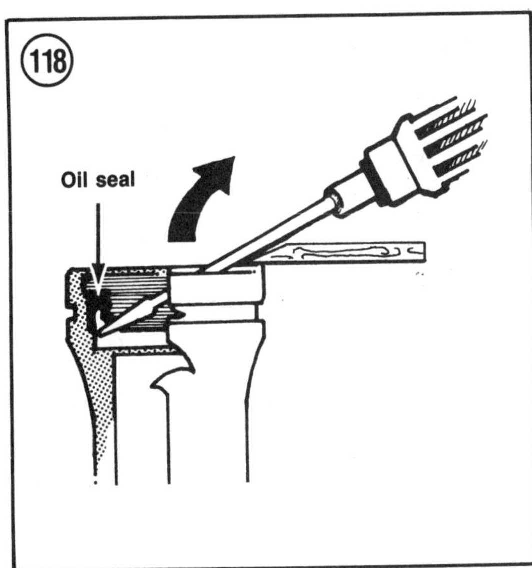

118

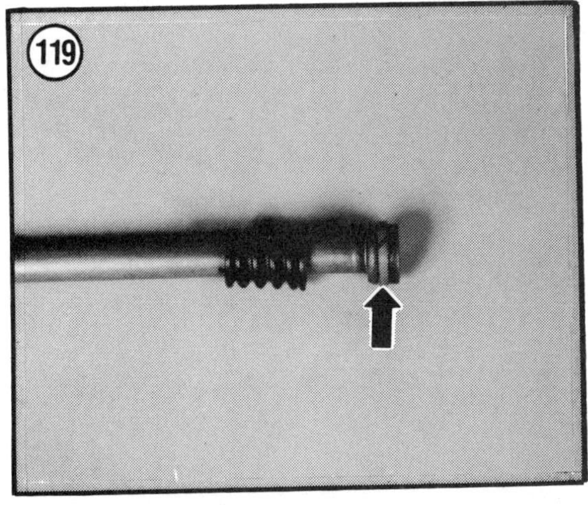

119

4. Check the fork tube for straightness. If bent or severely scratched, it should be replaced.
5. Check the slider for dents or exterior damage that may cause the upper fork tube to hang up during riding conditions. Replace if necessary.
6. Measure the uncompressed length of the fork spring with a tape measure and compare to the specification in **Table 1**. On 1979 YZ80 models, place both springs together with the spring seat placed between them for total length. Replace any spring(s) that is approximately 4 mm (0.15 in.) shorter than the standard dimension in **Table 1**.

NOTE

If one fork spring is replaced, it is best to replace both springs to keep the forks balanced. On 1979 YZ80 models, replace all 4 springs.

7. Replace the fork cap O-ring (**Figure 120**) if damaged.
8. Any parts that are worn or damaged should be replaced. Simply cleaning and reinstalling unserviceable components will not improve performance of the front suspension.

Assembly

1. If the oil seals were removed, install new seals as follows:
   a. *1981-1982 YZ80 models:* Install the O-ring.
   b. Install a new oil seal by driving it into the slider with a suitable size socked placed on the top of the seal. Drive the seal in until it bottoms.
   c. *1981-1982 YZ80 models:* Install the washer.
   d. Install the circlip. Make sure it seats in the slider groove completely.

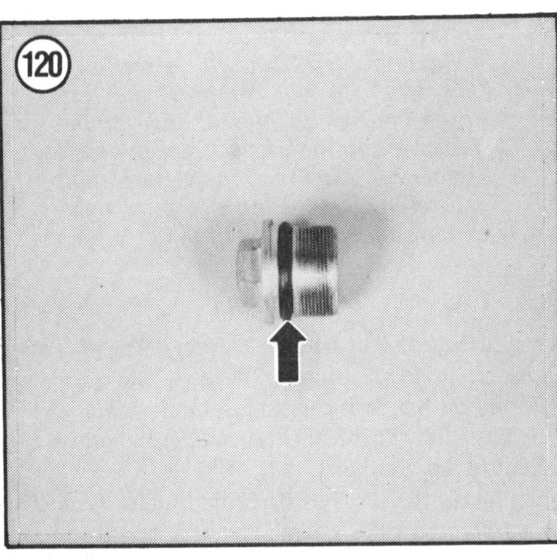

120

2. Coat all parts with fresh fork oil prior to installation. Refer to Chapter 3, **Table 4** for the correct oil weight.
3. Install the rebound spring onto the damper rod and insert the damper rod into the fork tube (**Figure 116**).
4. Install the oil lock piece (**Figure 115**) onto the end of the damper rod.
5. Slide the fork tube into the slider (**Figure 114**).
6. Make sure the gasket is on the Allen bolt (**Figure 121**).
7. Apply Locite 242 (blue) to the threads on the Allen bolt. Install the Allen bolt (**Figure 113**) and tighten securely.

NOTE

If the damper rod turns when tightening the Allen bolts, perform Step 8. Then after the fork cap is installed, tighten the Allen bolt.

8A. *YZ50 models:* Install the fork spring, spacer and washer.
8B. *YZ60 models:* Install the fork spring.
8C. *1978 and 1980 YZ80 models:* Install the fork spring.
8D. *1979 YZ80 models:* Install the following parts in order:
   a. Install the lower long spring (**Figure 112**) into the upper fork tube.
   b. Install the spring seat (**Figure 112**).
   c. Install the upper short spring (**Figure 111**) into the fork tube.
   d. Install the spacer.
8E. *1981-1982 YZ80 models:* Install the spring and spring seat.

NOTE

If the Allen bolt was not tightened securely in Step 7, install the fork cap. The fork cap will compress the fork spring enough to prevent the damper rod from turning when the Allen bolt is tightened. Tighten the Allen bolt securely. After the Allen bolt is tight, remove the fork cap and perform Step 9.

9. Fill the fork tube with the correct type and quantity fork oil. Refer to Chapter Three.
10. Install the fork cap and tighten securely.
11. Install the dust seal (**Figure 122**) and brake cable clamp if so equipped.
12. Install the forks as described under *Front Fork Installation* in this chapter.

FRONT FORK (1983-ON)

If the front forks are going to be removed without disassembly, perform the *Removal/Installation* procedures in this chapter. If the front forks are going to be disassembled, refer to *Disassembly* in this chapter as the fork tubes are partially disassembled while installed on the bike.

Refer to **Figure 123** for this procedure.

Removal/Installation

1. Remove the front wheel as described in this chapter.
2. *Disc brake models:* Remove the brake caliper as described under *Front Caliper Removal/Installation* in Chapter Thirteen.

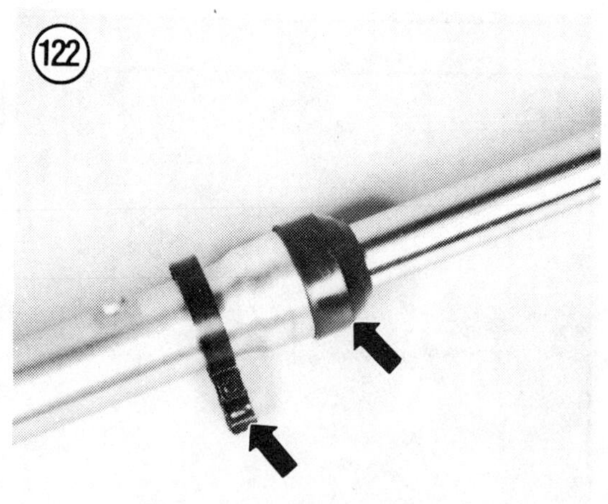

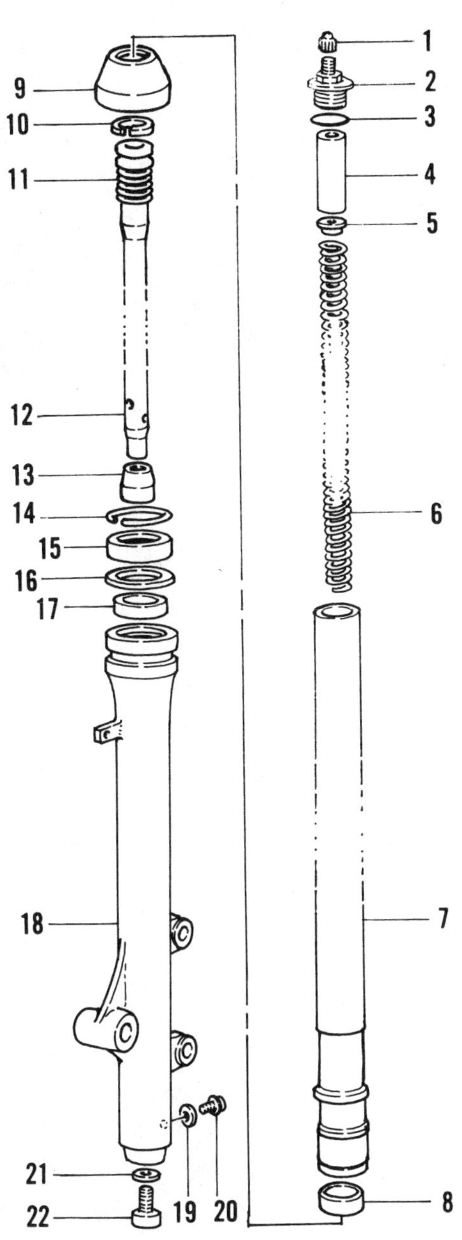

FRONT FORK
(1983-ON YZ80)

1. Air cap
2. Fork cap
3. O-ring
4. Spacer
5. Spring seat
6. Spring
7. Fork tube
8. Bushing
9. Dust cap
10. Piston ring
11. Spring
12. Damper rod
13. Oil lock piece
14. Clip
15. Oil seal
16. Washer
17. Bushing
18. Slider
19. Washer
20. Drain screw
21. Washer
22. Allen bolt

NOTE
Insert a piece of wood in the calipers in place of the disc. That way, if the brake lever is inadvertently squeezed, the piston will not be forced out of the calipers. If it does happen, the calipers might have to be overhauled to reseat the piston.

3. Remove the air valve cap and depress the valve (A, **Figure 124**) to release fork air pressure from both fork tubes.

NOTE
*Measure and write down on a piece of masking tape attached to the fork, the distance (**Figure 125**) from the top of the fork tube to the top of the upper fork bridge. This will enable the fork tube to be reinstalled in the same position.*

4. Loosen the upper and lower fork bridge bolts (**Figure 126**).
5. Twist the fork tube and remove it.
6. Install by reversing these removal steps. Note the following.
7. Install the fork tubes in the same position as noted after Step 3.
8. Tighten the fork bridge bolts to the torque specification in **Table 2**.
9. *Disc brake models:* Install and tighten the brake caliper as described in Chapter Thirteen.
10. *Disc brake models:* After installing the front wheel, squeeze the front brake lever. If the brake lever feels spongy, bleed the brake as described under *Bleeding the System* in Chapter Thirteen.
11. Refill the front fork air pressure as described under *Suspension Adjustment* in Chapter Fourteen.

Disassembly

Refer to **Figure 123** for this procedure.

1. Perform Step 1 and Step 2 described under front fork *Removal/Installation.*
2. Depress the air valve(s) to release all fork air pressure.

NOTE
The slider Allen bolt is normally secured with a locking agent and can be very difficult to remove because the damper rod may turn inside the lower fork tube. The Allen bolt can be removed easily with an air impact driver. If you do not have access to an air impact driver, it is best to loosen the Allen bolt before removing the fork tube cap and spring. This method allows the fork spring to apply pressure to the damper rod and keep it from turning when the Allen bolt is loosened.

3. Place a drain pan underneath one of the fork tubes.

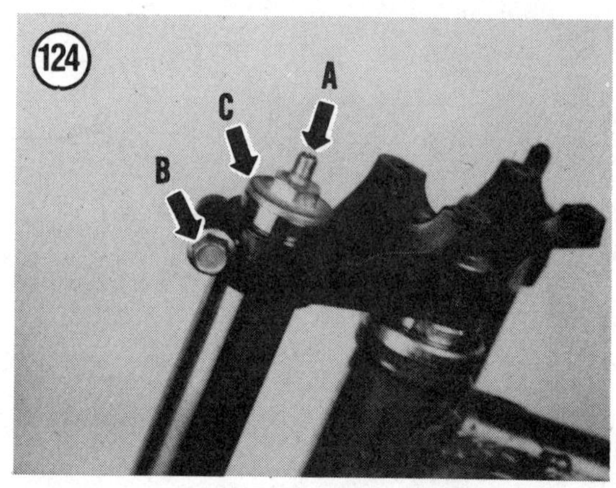

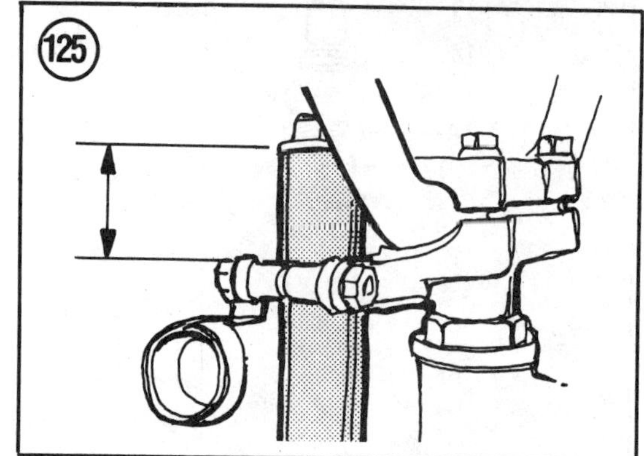

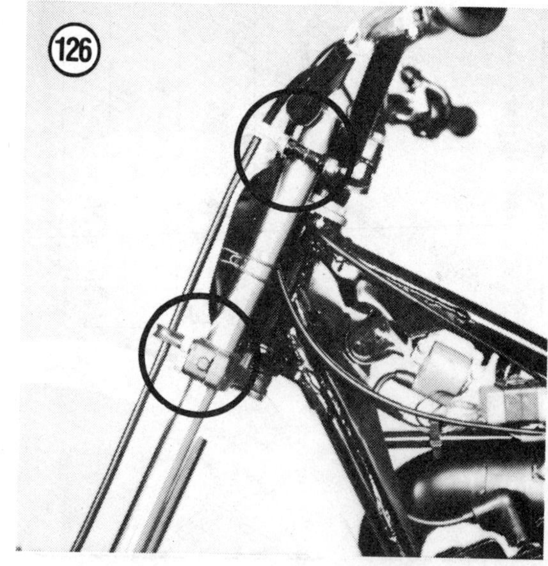

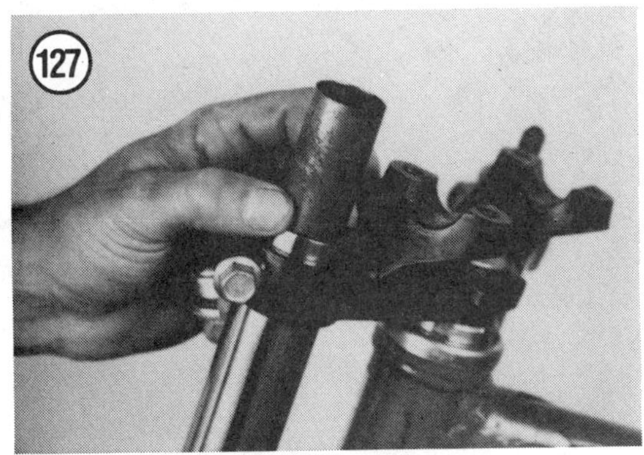
127

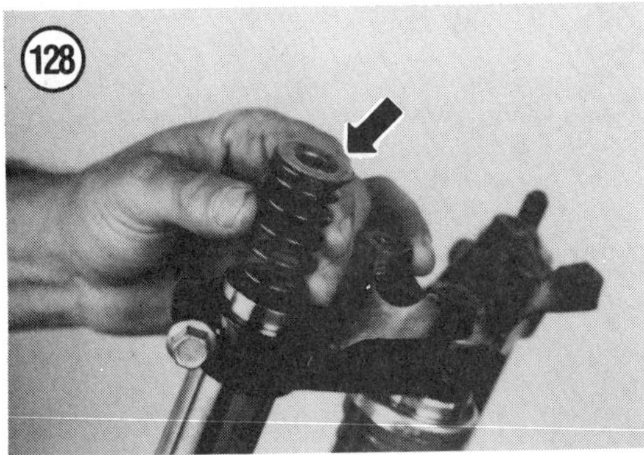
128

129

130

NOTE

When loosening the fork tube Allen bolt in Step 4, the fork tube will turn with the wrench. To prevent the fork tubes from turning, lock them together with the front axle.

4. Using an Allen bit fixed to a socket, loosen but do not remove the fork tube Allen bolt.

WARNING

The fork caps are held under spring pressure. Take precautions to prevent the fork caps from flying off and into your face during removal. If the fork tubes are bent in a compressed position, the fork caps will be under considerable pressure.

5. See **Figure 124**. Loosen the upper fork bridge pinch bolt (B) and remove the fork cap (C). Retighten the pinch bolt after removing the fork cap.
6. Remove the spacer (**Figure 127**).
7. Remove the spring seat (**Figure 128**).
8. Remove the fork spring (**Figure 129**). Cover the bottom of the spring with a shop rag as it is removed to prevent oil from dripping down the steering stem and fork tube.
9. Remove the Allen bolt loosened in Step 4.
10. Work the dust seal out of the slider and slide it up the fork tube.
11. Carefully pry the snap ring (**Figure 130**) out of the slider.
12. There is an interference fit between the bushing in the fork slider and the bushing on the fork tube. In order to remove the slider from the fork tube, pull hard on the slider using quick in-and-out strokes (**Figure 131**). Doing this will remove the oil seal, washer and bushing (**Figure 132**).

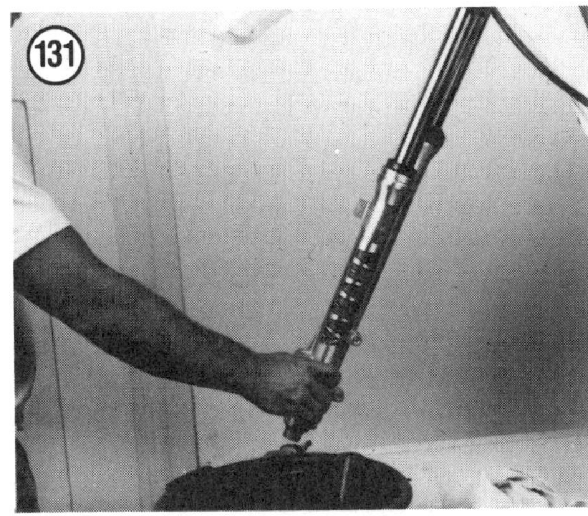
131

13. Loosen the upper and lower fork bridge pinch bolts and remove the fork tube assembly.
14. Remove the oil lock piece from the end of the damper rod (**Figure 133**).
15. Slide the damper rod and spring (**Figure 134**) out of the fork tube.
16. See **Figure 135**. Slide the following parts off the fork tube:
   a. Dust seal (A).
   b. Circlip (B).
   c. Oil seal (C).
   d. Washer (D).
   e. Bushing (E).

Inspection

1. Thoroughly clean all parts in solvent and dry them.
2. Check both fork tubes for wear or scratches. Check the fork tube for straightness. If bent, refer service to a Yamaha dealer.
3. Check the fork tube for chrome flaking or creasing; this condition will damage oil seals. Replace the fork tube if necessary.
4. Check the slider oil seal area for dents or other damage that would allow oil leakage. Replace the slider if necessary.

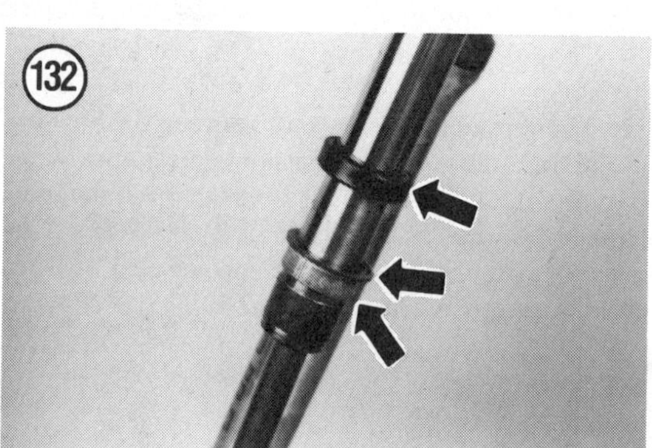

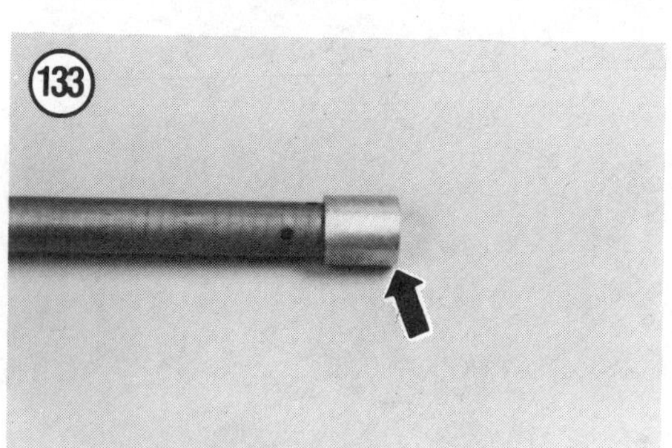

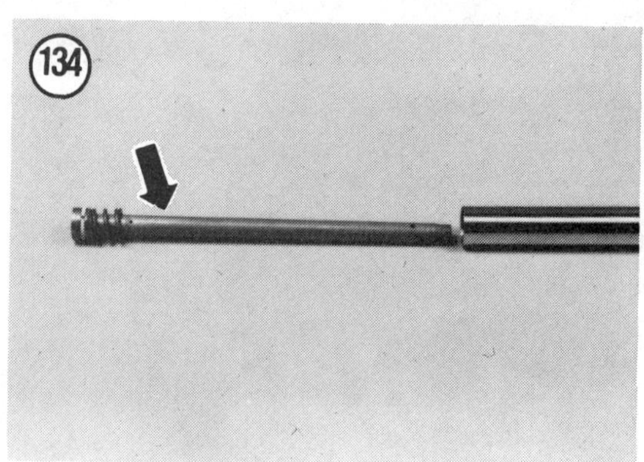

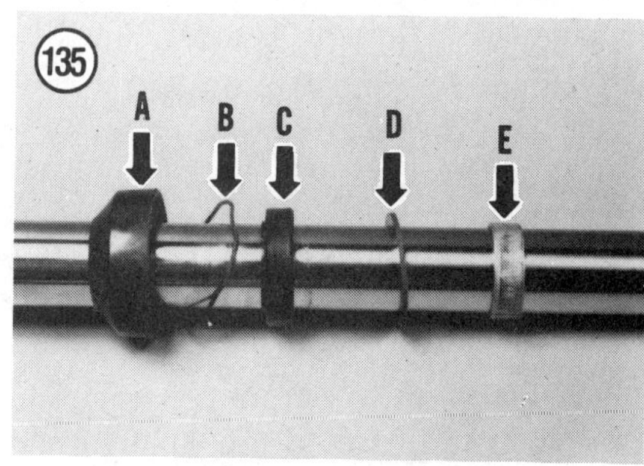

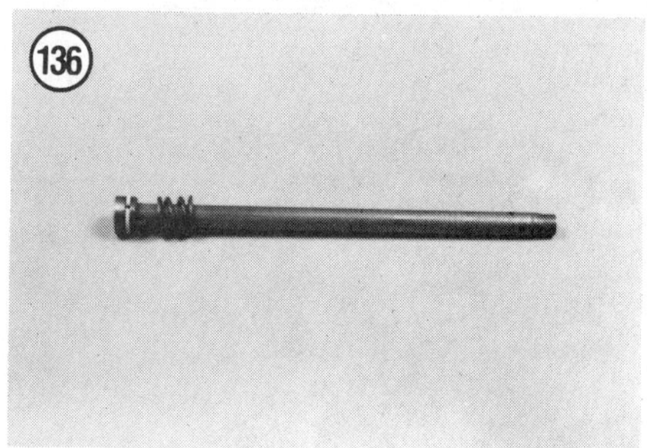

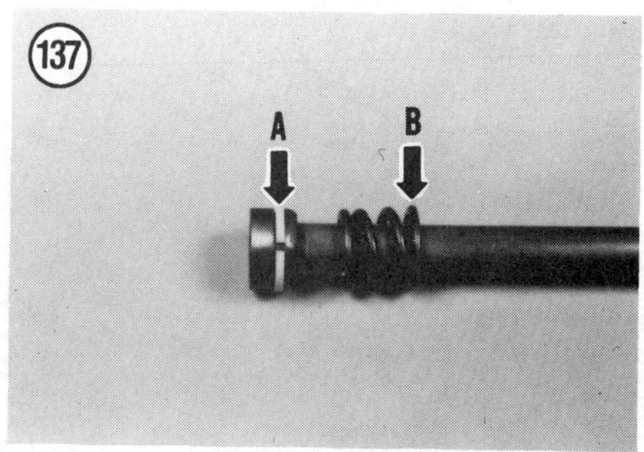

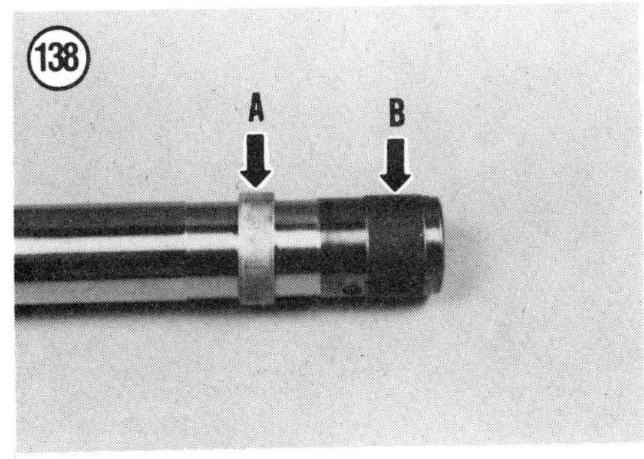

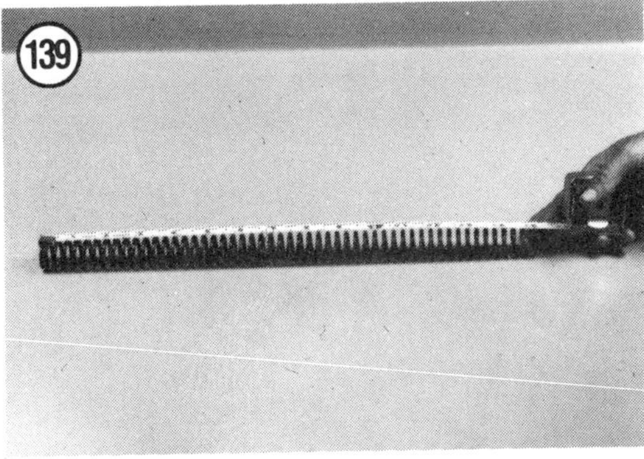

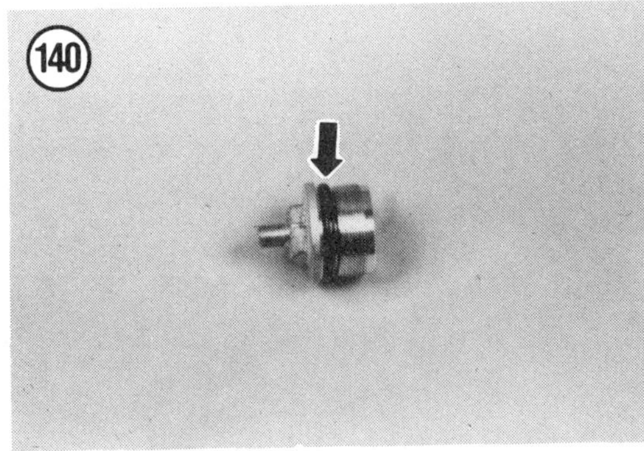

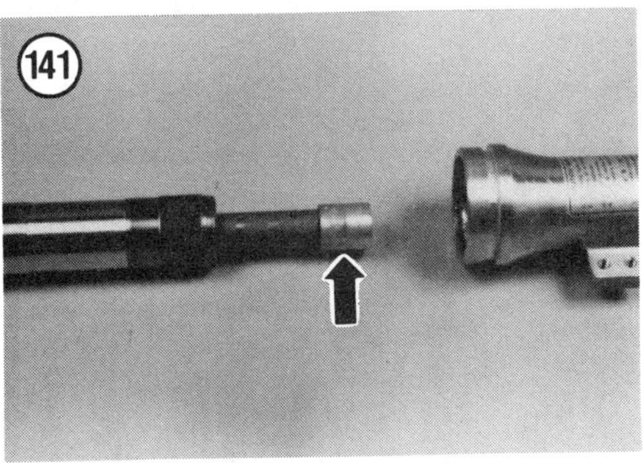

5. Check the damper rod for straightness (**Figure 136**) by rolling it on a surface plate or thick piece of glass. Any clicking noise indicates a bent rod.
6. Check the damper rod piston ring (A, **Figure 137**) for tearing, cracks or damage.
7. Check the guide bushing on the fork tube (A, **Figure 138**) for scoring, nicks or damage. Replace if necessary by pulling off the fork tube.
8. Check the mating guide bushing (B, **Figure 138**) for scoring, nicks or damage. Replace if necessary.
9. Measure the uncompressed length of the fork springs (**Figure 139**) with a tape measure and compare to specifications in **Table 1**. Replace any spring(s) that is approximately 4 mm (0.15 in.) shorter than the standard dimension in **Table 1**.

NOTE
If one fork spring is replaced, it is best to replace both springs to keep the forks balanced.

10. Replace the fork cap O-ring (**Figure 140**) if damaged.
11. Check the oil and dust seals for wear or damage. Replace if necessary.

Assembly

Refer to **Figure 123** for this procedure.
1. Slide the rebound spring (B, **Figure 137**) onto the damper rod and spring into the fork tube (**Figure 134**).
2. Slide the oil lock piece (**Figure 133**) onto the end of the damper rod.
3. Insert the damper rod/ fork tube into the slider (**Figure 141**).
4. Make sure the gasket is on the Allen bolt (**Figure 142**).

5. Apply Loctite 242 (blue) to the threads on the Allen bolt. Install the Allen bolt (**Figure 143**) and tighten securely.

NOTE

If the damper rod turns when tightening the Allen bolt, install the fork spring, spring seat, spacer and fork cap. Then tighten the Allen bolt securely. After the allen bolt is tight, remove the fork cap and remove the spacer, spring seat and spring.

NOTE

The guide bushing can be installed with a piece of pipe or other piece of tubing that fits over the fork tube. If both ends of the pipe are threaded, wrap one end with duct tape to prevent the threads from damaging the interior of the slider.

6. Slide the guide bushing (**Figure 144**) over the fork tube. Tap the guide bushing into the slider until it bottoms (**Figure 145**).
7. Slide the washer (**Figure 146**) down the fork tube until it rests against the bushing.
8. Position the oil seal with the marking facing upward and slide down onto the fork tube (**Figure 147**). Drive the seal into the slider with the same tool used in Step 6. Drive the oil seal in until it rests against the washer.

NOTE

Make sure the groove in the lower fork tube can be seen above the oil seal. If not, the bushing and oil seal will have to be driven farther into the slider.

9. Slide the circlip (**Figure 148**) down the fork tube and seat it in the slider groove. Make sure the circlip is completely seated in the groove.

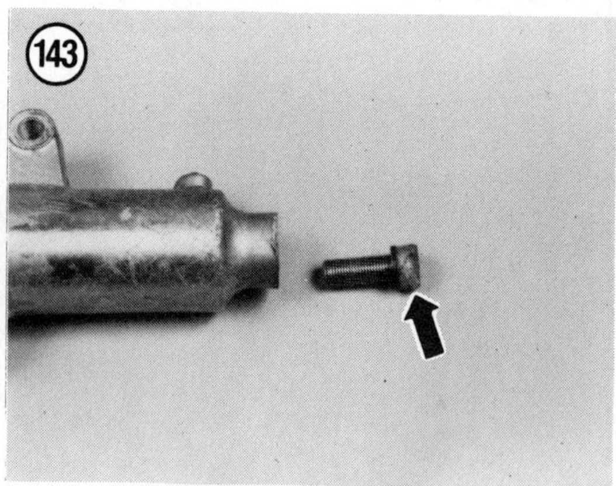

143

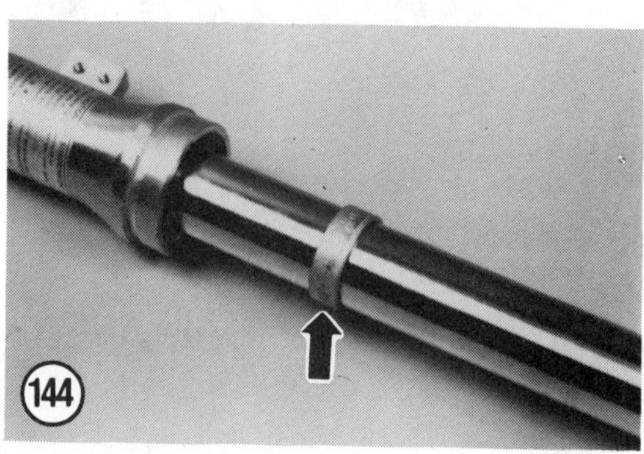

144

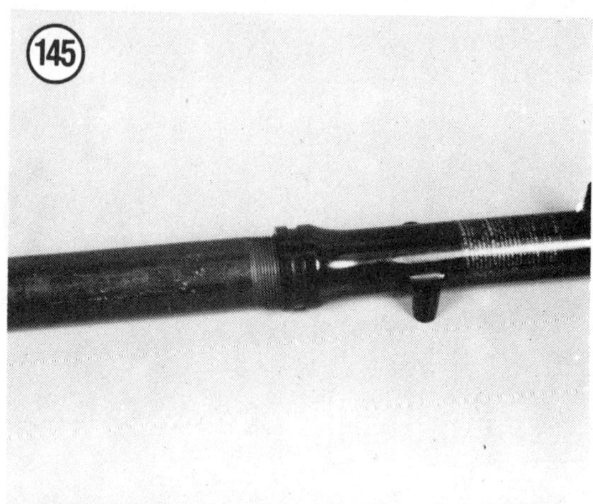

145

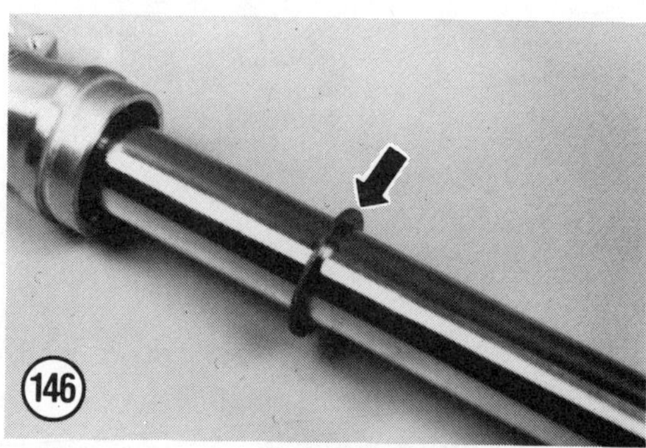

146

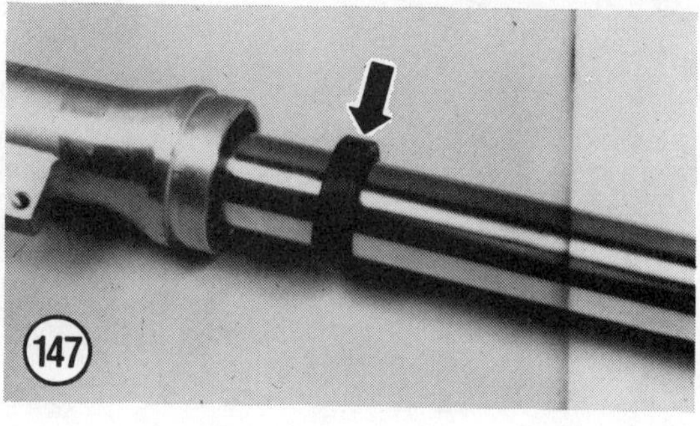

147

10. Slide the dust seal down the fork tube and seat it in the slider (**Figure 149**).
11. Fill the fork tube with the correct quantity and weight fork oil as described in Chapter Three. Check the oil level as described in Chapter Fourteen.
12. Install the fork spring with the closer wound coils toward the top of the fork.

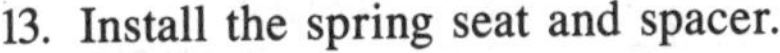

13. Install the spring seat and spacer.
14. Pull the slider and fork tubes as far apart as possible. Apply a light coat of oil to the fork cap and install it by slightly compressing the fork spring. Once the fork cap is installed, it can be tightened after installing the fork tube onto the motorcycle. See *Front Fork Removal/Installation* in this chapter.

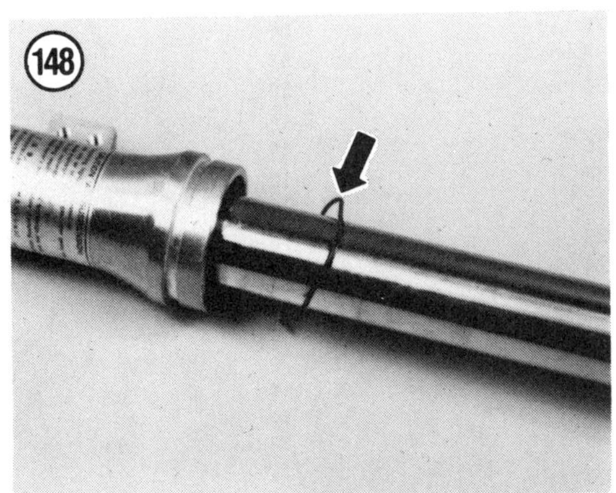

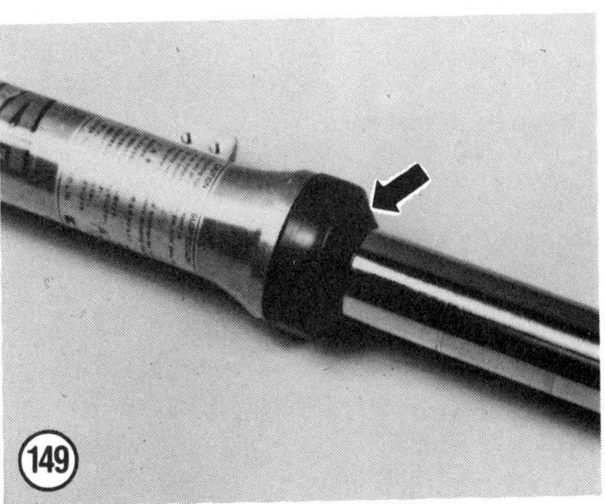

Table 1 FRONT FORK AND STEERING SPECIFICATIONS

	mm	in.
Front fork travel		
YZ50	110	4.3
YZ60		
1981	150	5.9
1982	165	6.5
YZ80		
1978	140	5.5
1979	165	6.5
1980	180	7.1
1981	215	8.46
1982	225	8.86
1983	240	9.45
1984-on	255	10.04
Front fork spring free length		
YZ50	417.9	16.5
YZ60		
1981	466.5	18.37
1982	467.5	18.41
YZ80		
1978	490.6	19.3
1979*	515.2	20.3
1980	541.7	21.3
1981	564.7	22.23
1982	564.7	22.23
1983	554	21.81
1984-on	461	18.1

* The dimension on 1979 YZ80 models is for both spring A and spring B placed together with the spring seat placed between them for total length.

Table 2 FRONT SUSPENSION TORQUE SPECIFICATIONS

	N•m	ft.-lb.
Front axle nut		
YZ50	35	25
YZ60	35	25
YZ80		
1978	60	43
1979-1980	75	54
1981	70	50
1982-1987	74	53
1988-on	70	50
Handlebar holder bolts		
YZ50	15	11
YZ60	16	12
YZ80		
1978	20	15
1979-1980	24	17
1981	26	18
1982-on	27	19
Fork bridge bolts (upper and lower)		
YZ50	15	11
YZ60	16	12
YZ80		
1978	24	17
1979-1979	23	16
1980-1981	15	11
1982	18	13
1983-1985	23	17
1985-on	18	13
Steering bolt or nut		
YZ50	60	43
YZ60	60	43
YZ80		
1978	58	42
1979-1981	60	43
1982	122	90
1983-on	60	43

CHAPTER TWELVE

REAR SUSPENSION

This chapter contains procedures for repair and replacement of the rear wheel and hub and rear suspension components. Service to the rear suspension consists of periodically checking bolt tightness, replacing swing arm bushings, and checking thecondition of the spring/gas monoshock units and replacing them as necessary.

Tire changing and tire repairs are covered in Chapter Eleven.

Rear suspension specifications are listed in **Tables 1-4** at the end of the chapter.

REAR WHEEL

Removal/Installation (1978-1979)

Refer to **Figure 1** for this procedure.

1. Place a workstand under the frame so that the rear wheel is off the ground.
2. Unscrew the rear brake adjusting nut completely from the brake rod (**Figure 2**). Withdraw the brake rod from the brake lever and pivot it down out of the way. Reinstall the adjusting nut and lever end onto the rod to avoid misplacing them.
3. Remove the bolt and nut (**Figure 3**) securing the rear brake torque link. Let it pivot down out of the way.
4. Remove the cotter pin (if so equipped) and axle nut (**Figure 4**). Discard the old cotter pin.

NOTE
On YZ50 models, also remove the axle adjuster on the left-hand side.

5. Remove the master link (**Figure 5**) from the drive chain and remove the chain from the drive sprocket.
6. Withdraw the axle (A, **Figure 6**) from the right-hand side of the wheel. Do not lose the spacer (B, **Figure 6**) or the right-hand axle adjuster YZ50 models.
7. Pull the wheel to the rear and remove it.
8. On YZ80 models, leave the axle adjusters on the swing arm. If they are loose, remove them, tap the open end slightly with a hammer and reinstall on the swing arm.

NOTE
On YZ80 models, don't lose the bushings inside the axle adjusters.

9. Install by reversing these removal steps, note the following.
10. Be sure to install the axle spacer on the left-hand side of the wheel (**Figure 7**).
11. If the drive chain was disconnected, install the clip on the drive chain master link and install it so

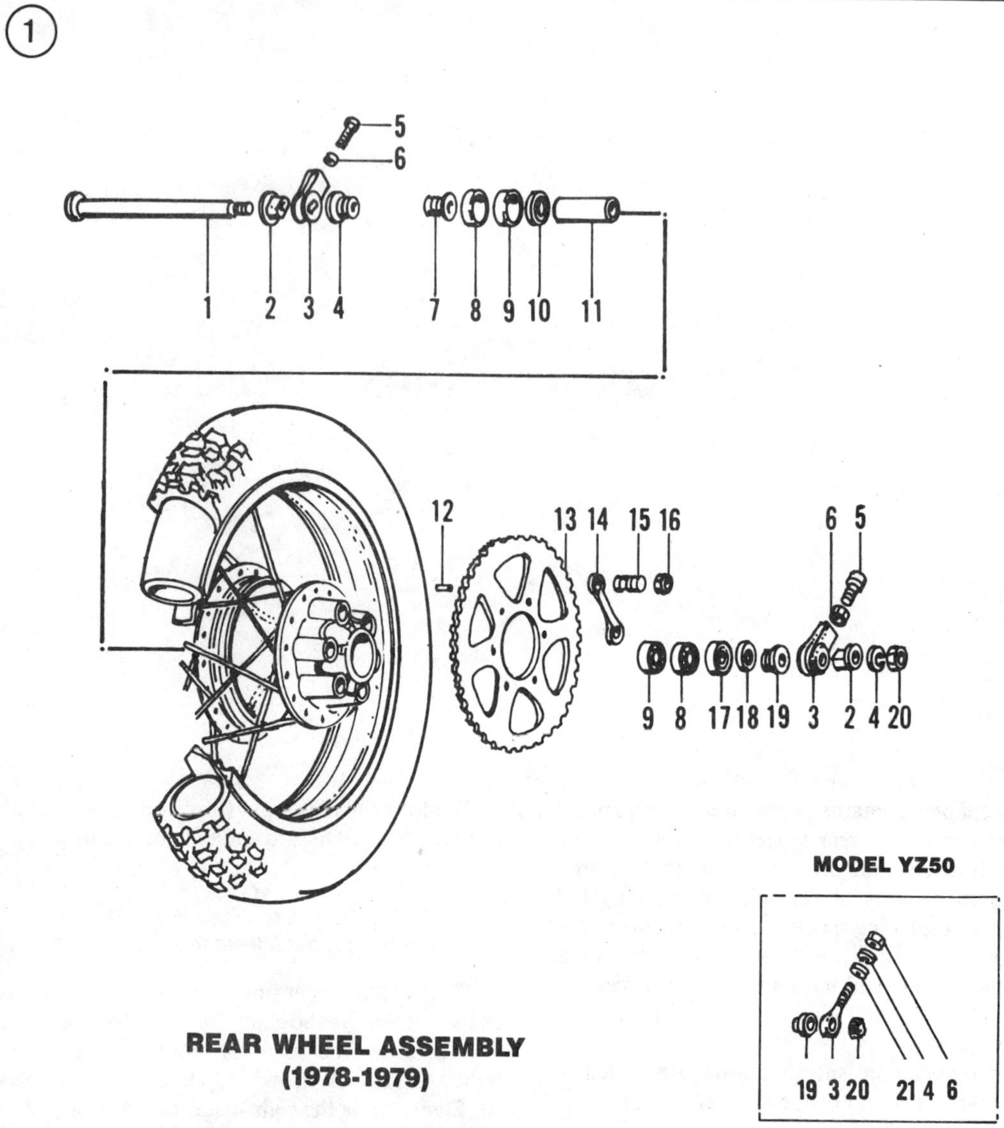

1

MODEL YZ50

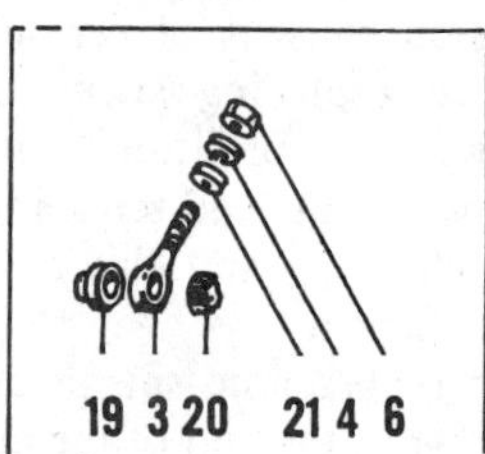

REAR WHEEL ASSEMBLY (1978-1979)

1. Rear axle
2. Bushing
3. Axle adjuster
4. Lockwasher
5. Adjuster bolt
6. Locknut
7. Seal
8. Bearing
9. Wheel bearing
10. Spacer flange
11. Distance collar
12. Stud
13. Sprocket
14. Lockwasher
15. Bolt
16. Nut
17. Oil seal
18. Dust seal
19. Seal
20. Axle nut
21. Washer

2

5

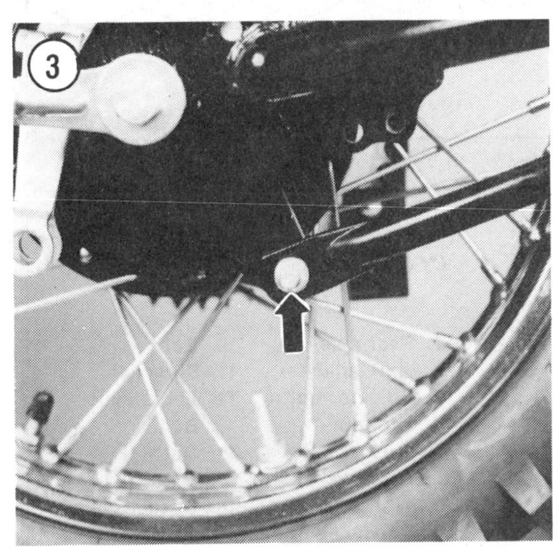
3

6
A
B

4

7

that the closed end of the clip is facing the direction of chain travel (**Figure 8**).

12. Install the axle from the right-hand side.

NOTE
On YZ50 models, don't forget to install the axle adjuster onto the right-hand end of the axle prior to installation. Also install the other one prior to installing the axle nut.

13. Adjust the drive chain tension as described under *Drive Chain Adjustment* in Chapter Three.

14. Tighten the axle nut to the torque specifications in **Table 3**. Tighten the brake torque link nut securely.

NOTE
If equipped, install a new cotter pin on the axle nut. Never reuse an old one as it may break and fall off.

15. After the wheel is completely installed, rotate it several times to make sure it rotates smoothly. Apply the brake several times to make sure it operates correctly.

16. Adjust the rear brake as described under *Rear Brake Pedal Adjustment* in Chapter Three.

Removal/Installation (1980-on)

Refer to the illustration for your model when servicing the rear wheel:

a. **Figure 9**: YZ60 and 1980-1983 YZ80.
b. **Figure 10**: 1984-1985 YZ80.
c. **Figure 11**: 1986 YZ80.
d. **Figure 12**: 1987-on YZ80.

8

Master link clip
Direction
of chain travel

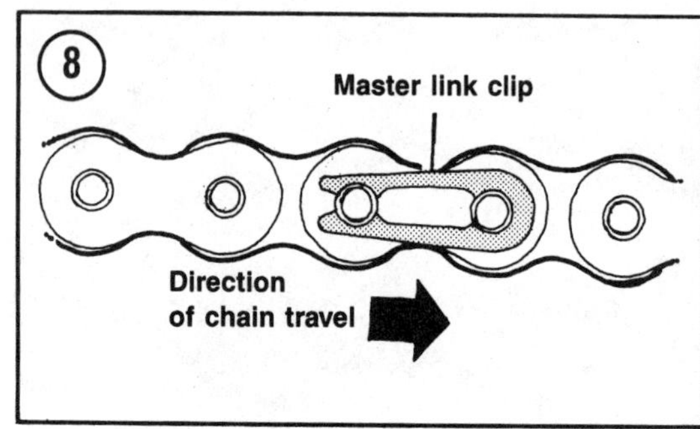

9

REAR WHEEL ASSEMBLY
(YZ60 AND 1980-1983 YZ80)
1. Rear axle
2. Axle adjuster
3. Adjuster bolt
4. Locknut
5. Washer
6. Lockwasher
7. Wheel bearing
8. Spacer flange
9. Distance collar
10. Bolt
11. Sprocket
12. Lockwasher
13. Bolt
14. Nut
15. Oil seal
16. Spacer collar
17. Axle nut
18. Seal
MODEL YZ60

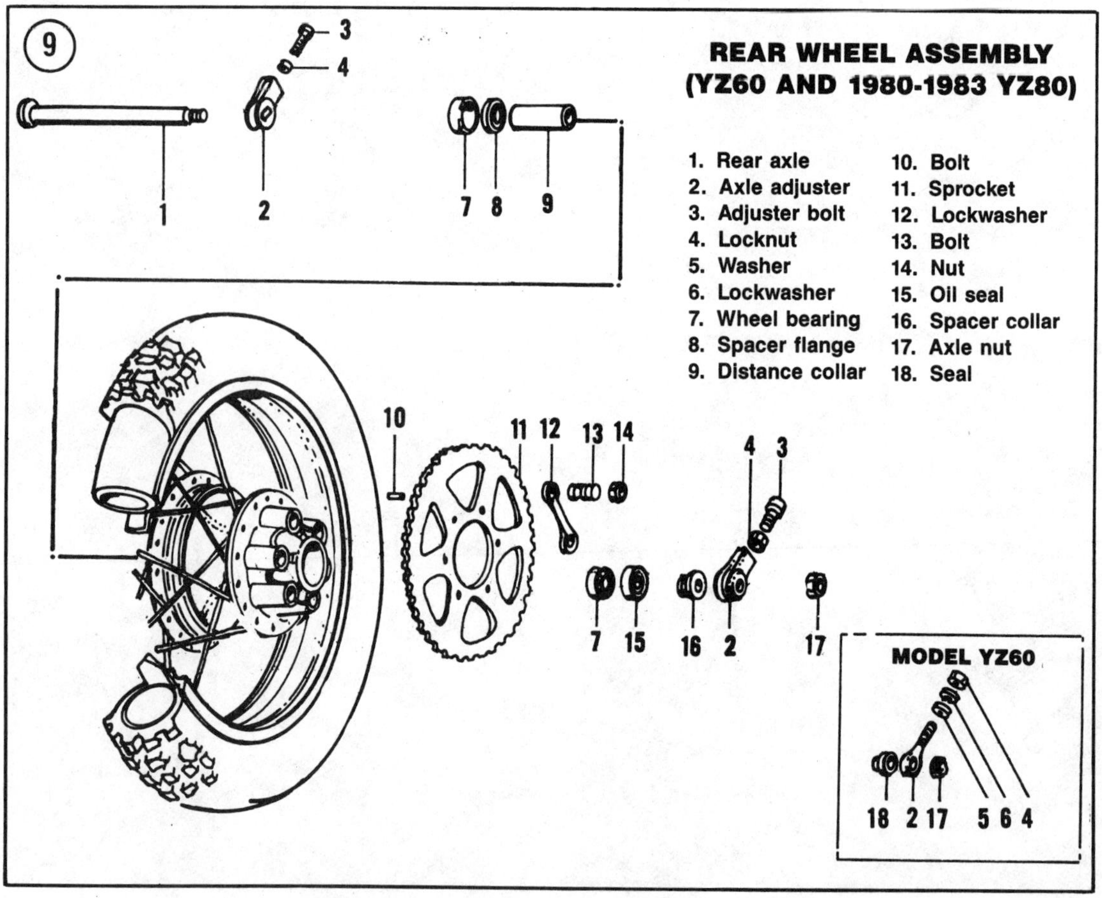

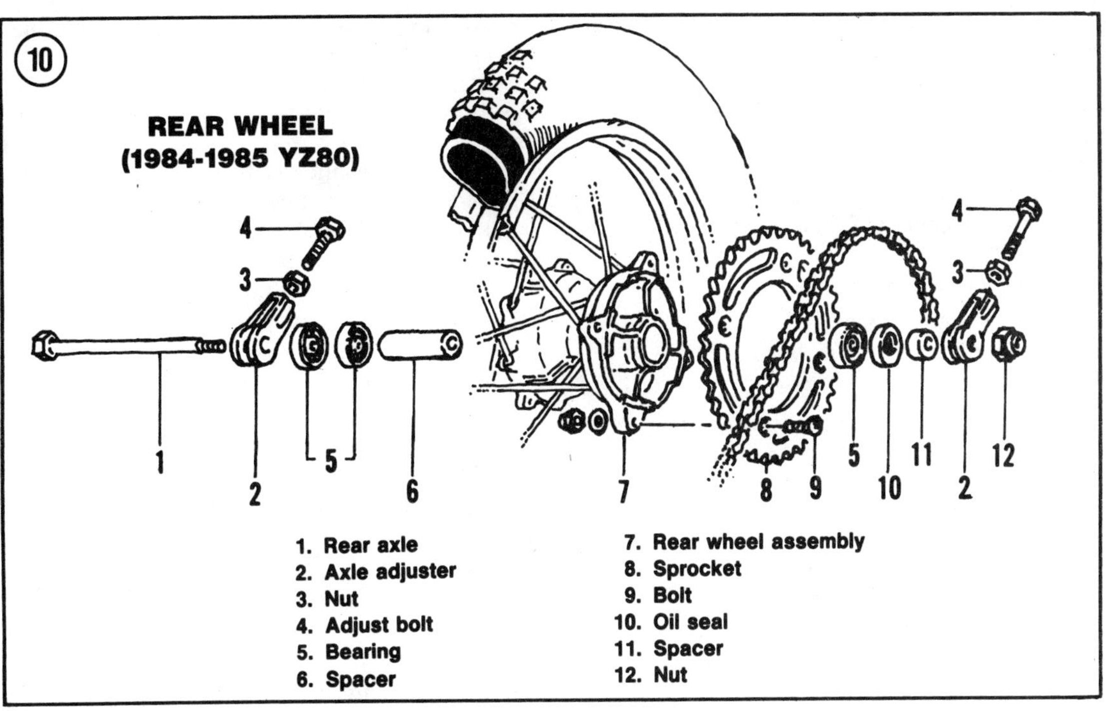

(10)

REAR WHEEL (1984-1985 YZ80)

1. Rear axle
2. Axle adjuster
3. Nut
4. Adjust bolt
5. Bearing
6. Spacer
7. Rear wheel assembly
8. Sprocket
9. Bolt
10. Oil seal
11. Spacer
12. Nut

(11)

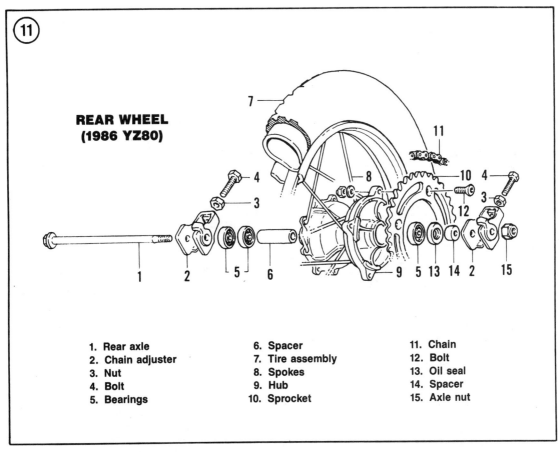

REAR WHEEL (1986 YZ80)

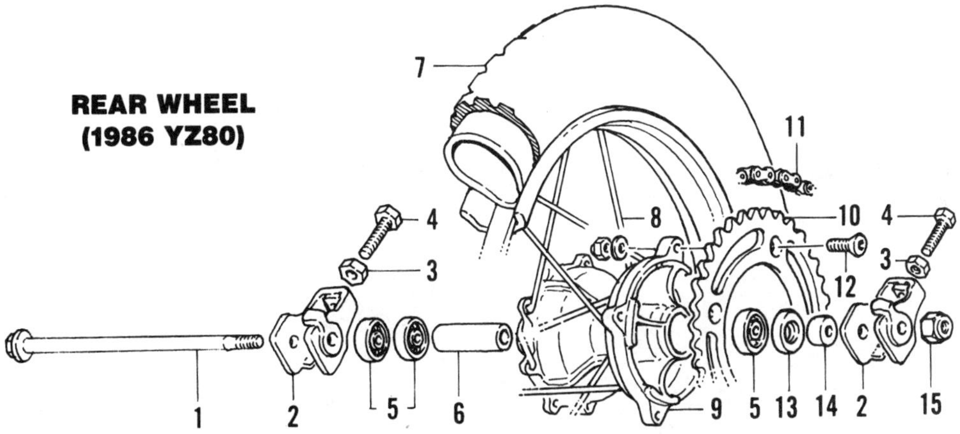

1. Rear axle
2. Chain adjuster
3. Nut
4. Bolt
5. Bearings
6. Spacer
7. Tire assembly
8. Spokes
9. Hub
10. Sprocket
11. Chain
12. Bolt
13. Oil seal
14. Spacer
15. Axle nut

1. Place a workstand under the frame so that the rear wheel is off the ground.
2. Unscrew the rear brake adjusting nut completely from the brake rod (**Figure 2**). Withdraw the brake rod from the brake lever and pivot it down out of the way. Reinstall the adjusting nut and lever end onto the rod to avoid misplacing them.
3. Remove the cotter pin (if so equipped). Discard the cotter pin.
4. Loosen and remove the axle nut.

NOTE
On YZ60 models, also remove the axle adjuster on the left-hand side.

5. If necessary, remove the master link (**Figure 5**) from the drive chain and remove the chain from the drive sprocket.
6. Withdraw the axle from the right-hand side of the wheel. Do not lose the spacer (**Figure 13**) or the right-hand axle adjuster on YZ60 models.
7. Pull the wheel to the rear and remove it.
8. On YZ80 models, leave the axle adjusters on the swing arm. If they are loose, remove them, tap the open end slightly with a hammer and reinstall on the swing arm.
9. Install by reversing these removal steps.
10. Be sure to install the axle spacer on the left-hand side of the wheel (**Figure 13**).
11. Make sure to align the groove in the brake panel (**Figure 14**) with the rib welded to the swing arm.
12. If the drive chain was disconnected, install the clip on the drive chain master link and install it so that the closed end of the clip is facing the direction of chain travel (**Figure 8**).
13. Install the axle from the right-hand side.

NOTE
On YZ60 models, don't forget to install the axle adjuster onto the right-hand end of the axle prior to installation. Also install the other one prior to installing the axle nut.

14. Adjust the drive chain tension as described under *Drive Chain Adjustment* in Chapter Three.
15. Tighten the axle nut to the torque specifications in **Table 3** or **Table 4**.

NOTE
If a cotter pin is used to secure the rear axle nut, install a new cotter pin. Never reuse an old one as it may break and fall off.

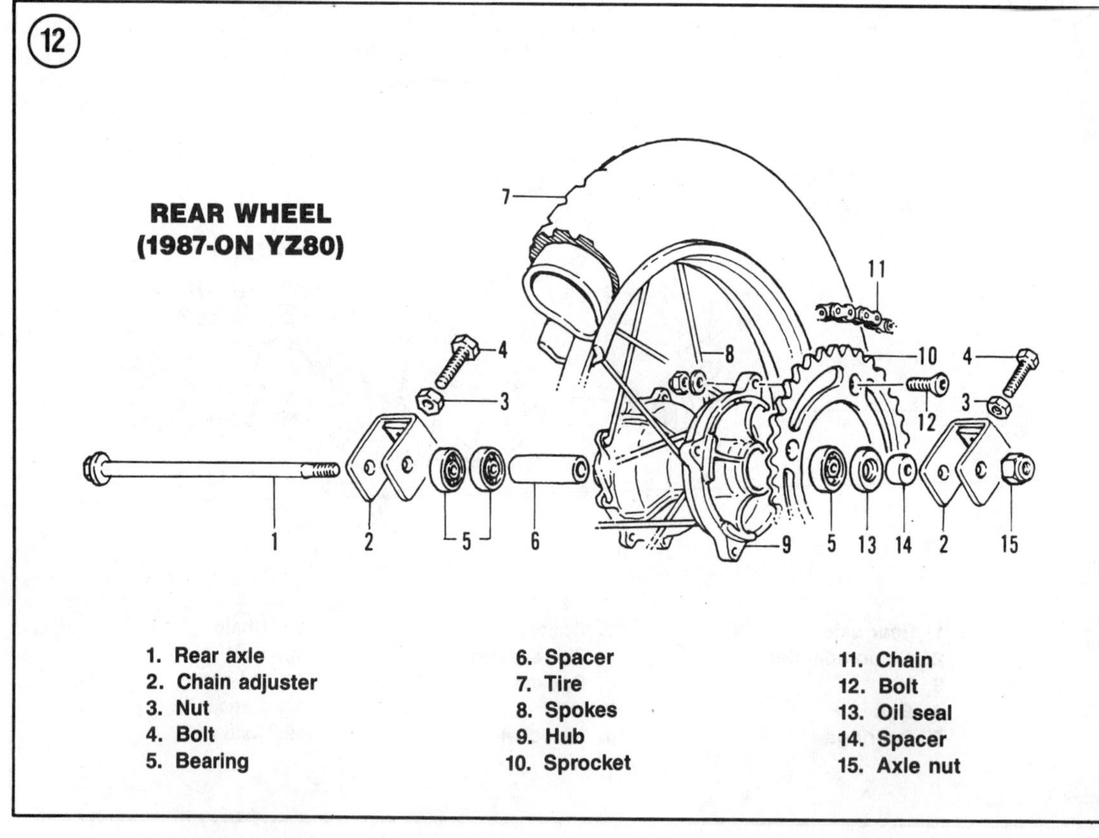

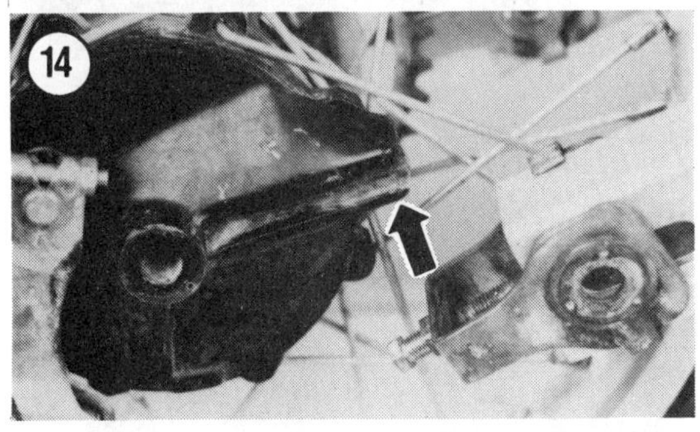

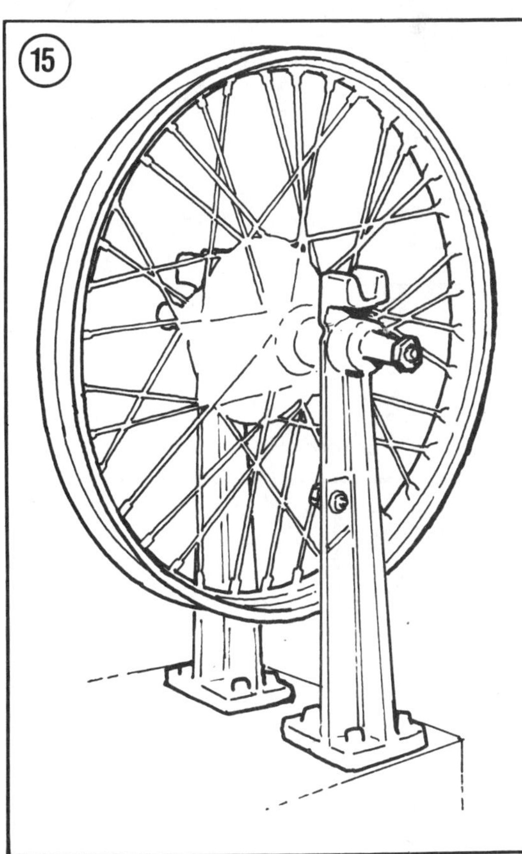

16. After the wheel is completely installed, rotate it several times to make sure it rotates smoothly. Apply the brakes several times to make sure it operates correctly.
17. Adjust the rear brake as described under *Rear Brake Pedal Adjustment* in Chapter Three.

Inspection (All Models)

The easiest way to check wheel rim straightness is with a truing stand (**Figure 15**). If a stand isn't available, you can make one yourself with some 2×4 wood scraps and 16 penny nails.

After mounting the wheel in a suitable stand, fix a pointer so that you can check radial (up and down) and axial (side-to-side) play (**Figure 16**).

Spin the wheel and check radial and axial play. When determining wheel play, it is more important to clean up the axial play. Since the wheel is bouncing up and down on a motocross track, radial play isn't as critical. It's more important for the wheel to be vertically straight, so it isn't wobbling around between the swing arm.

Tighten or replace any bent or loose spokes. Refer to *Spoke Adjustment* or *Spoke Inspection and Replacement* in this chapter.

Check the axle runout as described under *Rear Hub Inspection* in this chapter.

REAR HUB

Refer to the illustration for your model when servicing the rear wheel:

a. **Figure 1**: YZ50 and 1978-1979 YZ80.
b. **Figure 9**: YZ60 and 1980-1983 YZ80.
c. **Figure 10**: 1984-1985 YZ80.
d. **Figure 11**: 1986 YZ80.
e. **Figure 12**: 1987-on YZ80.

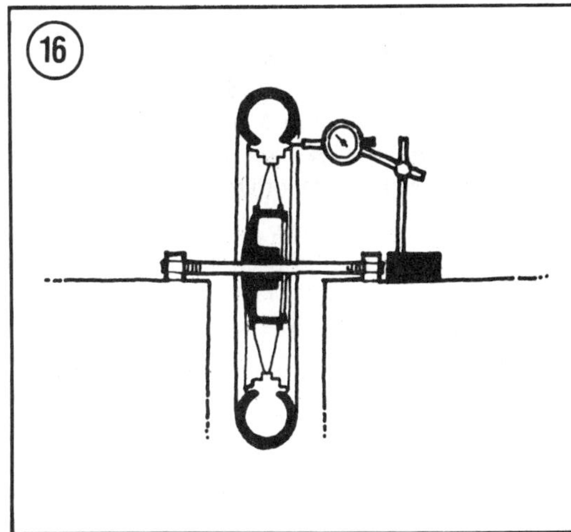

Disassembly

1. Remove the rear wheel as described under *Rear Wheel Removal/Installation* in this chapter.
2. Remove the axle spacers from the wheel.
3. Pull the brake assembly straight up and out of the drum.
4. Remove the oil seals (**Figure 17**) by carefully prying them out of the hub with a long screwdriver. Prop a piece of wood or rag underneath the screwdriver to prevent from damaging the hub.

NOTE
If the seal is tight, work the screwdriver around the seal every few degrees until the seal pops out of the hub.

5. Remove the left- and right-hand bearings (**Figure 18**) and distance collar. To remove them, insert a soft aluminum or brass drift into one side of the hub. Push the distance collar over to one side and place the drift on the inner race of the lower bearing (**Figure 19**). Tap the bearing out of the hub with a hammer, working around the perimeter of the inner race.
6. Remove the distance collar and tap out the opposite bearing.

17

18

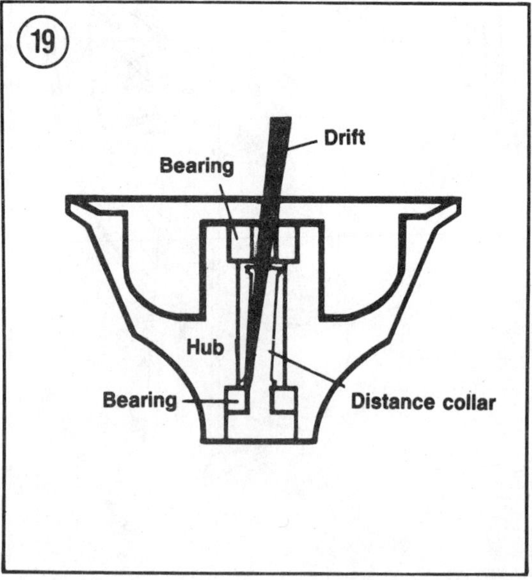

19

Inspection

1. Thoroughly clean out the inside of the hub with solvent and dry with compressed air or a shop cloth.

NOTE
Avoid getting any greasy solvent residue on the brake drum during this procedure. If this happens, clean it off with a shop cloth and lacquer thinner.

2. Do not clean sealed bearings with solvent as this will liquefy the grease and cause bearing damage. Wipe sealed bearings off with a lint-free cloth or rag. If non-sealed bearings are installed, clean them in solvent and thoroughly dry with compressed air. Do not let the bearing spin while drying.
3. Turn each bearing by hand (**Figure 20**). Make sure the bearings turn smoothly.

NOTE
Some axial play is normal, but radial play should be negligible. The bearing should turn smoothly.

4. On non-sealed bearings, check the balls for evidence of wear, pitting, or excessive heat (bluish tint). Replace bearing if necessary; always replace as a complete set. When replacing, be sure to take your old bearings along to ensure a perfect matchup.

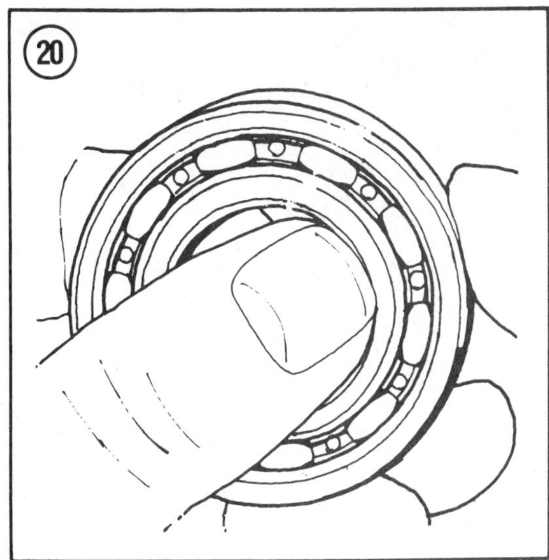

20

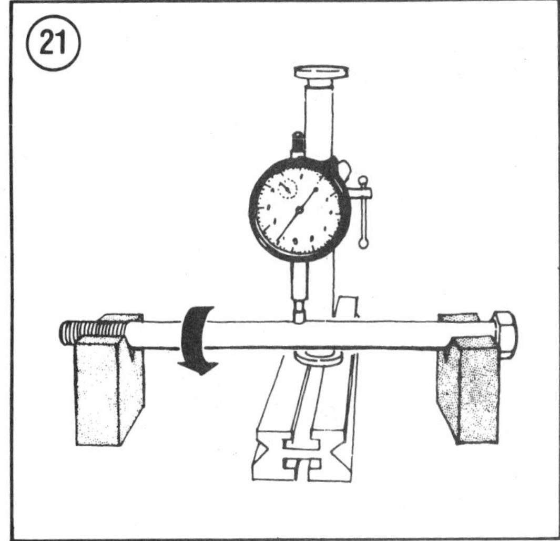

21

22

NOTE
Fully sealed bearings are available from many good bearing specialty shops. Fully sealed bearings provide better protection from dirt and moisture that may get into the hub.

5. Check the axle for wear and straightness. Use V-blocks and a dial indicator as shown in **Figure 21**. If the runout is 0.2 mm (0.008 in.) or greater, the axle should be replaced.

Assembly

1. If cleaned, pack the non-sealed bearings with a good quality bearing grease. Work the grease in between the balls thoroughly. Turn the bearing by hand a couple of times to make sure the grease is distributed evenly inside the bearing.
2. Pack the wheel hub with lithium waterproof wheel bearing grease.

CAUTION
*When installing the bearings in the following steps, tap the bearings squarely into place by tapping on the outer race only. Use a socket (**Figure 22**) that matches the outer race diameter. Do not tap on the inner race or the bearing will be damaged. Be sure that the bearings are completely seated.*

3. Install the left-hand bearing.
4. Install the distance collar.
5. Install the right-hand bearing.

NOTE
Install the wheel bearings with the sealed side facing out.

6. Lubricate the new grease seal with fresh multipurpose grease and tap it gently into place in the hub.
7. Install the rear wheel as described in this chapter.

DRIVEN SPROCKET

Disassembly/Assembly

1. Remove the rear wheel as described in this chapter.
2. If your model uses nuts and lockwashers to secure the driven sprocket, straighten the locking tabs on the lockwashers and remove the bolts and lockwashers (**Figure 23**). If your model uses Allen

bolts to secure the driven sprocket (**Figure 24**), loosen the nuts at the back of the sprocket. Then remove the nuts, washers and bolts. Do not loosen the Allen bolts by turning the bolt; this will damage the Allen head.

3. Remove the driven sprocket.
4. Assemble by reversing these disassembly steps, noting the following:
   a. If so equipped, install new lockwashers.
   b. Tighten the nuts securely.

Inspection

Inspect the sprocket teeth. If they are visibly worn as shown in **Figure 25**, replace the sprocket.

If the sprocket requires replacement, the drive chain is probably worn also and may need replacement. Refer to *Drive Chain/Cleaning, Inspection, and Lubrication* in Chapter Three.

23

24

DRIVE CHAIN

Removal/Installation

1. Place a workstand under the frame so the rear wheel is off the ground.
2. Turn the rear wheel and drive chain until the master link is accessible.
3. Remove the master link clip (**Figure 26**) and remove the master link.
4. Slowly rotate the rear wheel and pull the drive chain off the drive sprocket.
5. Install by reversing these removal steps.
6. Install the clip on the master link so that the closed end of the clip is facing the direction of chain travel (**Figure 8**).

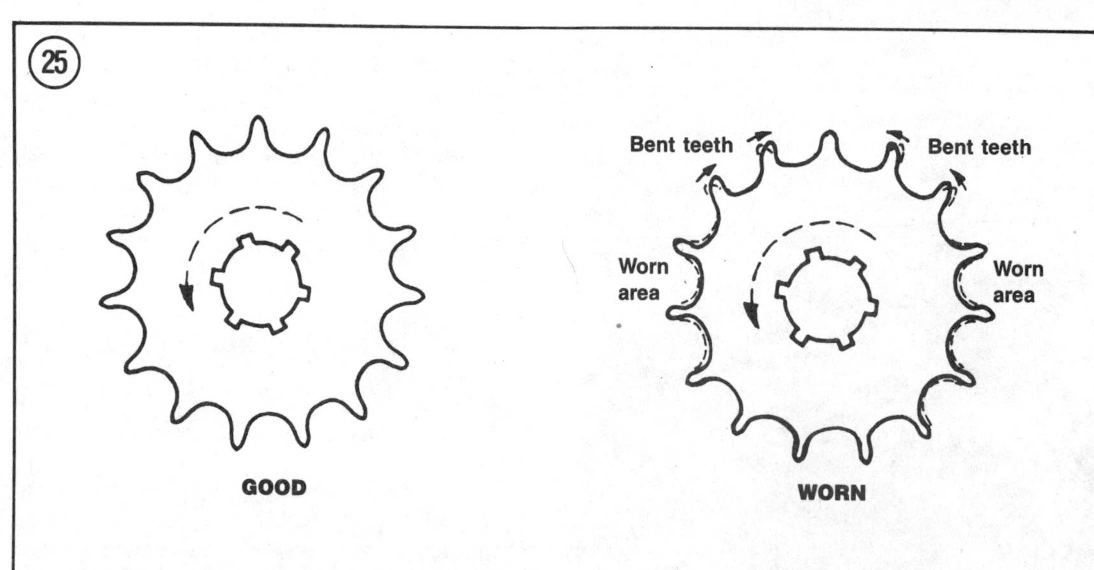

25

Service and Inspection

For service and inspection of the drive chain, refer to *Drive Chain/Cleaning, Inspection and Lubrication* in Chapter Three.

REAR SUSPENSION (DECARBON MONOSHOCK SYSTEM)

WARNING

*The monoshock unit contains highly compressed nitrogen gas. Do not tamper with or attempt to open the damper/cylinder assembly (**Figure 27**). Do not place it near an open flame or other extreme heat. Do not weld on the frame near it. Do not dispose of the damper subassembly yourself. Take it to a Yamaha dealer where it can be deactivated and disposed of properly.*

26

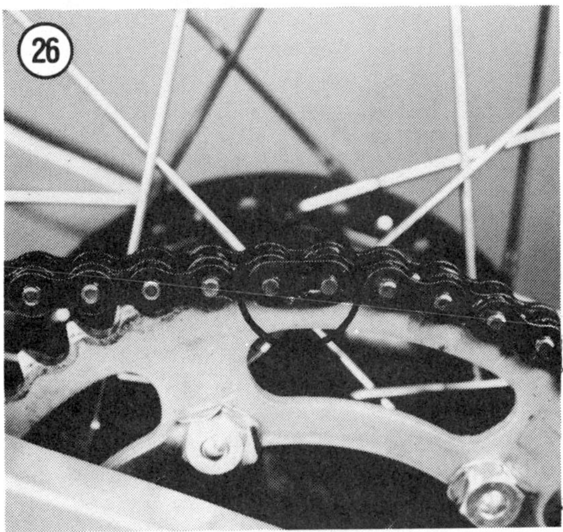

27

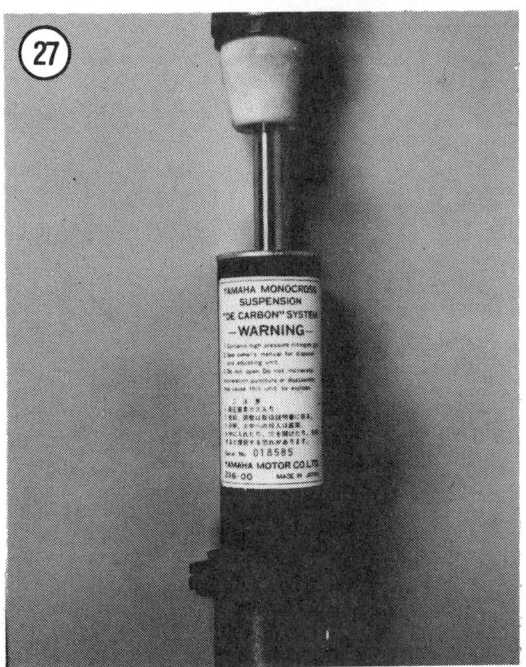

Monoshock Removal/Installation (YZ50, YZ60 and 1978-1980 YZ80)

Refer to **Figure 28** or **Figure 29** for this procedure.

1. Place a workstand under the frame high enough to lift the rear wheel off the ground by at least 10 to 12 inches.
2. Remove the seat.
3. Remove the fuel tank as described in Chapter Eight.
4. Remove the cotter pin and flat washer (A, **Figure 30**) securing the upper monoshock mount to the frame. Remove the pivot pin and discard the cotter pin.
5. Remove the cotter pin and flat washer (B, **Figure 30**) securing the lower monoshock mount to the swing arm. Remove the pivot pin and discard the cotter pin.
6. Pivot the rear wheel and swing arm down. Do not lose the 2 cover washers (**Figure 31**) on each side of the monoshock at the lower mount.
7. Carefully withdraw the monoshock assembly out through the rear of the frame and over the rear wheel.

NOTE

If you cannot withdraw the monoshock over the rear wheel, either block up the frame higher or remove the rear wheel.

8. Install by reversing these removal steps, noting the following.
9. Insert the monoshock with the spring pre-load adjuster end in first toward the front of the bike.

NOTE

Make sure that both cover washers are installed. They are necessary to maintain the proper clearance between the monoshock and the swing arm. If they are slightly flattened out, replace them.

10. Install the cover washers (**Figure 31**) on each side of the monoshock at the lower mount.
11. Insert the upper pivot pin from the left-hand side and the lower from the right-hand side. Apply

12

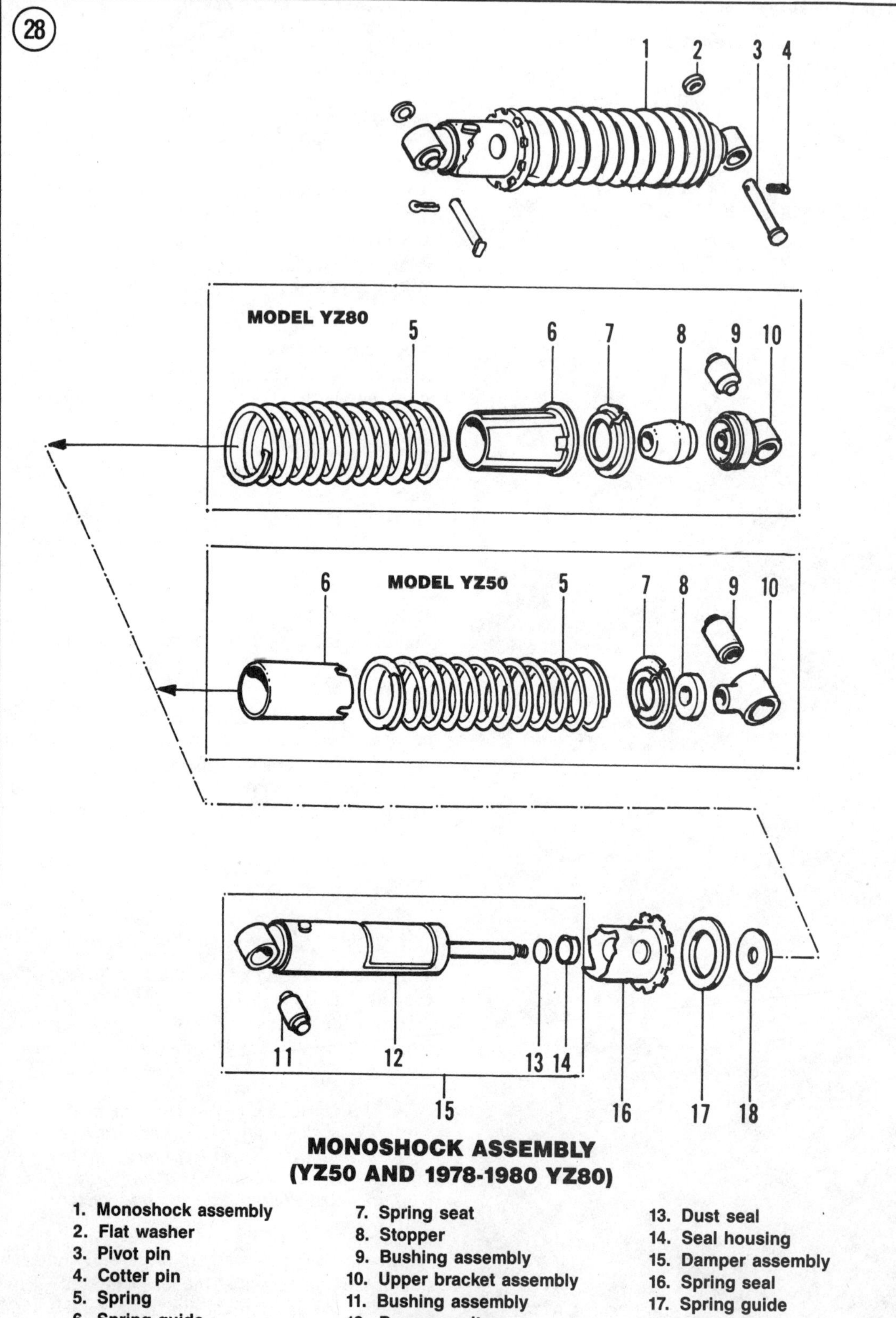

MONOSHOCK ASSEMBLY (YZ50 AND 1978-1980 YZ80)

1. Monoshock assembly
2. Flat washer
3. Pivot pin
4. Cotter pin
5. Spring
6. Spring guide
7. Spring seat
8. Stopper
9. Bushing assembly
10. Upper bracket assembly
11. Bushing assembly
12. Damper unit
13. Dust seal
14. Seal housing
15. Damper assembly
16. Spring seal
17. Spring guide
18. Case cap

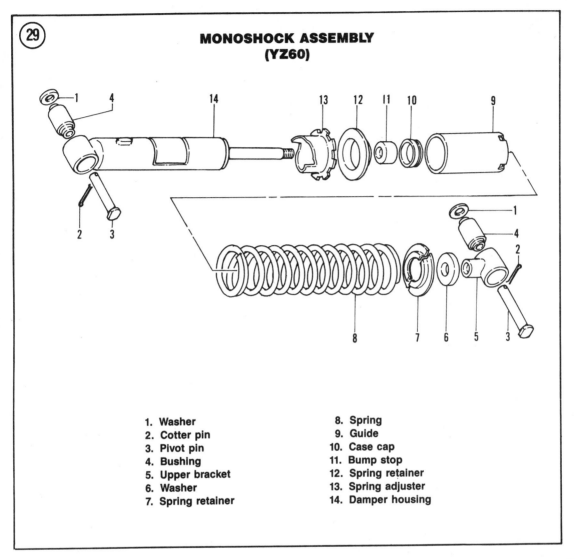

29

MONOSHOCK ASSEMBLY (YZ60)

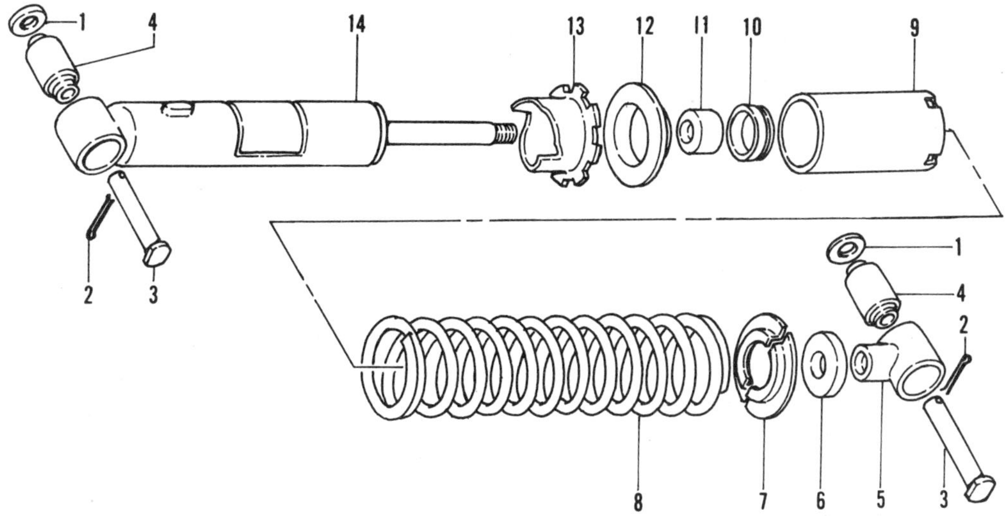

1. Washer
2. Cotter pin
3. Pivot pin
4. Bushing
5. Upper bracket
6. Washer
7. Spring retainer
8. Spring
9. Guide
10. Case cap
11. Bump stop
12. Spring retainer
13. Spring adjuster
14. Damper housing

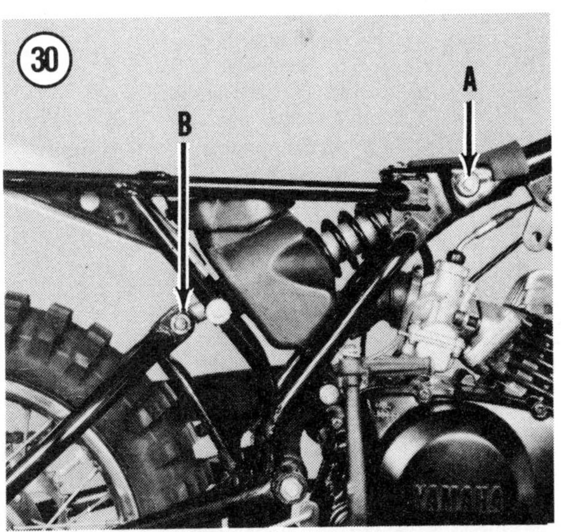

30

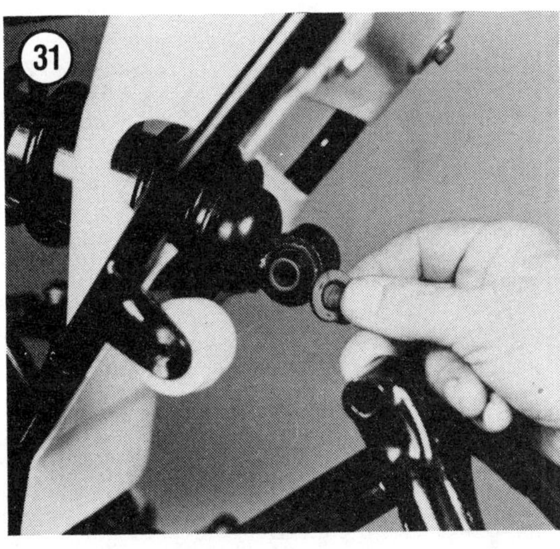

31

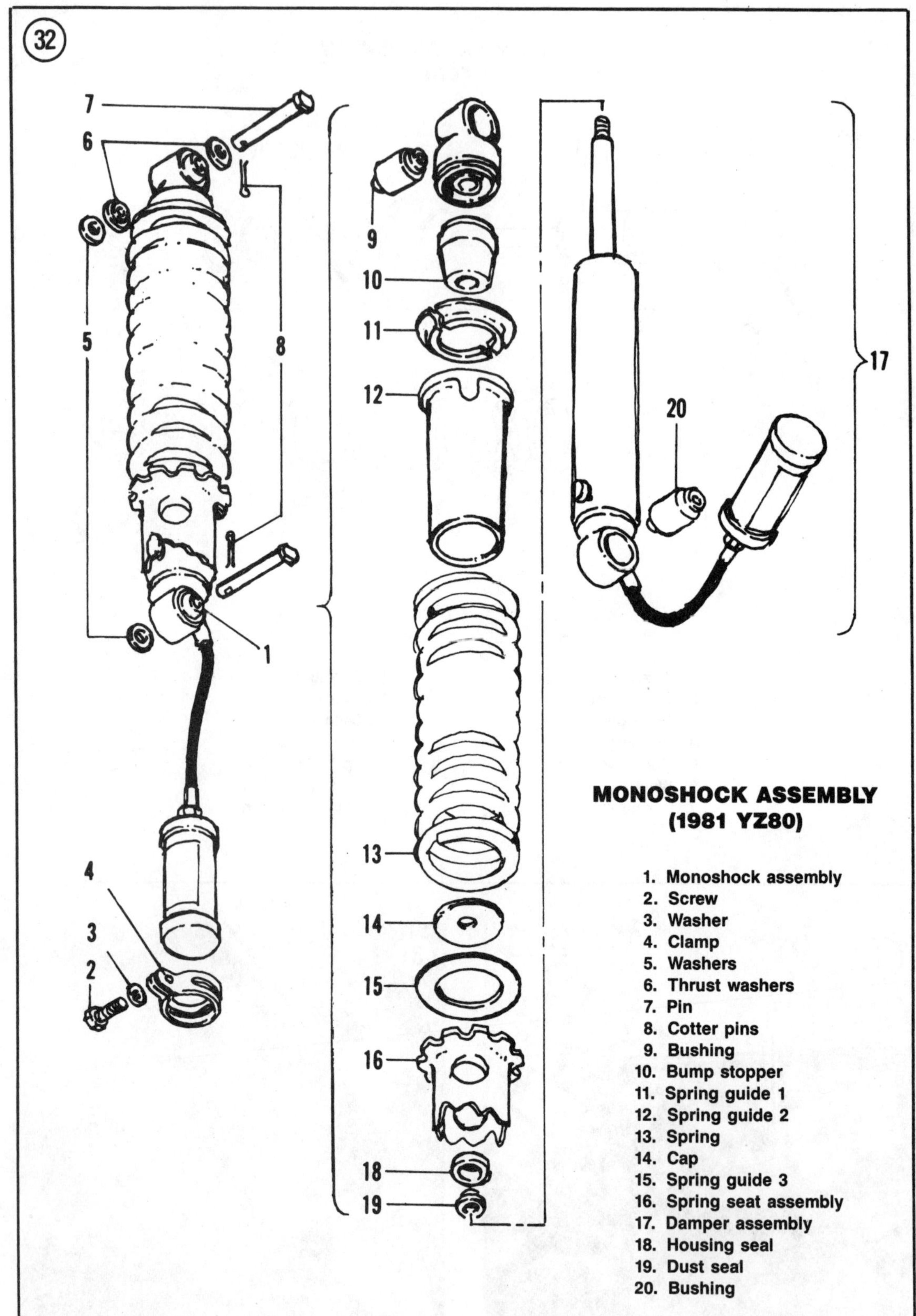
32
7
6
5
8
1
4
3
2
9
10
11
12
13
14
15
16
18
19
17
20
MONOSHOCK ASSEMBLY
(1981 YZ80)
1. Monoshock assembly
2. Screw
3. Washer
4. Clamp
5. Washers
6. Thrust washers
7. Pin
8. Cotter pins
9. Bushing
10. Bump stopper
11. Spring guide 1
12. Spring guide 2
13. Spring
14. Cap
15. Spring guide 3
16. Spring seat assembly
17. Damper assembly
18. Housing seal
19. Dust seal
20. Bushing

a light coat of grease to each pivot pin prior to installing it.

12. Install the washer and a new cotter pin on each pivot pin—never reuse a cotter pin as it may break and fall out. Hold one end of the pin with a wrench and bend over the end of the cotter pin completely.

Removal/Installation (1981 YZ80)

Refer to **Figure 32** for this procedure.

1. Place a workstand under the frame high enough to lift the rear wheel off the ground by at least 10 to 12 inches.
2. Remove the side covers.
3. Remove the screws securing the reservoir to the frame (**Figure 33**). Place the reservoir on the cylinder head.
4. Remove the cotter pin and washer from the rear monoshock-to-swing arm mount. Remove the pivot pin and discard the cotter pin. Remove the 2 cover washers from the swing arm.
5. Pivot the rear wheel and swing arm down after disconnecting the shock absorber.
6. Remove the cotter pin and washer from the upper monoshock-to-frame mount.
7. Carefully withdraw the monoshock assembly out through the rear of the frame over the rear wheel. When removing the monoshock, guide the reservoir and its hose by hand to prevent damage.
8. Install by reversing these removal steps, noting the following:
   a. Install the cover washers on each side of the monoshock at the lower mount.

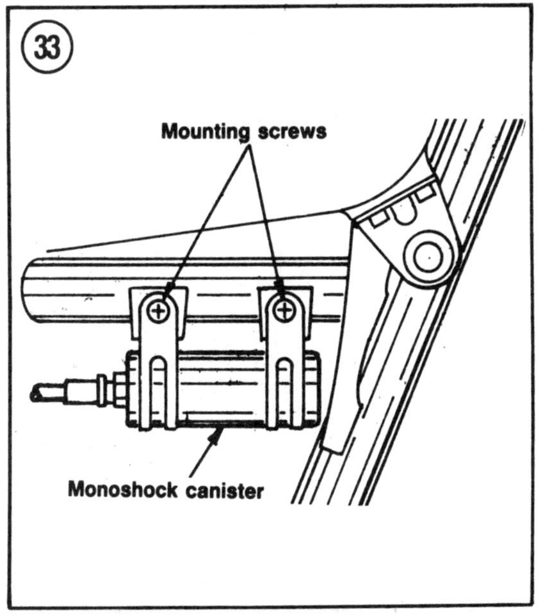

NOTE
Make sure both cover washers are installed. They are necessary to maintain the proper clearance between the monoshock and swing arm. If they are slightly flattened out, replace them.

   b. Insert the upper and lower pivot pins from the left-hand side. Apply a light coat of grease to each pivot pin prior to installing it.
   c. Install the washer and a new cotter pin on each pivot pin—never reuse a cotter pin as it may break and fall out. Hold one end of the pin with a wrench and bend over the end of the cotter pin completely.

Removal/Installation (1982 YZ80)

Refer to **Figure 34** for this procedure.

1. Place a workstand under the frame high enough to lift the rear wheel off the ground by at least 10 to 12 inches.
2. Remove the side covers.
3. Remove the seat.
4. Remove the fuel tank as described in Chapter Eight.
5. Remove the remote shock reservoir top clamp (**Figure 35**) and pull the reservoir up and away from the frame.
6. Remove the cotter pin and washer from the rear monoshock-to-swing arm mount (**Figure 36**). Remove the pivot pin and discard the cotter pin. Remove the 2 cover washers (**Figure 37**) from the swing arm.
7. Pivot the rear wheel and swing arm down after disconnecting the shock absorber.
8. Remove the cotter pin and washer from the upper monoshock-to-frame mount (**Figure 38**). Discard the cotter pin.
9. Carefully withdraw the monoshock assembly out through the rear of the frame over the rear wheel. When removing the monoshock, guide the reservoir and its hose by hand to prevent damage.
10. Install by reversing these removal steps, noting the following:
    a. Install the cover washers (**Figure 37**) on each side of the monoshock at the lower mount.

NOTE
Make sure both cover washers are installed. They are necessary to maintain the proper clearance between the monoshock and swing arm. If they are slightly flattened out, replace them.

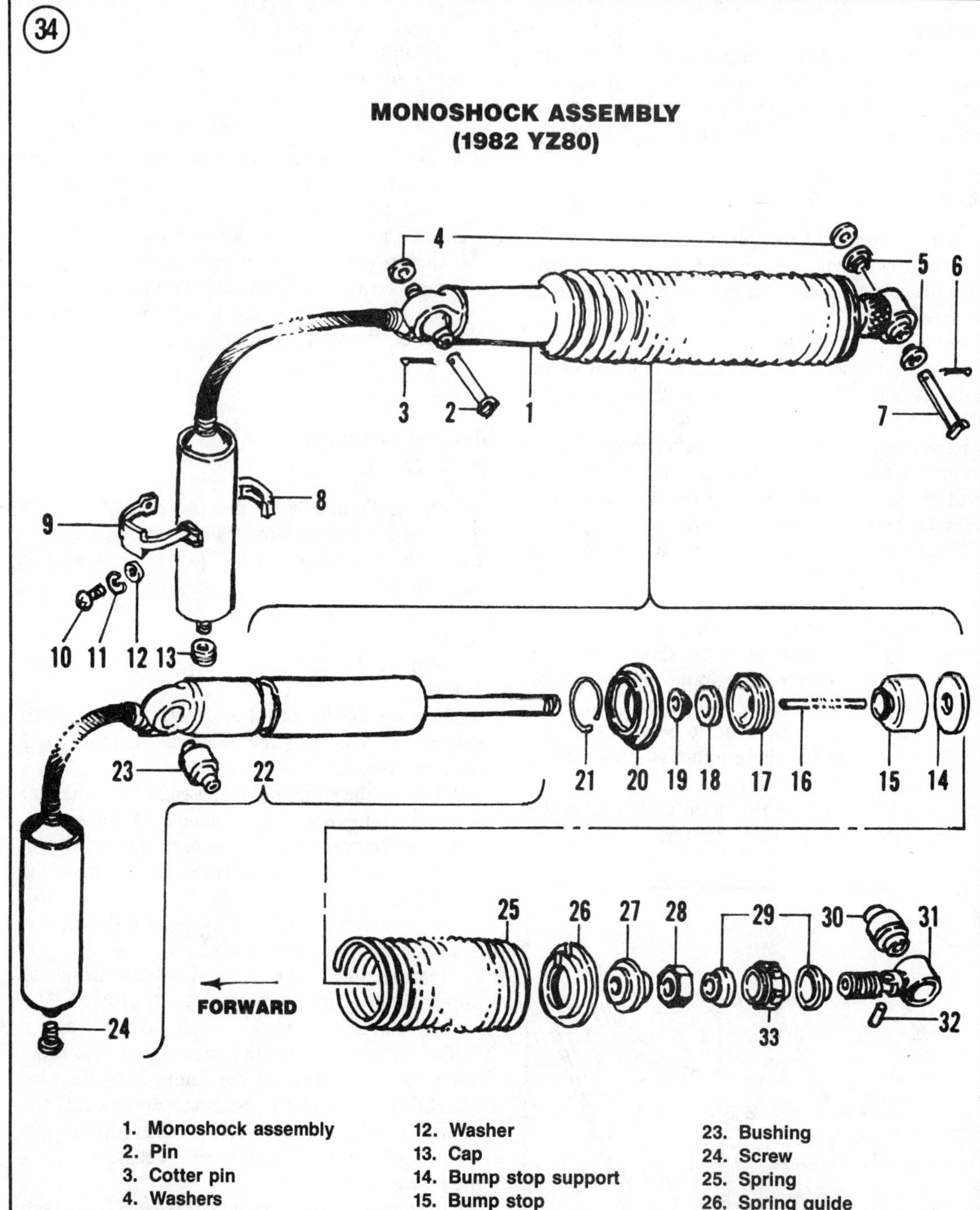
34
MONOSHOCK ASSEMBLY
(1982 YZ80)
4
5
6
3
2
1
7
8
9
10
11
12
13
23
22
21
20
19
18
17
16
15
14
25
26
27
28
29
30
31
FORWARD
24
33
32
1. Monoshock assembly
2. Pin
3. Cotter pin
4. Washers
5. Thrust cover
6. Cotter pin
7. Pin
8. Damper
9. Holder
10. Screw
11. Lockwasher
12. Washer
13. Cap
14. Bump stop support
15. Bump stop
16. Pushrod
17. Cap
18. Seal housing
19. Dust seal
20. Spring seat
21. Circlip
22. Damper subassembly
23. Bushing
24. Screw
25. Spring
26. Spring guide
27. Spring seat
28. Nut
29. Covers
30. Bushing
31. Bushing support
32. Pin
33. Adusting nut

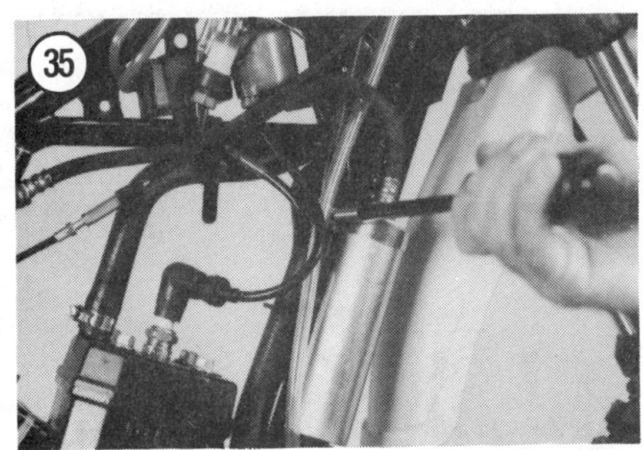

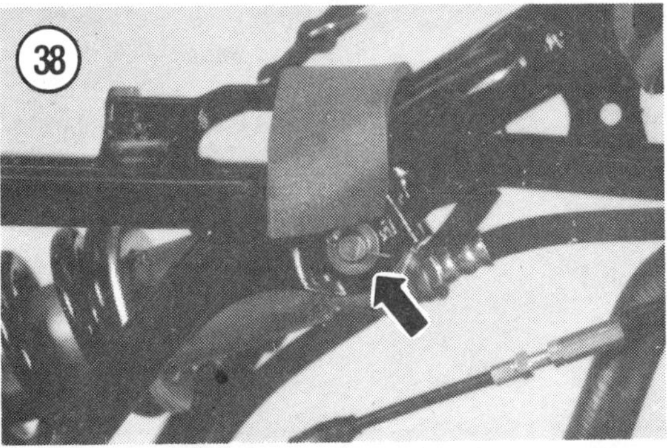

b. Insert the upper and lower pivot pins from the left-hand side. Apply a light coat of grease to each pivot pin prior to installing it.
c. Install the washer and a new cotter pin on each pivot pin—never reuse a cotter pin as it may break and fall out. Hold one end of the pin with a wrench and bend over the end of the cotter pin completely.
d. Make sure the rubber damper is secured on the frame down tube (**Figure 39**).
e. When installing the reservoir, make sure to insert the end of the reservoir nitrogen fitting into the welded joint on the downtube as shown in **Figure 40**.

Monoshock Removal/Installation (1983-on YZ80)

Removal/Installation

Refer to **Figure 41A** (1983) or **Figure 41B** (1984-on) for this procedure.

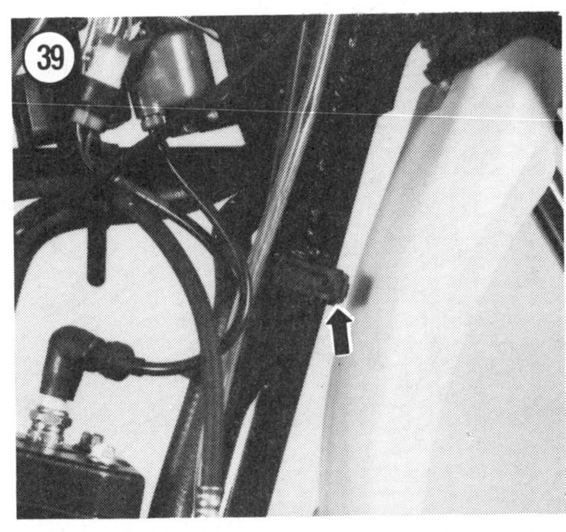

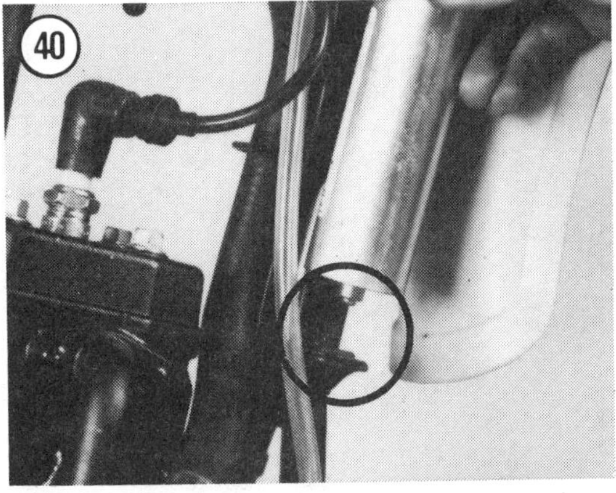

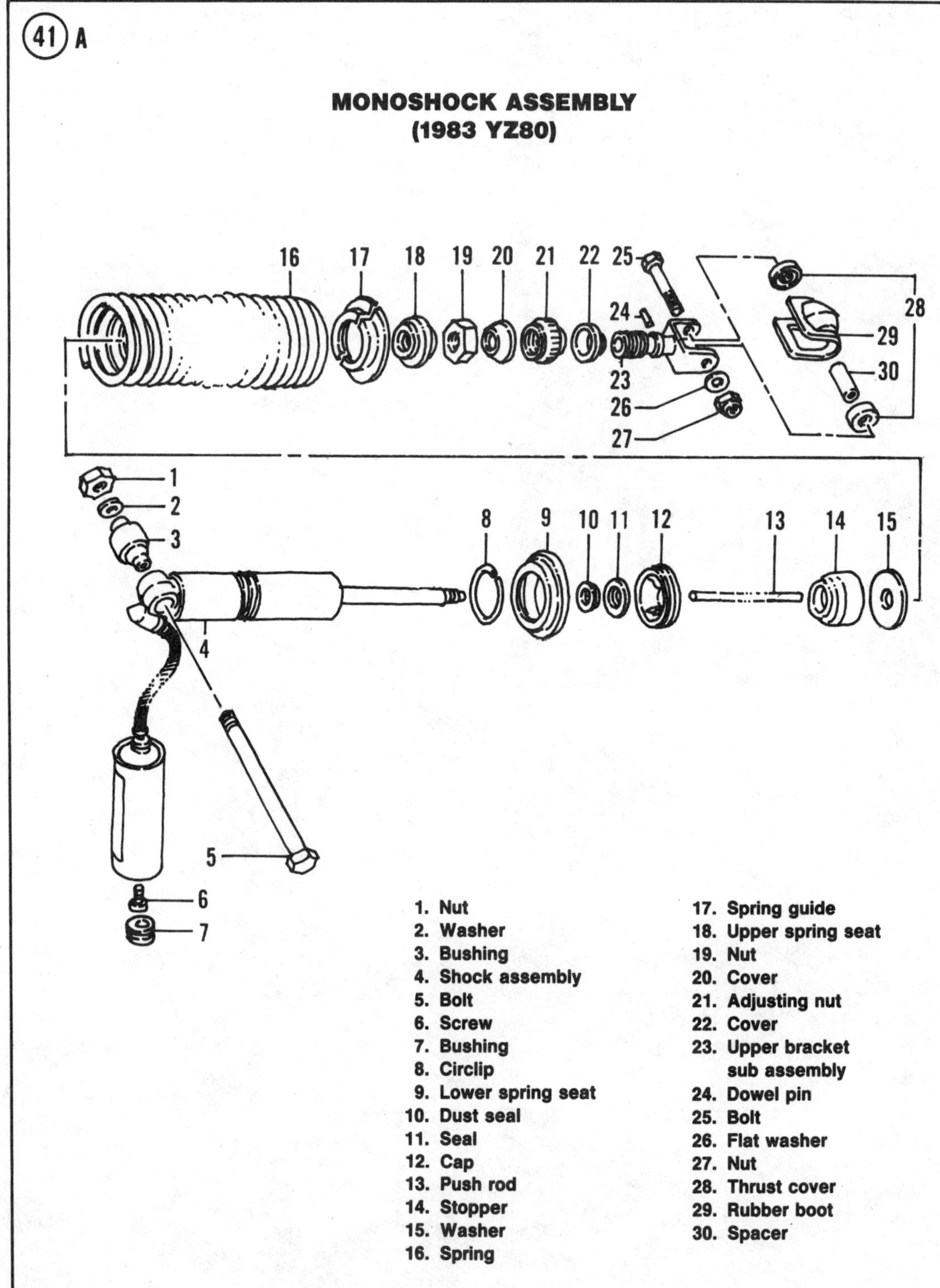
41 A
MONOSHOCK ASSEMBLY
(1983 YZ80)
1. Nut
2. Washer
3. Bushing
4. Shock assembly
5. Bolt
6. Screw
7. Bushing
8. Circlip
9. Lower spring seat
10. Dust seal
11. Seal
12. Cap
13. Push rod
14. Stopper
15. Washer
16. Spring
17. Spring guide
18. Upper spring seat
19. Nut
20. Cover
21. Adjusting nut
22. Cover
23. Upper bracket sub assembly
24. Dowel pin
25. Bolt
26. Flat washer
27. Nut
28. Thrust cover
29. Rubber boot
30. Spacer

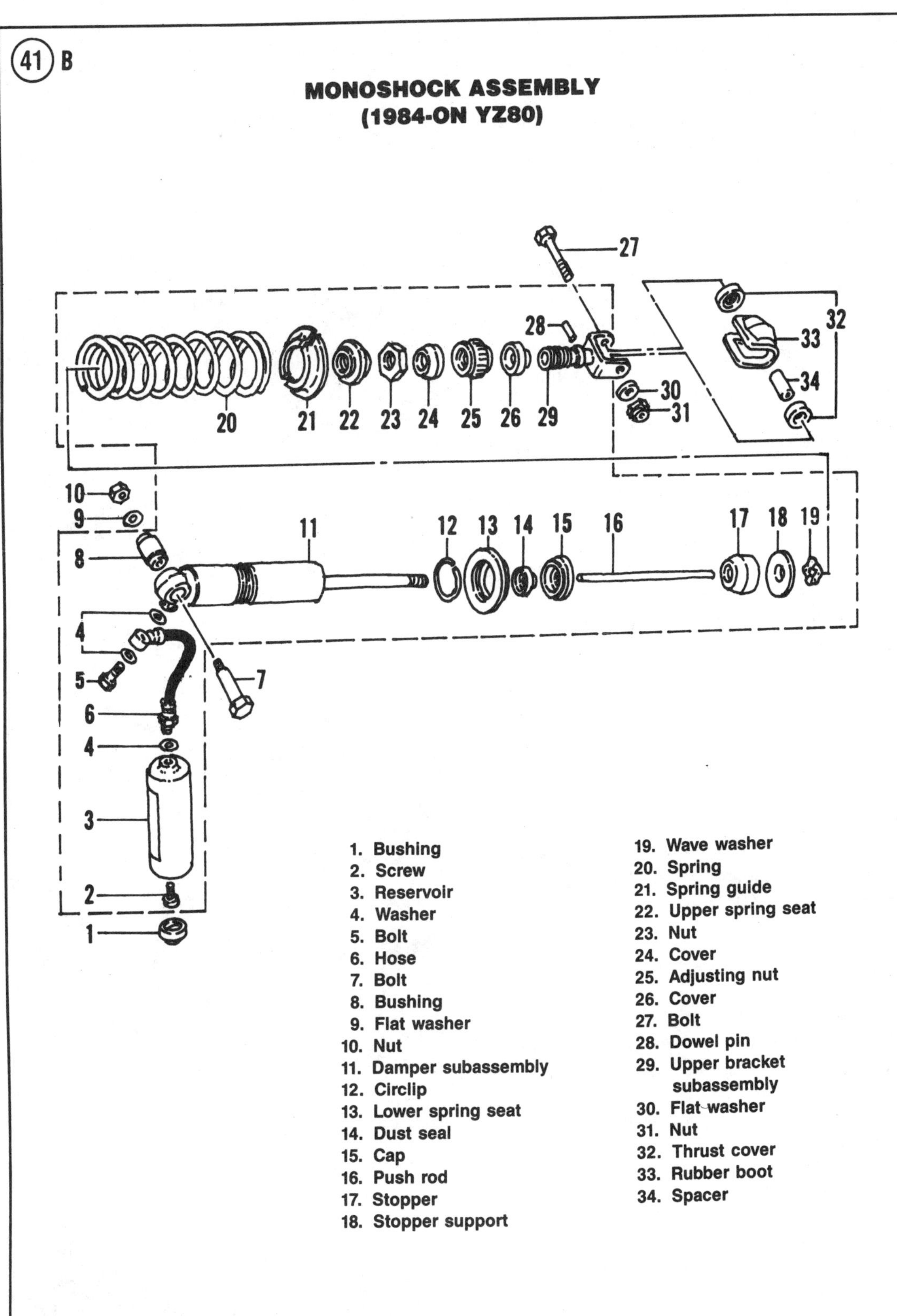
41 B
MONOSHOCK ASSEMBLY
(1984-ON YZ80)
1. Bushing
2. Screw
3. Reservoir
4. Washer
5. Bolt
6. Hose
7. Bolt
8. Bushing
9. Flat washer
10. Nut
11. Damper subassembly
12. Circlip
13. Lower spring seat
14. Dust seal
15. Cap
16. Push rod
17. Stopper
18. Stopper support
19. Wave washer
20. Spring
21. Spring guide
22. Upper spring seat
23. Nut
24. Cover
25. Adjusting nut
26. Cover
27. Bolt
28. Dowel pin
29. Upper bracket subassembly
30. Flat washer
31. Nut
32. Thrust cover
33. Rubber boot
34. Spacer

12

1. Place a workstand under the frame high enough to lift the rear wheel off the ground.
2. Remove the seat and fuel tank.
3. Remove the rear wheel.
4. Detach the shock absorber reservoir strap and lift the reservoir (**Figure 42**) away from the frame.

WARNING
Do not disconnect the shock absorber-to-reservoir hose. The reservoir and shock absorber body is pressurized with nitrogen gas and could cause personal injury.

5. Remove the nut and bolt (**Figure 43**) securing the upper shock absorber mount to the frame.
6. Remove the nut and bolt securing the lower shock absorber mount (**Figure 44**) to the relay arm.
7. Pull the shock absorber away from the relay arm (**Figure 45**) and lift it out of the frame, making sure not to damage the reservoir.
8. Installation is the reverse of these steps, noting the following.
   a. Apply a coat of molybdenum disulfide grease to the upper and lower mounting bushings on the shock absorber and connecting rod.
   b. Place the shock absorber in the frame with the reservoir to the right-hand side of the frame. Be careful not to damage the reservoir hose or reservoir body.
   c. Tighten the shock bolts and nuts to the torque specification in **Table 4**.

Spring Replacement (All Models)

Refer to the illustration for your model when removing and installing the shock spring:
   a. **Figure 28**: YZ50 and 1978-1979 YZ80.
   b. **Figure 29**: YZ60.
   c. **Figure 32**: 1981 YZ80.
   d. **Figure 34**: 1982 YZ80.
   e. **Figure 41A**: 1983 YZ80.
   f. **Figure 41B**: 1984-on YZ80.

Disassembly of the monoshock is not possible. This procedure describes how to replace the monoshock spring.

The spring on these models is not under the same amount of pressure as those used on a dual-shock rear suspension. Therefore a spring compression tool should not be needed.

WARNING
*The monoshock unit contains highly compressed nitrogen gas (**Figure 46**). Do not tamper with or attempt to open the damper/cylinder assembly (**Figure 47**). Do not place it near an open flame or other extreme heat. Do not weld on the frame near it. Do not dispose of the damper subassembly yourself. Take it to a Yamaha dealer where it can be deactivated and disposed of properly.*

1. Remove the monoshock as described in this chapter.

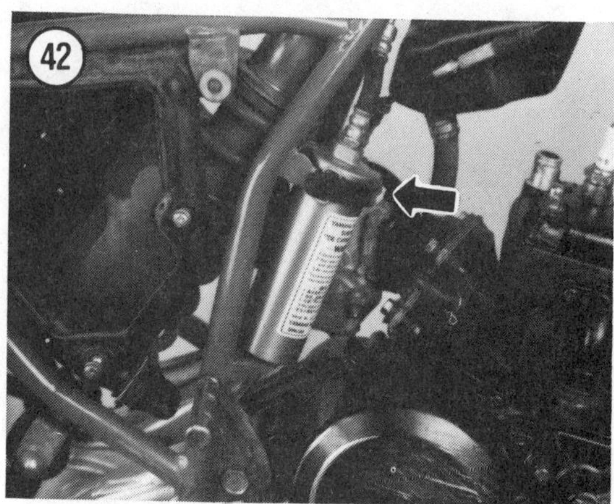

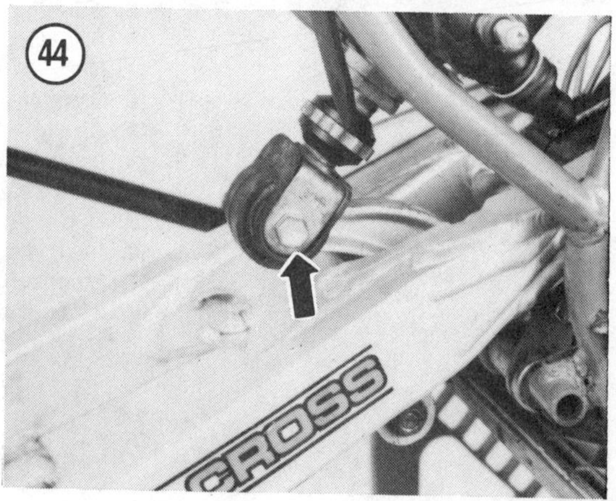

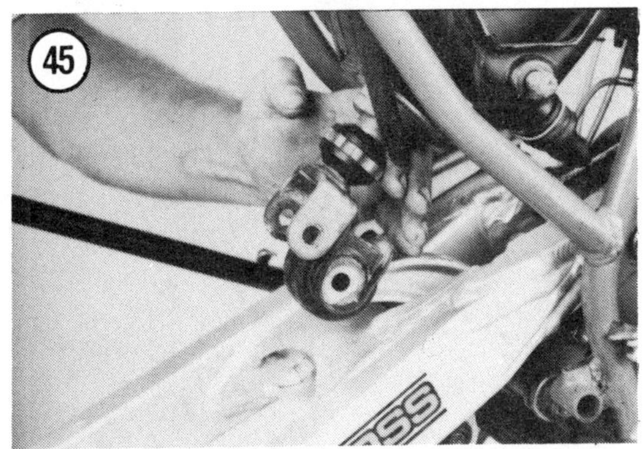
45

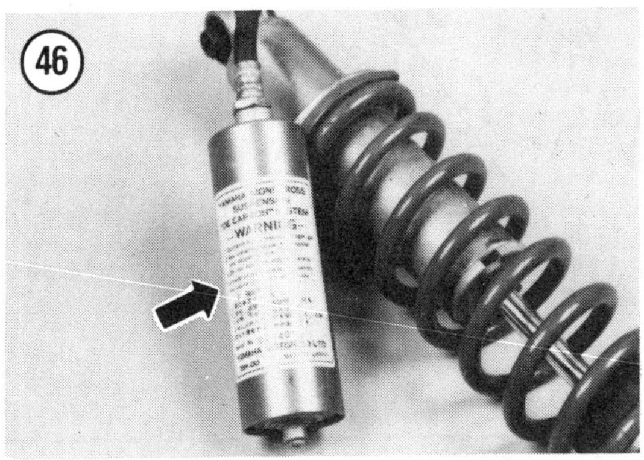
46

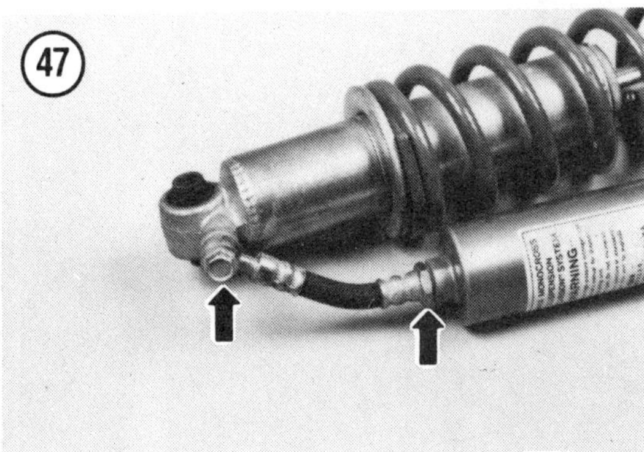
47

48

NOTE

In order to maintain the same spring pre-load adjustment, record the notch position prior to performing Step 2A.

2A. *1978-1981:* Turn the spring pre-load adjuster to the softest setting.

NOTE

In order to maintain the same spring preload, measure the installed spring length with a tape measure before performing Step 2B.

2B. *1982-on:* See **Figure 48**. Loosen the adjuster locknut (A) and loosen the adjuster (B).
3. Push down on the spring with your hands and the spring seats (keepers) will become loose. Remove the spring seat.
4. Slide the spring off the shock.

NOTE

The damper unit cannot be rebuilt; it must be replaced as a unit.

5. Install the spring. If the spring guide was removed, make sure it is installed properly.

NOTE

There may be springs available from Yamaha in different spring rates. See your Yamaha dealer for availability.

6A. *1978-1981:* Install the spring seats (retainers) and tighten the spring pre-load adjuster. If the same spring (spring rate) is installed return the adjuster to the same position as noted in the NOTE before Step 2A.
6B. *1982-on:* Install the spring seats (retainers) and tighten the adjuster (B, **Figure 48**) so that it rests against the spring. Tighten the adjuster so that the installed spring height is the same as noted in the NOTE before Step 2B. Tighten the locknut (A, **Figure 48**) securely.

NOTE

If a new spring with a different spring rate has been installed, readjust as described under ***Spring Pre-Load Adjustment*** *in Chapter Fourteen.*

7. Install the monoshock as described under *Monoshock Removal/Installation* in this chapter.

SWING ARM (1978-1982)

In time the bushings will wear beyond service limits and must be replaced. The condition of the bushings can greatly affect handling performance and if not replaced they can produce erratic and dangerous handling.

(49)

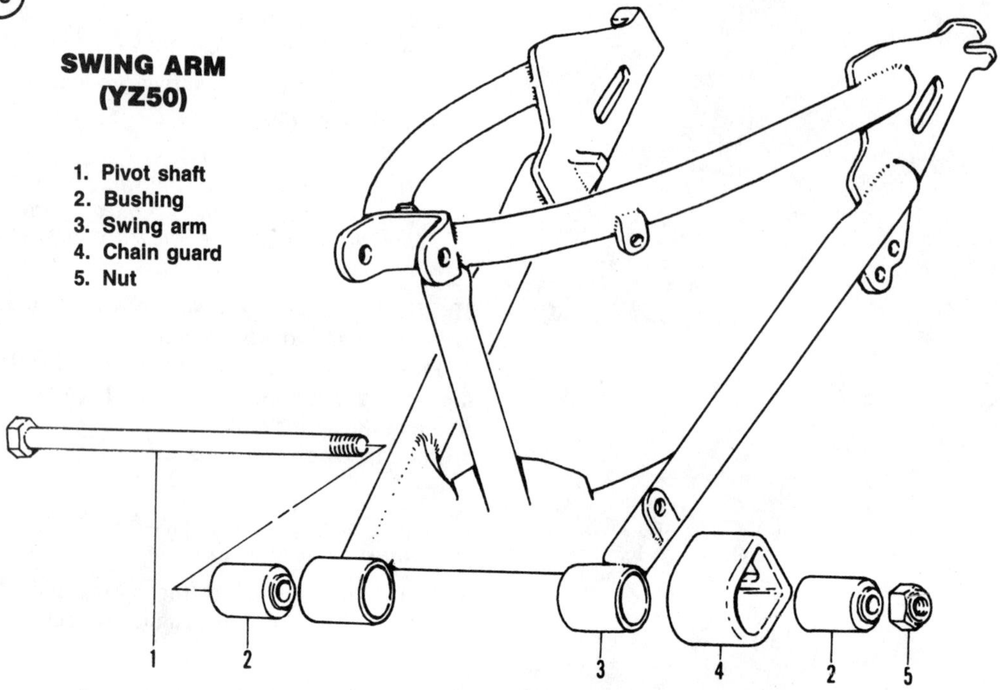

SWING ARM (YZ50)

1. Pivot shaft
2. Bushing
3. Swing arm
4. Chain guard
5. Nut

(50)

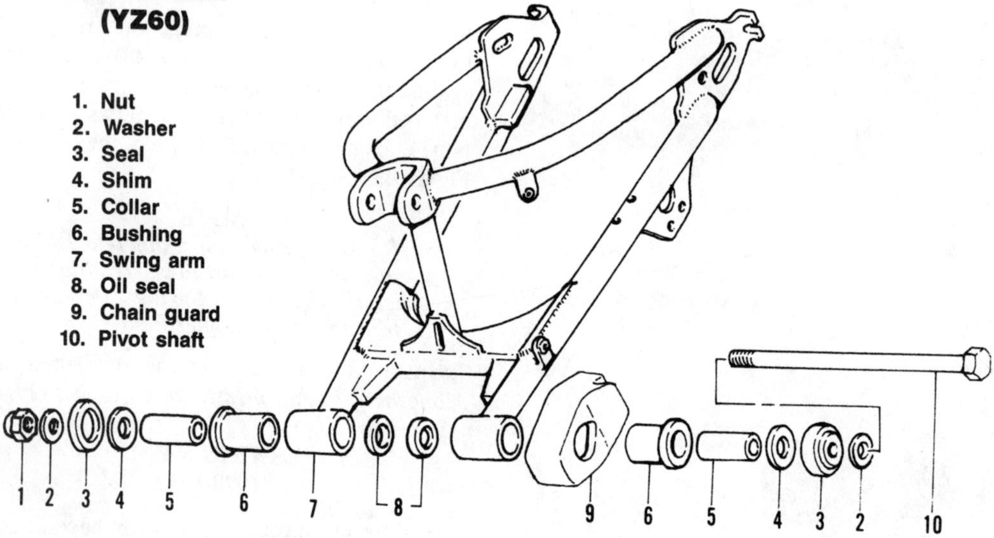

SWING ARM (YZ60)

1. Nut
2. Washer
3. Seal
4. Shim
5. Collar
6. Bushing
7. Swing arm
8. Oil seal
9. Chain guard
10. Pivot shaft

The swing arm used on the various models differ in construction and design. Service procedures for the various swing arm assemblies are covered separately. While bushing and bearing alignment differs between the various models, replacement is the same for all models.

Removal/Installation

Refer to the illustration for your model during removal and installation:

a. **Figure 49**: YZ50.
b. **Figure 50**: YZ60.
c. **Figure 51**: 1978-1980 YZ80.
d. **Figure 52**: 1981 YZ80.
e. **Figure 53**: 1982 YZ80.

1. Remove the bolts securing the seat and remove it.
2. Remove both number/side panels.
3. Remove the rear wheel and drive chain as described under *Rear Wheel Removal/Installation* in this chapter.

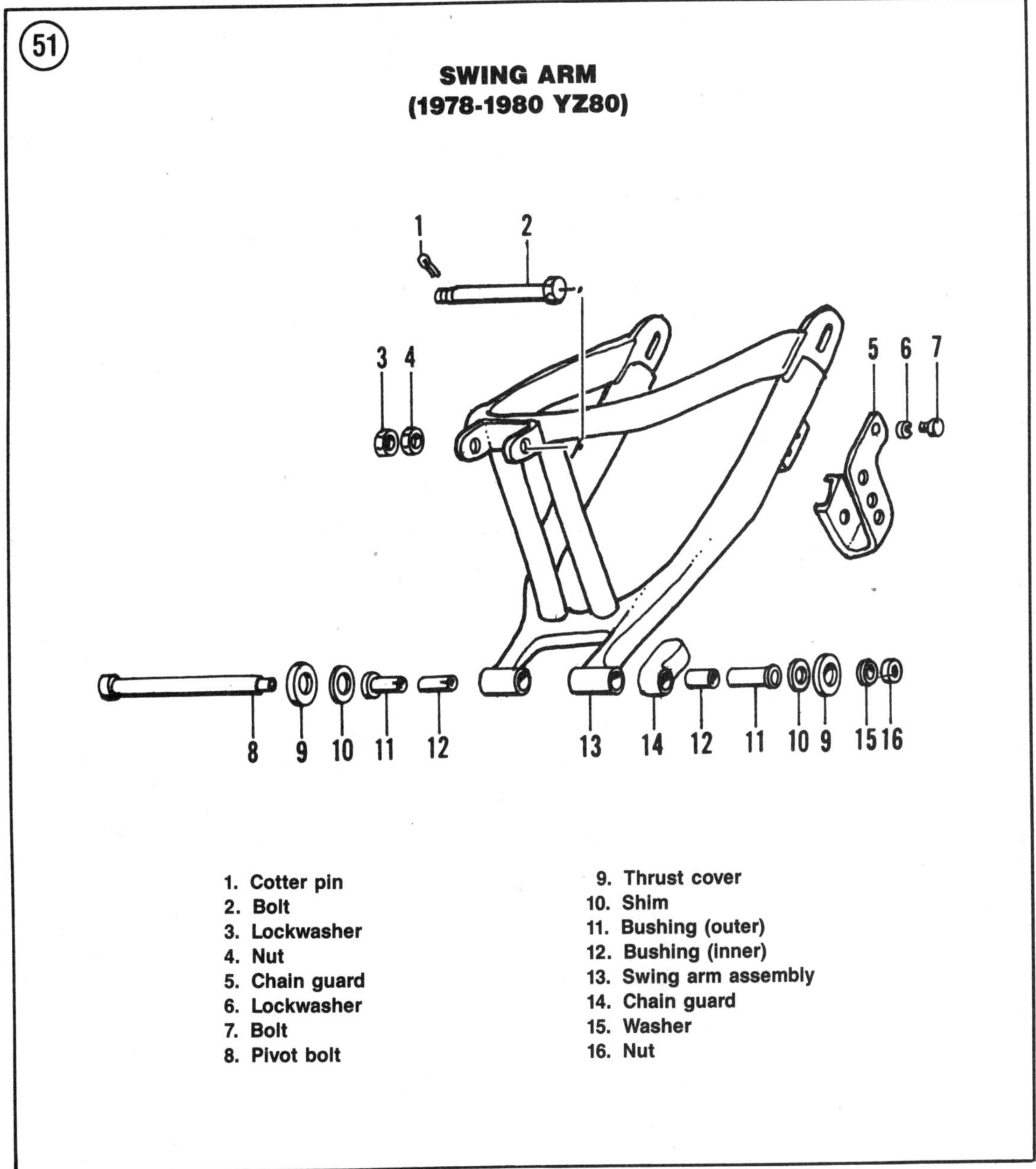

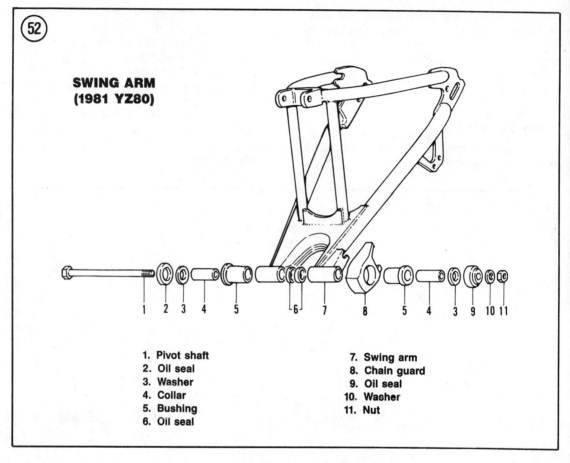

(52)

SWING ARM (1981 YZ80)

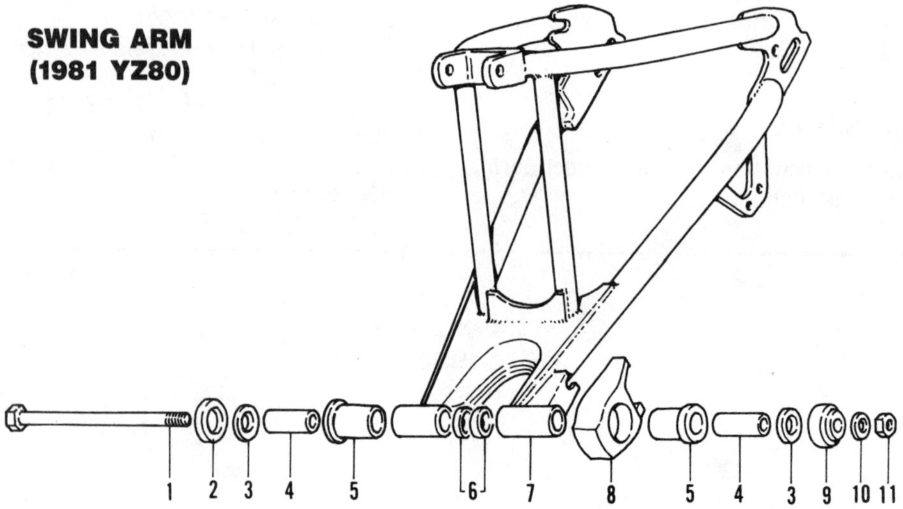

1. Pivot shaft
2. Oil seal
3. Washer
4. Collar
5. Bushing
6. Oil seal
7. Swing arm
8. Chain guard
9. Oil seal
10. Washer
11. Nut

(53)

SWING ARM (1982 YZ80)

1. Swing arm
2. Decal
3. Bolt
4. Spring washer
5. Chain support
6. Pivot shaft
7. Guard seal
8. Shim
9. Bushing
10. Collar
11. Collar
12. Oil seal
13. Guard seal
14. Bushing
15. Washer
16. Nut

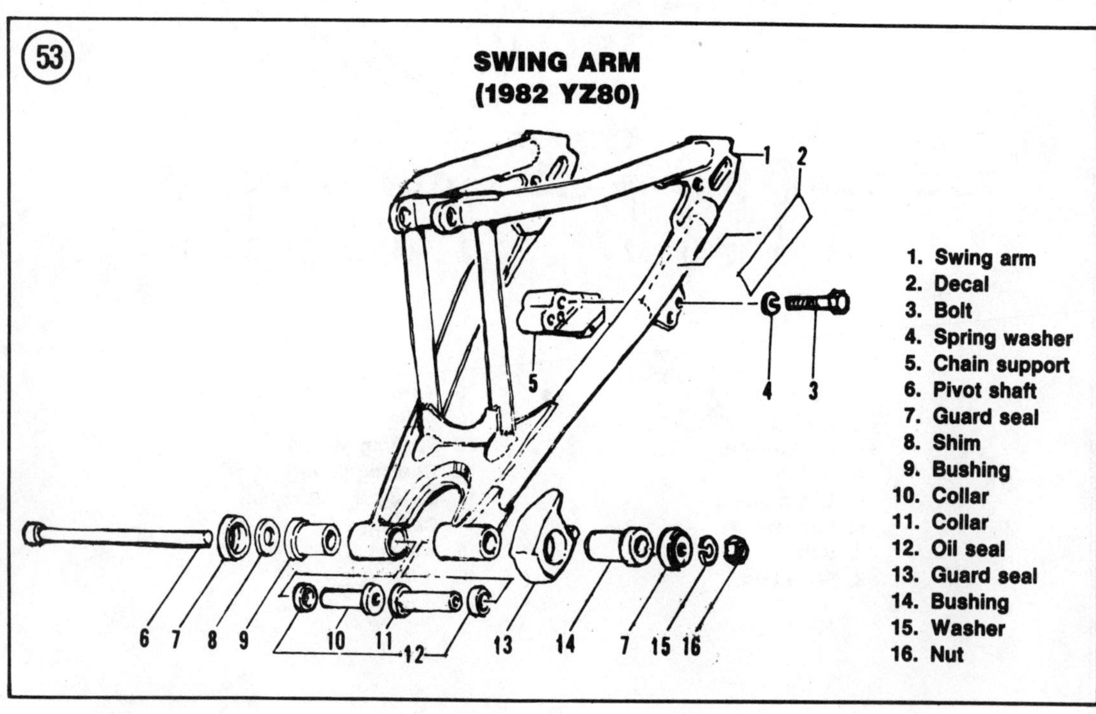

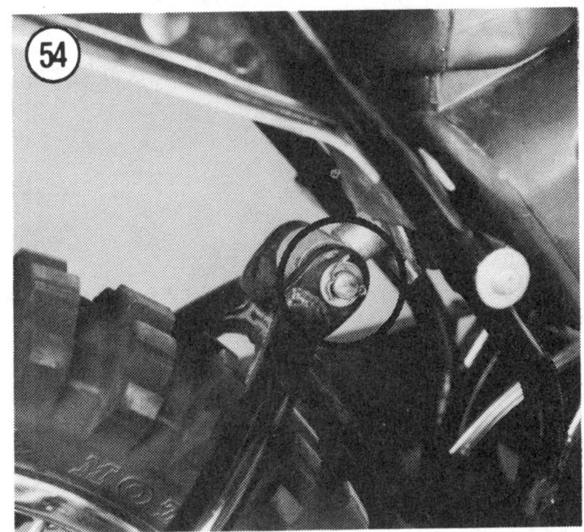

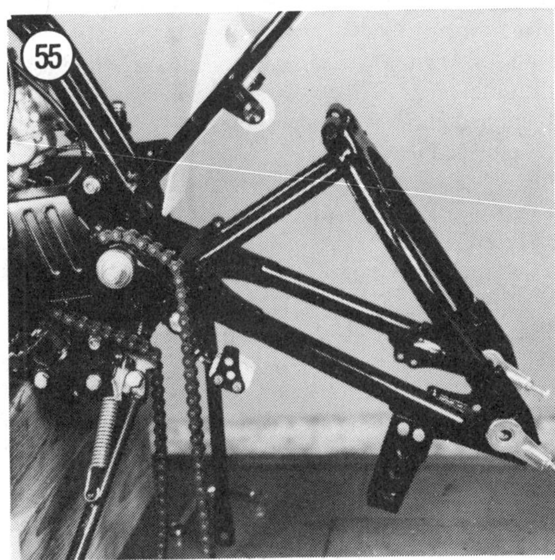

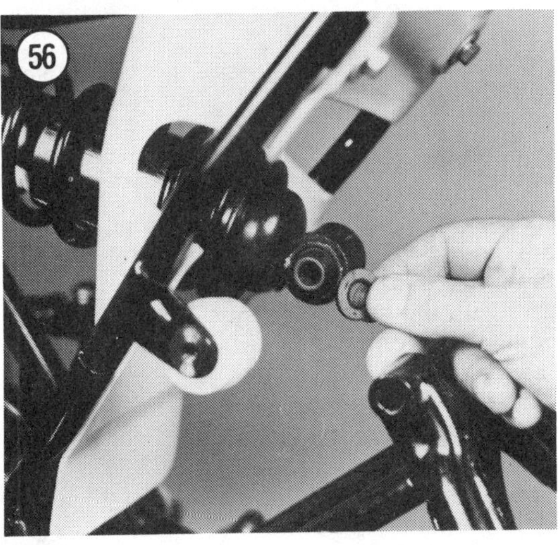

4. Remove the cotter pin and flat washer (**Figure 54**) on the end of the lower mounting pin.
5. Pull the pin out and gently let the swing arm pivot down (**Figure 55**).

NOTE
Don't lose the cover washers on each side of the monoshock rear mount.

6. After the upper end of the swing arm is disconnected, grasp the rear end of it and try to move it from side-to-side in a horizontal arc. Side play should be minimal. If play is excessive and the pivot bolt is tightened correctly, the bushings should be replaced.
7. Remove the nut and lockwasher and withdraw the pivot bolt from the right-hand side. It is not necessary to remove the engine to remove the swing arm.
8. Remove the swing arm assembly.
9. Clean the pivot bolt in solvent and dry thoroughly. Wipe all dirt and grease from the bushing area.
10. To install, position the swing arm into the lower mounting area. Align the holes in the swing arm with the hole in the frame. Insert a drift in from the side opposite where the bolt is to be inserted and align the holes.
11. Apply a light coat of lithium waterproof grease to the swing arm pivot bolt prior to installing it.
12. After all holes are aligned, insert the pivot bolt and install the lockwasher and nut. Refer to **Figures 49-53** for the correct side to insert the pivot bolt. Tighten the nut to the torque specification in **Table 3**.
13. Install the cover washers on each side of the monoshock (**Figure 56**).
14. Insert the upper mounting pin (**Figure 54**) from the left-hand side. Apply a light coat of grease to it prior to installing it.
15. Install the flat washer and a new cotter pin—never reuse a cotter pin as it may break and fall out. Hold one end of the pin with a wrench and bend over the end of the cotter pin completely.

NOTE
*Make sure that both cover washers (**Figure 56**) are installed. They are necessary to maintain the proper clearance between the monoshock and the swing arm. If they are slightly flattened out, replace them.*

16. Install the rear wheel as described in this chapter.
17. Install both number/side covers and the seat.

Disassembly/Inspection/Assembly

Refer to the illustration for your model during disassembly and reassembly:

a. **Figure 49**: YZ50.
b. **Figure 50**: YZ60.
c. **Figure 51**: 1978-1980 YZ80.
d. **Figure 52**: 1981 YZ80.
e. **Figure 53**: 1982 YZ80.

1. Remove the swing arm as previously described.
2. Secure the swing arm in a vise with soft jaws.
3. Remove the chain guard/seal.
4. Remove the dust seals from the swing arm.
5. Remove the shim if it was not stuck to the inside of the dust seals.
6. Remove the collars from the swing arm bushings.
7. Inspect the collars and the bushings. If they are worn or damaged they must be replaced. Refer to *Rear Suspension Bushing and Bearing Replacement* in this chapter.

NOTE
Always replace all bushings and collars as a set.

8. Wash all parts, including the inside of the swing arm pivot area, in solvent and thoroughly dry.
9. Apply a light coat of lithium waterproof grease to all parts prior to installation.
10. Install all parts in the reverse order of disassembly, noting the following.

CAUTION
Never reinstall a bushing that has been removed. During removal it becomes slightly damaged and is no longer true to alignment. If installed, it will damage the inner bushing and create an unsafe riding condition.

11. Replace the drive chain slider if worn severely or damaged.

SWING ARM AND RELAY ARM (1983-ON)

In time the bushings will wear beyond service limits and must be replaced. The condition of the bushings can greatly affect handling performance and if not replaced they can produce erratic and dangerous handling.

The swing arm used on the various models differ in construction and design. Service procedures for the various swing arm assemblies are covered separately. While bushing and bearing alignment differs between the various models, replacement is the same for all models.

Removal/Installation

Refer to the illustration for your model during removal and installation:

a. **Figure 57**: 1983 YZ80.
b. **Figure 58**: 1984-on YZ80.

1. Remove the bolts securing the seat and remove it.
2. Remove both number/side panels.
3. Remove the rear wheel and drive chain as described in this chapter.
4. Remove the nut and bolt securing the lower shock absorber mount at the relay arm and disconnect the shock absorber (**Figure 45**).
5. Remove the nut and bolt securing the connecting rod to the swing arm.

6A. *1983-1986 models:* After the shock absorber is disconnected from the relay arm and the connecting rod is disconnected from the swing arm, grasp the swing arm and try to move it from side-to-side in a horizontal arc. Side play should be minimal. If play is excessive and the pivot bolt is tightened correctly, the bushings and collars should be replaced.

6B. *1987-on models:* Perform the *Swing Arm Side Clearance Check and Adjustment (1987-on)* in this chapter.

7. Remove the nut and lockwasher and withdraw the pivot bolt (**Figure 59**) from the right-hand side. It is not necessary to remove the engine to remove the swing arm.
8. Remove the swing arm assembly.
9. Remove the relay arm (A, **Figure 60**) as follows:
   a. Remove the shock absorber-to-relay arm nut and bolt (B, **Figure 60**) if necessary.
   b. Remove the relay arm-to-frame nut and bolt (**Figure 61**) and remove the relay arm.
10. Remove the connecting rod-to-frame nut and bolt (A, **Figure 62**) and remove the connecting rod (B, **Figure 62**).
11. Installation is the reverse of these steps. Note the following.
12. Clean all pivot bolts in solvent and dry thoroughly.
13. Lubricate all pivot bolts with a light coat of lithium waterproof grease prior to installation.
14. To install, position the swing arm into the lower mounting area. Align the holes in the swing arm with the hole in the frame. Insert a drift in from the side opposite where the bolt is to be inserted and align the holes.
15. After all holes are aligned, insert the pivot bolt and install the lockwasher and nut. Tighten the nut to the torque specification in **Table 3**.
16. Tighten the connecting rod bolt to the torque specification in **Table 3**.

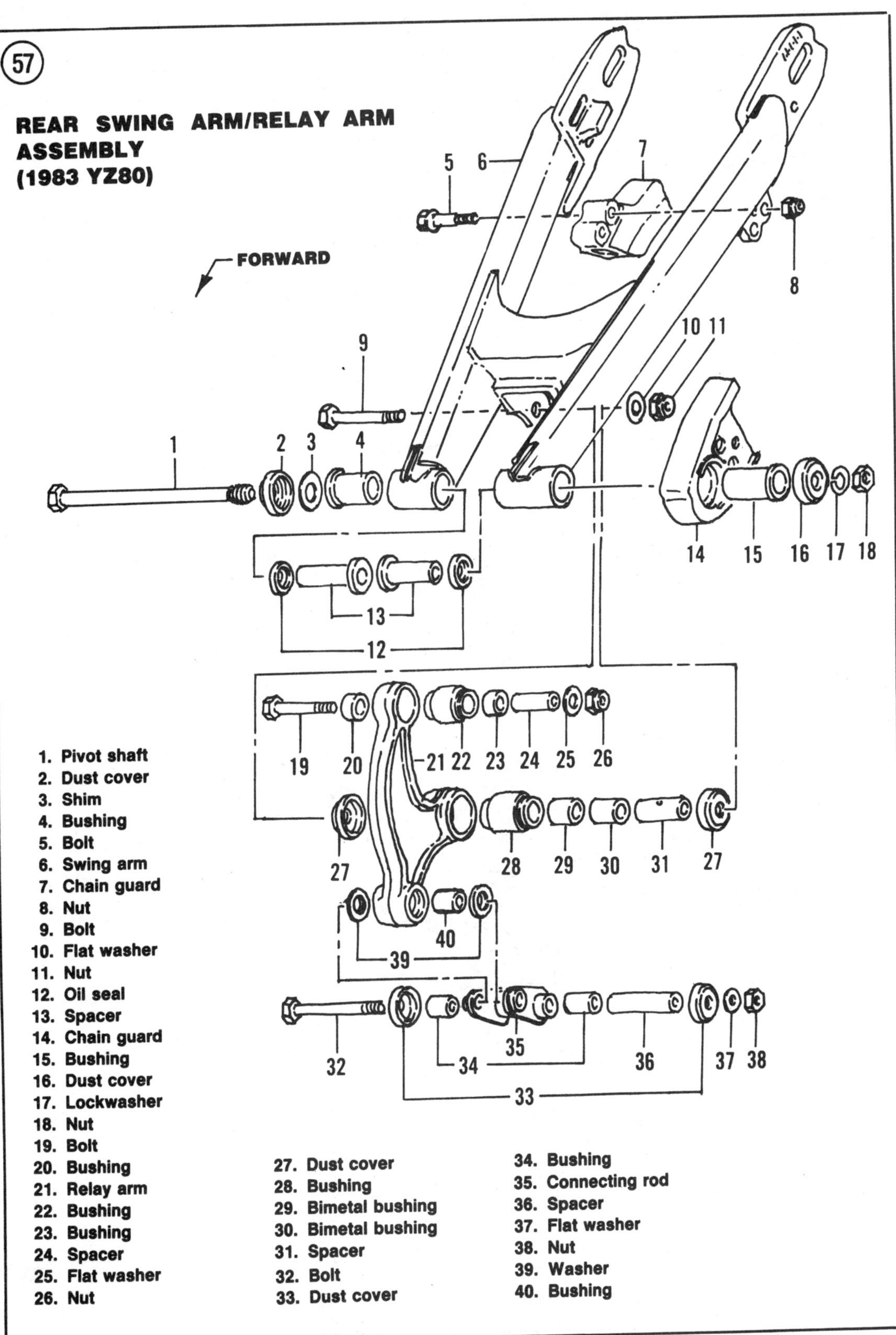

(57)

REAR SWING ARM/RELAY ARM ASSEMBLY (1983 YZ80)

1. Pivot shaft
2. Dust cover
3. Shim
4. Bushing
5. Bolt
6. Swing arm
7. Chain guard
8. Nut
9. Bolt
10. Flat washer
11. Nut
12. Oil seal
13. Spacer
14. Chain guard
15. Bushing
16. Dust cover
17. Lockwasher
18. Nut
19. Bolt
20. Bushing
21. Relay arm
22. Bushing
23. Bushing
24. Spacer
25. Flat washer
26. Nut
27. Dust cover
28. Bushing
29. Bimetal bushing
30. Bimetal bushing
31. Spacer
32. Bolt
33. Dust cover
34. Bushing
35. Connecting rod
36. Spacer
37. Flat washer
38. Nut
39. Washer
40. Bushing

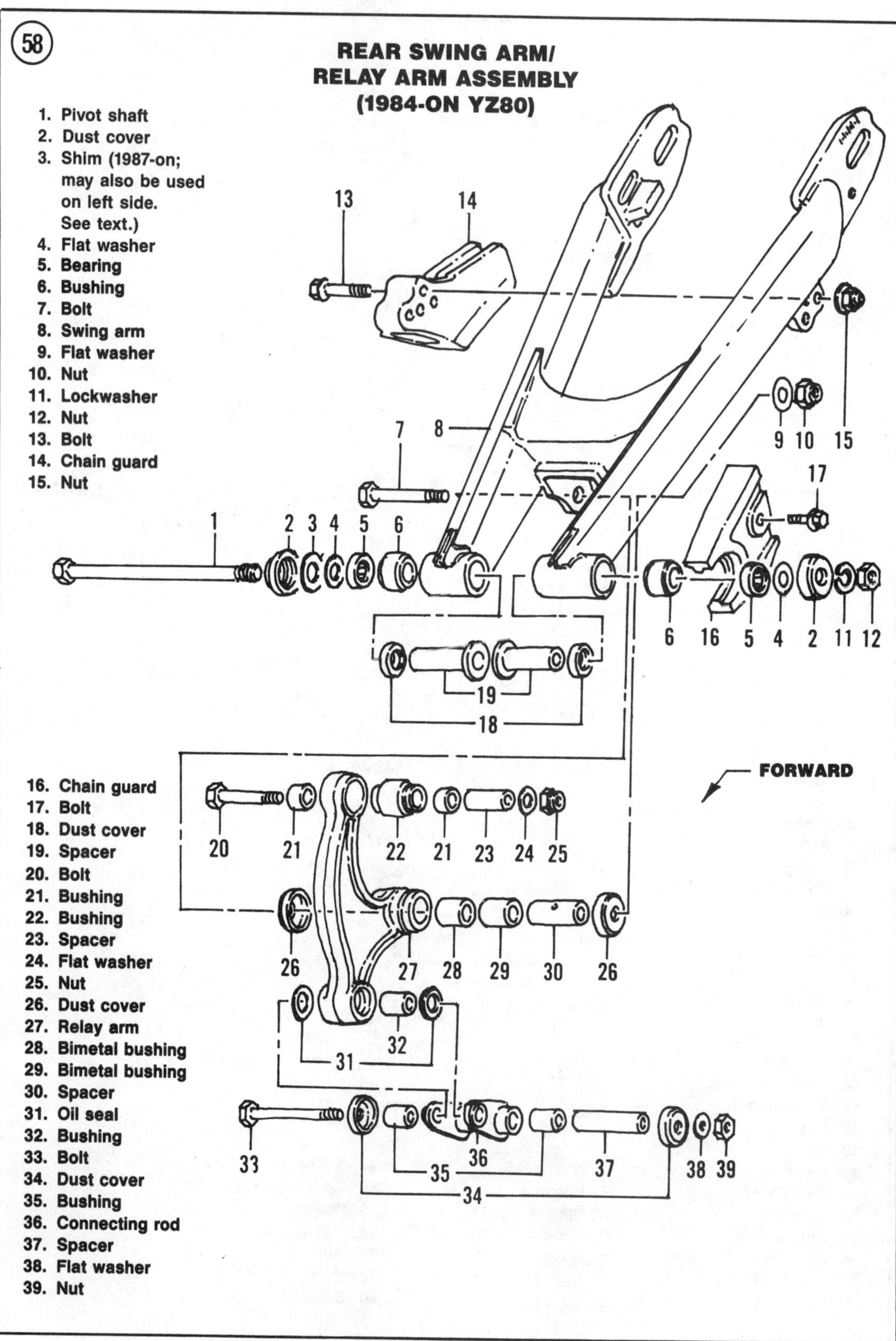
58
REAR SWING ARM/
RELAY ARM ASSEMBLY
(1984-ON YZ80)
1. Pivot shaft
2. Dust cover
3. Shim (1987-on; may also be used on left side. See text.)
4. Flat washer
5. Bearing
6. Bushing
7. Bolt
8. Swing arm
9. Flat washer
10. Nut
11. Lockwasher
12. Nut
13. Bolt
14. Chain guard
15. Nut
16. Chain guard
17. Bolt
18. Dust cover
19. Spacer
20. Bolt
21. Bushing
22. Bushing
23. Spacer
24. Flat washer
25. Nut
26. Dust cover
27. Relay arm
28. Bimetal bushing
29. Bimetal bushing
30. Spacer
31. Oil seal
32. Bushing
33. Bolt
34. Dust cover
35. Bushing
36. Connecting rod
37. Spacer
38. Flat washer
39. Nut
FORWARD

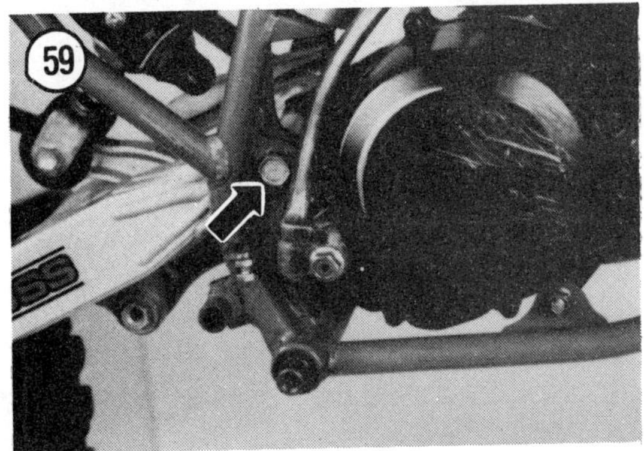

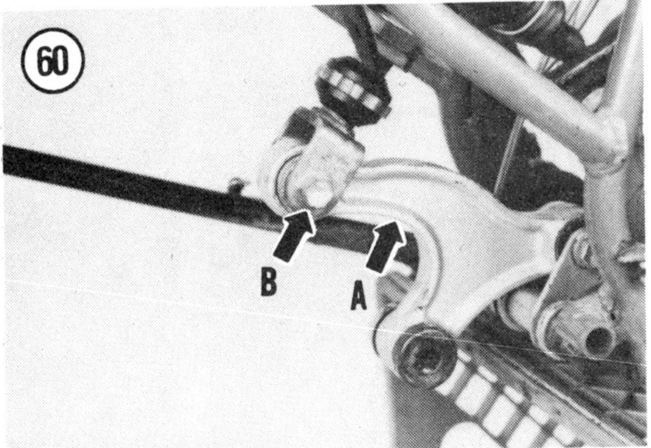

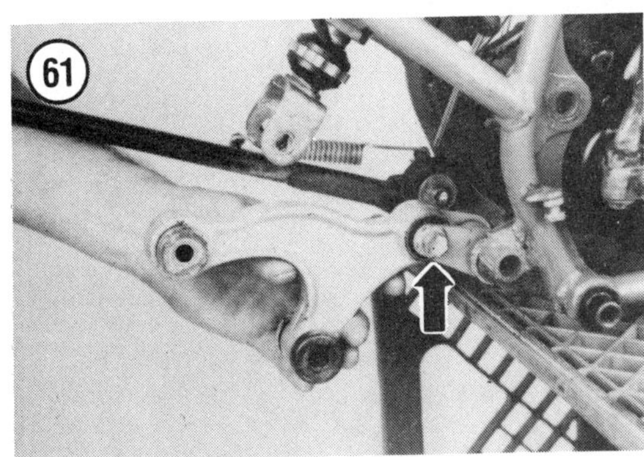

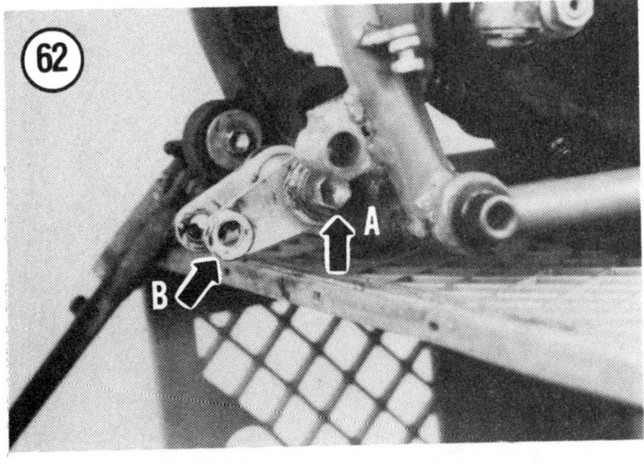

17. Tighten the relay arm-to-swing arm bolt to the torque specification in **Table 4**.
18. Tighten the shock absorber-to-relay arm bolt to the torque specification in **Table 4**.
19. Install the rear wheel as described in this chapter.
20. Install both number/side covers and the seat.

Disassembly/Inspection/Assembly

Refer to the illustration for your model during disassembly and assembly:

a. **Figure 57**: 1983 YZ80.
b. **Figure 58**: 1984-on YZ80.

1. Remove the swing arm as previously described.
2. Secure the swing arm in a vise with soft jaws.
3. Remove the upper and lower chain guards. See **Figure 63** and **Figure 64**.
4. Remove the dust covers (**Figure 65**) from the swing arm.

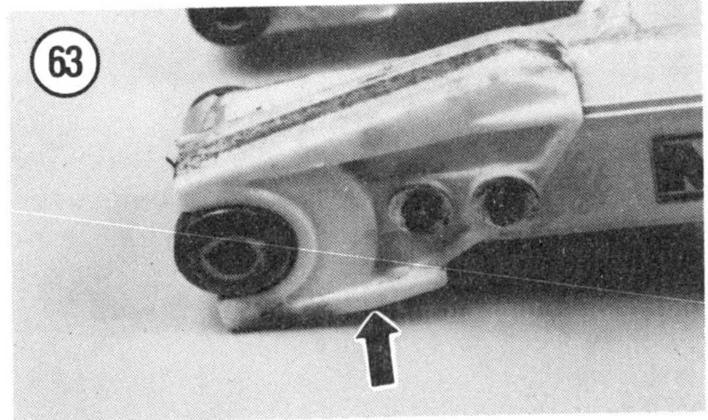

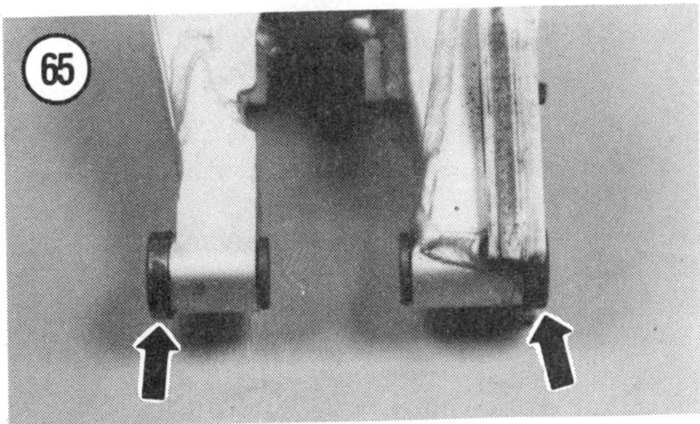

5. Remove the shims if they were not stuck to the inside of the dust covers.
6. Remove the collars (A, **Figure 66**) from the swing arm bushings (1983) or bearings (1984-on).
7. Disassemble the relay arm assembly (**Figure 67**).
8. Disassemble the connecting rod assembly (**Figure 68**).
9. Inspect the collars and the bushings (1983) or bearings (1984-on). See **Figure 69**. If they are worn or damaged they must be replaced. Refer to *Rear Suspension Bushing and Bearing Replacement* in this chapter.

NOTE
Always replace all collars and bushings or bearings as a set.

10. Check the connecting rod brackets on the swing arm (**Figure 70**) for cracks, damage or weld damage.
11. Wash all parts, including the inside of the swing arm pivot area, in solvent and thoroughly dry.
12. *1987-on models:* Perform the *Swing Arm Side Clearance Check and Adjustment* in this chapter.
13. Apply a light coat of lithium waterproof grease to all parts prior to installation.
14. Install all parts in the reverse order of disassembly. Refer to **Figure 57** or **Figure 58** when installing the collars and dust covers.

CAUTION
Never reinstall a bushing or bearing that has been removed. During removal it becomes slightly damaged and is no longer true to alignment.

15. Replace the drive chain guides if worn severely or damaged.

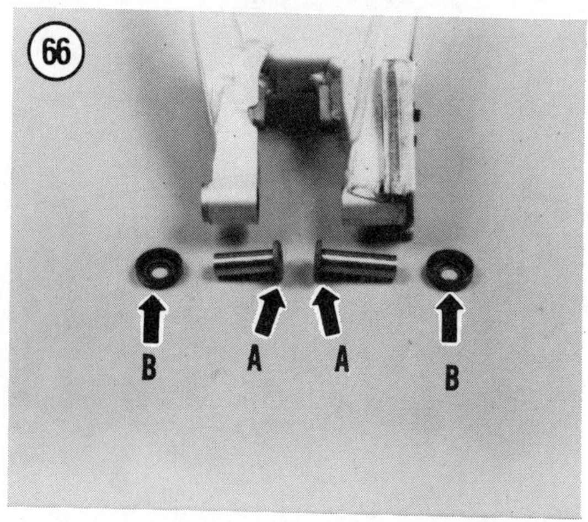

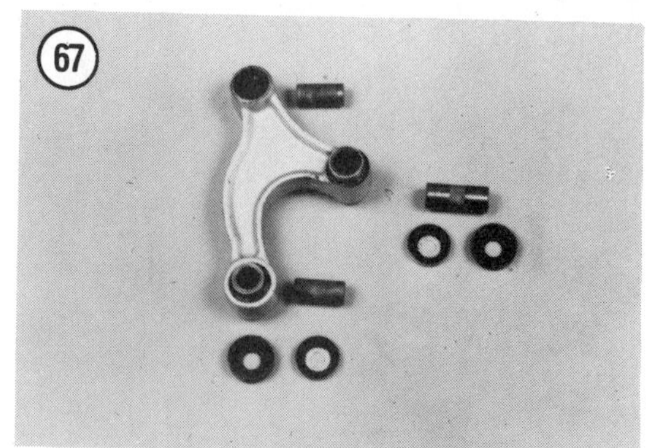

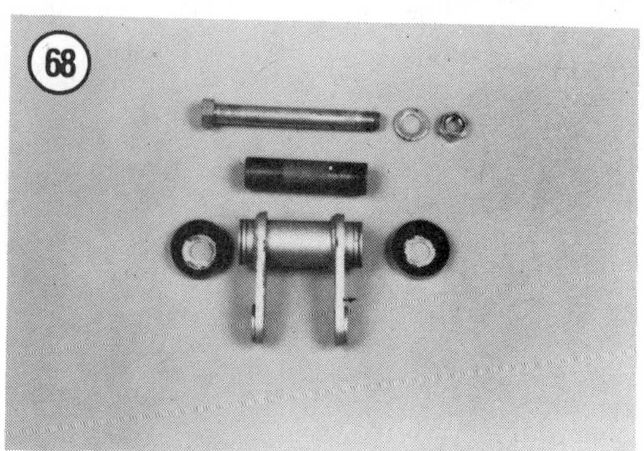

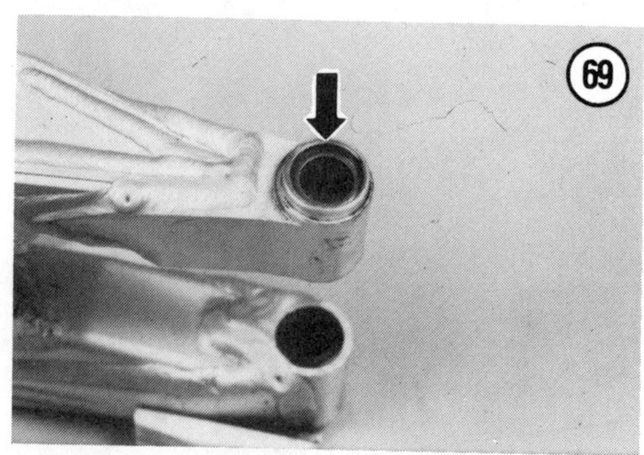

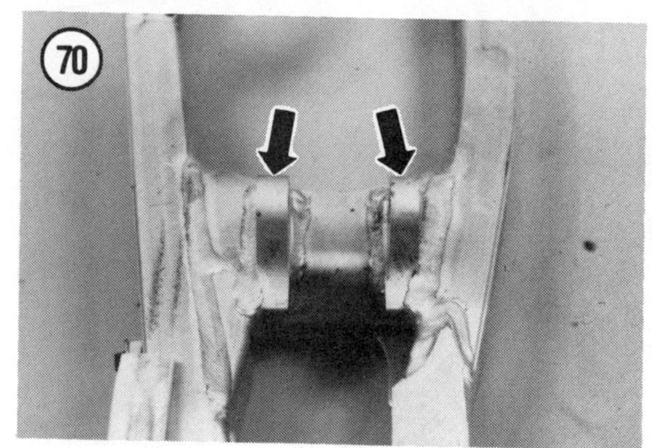

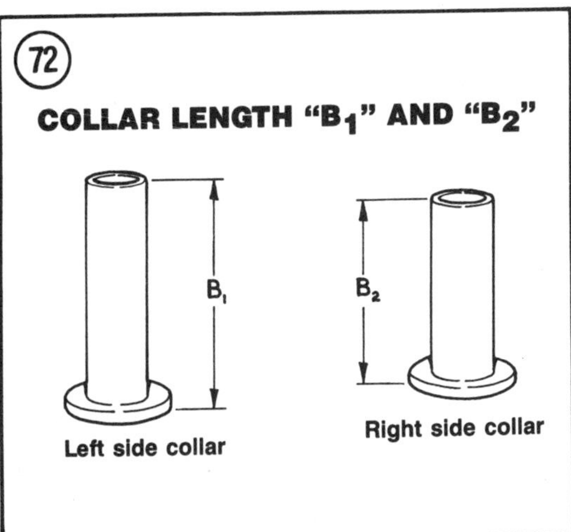

Swing Arm Side Clearance Check and Adjustment (1987-on)

This procedure describes how to check and adjust swing arm side clearance. A vernier caliper will be required to check side clearance. Refer to **Figure 58** when performing this procedure.

1. Remove the swing arm as described in this chapter.
2. Perform the following:
   a. Measure the width of the engine mount boss (A) with a vernier caliper (**Figure 71**).
   b. Measure the length of collar B1 (**Figure 72**).
   c. Measure the length of collar B2 (**Figure 72**).
3. Add the 3 measurements taken in Step 2.
4. Perform the following:
   a. Measure the width of the swing arm mounting boss (D). See **Figure 73**.
   b. Measure the thickness of plain washer E1 (**Figure 74**).
   c. Measure the thickness of plain washer E2 (**Figure 74**).
5. Add the 3 measurements taken in Step 4.
6. Subtract the measurement in Step 5 from the measurement in Step 3. Interpret results as follows:
   a. The correct swing arm side clearance is 0.2-0.4 mm (0.008-0.016 in.).
   b. If the side clearance is incorrect, 1 or 2 adjusting shims will be required. Adjusting shims are available in one thickness only: 0.3 mm (0.012 in.).
   c. If only one shim is required, install it on the right-hand side. If 2 shims are required, install 1 shim on each side.
   d. Install the shim(s) inside the dust cover (B, **Figure 66**).

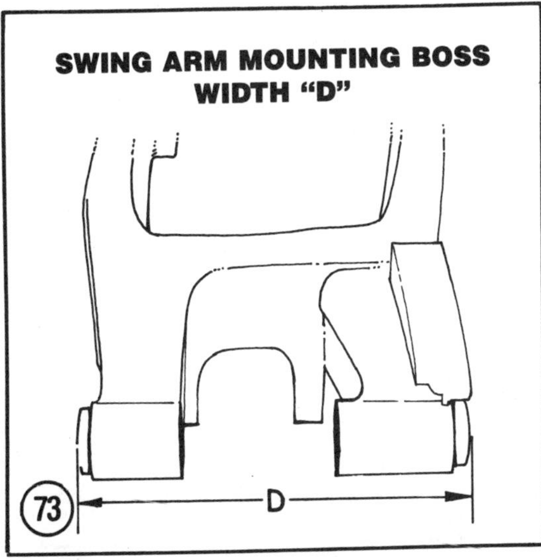

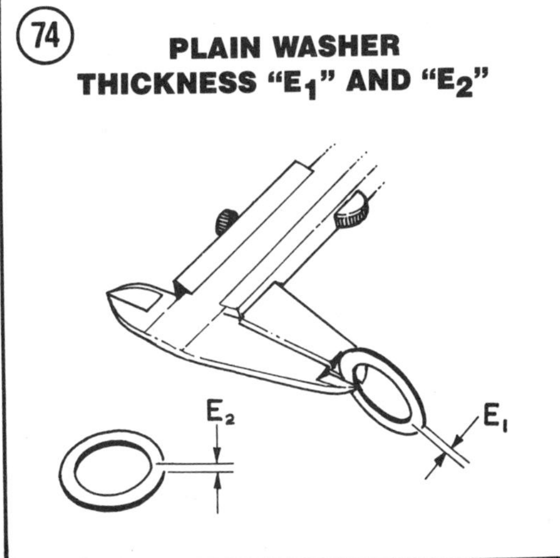

REAR SUSPENSION BUSHING AND BEARING REPLACEMENT (ALL MODELS)

1. Remove the swing arm as described in this chapter.
2. Secure the swing arm in a vise with soft jaws.

CAUTION
Do not remove the bushings or bearings just for inspection as they are usually damaged during removal.

3. Carefully tap out the bushing or bearing. Use a suitable size drift or socket and extension and carefully drive them out from the opposite end (**Figure 75**).
4. *1983-on models:* Repeat Step 3 when replacing bushings in the relay arm.
5. Clean the swing arm and relay arm (1983-on) thoroughly in solvent. Check the bushing and bearing mounting areas for cracks, wear or other damage.

NOTE
A press will be required to accurately and safely install the bushings and bearings.

NOTE
*On 1987 and later models, the swing arm bearings and bushings must be installed to the dimensions in **Figure 76**. Use a vernier caliper to check bearing and bushing positioning during installation.*

6. Apply a light coat of lithium waterproof wheel bearing grease to all parts before installation.
7. Using a press, install the new bushings and bearings.
8. After installing the bearings and bushings, liberally coat them with lithium waterproof wheel bearing grease.
9. Install the swing arm and relay arm (1983-on) as described in this chapter.

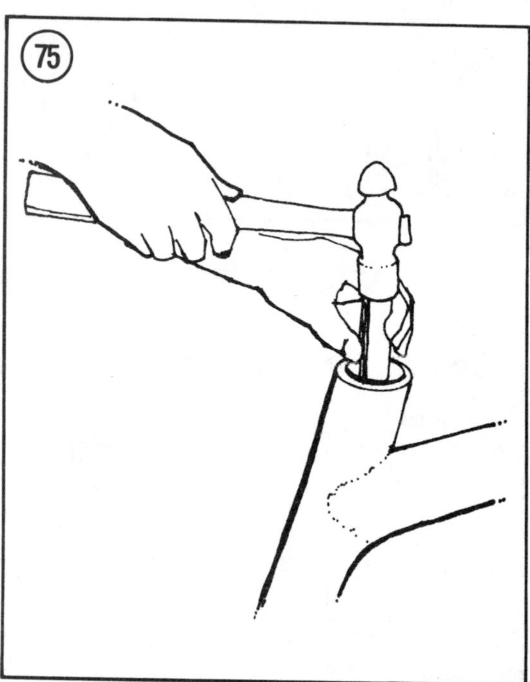

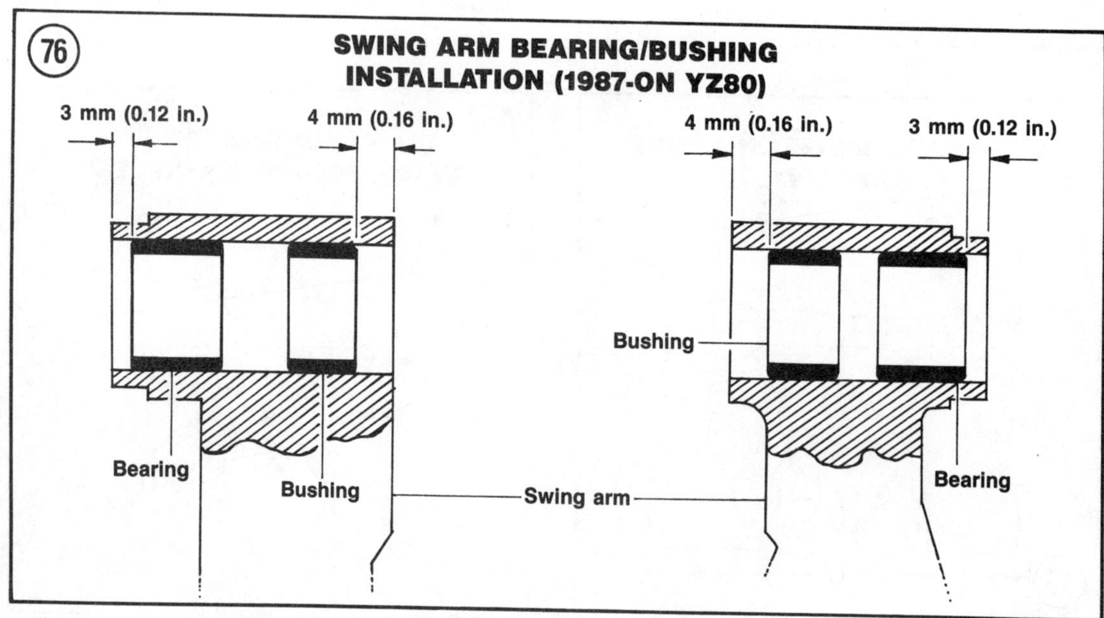

Table 1 REAR SUSPENSION SPECIFICATIONS

	mm	in.
Rear wheel travel		
YZ50	115	4.5
YZ60		
1981	163	6.4
1982	178	7.0
YZ80		
1978	120	4.7
1979	155	6.1
1980	170	6.7
1981	205	8.1
1982	230	9.1
1983	250	9.84
1984-on	260	10.2

Table 2 REAR SHOCK SPRING LENGTH

Model	Spring length installed mm (in.)	Free mm (in.)
YZ50	178 (7.01)	193 (7.60)
YZ60		
1980	214 (8.43)	219 (8.62)
1981	215 (8.5)	235 (9.3)
YZ80		
1978	*	*
1979	216 (8.5)	222 (8.74)
1980	226 (8.9)	236 (9.3)
1981	257 (10.1)	262 (10.31)
1982	*	283 (11.1)
1983	240 (9.45)	220 (8.66)
1984-1986	221 (8.70)	237 (9.33)
1987-on	211 (8.31)	233 (9.17)

* Not specified by Yamaha.

Table 3 REAR SUSPENSION TORQUE SPECIFICATIONS (1978-1982)

	N•m	ft.-lb.
Rear axle nut		
YZ50	40	29
YZ60	45	32
YZ80		
1978	70	49
1979-1980	75	54
1981	70	49
1982	85	61
Swing arm pivot nut		
YZ50	30	22
YZ60	50	36
YZ80		
1978-1980	43	31
1981	50	36
1982	53	38

Table 4 REAR SUSPENSION TORQUE SPECIFICATIONS (1983-ON)

	N•m	ft.-lb.
Rear axle nut	85	61
Swing arm pivot nut	53	38
Rear shock absorber nuts	32	23
Relay arm bolts	32	23
Connecting rod bolts	32	23

CHAPTER THIRTEEN

BRAKES

All models are equipped with drum brakes on the rear. On 1978-1985 models drum brakes were installed on the front. Starting with 1986 models, disc brakes are used on the front.

Brake specifications are listed in **Tables 1-3** at the end of this chapter.

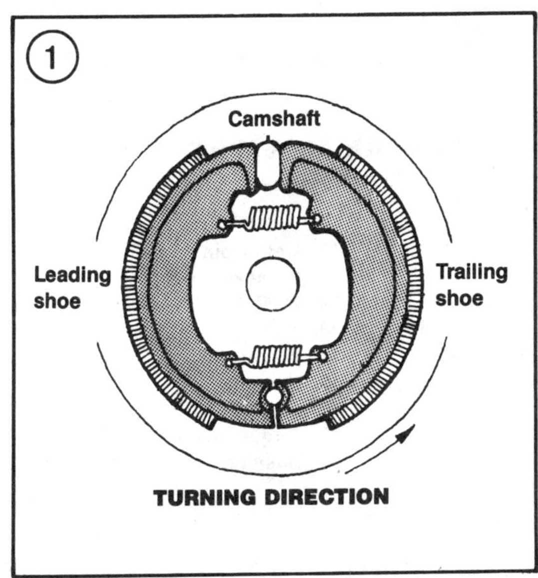

DRUM BRAKES

Figure 1 illustrates the major components of a typical drum brake assembly. Activating the brake hand lever or foot pedal pulls the cable or rod which in turn rotates the camshaft. This forces the brake shoes out into contact with the brake drum.

Lever and pedal free play must be maintained on both brakes to minimize brake drag and premature brake wear and maximize braking effectiveness. Refer to *Front Brake Lever Adjustment* and *Rear Brake Pedal Free Play* in Chapter Three, for complete adjustment procedures.

The front brake cable must be inspected and replaced periodically as it will stretch with use and can no longer be properly adjusted.

Disassembly

Refer to **Figure 2** (front), **Figure 3** (rear) or **Figure 4** (rear) for this procedure.

1A. Remove the front wheel as described under *Front Wheel Removal/Installation* in Chapter Eleven.

1B. Remove the rear wheel as described under *Rear Wheel Removal/Installation* in Chapter Twelve.

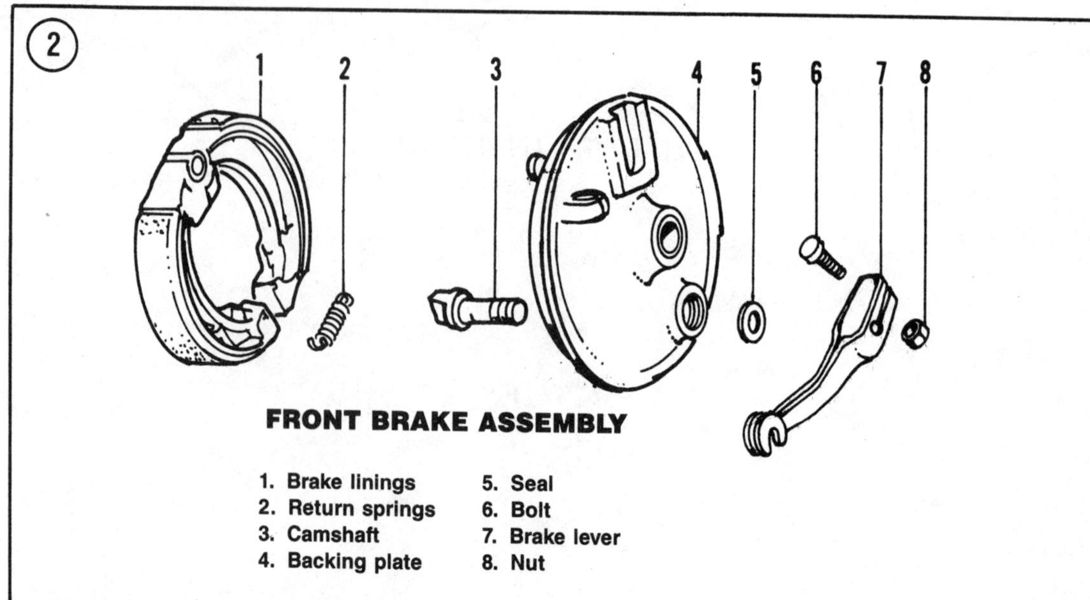

FRONT BRAKE ASSEMBLY

1. Brake linings
2. Return springs
3. Camshaft
4. Backing plate
5. Seal
6. Bolt
7. Brake lever
8. Nut

3

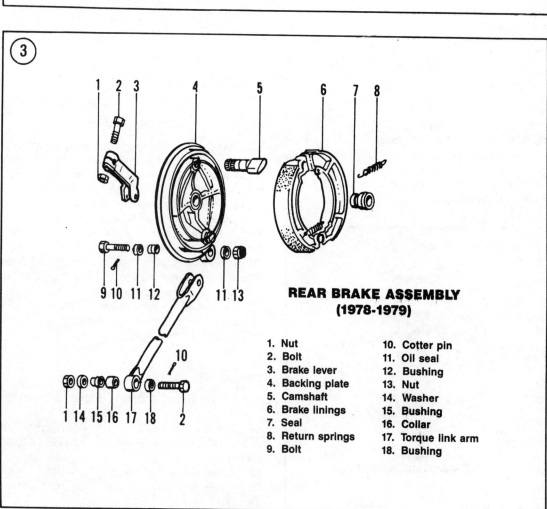

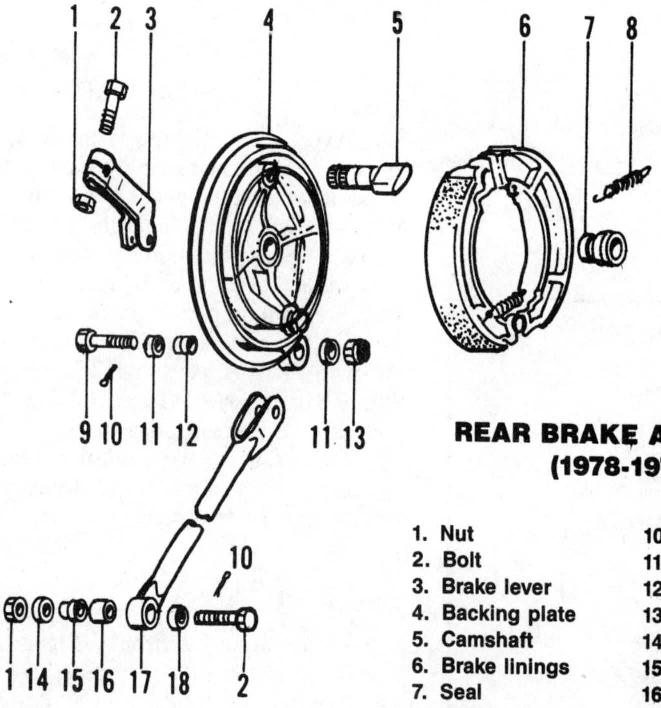

REAR BRAKE ASSEMBLY (1978-1979)

1. Nut
2. Bolt
3. Brake lever
4. Backing plate
5. Camshaft
6. Brake linings
7. Seal
8. Return springs
9. Bolt
10. Cotter pin
11. Oil seal
12. Bushing
13. Nut
14. Washer
15. Bushing
16. Collar
17. Torque link arm
18. Bushing

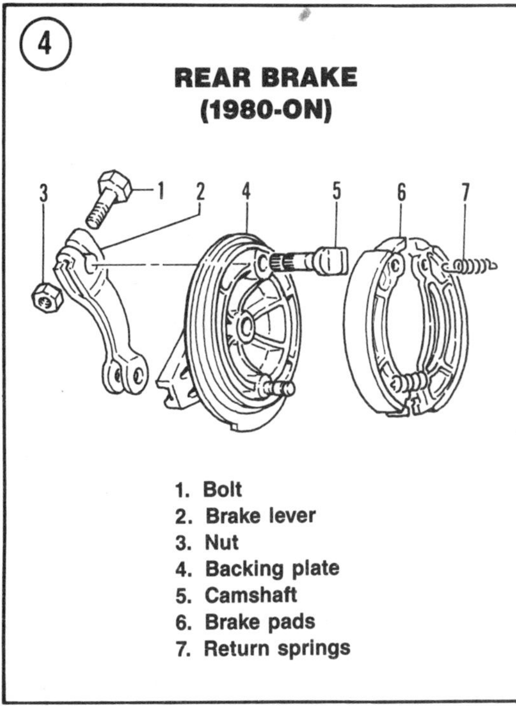

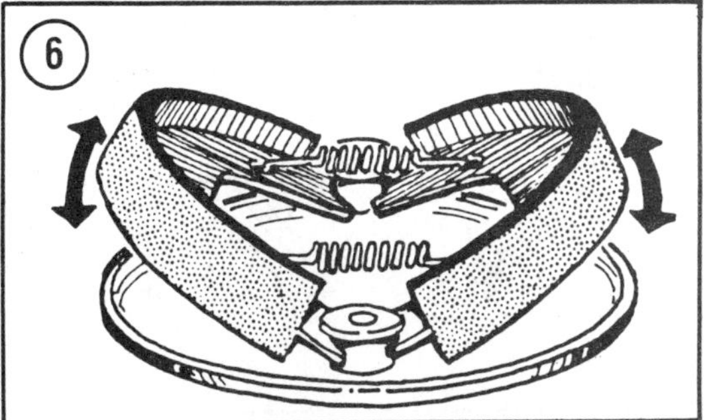

2. If still attached, disconnect the brake cable or rod at the brake assembly and remove it (**Figure 5**).

NOTE
Mark each brake shoe for position before removing them in Step 3.

NOTE
Place a clean shop rag on the linings to protect them from oil and grease during removal.

3. Remove the brake shoe assembly, including the return springs, from the backing plate. Pull both brake shoes from the backing plate (**Figure 6**).
4. Remove the return springs and separate the shoes.
5. Mark the position of the cam lever as it is installed on the camshaft so it can be reinstalled in the same position.
6. Loosen the bolt and nut securing the brake lever to the cam. Remove the lever and camshaft.

Inspection

1. Thoroughly clean and dry all parts except the linings.
2. Check the contact surface of the drum (**Figure 7**) for scoring. If there are deep grooves, deep enough to snag a fingernail, the drum should be reground and new shoes fitted. This type of wear can be avoided to a great extent if the brakes are disassembled and thoroughly cleaned after the bike has been ridden in mud or deep sand, or after each race.

NOTE
If oil or grease is on the drum surface, clean it off with a clean rag soaked in

lacquer thinner—do not use any solvent that may leave an oily residue.

3. Use a vernier caliper (**Figure 8**) and check the inside diameter of the drum for out-of-round or excessive wear. Refer to **Table 1** for brake specifications.
4. Inspect the linings for imbedded foreign material. Dirt can be removed with a stiff wire brush. Check for traces of oil or grease. If the linings are contaminated, they must be replaced.
5. Measure the brake lining thickness with a vernier caliper as shown in **Figure 9**. Replace the linings if worn to the wear limits in **Table 1**.

NOTE
Do not include the metal shoe thickness when measuring lining thickness.

6. *1978-1981:* With the linings installed on the backing plate, measure the brake shoe outside diameter (**Figure 10**) with a vernier caliper in the locations shown in **Figure 11**. Refer to **Table 1** for brake specifications. Replace as necessary.
7. Inspect the cam lobe and the pivot pin area of the shaft for wear and corrosion. Minor roughness can be removed with fine emery cloth.
8. Inspect the brake shoe return springs with a vernier caliper as shown in **Figure 12**. Compare length to **Table 1**. Replace the springs as a set if excessively stretched. If they are stretched, they will not fully retract the brake shoes from the drum, resulting in a power-robbing drag on the drums and premature wear of the linings.

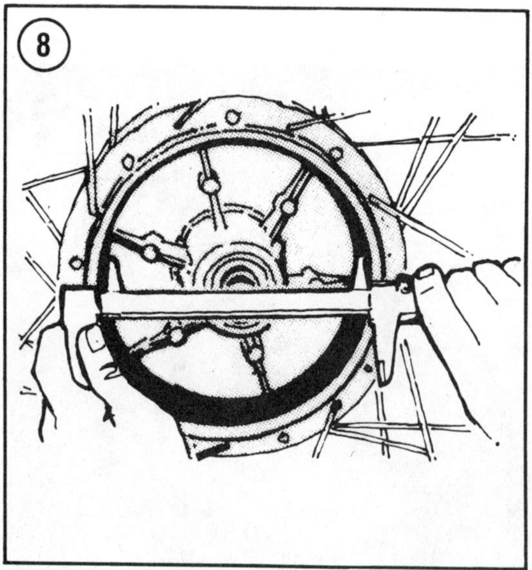

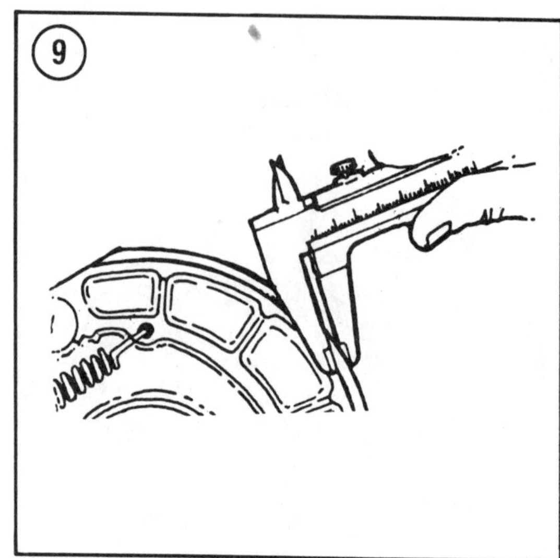

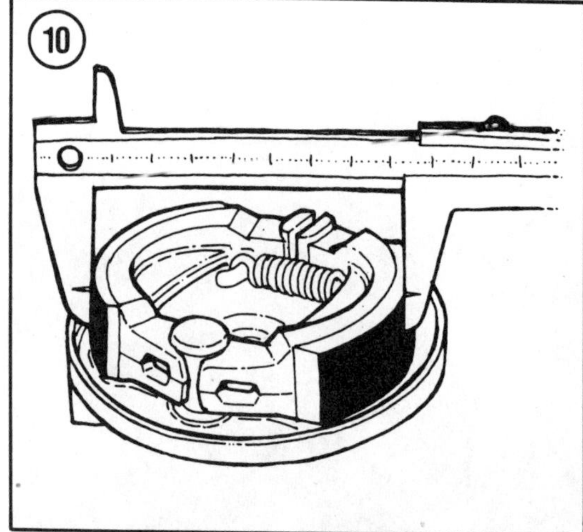

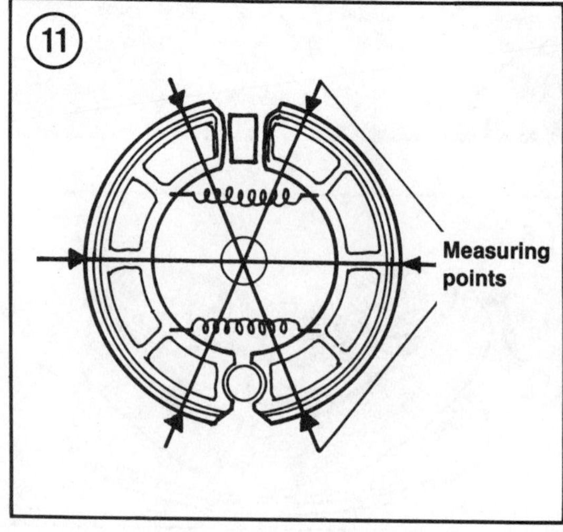

Assembly

Refer to **Figure 2** (front), **Figure 3** (rear) or **Figure 4** (rear) for this procedure.

1. Grease the shaft, cam and pivot post with a light coat of brake grease. Avoid getting any grease on the brake plate where the linings come in contact with it.

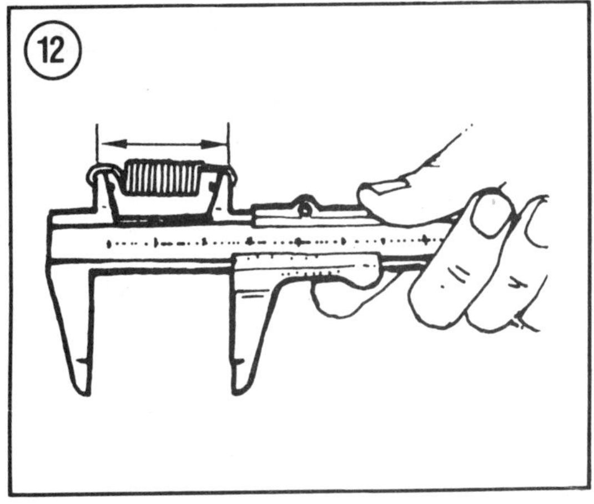

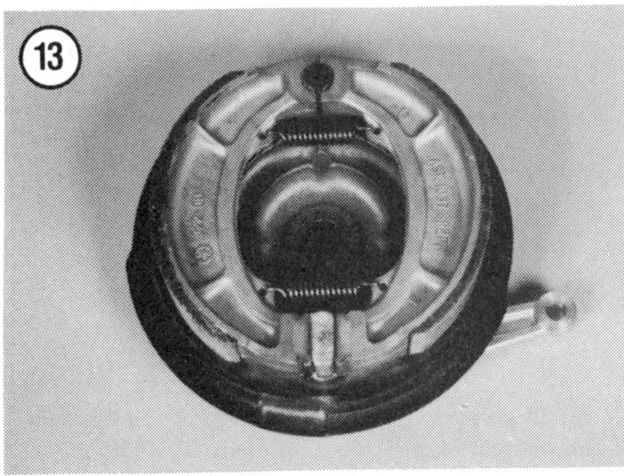

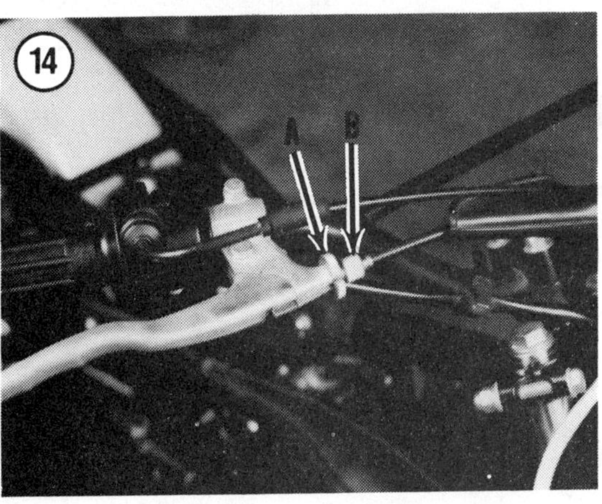

2. Install the brake lever onto the brake camshaft. Make sure to align the 2 marks made during disassembly.
3. Hold the brake shoes in a V-formation with the return springs attached (**Figure 6**) and snap them in place on the brake backing plate. Make sure they are firmly seated on it (**Figure 13**).
4. Install the brake panel assembly into the brake drum.

5A. Install the front wheel as described in Chapter Eleven.

5B. Install the rear wheel as described in Chapter Twelve.

6. Adjust the front brake as described under *Front Brake Lever Adjustment* in Chapter Three.

FRONT BRAKE CABLE REPLACEMENT

Brake cable adjustment should be checked periodically as the cable stretches with use and increases brake lever free play. Free play is the distance that the brake lever travels between the released position and the point when the brake shoes come in contact with the drum.

If the brake adjustment, as described in Chapter Three, can no longer be achieved the cable must be replaced.

1. At the hand lever, loosen the locknut (A, **Figure 14**) and turn the adjusting barrel (B, **Figure 14**) all the way toward the cable sheath.
2. At the brake assembly, loosen the locknut (A, **Figure 15**) and screw it all the way toward the cable sheath. Withdraw the pin from the end of the brake lever (B, **Figure 15**) and disconnect the cable from the receptacle on the backing plate (C, **Figure 15**).
3. Pull the hand lever all the way to the grip, remove the cable nipple from the lever and remove the cable.

4. Remove the band (**Figure 16**) securing the cable to the front fork leg.

NOTE
Prior to removing the cable, make a drawing (or take a Polaroid picture) of the cable routing through the frame. It is very easy to forget how it was once it has been removed. Replace it exactly as it was, avoiding any sharp turns.

5. Withdraw the cable from the plastic holders on the front fork clamps (**Figure 17**).
6. Install by reversing these removal steps.
7. Adjust the brake as described under *Front Brake Lever Adjustment* in Chapter Three.

FRONT DISC BRAKE (1986-ON)

The front disc brake is actuated by hydraulic fluid and controlled by a hand lever on the master cylinder. As the brake pads wear, the caliper pistons move outward and automatically adjust for wear.

When working on hydraulic brake systems, it is necessary that the work area and all tools be absolutely clean. Any tiny particles of foreign matter and grit in the caliper assembly or master cylinder can damage the components.

Consider the following when servicing the front disc brake.

1. Use only DOT 3 or DOT 4 brake fluid.
2. Do not allow disc brake fluid to contact any plastic parts or painted surfaces or damage will result.
3. Always keep the master cylinder reservoir and spare cans of brake fluid closed to prevent dust or moisture from entering. This would result in brake fluid contamination and brake problems.

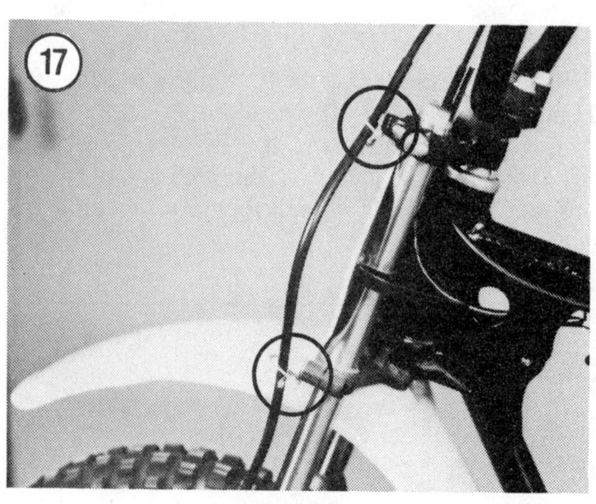

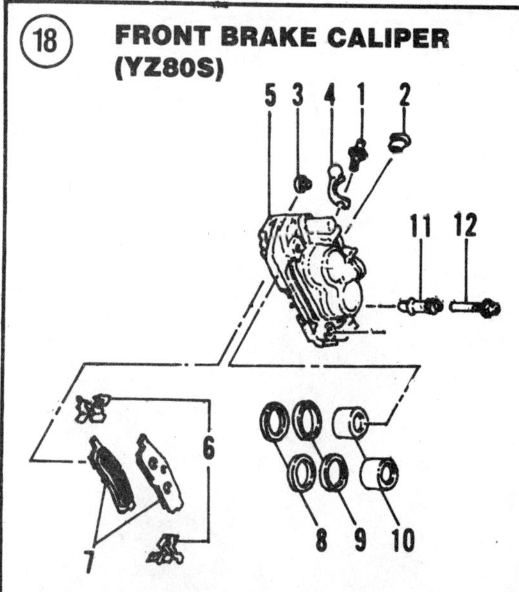

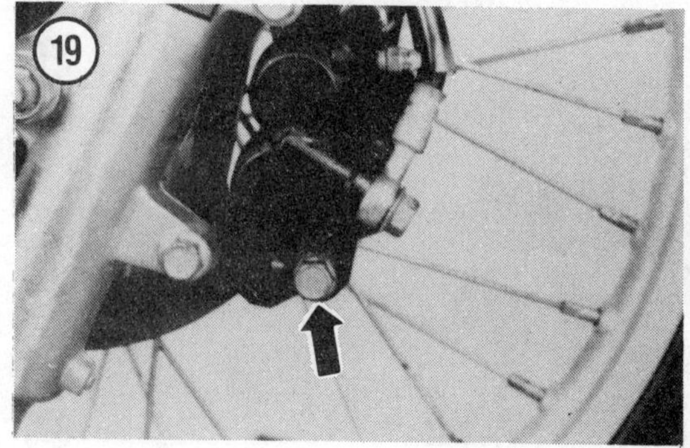

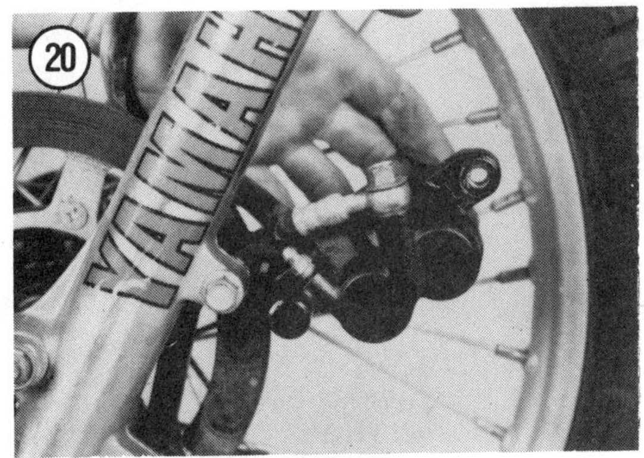

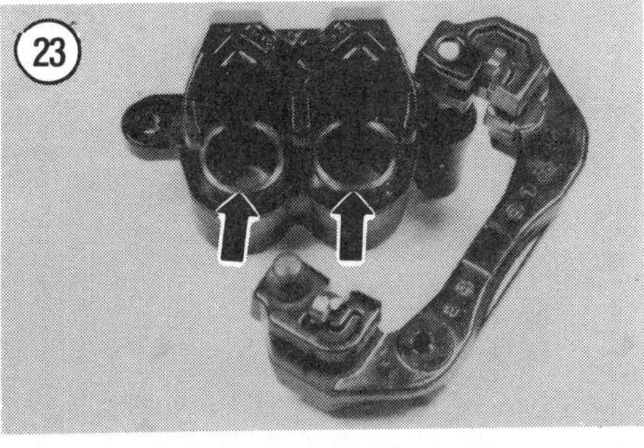

4. Use only disc brake fluid (DOT 3 or DOT 4) to wash parts. Never clean any internal brake components with solvent or any other petroleum base cleaners.

5. Whenever *any* component has been removed from the brake system the system is considered "opened" and must be bled to remove air bubbles. Also, if the brake feels "spongy," this usually means there are air bubbles in the system and it must be bled. For safe brake operation, refer to *Bleeding the System* in this chapter for complete details.

CAUTION

Disc brake components rarely require disassembly, so do not disassemble unless absolutely necessary. Do not use solvents of any kind on the brake systems internal components. Solvents will cause the seals to swell and distort. When disassembling and cleaning brake components (except brake pads) use new brake fluid.

FRONT BRAKE PAD REPLACEMENT

There is no recommended time interval for changing the friction pads in the front disc brake. Pad wear depends greatly on riding habits and conditions.

To maintain an even brake pressure on the disc always replace both pads in the caliper at the same time.

Refer to **Figure 18** for this procedure.

1. Place the bike on a stand so the front wheel clears the ground.
2. Remove the brake caliper bolt (**Figure 19**) and pivot the caliper housing up (**Figure 20**).
3. Remove the brake pads from the caliper bracket (**Figure 21**).
4. Remove the upper and lower (**Figure 22**) pad springs.

NOTE

***Figure 23** shows the caliper housing with pistons removed for clarity.*

5. Clean the pad recess and the end of the pistons (**Figure 23**) with a soft brush. Do not use solvent, wire brush or any hard tool which could damage the cylinder and/or piston.
6. Carefully remove any rust or corrosion from the disc.
7. When new brake pads are installed in the caliper the master cylinder brake fluid will rise as the caliper pistons are repositioned. Clean the top

of the master cylinder of all dirt. Remove the cover (**Figure 24**) and diaphragm from the master cylinder and slowly push the caliper pistons into the caliper. Constantly check the reservoir to make sure brake fluid does not overflow. Remove fluid, if necessary, prior to it overflowing. The pistons should move freely in the caliper bores. If they don't, and there is evidence of them sticking in the caliper, the caliper should be removed and serviced as described under *Front Caliper Rebuilding* in this chapter.

8. Push the caliper pistons in all the way to allow room for the new pads.
9. Install the anti-rattle springs. **Figure 22** shows the lower spring. The top spring is similar.
10. Place the new brake pads in the caliper bracket (**Figure 21**) and pivot the caliper housing clockwise and install it over the brake shoes (**Figure 25**).
11. Install the caliper bolt (**Figure 19**) and tighten to the torque specification in **Table 3**.
12. Spin the front wheel and activate the brake lever as many times as necessary as it takes to refill the cylinders in the caliper and correctly locate the pads.
13. Refill the master cylinder reservoir, if necessary, to maintain the correct brake fluid level. Install the diaphragm and cover.

WARNING
Use brake fluid clearly marked DOT 3 or DOT 4 from a sealed container. Other types may vaporize and cause brake failure. Always use the same brand name; do not intermix as many brands are not compatible.

WARNING
Do not ride the motorcycle until you are sure the brake is operating correctly with full hydraulic advantage. If necessary, bleed the brake system as described in this chapter.

FRONT CALIPER

Removal/Installation

1. Place the bike on a stand so the front wheel clears the ground.
2. Remove the brake pads as described in this chapter.
3. Disconnect the caliper brake hose and washers. See **Figure 26**.
4. Place the end of the brake hose in a clean container. Operate the front brake lever to drain the master cylinder and brake hose of all brake fluid. Dispose of this brake fluid—never reuse brake fluid. To prevent the entry of moisture and

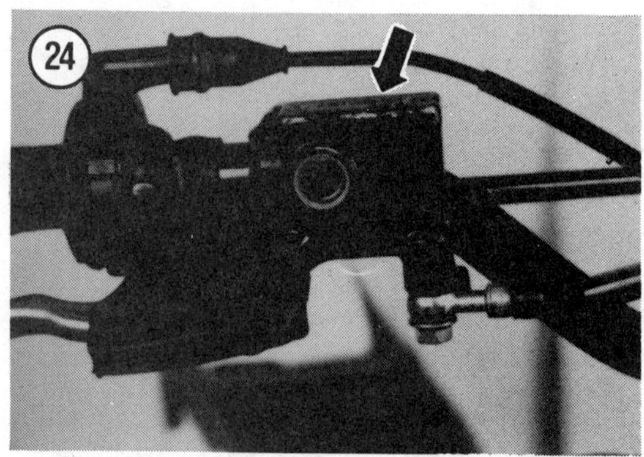

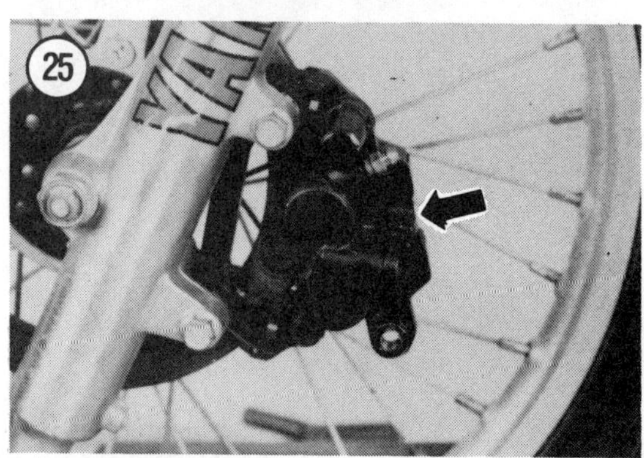

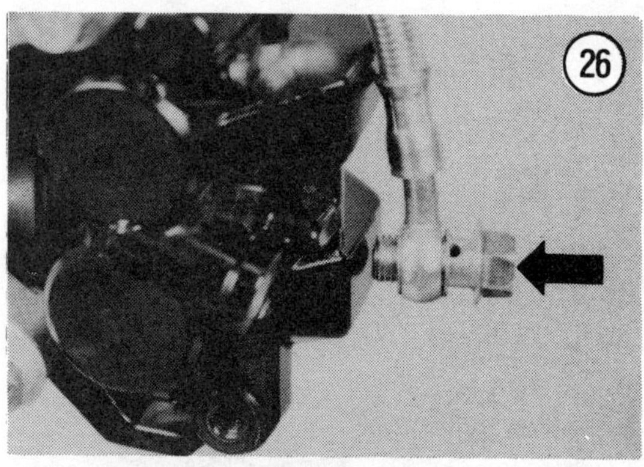

28

29

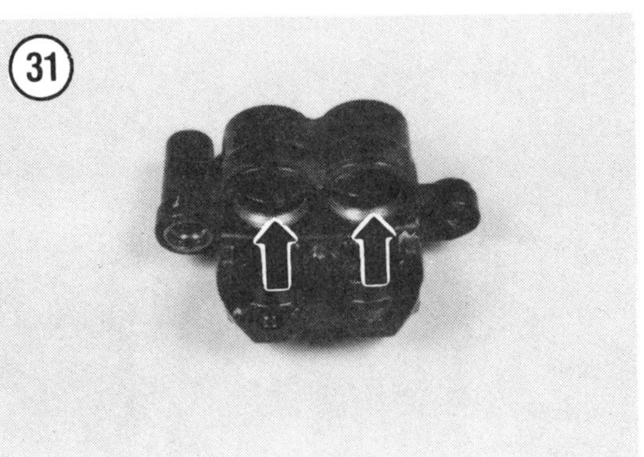

30

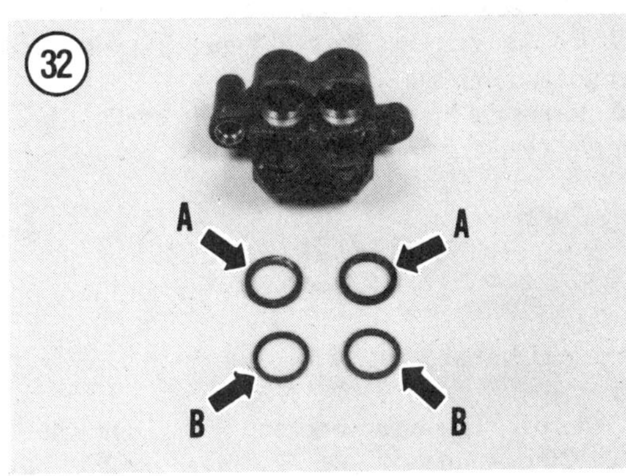

31

dirt, cap the end of the brake line and tie the loose end up to the forks.

5. Pivot the caliper housing counterclockwise (**Figure 25**) and slide if off the caliper bracket.
6. Remove the 2 bracket bolts and remove the bracket (A, **Figure 27**).
7. Install by reversing these removal steps, noting the following.
8. Install the bracket and the 2 mounting bolts. Tighten the bolts to the torque specification in **Table 3**.
9. Coat the bracket pivot rod (B, **Figure 27**) with high temperature grease.
10. Install the brake hose, with a new sealing washer on each side of the fitting, onto the caliper (**Figure 26**). Install the banjo bolt and tighten to the torque specification in **Table 3**.
11. Install the brake pads and tighten the caliper bolt as described in this chapter.
12. Bleed the brake as described in this chapter.

WARNING
Do not ride the motorcycle until you are sure the brake is operating properly.

Disassembly/Inspection/Reassembly

Refer to **Figure 18** for this procedure.

NOTE
Keep track of each piston position. They must be reinstalled in their original positions.

1. Cushion the caliper pistons with a shop rag. Then apply compressed air (**Figure 28**) through the brake line port to remove the pistons (**Figure 29**).

WARNING
Cushion the pistons with a shop rag. Do not try to cushion the pistons with your fingers, as injury could result.

2. Remove the dust (**Figure 30**) and piston (**Figure 31**) seals from each piston bore. See **Figure 32**.

32

3. Check the pistons (**Figure 33**) and piston bores (**Figure 34**) for deep scratches or other obvious wear marks. If either part is less than perfect, replace it.
4. Check the caliper housing for damage; replace if needed.
5. Remove the bleed screw (A, **Figure 35**) and check it for wear or damage.
6. Check the banjo bolt threads in the caliper (B, **Figure 35**). Check thread condition by screwing the bolt into the caliper.
7. Check the bracket bushing (A, **Figure 36**) for wear or damage; replace the bushing if necessary by pulling it out of the bracket. Check the bracket pivot rod (B, **Figure 36**) for cracks, scoring or damage; replace the bracket assembly if necessary.
8. Check the threads in the bracket (A, **Figure 37**) for damage. Repair threads if they are stripped.
9. Check the pad springs (B, **Figure 37**) for cracks or damage. Install each spring onto its bracket mounting position and check fit and tightness. Replace the pad springs as a set if any one spring is damaged.
10. Clean all parts (except brake pads) with DOT 3 or DOT 4 brake fluid.
11. Soak the new dust seals and piston seals in fresh brake fluid. Coat the inside of the cylinder with fresh brake fluid prior to the assembly of parts.
12. Install a piston seal (A, **Figure 32**) into the second groove in each cylinder bore. See **Figure 31**.
13. Install a dust seal (B, **Figure 32**) into the first groove in each cylinder bore. See **Figure 30**.

NOTE
Check that the seals fit squarely in the cylinder bore grooves. If the seals are not installed properly, the caliper assembly will leak and braking performance will be reduced.

14. The pistons (**Figure 33**) have one open and one closed end. Install the pistons in their respective cylinders so that the open end faces out (**Figure 29**).
15. Coat the bracket pivot rod (**Figure 36**) with high temperature grease.
16. Install the brake caliper assembly as described in this chapter.

FRONT MASTER CYLINDER (1986-ON)

Removal/Installation

1. Place the bike on a workstand so the front wheel clears the ground.

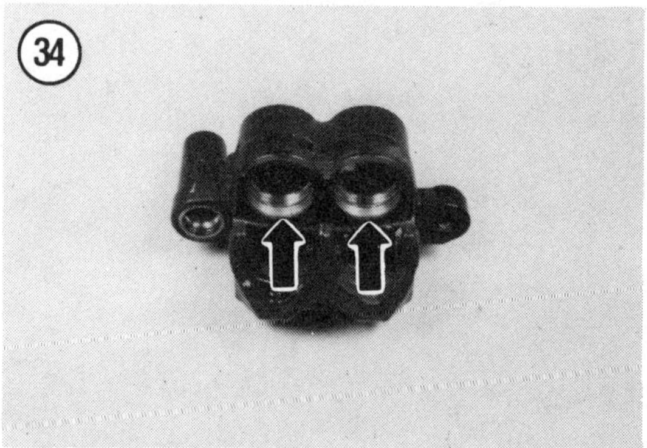

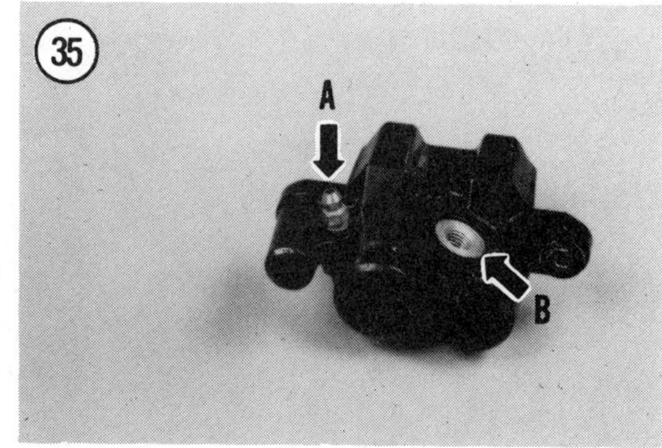

2. Remove the caliper banjo bolt and washers (**Figure 38**) and disconnect the brake hose at the caliper.
3. Place the end of the brake hose in a clean container. Operate the front brake lever to drain the master cylinder and brake hose of all brake fluid. Dispose of this brake fluid—never reuse brake fluid. To prevent the entry of moisture and dirt, cap the end of the brake line and tie the loose end up to the forks.
4. Remove the master cylinder banjo bolt and washers (**Figure 39**) and disconnect the brake hose. Wrap a plastic bag around the brake hose to prevent brake fluid from dripping onto other parts.

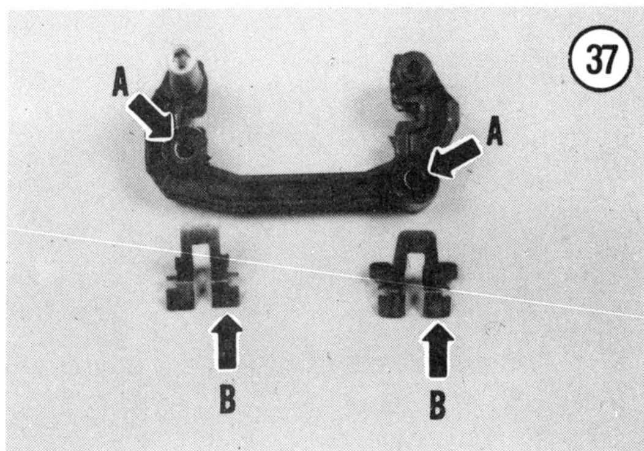

5. Remove the master cylinder clamp bolts at the handlebar and remove the master cylinder.
6. Install by reversing these removal steps, noting the following.
7. Install the brake hose, with new sealing washers on each side of the fitting, onto the master cylinder and caliper. Install the banjo bolts and tighten to the torque specification listed in **Table 3**.
8. Bleed the brake as described in this chapter.

WARNING
Do not ride the motorcycle until you are sure the brake is operating properly.

Disassembly/Inspection/Assembly

Refer to **Figure 40** for this procedure.

1. Remove the master cylinder as described in this chapter.
2. Remove the screws securing the cover and remove the cover and diaphragm. Pour out the

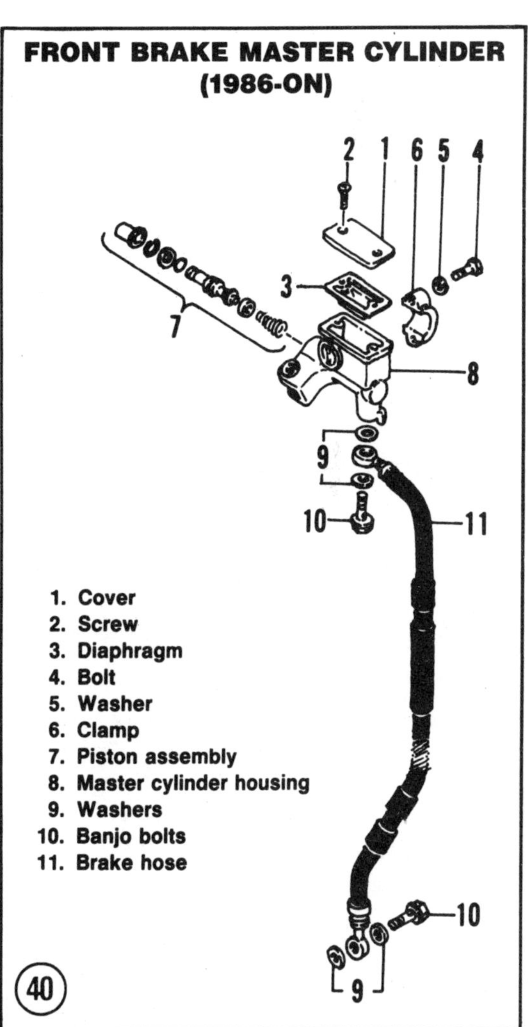

13

remaining brake fluid and discard it. Never reuse brake fluid.
3. Remove the hand lever nut (**Figure 41**). Then remove the pivot bolt (A, **Figure 42**) and hand lever (B, **Figure 42**).
4. Remove the hand lever spring (**Figure 43**).
5. Remove the dust seal (**Figure 44**). See **Figure 45**.
6. Using circlip pliers, remove the circlip (**Figure 46** and A, **Figure 47**) from the master cylinder.
7. Referring to **Figure 47**, remove the following parts in order:
   a. Washer (B).
   b. Piston assembly (C).
   c. Spring (D).
8. Clean all parts in fresh DOT 3 or DOT 4 brake fluid.

NOTE
All of the parts removed in Steps 5-7 are part of the piston assembly. If any one of these parts is worn or damaged, the complete piston assembly (7, ***Figure 40****) must be replaced.*

9. Inspect the cylinder bore and piston contact surfaces for scratches, pitting or rust. If either part is less than perfect, replace it.
10. Check the spring (A, **Figure 48**) for cracks or damage.

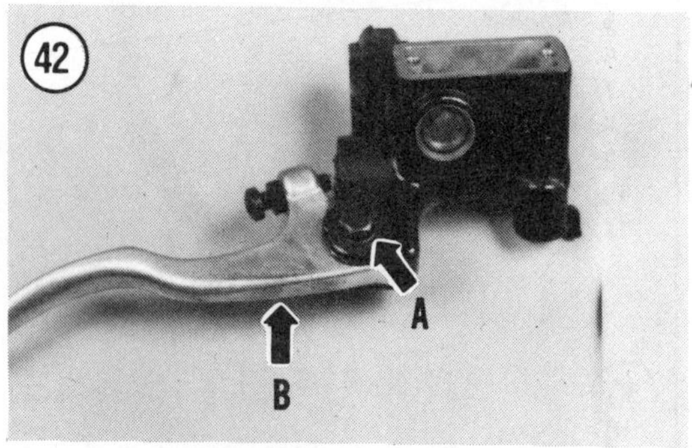

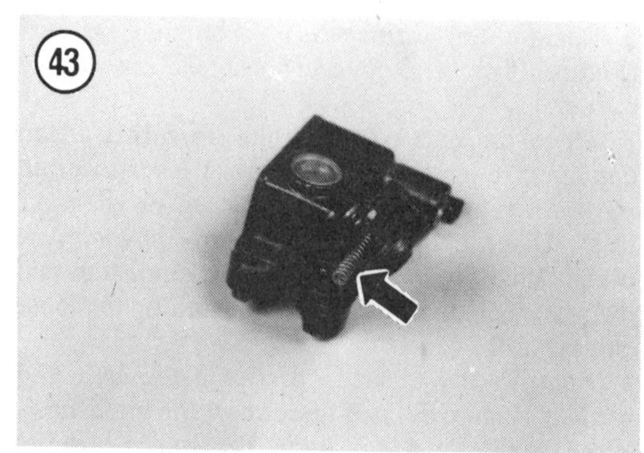

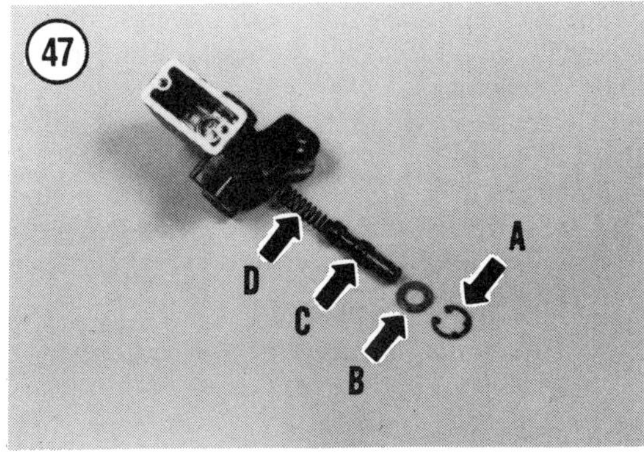

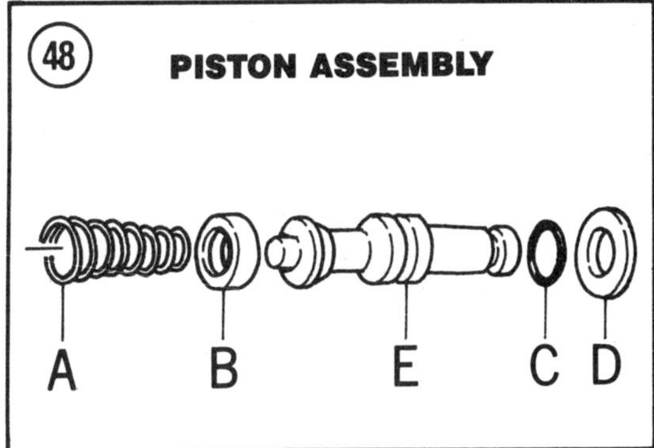

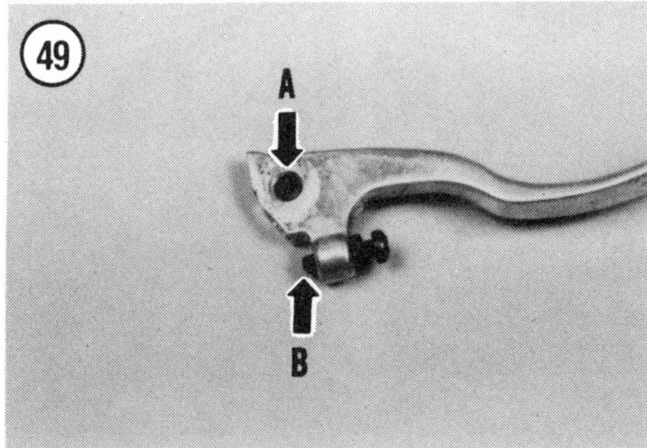

11. Check the primary cup (B, **Figure 48**) and the O-ring (C, **Figure 48**) on the piston. Replace the piston assembly if the cup or O-ring is worn, softened, swollen or damaged.

12. Check the washer (D, **Figure 48**) for cracks. If the washer is damaged and the other piston assembly parts are okay, measure the washer and take the measurements to a dealer for selection and purchase. If you cannot find a washer with the exact measurements, you will have to purchase and install a new piston assembly.

13. Check the end of the piston (E, **Figure 48**) for wear caused by the hand lever. Replace if worn.

14. Inspect the pivot hole in the hand lever (A, **Figure 49**). If worn or elongated it must be replaced. Also inspect the adjust bolt (B, **Figure 49**). Replace the bolt if the end is damaged or if the threads are stripped.

15. Make sure the passages in the bottom of the brake fluid reservoir are clear (**Figure 50**). A plugged relief port will cause the pads to drag on the disc.

16. Check the banjo bolt threads in the master cylinder housing (A, **Figure 51**) for damage. Also check the lever pivot hole and threads (B, **Figure 51**) for damage. If necessary, repair threads. If thread damage is severe, replace the master cylinder housing.

17. Check the reservoir cap and diaphragm (**Figure 52**) for damage and deterioration and replace as necessary.

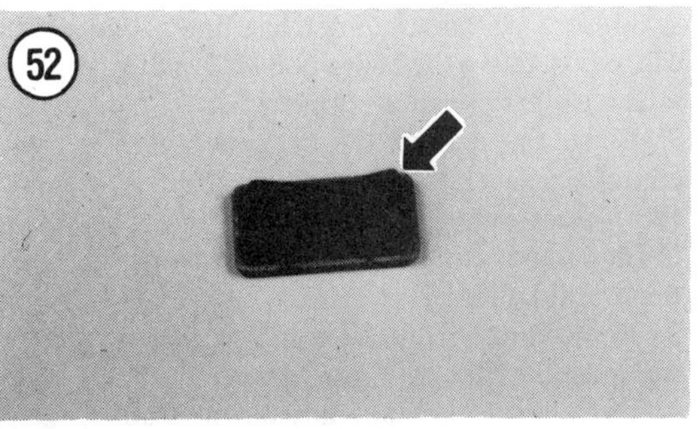

18. Assemble the master cylinder as follows.
19. Soak the piston assembly in fresh DOT 3 or DOT 4 brake fluid. Coat the inside of the cylinder with fresh brake fluid prior to the assembly of parts.
20. Referring to **Figure 47**, install the piston assembly as follows:
  a. Make sure the spring (A, **Figure 48**) is pushed onto the end of the piston.
  b. Insert the spring and piston into the master cylinder.

NOTE
*When installing the piston, the primary cup (B, **Figure 48**) should be slightly larger than the bore and will drag as the piston is inserted. If the cup appears loose and does not contact the cylinder bore correctly, replace the piston assembly.*

  c. Slide the washer (B) over the end of the piston and seat it squarely in the bore.
  d. Compress the piston assembly and install the circlip (A) in the caliper bore with circlip pliers. See **Figure 46**. Make sure the circlip seats securely in the groove.
  e. Install the dust seal into the end of the caliper in the direction shown in **Figure 45**. Make sure the seal seats securely around the piston and in the bore as shown in **Figure 44**.
21. Insert the lever spring (**Figure 43**) into the housing.
22. Install the lever into the housing (B, **Figure 42**). Lightly grease the pivot bolt and install it (A, **Figure 42**) and the nut (**Figure 41**). Operate the lever to make sure the pivot bolt is not too tight.

FRONT BRAKE HOSE REPLACEMENT

Under racing conditions, the brake hose should be replaced once a year or whenever it shows signs of wear or damage.
1. Place a container under the brake line at the caliper. Remove the banjo bolt and sealing washers at the caliper assembly (**Figure 53**).
2. Place the end of the brake hose in a clean container. Operate the front brake lever to drain the master cylinder and brake hose of all brake fluid. Dispose of this brake fluid—never reuse brake fluid.
3. Remove the banjo bolt and sealing washers at the master cylinder (**Figure 54**).
4. Disconnect the brake hose at the front fork.
5. Install a new brake hose in the reverse order of removal. Install new sealing washers and banjo bolts if necessary.
6. Tighten the banjo bolts to torque specification listed in **Table 3**.
7. Refill the master cylinder with fresh brake fluid clearly marked DOT 3 or DOT 4. Bleed the brake as described in this chapter.

WARNING
Do not ride the motorcycle until you are sure that the brakes are operating properly.

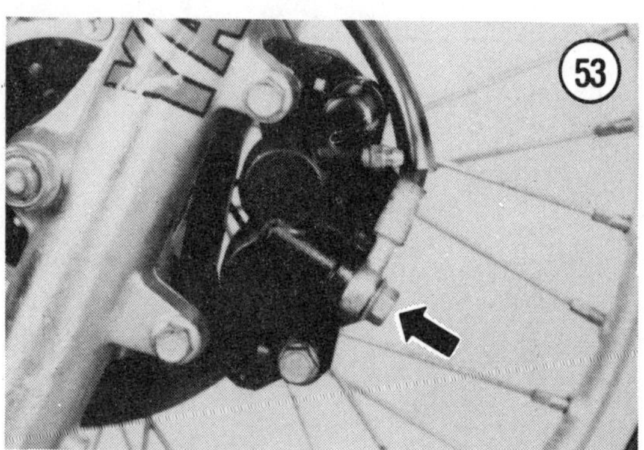
53

54

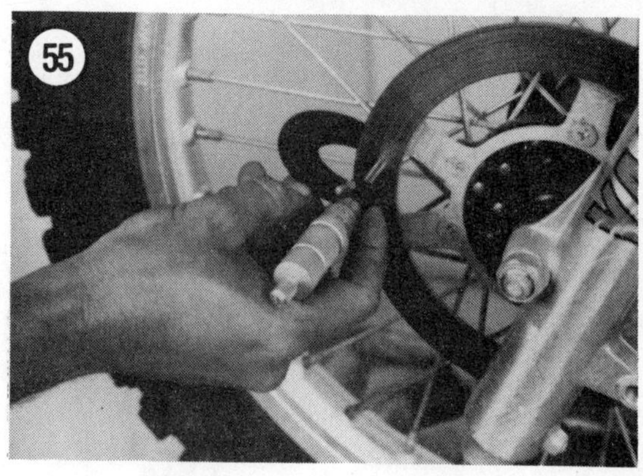
55

FRONT BRAKE DISC

Removal/Installation

1. Remove the front wheel as described in Chapter Eleven.

NOTE
Place a piece of wood in the caliper in place of the disc. This way, if the brake lever is inadvertently squeezed, the pistons will not be forced out of the cylinders. If this does happen, the caliper might have to be disassembled to reseat the pistons and the system will have to be bled.

2. Remove the bolts securing the disc to the wheel.
3. Install by reversing these removal steps. Tighten the bolts to the torque specification in **Table 3**.

Inspection

It is not necessary to remove the disc from the wheel to inspect it. Small marks on the disc are not important, but radial scratches deep enough to snag a fingernail reduce braking effectiveness and increase brake pad wear. If these grooves are found, the disc should be resurfaced or replaced.

1. Measure the thickness around the disc at several locations with vernier calipers or a micrometer (**Figure 55**). The disc must be replaced if the thickness at any point is less than specified in **Table 2**.
2. Make sure the disc bolts are tight prior to performing this check. Check the disc runout with a dial indicator as shown in **Figure 56**. Slowly rotate the wheel and watch the dial indicator. If the runout exceeds the limit in **Table 2**, the disc must be replaced.
3. Clean the disc of any rust or corrosion and wipe clean with lacquer thinner. Never use an oil based solvent that may leave an oil residue on the disc.

13

BLEEDING THE SYSTEM

This procedure is necessary only when the brakes feel spongy, there is a leak in the hydraulic system, a component has been replaced or the brake fluid has been replaced.

1. Flip off the dust cap from the brake bleeder valve (**Figure 57**).
2. Connect a length of clear tubing to the bleeder valve on the caliper (**Figure 58**). Place the other end of the tube into a clean container. Fill the

container with enough fresh brake fluid to keep the end submerged. The tube should be long enough so that a loop can be made higher than the bleeder valve to prevent air from being drawn into the caliper during bleeding. See **Figure 59**.

CAUTION
Cover the front wheel, fender and fuel tank with a heavy cloth or plastic tarp to protect it from the accidental spilling of brake fluid. Wash any spilled brake fluid off of any surface immediately, as it will destroy the finish. Use soapy water and rinse completely.

3. Clean the top of the master cylinder of all dirt and foreign matter. Remove the cover and diaphragm (**Figure 60**). Fill the reservoir to about 10 mm (3/8 in.) from the top. Insert the diaphragm to prevent the entry of dirt and moisture.

WARNING
Use brake fluid clearly marked DOT 3 or DOT 4 only. Others may vaporize and cause brake failure. Always use the same brand name; do not intermix the brake fluids, as many brands are not compatible.

4. Slowly apply the brake lever several times. Hold the lever in the applied position and open the bleeder valve about 1/2 turn. Allow the lever to travel to its limit. When this limit is reached, tighten the bleeder screw. As the brake fluid enters the system, the level will drop in the master cylinder reservoir. Maintain the level at about 10 mm (3/8 in.) from the top of the reservoir to prevent air from being drawn into the system.
5. Continue to pump the lever and fill the reservoir until the fluid emerging from the hose is completely free of air bubbles. If you are replacing the fluid, continue until the fluid emerging from the hose is clean.

NOTE
If bleeding is difficult, it may be necessary to allow the fluid to stabilize for a few hours. Repeat the bleeding procedure when the tiny bubbles in the system settle out.

6. Hold the lever in the applied position and tighten the bleeder valve. Remove the bleeder tube and install the bleeder valve dust cap (**Figure 57**).
7. If necessary, add fluid to correct the level in the master cylinder reservoir. It must be above the level line (**Figure 60**).
8. Install the cover and tighten the screws. See **Figure 60**.
9. Test the feel of the brake lever. It should feel firm and should offer the same resistance each time it's operated. If it feels spongy, it is likely that air is still in the system and it must be bled again. When all air has been bled from the system and the brake fluid level is correct in the reservoir, double-check for leaks and tighten all fittings and connections.

WARNING
Before riding the motorcycle, make certain that the front brake is working correctly by operating the lever several times. Then make the test ride a slow one at first to make sure the brake is working correctly.

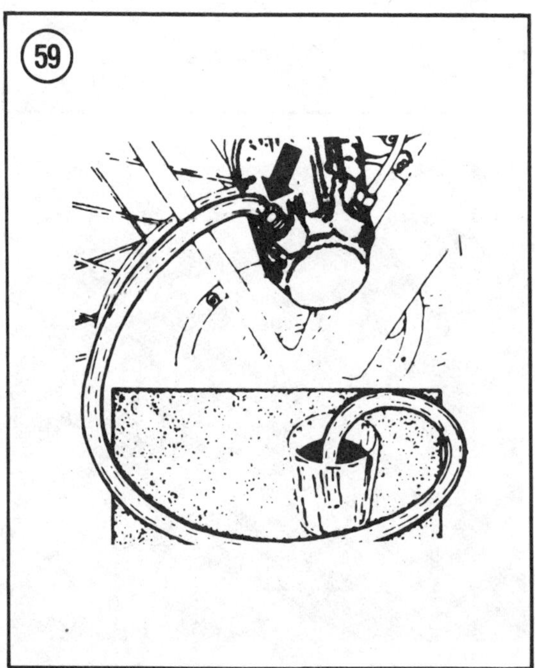

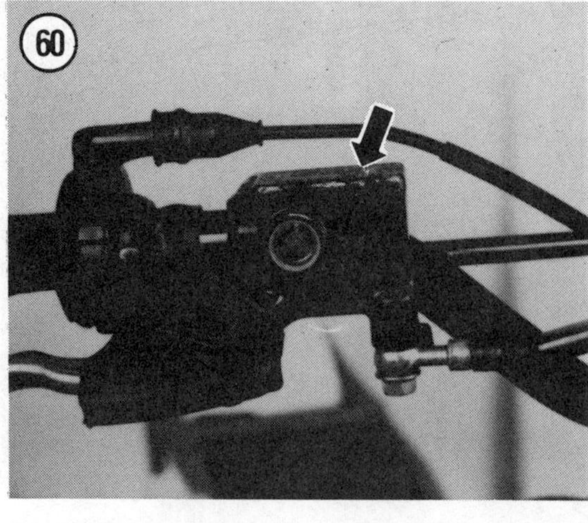

Table 1 DRUM BRAKE SPECIFICATIONS

	mm	in.
Brake drum inside diameter (new)		
Front		
YZ50	95	3.74
YZ60	95	3.74
YZ80		
1978	89	3.50
1979-1985	95	3.74
Rear		
YZ50	95	3.74
YZ60	95	3.74
YZ80		
1978	102	4.0
1979	110	4.33
1980-on	95	3.74
Brake lining thickness wear limit		
1978		
New	3.0	0.12
Wear limit	1.5	0.06
1979		
Front		
New	3.0	0.16
Wear limit	1.5	0.06
Rear		
New	4.0	0.20
Wear limit	1.5	0.06
1980-1982		
New	3.0	0.12
Wear limit	1.5	0.06
1983-on		
New	4.0	0.16
Wear limit	2.0	0.08
Brake shoe O.D. wear limit		
YZ50		
Front and rear	92	3.62
YZ60	*	*
YZ80		
1978		
Front	86	3.4
Rear	98	3.86
1979		
Front	92	3.62
Rear	106	4.17
1980		
Front and rear	92	3.62
1981	*	*
Return spring free length		
YZ50		
New	32.7	1.29
Wear limit	*	*
YZ60		
New	32.7	1.29
Wear limit	*	*

(continued)

13

Table 1 DRUM BRAKE SPECIFICATIONS (continued)

	mm	in.
YZ80		
1978	*	*
1979		
Front		
New	32	1.26
Wear limit	*	*
Rear		
New	34.5	1.36
Wear limit	*	*
1980		
New	32	1.26
Wear limit	*	*
1981		
Front		
New	32	1.26
Wear limit	*	*
Rear		
New	32.7	1.29
Wear limit	*	*
1982-1986	*	*
1987-on		
Rear		
New	32.7	1.29
Wear limit	*	*

* Not specified by Yamaha.

Table 2 FRONT DISC BRAKE SPECIFICATIONS (1986-ON)

	mm	in.
Brake disc		
Thickness		
New	3.0	0.12
Wear limit	2.5	0.10
Maximum runout	0.15	0.006
Brake pad thickness		
New	4.0	0.16
Wear limit	0.8	0.031

Table 3 DISC BRAKE TORQUE SPECIFICATIONS (1986-ON)

	N•m	ft.-lb.
Brake disc bolts		
1986-1987	7	5.1
1988-on	8.7	6
Brake caliper bolts	30	22
Banjo bolts	26	19
Master cylinder clamp bolts	9	6.5

CHAPTER FOURTEEN

SUSPENSION ADJUSTMENT

For the competitive motocross rider, no area of machine tuning is more critical than suspension adjustment. The Yamaha YZ models are sold as competition motorcycles designed to race over rough terrain. Thus a long travel suspension able to absorb bumps and maintain optimum handling and traction is required.

When adjusting your bike's suspension, consider the following:

a. Always make suspension adjustments in small increments. It's difficult to say how one adjustment will affect your bike's handling. Too big a change can have a big effect on the bike's handling and really confuse you.
b. Make the most of your practice time to learn the track's condition and then adjust the suspension accordingly.
c. Depending upon the weather and how many races are run during the day, track conditions may change drastically from the practice to the start of your race. Learn to recognize changes in track conditions and to adjust your suspension accordingly.
d. Once the suspension has been adjusted for a particular track, record the settings in a notebook. This information can be used as a reference when returning to that track.
e. If an adjustment change doesn't work once, it might under different conditions.
f. Perform weekly checks and maintenance to the suspension components as described in this book.

Tables 1-7 are at the end of the chapter.

YAMAHA FACTORY ACCESSORIES

To offer a wider range of tuning capabilities for stock front forks and the rear shock absorber, Yamaha dealers sell different front fork springs, fork spacers and shock absorber springs. The front fork and rear shock absorber springs are available in standard, softer and harder spring rates. The fork spacers are available in different lengths. See your Yamaha dealer for the availability of these items for your model.

NOTE

The list of accessory fork springs, fork spacers and shock absorber springs are not available for all models. Consult with your Yamaha dealer on availability.

SUSPENSION TRAVEL MEASUREMENT

Before tuning your suspension, you should know if the bike is using all of its front and rear travel. If the bike is bottoming heavily, you can probably feel it through the handlebars or on your legs; this is a good indication that you have to stiffen the suspension. On the other hand, if the bike is not bottoming, your suspension setup is too stiff and you are not using all of the bike's travel. To check suspension travel on the front forks or rear shock absorber, perform the following. **Table 1** lists suspension travel for stock suspension components.

Front Fork

Attach a cable tie around the fork tube and slide it down next to the dust cap. After riding a few hard practice laps, pit the bike and measure how far the cable tie traveled up the fork tube. If the cable tie traveled the full distance and the forks bottomed gently, your front forks are properly setup.

If the forks bottomed harshly, they are setup too soft. First install a heavier weight oil and/or increase the fork oil level as described in this chapter. If changing the fork oil does not help, install a heavier spring if available. If you are not using all of the travel, the front fork setup is too hard. Install a lighter weight fork oil and/or reduce the fork oil level.

Rear Shock Absorber

1. Before checking rear wheel travel, check the rear shock absorber's spring pre-load as follows:
   a. Place the bike on a workstand so that the rear wheel clears the ground.
   b. Measure the distance from the center of the rear axle to the center of a fender or seat bolt. Record this measurement.
   c. Take the bike off the stand. Have the rider (wearing complete riding gear) sit on the seat with both feet on the footpegs. Have an assistant lightly steady the front forks to keep the bike from falling. Measure the same distance and record the measurement.
   d. Subtract sub-step "c" from sub-step "b" to obtain your bike's spring pre-load measurement. The difference should be approximately 80 mm (3.1). If the difference is incorrect, adjust the spring pre-load as described in this chapter.
2. After adjusting your bike's spring pre-load, stick a piece of duct tape under the rear fender. Ride the bike a few hard practice laps and check the condition of the tape. If the tape has been lightly scuffed, rear wheel travel is perfect. If the rear wheel does not bottom out, the spring is too hard. If the bike bottoms severely, the spring is too soft.

FRONT FORK

The following adjustment procedures can be performed on stock YZ front forks covered in this manual:

a. Front fork oil level.
b. Air pressure.
c. Front fork tube height.

Troubleshooting

Front fork conditions are usually defined as perfect, too hard or too soft. If your forks are not perfect, they should be adjusted to best suit your

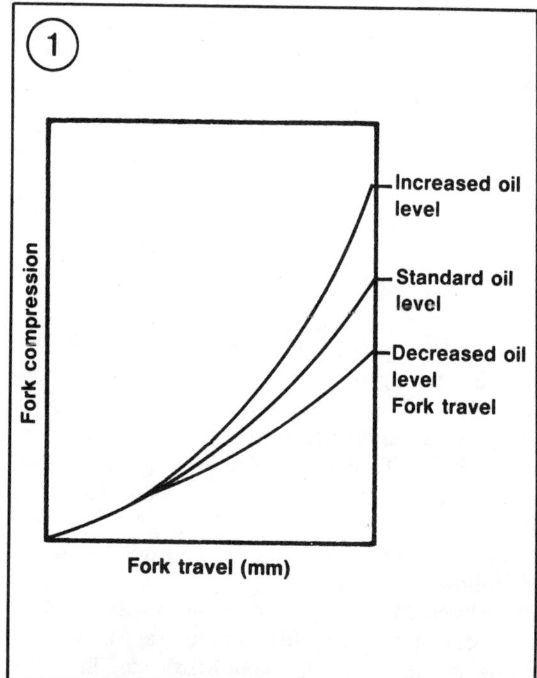

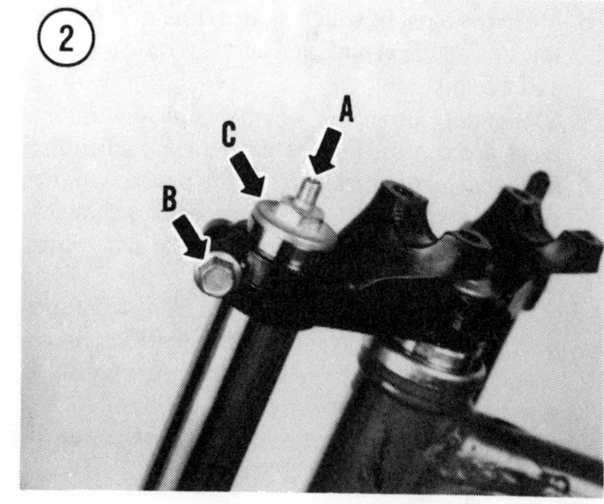

riding ability and track conditions. Consider the following before adjusting your forks:1. *Too soft:* If the front forks dive or compress quickly, especially when you are not using the front brake, note the following conditions:

a. The fork springs are too soft.
b. The fork oil level is too low.

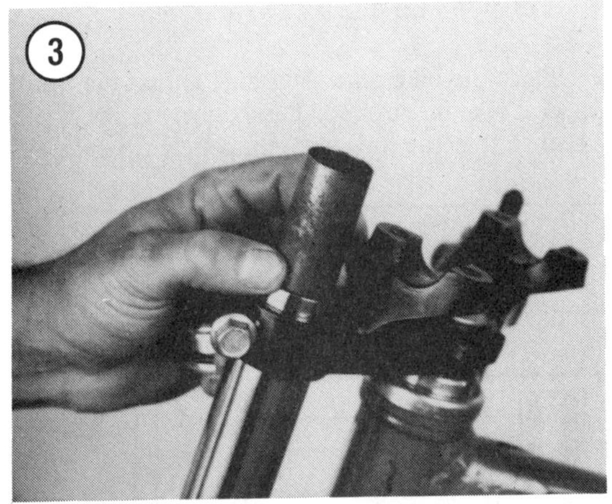

3

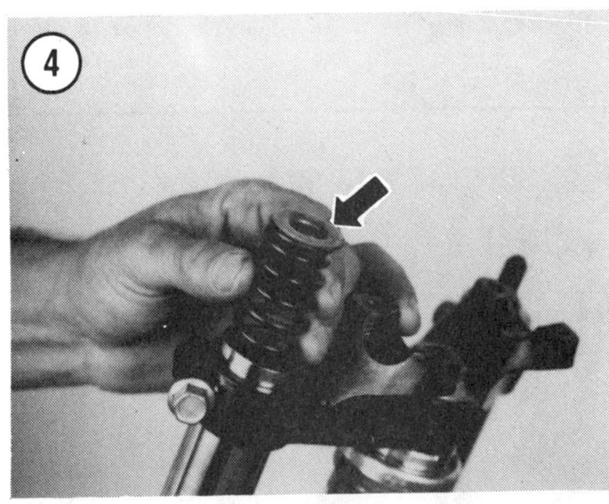

4

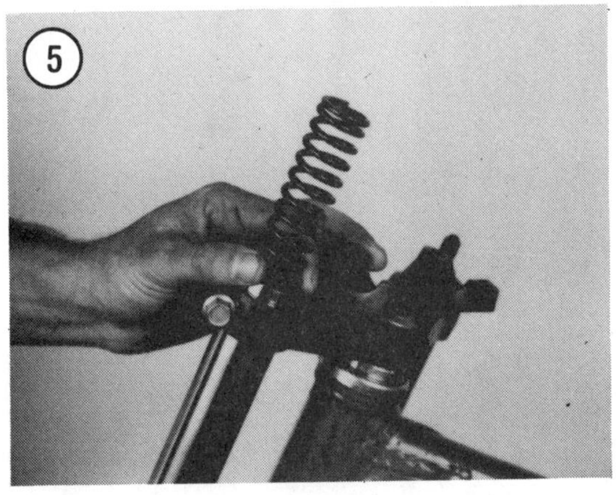

5

c. The spring pre-load is incorrect (not enough pre-load).

2. *Too hard:* If the fork forks operation seems harsh, note the following conditions:

a. If the front forks are too stiff, the springs are too hard.
b. If the front fork operation seems hard, the spring pre-load is excessive or air has built up in the fork tubes.
c. Hard fork operation can be caused by installing too much air pressure.
d. If the front forks stiffen at the second part of travel, the fork oil level is too high.

Front Fork Oil Level Adjustment (1982-on YZ80)

The fork oil level determines the fork tube air volume (**Figure 1**). When the forks are compressed, the air pressure inside the fork tube increases, making the fork action stiffer. If a fork tube has a lower oil level, the air pressure will not increase as quickly as for a fork tube with a higher oil level. Thus the fork oil level effects the fork operation during the second part of travel.

For maximum fork performance, it is necessary to measure the oil level in each fork. When changing the fork oil level, consider the following:

a. If the forks bottom, raise the fork oil level in 10 mm (0.4 in.) increments.
b. If the forks are too stiff over large jumps, reduce the fork oil level by 5 mm (0.2 in.).

1. Place the bike on a workstand so that the front wheel clears the ground.
2. Remove the handlebar as described in Chapter Eleven. It is not necessary to disconnect any cables or wires.
3. Remove the fork tube air valve cap. Use a small screwdriver or punch and release all air pressure in the fork (A, **Figure 2**).

CAUTION

Release the air pressure gradually. If released too fast, fork oil may spurt out with the air. Protect your eyes accordingly.

4. Loosen the upper fork bridge pinch bolts (B, **Figure 2**) and remove the fork cap (C, **Figure 2**).
5. *1983-on models:* Remove the spacer (**Figure 3**).
6. Remove the spring seat (**Figure 4**).
7. Remove the fork spring (**Figure 5**).
8. Repeat Steps 3-7 for the other fork assembly.
9. With an assistant's help, roll the bike off of the stand so that the forks are placed in a vertical position.

10. Using a fork oil level gauge (**Figure 6**) measure the distance from the top of the fork tube to the top of the oil (**Figure 7**). Refer to **Table 2** for the correct specifications. Repeat for the opposite fork. **Figure 8** shows a fork oil level gauge being used with the forks removed. If the oil level is too high, use the gauge to siphon some of the oil out of the fork tube. If the oil level is too low, pour some fork oil into the fork tube. Measure the fork oil level once again and adjust as required.

NOTE
A tape measure or ruler can be used to perform Step 9. However, to assure a precise oil level, you may want to invest in a fork oil level gauge offered by Yamaha or an accessory manufacturer. A fork oil level gauge works well when adjusting the suspension at the race track.

NOTE
Change the fork oil level in increments of 5-10 mm (0.2-0.4 in.) at a time.

11. Place the bike onto the stand so that the front wheel clears the ground. Push down on the front wheel so that the forks are completely extended.

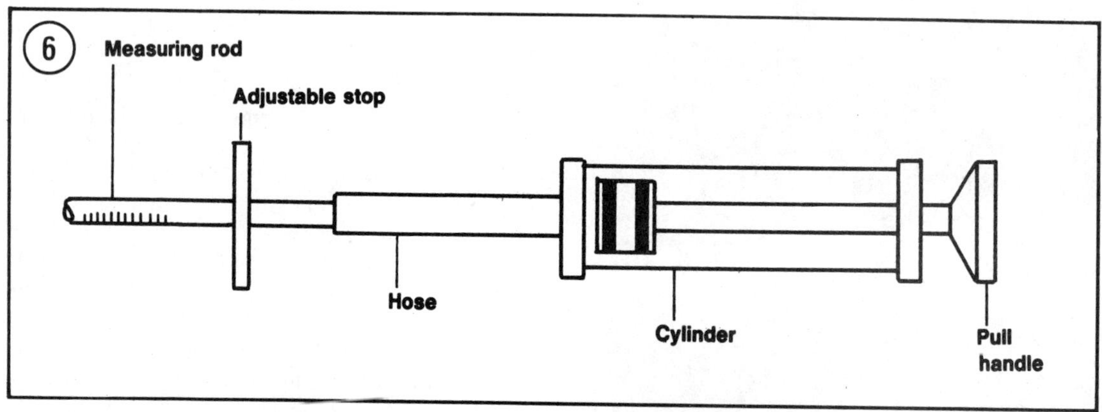

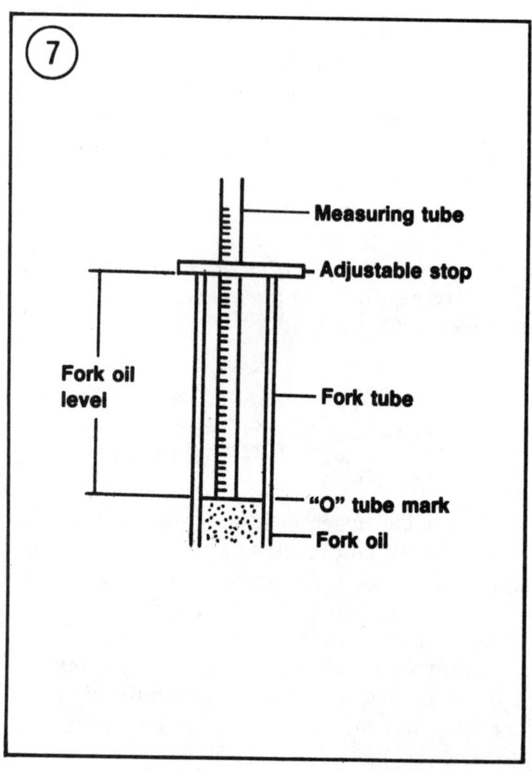

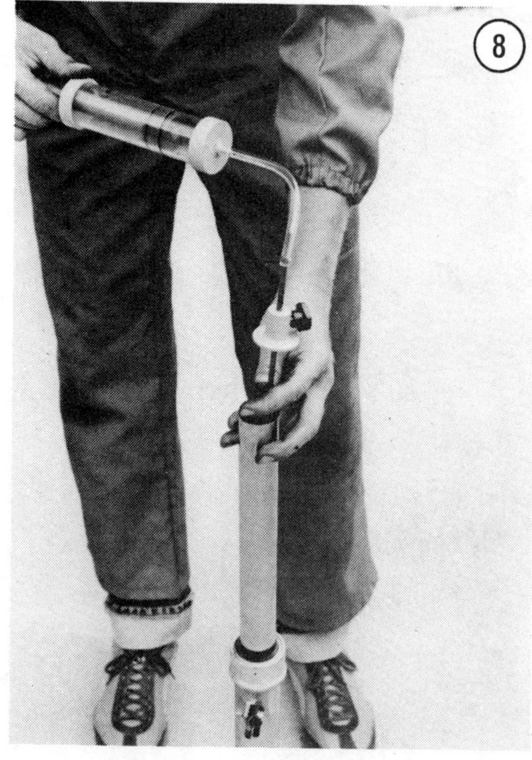

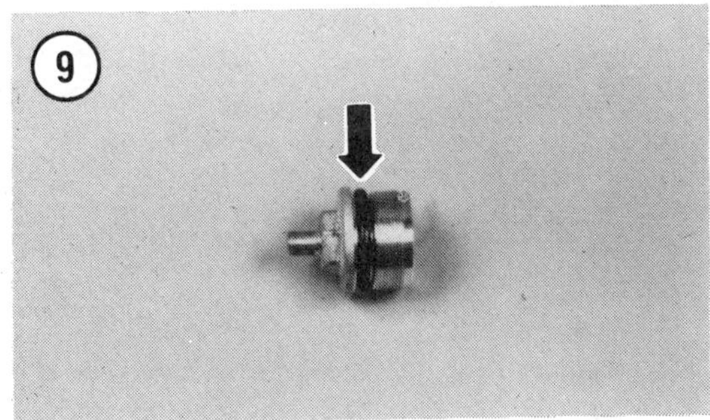

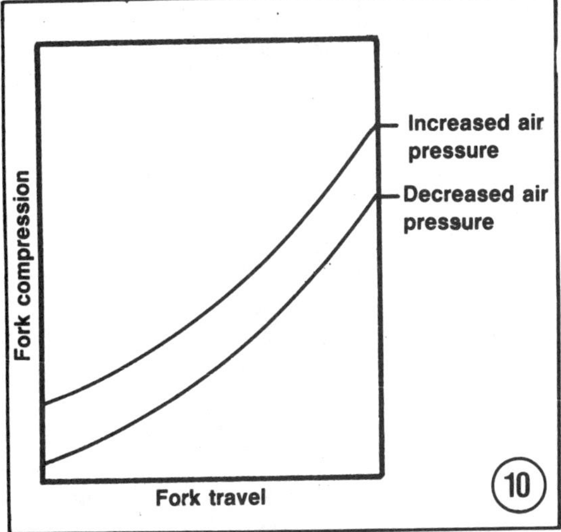

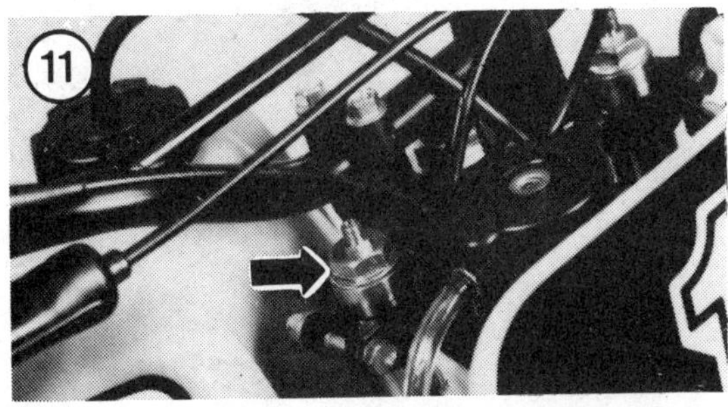

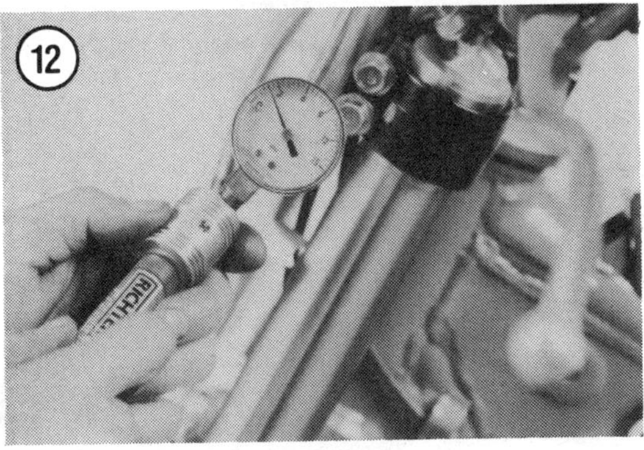

12. Check the O-ring in the fork cap (**Figure 9**). Replace it if worn or damaged.
13. Install the fork spring (**Figure 5**), spring seat (**Figure 4**) and spacer (**Figure 3**) (1983-on).
14. Place the fork cap on the spring seat and push it down with a speeder bar and socket. Install the fork cap by carefully threading it into the fork. Don't cross thread it. Tighten the fork cap securely.
15. Tighten the upper fork bridge bolts to the torque specification listed in **Table 5**.
16. If removed, install the handlebar assembly. Tighten the mounting bolts securely.
17. Inflate each fork tube to the correct amount of air pressure as described in this chapter.

Air Pressure Adjustment

Air pressure will increase or decrease pressure through the entire fork travel range (**Figure 10**). Because air pressure makes the forks hard, many riders do not pressurize their forks. Instead, they use the air valves on the fork caps to bleed off air that builds up inside the forks after each ride. When bleeding off air pressure, prop the bike up so that the front wheel clears the ground. Then depress the air valve (**Figure 11**) and bleed off all air pressure. Raising the front wheel off the ground prevents a vacuum from building in the fork tubes.

If your front forks seem soft and are bottoming harshly, you may want to add a small amount of air pressure. Consider the following when adjusting fork air pressure:

a. Decreasing air pressure will soften fork travel.
b. Increasing air pressure will stiffen fork travel.

CAUTION
*Do not exceed the air pressure specifications in **Table 3**.*

1. Place the bike on a stand so that the forks are fully extended and the front wheel clears the ground.
2. Remove the air valve caps.
3. Use a small manual air pump. Attach it to the air fitting and inflate the fork to the desired setting. See **Figure 12**.
4. Repeat for the opposite side.

WARNING
Use only compressed air or nitrogen—DO NOT use any other type of compressed gas as an explosion may result. Never heat the front forks with a torch or place them near an open flame or extreme heat.

14

NOTE
The air pressure difference between the 2 fork tubes should be 0.1 kg/cm² (1.4 psi) or less.

5. Reinstall the air caps.
6. Test ride the bike.

Front Fork Tube Height

Varying the fork tube height in the fork bridge will change steering characteristics. When the fork tubes are raised, the steering becomes quicker but is less stable on tracks with long straights. When the fork tubes are lowered, the steering is slower but the bike is more stable on tracks with long straights.

1. Place the bike on a workstand so that the front wheel clears the ground.
2. Loosen the upper and lower fork bridge bolts.
3. Raise or lower the fork tubes in 5 mm (0.2 in.) increments.

Maintain the fork height within the specifications listed in **Table 4**.

4. Tighten the upper and lower fork bridge bolts to the torque specifications in **Table 5**.

REAR SHOCK ABSORBER (1978-1981)

Adjusting the shock spring pre-load is the only adjustment provided on the stock monoshock unit. Before adjusting the spring pre-load, perform the *Suspension Travel Measurement* in this chapter.

This procedure will determine if the spring you are currently using is adjusted properly or if it is adjusted too soft or too hard.

Spring Pre-load Adjustment

NOTE
Adjustment should be made in increments of one adjusting notch each time. Select the adjustment that offers you the best riding condition. If the bike still bottoms out on the hardest setting, there may be an optional spring available from Yamaha. Refer to Chapter Twelve when replacing the monoshock spring.

1. Remove the seat.
2. Remove the fuel tank as described in Chapter Eight.
3. Use the ring nut wrench supplied in the owner's tool kit and turn the spring seat to the left-hand side to decrease spring pre-load or to the right to increase spring pre-load.

NOTE
On these models, there are 5 spring adjustments.

REAR SHOCK ABSORBER (1982-ON)

The monoshock on these models offers 4 adjustments to tune the rear suspension for different riding conditions. The adjustments are:

a. Spring pre-load adjustment.
b. Damping adjustment.
c. Spring replacement.
d. Nitrogen gas pressure (1982-1986).

Spring Pre-load Adjustment

Spring pre-load is the amount of spring compression before suspension movement. Adjusting spring pre-load will make the rear shock spring softer or stiffer. If there is too much preload, the shock spring will be too stiff and cause a hard ride over small bumps. If there is too little preload, the shock spring will be too soft and cause the suspension to bottom easily over small bumps.

The spring is held in position on the shock absorber between an upper and lower spring seat.

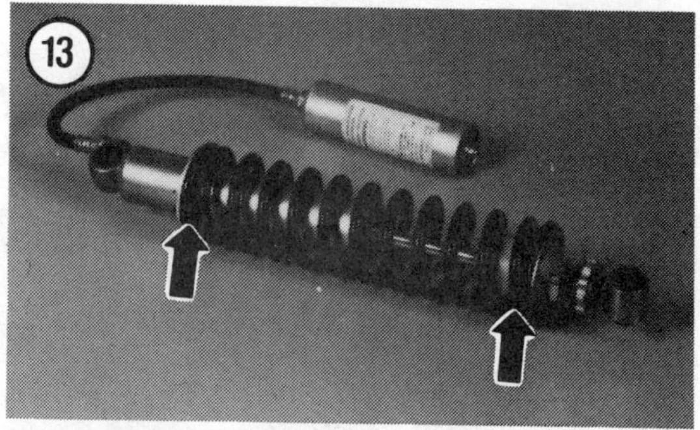

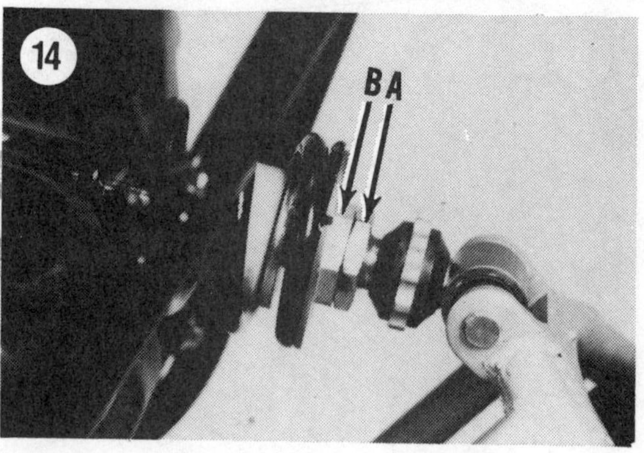

The distance between the spring seats is spring length (**Figure 13**). Spring preload is changed by varying the length of the spring between the upper and lower spring seats. To change spring preload, perform the following.

NOTE
Before adjusting the spring pre-load, perform the ***Suspension Travel Measurement*** *in this chapter. This procedure will determine if the spring you are currently using is adjusted properly or if it is too soft or too hard.*

CAUTION
Do not turn the spring pre-load adjuster in excess of the minimum or maximum length settings listed in ***Table 6****.*

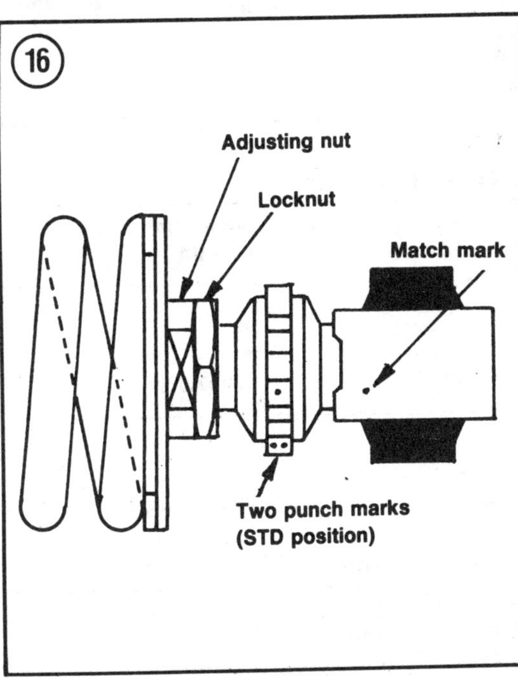

1. If necessary, remove the shock absorber.
2. Using the wrench provided in the owner's tool kit, loosen the locknut (A, **Figure 14**) and turn the adjuster (B, **Figure 14**) as required. Tighten the adjuster to increase spring pre-load or loosen it to decrease it.
3. The installed spring length must be within the range listed in **Table 6**.

NOTE
When changing the spring preload, work in increments of 3 mm (0.1 in.) at a time.

NOTE
One revolution of the spring adjuster is equal to 1 mm (0.04 in.) of spring preload change.

4. After adjustment, tighten the locknut against the adjuster to 55 N•m (40 ft.-lb).

Damping Adjustment

Damping adjustments can be performed without removing the shock absorber.

1. With your hand, turn the damping adjuster (**Figure 15**) clockwise to stiffen the damping or counterclockwise (as looking at the rear of the shock) to soften the damping. When the adjuster is turned, it will click into each position with each click representing one setting. Refer to **Table 7** for damping adjustment settings. Make sure the damping adjuster seats into one of the clicks and not in between 2 clicks.

NOTE
*On 1982 YZ80 models, the damping adjuster is initially set at 2 steps to the softer side. This is indicated by the alignment of the single punch mark on the damper adjuster with the punch mark on the shock body (****Figure 16****). Yamaha recommends that the adjuster be left in this position until the motorcycle is ridden for approximately 200 miles. After the break-in, turn the damper adjuster to the standard position (2 punch marks) as shown in* ***Figure 16*** *and test the motorcycle. Make further damping adjustments accordingly.*

NOTE
On 1982 YZ80 models, to bring the damper to the softest setting, turn the adjuster clockwise (as looking at the rear of the shock) until it bottoms. To bring to the standard setting, turn the

adjuster until the 2 punch marks on the adjuster align with the punch mark on the shock body.

Spring Replacement

Additional spring rates are available through Yamaha dealers. Consult your local dealer for details.

Nitrogen Gas Pressure Adjustment

The monoshock gas pressure is adjustable on some models. Refer this procedure to a Yamaha dealer as special tools and procedures are required.

WARNING
Do not attempt to adjust the monoshock gas pressure yourself.

Table 1 SUSPENSION TRAVEL (STOCK SUSPENSION COMPONENTS)

	mm	in.
Front fork travel		
YZ50	110	4.3
YZ60		
1981	150	5.9
1982	165	6.5
YZ80		
1978	140	5.5
1979	165	6.5
1980	180	7.1
1981	215	8.46
1982	225	8.86
1983	240	9.45
1984-on	255	10.04
Rear wheel travel		
YZ50	115	4.5
YZ60		
1981	163	6.4
1982	178	7.0
YZ80		
1978	120	4.7
1979	155	6.1
1980	170	6.7
1981	205	8.1
1982	230	9.1
1983	250	9.84
1984-on	260	10.2

Table 2 FRONT FORK OIL LEVEL (1982-ON)*

Model	Standard mm (in.)	Minimum mm (in.)	Maximum mm (in.)
YZ80 (1982)	160 (7.87)	**	**
YZ80 (1983)	173 (6.81)	**	**
YZ80 (1984-1987)	157 (6.18)	**	**
YZ80 (1988-on)	157 (6.18)	130 (5.12)	180 (7.09)

* Distance from top of fork tube.
** Not specified.

Table 3 FRONT FORK AIR PRESSURE

Standard	0 kg/cm² (0 psi)
Maximum	1.2 kg/cm² (17 psi)

Table 4 FORK TUBE HEIGHT

Model	Standard mm (in.)	Maximum mm (in.)	Minimum mm (in.)
YZ50	*	*	*
YZ60	*	*	*
YZ80			
1978-1983	*	*	*
1984-1986	7 (0.28)	*	*
1987	12 (0.47)	*	*
1988-on	7 (0.28)	*	*

* Not specified by Yamaha.

Table 5 FRONT FORK BRIDGE BOLT TORQUE SPECIFICATIONS (UPPER AND LOWER)

	N•m	ft.-lb.
YZ50	15	11
YZ60	16	12
YZ80		
1978	24	17
1979-1979	23	16
1980-1981	15	11
1982	18	13
1983-1985	23	17
1985-on	18	13

Table 6 REAR SHOCK SPRING PRELOAD SPECIFICATIONS

Model	Standard in. (mm)	Minimum in. (mm)	Maximum in. (mm)
YZ80 (1982)	10.9 (278)	10.2 (258)	10.9 (278)
YZ80 (1983)	8.66 (220)	8.35 (212)	9.13 (232)
YZ80 (1984-1985)	8.70 (221)	8.35 (212)	9.13 (232)

* One adjuster turn equals 0.04 (1 mm) spring preload change.

Table 7 MONOSHOCK DAMPING ADJUSTMENTS

	Standard	Maximum
YZ80 (1982)	4 clicks out	16
YZ80 (1983)	5 clicks out	10
YZ80 (1984-1986)	7 clicks out	10
YZ80 (1987-on)	5 (middle)	10

INDEX

D

E

F

H

I

K

L

M

O

P

R

S

T

V

W

WIRING DIAGRAMS

YAMAHA YZ80E (1978)

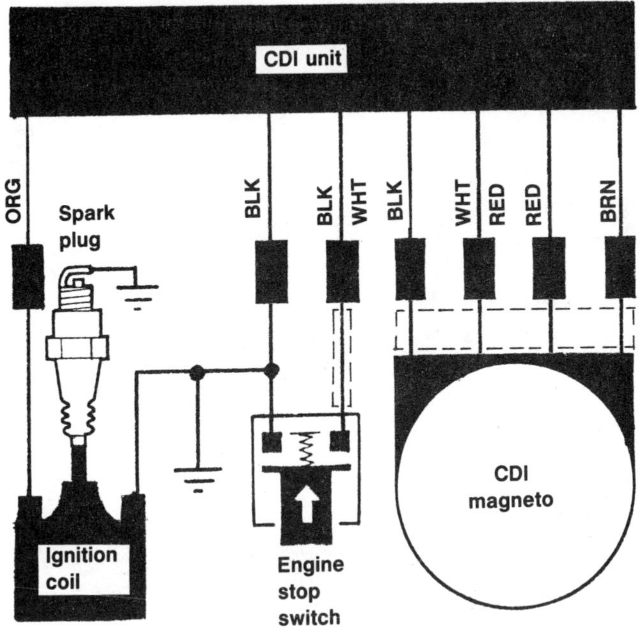

YAMAHA YZ80H, G, F (1979-1981)

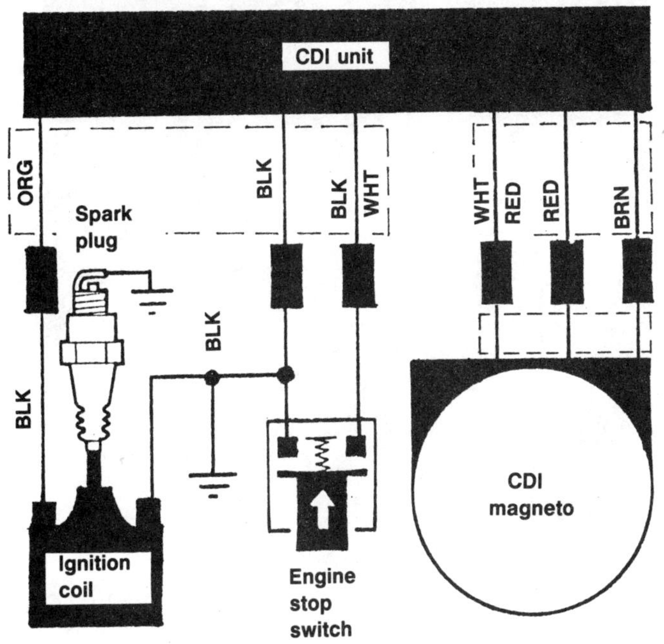

* ORG ON H (1981)

YAMAHA YZ50G (1980)

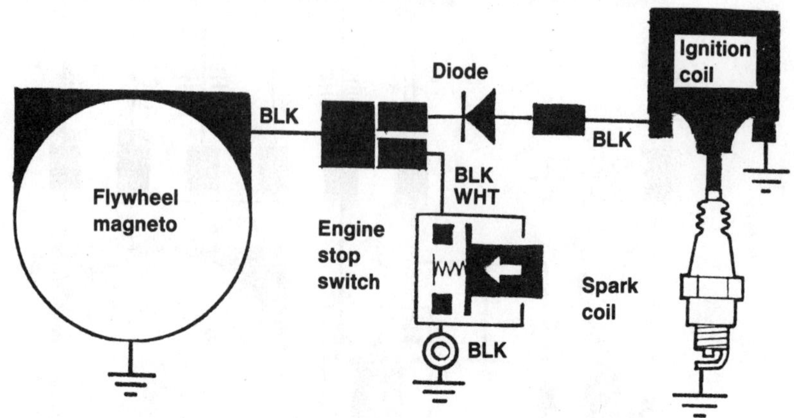

YAMAHA YZ60J, H (1981-1982)

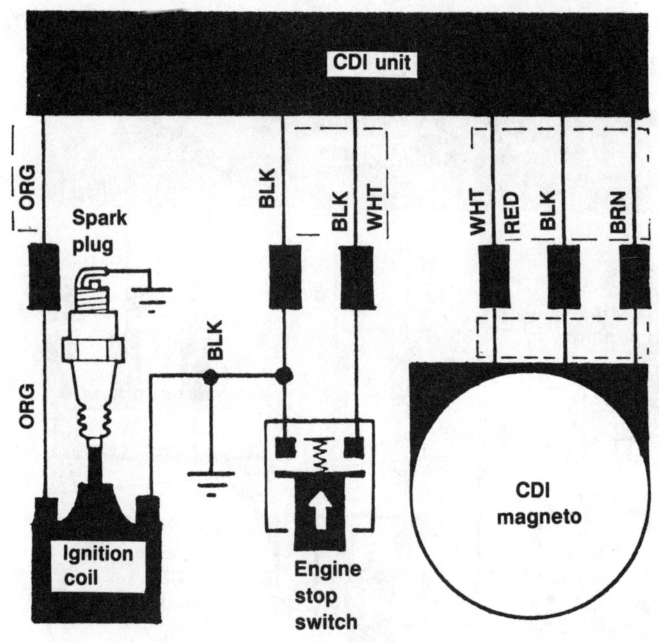

YAMAHA YZ80J, K, L (1982-1984)

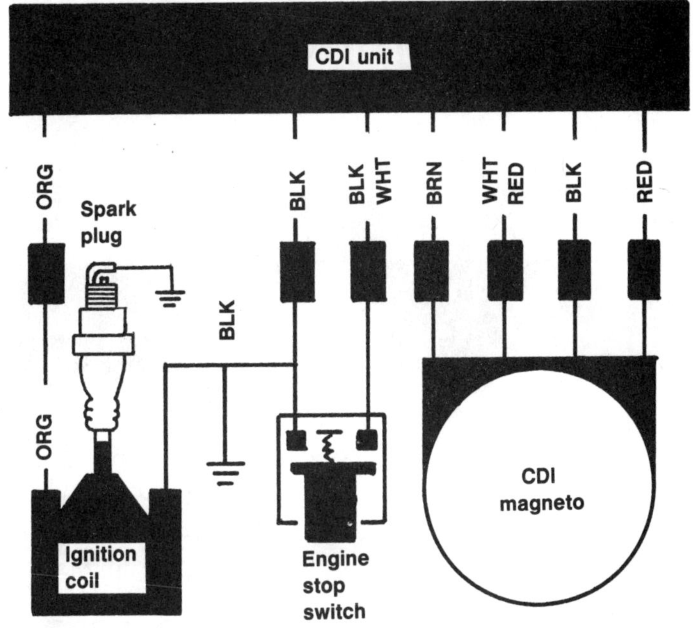

YAMAHA YZ80N, S (1985-1986)

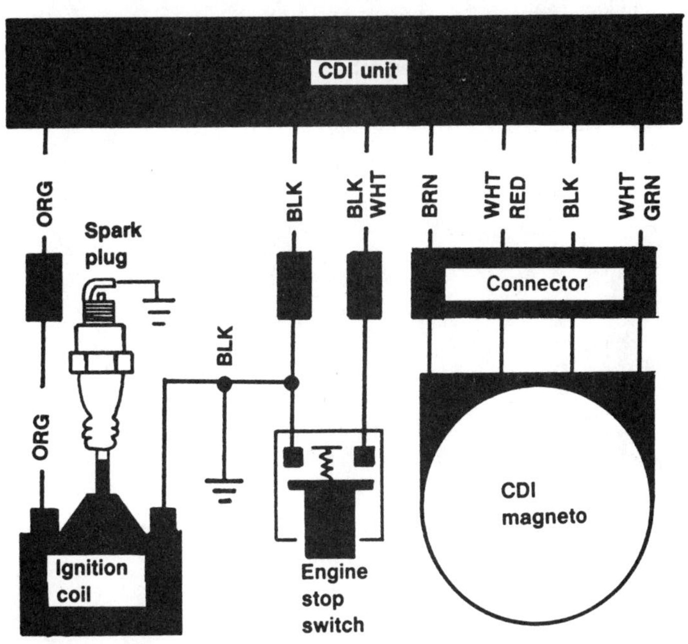

YAMAHA YZ80T, U, W, A (1987-1990)

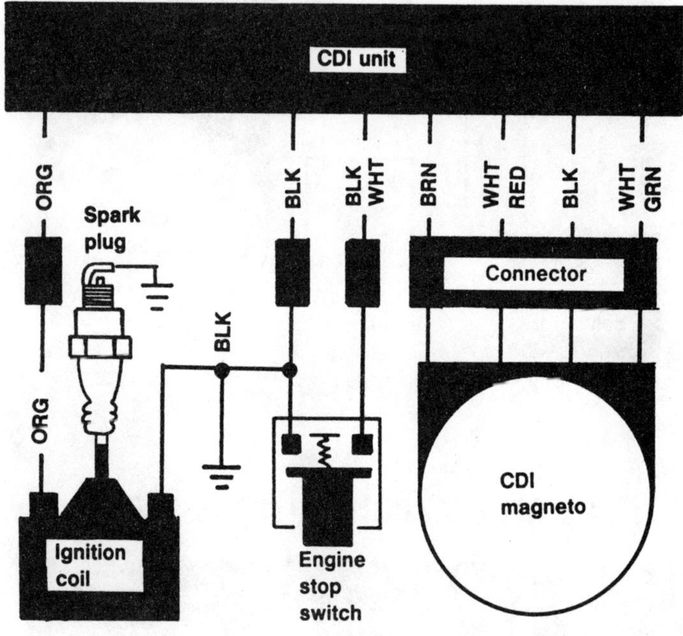

NOTES

MAINTENANCE LOG

Service Performed	Mileage Reading				
Oil change (example)	2,836	5,782	8,601		